D0504169

ACC. No: 05168744

DIANE ABBOTT

ROBIN BUNCE AND SAMARA LINTON

DIANE ABBOTT

THE AUTHORISED BIOGRAPHY

Biteback Publishing

First published in Great Britain in 2020 by
Biteback Publishing Ltd, London
Copyright © Robin Bunce and Samara Linton 2020

Robin Bunce and Samara Linton have asserted their rights under the Copyright, Designs and
Patents Act 1988 to be identified as the authors of this work.

All rights reserved. No part of this publication may be reproduced, stored in a retrieval system or
transmitted, in any form or by any means, without the publisher's prior permission in writing.

This book is sold subject to the condition that it shall not, by way of trade or otherwise, be lent,
resold, hired out or otherwise circulated without the publisher's prior consent in any form
of binding or cover other than that in which it is published and without a similar condition,
including this condition, being imposed on the subsequent purchaser.

Every reasonable effort has been made to trace copyright holders of material reproduced in this book,
but if any have been inadvertently overlooked the publisher would be glad to hear from them.

ISBN 978-1-78590-603-9

10 9 8 7 6 5 4 3 2 1

A CIP catalogue record for this book is available from the British Library.

Set in Adobe Garamond Pro

Printed and bound in Great Britain by
CPI Group (UK) Ltd, Croydon CR0 4YY

MIX
Paper from
responsible sources
FSC
www.fsc.org   FSC® C020471

For the women held at Yarl's Wood Immigration Removal Centre

CONTENTS

INTRODUCTION

A winter election is a sure sign of crisis. Like December 1923 and February 1974, December 2019 was a tumultuous time for politics. The political and constitutional crisis of 2019 was profound: an illegal prorogation of Parliament; a government ruling with no majority; and a constitution bent out of shape by Brexit. Despite this, the feeling in Hackney on election day was optimistic. Situated next to a hipster barbershop populated exclusively by men with monumental beards, and opposite a Lebanese deli, the mood in Diane Abbott's election office was focused, a little nervous, but definitely upbeat. The view a few hours before the polls closed was that the local campaign had been good, although it was agreed that the result of the national campaign was impossible to gauge.

In one corner a young computer scientist and social media influencer curates Abbott's Instagram. 'I usually use Lota Grotesque,' she explains. 'It's Labour's font, so it's part of the brand.' Apparently, while Abbott is routinely vilified on Twitter, her reception on Instagram is altogether warmer – presumably due to the demographic of the platform's users. Another staffer co-ordinates last-minute leafleting, while Abbott's agent is out of the office running people to and from polling stations. Electioneering in Hackney has none of the glamour of *The West Wing*, nor the muted chic of *House of Cards*. Boxes of campaign material lie here and there, activists come and go, some wearing bright red 'Vote Labour' hats provided by UNISON. Between the 'Vote Labour' posters, some Labour red tinsel adds a touch of seasonal cheer.

Abbott's arrival at 4 p.m. changes the atmosphere: the focused silence is replaced by a buzz of enthusiasm. It has been a long campaign, the phoney war having started in the summer, and, as far as Abbott is concerned it has been 'an exceptionally dirty campaign'.[1] Yet Abbott seems energised. At the end of November 2019, the Tories were something like twelve points ahead, but in the final fortnight the lead had narrowed. Moreover, the last few days of the campaign were dominated by the story of Jack Williment-Barr, the four-year-old boy who was forced to sleep on the floor of Leeds General Infirmary, which led to a 'car-crash interview' with Boris Johnson, a flurry of fake news stories and the unseemly sight of Johnson 'no-platforming' himself by hiding in a fridge. Six hours before the polls closed, Abbott's view was that the election was too close to call, a view shared by respected psephologist John Curtice, at least up until polling day. Although Labour was still behind in the polls, there was a chance of a minority government and, with it, Abbott's promotion to one of the great offices of state.

> We had a rally last night in Hackney, and when you see Jeremy up on the platform, and you realise he's on the brink of becoming Prime Minister, you want to cry. It's been thirty years, working on the left, this has been our Long March! Jeremy, John McDonnell and the rest of us. Today, we could be twenty-four hours away from having state power, and its extraordinary.[2]

While other politicians prevaricate and bluster, Abbott, even after a gruelling campaign, is focused, her answers sharp and clear.

There is no let-up. After our interview, Abbott is back on the campaign trail. Her brother is spending a few days in London to help on the campaign, and together they drive with a handful of activists to the Hawksley Court Estate in Stoke Newington. Abbott's focus, in the last hours before the polls close, is a council by-election in Clissold Ward. After all, all politics is local politics. Abbott's last few hours of campaigning are striking. A national figure, instantly recognisable, she canvasses the estate with no security. What is more, she treats this local council by-election with the same energy with which she fought the national campaign.

Corbyn's Labour Party has been caricatured as a rabid Marxist sect: Trotskyites, Stalinists, Maoists – the exact flavour depends on who you read – animated, according to Boris Johnson at least, by a 'vindictiveness not seen since Stalin persecuted the kulaks'.[3] The reality was much more prosaic and much more democratic. Abbott's office was full of people who believe that democracy can deliver change, that people inspired by hope rather than fear can vote for a better future. On this occasion their faith was not rewarded.

The journey back from Stoke Newington to central London highlighted what was at stake on election night. As shadow Minister for Public Health under Ed Miliband, Abbott made a great deal out of research which showed the drop in life expectancy as you travel east on the Central Line. The short trip south from Stoke Newington to Liverpool Street threw the difference between London's 'two cities' into sharp relief.[4] For all its proximity to the City, Stoke Newington is a different world in terms of wealth and privilege. In a way, Stoke Newington and Liverpool Street are two different utopias. Stoke Newington's council estates, each with its attendant green space, is the utopia of the Beveridge Report and the Parker Morris Committee; sincere attempts to ensure that working people benefited from economic growth in the mid-twentieth century. The glittering glass and steel towers of Liverpool Street, by contrast, represent a more recent utopia, the work hard, play hard utopia of market forces and financialisation. And hidden in each is a corresponding dystopia. For David Cameron, estates like those in Stoke Newington were 'concrete slabs dropped from on high, brutal high-rise towers and dark alleyways that are a gift to criminals and drug dealers'.[5] While the glass and neon skyscrapers around Liverpool Street, which are almost entirely devoid of greenery, are closer to the soulless materialism of Huxley's *Brave New World*. It's easy to see why politics is so polarised, when the country itself is divided into different worlds.

Abbott's politics are complex. She embraced socialism while an undergraduate at Cambridge University, studying black history for the first time with Jack Pole and Professor Robert Fogel. On returning to London, she became involved with the Organisation of Women of African and Asian Descent, an umbrella group of black and Asian women radicals which had grown out of the Black Power movement and embraced anti-imperialism and black womanism. In the 1980s Abbott was a councillor in Westminster where she fought for better housing, the provision of crèches, and honesty with the local population about their prospects in the event of nuclear attack – which led to her being labelled as a member of the 'loony left'. Since her time at Cambridge she has campaigned on issues of representation. And it was her work with the Labour Party Black Sections campaign that propelled her into Parliament. As an MP she has been a constant critic of unaccountable executive power; of the consequences of privatisation; of draconian immigration laws; and of illiberal measures which compromise civil rights in the name of security.

Abbott's politics may be complex, but her essential beliefs can be expressed simply. Speaking to a group of young people in Parliament in December 2013, she linked her politics to her background. 'I came down from Cambridge with my degree,' she recalls, 'and I really felt the world was my oyster. As a young undergraduate, I didn't have the debt, buying a home was perfectly in reach, and getting a decent job was perfectly within reach.'[6] Abbott regards herself as being a beneficiary of the 'enabling state'. She received the best education that money could buy for free. 'My education was completely free. From start to finish. There were no tuition fees, I got a maintenance grant, and it was very easy to get jobs in the holidays.'[7] Having left university, she bought a house in central London, with the help of a loan from her local council. Due to a buoyant labour market, she was able to gain well-paid work first in the civil service, then the National Council of Civil Liberties, and latterly in the media. In fact, her varied career was a testament to the numerous opportunities for young people in the years after she graduated. Abbott's early life was not without difficulties: 'I had to deal with a lot more overt racism than is around today, but, you know, some things were better.' However, almost four decades later, 'young people today face a very grim prospect'.[8] Debt, the housing crisis and the dwindling number of secure well-paid jobs mean that 'Generation Z' have few of the opportunities of those born before 1980. And while all young people have been disadvantaged by these changes, those who are likely to have been hit worst are young people of colour.

For Abbott, this narrowing of prospects is 'largely because of decisions made by politicians'. Abbott argues that there's a simple equation at the heart of politics: 'What you put into it is what you get out of it. If they [politicians] feel that people who look like you don't care, don't ask hard questions, and above all do not vote they will do what they like to you.'[9] In a country where democracy has become increasingly winner-takes-all, and progressively majoritarian, Abbott offers an important corrective. Minority representation at all levels of politics, and throughout civil society is crucial because it is the best way of defending and advancing minority rights. And democracy without minority rights is no democracy at all.

Election day on Thursday 12 December 2019 did not bring Labour's hoped-for breakthrough. The Conservatives swept to power with a majority of eighty, while Labour lost sixty seats, many in its traditional heartlands. Nonetheless, the election may well have been a breakthrough in a different way. The parliament that was elected in 2019 is the most diverse in British history, containing more black, Asian and female MPs than ever before. This achievement is part of Abbott's legacy. As the first black woman ever elected to the British Parliament, she changed the face of British politics for good.

* * *

This book was conceived in the months following the 2017 election. Research took place during the biggest political and constitutional crisis in generations. Writing began on election night 2019, and the first draft was concluded on 11 June 2020, which was by lucky hap the thirty-third anniversary of Abbott's election to Parliament. Writing, then, coincided with the Covid-19 pandemic and the period of lockdown. The final sections were written in the aftermath of the murder of George Floyd, during a renewed global campaign for racial justice.

This book emerges from a period that was characterised by both hope and pessimism. Hope among some that Brexit might allow Britain to 'take back control'; among others that Corbynism might lead to a fundamental restructuring of social and economic life. Pessimism about the environmental crisis, about rising populism and the capacity of democratic politics to deal with problems on a global scale. Yet, in the past few years, there have been genuinely innovative ideas about how we might begin to tackle inequality, the climate crisis, the refugee crisis and racial justice. Abbott and the project which she has helped lead have been at the forefront of offering radical solutions to contemporary problems, of imagining the politics of the future.

'Black' and 'white' are words that occur again and again in this book. We have tried to use the terms historically. That is to say, the book tries to reflect the shifting usage of these terms from the 1960s to the 1990s. Similarly, at the point where phrases such as 'black' and 'Asian' and terms such as 'BME' and 'BAME' became common this is also reflected in the text.

Attempting to sum up a life in the space of a book is an impossible task. Writing a biography is like trying to see London in a weekend. The best you can hope is to get a sense of the place and see some well-known landmarks. Early chapters try to fill in the context of Britain in the '50s and '60s. In later chapters, where the context is more immediate, we have taken more for granted. One way in which this book is incomplete is that it is essentially political, and therefore it is not a personal portrait nor an intimate history. Even though it is a political book, there is no extended treatment of Abbott's work as a constituency MP. There is clearly a need for other projects dealing with issues such as Black Sections, and Labour's reaction to Brexit. With any luck, this book will be a small help for those engaged in such tasks. We hope that the material included in this book will please as much as the omissions offend.

CHAPTER 1

THE DAUGHTER OF IMMIGRANTS

'I'm the daughter of those immigrants you've heard so much about...'[1]

Since the early 1980s, St Mary's Hospital in Paddington has been the birthplace of British royalty. William and Harry, Peter and Zara, George, Charlotte and Louis – with the exception of Archie, two generations of royals have now been born at St Mary's. Thirty years before it was fashionable, at least with the House of Windsor, Julia Addassa Abbott, formerly Julia Addassa McLymont, known to her friends as 'Little Lucille', gave birth there too. Her first child, Diane Julie Abbott, was born at St Mary's Paddington on 27 September 1953. Despite the establishment of the NHS five years earlier, St Mary's Hospital was segregated. Private patients were treated in St Mary's Lindo Wing on Wharf Street. NHS patients, by contrast, were treated across the other side of the Paddington Basin in the Victorian part of the hospital, which had opened on Michaelmas Day 1847, as the new Paddington workhouse. Needless to say, Abbott was born in the NHS part of the hospital.

Abbott's birth was recorded a fortnight later at the Paddington Register Office. Her parents were part of what is now known as the Windrush generation, migrants from the Caribbean who moved to Britain in the 1940s and 1950s to rebuild the mother country after the war, and in so doing made Britain their home. Abbott's parents had grown up in Smithville, a small village in Clarendon, Jamaica, known, at the time, for its dairy farming. Both of Abbott's grandfathers, John Abbott and Basil McLymont, are described as farmers on her parents' wedding certificate. Abbott attributes her success in politics, at least in part, to the spirit of her forebears. On Christmas morning 1987, Abbott, together with her uncles Charlie Brown and Frederick Russell, attended a service at the Baptist church in Smithville. Having given the notices, Sister Kate, the church elder, announced: 'I'm delighted to say that we have here in the congregation this morning an MP all the way from London in England, Little Lucille's daughter.'[2]

As she was leaving the church, Abbott was stopped by one of the congregants. Congratulating Abbott on her election, she said, 'When I hear that a black woman become an MP in England, I was so pleased. But when I hear that a black woman become an MP in England, I know it was someone from Smithville.'[3] While Smithville is a small community in the middle of rural Jamaica far from the centres of global power, the local people have a deeply rooted confidence in themselves, in their community, and believe that their voices should be heard where matters of state are discussed.

JULIA MCLYMONT AND REGINALD ABBOTT
Both of Abbott's parents left school at fourteen, although her mother had stayed on for a couple of years as a pupil-teacher, supervising younger students.

Julia Addassa McLymont travelled to Britain aboard SS *Ariguani*, arriving in Avonmouth, near Bristol, on 12 September 1950. Apparently, she moved first to Ashford in Middlesex and then quickly to Paddington. Abbott's mother was not the first in the family to seek work overseas. Her father, Abbott's maternal grandfather, had travelled to Panama prior to the First World War, to work on the Panama Canal. He returned to Jamaica having picked up some Spanish. Others in the McLymont family had travelled to the United States to work as fruit pickers.

As a concert violinist, Adrian McLymont, Abbott's great-uncle, was perhaps her most glamorous relative. It seems he studied the piano as a young man in Jamaica and picked up his love for the violin when he went to New York in the summer of 1920 to study at Weir's Conservatoire.[4] He must have done well during the roaring twenties, as he bought an eighteenth-century Guarneri violin, but on his return to Jamaica in 1929, he was unable to escape the ravages of the Great Depression. His son, Abbott's uncle Felix, recalls, 'He tried his hand at everything, just to make a living, because, of course, the Depression hit everywhere, including Jamaica.' On nights when there was nothing to eat, Felix remembers his father playing for them, 'We slept many a night on music, never hungry, always full of music.'[5]

Following in her great-uncle's footsteps, Abbott learned to play the piano as part of the BBC's *Play It Again* TV show, performing Frédéric Chopin's Prelude in E-Minor to an audience in London at the end of the show. According to Andrew Neil, this feat demonstrated that 'under that rough Labour exterior, she's very posh'.[6] Music was an important part of life in Abbott's mother's family. Abbott's uncle, Len, loved the piano music of Debussy and Chopin, due to the influence of his mother, Abbott's great-aunt, who played the organ in church.

Julia McLymont and Reginald Abbott came to Britain for a better life. Nonetheless, they continued to regard Jamaica as home. At weekends and on holidays, Abbott's parents would get together with friends from the Caribbean and talk about what was going on back home. 'They felt really engaged with Jamaica,' Abbott recalls. Family and friends in Jamaica were as much a part of their lives as their family and friends in London. They felt proud of Britain, and of what Britain represented, but Jamaica was home, not least as they planned to return.[7] The endless talk of home made Jamaica real for Abbott. So much so that on her first trip there she visited places that she had never seen but felt she had known all her life.

Looking back, Abbott sees the politics of her family's situation clearly. Her parents were black economic migrants.

My family came to this country as economic migrants in the 1950s, so they were at the bottom of the economic pile. In the 1960s, when I was a child, the Caribbean community was a very tightly knit community. People were very conscious of struggling to survive.

But it was a very warm community, so I had a real sense of community and place.[8]

The Windrush generation were undoubtedly at the bottom of the economic pile. Migrants from the 'coloured colonies' were routinely employed in the most menial of roles, regardless of experience or qualifications.[9] This may well have been McLymont's experience. Although the family recalls that she was recruited directly into the NHS, in the statement she provided on arrival in Britain she indicated that she hoped to work as a teacher. In the 1950s, teaching was relatively high status and well paid. However, she found work as a nurse, which required much longer hours and lower pay and was far more physically demanding than teaching. Moreover, McLymont joined the NHS as a state enrolled nurse (SEN), the higher grade of state registered nurse (SRN) being reserved for white women. Abbott's mother trained for two years as a pupil nurse. By the time of her marriage, she recorded her 'rank or professions' as 'formerly a hospital student nurse'. The sharpest division between the two grades related to their long-term prospects. SRNs could go on to become staff nurses or gain promotions to become ward sisters or matrons. SENs, by contrast, were unable to work their way up through the hierarchy. Writing in the pages of the radical journal *Race Today*, members of the Brixton Black Women's Group claimed, 'Those who work the hardest have the least status and the least wages.'[10] As wages rose with seniority, black women were consigned to a life of physically demanding, low-paid, low-status work. Beverley Bryan, Stella Dadzie and Suzanne Scafe point out the deep irony of the 'caring profession', in their seminal book *Heart of the Race*, detailing the health impact of 'long hours, shift work and the frequent need to hold down more than one job in order to support ourselves and our families'.[11] Abbott's mother was one of 3,000 black women, recruited as NHS nurses in the period between 1948 and 1954; the first of a generation of black women nurses who worked in the lower ranks of the NHS.

Abbott's mother never complained to her children about her work as a nurse. She took pride in nursing and had a fair degree of authority in her role. Abbott recalls that her mother was often the most experienced nurse on shift, and in those situations she would effectively run the ward. She also taught younger nurses, trainee SRNs, who would go on to make their way up the hierarchy. Abbott explains, 'She loved her job, she was very proud of being a nurse, as all of that generation was.'[12] Nonetheless, Abbott's mother stopped nursing once her first child was born. 'That's what my father wanted, and that's how it was, it was that era for women, and you were meant to subordinate yourself inside the family.' Abbott's brother Hugh was born in 1955. Once her children were at secondary school, Julia Abbott got a job in Sainsbury's, although 'the striking thing was, she wasn't allowed to serve on the counters; she was behind the scenes cutting meat'. Following her parents' separation when Abbott was fifteen, her mother moved to Yorkshire and returned to nursing. Notably, she worked in mental health. This too reflected the structure of the labour market: working as a mental health nurse was a relatively unattractive and low-status role, and therefore black women tended to be over-represented in the profession. Abbott's mother worked in the NHS until the 1990s and was never made a staff nurse.

The post-war Labour government, which fell just over a year after Abbott's parents arrived in Britain, was aware of the growing problem of racism. Letters to MPs from recent migrants, and representations from the governments of Trinidad, Jamaica, India and Pakistan, set out the position clearly. Indeed, the government's own research concluded that discrimination was widespread. In terms of employment, the Ministry of Labour reported in 1949 that black men in the Midlands were employed 'on dirty and rough finishing work', and that they were excluded from better jobs in 'building, [the] Post Office, transport, coalmining, railways, clerical, and draughtsmen's work'.[13] However, Attlee's Cabinet made a strategic decision to allow discrimination to continue. The Labour government calculated that protecting the rights of migrants would enrage white Britons, who were dealing with the consequences of post-war austerity. Worse still, they feared that tackling discrimination would make migration to Britain more attractive. Therefore, while the Attlee government issued statements

demanding 'tolerance', they deliberately refused to take action to protect the rights of migrants as part of a strategy to deter migration. The
government wanted enough migrant labour to help rebuild Britain's
shattered economy but believed that the British public were not ready
to accept migrants as equal citizens. There were plans for an act of
Parliament outlawing the incitement of racial hatred, but these were
conceived as an anti-fascist measure, and the government's prime concern focused on anti-Semitism rather than the rights of migrants from
the Caribbean or Asia. Indeed, at the top of government, it was felt
that racism was the result of too many migrants from the 'coloured
colonies' arriving too quickly.

The post-war Labour government was also under pressure from
its own MPs to curb immigration. A letter to the government from
eleven Labour MPs in 1948 claimed, 'An influx of coloured people
domiciled here is likely to impair the harmony, strength and cohesion
of our public and social life and to cause discord and unhappiness
among all concerned.'[14] Consequently, they asked the government
for 'legislation if necessary, [to] control immigration in the political,
social, economic and fiscal interests of our people'.[15] While ministers
resisted the call for legislation, they put pressure on colonial governments and behind the scenes to restrict the availability of passports, in
order to limit migration.

PADDINGTON

Reginald Nathaniel Abbott, clearly a man in a hurry, came to Britain
by plane and moved to Paddington to work in a factory. According
to the Abbotts' marriage certificate, Reginald Abbott was working
as a machine operator in an electric lightbulb factory at the time he
married Julia McLymont. By the time of Diane's birth, he was a sheet
metal worker, his job for the entirety of her childhood.

Abbott's parents had known each other in Smithville but made
their way to Britain separately, meeting again in Paddington. According to family lore, Reginald bumped into a family friend in north
London and learned that Little Lucille had moved into the area. The
couple got reacquainted and married at Paddington Register Office

on Saturday 4 August 1951. At first, the couple lived at 232 Harrow Road, before moving to 33 Edbrooke Road when they started a family.

A well-to-do area in the Victorian period, Edbrooke Road was decidedly down at heel by the time the Abbotts arrived. Several houses at the south-east end of the terrace had been destroyed by German bombing, and most of the houses in the street had suffered some blast damage. The Abbotts bought the house, taking in tenants to help pay their mortgage. The house was divided between three families, each living in a single room; Abbott remembers an Irish family living in a room in the basement. A single shared cooker stood on the landing.

At the time, Edbrooke Road appeared semi-regularly in the local press in relation to instances of crime, much of it petty, but including assault, GBH, stabbing and theft. The area was overcrowded, with much of the housing in a state of disrepair. While the politics of Paddington's housing situation were hotly contested, the roots of the problem were clear. Writing to *The Times* in August 1950, a local lawyer claimed, 'The trouble about Paddington is that before the war there was hardly any municipal housing done, while luxury flats sprang up on almost all the vacant sites. At the same time practically nothing was done to arrest the neglect and deterioration of large areas.'[16] Perhaps thinking of recent migrants from the Caribbean, the writer added, 'Another problem affecting Paddington is that people continue to come into the area from outside.' By the middle of the decade, London County Council announced that there were 160,000 people on the waiting list for council housing, of whom 3,000 were waiting for accommodation in Paddington. The 1961 census, taken shortly after the Abbotts had moved away, demonstrated that Paddington was the most overcrowded area in London, and that recent migrants were the group most likely to be affected.[17]

The Abbotts' decision to buy, rather than to apply for a council house, reflected the fact that they were unlikely to be allocated local authority housing. In the absence of regulation from central government, local authorities had a great deal of autonomy when selecting tenants. According to Mark Stephens, a specialist in housing policy, 'Housing officers would conduct household inspections to gauge the "respectability" of a household wanting to be re-housed.'[18] In London, housing was allocated according to 'sons and daughters' schemes which gave priority to the children of existing council tenants. Housing was also allocated to people who had homes which were demolished in slum clearance schemes. So, for a variety of reasons, the post-war Beveridgean welfare system was never truly 'colour blind'.[19] The Abbotts' decision to buy a house was not unusual. 'In that era,' Abbott explains, 'most, almost all, West Indians bought their homes, not least because councils just wouldn't house black people.' Necessity was not the only reason for the Abbotts' desire to buy. 'You are talking about a West Indian community which largely came from the countryside and believed passionately in owning something. Even though we could only live in one room, even though every other room had to be let; it was important, coming as you did from rural Jamaica, to own something.'[20]

Discrimination in housing was part of a broader trend within the welfare state. The Beveridgean welfare state created following the Second World War is often described as universal, in the sense that it was designed to support all who were in need. However, it did not function in a universalist way, and many white Britons did not regard welfare as being a universal entitlement. Camilla Schofield argues that many white Britons regarded the NHS, the benefit system and council housing not as a universal right, but as a reward for the public's sacrifices during the Second World War. They also assumed that black and Asian people had not made the same sacrifices and had not played a significant role in the victory against the Nazis. From this point of view, it was widely believed that migrants had no right to state support. This attitude may go some way to explain why black and Asian migrants faced discrimination in what was ostensibly a universal welfare system.[21]

By the mid-1950s, Paddington was a very diverse area, with migrants, mostly from Ireland and the Caribbean, making it their home from 1945 onwards. The majority of Paddington's black residents came from St Lucia and Dominica, part of the British Windward Islands until its independence in 1958. Roughly a quarter of Paddington's black population came, like the Abbotts, from Jamaica.[22] For all of the problems associated with living in Paddington, Abbott remembers it as a real community, and although life was hard, people looked out for one another.

During the 1950s, Paddington's politics changed as a variety of groups, some benign, others more sinister, responded to the area's changing demographics. The Paddington Project, launched in 1955, was the first of a multitude of initiatives started by liberal and philanthropic groups interested in 'community relations'.[23] The project was set up in order to give advice to recent arrivals. The Notting Hill race riots of 1958 led to a flurry of activity in north London. Statements were issued by the Mayor of Kensington, the Home Office issued reports on the need for integration, and charitable organisations descended on the area in a determined effort to foster goodwill. Historian John Davis notes, 'Race work became the new "slumming" as north London's black communities became the focus of charitable endeavour, much as the East End poor had been in the Victorian period.'[24]

Paddington, Kensington and Notting Hill also became the focus of more sinister activity. In the aftermath of the 1958 riots, Sir Oswald Mosley's Union Movement targeted the area. Mosley himself stood as a candidate for Kensington North in the 1959 general election. He was defeated, but in response, the sitting Labour candidate toughened his rhetoric on immigration. This, however, proved counter-productive. Black voters turned their back on Labour in the constituency, slashing Labour's majority, and giving a considerable boost to the Liberals.

One peculiar initiative set up in the aftermath of the Notting Hill race riots gives an insight into the way 'race relations' were perceived by well-meaning white people at the time. James MacColl, Paddington's Labour MP, co-ordinated efforts to remove phrases such as 'Europeans only' and 'no coloureds' from housing adverts in newspapers. The result was a very British compromise. On the basis that British people valued freedom of speech, and that landlords were paying for the adverts, there was no prohibition. Rather, newspaper staff would advise that phrases such as 'no coloureds' could be perceived as offensive and offer the opportunity to rephrase. Nonetheless, as long as the advert was not 'deliberately offensive' the wording was allowed to stand.[25]

In the absence of any meaningful support from the local authority or the voluntary sector, the Abbotts looked to the local West Indian community. In 1958, around the time of the riots, the family moved to Harrow. 'The banks weren't going to be a great deal of help,' explains Abbott, 'so the practice was to do something that we still call in the West Indian community, "throwing your partner," a form of saving. That's how, through these community savings schemes, people were able to accumulate enough for a deposit.'[26] 'Partners' were an established form of community saving which migrants brought with them from the Caribbean. They allowed a family, or an individual to draw on the savings of a whole group for purposes such as buying a house. As a result of the riots, the partner system, which had been run for the benefit of the West Indian middle class, was extended to support the whole community. Abbott's home in Paddington was located little more than a mile from the epicentre of the 1958 Notting Hill race riots. Her parents said nothing to their children about the riots, nor about the issue of racism.

> For that generation of West Indians who came here in the 1950s, Britain was the mother country, and they were proud to be here. They experienced racism, but they put that to one side. They would sometimes make oblique references to things, and you look back and realise what they were saying.[27]

Nonetheless, it may be that the Abbotts' decision to move was a response to the Notting Hill race riots, an idea borne out by a story Abbott recalls from her childhood. Abbott still remembers 'Uncle Jimmy', an Irishman who lived in the family's basement. When she was old enough, having had breakfast with her parents, she would go downstairs for a second breakfast with Uncle Jimmy and his family. 'Jimmy', she remembers, 'thought the world of me'. Around the time of the Notting Hill riots, white racists descended on Edbrooke Road and began banging on doors. Black people who opened their doors faced a real threat of violence. 'They came to our house, they came banging on the door, my mother was terrified, but Uncle Jimmy came up from the basement and said, "They're not getting our Diane."'[28] Jimmy opened the door and, seeing a white man, the hooligans moved on. It is an example of solidarity that moves Abbott to this day.

HARROW

Around the time Abbott started primary school, the family moved to 44 Somerset Road, Harrow, in what Abbott describes as 'a huge piece of upward mobility'. The impetus to move, Abbott recalls, came from her father, who was something of a pioneer: 'Daddy was very intrepid … [he] took it on himself to move out all the way to Harrow. His friends thought he was crazy, because there were no black people in Harrow. As far as they were concerned it was like moving to the dark side of the Moon!'[29]

As far as Diane could tell, the Abbotts were the only black family in that part of suburbia: 'If I went out and saw a black person on the street, I'd run home and tell my mother.' At the time the family moved to Harrow, white people who were born in Britain made up 95 per cent of the population. Of the 5 per cent of the population who were born overseas, the vast majority were Irish.[30]

The houses on Somerset Road had touches of the Tudorbethan, a style typical of Harrow. The Abbotts' neighbours included a teacher, a driver for the Gas Board, clerical assistants, an electrical engineer and a photographer based at Unilever's local research lab. Harrow Central, the Abbotts' constituency, elected Conservative MPs consistently from its creation in 1950 until its abolition in the 1980s. So in terms of the area's make-up, they had in some sense, as their family friends recognised, moved to an alien world.

Although houses in the area were cheap and the Abbotts were able to put together the deposit from the partner system, they had to take in a lodger to pay the mortgage. The house also became a base for the extended family and for friends. Abbott recalls, 'My mother and father came quite early on, so members of the extended family who decided to migrate subsequently, would often come to our house to stay there for a few weeks or a few months while they were finding their feet.'[31] Despite the move to the suburbs, the family's social life continued to revolve around Paddington, Willesden, Harlesden and Notting Hill. Abbott's uncles stayed in central London. Every Saturday, the family would drive to central London, do the family shopping, collect the rent on their house on Edbrooke Road and spend the evening at a friend's house.

Abbott attended Vaughan Primary School, which was a five-minute walk from the family home. Marilyn Macey, who was a year above Abbott, remembers that the two had coat pegs next to one another and as a result, they got to know each other and would skip together in the playground.[32] The headmistress at the time was a Miss D. M. M. Stenner, who had been in post since the early 1950s, had a reputation as a strong head and fought tirelessly for improvements to the school, including better lighting so that students could read until the end of the school day. Macey recalls that it was a small and pleasant school, but 'it was the 1950s, so there was a certain amount of discipline'.

Academically, Abbott stood out at primary school due to her essay writing. As a schoolgirl, this was a big thing, as her essays were regularly pinned up on the wall or read out to the rest of the class. Abbott stood out in other ways too. Despite this success, Abbott felt that in some way she did not fit in. 'My recollection of primary school is often feeling like an outsider. I never understood why that was, until I became an adult.'[33] Abbott, her brother and one other boy were the only black children in the school. 'Some of the teachers would single me out,' she explains. It was not just the teachers: Abbott was never invited to her best friend's house. The two were inseparable and spent every breaktime together, but Abbott was not even invited to her birthday party. 'I didn't understand at the time, although in retrospect you see what's going on.'

The late 1950s and early 1960s was a time of growing affluence, and the Abbotts were able to enjoy, to some extent, the consolations of consumerism. The family's Blue Spot radiogram was one piece of conspicuous consumption. Abbott recalls it as a massive piece of wooden furniture and, more than that, an object of which they could be proud. The family had a small collection of records. Julia Abbott was a fan of the Jamaican calypso star Harry Belafonte, particularly 'Scarlet Ribbons'. 'The theme of the song actually brings back my childhood. As a little girl, I had all these plaits which my mother used to religiously plait every morning, and every day I had fresh ribbons.'[34] Abbott's first record, which she bought as a teenager, was the more up-tempo 'Ain't Too Proud to Beg' by the Temptations, a Motown classic. The family also used the radiogram to listen to the 8 p.m. news on the BBC Home Service, which fostered an early interest in politics. While Abbott's parents were not particularly political, they had an international outlook. As a result, Abbott followed national and international news. Abbott also recalls engaging with the news and, even as a young woman, thinking, 'If I was Secretary General of the United Nations I would do this…'[35]

The Abbotts' other piece of conspicuous consumption was a cocktail cabinet. 'Basically, everyone that we knew who was West Indian had a cocktail cabinet, but I don't know a single one of them who ever drank a cocktail.'[36] In the Abbott household, the cocktail cabinet held sherry and Stones Ginger Wine, which came out on special occasions. Nonetheless, the Abbotts were not affluent. Family holidays were rare and would consist of occasional trips to Brighton or Blackpool. As far as Abbott could see, going on holiday was something that white people did. Government policy and the attitude of employers and unions meant black people were less likely to share in the growing prosperity of the 'long boom'.

HARROW COUNTY SCHOOL FOR GIRLS

Abbott did well at school. Having passed her eleven-plus she was allocated a place at Harrow County School for Girls, the local selective school. In the Tripartite System of the time, passing the eleven-plus was an important achievement, and the letter from W. H. J. Knight, director of education for the London Borough of Harrow, stressed its significance: at the age of eleven, Abbott had been selected to sit O Levels and A Levels.

This point was not lost on the young Abbott:

I thought it was very significant. I had this remarkably ugly uniform, navy and pink, and a felt hat in the winter, and a straw boater in the summer, because I was still wearing all these plaits, I was always losing my hats, they would just blow off. But I was so proud of my uniform, so proud of going to the school. It was a rite of passage going up to grammar school.[37]

The uniform is one of the first things that former pupils at Harrow County School for Girls remember. The school took the uniform extremely seriously, and it was policed vigorously. At the beginning of each term, girls were required to kneel so that the distance between the bottom of the skirt and the floor could be measured. Skirt length was monitored with particular rigour during Abbott's time due to the miniskirt craze of the 1960s. The uniform was monitored at the beginning of every day as girls filed into the school hall and there were spot checks in corridors. The school also had strict rules on shoes. Brown leather 'house shoes' were required to be worn inside the school to protect the parquet floors. Hats were an essential part of the uniform. Madeleine Watkins, one of Abbott's school friends, recalls, 'You didn't dare be seen outside without your hat on, that would have meant death!'[38] Girls who did not conform to the uniform rules were given an 'order mark'. Any girl who received three order marks was sent to see the headmistress. Remarkably, the uniform was also policed outside of school. According to Maxine Longmuir, 'We had an eccentric uniform mistress called Miss Buckley. If she caught you in the High Street and she thought your skirt was too short, she'd make you kneel on the ground, and get her ruler out!'[39] Fiona Santon, another of Abbott's contemporaries, concurs, recalling that the zealous Miss Buckley would sit in the local KKK café – which apparently had nothing to do with the Klan – 'watching the schoolgirls on their way home'. On one occasion, 'she accosted me in Station Road and gave me a thorough and humiliating dressing down in the street about the length (or rather lack of it) of my skirt and then sent me immediately back to the school to see the headmistress for a further dressing down'.[40] For much of her time at the school, Miss Buckley was Abbott's history teacher.

The emphasis on the uniform was part of the atmosphere of the institution. Ann West, who taught Abbott A Level history, explains, 'For a girls' grammar school in the 1960s and 1970s, it was very much of its time. There was a strict uniform code, high expectations of standards of behaviour, prompt handing in of homework, with "order marks" handed out for infringements.'[41] Longmuir recalls that the school was 'strict, very academic. There was no question that the girls were expected to go to university.'[42] Those girls who took the secretarial course were considered 'second-class citizens'. Similarly, students who left before sixth form were regarded as failures.[43] Several of the former students agree that the school was not a nurturing environment, certainly not towards the end of Abbott's time there. For Watkins, the school 'was, in its day, quite a posh school'.[44] According to Longmuir, few of the school's 550 students came from council house backgrounds. When they put on a production of *Pygmalion*, the one girl who spoke with a cockney accent was immediately cast as Eliza Doolittle. Nor was it ethnically diverse, Abbott being the only black student.

The atmosphere was heightened by the school buildings. Watkins remembers that the school, built in the Queen Anne style in 1913, still had a 'very oldy-worldy' feel, which was heightened by the wood panelling throughout. Despite the strict regulations, many of the girls warmed to the school's atmosphere. For Longmuir, 'the discipline of the school definitely spilt over into my private life. The discipline of that school is part of what made me who I am today, and I feel lucky and privileged to have been there.'[45] While primarily academic, the curriculum also included needlework and cooking. Abbott credits the school with teaching her how to make a good apple pie.[46]

Daily assemblies were presided over by the terrifying headmistress, Miss Robinson. Abbott's peers remember their headmistress as being short, fierce and elderly; for Watkins, she was 'way past her sell-by date!'[47]

The first year in the school was known as year three, and first year students were therefore known as 'Thirds', emphasising their diminutive stature. Each year was organised into three classes: A, B and C. The formula which was used to divide the girls between these classes was never made clear. Nonetheless, it was accepted that the girls in the 'A' class were the brightest, and those in class 'C' were the least academic. In 1965, to try to remove the stigma attached to the A, B, C classification, the classes were renamed: 3A, 3Alpha and 3Aleph. Abbott was allocated to the 3Alpha class. The girls quickly worked out that this was the equivalent of the B class. Once the allocation was made, there was no movement between the three classes.

As Longmuir remembers, 'all of our teachers were eccentric'.[48] Mrs Heather, well liked and remembered by Watkins as 'sort of mumsy', was Abbott's first form tutor. Abbott's first English teacher, Miss Platt, stands out. Catherine Wilkey, who was in Abbott's class, remembers her as 'an absolute tyrant'.[49] Abbott's first few English lessons at the school ended in humiliation.

> When I started at grammar school, we were given an essay writing assignment in my first English class. The second class, I came, and the teacher read out the grades, and I sat there complacently waiting for my A. She started at the top and went down to the bottom: she started with A+, A, A-, and she still hadn't called my name. I was a bit surprised, because I never got less than an A in my primary school. She read out everyone's name, and everyone's grade, and not my name. So I put up my hand and said, 'You haven't read out my grade,' and she said, 'Come and see me afterwards.' So I went up to her at the end of the class, and she was standing on a sort of dais, about six inches above. She held my essay between her thumb and forefinger, and she literally looked down on me and without missing a beat said, 'Where did you copy this essay?' She couldn't believe that a little chubby black girl with her pebble lenses and her plaits could have written that essay.[50]

Abbott was mortified. Notably, she did not think about what had happened in terms of race. Her parents and their friends had never discussed racism, or how prejudice expressed itself in Britain, and therefore Abbott did not have the conceptual framework for exploring what had happened, or why her teacher was so certain that the essay must have been copied. At the time Abbott assumed that the teacher had taken a dislike to her.

Abbott responded, quite naturally, by refusing to co-operate. Longmuir remembers, 'Diane got so fed up with Miss Platt that [when] we had to write a critique of a poem, Diane just wrote, "It's a load of old slush!" [For Diane] there was no point in doing the work if the teacher refused to mark it.' Predictably, the English teacher punished Diane for her response.

With Miss Platt refusing to mark her essays, and refusing to tolerate non-compliance, Abbott was forced to underperform. She recalls, 'I felt humiliated. But I didn't go home and complain to my parents, but for the remainder of that year, I wrote down, because I was frightened of being humiliated like that again. It wasn't until my second year that I had an English teacher who really believed in me that I was able to blossom again.'[51] Looking back on those English lessons, Longmuir concludes that Miss Platt was critical of girls who spoke with London accents, 'so you can imagine what she made of Diane', the only black student in the school.[52]

In September 1967, two years after Abbott joined the school, there was a changing of the guard. The fearsome Miss Robinson was replaced as head by Miss Joan W. Cartman. According to Longmuir, Cartman was just as strict but younger and 'more human' than her predecessor. Watkins recalls that around the time that Cartman took over 'we started to get a run of younger teachers', some of whom had come straight from teacher training college.[53]

With a new English teacher in her second year, once again Abbott began to flourish. Watkins remembers that she was 'a star in the English class'. While the new English teacher, Mrs Landy, liked Abbott, other students who did not perform well were subjected to her disdain; one recalls being called a 'stupid creature' before being excluded from the class.[54]

Abbott's parents supported her education in different ways. At the beginning of her time at secondary school, her mother enrolled her in the local library. From that point on, Abbott read incessantly. 'In my summer holidays, I'd get through a book a day. My mother would send me on an errand, and I'd walk along the street, reading a book.' Her university application, completed in October 1972, listed reading 'biography, science fiction and poetry' among her many activities, along with visiting art galleries and museums and playing tennis.[55]

Her father always attended school parents' evenings with

a brown shiny briefcase. He would change out of his work clothes and he wore a suit. But the briefcase was always empty. This was a working-class black man who spent his working day in overalls, and somehow he felt that if he had a briefcase those white teachers would take him seriously.[56]

School became part of the family routine, and Abbott remembers her mother's insistence that she should change into her 'home clothes' and do her homework as soon as she returned from school.

Abbott's parents had aspirations for their daughter – 'but their ambitions clearly had a ceiling. No one they knew had been to university. The British education system, for them, was uncharted territory.' With that in mind, her mother and father would have been happy had Abbott got a job as a staff nurse or a schoolteacher. She had other ideas. As a young woman, she wanted to be a 'Member of Parliament and a bestselling writer'.[57]

Her work for the school magazine, which began when she was fifteen, shows how seriously Abbott took writing. The 1968–69 edition, produced when Abbott was in the lower fifth, contains several of her pieces. '*Venimus vidimus vicimus!*', a play on Julius Caesar's 'I came, I saw, I conquered', tells of Harrow County Girls' first victory at the Classical Reading Competition, which was held at University College London. Abbott, who was studying Latin at the time, used the piece to press the school authorities to introduce Ancient Greek to the school curriculum.[58]

Abbott's second piece concerned the school production of *Romeo and Juliet,* which took place in March 1969. It was an important moment, bringing together students from Harrow County School for Girls with their counterparts from Harrow County Boys for their first major production. Abbott remembers that her first political impulse was towards feminism. This is clear in her article, which explores the disparities between the resources available to the two schools. The boys' school, Abbott reports, had a large and well-equipped stage. Moreover, the boys' school trained its students in the technical aspects of running a show. Neither was true for the girls. After the piece was written, a new lighting panel was bought for Harrow County Girls.[59]

Most of these pieces revolve around the concerns of school life. Abbott's cartoon strip, for instance, was a parody of a school which revolves around status, excellence and achievement. Her final piece was quite different. 'Timothy the Hermit' was a piece of creative writing which had no obvious connection to the school. It gives the fullest impression of Abbott's interests at the age of fifteen. The story is full of references to the concerns of the late 1960s and has an interesting political undertone. Abbott's protagonist wants nothing more than to be left alone. However, civilisation is hot on his heels. His quiet spot on a deserted beach is redeveloped as a seaside resort. 'The faster he fled civilization,' Abbott wrote, 'the faster it strove to keep up with him.' Then, years before J. G. Ballard's *High-Rise*, Timothy finds the solitude he craves in the flat at the top of a tower block. However, the flats are demolished, due to concerns that the buildings are leaving people isolated. 'Wherever he settled he was haunted by droves of welfare workers … food parcels were pressed on him … he was stifled by other people's concern.'[60] Finally, anticipating Ballard's *Concrete Island*, Timothy finds the peace he craves in a hole under the recently completed M1.

The story is full of counter-intuitive twists: the hermit finds solitude in a tower block, he finds serenity under a busy motorway and his life is bedevilled by the constant attention of welfare workers. Each aspect of the story reflects important debates that were taking place in Britain in the late 1960s. Many of the hermit's problems stem from the regeneration and urbanisation which characterised the 1960s. Indeed, the M1, which was completed shortly before the story was written, ran through Harrow. The impact of tower blocks, which is crucial to the story, reflects both London's changing urban environment after the building boom of the 1960s, and growing concerns about high-rise developments following the partial collapse of Ronan Point. Questions over the extent to which the hermit's desire to be alone is a form of madness may also reflect an awareness of contemporary debates over mental illness. Abbott does seem to have been interested in the issue of mental illness and it formed part of her voluntary work during her school years.

The most surprising aspect of the story, for a politician who has been a consistent advocate of the 'enabling state', is the scepticism of welfarism. The story is full of social workers 'grimly concerned for [the hermit's] welfare', who do more harm than good. The story also pokes fun at the bureaucracy of the welfare state, commenting that the hermit is bombarded with paperwork. Again, this reflects the kinds of debates that were going on in Britain at the time. During the 1960s there was an increasing concern that post-war welfarism had destroyed traditional communities, and that the welfare state was bureaucratic, inflexible and paternalistic. Significantly, these concerns came from the counter-cultural left, as well as the New Right. Researcher Richard Titmuss began exploring the problems of the welfare state in the late 1950s. In the early 1960s he criticised the 'assumption that the establishment of social welfare necessarily and inevitably contributes to the spread of humanism and the resolution of social injustice', noting that 'a multitude of sins may be committed in its appealing name'.[61]

It is unlikely that Abbott read Titmuss prior to writing 'Timothy the Hermit', but counter-cultural ideas were not restricted to academic writers. Records by the Beatles had an increasingly counter-cultural edge. While the Cold War became decidedly less dangerous in the years after 1963, counter-cultural anxieties about the threat of a nuclear apocalypse, and the political systems that might annihilate humanity, were still aired regularly in film and in print. 1968 was a year of revolution at home and abroad. The Prague Spring, the huge anti-Vietnam demonstration in London in March, riots in the US following the assassination of Martin Luther King, the student protests in Paris – known simply as 'May '68' – and student sit-ins at the London School of Economics among others, all in their different ways brought counter-cultural ideas into the mainstream.

By the late 1960s, politics was beginning to impinge on Abbott. At the end of the 1950s, the debate around immigration had become fierce. The Commonwealth Immigrants Act of 1962 was the first legislative measure which responded to concerns about mass migration. However, rather than restricting immigration, the Act led to an influx of migrants from the new Commonwealth, who moved to Britain in 1961 before the legislation was introduced. Nor did the Act quieten concern. Indeed, by the late 1960s there were demands for still tighter controls. At the same time, there was concern about Labour's new Race Relations Acts, the second of which outlawed discrimination in housing. It was in this context that Enoch Powell's 'Rivers of Blood' speech caused a political storm. Powell argued that in allowing continuing immigration Britain was 'busily engaged in heaping up its own funeral pyre'.[62] The growing number of immigrants, who in time, Powell argued, would occupy entire towns across the country, were making white Britons 'strangers in their own country', giving them a 'sense of being a persecuted minority'. Worse still, he predicted that immigrants had 'vested interests in the preservation and sharpening of racial and religious differences, with a view to the exercise of actual domination' over the white population, which would inevitably lead to violence.[63] The not-so-subtle subtext of Powell's speech was that black and Asian immigrants would soon be an occupying army; that immigrants were already displacing white people in the competition for jobs, hospital beds and school places; that they would soon have legal privileges denied to white Britons; and that in time they would go to war with the white population. Powell focused particular attention on the threat posed by black and Asian children, each of whom, in time, would have a family of their own, which would add to the 'growth of the immigrant-descended population'.[64]

Powell's speech was a sensation and was widely covered in the press. The *Daily Mirror*, the Abbott family paper, reported the story extensively, often devoting the front page to reactions to Powell. Edward

Heath, leader of the Conservative Party, dismissed Powell immediately. In reality, as Powell made clear in his speech, he was making a case for two existing Tory policies: strict immigration controls and financial incentives for repatriation. In that sense, there was little disagreement between Powell and the rest of the Tory frontbench. Heath sacked him on the basis that the speech was 'racialist in tone, and liable to exacerbate racial tensions', not due to any substantive policy disagreement.[65] But Powell had considerable public sympathy. Quickly, letters were written and marches and strikes organised protesting Powell's dismissal. Looking back to April 1968, Abbott comments, 'I remember going to school the next day, and everything seemed different. You felt a little scared, you felt that something had happened which carried a hint of menace, towards you personally.'[66]

Powell's speech certainly had an impact on Harrow. It was covered extensively in the local press. On 26 April, less than a week after Powell's speech, the front page of the *Harrow Observer*, was largely taken up with reactions to Powell's speech and his subsequent sacking. The MPs for the three seats in Harrow took quite different positions. John Page, Conservative MP for Harrow West, declared himself 'grateful that a man of the stature of Mr Enoch Powell has taken it upon himself to turn the spotlight on the subject of immigration', adding that he shared Powell's views. Page concluded that Heath had been right to sack Powell, simply because he had broken the principle of collective responsibility, not because there was anything inherently wrong with his message. Anthony Grant, Harrow Central's Conservative MP, explicitly endorsed Powell's sacking, while implicitly endorsing his message. Grant argued that MPs had a duty to do everything they could to stop Britain experiencing the kind of violence witnessed in America, and therefore should stop immigration as swiftly as possible. Neither of the MPs acknowledged that the population of Harrow was almost entirely white. Roy Roebuck, the Labour MP for Harrow East, demurred, arguing that the Race Relations Act was 'in tune with our British tradition of fair play' as well as 'the message of Christianity'.

Powell's intervention seems to have inspired an uptick in the activity of racist groups in Harrow, including the neo-Nazi Union

Movement, which fielded a candidate in a council by-election in July 1968. According to the local press, Union Movement activists spent a great deal of time in late June canvassing door-to-door. At the same time, the Racial Preservation Society leafleted the area. The reaction to Powell's speech rumbled on for some time. Powell was back on the front page of the *Harrow Observer* in November, backed by Harrow's two Conservative MPs who were advocating the repatriation of black and Asian Britons. Crucially, Powell's intervention gave racist views the veneer of respectability. Early in 1969, the National Front were given the *Harrow Observer*'s regular 'Opinion Column', in which they advocated 'the preservation of our British native stock ... by terminating non-white immigration and the orderly and humane repatriation of immigrants'. Harrow seems to have been spared the worst repercussions of Powell's speech; there are no reports in the local press of violence against black or Asian people, as there were in other areas of the country.[67] Moreover, local opinion was not uniformly Powellite. In fact, the *Harrow Observer* published numerous letters decrying racism, as well as reports of anti-racist marches in Harrow. But Powell had changed the debate fundamentally; he had politicised the very presence of black people in Britain in a new and ominous way.

The outside world certainly affected Abbott's school life, although not always in sinister ways. Although the school functioned as though it was still in the 1950s, the pupils were rooted firmly in the contemporary world. Longmuir recalls that before school and in breaks there were 'huddles of girls in the cloakroom looking at *Melody Maker* and the *New Musical Express*'. On one occasion, a group of girls smuggled a radio into a home economics lesson, hid it inside a cooker and listened to *Radio One Club* at the back of the lesson. At the beginning of the 1970s, pictures of Marc Bolan, David Bowie and David Cassidy began to appear in school. Abbott, however, had other interests. Catherine Wilkey remembers, 'She loved old film stars, Greta Garbo and Elizabeth Taylor. We used to sit at the back of the classroom and pluck our eyebrows; the fashion then was for very thin eyebrows.'[68]

Abbott began studying for her O Levels in the autumn of 1970. Longmuir, who was in her French class, remembers, 'She was definitely eccentric, loud, definitely had her opinions. But she was so clever, and so quick. She was almost a bit fearsome, you were a bit in awe of her.' Abbott was certainly a self-confident student. Towards the end of her O Levels, she stopped attending English lessons. Together with another student, she used the time to set up reading groups for younger girls, apparently telling her teacher, 'I don't think I'm learning anything in this class, it would be better if I studied on my own.'[69]

Abbott's O Level mocks revealed that at least some of her teachers thought she should be taken down a peg or two. Students at the school studied a science O Level which combined physics and chemistry. Having lost her mock timetable, Abbott arrived for what she thought was the physics exam, only to discover that she would be examined on chemistry. Exasperated, her teacher gave her an extra thirty minutes to revise. When the mock results were given out Abbott got straight As. But some of the teachers were not pleased, feeling that her disorganisation should have been reflected in her marks.

SIXTH FORM

Like most of the young women in the school Abbott took nine O Levels in her upper fifth year. She is recorded in the school magazine as one of many students who did well, and she qualified for the sixth form. Around the time that Abbott began her A Levels, her parents separated. A reference sent to Newnham College, written by her headmistress, notes that the separation caused her 'immense difficulties'. One of the more practical issues was the physical upheaval that occurred as a result of the separation. Abbott, together with her father and brother, moved from Harrow to Mount Grove in Edgware, and then to Turner Road in Queensbury. Her mother relocated to Huddersfield.[70]

Sixth formers had various responsibilities and privileges which marked them out from the rest of the students. They were made prefects and given responsibility for enforcing silence in the corridors. Abbott's classmate Rachel Kolsky remembers they were also entitled to use 'the white house'. Liz Turner, five years younger than Abbott, remembers the sixth form had a certain mystique:

They had this beautiful house, full of common rooms, an old white house like a manor house, that was on the site before the school. The sixth formers had the lower floor, which had French windows out on to the grass. If you think about St Trinian's, the way the girls change, you get these scruffy little oiks, and then they transform into these stylish beauties. The upper sixth were goddesses![71]

One of the sixth formers' responsibilities was looking after the tea and coffee machine. It was in this context that Turner met Abbott.

The sixth form were given the job of refunding money swallowed by the little drinks machine serving watery hot chocolate. As a nervous first year, I made my way to the sixth form common room and knocked on the door. Diane answered, when I said I'd come for my 3p, she told me imperiously that I had to come at lunchtime not break time and said something to the tune of, 'We don't hand out money just any time.'[72]

Abbott studied English, religious knowledge and history at A Level. She was also one of a handful of young women in her year to be allowed to take art as a fourth A Level. Taking four A Levels was unusual, and Abbott had to 'make a fuss' with her teachers to persuade them, but taking all four was important to her as she 'cared passionately about all of the subjects'. Taking an additional A Level meant working at lunchtimes, and more work during holidays and at weekends.

Abbott's history class was taught by Ann West, and focused on the period of the Renaissance and Reformation in Europe. West comments:

From what I can remember, Diane was an outstanding student. That particular A Level group, of about twelve girls, was a joy to teach. From my perspective, lessons were never dull as the girls were willing to engage in discussion and debate around whatever topic we were studying. Diane was especially good at that! She was willing to question a perspective, disagree sometimes, and offer a different critical opinion but never in a way that I could object to. Her written work was of a very high standard – mature, well-argued and presented, quoting different authorities and making a clear and coherent argument.[73]

Gillian Soulby, who studied art with Abbott, recalls, 'She was very good at art, we spent a lot of time in the art room together. She had a very distinctive style – like Henry Moore's drawings, lots of lines giving form to a shape.' Apparently, she signed her paintings 'Dabbott'. Together, with four others, Abbott helped paint a series of murals at Roxbourne Hospital for Geriatric Patients over the Easter holidays of 1971. The project was featured twice in the *Harrow Observer*, which carried photographs of the girls and two of their five murals. Abbott also wrote about the initiative in the 1971 edition of the school magazine in an article entitled 'Social Service'. Apparently, the murals were part of a broader initiative in the school which encouraged students to engage with the community. Abbott wrote:

> Recently there was a debate in school as to whether the school curriculum bore any relevance to life; this new Community Service scheme shows that some attempt, at least, is being made to relate the work done in school to life and the community, and that part of the school, at least, has the opportunity of discovering the reality of being part of a community.[74]

The opening line is almost certainly a reference to the school debating society. Gillian Soulby, who was one of the group who painted the mural, recalls Abbott was an active member of the society.

> Diane could be quite outspoken ... She wasn't popular with a lot of the staff. It was a very traditional girl's grammar school, and we weren't encouraged to discuss things – we didn't do much public speaking. The debating society was quite poorly attended, it wasn't a big thing at all. Diane did like debating, and she wasn't afraid to express her views, and she was the only black girl in the school. Diane wasn't afraid to put her head above the parapet, and that didn't go down well with the old female staff in the school.[75]

Abbott's willingness to speak her mind was noted in her school reference. Writing in late 1972, Abbott's headmistress stated:

> Diane Abbott has shown, from a relatively young age, powers of
> penetrating insight, mature understanding and a capacity for ab-
> stract reasoning which have marked her as a rare pupil. She has a
> quick mind and unusual independence of judgement, though the
> tenacity of her personality, not to say stubbornness at times, occa-
> sionally has led her to persevere in somewhat idiosyncratic views
> which she nevertheless, argues with great cogency … She is blessed
> with a sense of humour which makes her a witty and provocative
> conversationalist.[76]

The school magazine records that the debating society was in a
'dormant state' until Abbott entered the upper sixth, becoming its
vice-chair. The magazine records that in the first debate of the new
school year, 'the irrepressible Miss D. Abbott surprisingly opposed
the motion that "Oxford and Cambridge occupy a justifiable position
in the Educational System" but was characteristically victorious'.[77]
The school debating team also took on Harrow County Boys' School,
defeating them in a debate on the topic of women's liberation. Some
students joined the society opportunistically, in order to mention it
on their university applications. Abbott, by contrast, really shone in
the debates. Wilkey comments, 'She was flamboyant. She was really
good at debate, good at speaking up and speaking out.'[78]

Abbott's final years at Harrow County Girls seem to have been
extraordinarily active. The school magazine records that she wrote
the 'grand finale' for the Christmas show. The piece, 'Marylou', was
'loosely based on the Hollywood musicals (the theme being the rise
to fame of Marylou after she went to the big city and her consequent
romance with Irvine Oppenheimer)'. Abbott's finale

> brought the house down with laughter as many unrehearsed things
> happened, such as the continuous reintroduction of 'the little girl
> wonder' and 'the lunettes' while Diane, who played Marylou,

struggled into her dress, which eventually slithered down while she was singing the final song, and had to be hastily held up by someone behind her before it went any further![79]

Abbott also played a leading role in the sixth form society, organising 'a lavish tea' with some of the Harrow Boys' sixth form. 'The intrepid Diane Abbott and Catherine Wilkey' are credited with surpassing the students from the boys' school in terms of their organisation.[80]

Collaborations with the boys' school brought Abbott into contact with Michael Portillo and Clive Anderson. Decades before they shared a sofa on *This Week*, Portillo and Abbott starred as Lord and Lady Macduff in Portillo's first attempt to make a film. Indeed, Portillo claims that he gave Abbott her first ever screen test for the part. Students from the two schools got together as part of Convergence, a theatrical group formed while Abbott was still in the lower fifth. Looking back on the joint ventures, Abbott's contemporary Gill Cook recalls, 'Most of the girls went there because of the boys.' It was through the group, Cook says, that 'Diane became friendly with quite a few of the boys'.[81] From Abbott's point of view, the group was about the drama, but it was also 'a legitimate way for boys from the boys' school to meet the girls from the girls' school'.[82] Convergence put on a production of *Hamlet* in April 1971, which starred Clive Anderson as Laertes. Appropriately for a future Conservative politician, Michael Portillo was the show's business manager and head of the publicity team.[83]

Abbott also joined the editorial board of the school magazine in her final year. Cook, who was also on the magazine's board, recalls that the teachers helped, contacting sponsors such as NatWest Bank and the local paper to raise the money to produce the magazine, and liaised with the printers, but the students selected the articles and artwork themselves. The editorial, which Abbott co-wrote, had a clearly political tone:

The editorial committee considered putting forward its views on the situation in the Middle East, a solution to the Irish question, a cure for all our economic ills but unfortunately, those in the corridors of power are unlikely to hear about, still less to attend to and act on, any editorial opinion of ours.[84]

Abbott was just as active outside school. Her mother made sure that the children went to church. 'There was a period in my life when I was a Sunday school teacher,' Abbott recalls. 'Some might say that was the pinnacle of my achievements!'[85] She also wrote about religion twice in the school magazine. One piece on the Open Religious Society, a group open to Christians, Jews, all believers and non-believers at the school, indicates that she attended lectures from missionaries, theologians from London Bible College, as well as talks on the relationship between religion and science. The article praises 'invaluable social work the mission performs as the inevitable accompaniment of preaching the gospel'. The second piece, concerning a visit to the Radha Krishna Temple, concludes, 'The Radha Krishna cult does not appeal to me personally, but it has brought purpose and contentment into the lives of the people we saw.'[86]

Abbott was clearly fascinated by politics as a teenager. A school reference written late in 1972 notes that 'she has an informed interest in matters social, political and artistic'.[87] Nor was her interest merely academic. It was in her final years at secondary school that Abbott became politically active. 'My earliest participatory radicalisation was around the women's movement. I was reading *Spare Rib*, I was a feminist, so I joined a women's group in Edgware.'[88] However, this first experience of political organisation was not a happy one. Abbott attended regularly until a discussion turned to booking a black male stripper for a fundraiser. Abbott concluded that 'maybe I don't identify with *this* group of feminists' and stopped attending.[89]

The early 1970s was also a time when black politics achieved a new salience in Britain. Martin Luther King's visit in 1964 and Malcolm X's visit in 1965 led to the creation of transient political groups. However, Stokely Carmichael's visit in 1967 was the real turning point. Carmichael came to prominence as chair of the Student Non-violent Coordinating Committee, which emerged from the sit-in movement of 1960. By 1967 Carmichael was the honorary prime

minister of the Black Panther Party, and one of the leading expo-
nents of Black Power. His visit galvanised black radicals in Britain,
leading to the creation of a British Black Panther movement, as
well as groups such as the Black Unity and Freedom Party, and the
Fasimba.[90] The election of a Conservative government in 1970 led
to the enactment of legislation realising Enoch Powell's twin goals:
stricter immigration laws and provisions for repatriation. Although
the Immigration Act of 1971 was the third such act in a decade, it
broke new ground. For the first time in modern British history racial
categories were introduced into British law. The Act distinguished
between 'patrials', people whose grandparents were born in Britain,
and 'non-patrials', people who did not have British grandparents.
'Patrials' – which included white people living in Australia, Canada
and New Zealand – could come and go as they pleased. 'Non-
patrials', the vast majority of whom were black and Asian, faced
significant new restrictions. Moreover, 'non-patrials' could be repat-
riated within ten years of their arrival. The 1971 Act exposed what
was implicit in Powellite arguments: not all immigrants were equal.
White immigrants were welcome; black and Asian immigrants were
an existential threat to the nation.

The 1971 Immigration Act was not passed without a fight. In the
spring of 1971, Britain's new Black Power groups organised to protest
the new law, along with older groups such as the Supreme Council of
Sikhs, the Indian Workers' Association and the West Indian Standing Conference. Black Power groups also marched through central
London in August 1971 in protest at the killing of George Jackson,
and the imprisonment of Angela Davis. Black Power also scored a
notable victory at the end of the year. The Mangrove Nine, a group of
black radicals – including Altheia Jones-LeCointe, a leading figure in
the British Panthers; Darcus Howe, who would go on to become one
of Britain's best known black radicals; and Frank Crichlow, a beloved
and central figure in Notting Hill's black community – took on the
Metropolitan Police in court, which led to the first judicial acknowledgement that there was 'evidence of racial hatred' in the police. The
Mangrove campaign was not merely a legal fight, several of the group

toured the country making their case, and the Panthers organised demonstrations by black women outside the Old Bailey.[91]

'Community Relations' was a vexed issue in Harrow in 1971. Public meetings were organised by black locals in July and November, in an attempt to persuade local councillors that racism was a reality in the area. The second meeting was arranged by Tony Mathews, a migrant from Jamaica, in response to the ongoing activities of Oswald Mosley's Union Movement in Harrow. The local authority finally agreed to set up a community council in December 1971, despite the delaying tactics of two Conservative councillors. The local press also responded to local pressure by publishing a feature on recent migrants to the area under the title 'Peaceful co-existence'. Ominously, the term used by the *Harrow Observer* to describe the relationship between Asian families and their white neighbours was borrowed from the vocabulary of the Cold War.

Perhaps as a result of the heightened attention paid to race and immigration in public debate, perhaps as a result of the activities of Black Power groups, Abbott became interested in black politics in the early 1970s. Tommie Smith and John Carlos's Black Power salute at the 1968 Olympics was her first encounter with Black Power: 'I remember it very clearly, and it having a big impact on me.' Abbott was never a member of any of the Black Power groups, but she kept an eye on what was going on in the movement. 'There was nothing in the library about it, and nothing on the television, there wasn't an online world. So as a teenager before I went to university, I relied completely on the black bookshop movement, and *Race Today* to understand what was happening in the world of black politics.'[92] In the late 1960s, a number of radical black bookshops opened across London. New Beacon Books, founded by John La Rose and Sarah White, opened a shop in Finsbury Park, around the corner from the Black Panther's north London base in Tollington Park. Around the same time Jessica and Eric Huntley founded Bogle-L'Ouverture Publications. In the early days, Bogle-L'Ouverture was based in a room at the Huntley's west London home, before they established a shop in Chignell Place, West Ealing. Abbott remembers that New Beacon and Bogle-L'Ouverture were the places to go to find out what was going on in black politics in Britain. As well as publishing new work, the shops distributed flyers and magazines which promoted grassroots campaigns. In the early 1970s, Abbott also became a regular reader of *Race Today*. 'Race Today and *Spare Rib* were my Bibles for left activism. As a young woman, *Race Today* meant a lot to me. It let people know what was going on, it made ideas about race readily available and resonant.'[93]

The trial of the Mangrove Nine, which ran from September to December 1971, was covered extensively in *Race Today*, as well as other counter-cultural magazines such as *Time Out* and the *International Times*. The Mangrove campaign also gained significant coverage in the broadsheets.[94] Abbott was in the upper sixth at the time and made a trip to the Old Bailey to sit in the public gallery to watch the trial. Encouraging black people to attend the trial was part of the Nine's political strategy. In a democracy, justice must be seen to be fair. The power of the public gallery was not lost on the Nine, who determined from the outset of the trial to use the presence of black people in the courtroom, to signal to the judge and jury that the defendants had the support of the community, and that the black community would be scrutinising the trial and the verdict. Abbott attended the trial and remembers it as the first time that she saw Darcus Howe, who later became a friend. She also took her sketchbook and sketched strangers on the Tube, the defendants and the court officials.

In the summer after her A Level exams, Abbott and some friends took a holiday to the Isle of Wight. Abbott went with a group of young women, many of whom had worked with her either on the murals at Roxbourne Hospital or on the school magazine. Preparations were extensive. The plan was to get a train from Harrow on the Hill to Leatherhead, then to walk to Southampton, staying at youth hostels along the way before taking the ferry to the Isle of Wight. All did not go according to plan. The trip began badly, Wilkey recalls, when 'we were inappropriately clad and inappropriately shod! There were four or five of us, we all met at Harrow on the Hill station. We were all carrying way too much, so we jettisoned a lot of what we had when we realised we couldn't carry it.'[95] The walking element of the holiday was quickly abandoned and the group decided to rely on buses, a decision which ate into their meagre funds.[96] Nonetheless, they made it to the Isle of Wight and back, drawing a veil over their use of public transport when they recounted their exploits to family and friends back home.

At the end of the summer, Abbott's A Level results were good. The school magazine records that she was one of two young women to come joint top of the year, with four A Levels, for three of which she received distinctions, a result which set her up for an application to Cambridge.

Looking back, Abbott argues that her background and early experiences informed her politics. First, her commitment to decent education for all flows from her own experience of school.

> Education is really important. My parents left school at fourteen. The thing which enabled me to go further and higher was entirely my education. Education is a liberating force. Education gives you confidence, and if you are a black girl from north London, you have to have something that can enable you to walk into a room of white middle-class people without crumpling. I had a certain rural Jamaican confidence, but it was also the fact that I knew that I had as good an education as anyone.[97]

Improving education has been an important aspect of Abbott's work as an MP: in fact, she regards the opening of five secondary schools in Hackney during the New Labour era as one of her proudest achievements. It also explains why so much of the policy development that Abbott was involved in as shadow Minister for Public Health focused on schools and the life chances of children. London Schools and the Black Child, an initiative that Abbott founded in 1999, also reflects her conviction that education, particularly for black children, can be liberating.

On a deeper level, Abbott's politics are shaped by the experience of being the child of migrants. 'My parents were economic migrants, so whenever I take part in the debate about migration, I'm very aware, and sometimes some commentators aren't, these people are real people, just trying to do the best for their children.'[98] As the daughter of migrants, Abbott's presence in Britain, her access to education and healthcare, her experience in school were all politicised, particularly after Powell's 1968 speech and the 1971 Immigration Act, which translated Powell's rhetoric into law. The immigration debate, which often had racist overtones, has been part of British politics, part of western politics ever since, informing the electoral strategies of major political parties, accounting for the emergence of new political groups, and feeding into debates about Europe. The importance of immigration is clear from the flood of immigration laws passed, by Conservative and Labour governments. Since Abbott's parents arrived in Britain 1951, new immigration laws were introduced in the 1960s, 1970s, 1980s and 1990s, not to mention the swarm of laws passed under Blair and Brown.

In a sense, the immigration debates which have raged from the 1950s are merely a rehearsal for debates to come; debates which will reckon with the displacement of millions of people due to climate change and environmental degradation. Since entering Parliament in 1987, Abbott has consistently championed the rights of migrants as human beings, while some politicians have wanted to draw sharp distinctions between the rights of 'patrials' and 'non-patrials', between 'aliens' and 'citizens', or between 'the native Anglo-Saxon stock' and the 'swarm of people' who have no right to a safe haven. In a world where migration is shaped by extreme scarcity and a growing climate crisis, Britain has a choice between the politics which Abbott has championed, which recognises the humanity of migrants; and the rhetoric of walls and permits, of sprawling detention centres and barbed wire refugee camps.

CHAPTER 2

CAMBRIDGE: THE MAKING OF DIANE ABBOTT

The essential shape of the Cambridge history degree was determined in the 1870s. Cambridge University, unlike almost any other in the world, chose to teach political science through history. Consequently, history students could study not only the history of political thought but also theories of state and, by the early 1970s, modern political philosophy. It was this combination of history and politics that attracted Abbott. 'I'd always loved history, but history at Cambridge enabled me to read about, to talk about, and to study politics. There was no PPE [philosophy, politics and economics] at Cambridge, so history was the degree that allowed me to do that.'[1]

Deciding to study history was one thing; deciding to study at Cambridge was another. In part, Abbott's decision was motivated by her reading. From her early teens, she had been a voracious reader and the novels she read were full of characters who went to Oxford or Cambridge. Swift's Gulliver, Austen's Mr Darcy and Mr Wickham all went to Cambridge, while Wodehouse's Bertie Wooster, Fitzgerald's Gatsby and a host of others went to Oxford. So, Abbott picked up the message that anybody who was anybody went to one of Britain's two ancient universities. The choice of Cambridge was influenced by a school trip. Every year, older students at Harrow County School for Girls could choose from a number of excursions. Abbott opted for Cambridge, with the express purpose of touring the university. It made a major impression: 'subconsciously I was swept up by the architecture and the look of the place'.[2] Great St Mary's Church, the geographical centre of the university, stands on King's Parade, and the area is quintessentially Cambridge, with King's College Chapel and Senate House dominating the scene. For Abbott, visiting King's Parade for the first time, there was also something about the students, who in their stripy scarfs seemed like 'gods and goddesses', or at least 'people from another state of being'.[3] The place, the idea of the place, and joining the community of scholars were all enormously attractive to seventeen-year-old Abbott. However, Cambridge was not the only university on her radar. Her second choice was Oxford – to study history at either Wadham College or St Hugh's – where she would have been a near contemporary of Theresa May.[4]

Then, as now, getting into Cambridge was no mean feat. Abbott, however, faced more obstacles than most. There was no formal prohibition on young black women from the working class gaining a place at Cambridge, but the nature of the school system, as well as the nature of the Cambridge entrance exam, favoured white men from private schools. First, in 1973, only six of the university's thirty colleges admitted women: Newnham, Girton, and Newhall admitted women only, while King's, Clare, and Churchill were 'co-residential'. Consequently, only 16 per cent of Cambridge undergraduates were women.[5] The proportion of female undergraduates had risen in the late 1960s, but as Edward Heath's government cut university funding in the early 1970s, Cambridge responded by halting initiatives to increase female recruitment. The fact that Cambridge was so male-dominated had a knock-on effect on secondary schools and sixth forms. This was clear enough in Harrow. While Harrow County School for Boys had a long history of sending students to Oxford and Cambridge, and therefore had teachers who were well versed in guiding their students through the process, there was no tradition and little expectation that students at the girls' school would go on to Oxbridge. As a result, Abbott's teachers had nothing like the expertise of their counterparts at the boys' school. Indeed, their understanding of Cambridge would prove decades out of date.

Turning to class, in 1973 around 5 per cent of working-class young people went to university, compared to just over 30 per cent of those from higher status socio-economic groups.[6] This percentage of working-class students was much smaller at Oxford and Cambridge. Latin was one of the barriers to admittance. All students applying for arts subjects sat a compulsory Latin paper as part of the entrance exam. Abbott opines that it was 'one of the methods by which Oxford and Cambridge keep most working-class students, and many state school students out'. Students from private and public schools had a huge advantage. In the early 1970s, although only around 7 per cent of students in the country were privately educated, private school students made up around 60 per cent of Cambridge undergraduates.[7] Fortunately, Abbott had studied Latin at O Level.

Finally, Abbott had to persuade her school to support her application. This was essential, as in the 1970s students from state schools stayed on for a term after their A Levels to prepare for the Oxford and Cambridge entrance exams and for the interview process. Academically, Abbott was one of the best students in the school, but in spite of this she faced an uphill struggle.

> I remember going up to my head of year and saying that I wanted to do the Oxford and Cambridge entrance. My teacher looked at me in horror and said, 'I don't think you're up to it.' And this was a fateful moment for me. Fortunately, my quite assertive Jamaican heritage kicked in and I said, 'But I do, and that's what matters, isn't it?' It changed the course of my life.[8]

This was one of the clearest examples of racism that Abbott experienced at school. With the utmost reluctance, Abbott was allowed to stay on for the 'seventh term', which she spent revising and extending her command of Latin. One other young woman, a white student, also stayed on for the autumn term of 1972. Abbott recalls that her head of year lavished attention on the white student and 'only taught me under duress'. The advice given to the two students underlines the attitude of the school: Abbott was told to apply to Newnham College, whereas the other student was groomed for the more prestigious

Girton. Gill Sutherland, director of studies for history at Newnham in the early 1970s, suggests that this was an extremely dated mis-apprehension: 'Folklore had it, in the late nineteenth century, that Girton was for ladies and Newnham was for governesses.'⁹ There was little basis for this perception, but before 1914 it was easier for young women of slender means to go to Newnham, leading to gossip among the anxious middle classes about what kinds of students went to the two colleges.

In mid-December 1972, Abbott went to Newnham for her inter-view, which was conducted in the study of one of the college's history scholars. The interview was both intimidating and inspiring. 'I re-member my interviewer was wearing these smart blue shoes, because for a lot of the interview I was looking at her feet, because it's an intimidating thing, an Oxbridge interview.'¹⁰ It was a new experience in other ways too. The interviewer was a writer, and her books were on display. For the first time in her life Abbott, who harboured an ambi-tion to write, came face to face with an author. The interviewers were impressed, one noting, 'I thought this girl a definite possibility. Eager – a bit sprawling. But might come on quite well. Definitely interested in art history. Talked intelligently about it.'¹¹ Her second interviewer concurred: 'Passionate enthusiasm, v. good on uses of RK [religious knowledge] to historian. Is stubborn – but determined. Worth having a go at.'¹² In early 1974, Abbott received an offer to study history at Newnham College.

Newnham College was founded in 1871 by suffragist Millicent Faw-cett and utilitarian philosopher Henry Sidgwick as part of a campaign to gain equal rights for women within the university. Although the college was founded with radical intentions, it embodied a particular view of a woman's place in the world. Newnham was designed and built on the model of the home. Rather than being designed as a large single institution, the college was conceived as a series of buildings. According to the original plan, each of these houses had a sitting room and a communal dining room, in an attempt to create an intimate family atmosphere. By the time Abbott joined the college, Newnham was made up of Old Hall, Sidgwick, Kennedy and Peile Hall, where

Abbott lived for her three years as an undergraduate. Each of the student rooms had a small gas fire and students shared a small kitchen and a bathroom. Covered corridors connected the different parts of the college. These were conceived to protect the young women from the elements and to ensure privacy. This sense of seclusion was heightened by the layout of the buildings which faced onto central gardens, again creating a private sphere cut off from the outside. While the college had been extended and modernised since the First World War, it still embodied a Victorian conception of architecture for women.[13]

One aspect of getting into Cambridge was straightforward: having won a place Abbott received a full grant, covering her university fees, college fees and a living allowance. Tuition fees for all students were paid by local authorities. The maintenance grant was means-tested, and due to the level of her parents' income Abbott received a full grant. This was crucial, as without the grant Cambridge would have remained out of reach. Certainly, her father would never have countenanced taking on the debt. The Abbotts, after all, had no credit card. If they did not have the money, they saved. In addition to the grant, Abbott recalls that it was easy to pick up a job in the holidays, and that if that proved impossible, undergraduates could sign on and get unemployment benefits over the summer break. All in all, it was a wholly different financial regime.

Abbott was one of 110 freshers who matriculated at Newnham in October 1973. For much of its history, the college made no attempt to monitor the ethnicity of its students. Nonetheless, based on a careful reading of college records, Abbott appears to have been the second black student ever to have attended. Eight of Newnham's first year students in Abbott's year studied history.

University life was a culture shock. Comparing Cambridge with the world she had left she was 'struck by the contrast between the people with nothing, and the people at the top', which taught her that 'the world is a wildly unfair place'. Some of Abbott's school friends remember Harrow County School for Girls as being 'a bit posh', but Newnham was something else again. As far as Abbott was concerned a great deal of college life was simply baffling. 'Cambridge was a law unto itself. There were endless rules and regulations, like when you had to wear your gown.'[14] Her first meeting with her tutor also caught her off guard. Arriving at her tutor's rooms at noon, she was offered a glass of wine. 'This was a new life. In our house we had a bottle of Cyprus sherry, which lasted for months.'[15] Formal college dinners began with toasts to the Queen, and the founders and benefactors of the college, there were regular formal dinners at which students and fellows wore gowns, and the students themselves organised sherry parties. Jill Lewis, who was a graduate student at Newnham at the time recalls, 'There was a sense of being among women from wealthy backgrounds. The woman in the room beside me spoke a bit like the Queen, obviously had money and knew the Duke of Marlborough.'[16]

Newnham's student magazine gives an impression of the activities available to students at the time. The Junior Common Room (JCR) Committee, which looked after the welfare of the college's undergrads, organised punting, university challenge trials, a croquet club, a squash club and a student fiction library. The college also had a boat club, which organised competitive rowing and sculling, as well as tennis courts, a cigarette machine and a Victorian observatory, which were available to students.[17]

'One of the rules', Abbott recalls, 'was that we weren't allowed to have any man – boyfriend or otherwise – in our room overnight. We were allowed male guests during the day, but they had to be out by 10 p.m. There was only one entrance, so it was well-nigh impossible to sneak a man in at night, and I certainly never tried.'[18] Newnham undergraduates speculated that the narrow single beds and thin walls were further deterrents for overnight guests. Perhaps the prohibition against male guests is overstated; certainly, Sutherland comments that the rule tended to be 'honoured in the breach'. In any case, Newnham was a different world to the one Abbott had known in north London.

I had led a relatively sheltered life. I was part of a working-class West Indian family who mostly, if not entirely, socialised with other working-class West Indians. My reading ranged far and wide, but my personal experience was relatively sheltered. So you go up to

Cambridge, and Jesus Christ almighty! There's all these posh white girls. I remember sitting in hall and hearing a girl talk about her family's country cottage, my head nearly fell off! Most people I knew lived in a flat.[19]

Before going to university, Abbott's world view was shaped, in part, by the *Daily Mirror*, which presented Britain as 'a wide egalitarian world where anything is possible'. The reality of Cambridge, which exposed the limits of British egalitarianism, was beyond Abbott's experience.

This alien world caused Abbott to retreat, at least in her first term. Her abiding memory of the early days is eating toast alone in her room in Peile Hall. Being 'effortlessly top at Harrow' did not prepare her for Cambridge, where she was one of many brilliant students. During the Christmas holiday of 1973–74, she seriously considered leaving, but a friend encouraged her to keep going. Having returned at the beginning of 1974, Abbott began to find her feet. Nonetheless, there were fewer opportunities for her to contribute to university life than there had been at school. During her Harrow County Girls days, she had written for the school magazine, written and starred in plays, been part of the debating society and taken every opportunity to mix with boys from the neighbouring school. Things were different at Cambridge, where in spite of their privileges, female undergraduates were at a considerable disadvantage. Judith Kampfner, a history student at Girton and friend of Abbott, recalls:

There was a huge gap between the women and the men. There was a huge sense that the men, even if they came from comprehensives, were part of the inside world, and we were the outsiders. Our colleges didn't have anything like their endowments and didn't have anything like their facilities. As a woman who was there at the time, you had to be quite pushy. Things were stacked against you, and you had to fight.[20]

Female students, Kampfner argues, had to work around the university and college authorities to get the best supervisors, or to get funding to put on plays, in a way that male students never had to. Kampfner's recollections chime with the 1974 *Alternative Prospectus*, which states simply:

> Cambridge University is a sexist institution ... Women are discriminated against when they try to get into it, and, once in, are often made to feel that they don't really belong here but must work exceptionally hard to justify their place. The women's colleges ... [are] the poor sisters of the richer men's colleges.'[21]

The sexism of university life was clear from the predominance of all-male university societies, from the behaviour of members of the Pitt Club, which was notorious for hiring black female strippers, and from what *Alternative Prospectus* describes as the 'male-cultural ethos of large sections of the university which thrive on the football/cricket teams, [and] drunken parties in college bars'.[22] There were also obstacles to writing for at least some of the student newspapers. Kampfner remembers writing a book review for the magazine *Broadsheet*, only to be told 'that I didn't have a "male sense of humour" and therefore I was fired'.[23]

Whatever the drawbacks of being at a women's college, Abbott doesn't regret the experience. 'It helped to strengthen and reinforce my feminism. The thing about a women's college is that you see women in leadership roles, in a way that I wouldn't have seen had I gone to King's or one of the mixed colleges.'[24]

UNIVERSITY POLITICS

Abbott did get involved in a number of initiatives during her time at Cambridge, but a great deal of the political life of the university left her cold and she tended to steer clear of student politics, which had a dual character. Traditional societies, such as the Cambridge Union Society, were male dominated and conservative. The fact that Enoch Powell was honorary president of the Cambridge University Conservative Association is an indication of the nature of at least some aspects of student politics at Cambridge. The Cambridge Union Society was the university's largest political society. It hosted regular debates, and during Abbott's time at Cambridge speakers included Edward Heath and Margaret Thatcher.

While the Cambridge Union has never been as prestigious as its Oxford counterpart, many of the union's presidents have gone on to have successful political careers. Former presidents include Rab Butler, Michael Howard, Ken Clarke, Leon Brittan, Baroness Hayman and Vince Cable. Abbott attended a few debates at the Union Society and spoke from the floor during the course of one of the debates in her first term. It was an unpleasant experience: 'Everyone got quite frenzied because a black woman was speaking. I found it off-putting.' Although she was not a regular at debates, one of her interventions made quite a stir. Abbott challenged Max Beloff, the Liberal politician and principal of the privately owned University of Buckingham. Her director of studies later cited this as an example of Abbott's 'assured, lively and enterprising' approach to her studies.[25] However, she rarely took part in Union Society debates. 'You have to have quite a strong stomach for it. It's full of people preparing to give speeches in the House of Commons and be important people in the outside world.' Union Society debates were essentially detached from reality; the political debates were for show. 'I observed it, but that self-important preening has never appealed to me.'[26]

Away from the traditional societies, however, Cambridge was also a radical place in the early 1970s. Beginning in earnest the year before Abbott arrived at Newnham, there were protests around the Conservative government's refusal to increase the student grant. Margaret Thatcher fought back with proposals to cut the expansion of universities, as well as to regulate and defund student unions. The early 1970s were also dominated by the fallout of a series of sit-ins demanding curriculum reform and student representation, particularly that the university recognise the newly formed Students' Union. There was also the beginning of a rent strike movement. These issues remained unresolved when Abbott arrived at Cambridge.

In Abbott's first term, university politics also swung left. A student squatter's movement took over the Owl Croft buildings, and in so doing saved them from demolition. Left-wing candidates won control of the Students' Union. While the Union Society had been founded in 1815 and had a very establishment feel, the Students' Union, which represented all students in higher education in the city, was only a couple of years old and was much more amenable to the radicalism of the early 1970s. The student magazine *Stop Press*, later *Stop Press with Varsity*, gives a flavour of early 1970s student radicalism, with opinion pieces on women's rights, gay rights and the evils of apartheid.

Enoch Powell's visit to Cambridge in October 1974 reignited debate over the toleration of racist speakers on campus. In April, the National Union of Students (NUS) had agreed a motion that 'fascist or racist' speakers should be barred from universities by 'whatever means are necessary'. However, the Cambridge Students' Union had refused to implement the ban and Powell's visit sparked protest. In response, the Conservative students decided to hold the meeting at a secret location, to avoid disruption. Speaking to *Stop Press with Varsity*, Archie Norman, who would later become a successful businessman and Tory MP, defended Powell's visit on the basis that he would be talking about the common market rather than immigration, adding that 'it is nonsense to describe Enoch Powell as a racist'.[27]

There was undoubtedly some interest in race in Cambridge student politics, though it had little to do with black people who lived in Britain, generally focusing instead on opposing apartheid. Cambridge students protested over the university's rugby team's 1974 South Africa tour. There was also a sustained campaign to expose the university's financial ties to South Africa. In 1974 Action for South Africa scored its first victory by forcing Churchill College to divest themselves of their shares in South African companies and to commit to making no further investments until apartheid was abolished. At the same time there were campaigns against Barclays Bank in protest at their ties to the regime. Similar protests were organised about university ties to Ian Smith's regime in Rhodesia. Notably, there was little enthusiasm for the battle against apartheid at Abbott's college. The Newnham College magazine reports that its students had not sent a representative to the Action for South Africa committee.

Students concerned with race also campaigned for Cambridge colleges to offer scholarships to black students. Notably, these were exclusively for black students who lived in Britain's former African colonies. Four Cambridge colleges had scholarship schemes for black students from South Africa at the time Abbott arrived in Cambridge. Following pressure from the Students' Union, similar schemes were set up in two other colleges in Abbott's second year. The creation of scholarships for black students from South Africa and Rhodesia was less radical than it looked, however. First, as the scholarships were awarded to 'suitably qualified students' and black people in South Africa and Rhodesia were routinely denied a decent education, these schemes rarely led to black students attending Cambridge. Existing research indicates that no black student was awarded any of these fellowships during the 1970s.[28] Second, the scholarships were conceived for students who came from and would return to Africa. This kind of arrangement was explicitly endorsed by Powell. As Powell said in his 'Rivers of Blood' speech, he objected to the 'settlement' of black and Asian people in Britain but had no objection to 'the entry of Commonwealth citizens ... for the purposes of study or of improving their qualifications' as these students 'are not, and never have been, immigrants'.[29] The notion that a small number of black people from the Caribbean and Africa would be educated in Britain and then return to the colonies and take up positions in the colonial administration was accepted practice.

In Abbott's experience, there were hardly any black people at the university. In her three years at Cambridge she met one other black student, a chance meeting in the stacks at the University Library. 'It was extraordinary, for three years at Cambridge University and you just didn't see any black people. You certainly didn't see any British black people; the guy I met was a postgraduate from overseas. It was an extraordinarily white environment.'[30]

During Abbott's first year, there seems to have been an increase in feminist activity on campus. The first issue of *Stop Press with Varsity* published during Abbott's time at Cambridge contained a long piece, simply entitled 'Women', written by four female students, which dealt with the prejudices that young women encountered. These included the assumption that they were 'gifted in intuitive response, fluid, irrational, imprecise in our thought', and how female undergrads were expected to be 'womanish coquettes' by their male counterparts on campus. In response to the growth of the Society for the Protection of Unborn Children, the Students' Union organised campaigns to defend abortion rights. There were protests against Roy Jenkins's white paper 'Equality for Women', the precursor to the Sex Discrimination Act 1975, which contained exemptions allowing Oxford and Cambridge colleges to remain single sex. Protests took the form of street theatre, male students marching through the city dressed as women, and occupations.

Jill Lewis's election as president of the Cambridge Students' Union in November 1973 was an important victory for women in the university. Lewis went on to be the first female student to speak at the university's Senate House. The first woman to win the presidency, her time in the role was short, not least because of the abuse she received. There was also a direct-action campaign against colleges which refused to admit women. Lewis was involved in the occupation of Christ's College. She explains:

> Discussions were going on in the men's colleges about whether to admit women. The fellows of Christ's College had this discussion, and voted not to let women in. We had a mole in the meeting, and they cited not only the classic reason that women would distract men, but that it would cost too much to fit mirrors and hairdryers in the bedrooms! … They all went that evening to Formal Hall, and we burst in and started singing songs. Judy [one of the protestors] marched up to the front to the elderly Dons and shouted at them, 'Just because you've got fucking balls!' I remember thinking, 'Oh my God there's no going back on this.'[31]

Having interrupted dinner, the activists occupied the junior common room and barricaded themselves in. During the occupation the whole college was surrounded by the police. Following the occupation of

Christ's College, even the rumour that student activists were planning an event would bring police out onto the streets. Newnham's students were at the forefront of women's liberation in Cambridge. Their student magazines *Next to None* and *Nimfo* ran vociferous campaigns to persuade recalcitrant colleges to admit women and to end all-male university societies.[32]

Sexism was hardwired into almost all areas of university life. Lewis explains:

> As a woman, you had to work bloody hard to prove yourself. There was nothing covert about the sexism of some of the academics. As an undergraduate, I had overworked dons screaming at me, 'They should never have let women in. It's a waste of money, in a few years' time you'll be slaving over a washing machine. Women can't think!' The fact that you were a woman was used to delegitimise you.[33]

Early in her time at Cambridge, Abbott joined a college women's group, but her experience was not encouraging. The group, as was common for small university societies, met in a student bedroom. Needless to say, Abbott was the only black member. Abbott attended regularly for a while, until at one meeting the group met with a working-class woman who was introduced as being 'from the town', a local, rather than someone involved in the university. Abbott recalls that the feminists looked at this working-class woman 'like she was a fucking laboratory specimen'. 'That was my second encounter with white feminism, and that was enough. My experiences with white women's groups were not auspicious. They didn't put me off feminism, but these weren't a form of feminism I could relate to.'[34] Though she quit the group, Abbott kept reading, and remembers Kate Millett's *Sexual Politics* and Germaine Greer's *The Female Eunuch* as being important in her intellectual development.

Cambridge politics was also very insular. Student magazines devoted pages to the controversies between different campus groups and to student union elections. But they only covered the political issues of the day in so far as they impinged on student life, or if frontbench politicians spoke at the Union Society. To give one example, *Stop Press with Varsity* barely covered the Common Market referendum of 1975. Again, this did not make university politics attractive to Abbott, who was, as Sutherland recalls, 'very alert and alive to a host of current political issues'.[35]

For all of Abbott's distaste for the preening and theatricality of the Union Society, and the privilege of middle-class campus feminism, there may have been another reason why she did not get involved in student politics. Lewis's time as president of the Students' Union shows just how much abuse politically active women received on campus. Four weeks after her election as president she stepped down. Looking back, Lewis recalls the abuse starting during the election campaign, when her right-wing opponents put out leaflets stating 'VOTE FOR THE LEFT and you'll get to FUCK JILL LEWIS'. Having been elected, her right-wing critics refused to recognise her legitimacy, insisting that she had been elected on her looks alone. Writing in *Stop Press with Varsity* shortly after her resignation, Lewis explained that as president her opponents dismissed her because she was a woman, ogled her because she was a woman, or patronised her because she was a woman. Even among her male allies, there were some who struggled to recognise her authority. What is more, there was constant speculation and continual enquiries, from male students and academics, about the nature of her sex life.

While Abbott played little part in student politics, she was active within the Faculty of History. Debates in the Union Society were purely theatrical. Working within the structures of the university, by contrast, had the potential to lead to real change.

STUDENT MEMBER OF THE BOARD

Calls for student representation in Cambridge picked up in 1970, with a mass demonstration outside Senate House, and the beginnings of negotiations between radical students and the Vice-Chancellor Owen Chadwick. The university moved slowly. Within the history faculty, the possibility of student representation was first discussed in October

1968, but it was not until 1974, after six years of protest and negotiations, that it was agreed that three student representatives would be elected annually to the history faculty board. In January 1975, Abbott was one of the first undergraduates to confirm her intention to stand.

Judith Kampfner, who seconded Abbott's nomination, remembers her as 'strong and bold, ambitious and excited by interesting ideas. She really stood out as someone who had a sense of mission, someone who was determined not to go quietly.'[36] Kampfner's experience of Cambridge was that these were the kinds of qualities that female undergraduates needed to succeed in a university which was largely run by and for men. 'She was very aware of being in a minority, and quite vocal about it, quite angry about it, and determined to change things. I think there were two things that made her angry, the lack of representation of women of colour, and the way that women were put down.'

On 27 January 1975, following a short campaign, Abbott topped the poll and was elected the first student member to the history faculty board – her first election victory.[37] Turnout across the university was low, rarely exceeding 30 per cent, and Abbott was elected on a 15 per cent turnout. *Stop Press with Varsity*, which had been monitoring the elections keenly, argued that this was not to do with student apathy but could be blamed on the university authorities, which had done nothing to alert students to the process, and in some instances, had hidden ballot boxes in inaccessible locations. Abbott won her election convincingly, topping the poll with forty-five of the ninety-eight votes cast.[38]

Serving as student member of the history faculty board involved none of the theatrics of union debates and none of the grassroots activism of union politics. Mark Goldie, who was elected as a student member at the same time, recalls the board meetings as extremely formal occasions. Geoffrey Elton, who was professor of modern history, dominated the board, 'still wearing a gown for such occasions, and chain smoking'.[39] Much of the work of the board was routine: lecture lists were approved, reports from the history faculty library were noted, funds were granted to buy a new photocopier and leaves of absence were granted to various lecturers. However, at the same time, the board took some radical steps.

In December 1974, they took the decision to adopt anonymous marking for first year students, so neither the name nor the college of the candidate would be known to the examiner. This was one of the key demands made by feminists on campus, who believed that women were being marked down due to the prejudice of examiners. There were also steps taken to reform the curriculum and introduce a dissertation, in a course which had historically rested wholly on exams. None of these reforms were revolutionary. But they were all meaningful, and every one of them reflected the demands made by student radicals.

The reforms were all the more significant given the nature of the board. Student radicals regarded the history faculty as one of the more conservative parts of the university. According to *Alternative Prospectus*, 'Most of the professors ... are reluctant to consider any reforms.'⁴⁰ Goldie recalls that these reforms were won without much confrontation between the student representatives and the academics on the board.⁴¹ That said, Abbott seems to have developed a style of her own. An internal college note describes her approach to working on the board as 'that of the ingénue, asking outrageous questions in a little-girl voice'.⁴² Gill Sutherland, Abbott's director of studies, opines that Abbott learned a great deal from her time on the board: 'Student involvement in college government gives a thorough political education, about what it is to sit on a committee, how a committee works, what are the right moments to intervene.'⁴³ Student union documents stress the uniquely Machiavellian nature of the history dons, who brought the 'practical lessons from lifetimes of studying double-crossing and manoeuvre in political history' to bear at every committee meeting. For Abbott, it was the first of innumerable occasions when she was the only black person and the only woman on a committee dominated by white men.

Nonetheless, the early 1970s were an exciting time to be studying history at Cambridge. Abbott recalls, 'There were a group of young guns, like Simon Schama, Roy Porter, John Brewer and Jack Pole who really cut a dash.'[44] Pole made a big impact on Abbott. His course, entitled 'The Idea of Equality in America 1760–1965', began with a focus on the development of US democracy in Massachusetts, Pennsylvania and Virginia, tracing the pursuit of equality through to the Civil Rights movement and women's movement. Schama's lectures dealt with 'Political Revolt and Social Disorder in Europe 1750–1848'. This too looked, at least in part, at aspirations for representative government in Europe. In that sense, the politics of representation was part of Abbott's academic study, as well as being central to radical campus politics. In addition to learning from this new generation of scholars, Abbott's first two years focused on British social, economic, political and constitutional history.

The supervision system, which is unique to Oxford and Cambridge, placed a considerable burden on the students. *Alternative Prospectus* explained the system in the following way: 'While one of the main faults of the course is that it provides insufficient opportunity for the student to develop his own ideas, the main fault of the teaching, paradoxically, is that it forces the student to work too much in isolation.'[45] In essence, history students were given a reading list and a set of questions and were asked to produce essays for weekly supervisions. Supervisions were usually hour-long one-to-one meetings between student and supervisor, where the student would discuss their work. The key to the supervision system, as students learned quite quickly, was to secure one of the better supervisors. In theory, supervisors were allocated by each college. Nonetheless, enterprising students could work around the system, approach academics directly and organise supervisions of their own. Student representatives could also approach members of the board for supervisions. Abbott was also fortunate to have Kathleen Hughes and Gill Sutherland as her directors of studies. Both were able to secure excellent supervisors for Newnham's history students.

In addition to history, Abbott spent her first year learning German. She appears to have done well: Kathleen Hughes, one of her directors of studies, described her as 'a vital sort of person, definitely intelligent. She has a vivid prose style, too wordy, but her attraction as a historian is that what she reads makes an imaginative impact on her.'[46] Supervision reports describe her variously as 'an intelligent girl with a talent for challenging everyone and everything in sight', 'able and hard-working' and 'perhaps inevitably, rather wary of the world; although she does have a number of passionately held views'. Abbott passed her first-year exams, known as prelims, without any difficulty.[47]

Abbott's second year was blighted by the Cambridge Rapist, who targeted halls of residence, raping six female undergraduates and assaulting several more during his six-month rampage. At the time, Newnham introduced the biggest security clampdown in its history, which made socialising difficult.

FIRST TRIP TO JAMAICA

During the second year's Christmas break, Abbott made her first trip to Jamaica. The holiday was her mother's idea, and initially Abbott was keen. 'As it got closer, I thought, I don't want to go on holiday with my mother, this is ridiculous.'[48] The holiday also meant missing the first few days of term. Even so, Julia Abbott insisted, telling her daughter that her brothers had put the money together to buy her ticket and that the family were eager to meet her.

On arrival in Jamaica, Abbott stayed with her uncles in Kingston. After a few days, she travelled to Smithville in Clarendon, where her parents had lived. 'Clarendon is what unkind people call "bush". It's rural Jamaica, it's not Ocho Rios, it's not Kingston, it's not somewhere where tourists go, it's rural Jamaica. Very green, very lovely.' Here, she met and charmed Dinah Dale, her grandmother, one of the highlights of her trip. Her place at Cambridge made her something of a star in the eyes of her family, but Abbott's grandmother was particularly smitten.

> She thought I was charming beyond belief, and in particular she was impressed by my British accent. I was sitting on the steps, she had a little house, and I was talking to my cousin, and my grandmother was in the doorway listening to us, and she said, to herself, not to us, 'Lord, she's refine!'[49]

Her grandmother was a central part of family life, having been involved with the upbringing of most of Abbott's maternal cousins and uncles. More than that, she had a grace and pride that Abbott took to heart.

> I always remember, when we came back from Smithville ... my mother and I were lugging these suitcases, but my grandmother said, 'No, no, no, no,' and she took them and put them on top of her head. Because that's the generation of West Indian women who carried stuff on their head, and she just looked extraordinarily graceful, extraordinarily at ease, extraordinarily proud, and that's always been an example for me: my grandmother's ease, grace and inner strength.

FINAL YEARS

Abbott's second year was intellectually fruitful. A group of historians at Cambridge including Quentin Skinner, Richard Tuck, and John Dunn were doing work which would reshape the study of political thought for decades to come. Abbott worked with Tuck in her second year and Dunn in her third. One supervision report describes her as an 'intelligent but somewhat wayward student' who followed her own interests rather than the topics most likely to appear on the exam paper. Another notes that she was 'particularly interested in those larger issues which seem most relevant to contemporary social and political questions', but that this approach could lead to interesting results, as she had 'more than once dug up out-of-the-way old books to illustrate contemporary attitudes' and in so doing demonstrated 'both enterprise and genuine interest'.[50]

Outside of supervisions, students usually worked in one of the university's many libraries. Lectures, according to *Alternative Prospectus*, were 'generally of poor quality' and attracted only small groups of students. The Students' Union appears to have accepted grudgingly that 'the excellence of the Faculty in certain fields cannot be denied', noting that this led to 'amazing smugness'. Although there were various shades of opinion among the history lecturers, *Alternative Prospectus* warned that anyone who was 'left-wing or Marxist' would have to 'fight against the current' of the faculty. The faculty organised very few undergraduate seminars, and as a result there was little scope for students to meet with academics to discuss ideas. The history course was also considered to be exceptionally exam-oriented, compared to other courses in the university.[51]

In her final year, Abbott took Jack Pole's special subject 'Race Relations in the United States 1863–96', which dealt primarily with the period of Reconstruction. 'I took it because it was the only special subject that enabled you to look at race.'[52]

Professor Robert Fogel, an economic historian based in Harvard, was another important influence in Abbott's final year. From 1975 to 1976, Fogel held the Pitt Professorship of American History at Cambridge. The year before taking up the professorship, Fogel and Stanley L. Engerman published the groundbreaking and controversial *Time on the Cross: The Economics of American Negro Slavery*, which contained counterfactual projections estimating the economic consequences had slavery continued after 1865. 'Diane', comments Sutherland, 'properly got very interested in this. She set up a debate between Bob Fogel and Geoffrey Elton about counterfactual history, which we housed in Newnham.'[53] Elton, whom Abbott knew through the history faculty board, was a historian of the Tudor period and was known as a combative debater. Sutherland remembers that the debate 'was attended by a vast number of students. It was a very ambitious and interesting thing to do.'[54] A decade later, Fogel and Elton would describe the debate in the following way:

> We recall an occasion at Newnham College, Cambridge, when a vastly overcrowded lecture room, full of people come to witness a fight to the death between King Kong and the Giant Lizard, grew more and more restive as it listened to two woolly lambs peacefully lying down side by side.[55]

During his year as Pitt Professor, Fogel was based at the 'Pitt Palace', an apartment on Chaucer Road, Cambridge, a twenty-minute walk from Newnham College. Sutherland recalls, 'Diane got to know the Fogels very well. Bob's wife Enid is one of the most formidable black matriarchs I have ever met. I think she was an enormously powerful and positive influence on Diane.'[56] Enid Fogel was also an academic and had worked as assistant director of admissions at the University of Chicago, before moving to Harvard, where she was the dean of the university's summer school. After her year in Cambridge, she published two books, with her husband, on economic history. Enid Fogel was the only black intellectual associated with the history faculty at the time. She and Abbott also shared an interest in the arts. The Fogels were clearly impressed by Abbott and were keen for her to take a higher degree. In the autumn of 1975, Fogel recommended Abbott to Professor Laurence Glasco at the Department of History at the University of Pittsburgh. Glasco, who was working on the history of American ethnic minority groups, was keen to put Abbott forward to the department's selection committee. In a letter to her director of studies, Abbott claimed that Fogel and Glasco were both very excited at the prospect of her taking a higher degree in the US. However, she wrote, 'of all the participants I am the least thrilled'. At the beginning of her third year, Abbott still wanted to keep her options open.[57]

Studying with Pole and Fogel was a stimulating experience, but even so, one of the lessons she learned at Cambridge was

> the extent to which black people had been written out of the history of Britain. I studied in the country from the age of five to my early twenties, and I had the finest education that money could buy. But there was no sense, either when I was studying history at sixth form, or at university, of any black presence in this country or any black contribution at all.[58]

Abbott seems to have adopted a more methodical approach to her work in her final year. One of her supervisors began the year predicting her a 2:1, noting that 'her usual gusto and enthusiasm is being more systematically translated into hard work' than in previous years. John Dunn, who taught Abbott on a political philosophy course was less impressed. According to Dunn, Abbott's 'grip on the subject remains a little erratic'. He concluded his final report saying, 'I shall remember her … as the only student who has ever stamped their foot at me in the course of a supervision (and managed to do so sitting down too).'[59] Another supervisor concluded her final report on Abbott with the thought that whatever else the historians at Cambridge had done for her, 'we have given her a political education'.[60]

The college May balls are one of the big events of the university year. Most colleges have a ball or an event once every two years, in early June, shortly after the exams have finished. Of the three balls that Abbott went to in her third year, one stood out.

> I remember going to a Cambridge May ball as an undergraduate. I was dressed up in a long evening dress and made up and bejewelled to within an inch of my life. Yet as soon as I came in through the gate someone rushed up to me and said, 'Oh good, you must have come to do the washing up.' He did not ask himself why I would wear an evening dress and diamante to do so. He only knew that I was a black woman and therefore must belong in the kitchen.[61]

Abbott was coming to the end of her time at Cambridge. She had served on the history faculty board, organised a debate featuring two of the university's most distinguished historians, and successfully passed her exams. But the experience at the May ball was telling. 'It pricked any notion I might have had that I was really one of them.'[62] Some working-class people who study at Oxford and Cambridge, Abbott opines, quickly lose their accents, adopt the clothes, habits and intellectual conservatism of their more privileged peers, and ingratiate themselves with the sons and daughters of the elite. Although the term 'young fogey' would not be coined until the 1980s, this kind of attitude was already emerging while Abbott was a student. Abbott never wanted to be accepted by rich young people at Cambridge, but even if she had, the fact that she was black meant that she could never be an insider.

Abbott graduated with a 2:2 in history in June 1976. Today, Abbott refers to her result, ironically, as 'the gentleman's grade', the grade obtained by young men who attended Cambridge for the social life, the connections and because it was part of the family tradition. Sutherland comments, 'grade inflation being what it is, the 2:2 class has virtually disappeared. In those days it was a respectable class.'[63] Abbott also took her final exams in a time before anonymous marking was introduced for second- and third-year students, so her name and college would have been clear at the top of her exams. When anonymous marking was finally introduced, the grades of female students shot up.

Cambridge was the making of Diane Abbott in two senses. First, it was at Cambridge that she became a socialist.

> If you are a thinking working-class person, and you go to Cambridge and you are surrounded by white people who, left or right, have that massive sense of entitlement, it will turn you into a socialist. The contrast with my family life could not have been more drastic. With Oxbridge, you can go two ways. You can run towards it, want to be absorbed by it, or you can become a socialist, that's my view.[64]

Abbott's radical orientation was clear to her supervisors, one of whom noted, at the end of her course, 'She says she is a committed Marxist,' adding disparagingly, 'but had never, quite frankly, done the work to be a really sophisticated one.'[65]

Before leaving Cambridge, Abbott's socialism remained largely theoretical. She did not get involved in grassroots politics until she returned to London. The contrast between the white middle-class feminism that she experienced in Cambridge and the black womanism she became involved in on her return to London was huge: 'It was like a miracle to come down from Cambridge and get involved with the black women's movement.'[66]

Much the same was true of her interest in race. 'In terms of my radicalisation around race, until I left university, it was all about reading.'[67] Through working with Fogel and Pole, she had studied the history of racial politics in the US, as well as debates around the origins of democracy and representative government, and the ways in which black people and women had to fight to win democratic rights on the same terms as white men. At the same time, she used the resources of the university to read work by Angela Davis, Stokely Carmichael and other leading intellectuals of the American Black Power movement. It was only after her return to London that she became involved in black activism, first around the campaign against the stop and search law, and then through the Organisation of Women of African and Asian Descent.

Cambridge made Abbott in a second sense too. Having been educated at one of the world's top universities, it gave her a sense of confidence. Whoever she worked with, whoever her opponents were, whatever their privileges were, her education was as good as theirs. After Cambridge, Abbott continued to pursue history. 'Having left, much of my reading has been around trying to educate myself about black history, black politics, black writing and black literature.'[68] More generally, Abbott argues,

> I took away from it the importance of history. When I went up for selection in Hackney North, one of the things I did before I went to my selection meeting was I went to a library in Hackney and went through the archives. History is really important, you have to situate yourself in history before you project yourself forward.

Cambridge also highlighted a problem which would recur throughout her career. One of the challenges Abbott faced was how to navigate the male-dominated and ferally competitive institution. A note from her director of studies, written at the end of her final year, states that Abbott was critical of female academics who were 'absorbed into the establishment' and who imitated 'male models of intellectual aggression'. Rather, Abbott attempted to make her own way at Cambridge, to avoid being swallowed up by the establishment or being exploited tokenistically.

The importance of education also stayed with her. Abbott was one of a generation of frontbench politicians who benefited from an excellent higher education system, with a generous state grant. Whereas many of the politicians who benefited from this system in the 1970s and 1980s voted to charge later generations thousands of pounds for the privilege, Abbott is on record as saying that she has never supported 'pulling up the ladder'.

CHAPTER 3

'BECAUSE I WANT POWER'

Abbott's move from Cambridge to London was a move from theory to practice. At Cambridge she had studied political history, the history of the British state and political philosophy. In London she began a life of activism, taking up politics as a vocation in pursuit of power.

Having decided not to continue her academic study at the University of Pittsburgh, Abbott sought career advice from the university appointments board. Abbott remembers that 'Cambridge's approach to career development was a bit rudimentary'. Nonetheless, her career adviser offered some words of wisdom. 'Whatever you do, don't learn to type, and if you do learn to type, don't tell anyone.' Abbott understood immediately that as a woman entering the workforce she risked being relegated to a secretarial role. Whatever else she learned at Cambridge, this advice stuck.[1]

Approaching the end of her time at university, Abbott became determined to make a difference. When asked by her college tutor about her career aims, Abbott replied simply that she wanted to 'do good'. In an incredible feat of lateral thinking, her tutor suggested the civil service. After some discussion Abbott opted to apply to the Home Office, as the arm of government which was involved in issues of 'race relations'. Roy Jenkins, who was Home Secretary at the time, had been an early advocate of 'multiculturalism' and in 1975 he had established a committee of academics to advise the Home Office on 'race relations' policy. Even so, Abbott had to think long and hard about working in the heart of the British state. A note from Abbott's director of studies Gill Sutherland to Jean Floud, Newnham's principal, states that Abbott 'is rather interested in the mechanisms of power but is inhibited in her approach to them by the fear that she will be swallowed up by the establishment, the more so as she is black and female'. Abbott wanted to use state power but did not want to be assimilated by Whitehall. What is more, Sutherland argued that Abbott was still unsure of her essential political commitments, arguing that she 'really has got to make up her mind whether she rejects or accepts social democratic politics pretty soon'.[2]

HOME OFFICE

Whatever her concerns about Whitehall, Abbott submitted her initial application in January 1976. Civil service selection had three stages. By April she had completed the initial written test and the selection board successfully and gained an invitation to the final interview. Mary Warnock, the noted philosopher, chaired the final interview panel. Abbott appears to have clinched the job at the very beginning of the interview. Asked by Warnock why she wanted to join the civil service, Abbott responded, 'because I want power'. It was a bold answer. The adage, sometimes attributed to Plato, that 'those who seek power are not worthy of that power' has a peculiar grip on the English political imagination. Abbott's desire to gain power to do good appears to have struck a chord with Warnock and she was offered a position as an administrative trainee at the Home Office.

Abbott moved back to London, this time to a bedsit near Sloane Square, which she had heard about through a friend at Cambridge. Her landlady was a dreadful cook. As a result, for the first time Abbott, who was always a voracious reader, turned her attention to cookbooks and began to master the art and science of casseroles.

Abbott was based in the Home Office headquarters, a post-war office block on Eccleston Square in Victoria. As a civil servant, Abbott worked alongside dedicated public servants, scrupulously committed to the ideal of meritocracy. Consequently, she rarely experienced racism in Whitehall. Assignments, to take one example, were given out on the basis of talent and interest. 'The civil servants at the Home

Office are some of the nicest people I have worked for, not earning a fortune, going home to Cheam at the end of the day, and doing what seems to be their duty.'³

At the same time, the Home Office was the epitome of structural racism. 'There I was, the only black woman in an eight-storey building, having to absorb the knowledge that the Home Office was intervening in black people's lives in a negative way, through the prisons, through the courts, through the immigration service.'⁴ On top of this, the ethos of the Home Office ran counter to progressive reform, particularly when it came to prisons. Roy Jenkins, known at the time as a progressive who was committed to civil liberties, turned out to be a remarkably authoritarian minister. Jenkins was criticised by the National Council of Civil Liberties in a report published around the time that Abbott entered the Home Office. The report excoriated Jenkins for his failure to deal with 'injustice in the courts, the abuse of police powers, repression in the prisons, the harsh operation of racialist immigration laws, intrusion into the individual's private life and the obsessive secrecy which covers the operation of government'. The report was particularly critical of Jenkins's record on prisons, claiming, 'Mr Jenkins prides himself on being a civilised man. There is nothing civilised about his decision to go ahead with the introduction of six months' solitary in the control units for recalcitrant prisoners', or his decision to increase the punitive power of unaccountable prison governors.⁵

Abbott quickly began working in the Home Office's prison department. In large part, her decision to work in the department was based on the fact that significant numbers of black men were given custodial sentences. The general conservatism of the Home Office was heightened in the prison department. As far as possible the Home Office kept conditions in prisons a closely guarded secret. Political scientist Marie Gottschalk argues that British prisons received little media attention at this time 'because of the extreme centralization and extreme culture of secrecy of the prison system. As one prisoner put it, borrowing from Oscar Wilde, "Prison walls are built not to keep prisoners in but prying eyes out."'⁶ Prisons were controlled by central, rather than local government, and much of what happened in Britain's jails was covered by the Official Secrets Act, which meant that there was no general public right to information. Civil servants could face criminal charges for revealing information about prisons. Abbott's duty to remain silent under the Official Secrets Act was reinforced by her employment contract, which expressly prohibited contact with the press. Historically, the Home Office had refused to release information on conditions in prisons, or prison riots. While this began to change in the 1970s, it was only in the 1980s that the Home Office released data on the number of black people who were incarcerated. The Home Office was also able to keep information about the conditions in prisons secret as prisoners had no right to consult lawyers without permission of the Home Secretary. Moreover, other than the rights granted under the European Convention on Human Rights, which were extremely hard to enforce in Britain at the time, prisoners had practically no meaningful legal rights under English law. Consequently, the only way for prisoners to make their voices heard was through direct action, such as the riots which were taking place in Hull Prison around the time that Abbott entered Whitehall. Notably, one of the demands of the prisoners in Hull was for a public inquiry, to expose the conditions in England's jails.

The prison riots of the 1970s led to greater scrutiny of the problems in Britain's prisons. Even so, reform was slow. Merlyn Rees, who replaced Jenkins as Home Secretary in September 1976, rejected proposals for modest changes in the legal advice available to prisoners, and refused to co-operate with an independent judicial inquiry into the Hull prison riots. What is more, in the difficult economic circumstances of the period budgets were cut. As a result, the number of prison officers on duty was reduced, the length of time that prisoners were confined to their cells increased, young offenders were housed in adult prisons and nothing was done to alleviate growing overcrowding.

Abbott's desire to reform the system quickly ran into the institutional conservatism of the civil service. Having tried, and failed, to push through reform Abbott registered her protest. 'I decided to join the Labour Party. It was a form of rebellion against the Home Office.'[7]

Policy demanded that she had to seek permission from the permanent secretary, so the move was a significant statement. While permission was granted, joining the Labour Party was a challenge to the ethos of Whitehall and a way of demonstrating to her bosses that she refused to accept the culture of the civil service. After eighteen months in the service, Abbott began to see worrying evidence that her peers were beginning to assimilate. 'Many of them, when they were new to the service, did want to see reform, but by the time they had got senior enough to implement such reform, they had absorbed so much of the ethos of the service they were no longer capable of carrying them out.' Over time, it dawned on Abbott that to get promoted 'I would have to internalise a culture and norms that I didn't want to internalise'.[8] The paradox of the civil service was that the people with the power to make change were the least likely to do so. The threat of becoming absorbed by the system had troubled Abbott from the outset. What is more, her experience confirmed that the civil service, as it was constituted in the late 1970s, was not a vehicle for radical reform. Abbott joined in search of power. Finding that the civil service's power consisted of upholding the status quo, she decided to leave.

With hindsight, joining the Labour Party in 1978 was the first step out of Whitehall. 'It was a rebellious thing to do. It's clearer to me now than it was then that it wasn't going to do my career any good.'[9] Events in the winter of 1978 and spring of 1979 also played a role in her decision to leave. The Winter of Discontent, as it became known, ended hopes of a Labour victory at the next election, as from January 1979 Margaret Thatcher's Conservative Party gained a decisive lead in the polls. If reform was difficult under Labour, Abbott calculated that it would be impossible under the Tories. Therefore, with a Conservative victory on the horizon, it was time to leave the civil service.

NCCL

Given Abbott's frustrations with the Home Office, a move to the National Council for Civil Liberties (NCCL) seemed perfectly natural. Unlike the civil service, progressive reform was at the NCCL's heart. The NCCL, after all, had done significant work highlighting the problems of the prison service, and campaigning for the kind of prison reform that Abbott had hoped to effect during her time at the Home Office. Leaving for the NCCL was also a final act of rebellion as Abbott recalls the NCCL was 'something of a bête noire as far as the Home Office was concerned'.[10]

Abbott joined the NCCL as race relations officer in February 1979. The role had been newly created through funding from the Gulbenkian Foundation and the Commission for Racial Equality in partnership with the Cobden Trust and had a starting salary of £10,000.[11] The role initially received little interest from applicants due to the small salary being offered. However, when the role was advertised for a second time in January 1979, Abbott was by this time keen to leave the civil service and applied. She began working at the Cobden Trust in February 1979.

The speed of Abbott's departure from the civil service was unusual. Normally a civil servant would work out a more extended period of notice. From what Patricia Hewitt remembers Abbott's decision to quit and join the NCCL caused such a stir in the Home Office that they let her leave all but immediately. 'She was one of their few, perhaps their only, high-flying black graduate recruits and they weren't at all happy that she was leaving – and, especially, that she was going over to an organisation they thoroughly disapproved of.'[12]

The Cobden Trust was largely concerned with the rights of young people. The fact that it, rather than the NCCL, led on race relations may well have reflected the history of the NCCL's engagement with race. By the time of Abbott's appointment, the NCCL's race relations subcommittee was almost two years old. Established in March 1977, the subcommittee's initial focus was the 'SUS' laws, the legal basis for a rampant stop and search culture which targeted young black men. At the same time Abbott and the NCCL wanted to broaden their focus on the rights of black and Asian people. Indeed, the NCCL wanted the subcommittee to examine the 1976 Race Relations Act, which, for the first time in law recognised legally defensible rights in areas such as employment. Consequently, although Abbott was employed by the Cobden Trust, she was based at the NCCL offices, at 186 Kings Cross

Road. By early 1979, the race relations subcommittee included Paul Boateng, Trevor Phillips and Hewitt. *Rights!*, the NCCL's magazine, announced Abbott's appointment in March 1979, reporting that 'she will be working closely with NCCL, preparing a report on the failures of the new race relations law, advising people who have suffered discrimination and following up cases'.[13]

'Race relations' is now considered a problematic term. Nonetheless, for several decades, beginning in the 1960s, the language of 'race relations' was widely used. The Wilson administration of the 1960s had given it a legal basis in the 1965 Race Relations Act, which outlawed the incitement of racial hatred. Two further Race Relations Acts passed in 1968 and 1976 had established a number of important rights in law, outlawing racial discrimination in the housing market, in employment, education and in the provision of goods and services. The 1976 Act also outlawed indirect discrimination: discrimination that was not based primarily on race or ethnicity but had the effect of disadvantaging racial minorities. Together with legal rights, by 1976 the government had established the Commission for Racial Equality, which was tasked with using its legal powers to stamp out racial discrimination and harassment. The significance of the 1976 Race Relations Act was not lost on the NCCL. A press release, dated 30 September 1977, noted, 'The coming into force of the 1976 Race Relations Act has provided the opportunity for a renewed drive against racial discrimination in this country.'[14] The NCCL responded by establishing its race relations subcommittee, and employing Abbott as its first full-time race relations officer.

The 1970s was also a new era in the debate over civil liberties. If the 1960s was a period of widespread social liberalism, the 1970s was quite different. Stuart Hall's *Policing the Crisis*, published shortly before Abbott joined the NCCL, was one of the first scholarly works to analyse the growing 'authoritarian consensus' that characterised the 1970s.[15] Starting with media hysteria over mugging, Hall argued that a series of moral panics during the 1970s had led to the emergence of a 'law-and-order society', in which there was widespread public sympathy for increased police powers and repressive legislation.[16] Antipathy towards the work of the NCCL was evident from death threats sent to leading members in the 1970s, and the beating of Graeme Atkinson, an NCCL member who received eighteen stitches as a result of a violent National Front attack.[17]

In spite of growing hostility toward civil liberties, the NCCL was clearly a dynamic organisation at the time Abbott joined. The NCCL was beginning to embrace the politics of women's liberation, black rights and gay and lesbian rights. Indeed, there was a growing consensus that the discourse of rights could unite these disparate campaigns into a national movement. In spite of its ambitions, the NCCL was a small organisation with around 5,000 members, fourteen staff and two lawyers at the time that Abbott joined.

Abbott's first month at the NCCL was devoted to organising a race relations conference. The race relations and racial discrimination one-day conference was an important part of the NCCL's strategy of reaching out to minority groups. The programme included sessions on immigration and nationality, discrimination in housing, local government and education, policing and SUS. Speakers included Paul Boateng, who was based at the Paddington Law Centre, Ann Dummett, one of the founders of the Joint Council for the Welfare of Immigrants, Trevor Phillips, President of the National Union of Students, and Pranlal Sheth, barrister and deputy chair of the Campaign for Racial Equality.

Anticipating controversy, Abbott invited Asquith Gibbes to chair the conference. Labour's Race Relations Acts were treated with considerable suspicion in black radical circles. They were viewed as part of a government strategy to neutralise black radicalism by co-opting young radicals. Farrukh Dhondy, a radical who was part of the Indian Workers' Association, the British Black Panther Movement and latterly the Race Today Collective, described this new generation of race relations professionals as 'race relations wallahs', a term which suggests that they were happy to serve the state in return for payment.[18] As community relations officer for Lewisham Council, Gibbes could have been accused of being a 'race relations wallah'. Yet Gibbes had also been involved in the grassroots campaign against

SUS, therefore he was well placed to defuse the tension between the radicals and those who were working with established community relations organisations.

The conference, which took place at the LSE on 3 March 1979 appears to have been a success. Writing in the May/June edition of *Rights!* Abbott states that around 300 people attended, including a strong trade union contingent.[19] As Abbott had hoped, Gibbes chaired the day effectively, steering discussion away from the controversy between the different approaches to combating racism. Abbott spoke briefly about institutional racism in the probation service, her comments, no doubt, informed by her time at the Home Office. Abbott also invited Brojon Chatterjee, who was not included on the original list of speakers, to give the day's final speech, dealing with the Asian campaigns in east London. Their campaigns included 'sit-down protests outside Bethnal Green police station to protest against police inaction against racist attacks, patrolling and occupying areas used by the National Front to sell newspapers and plan racial attacks and organising the Black Solidarity Day which consisted of a day-long strike in Tower Hamlets in July 1978 to protest against racist violence'.[20] Abbott commented that his speech was 'the most impassioned of the day'. Abbott's decision to highlight the final session in her article also reflected her own commitments: 'I've always been absolutely passionate about the relationship between black people and the state, it's always been at the heart of my concerns.'[21]

Abbott's article in *Rights!* outlined her understanding of the changing issues around 'race relations' at the end of the 1970s. She claims that the period was witnessing a shift from 'the fight against racism developing from simple opposition to the National Front to the more complex battle against institutionalised racism'. Shifting focus to institutionalised racism was one of the successes of the day. The conference had been attended by many white left-wing radicals, and it had exposed them to the realities of institutional racism in Britain. Looking back, Abbott commented, 'the white left were fine to march against the National Front, but if you tried to say that there was institutional racism in the institutions where they worked, you got a certain amount of push-back. The classic response was "Are you calling me a racist?" and that's not the point, we were talking about the institutions.'[22]

Abbott's article pointed to two issues that loomed large on the horizon, the 'new nationality law and the vexed question of ethnic record keeping'.[23] The latter issue was a bone of contention within the NCCL. Abbott's reference to 'ethnic record keeping' concerned, in the first instance, the 1981 census and whether the government should collect data on ethnicity. Alex Lyon, Labour MP for York, favoured making a question on ethnicity a compulsory part of the census. Haringey Council had also piloted a census questionnaire including a question on ethnicity. However, the question had deeper implications about the right of institutions to collect data. Many in the NCCL were against the move, on the basis that it was an invasion of privacy and that the state had no right to hold information of that kind. Abbott took a different view. Data on ethnicity was essential in proving institutional and indirect discrimination because it could be used to show patterns of discrimination in areas such as policing, education, housing and employment.[24]

Research was a big part of Abbott's role. In fact, she used her time at the NCCL to explore the recent history of black people in Britain, which was a significant gap in her education. Abbott's files demonstrate that she read up on conflict between the Indian Workers' Association and the police in Southall; Powellism; black participation in the 1974 elections; the prospects of black candidates in the 1979 election; publications by the CRE, particularly on education, housing and employment, as well as immigration law. In so doing, she amassed the data necessary to start making the case that institutional racism was every bit as real as National Front 'Paki-bashing'.[25]

Abbott put her research to good use and persuaded the NCCL about the necessity of 'ethnic record keeping'. After several months of agnosticism, the NCCL reached a consensus on the issue in May 1979. Abbott's minutes record the agreement in the following terms:

The meeting discussed the draft document on ethnic record-keeping.

It was agreed that it should be re-drafted as a document on equal opportunities policies and ethnic record keeping. It was felt that this would put ethnic record-keeping in its place as a weapon in the fight against discrimination rather than an end in itself.[26]

Abbott organised a seminar on the subject which brought together members of the Cobden Trust and the Runnymede Trust, a think tank dealing with racial inequality. She subsequently wrote the NCCL's position paper on 'Equal Opportunities and Ethnic Record Keeping', demonstrating the breadth of her research and subsequent expertise on discrimination in Britain, and the campaign to fight for equal rights in the 1970s. The report summarises the available data on discrimination in the labour market and examines the economics of migrant labour. Abbott places a particular focus on the lessons of the Imperial Typewriters strike and the Grunwick dispute, two of the landmark confrontations between mainly Asian workers and British employers and trade unions in the 1970s. Abbott wrote:

Imperial Typewriters in Leicester, for instance, managed to treble its turnover between 1968 and 1972 and it achieved this not by investing in new machinery but by doubling the workforce while keeping wages down. White immigrant men were replaced by black immigrant men and they were finally replaced by black immigrant women, the cheapest labour of all … It must be remembered that, for those firms which made a practice of recruiting immigrant labour because it was cheap, it was also in their interest to foster racial divisions in the workforce. A fragmented workforce, after all, could not organise against them to raise wage levels.[27]

Abbott concluded the report by countering the objections against record keeping:

The liberal platitude that 'colour doesn't matter' is sanctified by time. But it has been exploded by a whole new generation of blacks who say that colour does indeed matter and ought to be a matter

of pride and joy. It is a sick joke to say to the Bengali in the East
End who cannot get decent council housing, and to the black kid
shunted from the school for the educationally sub-normal to the
dole queue, that 'colour doesn't matter'. While racism exists, colour
is an issue and unless records are routinely kept of job applicants
etc., the racists will always deny, and it will be impossible to prove,
that racial discrimination is happening.[28]

Looking back, Abbott argues that the differences within the NCCL
reflected 'the difference between having a theoretical civil liberties position and having to engage in the realities of racism on the ground.
If you have to engage with the reality of racism, whether it's policing,
whether its education, you have to have the data because people are
not minded to believe you.'[29]

Abbott's activities at the NCCL were many and various. Her appointment was covered in the *Evening Standard*, which published
her first press profile in March 1979. Her casework included supporting the Railton Road Youth Club, who were negotiating with a
local Methodist church over space to run activities. She spoke to the
Greenwich Council for Racial Equality and ran a workshop for the
National Association of Probation Officers. Abbott also worked with
Jack Dromey, who had supported the Grunwick campaign, laying the
groundwork for a race and employment conference. Following Margaret Thatcher's 1979 election victory, the race relations subcommittee
started working on new strategies more appropriate to the new regime.

Despite the success of the March conference, Abbott was unhappy
in her new post. Paul Boateng, then a lawyer at Benedict Birnberg and
executive member of the NCCL, recalls that 'Diane didn't flourish at
the NCCL'.[30] The first evidence in the NCCL files that Abbott was
finding life as race relations officer difficult is a letter from Asquith
Gibbes dated 22 June 1979. The letter ends, 'Hope you are finding life
bearable. Please do not hesitate to ring us if you think we can offer any
help or advice.'[31] Disagreements over ethnic record keeping were part
of the problem, but there were deeper issues. Abbott recalls:

Working for the NCCL was very formative. I studied at Cambridge, which meant that I engaged with a certain sort of social and educational elite. Then I worked for the Home Office, which meant I engaged with the state, and I knew that the state was often quite reactionary. But then I went to the NCCL, which initially I thought was going to be some kind of nirvana of liberal progressivism. It was the first time I had to confront institutional racism on the left, and it was a shock because I wasn't expecting it. If you are at Cambridge or at the Home Office you know the deal, but the NCCL was supposedly a left-wing institution and you are having to engage with institutional racism.[32]

From Abbott's point of view, the problems with the NCCL were both personal and professional. On a personal level, Abbott recalls an uneasy relationship with some of her colleagues:

Although they paid lip service to anti-racism, their world was a white world. I know some of them were a little bit suspicious of me, because as far as they were concerned, I was far too smartly dressed to be a suffering member of the black proletariat. They had no idea that working-class black people love to look smart, because they didn't know any. So there was this tension.

At the Home Office Abbott exercised little power, but she had been treated with respect. At the NCCL she was more accustomed to sympathy than respect. In general terms, the NCCL viewed black people as victims, and therefore Abbott's abiding memory of her time there was of 'white liberals oozing their patronising sympathy all over me'.

Professionally, things were little better.

Superficially, the NCCL was more radical than the Home Office, it usually took the opposite view to the Home Office on anything to do with law and order. But as a black person, I felt oddly vulnerable there. In the Home Office, there was a structure, everything was done on paper, and there was a process. Precisely because the NCCL wasn't structured in that way you felt oddly vulnerable.

Abbott's first experience of the white liberal left made her realise that there was a lot of ambivalence about race. They could feel outraged by racism in South Africa or in the US, but they found it much harder to face racism in Britain, harder still the racism of their own institutions.

Fortunately, the NCCL shared a building with the Institute of Race Relations (IRR). Although the IRR had once been an establishment think tank, Ambalavaner Sivanandan had organised a radical takeover of the institute in the early 1970s. From then on, the resources and prestige of the IRR were put in the service of radicalism. Jenny Bourne, who was central to the work of the IRR, recalls that Abbott 'was not happy at the NCCL, was not clear as to her brief and not sure of the support she was getting. So, she seemed to prefer to come downstairs to IRR and read in the library.'[33] The other attraction of the IRR was that, unlike the NCCL, Abbott could pop in and talk to other black people.

However, Abbott's time at the NCCL was not wasted. Her rather nebulous brief was to develop and 'maintain contact with minority groups'. Abbott spent her time working with radical groups, particularly those created by black women. She had been involved in the Scrap SUS Campaign prior to joining the NCCL. She was alerted to the campaign by a flyer in a black bookshop, and in 1978 she started attending meetings of Black People's Organisations Campaign Against SUS, which met in Evelyn Street, Deptford. A 1978 flyer entitled 'FREEDOM FOR BLACK YOUTH AND OTHERS FROM "SUS"' that survives among Abbott's NCCL papers sets out the objectives of the campaign as:

- Call for the repeal of the Vagrancy Act: Section 4 – 'SUS'
- Demand an Independent Inquiry into police black relationships[34]

The Vagrancy Act was an archaic piece of legislation which gave police the power to stop, search and arrest 'every suspected person', which is where the term 'SUS' came from. Although it was not repealed until the 1980s, it was rarely used for much of the twentieth century. Nonetheless, it was revived in the 1970s and used extensively against black men, particularly young black men. An information sheet circulated by the Black People's Organisations Campaign Against SUS in the late 1970s detailed a series of cases where young black men, some as young as eleven, were stopped, searched and detained under the 1824 Act.

It was through Scrap SUS that Abbott met Mavis Best, who initiated the campaign. Abbott 'attended meetings regularly, and lobbied MPs' as part of the campaign.[35] Lobbying MPs was central to the campaign against SUS. In fact, it was through putting pressure on MPs that the law was eventually changed. Scrap SUS was a genuine grassroots campaign that 'began in a Black woman's front room in Deptford and eventually swept throughout the Black community, uniting the generations in a call for the law to be scrapped'.[36] Abbott explains how 'this was a campaign that was started by a bunch of black mothers. It was a bottom-up campaign, we had to work out for ourselves how to lobby MPs.'[37]

Abbott's experience organising the NCCL race relations campaign was also put to good use, and she played a central role in organising the Scrap SUS national conference on 16 June 1979.[38] The event, which was reported in Organisation of Women of African and Asian Descent (OWAAD) newsletters, attracted 150 attendees. A central part of the conference was a session in which some of the black mothers and their children who were affected by SUS spoke.[39]

It was through Scrap SUS that Abbott first met Paul Boateng who provided legal support to the campaign. For Boateng,

The great strength of the Scrap SUS campaign was that it came from the grassroots experience of a group of black women in Lewisham, and came, in time, to embrace black people, white people, churches, political parties, all united in the belief that this was a law that had to change.[40]

OWAAD

Involvement with OWAAD was another formative experience for

Abbott. OWAAD was an umbrella organisation which aimed to unite black and Asian women and black and Asian women's organisations. Formed in 1979 by radicals including Olive Morris and Stella Dadzie, OWAAD emerged from a decades-long tradition of black resistance, which included the work of radicals such as Una Marston and Claudia Jones. The Black Power movement drew black and Asian women into a grassroots movement and mobilised 'hundreds of young Black women who had had no former contact with political organisations, but who felt that the message of Black Power spoke to their immediate situation'.[41] In one way or another Black Power groups helped organise young black and Asian people, particularly second-generation migrants, and to unify them politically. While black women often made up the majority of the membership, male leaders often expected them to play a supporting role. Beverley Bryan, Stella Dadzie and Suzanne Scafe, who were key figures in the movement, highlighted two issues with male domination. First, 'Although we worked tirelessly, the significance of our contribution to the mass mobilisation of the Black Power era was undermined and overshadowed by the men. They both set the agenda and stole the show.'[42] Second, 'We could not realise our full organisational potential in a situation where we were constantly regarded as sexual prey.' As a result, black women's caucuses were formed within Black Power groups. These would become the foundation of the black women's movement. The Brixton Black Women's Group, founded in 1973, led the way. In the mid-1970s, black women's groups organised locally against police harassment – particularly against SUS – campaigned for better housing and for access to childcare. At the same time, radical black women had a global perspective, and women's groups began studying liberation movements and making links with black and Asian women's groups across the world. Between the local and the global, OWAAD allowed black and Asian women to collaborate at a national level.

The national black women's conference, OWAAD's first major meeting, took place on 18 March 1979 at the Abeng Centre in Brixton and drew an audience of around 300 women, primarily from London, but also from Birmingham, Leeds, Manchester and Brighton. Among them was Abbott, who arrived early for the event. 'I came out of Brixton Tube, and I must have looked lost. Ricky Cambridge asked me if I was looking for the OWAAD meeting. That's how I got to know him.'⁴³ Alrick 'Ricky' Xavier Cambridge was one of the founders of the Black Unity and Freedom Party, and he and Abbott would go on to collaborate on radical projects in the coming years. Fittingly, the conference took place on Gresham Road, opposite Brixton Police station.

OWAAD was a revelation for Abbott.

> I remember going to that first OWAAD meeting in Brixton and being completely blown away. It was the first time I'd been in a room, a meeting, full of black people, of black women, and people who broadly shared my political perspective. I had an adolescence and a university life where I was completely isolated. I just remember my first OWAAD meeting felt like magic. OWAAD was my main black political connection in that era.

OWAAD was inspiring for a number of reasons. The post-colonial emphasis on unity between black and Asian women was one aspect that particularly appealed to Abbott. Looking back, she views this post-colonial orientation as one of the progressive aspects of the politics of the time.

> Political blackness meant a huge amount to us in the 1970s and the 1980s. This was a generation that had come out of the post-colonial era. Political blackness was based on the notion that whatever your cultural identity, you had a unified experience of British colonialism. That's what united people and brought them together.

The emphasis on political blackness was central to OWAAD's position. The introductory talk on 18 March began by addressing the term 'black'. 'For our purposes,' the speaker began, 'we will use the term "black" to refer to the two major ethnic groups of black people in this country, namely: those people who came originally from the

Indian subcontinent ... those people who have their origins in Africa.'
These two groups were united by common persecution by the police,
by white racists, by immigration laws and were disadvantaged by the
legacy of colonialism. They were also united in the experience of colonial 'divide and rule'. 'OUR UNITY IS OUR STRENGTH', one of
OWAAD's slogans, was the antidote.[44]

A common post-colonial experience allowed black and Asian women
to learn from and make common cause with women fighting oppression in the developing world. This, in turn, had an impact on the kind
of feminism or womanism that Abbott encountered in OWAAD. One
of the participants in the black women's movement explains:

> I think we were influenced ... by what was happening in the libera-
> tion movements on the African continent ... What Samora Machel
> had to say about women's emancipation made a lot more sense to us
> than what Germaine Greer and other middle-class white feminists
> were saying. It just didn't make sense for us to be talking about
> changing life-styles and attitudes, when we were dealing with issues
> of survival, like housing, education and police brutality.[45]

This difference between the white feminism that Abbott had experienced as a teenager and at university and the black womanism
she encountered through OWAAD was one of the most exhilarat-
ing aspects of the experience. Dadzie's reflections on OWAAD's first
conference indicate that Abbott was not alone. Dadzie recalls that
while many of the women had backgrounds in Black Power groups,
others 'were coming more from a sense of isolation in white women's
groups, and they were happy to find a niche where they interacted
with other people who had shared histories and shared experiences'.[46]
For Mia Morris, who was also at the first OWAAD conference and
went on to co-ordinate the Heart of the Race oral history project,
OWAAD was something different to feminism. 'I have never called
myself a feminist ... We see it as a middle-class, middle-aged, white,
exclusive club.'[47] This was certainly Abbott's experience: 'There were
some amazing black women in OWAAD. It was so energising for me,

to break out of the establishment and the education system and meet all these amazing women.'[48]

Hazel V. Carby argues that OWAAD's black womanism was different to mainstream white feminism in a number of ways. First, it was concerned with the triple oppression of gender, race and class. Second, it had a different take on the family. Whereas white feminists tended to see white families as sites of oppression, black womanists saw black families as places from which to organise resistance. Black womanists also wanted to downplay the extent to which black womanism saw black men as antagonists, recognising that black men had few of the structural advantages that white men had. Finally, OWAAD were sceptical of claims that black women should seek liberation through assimilation. Put another way, OWAAD were critical of the notion that the liberation of black women would come about through rejecting the 'backwardness' of traditional cultures and embracing 'civilisation', conceived as the norms of the white middle class.[49] In many ways, the Scrap SUS campaign reflected this approach to politics. As Margaretta Jolly argues, the Scrap SUS campaign was 'maternalist', as mothers, beginning with the resources of the home, organised together to protect young black men.[50]

Elizabeth Anionwu, who was friends with OWAAD founder Olive Morris, recalls Abbott contributing to the discussion at the conference: 'She was very enthusiastic, obviously incredibly intelligent, very articulate.'[51] Anionwu recognised Abbott from her profile in the *Evening Standard*, which had been published ten days before the conference. At first, Abbott's contribution was not well received. 'She was still young, she still had her Afro then,' Anionwu recalls. 'She was a little bit over-enthusiastic. One of the things she said was that she was at the NCCL, and if there was anything she could do for the group, she would. Now this group, these were really radical, afro-centred feminists, an incredible group. That offer went down like a lead balloon. I remember the sharp reaction. But it was quickly sorted out.' This momentary awkwardness did not stop Abbott. Mia Morris recalls Abbott talking about her time at Cambridge and 'telling people how important it was that black women united and worked together'.[52]

Abbott's excitement is easy to understand. A fortnight after the conference Abbott received the text of the six talks that comprised the day. The topics included education, the law, health care, employment and the anti-imperial struggle: issues that were central to Abbott's concerns. Moreover, this was a conference organised for black women and organised by black women. In that sense, it escaped one of the problems of earlier iterations of black politics. Abbott explains, 'The danger was, with black politics, that it was very patriarchal. Relating to the black women's movement meant that I wasn't just a "hand-maiden of the patriarchy".'[53]

Reflecting on OWAAD, Dadzie comments:

The influence was far greater than anyone realised at the time, I think. And of course, you see women like Valerie Amos, Diane Abbott, they all flirted with OWAAD – I wouldn't say they were major activists within it ... [but] they were all very influenced by that, and went on to become influential women.[54]

1979 GENERAL ELECTION

OWAAD's first conference took place ten days before James Callaghan was forced to call a general election following a vote of no confidence in the Labour government. Abbott joined the Labour Party as a gesture of protest against the civil service. Joining was certainly not an endorsement of the Callaghan administration. Nonetheless, Abbott was a committed member of the party, and when the election came, she worked hard to keep the Conservatives out.

Having moved to Belsize Park, Abbott threw herself into campaigning for a Labour victory in Hampstead. Ken Livingstone recalls, 'I first met Diane in the late 1970s, when I was the candidate for Hampstead. She was this bright young woman, quite ebullient, in the Hampstead Labour Party.'[55] Hampstead was a key marginal, Labour having lost it to the Tories by 2,000 votes in October 1974. Livingstone, then serving as a councillor in the London Borough of Camden, was selected as the prospective parliamentary candidate in 1977, narrowly beating Vince Cable. 'I remember saying to him,

"You should be in the Liberals!" The right wing in Hampstead were horrified that I beat him.'⁵⁶

Having lost his majority in Parliament, facing an unpopular Conservative leader and enjoying a bump in the polls, many expected Callaghan to call an election in 1978. His decision to delay and extend his controversial incomes policy exposed divisions between the party leadership and the Labour left. As the October edition of *Socialist Organiser* put it, Callaghan's 5 per cent pay limit showed that 'the Labour government [is] firmly on the side of the bosses'.⁵⁷ Consequently, the left were as opposed to Callaghan's economic policies as the Tories. Crucially, the left saw the industrial action which took place across the country as a legitimate response to Labour's iniquitous economic policy, whereas the Tories saw it as evidence of unbridled union power. Along with the issue of race, these debates formed the backdrop of the 1979 campaign.

During the election, Abbott acted as Livingstone's election agent in the Belsize Ward. 'Hampstead', Abbott recalls, 'was quite a middle-class party, and Ken was a surprisingly left-wing candidate. The Hampstead Labour Party … like a candidate who's special. Ken didn't fit the Hampstead Labour Party template.'⁵⁸ Livingstone was certainly a radical; as *Socialist Organiser* made clear, he was fighting with two goals in mind: he was fighting against the Tories, but also to build a socialist alternative to Callaghan within the Labour Party.

Race was a significant theme in both the politics of the period and the Hampstead campaign. Early in the campaign, Livingstone emphasised the likely consequences of a Thatcher victory on women and minorities. Speaking to the *Hampstead & Highgate Express* in early April, he stated that the Conservative's economic policies were 'repressive and reactionary' and would penalise minorities. 'It is not only black people that will suffer,' he commented. 'Women who have found their way into the labour market will be squeezed out.' Geoffrey Finsberg, his Conservative opponent, apparently no enemy of hyperbole, hit back by claiming that 'the Labour Party is aiming to destroy society'.⁵⁹ Where Livingstone emphasised the rights of minorities, the Conservative candidate spoke up for the 'liberties of the majority of people' which he claimed would be torn down by 'the forces of destruction' in the Labour Party.

Ireland was also an issue in the campaign. Writing in *Socialist Organiser* shortly after election day, Livingstone explained that he faced an 'uphill struggle to convince the Irish community' to vote Labour. Apparently, at the outset of the campaign local Irish groups were encouraging Irish voters to put an 'H' on the ballot paper, in protest at the incarceration of so many Republicans in the infamous H-Block prisons. As a result, Livingstone had to emphasise his commitment to pulling British forces out of Ireland, circulating a 'troops out now' leaflet in areas with a significant Irish population such as Kilburn. Livingstone's efforts were largely successful and of the 4,000 Irish voters in Hampstead only four spoilt their ballots with an 'H'.[60]

The Hampstead campaign took a great deal of work organising large numbers of volunteers. Speaking to his campaign team in 1978, Livingstone had hoped for victory. In the aftermath of the Winter of Discontent, things looked different. On election night Livingstone was beaten and Geoffrey Finsberg was re-elected with an increased majority and given the job of Minister for London. Nonetheless, Livingstone achieved a good result in a bad year. As John Carvel notes, the swing to the Tories in the capital was 7.1 per cent and in the neighbouring constituencies of Hackney and Islington the swing was around 10 per cent.[61] While Livingstone lost, he was perhaps 8 per cent up on the average inner-London Labour candidate, demonstrating that Labour could do well if it appealed to minorities as well as the white working class.

Writing in *Socialist Organiser*, Livingstone blamed Labour's 1979 defeat on 'the disastrous record of Callaghan'. Nonetheless, Livingstone was committed to fighting the new government. 'Local councils', he wrote, 'will constitute one focus of the fightback.' Livingstone's next target was the Greater London Council (GLC) and as he was impressed by Abbott in the campaign, he encouraged her to seek selection and stand. Abbott declined: 'I felt that I was too young, but that was the strategy, you identified people and you put them in position.'[62] 'I wish she had come on,' Livingstone opines. 'She would have enjoyed it.'[63]

MEETING CORBYN

Abbott's association with Livingstone led to an important meeting: 'It was Ken who introduced me to Jeremy Corbyn.'[64] Abbott, Livingstone and Corbyn were all delegates at the 1978 Labour Party conference, which took place in Blackpool. There was a considerable commonality of interest with Corbyn, who recalls, 'I first met Diane in 1978. At that time, I was a councillor in Haringey, and chair of the community development committee, which was responsible for race relations.'[65] As a result, Corbyn was involved in the campaign against SUS. Corbyn proposed a motion calling on the Home Secretary Merlyn Rees to repeal the SUS law and to hold a public inquiry into the police, which were the two central demands of the Scrap SUS campaign. The motion, which had the backing of councillor Basil Lewis – one of the Tory's few black councillors – passed with cross-party support in January 1979. In a statement to *West Indian World*, published in February 1979, Corbyn argued that 'the campaign for the repeal of SUS should be supported by anyone concerned about basic civil liberties'.[66] The reference to civil liberties may have been an indication of Abbott's influence. Although Abbott was friends with Corbyn and Livingstone and was working on the London left she 'wasn't grand or important enough', as she puts it, to be invited to the Independent Left Corresponding Society, which met at Tony Benn's house in Holland Park.[67]

During 1979, Abbott and Corbyn became involved romantically. The relationship was brief, lasting less than a year. During this time the couple were able to get away on a motorcycle holiday to France. Stories that circulated from the early 1980s shifted the location of the trip to Eastern Europe, but reports that they toured East Germany are inaccurate. Keith Veness, an activist in Islington who was expelled from the Labour Party in 1976 for his criticisms of the local Labour MP, claims that the relationship ended simply because Corbyn devoted so much time to politics. Apparently Veness and Bernie Grant, a Guiana-born trades unionist and Labour councillor in Haringey, helped Abbott move her furniture out of Corbyn's flat when the relationship ended. In any case, Abbott and Corbyn remained firm friends and political allies.[68]

The two worked together during the 1979 election campaign. Corbyn was Ted Knight's election agent in Hornsey. 'As a nearby campaign,' Corbyn recalls, 'we kept in touch. Diane told me how the campaign was going; I told her how ours was going.'[69] In both constituencies Labour faced an uphill battle. 'We were up against the Winter of Discontent strike of 1978 to 1979, in which Diane supported the National Union of Public Employees (NUPE).' Corbyn was working as a NUPE official at the time and remembers being kept busy. 'By day I was organising the union, and in the evening I was a councillor dealing with the consequences of the strike, because we couldn't get the rubbish collected. It wasn't a conflict; it was more of an interesting challenge. And I was election agent in Hornsey. I never did less than an eighteen-hour day!'[70]

THATCHER'S ELECTION

Margaret Thatcher's appointment as Prime Minister in May 1979 is usually understood as being a turning point in recent political history, the point at which the social democratic consensus of the post-war years finally came to an end. For Abbott, the Conservative victory was certainly a break with the past. 'I got involved in activist politics at a time where there seemed to be an upward trajectory. And then Thatcher was elected. It really did seem to be a reversal.'[71]

Abbott's view is close to that set out by Darcus Howe in *Race Today*. Writing in anticipation of a Conservative victory, Howe argued that 'the entire political atmosphere is transformed' by Thatcher.[72] He argued that since the 1960s black people had made great strides, standing up to police racism, winning employment rights through campaigns such as the Grunwick strike and building black organisations to advance the struggle. 'And just as we begin to see the end of the tunnel, enter Mrs Margaret Thatcher to put us back precisely where we were before.' For Howe, Thatcher's famous 'swamped' speech was a first step to recolonising black people.

OWAAD too were quick to spot the immediate dangers posed by the Thatcher government. Their third newsletter argued that sweeping cuts to social services, education and health care would have a 'devastating effect ... on both black and white working class', and that cuts to education, council-run nurseries and adult education would have a particular impact on young black mothers, forcing them back into the home.[73]

As she left Cambridge, Abbott's director of studies had commented that she urgently needed to make a decision about 'social democratic politics'. On her return to London, Abbott seems to have made that decision quickly. No fan of Callaghan, she joined the Labour Party and campaigned for a Labour victory at the ballot box. But electoral politics and party politics were not the sum of Abbott's vision of democracy. Unions, black women's groups, radical collectives, pressure groups, representative organisations of all kinds were central to her politics. Abbott knew that democracy meant more than regular elections. Elections are an inherently majoritarian mechanism. Consequently, minorities have to organise, to make their voices heard and to make sure that their interests are protected and advanced, and minority groups have to campaign, organise marches, write manifestos, lobby and educate, to use all of their rights as citizens to ensure that democracy works for them.

Perhaps Abbott had been inspired by the strategies of black radicals in America that she had studied in Cambridge. Perhaps it was Abbott's encounter with OWAAD and the Scrap SUS campaign, which demonstrated the effectiveness of people power. Or perhaps Abbott's thinking was influenced by the Labour left and Tony Benn's vision of the Labour Party as a movement that should draw on the strength of black movements, women's movements, as well as the trades unions. Whatever the source of the inspiration, by the late 1970s it was clear the power that Abbott sought was people power.

In the pursuit of power, Abbott consciously adopted a new strategy, which has shaped her politics ever since. 'I've always kept one foot in the organised Labour movement, and one foot in black politics.'[74] While Abbott felt more engaged in OWAAD and the campaign to Scrap SUS, she took Labour Party membership seriously. There was, after all, no contradiction between being involved in grassroots black politics and a mainstream political party. In fact, involvement in the former enriched her engagement in the latter.

The late 1970s was a period in which the notion of democracy was being contested. While Abbott wanted to unite parliamentary power with extra-parliamentary power, Thatcher took a different view. For Thatcher, democracy was problematic because it led to inflation, as unions and elected officials conspired to increase wages and public spending. As a result, democracy had to be tamed. For Thatcher, the democratic mandate gained at a general election was supreme. The policy of a democratically elected government should not be challenged by unions, grassroots organisations or local government. Indeed, these institutions needed to be constrained legally. Democracy needed to be protected from minorities. The tension between these two conceptions of democracy would play a large part in shaping the politics of the 1980s.

CHAPTER 4

THE FOURTH ESTATE

In the early 1980s, Abbott realised two long-held ambitions. She became a published writer and an elected politician. More often than not, these activities overlapped. In the context of rising inflation, rising unemployment, industrial strife and urban unrest, Abbott had her work cut out for her on both fronts. Economic problems were not the only cause of anxiety for British citizens in the early Thatcher years. For the first time since the 1960s there seemed to be a real chance of nuclear war. At the same time, the first Thatcher administration was a time of bold political experimentation and optimism. Thatcher, for a time at least, adopted monetarism, a radical, not to say experimental, set of policies that flew in the face of post-war economic orthodoxy. While monetarism was quickly abandoned, the commitment to markets remained, taking shape nationally and locally in the form of privatisation and outsourcing. On the left, new ideas were gaining ground, ideas that reached their fullest expression through the GLC. For feminists and black radicals too, the 1980s was a time of innovation in theory and in practice. This was the context in which Abbott established herself as a force to be reckoned with on the left.

Abbott left the NCCL in March 1980, after a little more than a year with the organisation. At the time unemployment, which had risen consistently for six months, reached 1.4 million. March 1980 also saw the publication of the Medium-Term Financial Strategy which contained significant cuts to public spending and led to more lay-offs. However, the economic downturn did not affect everyone equally. As a young professional living in the south-east of the country with a degree from one of Britain's top universities, Abbott was able to move from one job to another with ease. 'I really felt like the world was my oyster. There were a whole range of jobs available to me. If you didn't like a job, you could leave it on Friday and get another on Monday.'[1]

Seeking a change, and following advice from a friend, Abbott applied for a research job at Thames Television. She had first considered working in television around a year earlier. While working at the NCCL, she was approached by Michael Attwell, who was a producer based at London Weekend Television (LWT). Attwell, who had produced LWT's *Weekend World*, was developing the six-part series *Babylon*, which was aimed at young black viewers. Attwell and his team were looking for someone to front the show, and a roving interviewer. They considered Abbott for both roles. *Babylon*, the brainchild of John Birt, who was latterly director general of the BBC, was ground-breaking in a number of ways, particularly as 'there had never been a programme on British television presented solely by a black person'.[2] As a result, there were few black people outside children's television with experience as presenters. Abbott met LWT's team a couple of times to discuss working on the show but in the end LWT opted for Lincoln Browne.

A year later, Abbott was more successful. In the spring of 1980, she began work at the newsroom on Euston Road, on Thames Television's flagship news programme. *Thames News* went out twice every weekday, and Abbott worked on the team that put out the 6 p.m. show. As ever, Abbott was usually the only black person in the newsroom. Even so, she enjoyed the job. 'Every day was different, I liked the immediacy, and being at the centre of events.'[3] The job required an early start, and the deadlines were always tight. As a researcher, Abbott was attached to a roving news team who made short films, often interviews, which were slotted into the live broadcast. Each day began with a review of the papers, press releases and calls to press officers at emergency services. Producers met at 8 a.m. to establish a slate of stories, and shortly after, Abbott and the rest of the researchers were sent out to record interviews and contextual footage. The material was then rushed back and edited into a package lasting a few minutes.

Abbott worked as part of a crew, including a camera operator, director, sound technician, electrician and a driver. Around the time Abbott joined, Thames was changing to electronic news gathering and film cameras were replaced with video cameras which recorded on one-inch tape. Conducting interviews usually took place in the late morning and early afternoon. As a result, they spanned the mandated lunch break. 'It was the days when the unions really ruled in ITV,' Abbott explains.[4] On meeting her crew in the morning, the first issue was lunch: 'Before they asked the technical questions, they'd bring out a copy of the Michelin Guide and find the nearest three-star restaurant. Then they were happy, and they'd ask about the technicalities of the shoot.' Union regulations meant that the crew were entitled to lunch, and, quite reasonably, the crew were determined to ensure they got their due. Abbott was part of the union – she joined the Association of Cinematograph, Television and Allied Technicians (ACTT) and later became an ACTT rep – but she felt that some union rules were unnecessary. That said, 'the grip that unions had, had an upside, in that the technical quality of television was very good, and there was a route in for younger people'. In time, Abbott would work with the big television unions to ensure that the route in for younger people was also opened up to young black people, Asian people and women.

While working as a researcher Abbott was also writing for *London Labour Briefing* and *The Leveller*, publications far to the left of *Thames News*. *The Leveller* was a radical left newspaper which was issued fortnightly. Abbott became involved in late 1979 and continued writing for the paper through to the summer of 1981. She recalls 'attending their meetings faithfully. I was, of course, the only black person there, but I was used to that, so it wasn't a reason not to go.'[5] Tim Gopsill, a member of the collective which put out *The Leveller*, describes the group as 'a real collective, a completely open collective, and anyone who turned up could join in', claiming that all members took part in the decisions which shaped each issue.[6] Consistent with the principles of the collective, the magazine had no editor. Rather, the content of the magazine was agreed at weekly meetings. Then each issue was put together by two co-ordinators, one of whom was a professional and one who was not. Participation was voluntary, there was no formal hierarchy, and no one was paid. Initially, the collective was based in a squat on Drummond Street in Euston, but by the time Abbott became involved meetings took place in Caledonian Road, in the basement of the radical publisher Zed Books.

Looking back, Gopsill remembers Abbott, who was known as 'Di' within the collective, as 'so outgoing and upfront, you knew about her instantly. She asserted her presence very well. She announced she was going to be the first black woman MP the day she arrived, and we thought, "Great, we're with you!"' Gopsill rated her journalism: 'She was very good at explaining things, she would have made a good journalist. She's very good at putting a story across, and she had a very strong understanding of the world.'

Abbott's articles in *The Leveller* provide an insight into her political preoccupations and activities at the time. Her first piece concerned Labour Party reform. Published in October 1979 shortly after Labour's annual conference, Abbott presented an account of the first national Campaign for Labour Party Democracy (CLPD) Women's conference. Abbott's position was more radical than the mainstream CLPD as she advocated 'positive discrimination' in selection for parliamentary seats. Abbott was clearly enthused by the radicalism of the National CLPD Women's conference, for while noting that the conference was overwhelmingly 'young, white and middle class' she argued that it was finally 'beginning to reflect debates that have been going on in the women's movement for over a decade'.[7]

Abbott turned her attention to race in 'One battle won – but the war?', published in *The Leveller* in May 1980. Here, Abbott dealt with the violent clashes between police and young black people in St Pauls, Bristol, which took place in April 1980. While the mainstream media responded with disbelief, Abbott emphasised that the violence occurred for wholly predictable reasons. She argued that in a period where working people were under intense pressure and with 'capitalism in crisis', working-class people inevitably clashed with the police, 'the forces of the state'.[8] Where broadsheets and tabloids responded with moral horror, Abbott claimed the 'urban insurrection' was likely to be the most progressive event of the year as it 'posed a direct threat to [state] power'. Abbott's radicalism is also evident in her critique of established left-wing groups and activists. She found fault with Labour for introducing the 'monetarist and law-and-order policies' which led to the riots. She also criticised the white left, particularly the Anti-Nazi League for 'opportunism' and tokenism. Abbott predicted that the police would follow up the mass arrests with greater surveillance. Even so, she ended on an optimistic note, giving the last word to her mother:

> My mother is a black working-class lady nearing 60. Eminently respectable and conservative-minded, she was pleased and excited by the ITN film of policemen running away from black youth and said firmly: 'It shows they can't push us around anymore.'[9]

Years later, with free market assumptions widespread, talk of 'capitalism in crisis' can sound far-fetched. However, in the context of the early 1980s this was a wholly plausible argument. Inflation, which had been just under 10 per cent when Callaghan left office, reached 21.9 per cent in May 1980. According to the economic orthodoxy of the post-war years there was a trade-off between the rate of inflation and the level of unemployment, so that a rise in one would lead to a fall in the other. Thatcherism appeared to bring the worst of both worlds: soaring inflation accompanied by climbing levels of unemployment. The economy had also been in recession for about six months at the time Abbott was writing for *The Leveller*. Rather than reversing the 'stagflation' of the 1970s, Thatcherism initially made Britain's economic problems far worse. Thatcher's first recession also had palpable consequences, affecting Britons of all social backgrounds. The working class were hit by unemployment, and the middle class by inflation, which eroded the value of their savings. It is also worth recalling that Thatcher's policies, particularly the abolition of exchange controls and the decision to embrace deflation during a recession, were radical economic experiments. In a country that was widely regarded as 'ungovernable', it was impossible to predict the social consequences of the economic turmoil. In this context, Abbott was one of many who characterised the economic crisis of the early 1980s as a crisis of capitalism.

In February 1981, Abbott set out her views on television in *The Leveller*. Her article 'Who rules the airwaves?' was a response to a seminar on broadcasting that she had attended at the Institute of Contemporary Art featuring some big names, including Stuart Hood, a senior figure at the BBC. The article returns to one of Abbott's preoccupations, the ability of established institutions 'to absorb and/or control, and/or buy off mavericks'.[10] To some extent, the event was an opportunity to air grievances about BBC bias. However, it also allowed programme makers to express their concerns that interesting content, which might be deemed sexist or racist, was being cut. Reviewing the event in the *Financial Times*, Chris Dunkley described this as the 'totalitarianism of the new left'. Abbott was more concerned about another trend that Dunkley had missed. 'Curiously,' she wrote, 'he did not see anything noteworthy about the political vetting and blacklisting which Hood revealed went on at the BBC and which might reasonably be called the "totalitarianism of the old right".'

COUNTY HALL

Concerned that television was dominated by the 'old right', Abbott came up with a plan to bring a new kind of politics to the 6 p.m. news. Following Livingstone's campaign in Hampstead, Abbott joined the initiative to take control of the GLC. Believing that the coming election, Livingstone's planned takeover of the Labour group, and the left's agenda for London were newsworthy, Abbott made the case to her producer at Thames that she should be based permanently at County Hall. At first, Thames executives were unconvinced, but they agreed to a trial. When it became clear that Abbott had correctly predicted the outcome of the election and Livingstone's takeover of the Labour group, her bosses agreed, and Abbott spent the next year as Thames' correspondent at County Hall.

Michael Ward, initially chair of the industry and employment committee on the GLC, and latterly Livingstone's deputy, recalls, that in the late 1970s, 'County Hall was a place with terrific delusions of grandeur'.[11] In the 1970s, under the Tory leader Horace Cutler, the GLC developed a press corps, based at the GLC's subsidised bar. By the time Cutler left office, the GLC had dedicated studios to allow live radio and television broadcasts. These studios, Ward remembers, meant that Abbott could base herself at County Hall. While seconded to the GLC Abbott would begin every day in the County Hall Press Office, have lunch with the press pack and put together footage covering the GLC's exploits. What is more, she was able to spend time with Livingstone, John McDonnell, Paul Boateng and Jeremy Corbyn, who were all either Labour members of the GLC or used County Hall as a base.

Livingstone planned to use the considerable powers and financial resources of the GLC to introduce a form of 'municipal socialism'. This would both mitigate the economic damage caused by Thatcherism and showcase a radical alternative. Livingstone's municipal socialism was critical of Callaghan's economic policy, and of Wilson's willingness to compromise. However, Livingstone did not want a return to the Labourism of Clement Attlee. For all its successes, Livingstone argued that the Attlee government was essentially paternalistic. Indeed, paternalism was the common thread which ran through the post-war Labour governments. At their best, Labour administrations had improved the economic conditions of the working class. But they had taken a top-down approach. In the nationalised industries, in government, in the unions and in the Labour Party itself power remained centralised, out of reach of working people. Livingstone wanted to pioneer a decentralised, highly democratic form of socialism. In this sense, his vision was in line with the radicalism that was reshaping the Labour Party, albeit temporarily, at the beginning of the 1980s. The 1980 Labour Party conference had passed resolutions to extend 'public ownership with industrial democracy'.[12] Speaking at the 1980 conference, Tony Benn, the leading figure in this new wave of Labour radicalism, articulated this new position, arguing for 'self-management', which he held up as an alternative to both Thatcherism and 'the hideous bureaucracy of some of our nationalised industries'. Abbott's articles in *The Leveller*, her support for the Campaign for Labour Party Democracy and her endorsement of the proposals of the National CLPD Women's conference clearly locate her on this radical wing of the Labour Party.

The commonality between Abbott's concerns and those of Labour's new left went much further than a commitment to democratise public institutions. For radicals like Benn and Livingstone, empowering working people went hand-in-hand with a desire to work with minority groups and women's groups. Indeed, recognising the interests of marginalised groups was an essential part of breaking the stranglehold of central government and devolving power. This new approach chimed with Abbott's political commitments, as it recognised the legitimacy of black self-organisation, and accorded grassroots organisations an important role in building a more egalitarian and democratic society. In that sense, Abbott's commitment to grassroots black politics was wholly compatible with this approach to politics on the Labour left.

Livingstone had had his eye on the GLC from the late 1970s. Once the Hampstead campaign was over, he began planning for the 1981 GLC elections. But winning was not enough. Livingstone wanted Labour to put forward a radical manifesto, win the election, and then fulfil its promises. He was reflecting on the experience of the 1960s and 1970s where radical promises and election victories had been followed by compromise, which he blamed for electoral defeat. Determined to win and to establish a radical administration, Livingstone approached left-wingers at Labour's 1979 conference, encouraging them to stand for election to the GLC. At first it was an uphill struggle.

LONDON LABOUR BRIEFING

In February 1980, Livingstone's campaign took shape with the foundation of the magazine *London Labour Briefing*. According to Livingstone's first editorial, the new magazine aimed to keep 'active militants inside the Labour Party and the unions in London in touch with each other and up to date on what is happening in the various battles across the capital'.[13] At its inception the magazine had no fixed ideological line, and editorial meetings were open to all. Nonetheless, Corbyn recalls,

It was seen as outrageous by the higher echelons of the Labour Party. Whenever an issue came out, they were passed round the table at the executive of the London Labour Party. There would be points of order about some of the articles, allegations of libel, a lot of very loud figures in the party were on the executive, they'd get into rows about *Briefing*.[14]

During 1980, *Briefing* circulated details of Labour's radical agenda. This included the commitment to improve London transport services while cutting fares by 25 per cent, to renovate existing council homes, build more and freeze rents. *Briefing* also carried lists of candidates who had agreed to stand for the GLC elections, and news of selection battles. Years before Peter Mandelson professionalised Labour's national campaigns, *Briefing* was publishing lists of marginal seats and tables of statistics to help activists make calculations about where best to expend their energies.

By the end of 1980, *Briefing*'s campaign had expanded into the 'Target 82' campaign. Writing in the December issue, Corbyn explained:

THE LEFT NEEDS TO BEGIN NOW to build towards left control of Labour Councils in the 1982 London borough elections. In the fight against Thatcherism we need to ensure that our councillors will be people who accept that they have a political role in fighting the government.[15]

The huge programme of cuts planned by the Conservatives, Corbyn argued, would be forced through local government. Therefore, Labour needed to select councillors who were committed to a policy of resistance. In that sense, Target 82 was designed to 'extend the achievements in selection of GLC candidates to the control of local councils in 1982'.[16]

Abbott was involved in *Briefing* and Target 82. 'The point about Target 82,' she recalls, 'was to replace some of these centrist and right-wing councillors, and put left-wingers in. Target 82 brought all of us together across London, through meetings in different boroughs where you had to plot and scheme to get a left-wing person in.'[17] Abbott and Livingstone were both living in Westminster at the time. Livingstone stood for the GLC, and Abbott stood for Westminster City Council. While Target 82 was enormously exciting and ultimately very successful, it involved a great deal of hard work. Abbott remembers lots of evenings sitting in cold church halls with the likes of Livingstone, Corbyn, Graham Bash and Tony Banks drawing up plans to build left-wing representation across London, and Corbyn remembers that Abbott conducted interviews for *Briefing*. As a rule, interviews were unattributed, so it is difficult to know how many she carried out for the magazine.

Abbott describes herself as being 'on the fringes' of *Briefing*.[18] Livingstone, Corbyn, Bash, Ted and Chris Knight were at the heart of the magazine in the early days. Bash does not remember her as a regular at the editorial meetings, which took place at County Hall and were open to all. Equally, Abbott was active in Westminster, which was rarely featured in *Briefing*. The magazine paid considerable attention to Harringay, Brent, Ealing, Islington, Southwark and the activities of the GLC. In that sense the magazine focused on Labour administrations which were fighting government cuts. Westminster, which was under Conservative control, featured much less prominently, at least in the early 1980s. Paul Dimoldenberg, who was elected to Westminster Council in 1982 and went on to lead the Labour group, recalls, '*Briefing* were not at all active in Westminster in the early 1980s. They had very few active members locally.'[19]

Nonetheless, from 1984 *Briefing* backed Abbott in Labour Party National Executive Committee (NEC) elections, as a representative for the Women's section. Abbott was also one of the keynotes, together with Tony Benn and Livingstone, at the 'Target Labour Government' fringe meeting during the 1984 Labour conference, so although she remained on the fringes of the magazine she was on good terms with *Briefing*'s directing brains.

Briefing was not the only new political formation to emerge in the early 1980s. As Richard Heffernan and Mike Marqusee argue, while 1980 had been 'the high-water mark for the left', 1981 saw the beginnings of a backlash.[20] In January 1981 Shirley Williams, Roy Jen-kins, David Owen and Bill Rodgers issued the document that became known as the Limehouse Declaration. It marked the foundation of the Council of Social Democracy, which was quickly rebranded as the Social Democratic Party (SDP).

Abbott turned her attention to the new social democrats in *The Leveller* in February 1981, following Sue Slipman's decision to join the group. Slipman had first come to public attention in 1977 as the first woman to win election as president of the NUS, and had been a member of the Communist Party and area officer for the decidedly left-wing NUPE. For Abbott, Slipman had turned her back on the NUPE workers that she was paid to represent, and allowed herself to become the Social Democrats' 'token young feminist'.[21] In that sense, the article rehearsed Abbott's critique of the vices of middle-class student politics.

Abbott's attitude to the new SDP was equally scathing. She dismissed the claim that the founders were committed to creating a decentralised party, pointing to their trenchant opposition to decentralisation within the Labour Party. She also argued that they were on the side of their 'merchant banker backers' rather than on the side of NUPE members.[22] NUPE members had, after all, taken strike action in protest at Labour's incomes policy in the late 1970s, and had thrown their weight behind Bennite reform of the Labour Party in the early 1980s. Abbott, Corbyn recalls, had supported NUPE during the strike at the beginning of 1979, which meant she was well placed to garner reactions to Slipman's decision from within the union.

The article is also notable because it presents a brief interview with David Owen. Speaking to Owen on behalf of *The Leveller*, Abbott asked if there was 'not a contradiction between Slipman's past views and the right wingers she [was] now lining up with?' Abbott's question pointed to the fact that the SDP wanted to present themselves both as moderates and as radicals, and that in welcoming former communists into the party they had become vulnerable to accusations of leftist infiltration. Owen apparently had no comeback to Abbott's question.[23]

Abbott's early critique of the Social Democrats contained some of the major themes which *Briefing* took up repeatedly from the end of 1981. Writing in 1982, Tony Benn criticised the SDP's refusal to make policy on a democratic basis. Tony Banks and Jeremy Corbyn both critiqued the anti-union orientation of the SDP. In that sense, Abbott was one of the first on the London left to take on the Social Democrats, and her article anticipated some of the attack lines that would be used by the Labour left throughout the 1980s.[24]

Abbott's association with *The Leveller* came to an end around April 1981. Her final piece for the magazine was a review of *Sizwe Bansi is Dead*, a play by Athol Fugard, a white South African novelist, written in collaboration with John Kani and Winstin Ntshona, both black South African actors. Abbott's analysis of the play returns to one of her central concerns: the nature of racism. The problem with the play, according to Abbott, is that it deals with the Pass Laws, a single legal aspect of apartheid. Consequently, by 'focusing the audience's anger on the inanimate instrument of the system rather than the logic of the system he stops short of locating the roots of apartheid where they actually lie – in white racism'.[25] For Abbott, the play had missed the opportunity to examine the systemic nature of racism.

Abbott enjoyed writing for *The Leveller*, but the experience left her with an enduring suspicion of collectives. The desire to work in collectives, Abbott recalls, was well intentioned, but ultimately counter-productive. She argues:

> There was a tendency on the left to counter-pose capitalism and hierarchy with collectives. The argument was that collectives gave everybody an equal voice. But if you actually get involved in a collective, that's complete bullshit. In practice, the people with the most social capital and the most confidence dominate. A collective can be a harder system for a woman or a black person than an organisation where there is a structure and a system, where you can work your way up. What I learned is that collectives aren't the nirvana of social organisation they are meant to be.[26]

Over time it became clear that the dominant people on *The Leveller* were white men. Abbott's analysis of the pitfalls of collectives high-lighted a subtle distinction that was lost on many advocates of radical forms of organisation. Collectives, Abbott concluded, are not free of hierarchy and structure; they merely replace formal hierarchies with informal ones, where a lack of clearly articulated rules acts as a barrier to diversity.

Abbott regards writing for *The Leveller* and occasionally for *Briefing* as an important form of political engagement. Not only did writing for left-wing journals allow Abbott to indulge her passion for writing but activist journalism reflected one of Abbott's intuitions about radical politics: 'I've always felt that for someone on the left, communication is very important. A lot of our ideas, a lot of the things we are doing, don't get covered in the national media. Black activists were completely locked out of mainstream media.'

THE NEW CROSS FIRE

In the early hours of Sunday 18 January 1981, a fire swept through 439 New Cross Road in Deptford, south London. Thirteen young black people who had been attending a sixteenth birthday party died as a result of the blaze. Many more were injured.

The New Cross fire was a defining moment for black people in Britain. Looking back, Abbott argues that 'the fire symbolised the indifference of state institutions to black people, in the same way that the murder of Stephen Lawrence did'.[27] Gee Ruddock, who had organised the party to celebrate her daughter Yvonne's sixteenth birthday, was convinced that the fire was the result of a racist arson attack. Ruddock's belief fitted the facts. A car had been seen speeding away from the house before the fire took hold. Eyewitnesses described something being thrown through the living room window. Ruddock's view was all the more plausible in the context. National Front activity in southeast London was on the rise. Brian W. Alleyne argues, 'The New Cross area had seen numerous racist attacks on black people in the period leading up to the fire and there was a general atmosphere of tension in the area.'[28] Support for the far right was on the rise as groups such as the National Front sought to capitalise on the social unrest which accompanied soaring unemployment among young white people in Britain's towns and cities. Yvonne Ruddock died in the fire. Paul Ruddock, her brother, suffered extensive burns and died in hospital three weeks later.

In the aftermath of the fire, grieving families were faced with misinformation from much of the media, suspicion from the police and silence from the Thatcher government. A statement published by the New Cross Massacre Action Committee on 25 February, around six weeks after the fire, set out the family's grievances. The statement criticised the *Daily Mail* for deliberately spreading confusion. Indeed, on the morning of 25 February, the *Daily Mail* had reported, wholly inaccurately, that a group of black partygoers had been arrested by the police and charged with murder. The New Cross Massacre Action Committee also criticised the police. The immediate response of police investigators was to seek to blame the victims and other young people who were at the party. Equally concerning was the way in which the police announced arrests. The committee had predicted that the police would publicise the arrest of young black people to deflect attention away from claims that the fire was the result of racist violence. In the end, the New Cross Massacre Action Committee claimed that the arrests were timed in such a way as to 'divert attention from the demonstration' called to protest the official response to the fire.[29] Finally, the committee criticised government inaction. Specifically, they asked government and Parliament to show the same respect to families that had lost loved ones in New Cross as they had to families in Ireland who had lost relatives in the Stardust nightclub fire a few weeks earlier. 'If the same things happened today,' Abbott comments, 'the slogan would be Black Lives Matter. What we felt was that for the state, black lives didn't matter, and that was what was electrifying about the response to the New Cross fire.'[30]

The New Cross Massacre Action Committee emerged as black people began to organise to support the grieving families, to hold the police to account and to investigate the real causes of the fire in the absence of a meaningful police investigation. In the weeks following the fire, regular public meetings were held in New Cross. Soon,

Sybil Phoenix, a Methodist lay preacher who ran the Moonshot Youth Club; Darcus Howe, editor of *Race Today*; and John La Rose, an activist who had founded the radical publisher New Beacon Books, were joined by thousands demanding justice for the families. The first big public meeting took place a week after the fire. Around 2,000 people arrived from across the country, travelling from cities including Bradford, Manchester and Leeds to support those who had lost loved ones in the fire. The New Cross Massacre Action Committee emerged from these assemblies. Howe was tasked with the co-ordination of the Black People's Day of Action, a protest march in support of the families, which was designed to put pressure on the authorities to act.[31]

Abbott, who continued to combine collaboration with the white left and black grassroots politics, participated in the march, covering the event for *The Leveller*. Howe had argued that the Black People's Day of Action was conceived as 'a general strike of blacks'.[32] The idea of a black general strike had been circulating among black radicals since the late 1960s. Indeed, Abbott and Ricky Cambridge had discussed a similar idea in the late 1970s. For this reason, the New Cross Massacre Action Committee decided to hold the protest on the first Monday in March. This would otherwise have been a working day and a school day. This was a break with the traditional approach of the white left, which held mass protests at the weekend.

Abbott travelled from her home in Paddington to New Cross early on the Black People's Day of Action. As the number 36 bus made its way across London, white passengers got off to go to work while black people boarded heading to New Cross. On arrival at New Cross, Abbott saw coachloads of people 'from Manchester, Birmingham, Sheffield, Huddersfield' all arriving to join the march.[33] Organising the protest had been a national effort. Howe had toured the country, holding meetings, explaining the situation and making the case for a mass demonstration.

The march started in New Cross, headed over Blackfriars Bridge, through the City and Fleet Street, past Scotland Yard and the Houses of Parliament, before finishing in Hyde Park. The route was symbolic and took marchers from the location of the fire, past the offices of major newspapers, to the headquarters of the Metropolitan Police and on to Parliament. The fact that marchers would cross Blackfriars Bridge was also symbolic. It linked the Black People's Day of Action to a march organised by the Chartists in 1848 and in so doing linked the Black People's Day of Action to the country's tradition of democratic protest.

Many joined the march in New Cross, with others joining as it made its way through London. Writing in *The Leveller*, Abbott reported, 'Men in bookie shops left their betting and joined the march. People in doorways were drawn along ... Schoolchildren whose school gates had been locked specifically to stop them getting involved jumped over the walls to join the march.'[34]

For Abbott, what was particularly striking was the way black people united behind the march: 'West Indians of relentless respectability, people who had always sworn they weren't political, everyone you personally knew – they were all on the march.' Estimates at the time indicate that 20,000 people, the vast majority black, joined the demonstration, making the Black People's Day of Action the largest black march in British history. Abbott argued that the scale of the march and the unity of the people involved had an immediate political impact:

The march has had an effect on the political consciousness of the black community which cannot be overstated. The kind of black people who for nearly a generation have been unmoved by the best efforts of the white left to politicise them are still talking excitedly about it.

There is a feeling of strength. For everyone there it was the first time they had been on the streets of Britain surrounded by other black people in such numbers. It produced a sense of elation. It was as if white society's racist mystification, by which we are always the problem – always the passive object of other people's good works – suddenly cleared away and we realised what it was to feel powerful.[35]

Yet the event highlighted the racism they fought. From her vantage point in the Thames Television newsroom, Abbott could see that the march did not fit into any of the standard journalistic narratives. The Black People's Day of Action was not a story about mugging or 'mindless violence'. Nor did the large number of eminently respectable first-generation migrants lend itself to a story about black extremists. At the same time, there was no media template for a story about black people organising themselves. This was true on the left, Abbott argued, just as much as it was on the right. Rather than acknowledge that the march was organised by black people, the *Morning Star*, as Abbott noted, 'seemed to imply that most of the people on the march were white anti-racists'.[36] Nothing could have been further from the truth. The question of white participation caused controversy early in the planning process. Some argued that white people should be able to participate in the march on equal terms with black and Asian people; others argued that white people should be excluded. Howe's solution was to allow white people to join at the back of the march, symbolising the leading role of black people in the protest. Crucially, the demonstration was organised by Howe and the Race Today Collective, not white radicals.

Abbott's experience at Thames also illuminated the way the media reacted to stories about black people. Thames cameras were rolling throughout the march, and footage of the disciplined peaceful protest was screened that evening. The next day, print journalists published stories of mass violence and riots. *The Sun* covered the march with the headline 'Black Day at Blackfriars', devoting a double-page spread to stories of violence under the heading 'The Day the Blacks Ran Riot in London'. The following passage gives a flavour of *The Sun*'s coverage:

A cordon was thrown across the bridge in an attempt to halt the march. But militants angrily chanting 'Murder, murder, murder' bulldozed their way through with a five-ton truck. As it was driven relentlessly through the police ranks the mob charged across the bridge. Then the rampage began as thousands of blacks stormed up Fleet Street. Urged on by militants on the truck they hurled bricks and smashed shop windows.[37]

The *Daily Express* painted a similar picture under the heading 'The rampage of the mob'; the *Daily Mail* ran with 'When the Black Tide met the Thin Blue Line'. While the papers were right to point to some trouble on Blackfriars Bridge, the stories in *The Sun*, the *Daily Mail* and the *Daily Express* were wild exaggerations. As the *Thames News* footage showed, the march was almost entirely peaceful. Reports in the *South East London Mercury* that the marchers 'demonstrated their anger with dignity, their frustration noisily but peacefully, their sense of tragedy with emotion' corresponds more closely to eyewitness accounts. The seven-hour march through central London, which brought together 20,000 people, resulted in only twenty-five criminal charges. What is more, the press failed to record the fact that the trouble on the bridge was caused by the police issuing contradictory orders and deliberately obstructing a legal march.

The reaction in the Thames newsroom to the press coverage also made an impression on Abbott. Rather than believing the evidence of their own cameras, Thames producers took the stories of black mob violence seriously and assumed they had missed the story. Looking back, Abbott comments:

> If you had been on the march, and read the coverage the next day, you wouldn't have known it was the same event. Working for a mainstream media organisation made me very conscious of the role of the mainstream media and how it distorts reality, and how important it is to get your own version of events out there.[38]

Abbott concluded her piece in *The Leveller* with a warning: 'The kind of black people who have always rejected militancy before have come away from the march saying that perhaps violent confrontation is going to prove the only way the community can gain political recognition in British society.'[39]

Abbott's article appeared on 20 March. Three weeks later, it was clear how right she had been. Abbott was not the only black radical to detect a new sense of confidence among black Britons after the Black People's Day of Action. Howe, and others in the Race Today

Collective saw it too. The opposite was true of the police. As Paul Gilroy has noted, research into police attitudes to the Black People's Day of Action reveals that many in the Met saw the success of the march as 'a symbolic defeat'.[40] What is more, police officers were perturbed by the growing assurance of black people following the demonstration.

The police pushed back a month later with Operation Swamp 81, a new operation that appeared to echo Thatcher's anti-immigration rhetoric, which they justified in terms of identifying criminals. Ten police squads were instructed to use stop and search powers intensively over the course of the week beginning 6 April 1981. According to official instructions, 'The essence of the exercise is therefore to ensure that all officers remain on the streets and success will depend on a concentrated effort of "stops", based on the powers of surveillance and suspicion.'[41]

Almost half of the Swamp 81 officers were deployed in Brixton, where the operation led to 943 stops, the vast majority of which affected black people. Leila Hassan, deputy editor of *Race Today*, who lived on Railton Road, remembers that Swamp 81 transformed Brixton into something approximating the apartheid regime in South Africa, not least as the officers were in plain clothes and were not immediately distinguishable from white locals.[42]

Five days into Swamp 81, after a multitude of complaints about police behaviour and what appeared to be a growing number of scuffles between police and those they stopped, violence broke out. The ensuing uprising, often referred to as the Brixton Riots, lasted for two full days, during which the police lost control of the streets.

For Abbott, the riots were a turning point. Living in west London, she learned about them from television reports. However, even from a distance, she remembers the events of 10–12 April as being 'extraordinary because you saw streets in London on fire. You'd seen those sorts of scenes in Northern Ireland, but never on mainland Britain. It was both shocking and astonishing to see rioting on streets a few miles from Westminster. It was shocking personally, but shocking for the British state.'[43]

Abbott visited Brixton on 13 April, in the immediate aftermath of the riots. She remembers walking down Railton Road – 'the front line', as it became known – broken glass crunching underfoot. For two days, young black people, with the support of many in the community, had taken control of the streets. The George, a pub on Railton Road known as 'Rhodesia' due to the landlord's hostility to local black people, and a newsagent which refused to serve gay people had both been burned. Reflecting on the riots, Abbott argues, 'It was a defining political moment because it showed that the state could be challenged in a very comprehensive way.'

The Brixton Riots also challenged the British state in ways that the media and white audiences could understand. Newspapers were ready for stories of 'black violence' and black mobs on the rampage. As Howe argues, the riots were very disciplined, and one of the reasons that black protesters were able to run rings around the police was the sophistication of their tactics and organisation. With this in mind, stories of 'mobs' and 'mindless violence' missed the mark. But crucially, as papers ran well-rehearsed stories about black violence they inadvertently gave an opportunity for black radicals to make the case against the police, the case against the degradation of urban areas, and in so doing force an unsympathetic government to begin to recognise the reality of life for black people in Brixton.

Abbott argues that the Brixton Riots were also important as they marked a sea change in black radical politics:

> For people of my generation, the Brixton Riots were totemic. Up until then, a lot of black political activity had referenced a post-colonial reality, it was led by a generation who had been born overseas. After the riots, that post-colonial analysis still existed, but you had young people who were born here who wanted to shape the political narrative. They knew little of colonial Africa, or Jamaica, but they knew about the reality on the streets of Brixton or Bristol. So the riots were the dividing line between post-colonial politics and a very new politics. Although people like Darcus … still played a leading role, the new politics was based on the reality that young people faced on the streets.[44]

In the weeks and months after the riots, Abbott supported the Brixton Defence Committee (BDC) in its work to support those who had been accused of crimes after the riots. The BDC campaigned for an amnesty for all those arrested during the uprising. Rudi Narayan, a lawyer working with the BDC, justified an amnesty, not as a plea for clemency but on the basis that sooner or later black people were going to defend their community against an illegal police operation involving the unlawful stop and search of hundreds of innocent people.

ELIMU

Abbott was involved in other black community groups in this period. Following the 1979 election, she moved to Shirland Road in Paddington, and then to Lanhill Road. It was around this time that she joined the Elimu Carnival Band. Based in Harrow Road in Paddington, close to both Shirland and Lanhill Road, Elimu Carnival Band was founded by Ansel Wong in the late 1970s. It was the first carnival band to be founded in the area. Wong, a graduate of Hull University and founder of Britain's first full-time supplementary school, explains, 'We were a community education project; our concern was to try and educate young people about the history and heritage of the Caribbean.'[45] The educational aspect of the band was reflected in the name 'Elimu', which means 'knowledge' or 'education' in Swahili. Wong remembers that Abbott 'was a member of my carnival band for many years before becoming involved in politics'.

Elimu first performed at the Notting Hill Carnival in 1980. This was Abbott's first experience performing in Carnival. 'Carnival is not a Jamaican thing, they do it now, but it's an eastern Caribbean thing,' she explains. 'It was when I moved back to Paddington and made friends in the community that I did Carnival for the first time.'[46]

Wong recalls that Abbott joined Elimu in the early days. 'She was very dynamic, engaging and fully committed to the band. Like everybody else she contributed ideas, helping to develop the band in that way. It was before she was a prominent figure, but she was still an important influence on the band.' Reflecting on her time as part of Elimu, Abbott comments:

It was great. Carnival was a completely new phenomenon for me. It was an amazing experience because the eastern Caribbeans love their carnival. Other people, Jamaicans and white people would turn up on the day, but eastern Caribbeans spend months designing their costumes, and for weeks and weeks, people are there preparing. I enjoyed it on the day, but the whole cultural concept of carnival, of coming together was amazing.[47]

Abbott's election as a Labour councillor in 1982 changed her involvement with Elimu. Wong recalls, 'When she became a councillor, she still maintained an allegiance to Elimu, but she became involved in other bands in the area. She had to be able to demonstrate a commitment to supporting everybody else.'[48]

GLC ELECTION, 1981

Shortly after the Brixton Riots, Labour won control of the GLC. The 1981 election victory was the first fruit of *London Labour Briefing*'s efforts. In Paddington, where Abbott had campaigned for Livingstone, there was a 12.6 per cent swing to Labour. Across London, Labour won fifty seats, giving them a nine-seat majority.

The day after, Abbott was at County Hall covering events for Thames.

We had the election on the Thursday, and Friday was the GLC Labour group meeting, they all went in, a lot of them were new, there was Valery Wise, Michael Ward, everyone trooped in. I was outside with the other journalists, and when they came out Ken was leader. He looked completely different, it was the effect of power, suddenly he was transfigured! I knew he would win, because we had the numbers, but I wasn't expecting the transfiguring effect![49]

Livingstone's transformation was the prelude to a more profound change, which was to shape Abbott's approach to politics for years to come. Abbott comments, 'Ken has behaved in a problematic way in recent years. But when he was at the GLC he was at the height of his powers. He showed that you could take over a large institution and turn it to socialist ends.'[50] Since her time as an undergraduate, Abbott had been preoccupied by the problem of institutionalisation: the power of organisations to co-opt and assimilate radicals. She had witnessed this first-hand at the civil service, where organisational culture and institutional inertia transformed radicals into conservatives. The transformation of the GLC under Livingstone proved there was no iron law of institutionalisation. 'Institutions', Abbott argues, 'don't have to take you over, as a left-winger. You can take the institution over. That's what Ken showed us in the 1980s. It had a lasting influence on me.'

Taking over the institution was a deliberate strategy. Livingstone had been grappling with the problem of the County Hall bureaucracy long before becoming GLC leader. His initial plan was to push the institution in a progressive direction by replacing two thirds of the chief officers and by abolishing the post of director general. When this proved impossible, he worked department by department, replacing committee chairs and chief officers whenever the opportunity arose. Crucially, Livingstone was alive to the need to grapple with bureaucracy, to overcome institutional constraints, in order to reorient the County Hall machine.

Abbott's year covering the Livingstone administration coincided with a series of battles between GLC officials and the elected Labour administration. It allowed her to see, first-hand, how Livingstone's team learned to deal with institutional constraints. Writing in the wake of the GLC's abolition, Livingstone explained, 'The only thing we could do was change the rules of the game.'[51] Livingstone's team turned to new lawyers, often employing black barristers and female barristers. Having found sympathetic legal advice, they used this to force officials to implement radical policies. Michael Ward was one of the first to work out how to use lawyers to bolster rather than undermine the case for radical change.

There was an affinity between some aspects of the GLC's work and some of Abbott's political commitments. While working at the NCCL, Abbott had done a great deal of work exploring the potential of existing laws to effect progressive change. This became part of the GLC's practice. Ward argues, 'We were very good at asserting the moral case for these things. What we learned to do was to hook it on to a good statutory duty.'[52] The Sexual Discrimination Act of 1975 and the Race Relations Act of 1976 gave the GLC a legal basis for some of their progressive policies. Indeed, the Race Relations Act allowed the GLC to monitor the way in which GLC services were delivered, collect data and introduce initiatives to stamp out racial discrimination in areas such as housing. Like Abbott, Livingstone's team recognised the importance of 'ethnic record keeping'.

Another important law that allowed the GLC to introduce more radical initiatives was the Local Government Act of 1972. Passed by Edward Heath's Conservative government, radicals at the GLC made full use of its tax-raising powers. Linda Bellos, an officer for the GLC's women's committee who went on to become leader of Lambeth Council, recalls, 'It was discretionary expenditure, the product of a two pence in the pound rate that could be used for radical things. We wouldn't call them radical today; at the time they were called radical. Doing all kinds of things for the benefit of working-class people that Thatcher tried to stop.'[53]

The GLC also recognised its role as an employer. This too influenced Abbott. Rather than simply seeing the GLC as a provider of services, Livingstone's team recognised that it played an important role in the jobs market. By introducing fair employment practices, it could create opportunities for minorities in areas where they had traditionally been excluded. Ward argues, 'It's amazing to think how discriminatory public employment was, as recently as the 1980s.'[54] Opening up public service jobs to women and minorities was an uphill struggle. Ward recalls having to use the law to 'crowbar open' refuse collection and the fire service, which traditionally worked on a 'jobs for the boys' basis. These initiatives were ridiculed in the press. The *Daily Mail*, for example, complained that the GLC wanted to shut beauty parlours and make 'women strip down lorries instead'.[55] Equal opportunities policies were also lambasted by Tory ministers. Nonetheless, the GLC's example changed public sector recruitment for good. Although the

Thatcher government wanted to stop the GLC's equal opportunities initiative, the fact that the GLC grounded what it was doing in British, and latterly European, law meant that the Conservative government had very limited success countering equal opportunity initiatives.[56]

Abbott was also impressed by the shift she witnessed in the culture of County Hall. Prior to Labour's victory, Abbott had become accustomed to a building which was occupied almost entirely by middle-aged white men. In the wake of Livingstone's victory, Abbott recalls the corridors and committee rooms were populated by 'black people, women, there were a lot of younger people'.[57] This too was intentional. Livingstone introduced an 'open door policy'.[58] Any community group, excepting racist organisations, could hold meetings in County Hall free of charge. The change in atmosphere also reflected a change in personnel. Abbott recalls, 'There was a whole cadre of people, particularly women and ethnic minorities, who got their first toehold via the GLC. The left were able to bring people into the institution who went on to be highly influential, people like Herman Ouseley and Valerie Amos.'[59]

Changing the atmosphere of County Hall was another way of re-orienting the institution. It was also part of a broader understanding of the relationship between working people and government. John McDonnell explains, 'The basic theory that a number of us had when we went on the GLC was the concept of in and against the state.'[60] The theoretical discussions, McDonnell argues, taking place in the London left recognised that state institutions were characterised by a relationship of dominance. At best, he argues, working people were the passive recipients of services. Crucially, working people, were 'not involved in questions of how to deliver a public service or how to tackle social needs, so it's a relationship of dominance'. McDonnell argues that the GLC's programme was designed to 'change that relationship'. In practice 'in and against the state' meant, 'getting elected, and opening the doors and saying to people, "You come in, you tell us what's needed, you tell us how it should be delivered, and you participate in the delivery."' In and against the state meant democratising government institutions and treating people as citizens rather than consumers. 'It was revolutionary,' McDonnell comments. 'It's no wonder Mrs Thatcher closed us down. It challenged the establishment, the way the existing system operates, our politics, our economics. In addition to that, it was popular.'

Abbott made a similar point in 1985. Speaking to *Socialist Action*, she argued:

> Our approach is a challenge to all the Fabian assumptions that the state is a power for good as long as it is in the right hands. It is a challenge to the Morrisonian theory of nationalisation; to the idea that all you have to do is set up big bureaucratic corporations without any popular control.[61]

One way in which the GLC sought to engage with different communities was to have dedicated units based in County Hall which worked with community groups. Ansel Wong, whom Abbott had first met through the Elimu Carnival Band, was appointed principal race relations adviser and head of the GLC's ethnic minorities unit in 1982. Wong describes working at the GLC as being a 'Camelot experience. Everybody was involved, community activists engaging with us, people who were in receipt of GLC grant aid. There was a real engagement, a political and cultural engagement.'[62]

As well as covering the GLC for Thames, Abbott took part in the democratisation of County Hall, engaging in policy discussion. Wong recalls, 'There was a camaraderie, critical voices as well. Diane was very much part of that engagement, participating, criticising, supporting and making her views known.' McDonnell concurs: 'It was a dynamic period of new ideas being thrown in; she was part of that.'[63]

Livingstone's approach to retail politics also influenced Abbott.

> Ken had this view that you could get the white working class to agree to a progressive line on gay rights, or black rights so long as you deliver for them on a basic level. There were two things he was very insistent on in the early years of the GLC. One was cutting the price of school dinners, and the other was cutting fares.[64]

Abbott was right to predict that the GLC under Livingstone would be newsworthy. In the year that she was based at County Hall, Livingstone was constantly in the headlines. In May 1981, he offered food and accommodation to 500 protesters engaged in the People's March for Jobs. Years before County Hall was turned into a luxury hotel, the marchers slept on camp beds, originally intended for London's civil defence in the event of nuclear war. Shortly after, Livingstone was in the headlines again for turning down an invitation to the wedding of Charles and Diana. In July 1981, during the IRA hunger strikes Livingstone made himself the mortal enemy of the right-wing press by meeting Alice McElwee, the mother of hunger striker Tom McElwee. McElwee died the following month after sixty-two days on hunger strike. By October, the right-wing media narrative around Livingstone was neatly summarised by the *Sunday Express*, which described him as an 'IRA-loving, poof-loving Marxist'.[65]

Livingstone has been criticised for creating headlines which distracted from the central business of the GLC. However, Abbott takes a different view:

> When he was a little-known councillor in Camden he talked about exactly the same things: Ireland, women's rights, gay rights, and got no attention whatsoever. Then, suddenly, he was leader of the GLC, saying the same old things, and the national press was going crazy. It came as a bit of a surprise to him.[66]

What is more, Abbott points out that it was not just talk.

> He did advance those issues, and one of the reasons why London didn't have some of the types of race riots they had in the north of England was because we fought those battles about race in the 1980s. The left got hold of the GLC and used it to advance the anti-racist case. We fought those battles politically and we won them.

It's hard to overstate the ferocity of the right-wing press to the GLC's minorities agenda.[67] Many right-wing commentators simply refused to accept that systematic discrimination existed in Britain. Inequalities were often regarded as natural, inevitable or legitimate. Thatcher had a slightly more sophisticated approach. Writing in 1995, she argued:

> Nothing is more colour-blind than the capitalism in which I place my faith for Britain's revival. It was part of my credo that individuals were worthy of respect as individuals, not as members of classes or races; the whole purpose of the political and economic system I favoured was to liberate the talents of those individuals for the benefit of society.[68]

From this perspective equality of opportunity policies were at best unnecessary, because the market, ever hungry for profit, would automatically ensure that the best people, regardless of race or gender, would get the best jobs. At worst equality of opportunity policies were counter-productive, as they would impede the operation of the colour-blind market.

The response to the GLC's support for gay and lesbian rights was even more extreme. Indeed, for many right-wing commentators, the GLC's support for gay rights was taken as an indication that Livingstone and his supporters were moral degenerates who were seeking to corrupt youth by promoting forms of sexual deviance. The *Daily Mail* told its readers that thanks to the GLC, 'Children as young as five are being taught by lesbians and militant feminist teachers to question the traditional value of the sexes.'[69] The *Daily Telegraph*, albeit in a more sober tone, argued that the GLC was deliberately trying to confuse vulnerable young people 'by perverting all normal feelings and turning all accepted ideas upside down'.[70] Worse still, according to many right-wing columnists, the GLC was lavishing ratepayers' money on these deviant groups. In 1983, the *Daily Mail*, to take one example, castigated the GLC for giving millions of pounds of public money in handouts to 'militant lesbians, babies for peace, Irish and black extremists, prostitutes' collectives, left-wing theatre groups', not to mention revolutionary artists.[71] These attacks were repeated constantly until the GLC's abolition in 1986. Indeed, in March of that year the *Daily Mail* told its readers, 'The GLC has made London the laughing stock of local government by opening its doors to every no-hoper, Marxist trouble-maker, political scrounger, foreign terrorist and sexual pervert who wanted a public handout.'[72]

Right-wing outrage at support for LGB groups was not restricted to the press. Like the *Daily Mail*, the Thatcher government linked 'wasting' public funds with promoting 'alternative lifestyles'. Even within government, there were concerns that support for gay rights was an assault on the 'traditional family'. Therefore, the Thatcher government introduced Section 28 of the 1988 Local Government Act which banned the 'promotion of homosexuality' in schools and prohibited the teaching of the 'acceptability of homosexuality as a pretended family relationship'. In this context, the GLC's stance was radical indeed.

One of the remarkable things about this period is how quickly the hysteria around gay rights and equality of opportunity initiatives died down. By the late 1990s, inclusivity had become mainstream: front-benchers from both major parties had to pay lip service, at the very least, to the importance of diversity. However, as Abbott points out, 'at the time this seemed incredibly radical'.[73]

In the context of the 1980s, McDonnell emphasises Abbott's courage in advocating minority rights.

> At that time, raising anything around race inequality was intensely controversial, for most of the media. People like Diane, Paul Boateng and Herman Ouseley were raising issues and were immediately pounced upon for being ultra-left. She was courageously raising those issues, and the flack that she got was extraordinary, like a tsunami of bile. She was always a strong voice. I remember, during the GLC period, she was one of a number of people who wouldn't be silenced. She was a young woman, growing in stature in that period.[74]

More generally, Abbott argues that the GLC was a powerful counter to Thatcherism, which was all the more important as Labour's national leadership were failing to put up a meaningful opposition. 'We were across the Thames, with the unemployment figures up on the roof. It was exciting, it was about transforming reality, it was about changing the institution, not allowing the institution to change you … and about offering a real alternative to Thatcherism and neo-liberal ways of thinking.'[75]

The Coin Street development is one particularly successful example of the GLC's approach to government. By the early 1980s, the council housing of the 1960s and 1970s was under constant attack. The popular press presented brutalist developments like Trellick Tower and the Robin Hood Gardens estate as examples of failed social experiments. For many on the right, council housing was the cause of social problems. It was common for Conservative politicians to blame high-rise developments, slab blocks and sprawling estates for community breakdown, social isolation, the creation of a dependency culture, leading to family breakdown, delinquency and criminality. The Thatcher government looked to the market to succeed where the state had allegedly failed. Planners at the GLC did not accept the right-wing critique of post-war council housing in its totality. Nonetheless, they recognised that council housing was often the product of local councils working with property developers, and therefore that the voices of local people were rarely heard in the process of urban planning.

The Coin Street development was a radical alternative to both Thatcherite market solutions and traditional paternalistic approaches to council housing. It reflected the philosophy that McDonnell described as 'in and against the state'. First, the thirteen-acre Coin Street site, located on London's Southbank between Waterloo Bridge and Blackfriars Bridge, which had been earmarked for office blocks, was re-designated for housing. Next, GLC architects worked with the future residents to design the development. The resulting development mixed private spaces with communal gardens in innovative ways. The houses themselves were built by the Coin Street Community Builders, which provided training and employment to local people. Finally, the GLC bought the whole development and then sold it on to a community trust. The GLC's Coin Street development was an example of housing designed, built and managed by the community, a radical alternative to both Thatcherism and local authority paternalism.

Reflecting on the 1980s, Abbott argues, 'Target 82 and the campaign around the GLC were the defining campaigns for the white left.' Beyond the 1980s, the period had a lasting impact on her political imagination. Target 82 was an example of how the left could work through democratic institutions to lay a foundation for radical change. Livingstone's GLC, in turn, was a model of what a progressive government might look like: devolving power, using the resources of government to extend opportunities, empower people and improve the shared environment. Looking back on the experience of the GLC, Abbott argues, 'It gave people like myself, Jeremy and John the notion that you could organise and take over an institution. It then took us thirty-five years to do it to the national Labour Party! But Target 82 was the model.'[76]

CHAPTER 5

WESTMINSTER

At the age of twenty-nine, Abbott was elected to Westminster City Council. From 1982 to 1986 she represented Harrow Road, the ward in which she had been born. The battles she fought in Westminster Council were a microcosm of one of the new political divisions which emerged in the early 1980s. Abbott advocated a new left agenda. She wanted the council to engage with community groups and use the resources of the local authority to improve the lives of working people. The Tory majority, however, quickly embraced Thatcherism. Staff were laid off, local services were privatised and the council went to war with public sector unions. Council houses were sold off, laying the foundation for the aggressive gentrification that took place in Westminster in the late 1980s. Council assets were liquidated and services outsourced, culminating in 1987 in millions of pounds of public assets being sold for a few pence. Shirley Porter, leader of Westminster Council from 1983, was not merely fighting the council's Labour group: she was locked in battle with Ken Livingstone's GLC and vying with Wandsworth Council in a competition to see who could take municipal Thatcherism furthest.

Abbott's bid to become a Labour councillor started in earnest in 1981. Now living in Lanhill Road, Paddington, she sought selection as part of the 'Target Westminster' campaign, a local expression of the London-wide Target 82. Getting involved with the Labour Party in Paddington was an uphill struggle. Abbott recalls ringing the secretary of her local ward to enquire about the next party meeting and being politely brushed off. Phone calls to other officials in the local party had similar results. Having discovered the details of the next ward meeting from friends, she arrived at the leisure centre on the Mozart Estate only to be denied entry by an elderly white man. It was only after some persuasion that Abbott was allowed in. Abbott's experience was typical of many black and Asian people in the late 1970s and early 1980s who were either refused Labour Party membership or joined only to find that they were not welcome. 'At that point,' Abbott recalls, 'Labour was a virtually white party. Although much of the vote in Paddington came from black people, the idea of a black person joining the party aroused huge suspicion.'[1] Despite opposition from within, Abbott was determined to stand as Labour candidate for Harrow Road.

The selection meeting took place in early November 1981. Two of Harrow Road's three Labour councillors were standing down, and Abbott, Paul Dimoldenberg and three others put themselves forward. Dimoldenberg recalls that Joe Glickman, a semi-retired cab driver, had been a councillor for many years and was well liked. His reselection was a foregone conclusion. Consequently Abbott, Dimoldenberg and the other three candidates were effectively contesting the remaining two seats. Dimoldenberg first met Abbott at the selection meeting. Although the two lived in the same area, they were in different constituencies and therefore were active in different parties. Nonetheless, Dimoldenberg had heard about Abbott and was aware that she had ambitions to be an MP. By the end of the evening, Glickman, Abbott and Dimoldenberg had been selected to contest Harrow Road.[2]

Dimoldenberg remembers the selection taking place at a very exciting time for the local party. In May, Livingstone had won the GLC seat for Paddington. A traditionally marginal seat, Livingstone's victory was a sign that Labour could do well in the area. What is more, after six months, the GLC was showing the kinds of things that a radical Labour administration could do through local government. Thatcher also seemed vulnerable. Figures published in October 1981 showed that, due to high inflation and low wage growth, personal incomes were down by a fifth in the second quarter of the year, the sharpest fall in four years. At the Warrington by-election in June the Tories lost their deposit. They also lost the Croydon by-election in October, and in the same month Ivor Crewe, the respected co-director of the British Election Study, published research showing that Thatcher was the most unpopular Prime Minister since polling began. Looking back, Keith Veness argues that some in the local party thought that Labour were in with a shot of winning control of the council.[3] In this context, the selection contest was hard fought.

Six months later, Labour's position was weaker. The 1982 council elections took place a month into the Falklands War. Polling day occurred a week after RAF Vulcan bombers began the campaign to retake the Falkland Islands. 'The SDP', Dimoldenberg remarks, also 'had the wind in their sails'.[4] The SDP had won the Crosby by-election in November 1981 and the Glasgow Hillhead by-election of March 1982. What is more, the SDP–Liberal Alliance had been doing well in council by-elections since its formation in June 1981. As a result, the Harrow Road candidates found themselves fighting a rear-guard action in what had been a safe Labour area. In the end, the campaign in Harrow Road was contested with far more energy than was usual for a safe seat. Dimoldenberg remembers the three candidates canvassing the entire ward and mass-producing leaflets in an attempt to counter the threat of the SDP. By this stage the candidates did not expect to oust the Tory administration, but they hoped to make gains, to hold the SDP at bay, and to participate in what promised to be a good night for Labour in the capital.

There was clear-blue water between the SDP and Labour in the Westminster City Council elections of 1982. The SDP proposed cutting Westminster's financial contribution to the GLC and the Inner London Education Authority. This was not the full-throated condemnation of left-wing authorities that came from the Conservatives, but it was a clear dividing line between the SDP and Labour in London. What is more, the SDP's Westminster manifesto said nothing about women's rights or minority rights. Labour's manifesto was clearly in line with the municipal socialism of the GLC.

Abbott's election material promised that a Labour-led council would back the GLC's Fares Fair policy and make Westminster a nuclear-free zone.[5] The concept of nuclear-free zones was a part of the left's new radical agenda. As the 1980s progressed, Labour councils, particularly in London, used their power to stop nuclear material, whether fuel rods for reactors, nuclear waste or nuclear warheads passing through their areas. The promise reflected a commitment both to nuclear disarmament and to environmental protection. On housing, Abbott promised to renovate council houses and freeze council rents, as well as pledging, 'Tough action will be taken against landlords who fail to keep their property in good repair.'[6] The structure of Abbott's manifesto also reflected the GLC's approach to progressive politics: it began with issues central to the wellbeing of the working class as a whole and ended with the promise that 'Labour will promote racial and sex equality'. Here too, Abbott's manifesto was of a piece with the GLC's conception of 'in and against the state', promising that a Labour administration in City Hall would 'work in partnership with voluntary groups, such as tenants' associations and community organisations, to improve the council's services'. Had Labour won, no doubt the door of City Hall would have been opened to organisations representing women, black people, as well as groups organised by LGB people and people with disabilities. 'Equal opportunities' was one of eight commitments set out on the Labour leaflets distributed across Harrow Road.

According to the campaign literature, Abbott had two unique selling points. First, Labour leaflets billed her as 'Harrow Road's first black Labour candidate'. Second, they stressed her local connections: her campaign literature began with the fact that 'she was born in St Mary's Hospital Harrow Road'. The three candidates each had their own areas of interest. Labour leaflets quote Glickman and Dimoldenberg on the woeful state of council housing in Westminster. Abbott stressed her commitment to 'Giving Black People a Fair Share'. 'In the past,' she wrote 'black people have not had a fair deal when it comes to council services, particularly in housing. I want to fight that kind of racism.'[7] She was also concerned about opportunities for young people and women, arguing for 'training and workshops' as well as youth facilities in which 'young people [are] given more responsibility and control over their own activities'. No doubt the Elimu Carnival Band was a model for the kind of youth groups that Abbott had in mind. Abbott also advocated 'more day nurseries and support for childminders', another aspect of policy being pioneered by the GLC.

Abbott, Glickman and Dimoldenberg's emphasis on housing reflected one of the important local issues of the day. In the run-up to the election, the pages of the *Marylebone Mercury* were full of letters and stories about the disrepair of local housing. Unemployment was also an issue in the poorer areas of Westminster. Needless to say, Labour, the Conservatives and the SDP–Liberal Alliance took different approaches to these issues. The Tories' solution to the housing problem emphasised selling as much of the council's housing stock as possible. Notably, Labour, the Alliance and the Conservatives all agreed that spending had to increase. The Tories promised increased spending, and cuts in the rates; Labour, by contrast, wanted to increase taxes on local businesses. Labour's plan may seem like a typical left-wing anti-business measure. However, under previous Tory administrations, the council had subsidised business. For example, in 1981, it emerged that the council did not charge local businesses for rubbish collection. This cost local ratepayers £2 million a year. Although the district auditor declared this *de facto* business subsidy illegal, the Tory council refused to back down. It was only in 1986 that the council was forced to comply with the law. In the intervening period, Westminster Council had illegally handed a £10 million subsidy to local businesses.[8] In this context, Abbott's 1982 manifesto commitment to raise business rates was wholly reasonable.

At the end of the campaign, despite the 'Falklands Factor' and the rise of the SDP, Labour got a good result in Harrow Road: Glickman was re-elected with 1,588 votes, Abbott won her seat with 1,548 and Dimoldenberg was returned with 1,504. Turnout was high in Paddington, and the Labour vote was up on 1978. Abbott was one of two black councillors elected on the night; the other was Vince Allen, who was elected to represent Westbourne. As expected, the Conservatives retained control of Westminster Council, winning 49.6 per cent of the vote. Labour retained its second place with 30 per cent, and the SDP–Liberal Alliance won no council seats, gaining 18.6 per cent of the vote.

On 15 May, *The Guardian* reported Abbott's election, noting that she was 'the first black to win a seat on the strongly Conservative Westminster City Council'.[9] Here, she was cited as the exception that proved the rule. The 1982 council elections had done little to advance black and Asian representation in local government. Across London there were gains in Brent, Ealing, Hackney, Lewisham, Lambeth, Southwark and Tower Hamlets, taking the total number of black and Asian councillors in the capital to around fifty. Even so, black and Asian people were still significantly under-represented in local government. Outside the capital, there was even less progress. In Leeds, ninety-nine out of 100 councillors were white. Similarly, in Bradford eighty-seven of the ninety council seats were occupied by white councillors. Abbott, then, was a trailblazer in local government, as she would be in Parliament five years later. Something else emerged from the May 1982 election data, which would prove significant in ongoing debates about black representation: black and Asian Labour candidates in London tended to get a higher vote share than their white counterparts.

COUNCILLOR ABBOTT

Abbott's first council meeting took place on the evening of 17 May 1982. The first problem was getting into the building. Instinctively, security on the door at Marylebone Council House tried to turn Abbott away. Once inside, the Labour group nominated Abbott to the general purposes committee. The committee had one of the most wide-ranging briefs in the council and looked after local sports facilities, libraries, parks, swimming pools and the maintenance of public buildings and cemeteries and had a budget in excess of £15 million. Abbott was also nominated as Labour's spokesperson on the committee. As Dimoldenberg recalls, this reflected the view within the Labour group that Abbott had the makings of a successful politician. 'We all knew that Diane had a future, we knew she was ambitious, and that she was going to get there. She was a great speaker, she had lots of charisma, so it was only a matter of time.'[10]

With only sixteen out of sixty seats on the council, the Labour group had to think creatively about holding the Conservatives to account. Abbott scrutinised the activity and inactivity of the council vigorously. Her first intervention in the council chamber took place on 26 July, regarding the state of council housing. In other meetings, Abbott questioned the Conservative leadership on their job creation plans. Here, Abbott objected to the council's 'ill-conceived community programme', which involved enlisting unemployed young people to 'count the number of trees' on the city's streets, urging the Tory administration to find 'more useful ways of creating jobs' for Westminster's young unemployed.[11] Abbott also forced the Conservatives to acknowledge that the council was laying off a significant number of staff at a time of record unemployment. Rather than saving money, the redundancies would cost the council more than £500,000. Nonetheless, the lay-offs were part of a union-busting scheme whereby the council would outsource the provision of services to private companies. Abbott argues that this approach to local government was something new. While the GLC was pioneering a radical left-wing agenda on the Southbank, Westminster Council, under Shirley Porter, was developing an equal and opposite programme north of the river. Abbott recalls, 'Shirley Porter saw herself as a pathfinder for privatisation. She was the opposite of any *noblesse oblige* paternalist Tory, so there was an adversarial relationship between her and the Labour councillors.'[12] Dimoldenberg agrees, noting that this change in Tory politics in Westminster happened following the 1982 election: 'When we were first elected the council was run by the old school: paternalist Tories. They'd been on the council for twenty or thirty years' – and their politics had more in common with the Tory Party of the 1950s than that of the 1980s.[13]

CIVIL DEFENCE

Abbott's first exchange with Porter was in regard to the council's 'war plan'. The early 1980s was a time of heightened nuclear tension. Following the Soviet invasion of Afghanistan in 1979 détente had broken down, and the superpowers were plunged into 'the Second Cold War'. The announcement that US nuclear missiles would be stationed in

Britain, coupled with the publication of the apocalyptic public information booklet *Protect and Survive*, led to an increased sense of vulnerability to the nuclear threat.[14] Concerns about nuclear attack were heightened in 1981 when President Ronald Reagan remarked that he could envisage a limited nuclear war in Europe. The Thatcher government formally committed to purchase Trident, a new generation of American thermonuclear weapons, in July 1980. It was in this context that the government turned its attention to civil defence in early 1983. At the beginning of March, it announced new funding for local authorities but postponed a planned civil defence exercise due to opposition from Labour councils. This, in turn, led to widespread criticism of the government's nuclear strategy. Peace demonstrations took place at the nuclear submarine base at Faslane on the Clyde, and at the nuclear plant in Capenhurst, Cheshire. The press also sounded the alarm. As March wore on, articles appeared in the broadsheets arguing that official statements about the consequences of nuclear attack were profoundly unrealistic. Following a barrage of expert criticism, Sir Patrick Mayhew, then minister of state at the Home Office, was forced to acknowledge that government estimates of fatalities were grossly inaccurate. Nonetheless, Mayhew and the Thatcher government remained committed to the notion that Britain could survive a 200-megaton attack. Mayhew praised Westminster Council's civil defence planning in the House of Commons, and the Labour group at Westminster demanded an extraordinary meeting to discuss the council's unpublished 'war plan'.

The extraordinary meeting took place on 30 March 1983. Abbott's questions exposed many of the contradictions in the government's civil defence policy. Civil defence was the responsibility of the general purposes committee on which Abbott served, so she was well placed to challenge the council. First, despite being praised for their preparedness, Conservative counsellors repeatedly admitted that without details from central government they did not know how the council would respond to nuclear attack. Abbott's central line of attack concerned the council's openness and its willingness to be honest with the citizens of Westminster about the realities of the war plan. The council had demonstrated its desire for secrecy in the run-up to the extraordinary meeting by removing signposts to Westminster's civil defence headquarters, so Abbott had chosen her target wisely. Abbott challenged Porter to convince the Labour group, the press and local citizens of the efficacy of the council's civil defence plans by holding 'an "open day" to allow the press and public to inspect Westminster's bunker'.[15] Porter refused. Abbott also asked Porter to be honest with council tenants in flats and tower blocks, to let them know that 'the council will not help them and that they should "make arrangements now"' to ensure their survival. Again, Porter refused. This last question, in which Abbott quoted *Protect and Survive*, pointed to one of the open secrets of Thatcher's civil defence policy. For the vast majority of Britons, civil defence had been privatised; there were no public shelters, and there would be no state-run programme of evacuation. The government would provide no food, medicine or water in the aftermath of a nuclear attack. All the talk of civil defence exercises and local war plans masked the fact that survival, for all but a chosen few, was a matter of personal responsibility.

Abbott's appeal to Porter to be honest pointed to a larger truth: if London was hit by a bomb, the vast majority of Westminster's citizens would die. Many would be vaporised instantly, others crushed by the collapse of buildings, and those who might survive after the initial attack would die from dehydration or radiation shortly afterwards. This would be the case even if the attack comprised a single low-yield warhead in the kind of limited nuclear exchange envisaged by the Reagan White House. Of course – and Abbott knew this – Porter could not acknowledge this truth without undermining the founding assumptions of Britain's nuclear policy.

Abbott did force Porter, however, to acknowledge that the council simply did not have the information it needed to prepare for an attack. This exposed a paradox in Thatcher's approach to nuclear weapons. Thatcher was far more committed to the possession and use of weapons of mass destruction than previous Labour governments. Yet, compared to Wilson and Callaghan, her government did precious little to prepare for nuclear attack. During the 1970s, Labour had updated local authorities on the nuclear threat and survival plans every couple of months. The Thatcher government, by contrast, did not issue advice to councils at any point in 1983.

Porter's admission that the council could do little without advice from central government was all the more remarkable as a week earlier Mayhew had praised Westminster for having 'taken their community planning to an advanced stage' in the Commons.[16] He even commended the council for having 'made notable progress towards creating within communities the capacity to react spontaneously to an emergency rather than to await governmental response'. Abbott's questions demonstrated that Mayhew's estimate of the council was wholly wrong.

The exchange between Abbott and Porter took place in a forum known as Question Time, where councillors had an hour to put questions to the chairs of the various council committees. Dimoldenberg recalls:

Diane was really very good at Question Time. When she had her questions prepared, she was one of the star performers. She would really wind the Tories up. They'd never seen anything like her. It was a time when Labour politics was changing. They had one of the rising stars of the new politics in their midst. It was an exciting time.[17]

The Thatcher government's civil defence strategy emerged in greater clarity later in the year. Notably, the details of London's war plan were not revealed by the government.

After two years running London, Livingstone and his team hit upon a strategy for gaining access to the government's secret nuclear plans. Shortly thereafter, the GLC, working with the investigative journalist Duncan Campbell, published the government's war plans. In the build-up to a nuclear strike, peace protesters and other political radicals would be interned. Then fuel would be impounded and London closed off. The army, far from protecting British citizens, would be used to contain the population; as Livingstone put it, Britain's cities would be 'ringed by troops and police to prevent their populations fleeing to the countryside'.[18] The rationale was that anyone in London who survived the initial attack would be dead within two weeks due to injuries such as burns, disease due to the lack of clean water, or radiation sickness. Therefore, the rest of the country would have a better chance of surviving if Londoners died where they were, rather than escaping and putting pressure on the meagre food supplies of rural areas. The North East Thames Regional Health Authority War Plan described the strategy with the following metaphor:

> If all the great trees and much of the brushwood are felled, a forest may not regenerate for centuries. If a sufficient number of the great trees is left, however, if felling is to some extent selective and controlled, recovery is swift. In its way, a nation is like a forest and the aim of war planning is to secure the survival of the great trees.[19]

It was in this context that Abbott demanded that Westminster Council be honest with Londoners, and it was in this context that she advocated disarmament and making Westminster a nuclear-free zone – all policies derided as being those of the 'loony left'.

Porter was an implacable enemy of London's 'loony left'. Abbott recalls that Porter 'saw herself as a mini Margaret Thatcher'. This was certainly the way she presented herself to the press. An article in the *Marylebone Mercury* from 25 March 1983 claimed that 'the newly elected leader of Westminster Council, Mrs Shirley Porter, sees herself as a mini-Maggie Thatcher'. Thatcher was more cautious about the association. According to Porter's biographer Andrew Hosken, Thatcher 'appeared indifferent to Porter and gave the impression that she considered her something of a nuisance'.[20] Nonetheless, Porter wanted Westminster to be the trailblazing Thatcherite council, to show what could be achieved through running a local authority like a business. Her 'one-stop shop', which allowed locals to access all council services in one place, certainly streamlined access to services which survived the cuts and reflected her belief that ratepayers should be treated like consumers.[21]

Porter was also responsible for 'War Against Reckless Spending' (WARS). The WARS campaign was conceived to mobilise popular opposition to what Porter regarded as wasteful GLC spending. To that end she asked for £10,000 of council money to fund the campaign against the GLC. In the end the council contributed £250, but WARS carried on, with anti-GLC adverts appearing in the press and WARS banners draped across council buildings.

The Labour group's relationship with Porter's administration was fractious for Abbott's entire term. 'We were constantly pushing back at her attempts to advance a doctrinaire agenda,' Abbott recalls.[22] Labour clashed with the Tories over housing. In 1985 it became clear that Westminster Council were planning to sell off large swathes of council housing. The plan affected two estates in Abbott's ward. The Labour group in Paddington, of which Abbott was a member, mobilised popular opposition to the plan through the 'Save Westminster Services' newsletter. As Hosken argues, the Paddington Labour Party 'formed a base of resistance against Shirley Porter'.[23] As a result, a large group of council tenants attended meetings of the housing committee to express their opposition. Conflict over the sale of council homes came to a head at a meeting of the housing committee in October 1985. Patricia Kirwan, the architect of Westminster's 'new community' project, led the meeting. Kirwan, a highly intelligent and highly doctrinaire Thatcherite, faced a barrage of protest from the public gallery. Having lost control of the meeting she summoned the police who removed Dimoldenberg from the chamber and forcibly closed the meeting. Livingstone, the GLC member for Paddington, was in the public gallery and invited the protesters to continue their meeting across the Thames at County Hall.[24]

Another memorable council meeting took place a month later. In anticipation of the GLC's abolition, Westminster Council was preparing to take control of local services. Between 1981 and 1986 the GLC had significantly expanded funding for nursery places. At the time of abolition, the GLC was funding 3,000 nursery places across the capital through working with church groups, mothers' associations, women's groups, and disability rights groups. However, this expansion of state funding ran counter to the ethos of Thatcherism, which stressed scaling back state provision and cutting public spending. Some in the Thatcher government also regarded the GLC's nursery programme as morally suspect. Nurseries which received GLC funding were required to allow single mothers and gay couples to use childcare facilities on an equal basis to straight couples. Equally, some Conservatives felt that nurseries upset the established order, allowing mothers of young children to evade their natural responsibilities as carers. Concerns of this nature led to narratives that the GLC's nurseries were undermining 'family values' and promoting questionable 'alternative lifestyles' which, in the long run, would lead to juvenile delinquency and rising social problems. The right-wing press also castigated the GLC for giving grants to black women's centres in Southall and Brixton. So, for a variety of reasons, the Thatcher government was determined to stamp out what Sue Bruley describes as the GLC's 'municipal feminism'.[25]

As Westminster Council prepared to take over services that had been run by the GLC, it became clear that Porter would cut funding to crèches. Since becoming leader of the council in 1983, Porter had been constantly looking for ways to cut costs and to divest the council of expensive responsibilities. Abbott, by contrast, supported the provision of crèches: as a feminist she supported inexpensive, high-quality childcare as a matter of principle, but she also wanted to serve her constituents, and around 75 per cent of households in the Harrow Road Ward had children.

Anticipating cuts, the Labour group had invited mothers and representatives of women's groups to the council chamber to hear the announcement. News of the cuts was met with protest from the public gallery and police forcefully removed ten protesters from the meeting. Susan Kirby, who had made use of the Covent Garden Community Centre crèche, took matters into her own hands, giving her baby to Porter as she entered the Chamber, telling her, 'There's no one to look after him now, so you'll have to.' Porter was, by all accounts, an excellent baby wrangler.[26]

The involvement of community groups in conflicts over women's rights and housing shows a different face to the municipal socialism of the 1980s. At County Hall, where Labour was in power, the GLC could invite community groups to participate in developing policy. In Westminster, where the Conservatives were in control, Labour worked with community groups to create an effective opposition.

In the midst of this highly adversarial relationship, Abbott and Porter found some common ground. On one occasion, outside the council chamber, the issue of race came up. To Abbott's surprise, Porter acknowledged that she understood Abbott's concern about discrimination. She confided that the first golf club she had applied to join had turned her away because she was Jewish.

The battle over the GLC was another flash point. Porter was an outspoken advocate for the GLC's abolition, and she was not alone. At the same time Abbott was calling for Westminster to become a nuclear-free zone, Conservative councillor Teresa Gorman proposed making Westminster a 'GLC-free zone'. To that end, Westminster Council set up 'a GLC-Free Working Party', presumably to find ways to shield Westminster's citizens from lower bus fares and free nursery places. Abbott and the Labour group were determined to defend the GLC. Corbyn remembers that Abbott was 'very active in the campaign to defend the GLC. The GLC were absolutely iconic, and there was genuine popular support for the campaign.'[27] In September 1984, to take one example, Abbott supported Livingstone in a GLC by-election. A GLC election had been slated for May 1985 but was cancelled by the government ahead of the abolition. In the absence of a London-wide election, Livingstone resigned his seat, precipitating a by-election which he hoped would show public support for the GLC. Abbott took an important lesson from the campaign, which she explained to readers of *Tribune*: 'The turnout overall was less than some of us had hoped, but once again I was impressed with the unswerving loyalty that black people give the Labour Party.'[28]

While Porter was attacking the 'loony left', as Dimoldenberg recalls, Labour 'were on the attack against the extremism of Shirley Porter'.[29] One example of what Dimoldenberg calls 'Tory extremism' was to cost Westminster's ratepayers millions. Towards the end of Abbott's time on the council Porter initiated a policy that would lead to her undoing. In November 1985 Westminster Council approved the sale of cemeteries at Mill Hill, Hanwell and East Finchley. The cemeteries were sold for 5p apiece. From Porter's point of view, this was an excellent scheme. The cemeteries brought the council minimal income, but their upkeep was a constant drain on council resources, so moving them off the council's books made perfect business sense. The sale was possible because the cemeteries were attached to valuable land and properties. In fact, the three cemeteries came with three lodge houses, a flat and twelve acres of land that was ready for development in the heart of London.[30] The sale went through in 1987. Quickly, the former council properties were sold on. The three cemeteries were sold for £1.25 million, and Milespit Hill, the land attached to the Mill Hill cemetery, changed hands for £1.75 million.[31] Not only did this act of privatisation effectively give away millions of pounds worth of public property in 1987, but it also led to further losses for Westminster's taxpayers a few years later. The new owners had no legal obligation to maintain the cemeteries, so they quickly became derelict and attracted drug users and fly-tipping. In 1992 the council bought back the cemeteries for £4.25 million.[32] The houses and twelve acres of prime real estate were never recovered. The Labour group could make the case for using council assets for public good, for building council houses on the twelve acres of land, and for safeguarding public assets for the next generation, but as the Tories were in the majority, they were powerless to prevent an act of privatisation that cost Westminster's taxpayers dear.

According to Dimoldenberg, Abbott's time on the council can be divided into two. 'At some point, Diane's efforts went into trying to get selected as a parliamentary candidate.'[33] As a result, Dimoldenberg observed that Abbott began to 'put more of her effort into national politics and her own profile. One of the disappointments [for the Labour group] was that her council work didn't blossom at the same time.' As a result, Abbott was replaced as the Labour group's spokesperson on the general purposes committee.

Nonetheless, when Abbott put herself forward for selection as prospective parliamentary candidate for Westminster North, Di-moldenberg supported her. What is more, after Abbott decided not to contest the 1986 council elections she continued working with Target 86 to try to oust the Conservatives in Westminster.

MEDIA CAMPAIGNING

Election as a Labour councillor made life difficult for Abbott at Thames Television. Her bosses told her that following her election she could no longer work in news and current affairs and she was sent to work in the features department. Concluding quickly that her career at Thames was over, Abbott began the search for a new job. The early 1980s were an exciting time to be involved in television. After much anticipation, Channel 4 was launched at the end of 1982, and at the beginning of 1983 broadcasting hours were extended as the BBC and ITV both launched breakfast shows, so there were a whole range of new opportunities for Abbott to consider.

Abbott had kept a close eye on developments in television. Her general view was that black people should organise in order to make the most of new opportunities, both to get decent jobs and to influence the stories being told on television. There were hopes that Channel 4 would be a forum for new voices and a space to create content for minority audiences. As a result, in the run-up to Channel 4's launch a variety of events were held at which the public and media insiders could lobby the new channel's bosses. A year before the launch, to take one example, Jeremy Isaacs, the founding chief executive of the new channel, held a meeting to discuss its diversity policy. Jenny Bourne of the IRR recalls, 'Diane took control of the meeting from the floor, demanding in no uncertain terms that we had to meet with Jeremy Isaacs, then the head of Channel 4, and we did.'[34] Abbott, Bourne and Julian Henriques, Bourne recalls, had formed a 'black caucus lobbying within the media for more black representation'.

In 1981 Abbott was one of the founders of the Black Media Workers' Association (BMWA). Abbott explains, 'My response to racial injustice has always been to organise. When I was at the Home Office, I joined the Scrap SUS campaign, when I worked in the media and

perceived racial injustice, I set up the Black Media Workers' Association.'[35] Sarita Malik argues that the BMWA emerged from a small
group including Mike Phillips, Julian Henriques, Abbott, Parminder
Vir and Belkis Belgani which began meeting in 1980, before the official launch in February 1981. Lionel Morrison claims that the BMWA
'was one of the most important pressure groups to have emerged' in
the early 1980s media scene.[36]

The BMWA's strategy was twofold. First, it lobbied for equal
opportunities within the industry. One early achievement was the
publication of Marina Salandy-Brown's report 'Black Workers in the
Media' in 1983. The report showed that only 684 black people were
employed in the British media, which represented a mere 0.07 per
cent of media workers. In that sense, the report provided definitive evidence of chronic under-representation of black people in the media.
The BMWA also produced a directory of all black media workers.
Equipped with these documents, Abbott could approach media
unions and persuade them to do more to promote diversity in the
industry. The ACTT, for example, gave the BMWA money. From
Abbott's perspective the ACTT were a good example of how a radical
union should work: 'It was one of those craft unions which negotiated
really good deals for their members, so their members allowed them
to be quite radical on broader issues.' The second part of the BMWA's
strategy was to monitor depictions of black people in the media. As
'Black Workers in the Media' pointed out, racist depictions of black
people could only be tackled if black people were involved in programme making.

Abbott shared her perspective on the media at the inaugural session
of the first International Book Fair of Radical Black and Third World
Books in 1982. A letter of invitation to the fair informed potential participants that the event marked 'the new and expanding phase in the
growth of radical ideas and concepts and their expression in literature,
politics, music, art and social life'.[37] Abbott appeared on a panel discussion at the opening event, 'Forum on Black Films in Britain', with
the early part of the discussion focusing on black film-makers and
the problems of getting major studios to fund or distribute work by

black writers and directors. Abbott's first comment set issues relating to black people in the media in their historical context:

> My experience, both working in commercial television, and through my work in an organisation called the Black Media Workers, is that black people in film is becoming incredibly fashionable. It's as fashionable in the 1980s as race relations was in the 1970s. And a lot of people are generating a lot of money and work for themselves by bringing together the two concepts: black people and film.[38]

The crucial question, for Abbott, and she threw this out to the audience, was: 'What do black people want from their film-makers?' Most of the panel looked to independent film as the vehicle for black voices in the media. Abbott struck a different note, arguing that television, rather than film, was likely to be the best route into the media for black people. Abbott grounded this perspective in recent history, arguing, 'I don't think there is a black director in this country who hasn't passed through television, or very few.'

TV-AM

Having spent some time languishing in Thames Television's features department, Abbott applied for a job as a researcher and reporter with TV-am, soon to be Britain's first commercial breakfast broadcaster. TV-am, Abbott recalls, 'was less squeamish about employing a Labour councillor' than Thames.[39] Abbott began work for TV-am in the autumn of 1982, anticipating that the new company would start broadcasting in the summer of the following year.

Abbott remembers thinking that TV-am was a genuinely exciting prospect. The new time slot, the new building – known as 'Eggcup House' in Camden Town – the new production company, all created the impression that TV-am was a dynamic and innovative enterprise. There were also a lot of young people involved in the project, which distinguished the company from Thames. The informality of the company was emphasised by the post-modern architecture of its office which was designed around large open-plan spaces punctuated by palm trees. Managers' offices, Abbott recalls, had glass walls. This, and the presence of gantries, meant that the building was so contrived that everybody could be surveyed at any time. The openness backfired, Abbott recalls, when the company started losing money, as painful redundancy meetings took place in plain sight.

TV-am's first recruits were treated to a special welcome from Peter Jay, TV-am's founder, chairman and chief executive. Abbott's welcome took place in the crazily coloured atrium, an imposing space which took its inspiration from Mesopotamian ziggurats and classical temples. Jay's address fitted with the emerging 'work hard, play hard' rhetoric of the Thatcher period. Jay told his new recruits, 'The next weeks and months are going to be among the most hectic and demanding of your lives. We are asking one hell of a lot of you. In return and above all I want you to have fun.'[40]

Jay was not short on ambition, and told his new workforce that TV-am's mission was to make 'a new and different kind' of television, to pioneer 'a new and different kind' of journalism, to be 'a new and different kind' of company based on 'a new and different kind of management style and philosophy'. Jay's vision had a utopian flavour: he envisaged that TV-am would be not only a company but a community of friends, and that TV-am would 'in a very real sense' belong to its workers. Obviously, this was nonsense: the company belonged to the shareholders. But this was the utopianism of the Thatcher period: the utopianism that took private business as the model for all social life. In common with many who were swept up in the promise of the Thatcher period, Jay imagined that the relationship between boss and subordinate could be a meaningful form of friendship; he believed that 'the most hectic and demanding' working conditions could be the most fulfilling social life; and held that concentrating wealth and power in private hands was 'in a very real sense' a form of collectivisation. This was the free market at its most utopian. Jay's ambitions extended way beyond the walls of Eggcup House: he wanted TV-am to change British culture and become as indispensable to Britain's morning routine as the first cup of coffee.

Abbott recalls Jay's introduction with mirth. 'He gathered us all in the atrium and he handed out signed copies of his lecture "What is news?"' The essay's opening line, which began, 'Anyone trained in what was called "philosophy" at Oxford in the late 1950s', was so wonderfully self-important that it stuck in her mind.[41] 'I just thought, this guy's a complete fuckwit! Completely self-obsessed, a huge ego, which was one of the seeds of the company's problems.'[42]

The problems emerged quickly. At the end of 1982, TV-am was in a state of chaos. The company struggled to negotiate contracts with unions, which demanded additional pay for antisocial hours; there were problems with the computer system; Jay continued to speak in high-minded generalities when staff needed specifics; and there were problems filming early pilots. To make matters worse, TV-am's launch was brought forward from June 1983 to February.

The new television company was launched with great fanfare but was quickly plunged into crisis. Two weeks in, it became clear that TV-am was attracting less than a fifth of the audience of the rival BBC breakfast show, which had dire implications for the company's advertising revenue. Within a month of the launch, Jay was ousted in a boardroom coup, and TV-am got very political very quickly. 'It was all hanging by a thread. It was astonishing, it was the first and last company I ever worked for where they didn't pay you one month, they literally didn't have the money. But it was exciting.'[43] Jonathan Aitken took over as TV-am's temporary chief executive immediately after Jay's departure and set about rationalising the business. Bringing the costs down was relatively easy, Aitken recalls, as the business was massively over-staffed. In terms of the journalists, Aitken reckoned that TV-am only needed a fraction of those who were employed. It was in this context that Aitken first met Abbott, who represented the National Union of Journalists at TV-am. Abbott's first impression was that Aitken had 'all of Peter Jay's self-belief, but with charm'.[44] Aitken recalls that while Abbott was happy to denounce him vocally in public, in their private meetings she was

a very realistic sensible and sensitive trade union boss. She, first of all, realised that we really did have to survive as a station and make big cuts. She also realised that as part of the 'mission to explain' some very unsuitable people had been hired – Oxbridge theorists – when what we needed was people who could get the show out on time.[45]

On a personal level, too, Aitken remembers that he and Abbott communicated well. As a result, the redundancies were handled effectively and TV-am was able to continue making programmes throughout the negotiations. Despite feeling that Abbott was 'to the left of Karl Marx' and despite getting the feeling that she viewed him as being 'to the right of Genghis Khan', Aitken's abiding memory of Abbott was that she was 'intelligent and politically sensible', someone he could do business with.

Aitken's work at TV-am saved the company. He famously brought in Anne Diamond and Nick Owen, one of the great television partnerships of the decade. Abbott recalls TV-am lurching from one extreme to another: 'We went from Peter Jay's "mission to explain" to Greg Dyke and Roland Rat.'[46] Audience figures improved and advertising revenues followed. TV-am was safe for a while at least.

For all the excitement and headaches at TV-am, the job had one great advantage: Abbott could do the night shift, knock off around lunchtime and devote the rest of her day to council work. Evenings, more often than not, were taken up with political meetings. Abbott continued her activist journalism, writing occasionally for *Tribune*, and in October 1983 she staged a protest against racism in the press outside the offices of the *Daily Mail*.

It was in the mid-1980s that Abbott came to national attention. She became a regular speaker at political events. She gave her first speech to the Labour Party conference in 1984, as well as giving a keynote address at *London Labour Briefing*'s Target Labour Government fringe event. In June 1985 Abbott appeared alongside Harriet Harman and Glenys Kinnock, in 'Natural Selection or the Story of Why Men Run the Labour Party', a women's action committee review that took place at Bournemouth's Pavilion Ballroom.[47] She was one of fourteen candidates to stand for one of the five NEC women's section seats in September

1985. *Tribune* listed her, along with Betty Boothroyd, Margaret Beckett and Clare Short, as one of the main contenders. In November she was one of the main speakers at an Alliance for Socialism rally, where the promotional literature gave her equal billing with Tony Benn.

Abbott's 1985 Labour conference speech demonstrates why she was in demand as a speaker. Beginning in September, the conference took place six months after the end of the Miners' Strike. The debate on the strike was fractious. Neil Kinnock, Labour's leader, was booed as he stepped up to the platform at the beginning of the debate. Arthur Scargill, however, was welcomed with cheers, and was cheered again when he accused 'sections within our party' of aiding and abetting attacks on the NUM. Scargill proposed that a future Labour government should pass retrospective legislation to reimburse the NUM for the fines imposed on it during the strike. At the end of his speech Scargill was applauded by everyone on the platform except Kinnock and his deputy Roy Hattersley. The leadership opposed the resolution, claiming that it would set a dangerous precedent and leave the way open for future Conservative governments to pass retrospective legislation against trades unions. After a series of white men had spoken, the chair called Abbott, introducing her as 'a woman, you'll notice, a woman delegate with the blue blouse'.[48] The chair had been criticised a few days before by Irma Critchlow for his failure to call women to speak during the debate on Black Sections. Abbott was greeted enthusiastically by the conference, with shouts of 'Go on Diane!' as she stepped up to the microphone. Abbott made two arguments in support of the NUM. First, she rejected the idea that the law was sacrosanct. The law, she claimed,

> was not some impartial abstraction dealing with people in an even-handed way. The law was used in the Miners' Strike, as it has been used in Ireland, used against the black community, used in colonial struggles since time immemorial, the law was used as a weapon of the British state against working-class people.[49]

This argument was greeted enthusiastically by the conference. Benn applauded while shaking his head approvingly from the platform. Second, Abbott argued that rather than damaging Labour, the strike had caused a revival in the party. 'In my constituency in London', Abbott informed the conference, 'and in thousands of constituencies up and down the country the Miners' Strike regenerated our constituencies, and to my mind has been a crucial element reconstructing and re-energising the Labour Party as a genuine alliance of working-class people, black and white.'[50] This too precipitated prolonged applause, and television cameras zoomed in on Scargill, who was clapping vigorously. The resolution to support the miners was passed, gaining 55 per cent of the conference vote. However, the resolution did not receive the two-thirds majority necessary to ensure it was adopted in the party manifesto.

Abbott left TV-am in March 1985 to take up the job of equality officer of the ACTT. Abbott had been working with the union since the early 1980s. Posts dedicated to dealing with equality policies and minority rights were beginning to emerge in unions in this period, partly due to the demands of union members and partly due to equality legislation passed by the Wilson and Callaghan Labour governments, which gave a legal basis for protecting at least some minority rights. The ACTT had been an early adopter and had created the post of equality officer in 1982. At the time the ACTT represented around 25,000 members, a fifth of whom were women. Reflecting the structure of the industry, the ACTT's male members tended to be highly skilled workers dealing with technical aspects of programme making, whereas the women tended to work in lower-paid, lower-skilled supporting roles.

Abbott set out her plans at the ACTT in an interview with the *Equal Opportunities Review*. Building on the work done by BMWA, her strategy was to create an 'open and fair system of entry' to the profession through setting up technical training programmes specifically for women and minority groups.[51] She also ran seminars for equality officers, which suggested practical ways in which union officials could put pressure on management to adopt improved maternity and paternity leave, support childcare provision, embrace job sharing and institute equal opportunity recruitment policies. This was part of a broader objective, the *Equal Opportunities Review* reported: 'Ms Abbott believes that the path to change within the union and in the industry lies in substantially altering the pattern of employment in the industry.'

Abbott's predecessor Sandra Horne had worked to ensure that female members exercised political power within the union. Abbott wanted to take this further 'to translate the political power which women now have in the union into economic gains'.[52] Her plan, which developed BMWA's pioneering initiatives within ACTT, reflected the approach of black radical groups in Britain at the time. The strategy of the Race Today Collective, which for over a decade was at the centre of black liberation in Britain, was twofold. First, they worked with autonomous black groups, creating strong grassroots institutions that genuinely reflected the concerns of black people. Second, from this position of strength, black radical groups put pressure on existing trades unions to admit black members, recognise the legitimacy of their demands, and to support their black members in their campaigns for justice. Abbott took much the same approach. The BMWA quickly became a strong base from which she could work with unions to support racial justice. Abbott's emphasis on training was also similar to initiatives pioneered by Haringey and Hackney councils and Haringey Women's Training and Education Centre, which offered training opportunities particularly targeted at black people and women.

Such strategies were wholly different to the caricature of 'loony left' equality policies presented by right-wing newspapers. The best-known examples of tabloid coverage of equality policy are the 'Baa-Baa Black Sheep' stories which circulated in 1986. One version of the story, published by the *Star* in February 1986, implied that Hackney Council had banned toddlers at the Beavers Nursery from singing the traditional nursery rhyme 'Baa-Baa Black Sheep'. A similar story, initially published in the *Daily Mail* in October 1986, claimed that playgroup workers in Haringey had been ordered by the local council to sing 'Baa-Baa Green Sheep' following a ban of the original lyrics. A few days later the story was picked up by the *Sunday People* and the *News of the World*, and the alleged new rhyme was condemned by Education Minister Kenneth Baker at the Conservative Party conference. Notably, the stories were untrue. Neither Hackney nor Haringey Council had ever banned the singing of 'Baa-Baa Black Sheep'.[53] But these, along with stories about 'loony left' officials banning manholes, are typical of the way equality policies were presented by the tabloids. For right-wing tabloids, and other papers which followed their lead, equality of opportunity policies were presented as draconian diktats, handed down by know-it-all do-gooders, which posed a chilling Orwellian threat to the English language. Moreover, these stories had a tendency to circle back to homosexuality. For the *Yorkshire Evening Courier* the most worrying aspect of 'loony left' equality policies was not that they banned harmless nursery rhymes; it was that they insisted that children should be indoctrinated with the idea that 'abnormal sexual quirks' were acceptable. Tabloid coverage of equality policies often presented such a caricature that it was barely distinguishable from *Viz*'s comic strip Millie Tant, the self-proclaimed champion of 'wimmin's rights'. Tabloid stories completely misrepresented the serious work being done by local authorities and through unions to provide training and childcare and to open professions that had traditionally been dominated by white men.

The early 1980s were a time of competing political visions and radically different forms of political organisation. Of the various political groups and projects that Abbott engaged with, the GLC was by far the best model. Under Shirley Porter, Westminster Council pioneered municipal Thatcherism. This model of local government was secretive; local citizens were, as far as possible, excluded from decision making. Conservative councillors proceeded on the basis that they knew best, that community groups, particularly unions were the enemy, and that the relationship between government and citizen should be identical to the relationship between a privately owned business and a consumer. Indeed, by 1986, it became clear that Westminster Council's target market was wealthy consumers, and that poorer customers should shop elsewhere. Abbott rejected this form of politics as a model for local and national government.

The SDP took a different approach, but again, Abbott found fault with their style. The SDP centralised policy making in the hands of its leadership. The Limehouse Declaration, whatever its virtues, was the product of a small group of politicians who could not be described as representative of Britain as a whole. For Abbott – committed as she was to a genuinely democratic politics – the SDP offered nothing new.

The informal hierarchies of *The Leveller* collective were problematic in different ways. Abbott quickly learned that the informal nature of the organisation allowed white men to dominate and to hide their power behind radical rhetoric.

Conversely, rather than treating citizens as passive consumers, the GLC invited Londoners to play an active part in governing themselves. Rather than centralising power and taking a top-down approach to government, it worked with grassroots organisations to develop policy and to deliver change. Rather than pretending that there were no institutional hierarchies, black people and women – such as Paul Boateng and Linda Bellos – exercised power within an authoritative institution. By working through community groups, black people and women could engage with the GLC from a position of strength. In that sense, rather than rejecting hierarchies and formal structures, the GLC was attempting to democratise them and to use them to progressive ends. It was this model that Abbott championed for the rest of her political career, and this kind of politics that she determined to fight for in Parliament.

CHAPTER 6

THE REPRESENTATION
OF THE PEOPLE

Abbott was up early on election day in 1983. It was almost two months since Peter Jay had resigned as TV-am's chief executive, and the serious-minded 'mission to explain' had given way to a more folksy approach to breakfast news. Abbott was on the English Riviera with a film crew as Torbay held the record as the fastest constituency to declare. Abbott interviewed the local returning officer, enquiring after Torbay's secret, and she was shown a pair of Victorian brass scales. The returning officer explained, 'First, we count the votes in the normal way, but when we check the result ... we weigh them.'[1] As the Conservatives had won by a margin in excess of 20,000 votes in 1979, weighing the vote seemed wholly appropriate. On the night, Torbay declared first, beating its perennial rival Guildford. Despite a 9 per cent swing to the SDP–Liberal Alliance Torbay's Tories weighed in with the winning vote.

The 1983 election was a disaster for Labour. The Conservatives won 42.4 per cent of the popular vote, down a little from 1979. Labour's vote share dropped by more than 9 per cent. Gaining a mere 27.6 per cent of the vote, it was the party's worst result since the end of the First World War. Due to the vagaries of the electoral system, Thatcher won a majority of 144 seats, a landslide. Labour lost sixty seats in the Commons; Labour candidates lost their deposits in 112 seats, coming third or worse in 292 constituencies.

The result posed two important questions which would be crucial

to the politics of the coming years. First was the issue of representation. Speaking to ITN as the votes were being counted, Liberal leader
David Steel claimed, 'The millions of people who voted for us have
been cheated.'[2] Steel had a point. The SDP–Liberal Alliance had won
more than a quarter of the votes in the country, but less than 5 per
cent of the seats in the House of Commons. Shirley Williams and
Bill Rodgers, two of the SDP's original Gang of Four, had lost their
seats. But representation was also an issue in another sense. The 1983
election, like every election in the post-war period, returned an entirely white House of Commons. More than 2 million black and Asian
Britons, almost 5 per cent of the population, were not represented in
Parliament.

The second question concerned the reasons for Labour's historic
defeat. Remarkably, there was a consensus between the Conservative
frontbench and many in the Parliamentary Labour Party. One theme
of the Conservative election campaign was Labour's 'extremism'. The
Conservatives, by contrast, presented Thatcherism as moderate and
pragmatic. Writing in 1993, Thatcher argued that attacking Labour's
'extremism' was 'the real underlying theme of the 1983 general election'. Shortly after the election, Labour frontbencher Gerald Kauf-
man made much the same point, describing Labour's manifesto as 'the
longest suicide note in history'.[3] For many Labour MPs, the party's
commitments to nuclear disarmament and to leave the European
Economic Community were too far to the left of public opinion.
The left had an alternative view. Labour's vote had been declining
since 1966, and many voters judged the party not on its manifesto
but on the record of the last Labour government, which had been
led by the Labour right. What is more, prior to the campaign senior
figures on the right of the party, including Callaghan, Denis Healey
and Roy Hattersley, had spoken out against party policy. The fact that
senior figures in the party regarded their own programme as 'extreme'
made it easier for the Conservatives and the Alliance to persuade the
public that the party had been overrun by Trotskyites. There were
also immediate issues which had nothing to do with Labour's policy
offer. The Tories' fortunes had revived significantly following the

Falklands War. Labour's campaign had been, all agreed, a shambles. Equally, Michael Foot, Labour's septuagenarian leader, was hardly telegenic. Thatcher, by contrast, radiated a certain steely charisma. Foot looked as if he was stuck in the past, indecisive and distant from reality; in many ways, he embodied all that appeared to be wrong with the Labour Party. Abbott's allies in *Briefing* laid the blame for defeat with the backward-looking leadership, not the future-facing manifesto.[4]

The two issues of black representation and Labour's 'extremism' became inextricably linked in the middle of the 1980s. In general terms, Labour's right argued that the party had to cleave to the centre ground to see off the SDP and become electable. This meant rejecting 'extremist' demands for black representation. The left of the party rejected the label 'extremist'. They argued that a 'radical' Labour Party could win in an election, and that black representation in the party, and at all levels of government, was crucial to Labour's success as an electoral force. The divide between left and right did not fit divisions over Black Sections perfectly, however much the right-wing press conflated 'black extremism' with 'Militant Tendency'. Nonetheless, Labour's rivals seized on accusations of 'black militancy' as evidence that Labour was enthral to the 'loony left'. In short, the dispute over Black Sections soon became central to the politics of the 1980s.

It was in the wake of the 1983 defeat, and years before Tony Blair, that Abbott called for 'a new Labour Party'.[5] What Abbott meant in the 1980s and what Blair meant a decade later were quite different, but it is worth noting that across the Labour Party there was a recognition that change was needed. For Abbott, a 'new Labour Party' would be different from the old in the sense that it would be more democratic and more responsive to the voices of women and minorities. This, Abbott argued, required the representation of black people at every level of the Labour Party. Put another way, it meant that black representatives, who were responsive to the grassroots and independent of the leadership, should have voting rights on all party committees. This was one of the central demands of Black Sections: the campaign for black representation in the Labour Party.

BLACK SECTIONS

The campaign for Black Sections emerged in the summer of 1983. It built on an ongoing post-war campaign for black representation in and around the Labour Party. David Pitt was a pioneer. Standing for Labour in Hampstead in the general election of 1959 and for Clapham in 1970, he was beaten by Conservatives on both occasions. The events of 1979 also fed into the campaign. During the 1979 election a variety of minority groups seized the opportunity to make an impact through the ballot box. The Standing Conference of Pakistani Organisations, for example, advised its members to back either the Liberal Party or Labour, depending on which had the best chance of winning.[6] The Standing Conference of Afro-Caribbean and Asian Councillors (SCACAC) was another initiative founded in the late 1970s, formed in south-east London by Russell Profitt and Phil Sealey, Labour councillors in Lewisham and Brent respectively. Born in Georgetown, British Guiana in the 1950s, Profitt moved to London in the 1960s, where he became involved in student politics and latterly the Labour Party. Having become a councillor in Lewisham in the mid-1970s Profitt recalls being 'frustrated with the lack of action on equality issues generally in local government and elsewhere', and therefore reached out to black and Asian councillors.[7]

In time, Profitt and Sealey's informal network became SCACAC. A fortnight before the 1979 election, SCACAC convened the Black People's Manifesto conference, quickly issuing the Black People's Manifesto, which set out sixteen demands representing the interests of black and Asian voters. The Black People's Manifesto received a great deal of press coverage in the run-up to election day and would become the basis of the Black Sections Manifesto, which launched in 1987. Members of SCACAC would later play an important role in the campaign for Black Sections.

While Profitt was organising in south London, Ben Bousquet was working along similar lines north of the river. Born in St Lucia, Bousquet had arrived in Britain in 1957 at the age of eighteen. By the late 1970s, he was a NALGO shop steward in Charing Cross Hospital, and a Labour councillor for North Kensington. Together with Labour councillors Ray Philbert and Billy Poh, Bousquet established a group which, he argued, would 'create the proper atmosphere' to support black people in the Labour Party, encourage black people to join the party and to advance a black agenda.[8]

In the winter of 1982 Bousquet, Philbert and Poh expanded what they were doing. They decided to write to every black and Asian councillor in the country and invite them to participate in the initiative. Although the three were working within the Labour Party, their letter went to all members of the SCACAC, and therefore to the small number of Conservatives, Liberal and independent councillors who were part of the organisation. As the first letter elicited no response, they sent a second in the spring of 1983, prior to the general election. On this occasion, Bousquet recalls, there was more enthusiasm, notably from Paul Boateng. Abbott, however, did not respond. In the spring of 1983, she had good reason to wait and see. She was already a member of the SCACAC, and she was aware of several initiatives from the Confederation of Indian Organisations, the West Indian Standing Conference and the Federation of Bangladeshi Organisations, which were gearing up for the 1983 election. With her time already tight due to her work at TV-am and on Westminster Council, she wanted to see which of the initiatives bore fruit before getting involved.

Notably, neither Profitt nor Bousquet was advocating the agenda that later became central to Black Sections. They were pioneering initiatives which crossed party lines. Although their work laid a foundation for Black Sections, properly speaking Black Sections emerged in the latter part of 1983.

The 1983 election, and its aftermath, gave further impetus to the campaign for black representation. Five black or Asian candidates stood for election in 1979. In 1983 the figure rose to twenty-one, six of whom stood for Labour, four representing the other three major UK parties, and three independents. Despite the increase, Boateng argues that one of the lessons that he took away from 1983 was 'just how difficult it was to get black people selected in winnable seats'.[9] Boateng's campaign in Hertfordshire West was dispiriting. Not only were doors slammed in his face and dogs set on him and his black volunteers but he placed third, 15,000 votes behind the victorious Conservative candidate.

In protest at what they regarded as Labour's ambivalence toward black and Asian voters, the Confederation of Indian Organisations, in conjunction with the West Indian Standing Conference and the Federation of Bangladeshi Organisations put up three minority ethnic candidates.[10] The independent black and Asian candidates did not win, but they made their mark. In Leicester East, RV Ganatra won almost 1,000 votes. In a seat where the Tories won by just over 900 votes, Ganatra's candidacy demonstrated that the Asian vote could be decisive.

In the aftermath of the 1983 election, the Black Sections campaign began to emerge. Bousquet's initial vision was to establish informal black caucuses within the Labour Party across the country. However, by the autumn of 1983 Abbott and other black activists in the Labour Party had coalesced around a more radical proposal, not for informal caucuses but for formal Black Sections within the Labour Party. Although Bousquet and Profitt had been organising black councillors prior to 1983, Abbott argues that something new happened after the election:

> It wasn't that somebody set up Black Sections and asked us to join. There were a group of us who were individual black activists in our parties, but who were also informed by the politics of race and also post-colonial politics. We didn't start with the demand for Black Sections. We started by coming together and saying, 'How can we support each other, how can we get the left to pay attention to black struggles?'[11]

Boateng agrees: 'Black Sections was a genuine bottom-up, grassroots movement of activists.'[12]

The campaign for Black Sections began to take shape in Westminster in the late summer of 1983. Looking back Profitt recalls, there were 'a series of discussions in Paddington'.[13] These led to the establishment of the steering committee of Black Sections, and Profitt's appointment as chair. Marc Wadsworth, black activist and journalist, and Narendra Makanji, Labour councillor in Haringey and anti-racist campaigner, remember that 39 Chippenham Road, Labour's office in Westminster North, became the unofficial headquarters of Black Sections in the early days, so Abbott was at the heart of the new campaign. Makanji argues that Abbott's local party was 'one of the very few that was broadly supportive and could see that the black community in the area had very little representation'.[14] Westminster North was sympathetic because of groundwork that Abbott had been laying since the summer of 1982. Shortly after Abbott was elected as councillor, she had organised an informal black caucus. Writing in *Socialist Action* two years later, she explained:

> When I was first selected as a Labour councillor in my area, Paddington, I was very concerned not to fall into the trap that many other black people elected to such positions had fallen into. That is to become cut off from other black people. I wanted to be accountable to black people in the area … So I organised a black caucus of party members in Paddington constituency, as it was then. Since then Westminster North, as it now is, has become one of the CLPs fighting for the formal recognition of black section.[15]

Together with Elaine Foster and Sharon Hunte, Abbott was one of three black women from across England on the initial seventeen-strong committee, and the only black woman from London.[16]

The steering committee acted quickly, formulating a resolution to present to the annual party conference. With the help of the Labour Race Action Group the resolution was circulated to activists across the country in September 1983, weeks ahead of the Brighton conference. Abbott's constituency party was one of those to propose the first Black Sections resolution to conference. The resolution asked that the 'conference recognises that in this unequal society there is no real equality of opportunity and that working-class people, women and ethnic minority groups suffer severe discrimination'.[17] Closer to home, the resolution also asked conference delegates to recognise that 'our party itself is unfortunately not free from this' and therefore to embrace 'the principles of positive discrimination in favour of disadvantaged groups'. In concrete terms, the resolution proposed that Labour should establish a working group to make recommendations to the 1984 conference on constitutional changes to the party to 'ensuring greater involvement and more equal representation of disadvantaged groups at all levels of the party', as well as asking the NEC to consider 'mandatory inclusion of members of disadvantaged groups on parliamentary shortlists'.[18] The resolution also proposed that the party should recognise the right of black and Asian people to organise themselves 'in the same way as women's sections and young socialist branches', and that representatives of minority groups should play a major role in the proposed working party.

Abbott recalls that at the point these demands were formulated, they seemed entirely reasonable.

> We started off wanting Black Sections because we felt there was a precedent in the party: women's sections and youth sections, therefore why not Black Sections? It seemed to us that was a way of framing it so that the party could understand, rather than talking about black self-organisation.[19]

Jim Thakoordin, a member of the steering committee of Black Sections, who proposed the motion, told the conference that black and Asian voters were 'cheesed off with Labour'. Pointing to the wholly white platform, he told the conference that the party would lose black and Asian voters altogether unless it took a decisive step 'away from being a white and male dominated, chauvinistic and an often racist and sexist Labour party'.[20] In practical terms Thakoordin demanded that a woman and a black or Asian person should be on every shortlist.

The 1983 conference was the first victory for Black Sections and led to the establishment of a Positive Discrimination Working Party.

For Abbott, the creation of the Black Sections campaign in the Labour Party was part of a series of broader social and political changes. First, Abbott recalls that the group who came together to form Black

Sections were similar in that they were active in the Labour Party, but also similar in that they were also involved in black grassroots politics. Significantly, black grassroots politics had been radicalised by the riots in the early 1980s.

Second, with some notable exceptions, Abbott argues, the people who formed Black Sections were part of a new generation. For Abbott, the Black People's Day of Action and the subsequent riots were a sign that a new generation of black radicals was emerging. Black Sections was one of the first political campaigns run by this new generation. In part, this reflected a generational shift in perceptions of the Labour Party. First-generation migrants had known Labour under Hugh Gaitskell and remembered the party's principled opposition to immigration controls of any kind for British subjects from the former colonies. However, the experience of second- and third-generation migrants was very different. Wilson and Callaghan had treated immigration as a matter of electoral expedience, not moral principle. Therefore, from 1964 to 1979 Labour, in opposition and in government, had followed the Tory lead, making ever-tougher statements and passing ever more draconian laws against immigration from the 'new Commonwealth'. Indeed, one of the reasons that black and Asian people started joining the Labour Party in the early 1980s was that it was clear that the era of Wilson and Callaghan was over.[21]

This new generation also had different political objectives than the leaders of the struggle in the 1960s and 1970s. Bill Morris, a prominent black union leader in the 1980s, summed up the new orientation by arguing, 'We are moving from protest to politics. We are moving from protest to power.'[22] During the 1970s, black radicals had formed small organisations, and challenged authoritative institutions, often with considerable success. But from the early 1980s, black radicals increasingly wanted to exercise real power within existing institutions, rather than exerting influence from without. As the sociologist Hilary Wainwright has argued, by the early 1980s black people, 'had had enough of petitioning, lobbying, pressuring white politicians; they wanted direct representation of their own. Consequently, when they joined the Labour Party many of them were interested in power.'[23]

Although there was a great deal that was new about the emerging Black Sections, the new generation of activists continued the post-colonial orientation of the older generation. Specifically, they embraced a 'universal' notion of 'political blackness'. In 1985 Black Sections clarified the position in the following terms:

> 'Black' is a political concept. It is used to include all racially oppressed minorities. Each geographical area, therefore, is likely to reflect its own 'black' communities. In most areas this will inevitably mean people of Afro-Caribbean or Asian descent. However, in Haringey, for example, Cypriots have chosen to be, and are, involved in local Black Sections.[24]

This orientation reflected the dominant view among black and Asian radicals, and the campaigns that they had run in the 1960s and 1970s. It also reflected the basic reality that black and Asian people faced the same problems in terms of immigration law, similar problems in terms of access to public services, racist violence and exclusion from centres of power.

Third, Abbott argues that changes in Labour politics were also important in the development of Black Sections. While the riots highlighted the problem, the influence of the London left in the early 1980s held out the prospect of a solution. Much of the left was unsympathetic to black self-organisation. Radicals associated with *Tribune*, to take one example, were sympathetic to black rights conceived as anti-racism, in theory, but saw no reason why black people should lead the fight for racial justice in practice. Militant Tendency were even less sympathetic. Wedded to a politics of class, Militant was openly hostile to black self-organisation, which they saw as an attempt to distract and divide the working class. That said, radicals associated with *Briefing* and the CLPD, who were in the ascendancy in the London left, supported black self-organisation, and quickly threw their weight behind Black Sections.

The new Labour left was attractive to black people for a number of reasons. Like many black radicals, *Briefing* was critical of the compromises made by Wilson and Callaghan on immigration. *Briefing* and the CLPD were also committed to the democratisation of the Labour Party. This meant that black people could join the party and expect to make their voices heard. Finally, many on the London left were engaged in a new form of community politics which threw the party's support behind grassroots campaigns. Wainwright has argued that traditionally Labour councillors and MPs were remote from the communities they represented, except for brief periods of campaigning at election time. Jeremy Corbyn and Bernie Grant, to take two notable examples, pioneered a new kind of politics, using what power they had to actively support local campaigns. In so doing they built connections between local activist groups, including trades unions, women's groups, black groups, LGB groups, the peace movement and the Labour Party.[25]

Although Black Sections had support from the left, activists involved in the movement came from across the party. Russell Profitt, for example, was regarded as a moderate; Sharon Atkin as a radical. Keith Vaz, who became involved in Black Sections around the time of the 1984 European elections argues, 'It was never about policy, at the start, it was all about representation, the total and utter lack of representation.'[26]

While there were many good reasons to fight for Black Sections in the Labour Party, there were significant obstacles. Labour's record on fighting racism was far from encouraging. Immigration was not the only issue where the party leadership had demonstrated a willingness to tolerate racism. As Paul Boateng recalls:

> The two most obvious issues, which brought things to a head for me were SUS, the Vagrancy Acts, the problems we had with the Labour government who rejected any review of the SUS laws in no uncertain terms. The first time we got a parliamentary discussion of these concerns we had support from David Pitt and Eric Lubbock [a Liberal], but no support at all from Labour, who were in government. The minister for police answered the debate in the Lords, and was actively hostile. It was clear therefore that we weren't making

any headway despite the fact that the issue was big in many Labour seats.[27]

Much the same was true with housing. Boateng remembers hearing Labour Chief Whip Bob Mellish telling his black constituents, 'Don't push your luck, mate.'

Stories of racism in the Labour Party in the 1970s and 1980s are legion. Anecdotally, several black activists recounted stories of black people trying to join the Labour Party being turned away on the pretext that the party was 'full'. In 1984, the *Caribbean Times* reported that white members of the party in Birmingham refused to allow black people to join unless they could produce their passport and their union membership card. James Hunte, the black Labour councillor who broke the story, and accused the party of 'blatant racism', was quickly suspended.

Black people and Asian people who did make it into the party were met with prejudice. Boateng recalls that within the Labour Party, 'there were individuals in positions of power who were racist. There was institutional racism, but there was also individual hostility towards black people. The trades union movement was shot through with racism, so why would one be surprised to find individual racists in the party?'[28] Speaking in 1986, Narendra Makenji described his experience:

> In 1979 I wasn't allowed to go out canvassing … People mustn't underestimate the level of racism in the Labour Party … You'd go in at election time and say, 'I want to go out canvassing.' 'Oh, no, no, no. We've got better things for you to do,' they'd say. We'd spend the time indoors, out of sight, sitting stuffing envelopes.[29]

Makenji moved from Zimbabwe to Britain in 1974 and joined the Labour Party a year later. He subsequently became a Labour councillor in Haringey and a leading figure in Black Sections. He argues that 1983 was a turning point for black people within the Labour Party. While he recalls that there had 'always been informal black caucuses' in the party, he claims that the analysis of the 1983 election was one of the reasons behind the formation of Black Sections.

> It came out of the analysis of what happened at the 1983 election. The black vote was fairly solid for Labour. If the black vote had collapsed to the SDP and the Tories as the white working-class vote collapsed, Labour would have definitely been the third party, we would have lost possibly another thirty parliamentary seats, at least. And if Labour was the third party, defections [to the SDP] would grow, because very often black people were voting anti-Tory. If the Liberals and the SDP had the best chance of defeating the Tories, that's where they'd go.[30]

Makenji argues that the Runnymede Trust's analysis of the 1983 election persuaded a number of black and Asian activists that ethnic minority voters had made a significant difference to the outcome of the election, and that the time was right to turn this electoral power into institutional power within the Labour Party. Makenji was certainly right about the significance of the black vote. Of the 8 million votes that Labour received in 1983, 1 million came from black and Asian voters. What is more, the Runnymede Trust's figures showed that Labour's share of the black and Asian vote had slumped from around 90 per cent in 1979 to around 70 per cent in 1983.[31] But this decline was nothing compared to the collapse of Labour's white working-class vote. Support for Labour among skilled manual workers dropped from 42 per cent in 1979 to 32 per cent in 1983, and support among semi-skilled and unskilled white workers dropped from 49 per cent to 41 per cent in the same period.[32] Based on these figures, Makenji argued that black voters were a crucial part of Labour's coalition and therefore deserved a voice in policy-making and the selection of candidates.

Makenji's analysis suggested that despite racism within the party, Labour had an interest in being more responsive to black and Asian voters. Therefore, black and Asian activists took their resolution to the 1983 conference with a fair degree of optimism. Indeed, at first, the 1983 Labour conference's decision to establish the working party appeared to be a step forward for Black Sections. However, unbeknownst to black and Asian activists, in the longer term, the conference placed two obstacles in the way of Black Sections. The conference elected Neil Kinnock as the new party leader, with Roy Hattersley as his deputy. At the time, this was not an obvious setback for Black Sections. Kinnock was a passionate opponent of apartheid and he was regarded as sympathetic to the democratisation of the party. Equally, although the left regarded Hattersley as the 'standard-bearer of the old parliamentary right',[33] he represented Birmingham Sparkbrook, where minority ethnic voters made up more than 35 per cent of the population, and where historically as many as 90 per cent had voted Labour.[34] Therefore, it might have been assumed that Hattersley had an electoral interest in listening to black and Asian voters. The extent of Kinnock and Hattersley's opposition to Black Sections only became clear six months later.

Abbott made her position on Black Sections clear in the African-Caribbean paper *The Voice* in March 1984. Characteristically, she stressed the need to organise. The problem she identified was simply that 'white members of the Labour Party are not going to give blacks safe seats. People don't give away what they've got.'[35] Organisation was the solution: 'a black group within the Labour Party representing black interests' was the first step to winning safe seats for black people. Abbott struck a different note to Bousquet, who argued that Britain needed a Martin Luther King or Jesse Jackson to push forward the fight for black rights. Abbott, by contrast, put her faith in black people organising themselves, arguing that they would achieve nothing if they 'stand around waiting for a Moses to lead them out of the wilderness. If someone wants to see political changes, the thing to do is to get involved and bring those changes about.'

In addition to being part of the steering committee, Abbott was a founder member of the Westminster North Black Section. Formed in the autumn of 1983, it was one of the first Black Sections to be established. The other early adopter was Vauxhall, where a Black Section was formed in November 1983, and it was the actions of the Vauxhall party which forced Labour's new leadership to reveal their hand.

THE CAMPAIGN FOR BLACK REPRESENTATION

April 1984 was a crucial month for Black Sections. Wadsworth persuaded the Vauxhall Labour Party to formally recognise the local Black Section. As a result, black party members in Vauxhall were guaranteed representatives on the party's executive committee and general management committee. This was precisely what Black Sections had been campaigning for at a local level, but it was against Labour Party rules.

The following day, Kinnock set out his opposition to Black Sections. This was a significant change of heart, as for six months Kinnock had claimed to have an 'open mind' on the issue. Speaking to reporters at the House of Commons, Kinnock set out his objections. First, he claimed, an important matter of principle was at stake: 'The moment that we move, for whatever benevolent reasons to some form of segregated membership in the Labour Party that invites a major regression in our efforts to change attitudes in society, and indeed within the Labour movement.'[36] Second, pointing to the increased number of black councillors, Kinnock argued that Black Sections were unnecessary, adding that he anticipated that 'as many as six or seven' black MPs would be returned to Parliament at the next election.

Third, he argued that the mandatory inclusion of black people and women on shortlists would be counter-productive and would be an obstacle to black people and women being selected, as it would 'turn a selection conference into rivalry between people with different attributes'. This, in turn, would shift focus away from the merits of the candidates.

Kinnock's arguments against Black Sections were made prior to the first meeting of Labour's Working Party on Positive Discrimination, indicating, perhaps, that the leadership had prejudged the matter and were unlikely to be swayed by the working party's findings.

Kinnock's intervention led to a slew of articles on Black Sections. Needless to say, black activists responded. Opinion pieces appeared in *The Times*, *The Guardian*, the *Telegraph*, the *Daily Mail*, *The Voice*, *West Indian World*, *New Life*, *Tribune* and the *New Statesman*, and debates took place on television and radio. If Kinnock's intervention was calculated to settle the issue, it failed. By June 1984, positions were utterly polarised. Remarkably, the *Daily Mail* was initially quite sympathetic to Black Sections. Writing for the *Mail* in June, Kim Sengupta argued that the aspirations of 'Black activists, who, year after year, have delivered votes, the ethnic votes so crucial in marginal constituencies' were being denied by 'an unholy alliance of the party hierarchy, the trade unions and extreme left supporters of Militant Tendency'.[37]

In June, Kinnock's handling of the debate also provoked controversy. Having agreed to speak to Channel 4's *Black on Black* and BBC Two's *Ebony*, he failed to participate in either show, leading to claims in *The Voice* that he had snubbed black viewers, and criticisms of leadership arrogance in *Labour Weekly*.

It was in this context that Abbott announced her candidacy for the NEC. She was in a reasonably strong position: she had the backing of the women's action committee, *Briefing*, and was on the CLPD slate for the women's section. She used her June 1984 interview with *The Guardian* to spell out what she believed was at stake. Labour's racism, she argued, was 'shown not only by the party's support in the past for racist immigration measures, but also by the bad deal black people get from too many local Labour authorities in areas like housing and social services'.[38] Abbott coupled this critique of institutional racism with a message for Labour's leaders: 'White men have to learn that it's not enough to say how sorry you are for black people. We want real political power at all levels.' Black Sections was about power, and for many of its opponents this was the real sticking point.

The Black Sections debate lost none of its intensity over the summer's 'silly season'. Kinnock set out his position again in an open letter published at the end of June. Prior to this, Kinnock had made a series of scattered statements, but the letter was his first attempt to set out his objections to Black Sections in a systematic way. The letter changed the presentation of his arguments, as he did much more to stress his commitment to increased black participation in the party. It also introduced a new argument against Black Sections, which had been missing from his first interviews. Kinnock claimed that establishing Black Sections 'would create significant problems of racial definition which could lead only too easily to endless unproductive acrimony'.[39] Whatever else the letter achieved, it made it clear that the leadership were implacably opposed to Black Sections, regardless of the findings of the working party.

The working party was due to submit a report to the NEC ahead of the annual conference on 27 September. However, the NEC voted to delay publication of the report for twelve months. Instead of publishing positive recommendations, Jo Richardson's committee published a 'consultative document' which presented arguments for and against Black Sections. *The Times* claimed that this was a tactical delay, *The Guardian* agreed stating that the leadership wanted to 'keep the potentially embarrassing issue' of Black Sections, 'off the Blackpool agenda'.[40]

If the leadership had planned to stop Black Sections being discussed at conference, their plan failed. The leadership, it appears, acted far too late. Model resolutions demanding Black Sections had been circulated to constituency parties in early July, following the first annual Black Section conference, which took place in Birmingham and was chaired by Russell Profitt and Irma Critchlow. By the time the conference opened in September 1984, twenty-six constituency parties had established Black Sections. What is more, by lobbying local parties and trades unions, Black Sections activists ensured that twenty-five constituency parties and the Electricians Union submitted resolutions demanding Black Sections to the conference. Ahead of the conference, Black Sections had organised to ensure that the issue was debated, and to put the party under pressure to support the call for black self-organisation. Kinnock, by contrast, appears to have been caught out and forced to engage in some hasty improvisation ahead of the conference. Kinnock's disarray was not lost on senior figures in the party; indeed, a week before the conference opened thirty Labour MPs signed a letter published in *Tribune* which criticised Kinnock's approach as 'ill-considered, hasty and potentially divisive'.[41]

LABOUR PARTY CONFERENCE, 1984

The resolutions presented to the 1984 Labour conference codified the demands of Black Sections. First, resolutions called for a change in the Labour Party constitution to allow black and Asian activists to set up formal sections within the party. That representatives of each black section would be represented by right on the management committees of local parties, in selection meetings, on regional executives and on the NEC. These demands would give black and Asian members of the Labour Party who formed Black Sections the same rights as young people in the party's youth wing, and women in the party's women's section. In addition, the resolutions demanded the creation of all-black shortlists and all-women shortlists in some safe seats, in order to promote more diverse representation in Parliament. This was a change from the previous conference. In 1983, the resolution had demanded that a black person and a woman should be included on every shortlist. This, Wadsworth recalls, had the advantage of being acceptable to many of the big unions. It also had the disadvantage that it did nothing to guarantee a change to the makeup of the party. The revised demand, Wadsworth argues, was an indication of the audacity of the campaign and its refusal to accept half measures.

Abbott's influence on the debate is easy to see. ACTT was one of the first unions to establish Black Sections and pledge their block vote to the cause. Moreover, as delegates arrived at the conference, they were offered copies of 'Black Sections Yes!' a pamphlet outlining the central arguments for Black Sections. Abbott had contributed an essay, which summarised her thoughts thus:

In my view there are four main aims to Black Sections. Firstly … they encourage black people to feel confident and able to talk. Secondly it gives them a framework to discuss and form policy on things of concern to black people. Thirdly they allow black people to organise to fight for those things in the mainstream of the Labour Party. And fourthly through them we can organise for more black councillors, MPs, school governors and so on. But to get more in a framework where they are accountable to black people.[42]

Abbott was also one of the main speakers sent by Black Sections to make the case at conference. The afternoon of the debate started with procedural wrangling. The debate was scheduled to take place after a routine discussion of subscription fees. However, several white delegates raised points of order requiring successive formal votes. After fifteen minutes of procedural disruption and protests from Abbott and Sharon Atkin, the chair, Eric Heffer, recognised this for what it was: an attempt to prevent the question of Black Sections from reaching the conference floor.

Bernie Grant representing Tottenham spoke first and drew on centuries of history to make his case for Black Sections. Elaine Foster, from Birmingham Ladywood, seconded. Foster's speech countered Kinnock's objection to Black Sections on the basis that black people wanted to participate in the Labour Party but on their own terms.

Abbott was third to speak. She, Foster and Vaz all wore black and white Black Sections T-shirts, which helped the speakers grab the attention of the press. Abbott began with the local experience in Westminster North.

> Contrary to all the talk we've had about Black Sections being divisive, being ghettos or whatever, our experience in Paddington is that our black section has brought existing black members into the party, it's attracted new black members, and it's galvanised the entire party black and white on race issues.[43]

Abbott's strategy was to turn the debate away from fruitless discussion of abstract principle, which could never be resolved, to the reality of what Black Sections had achieved, which was far harder for the leadership to contest: 'The actual experience when you set up Black Sections, is far from being ghettos, far from being apartheid, they draw black people into the party and they maximise black involvement. That's the actual experience.'

Abbott was also willing to appeal to the leadership's strategic interests. Addressing 'readers of a certain newspaper, which I don't actually want to mention ... It's not as if they object to Black Sections as such, they object to Black Sections they don't control.'[44] This was one of the most explosive moments of the debate. The conference erupted in laughter. Kinnock was also moved. Having sat impassively through the first two speakers, he suddenly beamed, before bursting into laughter. Abbott's target was Militant Tendency, whom the leadership were trying to expel from the party. Abbott's reference to the group was a shrewd move in any number of ways. First, it was a reminder that Black Sections and the leadership had common ground. Second, it exposed the leadership's vulnerability: in opposing Black Sections, Kinnock had allied himself with Militant Tendency, a move that had resulted in some bad press.

Abbott's dig against Militant Tendency gained her prolonged applause from the floor, as well as some nods of approval from Tony Benn and Dennis Skinner, who were sitting behind her on the platform. Having garnered applause and laughter, Abbott concluded with some hard truths. 'Some opponents of Black Sections are straightforward racists. We've been told this week, "We don't want you in this party." White MPs have told us that.' Abbott was jeered from the floor.

> We've been accused of apartheid. I'll tell you what's apartheid: all white parties in multi-racial constituencies, that's apartheid. An all-white House of Commons, that's apartheid. We are providing a remedy for this apartheid, and there are no practical alternatives coming forward.

This was clearly not what white activists wanted to hear, but Abbott was exposing a problem with Labour's anti-racism. Speeches against racism in South Africa and appeals to high-minded principles did nothing to increase black representation in the party or in government.

Abbott closed with a unifying appeal.

> Black Sections are about a new Labour Party with a place for all its constituent parts. It's about a party which will end the special treatment it has always given to white middle-class men, it's about the renewal of the party, because ... a party united in genuine equality can never be defeated.

While much divided, Labour activists were united about the need for renewal, and in the desire for victory. In this sense, Abbott ended on a note which should have drawn delegates together.

Looking back, Boateng comments, 'It was a powerful speech, and an important intervention. Did it change the Labour leadership's attitude to us? Not one bit. On the contrary, if anything they intensified their opposition. But it was a good speech, and an important one.'[45]

Black Sections lost the vote. Far from being a setback, Wadsworth recalls that the steering committee had anticipated defeat and it was part of the strategy. First, while the leadership won the vote, the debate exposed the difficulty of their position. For example, two of the five speakers against Black Sections came from Hattersley's constituency. This was not lost on delegates, and was an indication that the speakers from Birmingham, far from representing black and Asian people from across the country, represented far narrower interests. Second, Wadsworth recalls being told that the leadership had implored Bill Morris to speak against Black Sections. Morris was highly respected and could claim to speak on behalf of many black workers. His refusal to oppose Black Sections in public was clearly a setback for the leadership. Additionally, the defeat caused Kinnock problems in the press. Reports that Abbott was jeered and heckled by white members of the Labour Party did not make good publicity. Nor did reports that Stan Orme, shadow Energy Secretary, had tried to silence Abbott. The *Caribbean Times* castigated Kinnock for taking black voters for granted. Then, a couple of days after the debate, Enoch Powell spoke to the press. Using Kinnock's own arguments, Powell demanded the repeal of all race relations legislation. The leadership had won the vote, but in so doing they found themselves on the same side as Powell and Militant Tendency – hardly a good look.

Kinnock was also up against the SDP–Liberal Alliance. Immediately before Labour's conference, Zerbanoo Gifford was elected to the Liberal Party's council. The Liberals made a great deal of the fact that while Labour's NEC remained all white, Gifford, a British Asian, had voting rights on the party's most senior policy making committee. The

Liberals kept up the pressure on Labour by announcing a recruitment drive for ethnic minorities and a commission to look into representation within the party.

The selection of Trinidad-born Peter Hamid, a member of the Black Sections steering committee, to stand for Labour in the Enfield Southgate by-election was greeted as a step forward for Black Sections by *West Indian World* and *New Life*. Moreover, toward the end of 1984 black and Asian candidates were performing well in by-elections for council seats, which gave Makanji the confidence to tell *The Voice* that Hamid had a good chance of overturning the Tory's 15,000 Enfield Southgate majority.

Hamid's candidacy was a turning point for press coverage of Black Sections. At the by-election in December, Michael Portillo retained the seat for the Tories. The majority was down more than 10,000, but, significantly, the main beneficiaries of the turn against the government were the SDP–Liberal Alliance, who came second in the polls. The Labour vote had been cut in half. Soon after Hamid's defeat, Nicholas Harman, writing in the *Sunday Times*, presented what he claimed was the view from Labour high command. 'Lots of Labour professionals, some of them sincerely anti-racist, are blaming Hamid's wretched performance on the fact that he is black.'[46] The result, Harman predicted, 'will make local Labour parties even more unwilling than previously to adopt black candidates'. Harman opined that the problem was that the black voters that Labour would pick up by endorsing black candidates would be significantly outweighed by the white voters that Labour would lose. Wadsworth recalls hearing that exactly this kind of analysis was influential at the top of the party. Kinnock's papers provide some evidence to bear this out. Kinnock consulted Marian Fitzgerald's 'Political Parties and "the Black Vote"', which looked at the role of race in the 1983 election.[47] The report, which was sent to the Labour leader at the end of 1983, presented the following analysis of the Tory strategy. The Tories had run an advert stating, 'Unlike Labour, we won't make a special case of black.'[48] In condemning this advert, the report concluded, 'The Labour Party itself walked straight into the trap the ad had set for it … The Tories had not needed to run a racist campaign against Labour; they simply provoked Labour into making statements from which white racists might safely be left to draw their own inferences.' Kinnock's letter to Jo Richardson, the chair of the Working Party on Positive Discrimination of 23 July 1984 stressed that while taking positive action to improve opportunities for black people, this was 'NOT to discriminate against white people'.[49] Fitzgerald's report also concluded by dismissing the notion that there was a 'black vote' or that it would remain cohesive in the future. On this basis, Kinnock could conclude that attracting black voters would give an electoral advantage to the Tories.

The formation of the Black Activist Campaign (BLAC) kept the issue of black representation on the agenda at the end of 1984.[50] BLAC published the 'Black List', a list of seats with significant minority populations, where they demanded the selection of black Labour candidates. In January 1985, Black Sections was in the headlines again following a report by the steering committee which pointed to institutional racism in the Labour Party. Indeed, Black Sections was rarely out of the headlines. Every time a black or Asian person won a council seat, every time a black or Asian person stood for selection, regardless of the political party involved, Black Sections returned to the headlines.

BRENT EAST

It was in this context that Abbott started her own campaign for selection. In February 1985, Abbott was approached by activists in Brent East. It was widely assumed that Livingstone would win the selection for the seat. Nonetheless, Abbott recalls, 'Everyone, including Ken, thought he had Brent East stitched up. But there were elements on the left who did not want to see a stitch-up, and they approached me to run. It was a bit of a kamikaze mission, more so than I appreciated at the time.'[51]

Around 30 per cent of Brent East's voters were classified as being first- or second-generation migrants from the new Commonwealth or Pakistan, and therefore the constituency was on the Black List. Nonetheless, Abbott's campaign in Brent was highly controversial.

Corbyn recalls, 'You had this mad competition between those two.'⁵²
Livingstone, he recalls, was horrified by Abbott's candidacy. Apparently, he contacted Corbyn demanding to know 'What's her game?'
Corbyn recalls, 'Ken was then, in a sense, the doomed leader of the
GLC, because abolition was on the way.' Livingstone was convinced
that he should be in Parliament after the next election, and therefore
would not back down. Looking back, Corbyn remembers:

> *Labour Briefing* were very torn between Diane and Ken. They
> thought a black woman should be in Parliament, they thought Ken
> should be in Parliament. Ken and Diane both wanted support from
> the group, so it was quite a difficult time … Diane did not succeed
> mainly because of Ken Livingstone and his mates.

Divisions over rate-capping were an important issue in the selection.
The Thatcher government had introduced new legal powers which
allowed Whitehall to limit local government power to raise and spend
money. Some left-wing councils rebelled by setting illegal rates. Livingstone, however, advocated abiding by the law, a strategy which
brought him into conflict with his deputy, John McDonnell. This
controversy meant that Livingstone no longer enjoyed the undivided
support of the London left.

As Abbott recalls, 'Ken was not amused by somebody having the temerity to challenge him. He didn't make life easy for me.'⁵³ According
to *The Guardian*, Livingstone feared that Abbott had done a deal with
his opponents in the Brent party to keep him out. Livingstone appears
to have resorted to black propaganda to defeat Abbott during the selection battle. In December 1984, Abbott wrote a discussion paper
for a Target Labour Government conference. A partially rewritten
version of the document attributed to Abbott was leaked to the press
at the time that Abbott was considering her candidacy. The altered
document included a commitment to abolish the monarchy, disband
the police force and take over public buildings. The language was also
immoderate and called for the 'elimination' of the Labour leadership.⁵⁴

Abbott, who was working on a freelance basis as GLC press officer at the time, confronted Livingstone over lunch at County Hall. *The Guardian* reported that Abbott forced the GLC leader to concede 'that maybe his supporters had been getting a little over-enthusiastic'.[55] In the spirit of plausible deniability, Livingstone denied any knowledge of dirty tactics. But when pressed by journalists, he refused to deny that he was behind the counterfeit document. Abbott told *The Guardian* that Livingstone's tactics strengthened her resolve to stand.

The Brent East contest was hard fought. Abbott recalls that she did not even win the vote of the women's section. The selection meeting lasted six hours, most of which was given over to Livingstone's decision to set a legal rate at the GLC. When the vote finally took place, the first round was closer than Livingstone might have liked. He won thirty-one votes to Abbott's twenty-six. The second round, however, was clear cut, Livingstone taking fifty votes to Abbott's twenty-five.

The day after the selection battle, Abbott bumped into Corbyn on Westminster Bridge. She was heading home; Corbyn was walking from the Commons to County Hall. Corbyn recalls seeing her from a distance looking uncharacteristically downcast. As the two met, Abbott remembers bursting into tears. The Brent East selection battle was Abbott's first experience of politicking on the left, and the lengths that her allies would go to in order to win. 'One of the things about Brent East is it knocked off some of my naïve corners.'[56] Corbyn offered a few words of consolation, telling her, 'I'm really sorry. But never mind, ducks, these things happen. Get your head up, do it again, and you'll get elected.'[57]

In the early months of 1985, the debate on Black Sections was becoming, if anything, more divisive. In March, Abbott found herself at loggerheads with others within Black Sections for refusing to back constitutional changes to the Westminster North party. Some in Black Sections proposed that constituency parties should make constitutional changes at a local level, ensuring that Black Sections had guaranteed seats on key local committees and a guaranteed vote in selection battles. However, the legality of such a move was questionable. Speaking to *The Voice* on 2 March 1985, Abbott explained that she cast her vote against the changes on the instructions from her local party. Later in the month, Labour's NEC mooted an 'oath of allegiance', which would require officials in constituency parties to swear not to allow representatives of Black Sections to take part in selection meetings.

March also saw a new media narrative emerging around Black Sections. At the end of the month, the *Daily Mail* linked Black Sections with the 'loony left', with the headline 'The Left's ideal MP: A black lady road digger'. This gave Kinnock another reason to oppose Black Sections. Abbott recalls:

> Kinnock was in a bind. He was the kind of politician who thought he was anti-racist. His grasp of the politics of race was very limited. At that point, he was trying to rebrand and purify the party and the idea of black people organising would have been an anathema. He was taking the Labour Party on a journey to the centre and he felt that black self-organisation would deter voters.[58]

With relations between Black Sections and the Labour leadership increasingly fraught, Abbott set out her reasons for continuing her work within the Labour Party in a March edition of *West Indian World*. Beginning with the acknowledgement that 'black people are, quite rightly deeply cynical about the Labour Party', Abbott defended continued engagement in terms of power: 'For too long black people have been willing to hang around outside the political mainstream as "clients", reliant on white people to be nice to us and dole out favours.'[59]

Abbott's alternative to this patron-client relationship was Black Sections, which would allow black people to take 'part in the decision making as equals. Black people should stop being clients and start wielding real political power.'

Abbott's argument exposed one of the weaknesses in Kinnock's position. His thinking was based on a simplistic distinction between integration and segregation. Abbott pointed out that integration was more problematic than Kinnock realised. Abbott backed Black Sections as a method by which black people could integrate from a position of strength, and in so doing integrate as equals, rather than clients.

Abbott concluded her piece with an analysis of the problems of the Labour Party:

> I find white people will actually tolerate and even encourage any black person who they think they can control or who they do not regard as intelligent, but if they think you have a mind of your own they feel very threatened. This is because too many white people think that anti-racism is all about going on marches and have not really come to terms with their own racism. Too many white radicals are only comfortable with black people if they are some sort of client. They find it difficult to deal with black people as equals. As a black woman you come under particular pressure. Most white people find it very difficult to accept a black woman in a position of authority.[60]

Despite hostility from the leadership, Black Sections took another step forward in April 1985. Bernie Grant was elected leader of Haringey Council, becoming Britain's first black council leader.

The media narrative in late April and early May was that the Labour Party was being 'hijacked' by black radicals. On 5 May, Ian Walker, the *Sunday Telegraph*'s political commentator advised Kinnock to 'appeal directly to the ordinary party member – both black and white – before the party is swamped by a specious but superficially plausible and highly emotive challenge to his authority'.

WESTMINSTER NORTH

Abbott's second attempt to win selection took place in May, this time for Westminster North. While Brent East had been a 'kamikaze mission', Abbott had a genuine opportunity to win in Westminster. Vaz, who also put himself forward for the seat, remembers that going into the selection Abbott was the favourite. 'I did it for practice,' Vaz explains. 'That was the seat that she wanted, because she was the local councillor, and I was very conscious of saying to her, "By the way, I don't want this seat, I just want to learn how to do this."' Vaz was knocked out early in the process.[61]

Abbott recalls that there was an understanding between herself, Boateng, Grant, Atkin and Profitt that they would not stand against each other. Makanji also recalls tactical discussions within Black Sections concerning who would run where.

> In 1985 and 1986 people started being selected for parliamentary seats. The kind of meetings we were having between 1983 and 1985 in preparation for that involved quite a lot of strategic discussion, which hadn't happened before. We said, OK, we're now going to go for a number of seats which are winnable, and a number of seats which are practice runs for up-and-coming people. When we went for selection meetings, we were as organised as you could be.[62]

In London, there was also an understanding about who would run where, Grant would run in Tottenham, Boateng would run in Brent South, and Profitt in Lewisham. By the same token, it was understood that Abbott would run in Westminster North. Westminster North constituency party, Abbott recalls, was also sympathetic to the politics of representation. There was also a realistic chance that Westminster North would fall to Labour at the next election, as the Tories had won the seat in 1983 with a majority of less than 2,000.

Jenny Edwards's decision to stand was the first indication that selection would not go Abbott's way. Abbott and Edwards were friends from Cambridge and socialised outside party meetings. Abbott's intention to seek selection was well known in the local party. Edwards's decision, however, was a bolt from the blue. Like Livingstone's reaction in Brent East, this was a shock. In both cases it turned out that politics trumped friendship.

Edwards's CV was similar to Abbott's: both had been to Cambridge; both had begun their careers in the civil service; and both had moved into the world of pressure groups, in Edwards's case the Campaign for Nuclear Disarmament (CND); before involvement in local government. At the time of the selection battle, Edwards was the nuclear-free zone officer for the London Borough of Camden.

Edwards, then, was eminently qualified to represent Westminster, and was genuine competition.

Westminster North, as Abbott had anticipated, used an all-women shortlist. Five stood and Abbott and Edwards were the frontrunners. Edwards, Abbott recalls, picked up the support of many of the young professionals who had joined the Westminster party in the early 1980s. In the end, Edwards won forty-eight votes to Abbott's twenty-five. The experience taught Abbott the truth of the saying, sometimes attributed to Aristotle, 'Oh friends, there are no friends' – or, as Harry Truman put it, 'If you want a friend in politics, buy a dog.'[63]

Abbott's failure in Westminster North meant that halfway through 1985, Labour had not selected a single black candidate for the next election. Russell Profitt had won a selection meeting in East Lewisham, only for the NEC to declare the result invalid, as representatives of the local Black Section were involved in the meeting.

The Westminster North selection committee took place in the same week that Labour's Working Party on Positive Discrimination finally reported. The report concluded that there should be greater black representation in the Labour Party. The majority on the working party supported the call for Black Sections. However, a minority report supported Kinnock.

Kinnock's alternative to Black Sections was to establish an anti-racist organisation in the party that would be open to all members. Once again, Kinnock appeared to have been on the back foot. *The Observer* reported that the submission came at the last minute in an attempt to counter the working party's support for Black Sections.

Kinnock returned to the problem of definition in June. Black Sections had worked on the assumption that people who defined themselves as black and had suffered historic oppression through colonialism and racism could join the movement. Kinnock responded by asking, 'Can I consider myself to be black?' On being told that he was not black, Kinnock told *The Times* that he considered Black Sections 'repellent' and the campaign's leaders 'bankrupt'.[64] Kinnock's immoderate language derailed a meeting with Atkin and Abbott about the definition of black. Abbott, having worked on race relations legislation for the NCCL, was well placed to talk Kinnock through the legal understandings of race, thus solving the problem of definition. Abbott and Atkin gave a press conference in the wake of the meeting, in which they attacked Kinnock for being unwilling to seek reconciliation. Nonetheless, there was good news for Black Sections towards the end of June, as Boateng became the first black person to win selection in a Labour safe seat, and the annual national conference of Labour women endorsed the call for Black Sections.

For eighteen months, Kinnock's approach to Black Sections had been criticised as reactive, hasty and poorly thought through. A recording, preserved in Kinnock's archive, which contains a series of off-the-record comments on Black Sections helps explain Kinnock's approach. Speaking to *Tribune* in September 1985 just ahead of the annual conference, Kinnock stated,

> This is off the record now. I've had most of the leaders of Black Sections in … The first thing was, they didn't realise how long I'd been involved with black communities ever since the early 1960s down in Cardiff, and when I say I've got some good mates among black people, I have. I played football with them, the whole thing. Bill Morris, of course, is quite special. He was a student of mine in the transport and general workers' schools, and a very fast friend from day two.[65]

Kinnock, it appeared, assumed that his trouble with Black Sections was based on ignorance. Having assured the leaders of Black Sections that he had good black friends, he hoped that they would begin to trust him and back the leadership. The events of the 1985 conference would prove Kinnock wrong.

During 1985 Hattersley became more prominent in the fight against Black Sections. Indeed, Hattersley led the leadership's attack on Black Sections at the party's annual conference. Prior to the conference, he wrote to Kinnock. His letter shows that the suspicions of black activists were well-founded.

I, however, counsel caution about finding some common ground with black section supporters. We are in no danger of losing the ethnic minority vote. Indeed, as far as the Asian community is concerned, they are more likely to desert us because they fear extreme infiltration than because they resent the absence of positive discrimination within the party. The black section issue has become a dispute between the mainstream of the party and the same groups that have caused so much trouble in the past. Black Sections and what goes with them are a product of middle class careerism, not genuine concern for equality.[66]

As Black Sections alleged, Hattersley appears to have taken the black vote for granted. More surprisingly, he seems to have believed that Black Sections were both left-wing extremists and middle-class careerists.

At the 1985 conference, Atkin gave a memorable speech. Prior to the conference, Hattersley had referred to his Asian constituents as 'my Asians', a comment which had been ridiculed by supporters of Black Sections. Atkin made the most of Hattersley's discomfort by commenting, 'Roy Hattersley relies on the black vote [in Birmingham Sparkbrook] to return him to Parliament. Yet he has this patronising, condescending attitude which talks about "my Asians". And what do they call him there? "Hatterjee!" Well he's not my Guru.'[67] Turning to the definition of black, Atkin continued:

People here say they don't know the definition of black. Well, I'll address that problem. The National Front know the definition of black. The police know the definition of black. The [Department of Health and Social Security] know the definition of black ... So why is it such a problem for the leadership of our party?

Hattersley's speech was unprecedented in the history of Black Sections. Kinnock never addressed the conference during a Black Sections debate. Indeed, after 1985 he stopped attending the debates. Hattersley opened by telling the conference that no one, on either side of the debate, should question their opponents' motives. This was quite a change of heart, given that his letter to Kinnock had written about Black Sections as a group of troublemakers, and careerists. Hattersley refused to countenance Black Sections, and offered instead the black and Asian advisory committee, a group within the Labour Party with no constitutional power, which would be open to all, and could advise the party on matters of race. His speech rehearsed much of what Kinnock had said to the press. However, Hattersley went further by redefining the word 'black'. For Hattersley, the correct term was 'the black and Asian British' or 'the ethnic minorities'.[68] His reasoning was that he could not accept the notion that,

> a group of men and women, of very different origins, with very different cultures, can be lumped together and generically and vacuously called 'the blacks' or the 'black and Asians', as if they all had the same problems, all had the same cultural background, all had the same aspirations, and all had the same interests. To lump the ethnic minorities together in that way is a deeply patronising view of those of our citizens.[69]

Linda Bellos who was standing with Abbott directly in front of the podium, was clearly not persuaded. Like many in Black Sections, she regarded it as a strategy of divide and rule. Equally, Hattersley's assertion that black and Asian people had significantly different interests and experiences sat uncomfortably with his view that the concerns of black and Asian people were essentially the same as those of the white working class. Hattersley's claim that he wanted to see Russell Profitt selected and elected was also treated with scepticism. After all, Hattersley had argued that Profitt's selection to represent Lewisham was invalid.

Hattersley's speech left a great deal unsaid. His claim that the vast majority of black and Asian Britons did not want Black Sections drew a veil over attempts to set up a black section in his own constituency. His claim that the NEC had decisively rejected Black Sections ignored the fact that the vote had been incredibly close: fourteen to twelve.

Crucially, Hattersley made no reference to the damaging revelations about his relations with Birmingham's Asian community which had been broadcast on Channel 4 days before his conference speech. *The Bandung File*, a show created by the radical intellectuals Darcus Howe and Tariq Ali, exposed evidence that Hattersley relied on the support of local 'godfathers' in the Asian community. Apparently, Hattersley prioritised the immigration cases that they presented to him, and in return they supported him in important votes; exactly the kind of patronage-based politics Abbott had criticised in *West Indian World* earlier in the year. The formation of a black section in Hattersley's constituency threatened to undermine his position, as the black section would not be loyal to the local 'godfathers'.

In many ways Hattersley's conference speech was an impressive performance. But for members of Black Sections, his appeal to high moral principle rang hollow considering the revelations from his own constituency. Behind his rhetoric, Hattersley's rejection of Black Sections appeared to be based on a calculation of his own political interest.

Hattersley's position at the conference may have been even weaker than supporters of Black Sections realised. Farrukh Dhondy, commissioning editor for multicultural programming at Channel 4, recalls meeting Kinnock at a party at the Indian High Commissioner's residence shortly after the programme aired. On establishing that Dhondy was behind the show, Kinnock simply said 'Roy' and mimed steam coming out of his ears.[70] The Labour leader appeared to be enjoying his deputy's discomfort.

The set-piece debate was only the most visible part of the campaign for Black Sections. Behind the scenes, Abbott and other activists were lobbying union bosses, MPs and other prominent figures. Makanji recalls:

From 1984 onwards, when we went to the conference, we'd go there together as a group ... and stay in the same hotel. We'd meet three times a day to discuss what we were going to do in the next session, who do we need to talk to, who do we need to persuade, where are the key fringe meetings where we need to inform people, who is going to speak in the next debate? Because if we didn't speak about it, no one else will.[71]

For Abbott and the others in the Black Sections campaign, lobbying at conference was a round-the-clock activity. On one occasion, Makanji remembers a discussion among the Black Sections group going on late into the evening. Eventually, once they had agreed a position and written up their proposals, Makanji rushed the notes to Bill Morris, slipping them under his door at 4.30 a.m. Despite these exertions, Black Sections were defeated again. But the result was closer than it had been a year earlier.

Abbott played an active role in the 1985 conference, lobbying behind the scenes for Black Sections and speaking in the debate on the NUM. However, this activity belied a certain disenchantment. Having sought selection twice, been involved in bruising selection battles twice, and having lost in Westminster North, her home seat, Abbott had given up on parliamentary selection. What is more, Abbott concluded that the battle in Brent East meant that she would never win in London. At the time Livingstone was the most powerful figure in the London Labour Party, so challenging him had been no small matter. Nonetheless, Abbott's secretary at ACTT alerted her to a selection contest in Hackney North and Stoke Newington. Initially, Abbott wanted nothing to do with it. However, her secretary would not take no for an answer and presented Abbott with a letter of application and an updated CV. Reluctantly, Abbott signed and took little comfort from the fact that her secretary 'had a feeling' that this time Abbott would win.

HACKNEY NORTH AND STOKE NEWINGTON

Hackney North and Stoke Newington had featured on the Black List, as it was a constituency in which ethnic minority voters made up almost 40 per cent of the electorate. As Abbott researched the area, another fact stood out: the constituency had the largest number of single mothers in the country. Hackney North and Stoke Newington also had an active Black Section. Significantly, Hackney's Black Section had evaded the wrath of the NEC. That said, selection would be an uphill battle. The smart money was on Ernie Roberts, the sitting MP, who was popular in the area and had a good track record on local issues. Significantly, Roberts was on the left and had the support of Livingstone and *Briefing*.

However, Roberts's victory was not assured. The left was strong in the constituency, and there was a feeling that it was time for a change. Roberts was in his early seventies, and although he was on the left he did not represent the new left which had emerged in London in the previous decade. Indeed, Roberts had been selected in 1978 as a stop-gap candidate. The constituency was divided on the issue and Roberts emerged as the compromise candidate, not least because he was in his late sixties and therefore it was assumed that he would serve no more than a single term. Roberts, however, surprised everyone by standing again in 1983, and in 1985 he was determined to serve a third term. Looking back, Peter Kahn, who had been deputy leader of Hackney Council, recalls, 'Ernie was a good solid anti-European, a solid trade unionist. Ernie had done nothing wrong, but it was felt that he was getting on and time was up.'[72]

Roberts was not Abbott's only competition. She was also up against Sunhail Aziz, an Asian trade unionist. The strongest local challenger, however, was Hilda Kean, who had triggered the contest. Going into the contest, Abbott learned that the white left in the constituency were backing Kean. The Labour left had won control of the local council in 1982, and Kean had come to the fore as a radical and principled council leader.

Abbott had supporters in the area. Patrick Kodikara, a local councillor and chair of the Campaign for Black Representation in Hackney, threw his weight behind her. Working with the local black section he secured Abbott five nominations. The Campaign for Black Representation in Hackney had been launched in October 1984. The organisation was working for the 'Hackney 28', to get twenty-seven black councillors elected, as well as a black MP. At the time the campaign was launched, only five of Hackney's sixty councillors were black. Kodikara's campaign was influential in the area, as Cathy Warnock, one of Abbott's backers in the local party remembers:

> The general consensus was that Ernie was a really good MP, and everybody was really fond of him. But there was quite a group of us who were saying that if a black candidate, particularly a black female candidate, came along who we thought was really good, then that is who we would all vote for.[73]

Kahn agrees; he remembers thinking that the 1983 election had been a huge disappointment in terms of black representation. In that light, Abbott's candidacy was 'manna from heaven'.[74]

Going into the selection, Roberts was in a strong position, having secured twenty-two nominations. Kean did less well than expected and gained only three. Warnock remembers that Roberts was determined to triumph, and so 'the lead-up to the selection involved Bernie's family going round to lots of [Christmas] parties that were taking place'.[75]

In the run-up to the selection meeting, there was a great deal of discussion about the merits of the front-runners. Graham Bash, who was central to the production of *Briefing*, recalls, 'My inclination was to vote for Ernie against Diane.'[76] In the first round, he intended to vote for Kean, whom he describes as 'a quasi-revolutionary leader of the council, did her best on rate-capping'. For Bash, Kean was the true left-wing candidate. However, prior to the meeting Bash spoke to Wadsworth. Bash recalls, 'He said, "If your words about supporting Black Sections and black representation are serious, you've got to support Diane Abbott, because she's on the left, she's a black woman, and this is a black area." I remember, as I was voting, he was sat on my shoulder.' On the night, with Wadsworth's words echoing in his ears, Bash voted for Abbott in the second round and brought at least one other on board with Wadsworth's reasoning. Bash continued to have his reservations – as far as he was concerned, Abbott's economic philosophy was 'Hattersleyite' – but Wadsworth's argument had won him over.

Wadsworth recalls that campaigning for Abbott was an uphill struggle. Some local activists did not think she was truly on the left; others thought that her time at Cambridge and working in the media meant that she could no longer represent the working class. The idea that she was not left enough struck Abbott as ridiculous. Even so, from what Wadsworth recalls there was always a reason not to support a black candidate. Nonetheless, the groundwork done by Black Sections over the previous three years played a part in swinging support behind Abbott.[77]

During the selection campaign, Abbott addressed the Hackney Trades Union Council on 5 October. According to the minutes of the meeting, 'The vote for our preferred candidate was taken and the result was: Roberts 14, Abbott 5, and Kean 1. Therefore our preferred candidate is Brother Roberts MP.'[78]

However, the minutes of the next meeting showed a change of position. On 7 November, Hackney Trades Union Council agreed that their delegates could support either Roberts or Abbott.[79]

The selection meeting took place on Sunday 9 December in the council chamber of Hackney Town Hall. Warnock, who was representing Hackney's Clissold Ward, remembers that it was a big event, with over 100 people in the chamber. Roberts had his people in place. 'Some of the tellers, the people who volunteered to count the votes, were very pro-Ernie Roberts. We were quite worried by that.'[80] As the meeting began, Abbott was tapped on the shoulder by a well-wisher, who reassured her, 'If you come a good second, that would be great.'[81] Abbott's supporters had good reason for their pessimism. The majority of delegates had arrived with a mandate to vote for Roberts. Based on the mandates issued before the meeting it was assumed that Roberts would win with sixty votes, Abbott would come second with nineteen, and Kean would place last with eight.

The selection meeting comprised a series of stages. Abbott was interviewed and Warnock remembers the interview going well. Crucially, Abbott announced her intention to relocate to Hackney if she was successful. She also agreed to use part of her MP's salary and her secretarial allowance to fund the creation of a constituency office.

These were significant promises, as Roberts, who had represented the area since 1979, had always lived outside the constituency.

Kean and Azis were knocked out in the first round, leaving delegates with a straight choice. The meeting turned on Abbott's speech. In the full knowledge that Roberts had the votes to win, Abbott recalls, 'I gave the speech of my life.' She confronted the delegates with a choice: would they look to the past, and continue as the party of white working men, or embrace the future by selecting a candidate who represented Hackney's growing black community? As she spoke, she could see the audience struggling, caught between the obligation of their mandate and the conviction that the party needed change. Abbott concluded with the words of Maya Angelou:

> Bringing the gifts that my ancestors gave,
> I am the dream and the hope of the slave.

The first indication that Abbott had won, Warnock recalls, were the tellers' downcast faces. The result was tight, but Abbott was victorious, winning on the second ballot by forty-two votes to Ernie Roberts's thirty-five.

Abbott was elated. Her first duty after the meeting was to thank the party officers. 'They looked like their dog had died,' she remembers. This was not the result that party managers had anticipated, nor the result they wanted. In the coming months, Abbott would see this look again and again, as she greeted local party workers. Formalities concluded, Abbott went to Warnock's house, where she called family and friends. The evening ended with a celebration with her supporters at Steptoe's, a pub on Stoke Newington Church Street.

Abbott was magnanimous in victory, telling *The Times* that she regarded Roberts as 'an excellent MP'.[82] Roberts, however, did not take the result at all well. Abbott learned later that he assumed that she stood no chance and therefore did little to try to discredit her. That changed as soon as the selection meeting was over. Over the next week Roberts went on the attack. Having learned, no doubt, from the experience in Lewisham, where the selection of a black candidate had been overturned by the NEC, Roberts alleged foul play. Speaking to the *Hackney Gazette* immediately after the vote, he said:

> It was an unfair result that underlines the need for one member, one vote. I was rejected because I am not black and I am not a woman. But if the party is going to be divided on the basis of colour, sex and witch-hunts then we shall lose the next election.[83]

Roberts, an MP who had been consistently on the left of the party, was not shy in deploying the leadership's arguments against black representation when it suited him. The *Gazette* also reported talk of 'a black woman being an electoral liability', although it stopped short of attributing this view to Roberts.

Roberts repeatedly questioned the legitimacy of the vote. Reported under the headline 'Black Diane "won after vote swap"', he told *The Sun* that some of his supporters were considering appealing to the NEC.[84] While Roberts said nothing that was technically untrue, his language implied that Abbott had engaged in vote tampering. He used much the same tactic a day later, telling the *Daily Express* he attributed Abbott's victory to 'mystery vote switching', and said he was considering a legal challenge.[85] *The Times* took Roberts's line, presenting Abbott's victory as 'a coup'. Together with *The Sun*, *The Times* emphasised that Abbott was an extremist. The *Express* went further: not only was she a 'black extremist'; she was part of the '"illegal" Black Sections movement'.[86]

Roberts's various references to 'vote switching' reflected the fact that delegates who were mandated to vote for him changed their minds during the meeting. According to Mike Graham, one of Roberts's supporters who wrote to the *Hackney Gazette* in protest at Abbott's victory, ignoring a mandate turned the selection process into a 'sham'. He claimed the whole meeting had been a 'kick in the teeth for democracy'.[87] Nonetheless, as Abbott told *The Times*, delegates were free, according to party rules, to make their own judgements.

In the week after her selection, Abbott went from not being left-wing enough for the likes of Bash to being a 'black extremist'. Roberts, by contrast, went from being the authentic voice of the left to being a 'veteran Labour MP' who was standing up for ordinary Labour voters against sectarian extremists. Roberts's talk of legal action came to nothing, and nor did the NEC come to his rescue – there was, after all, nothing irregular about the vote. In the aftermath of the controversy, one thing became clear: Abbott was set to become the first black woman to enter Parliament.

CHAPTER 7

IN THE BELLY OF THE BEAST

It was 10 p.m. and the campaign was over. Labour had had the better of it, but as the votes were counted a small Tory lead became a land-slide. The jubilant crowd packing Smith Square roared and struck up a chant of 'Here we go!' as the Prime Minister arrived at Tory headquarters. Margaret Thatcher's 1987 election victory, her third in a row, made her the most successful political leader of the century. Ex-hausted, Labour politicians toured television studios spinning defeat as best they could, their faces unable to hide the magnitude of their disappointment. Labour had gained twenty seats, but with only 31 per cent of the vote, Kinnock had done little better than Foot four years earlier.

Pundits were quick to call Thatcher's second landslide historic. But in centuries past others had won as big and as often. The truly un-precedented victory belonged to Abbott, the first black woman to win election to the House of Commons.

At 3 a.m. Hackney declared. For a moment the formalities of the count were suspended, the returning officer stopped dead by shouts of victory. Even her opponents, who formed a wall of grey behind her, appeared to be swept up in the moment. As soon as his duties were concluded, the returning officer, one of Britain's few Asian mayors, joined in the celebration. Abbott was elated. Speaking to an excited crowd, many of whom had worked tirelessly for years to win parlia-mentary representation for black people, Abbott was clear: hers was 'a victory for faith, a victory for principle, and a victory for socialism'.[1]

It was also a personal victory after a difficult journey from selection in 1985 to election in 1987.

From what Abbott could tell, the Labour leadership were not pleased with her selection. Looking back, she argues that she slipped through the net. It was widely assumed she would be beaten, so nothing was done. A week after her selection the *Daily Express* reported that Kinnock 'strongly repudiated Labour's prospective black woman parliamentary candidate Diane Abbott for claiming that Labour should dismantle the police, the forces, and the monarchy'.[2] The fact that Abbott had made none of these demands troubled neither the *Express* nor the Labour leader.

Abbott's selection meant that by the end of 1985 Labour had selected three black candidates for safe seats: Abbott in Hackney, Boateng in Brent and Grant in Tottenham. There were also three Black Sections candidates fighting marginals, Vaz in Leicester East, Profitt in Lewisham East and Ben Bousquet in Kensington. Even so, Kinnock made no concessions to Black Sections. Michael Leapman argues that the Labour leader had an unstated reason for refusing compromise: 'He thought Black Sections would prove an additional divisive force in a party he was trying to unite. Like the Labour Party Young Socialists, now dominated by the Militant Tendency, they could turn into a Frankenstein's monster, striking out against the body that created them.'[3] Perhaps for this reason, the Labour leadership were unwilling to work with Abbott. In June 1986, she was invited to appear on the BBC's flagship current affairs show *Question Time*. Four weeks ahead of the broadcast, she contacted Peter Mandelson to get the latest briefing. Weeks passed, and nothing arrived. With a week to go, she contacted him again, but once more, nothing arrived. The day before filming, Abbott called again, and recalls having a perfunctory conversation. Consequently, Abbott arrived at Television Centre having had no briefing, no coaching and no support from the Labour head office. She concluded that

> Mandelson didn't care if I fucked up. That was the issue with the
> Labour leadership all along, they would rather I fucked up than

have any credibility at all. Mandelson was horrified by the rise of the left in London, horrified by black politics and what it meant. It showed me that these people weren't on my side.[4]

Question Time had been running for almost a decade by the time Abbott first appeared. Profitt and Boateng had both been guests once. But in the era of Black Sections, Abbott was the first black politician to appear on the show. Before the broadcast Abbott went to dinner with Robin Day and the other panellists. Day 'was very patronising', Abbott recalls, and the meal had a gentlemen's club feel. Most of the other panellists, after all, were white men from the same privileged background. Abbott was joined by Jeffrey Archer, the deputy chairman of the Conservative Party; Alan Watson, former president of the Liberals; and Bill Jordan, the president of the Amalgamated Engineering Union. Abbott managed to be loyal to the Labour leadership, claiming that Kinnock's recent bump in the polls was 'well deserved', while advancing left-wing arguments, including arguing for the imposition of sanctions on South Africa, criticising members of the SDP for opposing the democratisation of the Labour Party and condemning government policy for failing people in inner cities.[5] On the subject of Black Sections, Archer claimed that there was nothing remarkable about Abbott's selection as there had been 'many black MPs in the past'.[6] Black radicals had pointed to Dadabhai Naoroji, Mancherjee Bhownaggree and Shapurji Saklatvala as their parliamentary forebears, but to claim that there were 'many' was a stretch. Archer's comments reflected the notion that racism simply was not a feature of British politics, and by implication that Black Sections were entirely unnecessary. Whatever the hopes of the Labour leadership, Abbott gave an assured performance.

SEPARATIST ACTION

Although Abbott had little support from the party leadership, her public statements in the mid-1980s were, as far as possible, conciliatory. Nonetheless, she was still willing to endorse radical positions. In March 1987, the Black Sections annual general meeting in Nottingham agreed that any successful Black Sections candidates would form a Parliamentary Black Caucus. The prospect of a caucus clearly aggravated the leadership. A week after the meeting, *The Guardian* reported that Kinnock 'cracked the whip against the black activists' involved.[7] Kinnock secured the backing of the NEC for a measure to discipline party members engaged in 'separatist action'. Notably, 'separatist action' encompassed Black Sections and even informal caucusing of black and Asian party members. In that sense, it banned even the kinds of initiatives that Profitt and Bousquet had pioneered years earlier.

Following the NEC's decision, Sharon Grant recalls that the candidates associated with Black Sections agreed on a collective strategy.[8] Conscious of their precarious position all agreed that they should give the leadership no excuse for deselections or expulsions.

In one way or another, the leadership made it clear that prospective black candidates needed to keep quiet in the run-up to the election. Abbott recalls receiving messages from people in Mandelson's office. Grant received a series of formal letters in relation to a Black Sections meeting which was due to take place after the NEC ban on 'separatist action'. The first, from Dick Knowles, leader of Birmingham City Council, asked him to persuade Black Sections to cancel the meeting. The second, which was much more belligerent in tone, came from Hattersley writing on behalf of local MPs:

> We understand that you are coming to Birmingham on Tuesday 7 April to attend a meeting organised by a small, unrepresentative group of people who claim to be concerned about the problems of some ethnic communities within our city. As Labour MPs in Birmingham, fully committed to racial equality and ending discrimination, we want to make it clear that neither Birmingham district Labour Party nor the city council needs any advice from you or Haringey and Lambeth councils ... But if you do have spare time, you should come to Birmingham to learn how a sensible and progressive council – the largest Labour-led council in Britain – is dealing with this problem instead of coming to give us the doubtful benefit of your advice.[9]

Grant was welcome to learn about issues of race from Hattersley, but he was not welcome to advise, much less exercise real power. Grant withdrew from the conference on grounds of ill health, a decision which may well have saved his candidacy.

Atkin, however, went ahead with the meeting. A fortnight after the prohibition of 'separatist action' she addressed around 250 people at the formal launch of the Birmingham black section. Hattersley and his caucus of Midlands MPs went public, telling Atkin and Linda Bellos that the good people of the Midlands did not want advice from Londoners. Neither Hattersley's Midlands caucus nor his anti-London language were viewed as 'separatist' by the NEC. White Labour activists who jeered Bellos, demanding that she 'go home', also evaded party discipline. The speeches by Bellos and Atkin, however, moved the NEC to action. The NEC focused on the following part of Atkin's speech:

> I was told not to come to this meeting tonight if I wanted my parliamentary seat. Well, I don't want a parliamentary seat if I can't represent black people. If I'm not a candidate at the next election I don't give a damn. Mr Kinnock can hear that again and again. I don't give a damn. Because what I'll always do is fight for black people, with black people, and first of all for myself and all of my kind. So I don't give a damn about Neil Kinnock and the racist Labour Party.[10]

A recording of the BBC *Today* programme report on the event is preserved in Kinnock's archive. Notably, while the audio of Atkin's speech is there in full, the BBC account of white violence was edited. A transcript of the edited report was presented to the NEC on 29 April.

Kinnock appears to have been involved in building the case against Atkin: his files contain records of Atkin's statements, copies of letters exchanged with Atkin, accounts of phone calls with Atkin, and an analysis of how the NEC was likely to vote on the issue. The papers indicate that Kinnock personally endorsed plans to deselect Atkin.[11]

An account of the NEC's deliberations was leaked to leading figures in Black Sections and appeared in the June edition of the *Campaign* newsletter. Dennis Skinner and Tony Benn moved that no action should be taken against Atkin, but the majority of the NEC voted with Kinnock and Hattersley to discipline her. Hattersley apparently justified acting against Atkin on the basis of the electoral consequences of inaction. Benn argued that the NEC should recognise that Atkin was responding to belligerent hecklers. He also argued that there was a double standard at work, as Frank Field had made critical comments about the Labour Party, going so far as to say that voters should vote for other parties, and had not been disciplined. This argument cut no ice and the NEC agreed to proceed against Atkin. Although the NEC had yet to find Atkin in breach of party rules, Kinnock moved that as she was under investigation she should be deselected. The NEC agreed. Notably, at no point in the NEC's three-hour discussion did Kinnock propose disciplining violent white members.

In the ensuing controversy, black radicals such as Darcus Howe gave Atkin their full support. Crucially, the NEC's decision put huge pressure on the remaining black and Asian candidates. Atkin was deselected at the end of April; Parliament was dissolved in early May ahead of a general election in June. Even if the NEC found in Atkin's favour, it would not be in time to fight the election. Moreover, the NEC ruling showed that black candidates could be deselected merely for being under investigation. The position of Labour's black and Asian candidates was extremely precarious.

Sharon Grant remembers the pressure that it put on the remaining black and Asian candidates. Grant had already had to fight off deselection. In this context, she recalls that Atkin 'expected the other black candidates to support her. It was awkward because she broke the agreement they had had and she suffered for it. They didn't want to fall into the trap of supporting her and getting into grief with Kinnock.'[12] Abbott recalls, 'Sharon and I were good friends, we were all good friends – black women activists of the time. We were given to understand that if we spoke up for Sharon it would happen to us. Although I didn't speak to Mandelson himself directly about this, he sent us messages about Sharon's situation.'[13]

1987 ELECTION

The 1987 election campaign was the first outing of Labour's new campaign team. Opinion polls put Labour ahead for almost half of the campaign. However, Abbott was convinced that as far as head office was concerned, 'they would rather that Keith, Bernie, Paul and I didn't exist'. Abbott got the impression that the leadership wanted her to be invisible and silent. 'The national party thought we were an embarrassment and they offered no support of any kind.' Certainly, Labour's party political broadcasts featured practically no black people. In *Thatcher's Glorious Reign 1979–1987*, shown on BBC One during the campaign, Kinnock was shown addressing all-white crowds in the Midlands and he was surrounded by Denis Healey, John Smith, Hattersley and Robin Cook. The broadcast also featured stills of white pensioners and white schoolchildren. Other than a black man in a crowd, the only person of colour in the broadcast was Colonel Gaddafi. Labour's best-known election broadcast of the campaign, which became known as 'Kinnock the Movie', featured no black people at all.

The Tories saw Abbott as an electoral asset, but not for Labour. Together with Livingstone and Corbyn, she featured on their 'So this is the new moderate militant-free Labour Party' advert. There were two versions: one which featured twenty-four faces and one which featured six; Abbott was on both. Abbott remembers getting more recognition from the Tory posters than from any Labour material.

Abbott and her team decided to go for broke. Dissatisfied with the official Labour posters, Abbott hired designers and asked them to come up with something better. Rather than hiding the fact that she was black – the preferred option of the party leadership – Abbott told her designers to put her face front and centre, 'so no one could be in any doubt'.[14] The design pushed the Labour logo to the bottom of the page. Abbott and her team opted for a colour scheme of black, white and silver, with only a flash of red. They also avoided Labour's standard typefaces, opting for a combination of Futura and Gill Sans, which gave the poster a hint of 1980s futurism. The design reflected Abbott's determination to run as herself, not as an identikit Labour candidate. This was a bold move. Although Hackney had been a safe Labour seat, politicians of all stripes assumed that white voters would not turn out for black candidates, and certainly not for black women. For her opponents, Abbott's candidacy had put the seat into play. As a result, the fight for Hackney was fierce.

None of Labour's big names joined Abbott on the campaign trail. An event with Bryan Gould was indicative of the leadership's attitude. During the campaign, the Transport and General Workers' Union (TGWU) invited Abbott to speak to Ford workers in Dagenham. Gould, Dagenham's MP and Labour's national campaign organiser, was horrified and tried to block the event. Abbott heard he initially refused to share a platform with her. Joe Gordon, the TGWU's convenor, went ahead with the meeting regardless. As a black man, he told reporters from *The Bandung File* that Abbott's candidacy was 'a tremendous step forward, as far as black people are concerned, for the Labour Party'.[15] In the end, Gould attended, but footage shows that he sat at the opposite end of the table to Abbott.

There were also problems with support from her local party: 'It was a tricky campaign, because some of the white activists wouldn't work for me.'[16] Whether they remained loyal to Ernie Roberts or whether they refused to work for a black candidate, Abbott was unable to tell. Consequently, she recruited volunteers from local black organisations. Corbyn recalls learning of the problems in Hackney and sending volunteers from Islington North to help with Abbott's campaign.[17] Nonetheless, there were a group of 'over a dozen key activists' from the constituency party who dedicated themselves to Abbott's campaign.[18] John Burnell, who was selected as Abbott's campaign manager, was central to the effort. He recalls, 'We knew that with Diane being black, and a woman it was going to present challenges, so we decided to fight the campaign as if it was a marginal seat.' Another activist named Peter Kenyon, who worked tirelessly for Abbott's election, recalls that Burnell ran the campaign 'like a military operation to maximise [Abbott's] vote'.[19]

The difficulties that Abbott had with the white working class were not lost on the SDP–Liberal Alliance. During the campaign, Simon

Taylor, the SDP's candidate, told the *Hackney Gazette* that 'Abbott had emerged as one of the issues on which his campaign would be fought because of her extreme views'.[20] Taylor was not the only person to link Abbott with extremism. He claimed that he had 'received considerable support among traditional Labour voters' who felt that Abbott did not represent them. Her Conservative opponent, Oliver Letwin, made much the same point, claiming, 'If Labour had put up a sensible moderate candidate then I don't think I would have stood a cat in hell chance.' John Young pointed out in his 'constituency profile', published during the campaign, that Abbott was 'regularly categorised as one of the new black extremists'.[21] In addition to Abbott's 'extremism', Letwin claimed that Abbott simply could not represent 'ordinary voters'.[22] These criticisms were always couched in terms of Abbott's extreme views. However, as Abbott was replacing a fellow left-winger, these attacks seem to have been an example of dog-whistle politics.

The campaign started traditionally enough. Abbott helped judge a cutest baby contest and took part in set-piece debates. However, the campaign soon became chaotic. The Conservatives' Hackney office was firebombed, Abbott's campaign headquarters had its windows smashed, and there was an abortive march by the National Front in protest at her candidacy. Early in the campaign, Abbott issued a libel writ against Letwin for claims made in his literature. Norman Tebbit visited the constituency during the campaign and blamed the firebomb on 'extremists'. Given the slew of claims that Abbott was an 'extremist', this could have been an attack on Abbott herself.

Abbott was also assisted by Terri Sewell, who acted as her intern. Sewell had graduated from Princeton in 1986 and had started a master's degree in politics at St Hilda's College, Oxford, looking at black representation in British politics. Her mother was the first black woman to be elected to Selma City Council in Alabama. Sewell remembers hitting on the theme when she discovered that Britain had never elected an Afro-Caribbean MP. She was struck by the contradiction that while Britain had abolished slavery before the US, and never introduced formal segregation, the country had never had an Afro-Caribbean MP. She was intrigued: 'How could England be so behind the times? We elected our first black woman to Congress, Shirley Chisholm, in 1968.'[23]

Sewell wrote to several candidates and was invited to work on both Abbott and Boateng's campaign. She recalls Abbott on the campaign trail as being 'this enthusiastic wonderful woman'. Sewell's research had led her to believe that British politics was divided on class lines and, unlike the US, race played a minor role. Her experiences in the 1987 election drew her to a different thesis. It was clear from the reaction of some white working-class voters in Hackney that race would determine their vote. Sewell had interviewed Chisholm during her time at Princeton and saw parallels between Abbott and America's first black female lawmaker.

ELECTION NIGHT

On election night, Sewell travelled to Brent South: she had been told that Boateng's constituency would declare first, and she wanted to see the first black election victory. As the polls closed, there was no telling who had won. The news from Brent South was good. Addressing a jubilant crowd, Boateng declaimed, 'There are some of us who have been waiting 400 years for this result, 400 years!'[24] At the same time, Boateng acknowledged that there was a great deal more to do. His famous statement, 'Today Brent South, tomorrow *Soweto*', reflected this. One of Boateng's guests on election night was Adelaide Tambo, who Boateng had known since childhood. She was the wife of Oliver Tambo, the deputy president of the African National Congress (ANC), and the couple were living in exile in London. 'I wasn't going to be triumphalist,' Boateng recalls, 'I was only too well aware that the struggle against racism was an ongoing struggle, and a global struggle. Adelaide was right in front of us, and it was important to remind people that there were places in the world where black people were prevented from voting.'[25] Vaz took Leicester East from the Tories, while Grant won in Brixton with a reduced majority. Profitt was defeated heavily in Lewisham – in fact, the Conservatives doubled their majority. Abbott won Hackney North and Stoke Newington, but Labour's majority went down by almost 1,000. Nationwide, there had been a 3.2 per cent swing to Labour, but in Hackney Labour's vote share declined by 3.3 per cent. Abbott lost almost 2,000 votes to the SDP, which she attributed to white Labour voters refusing to back a black candidate.

TV-am's Anne Diamond was one of the first to congratulate Abbott publicly on her victory. Abbott also participated in a TV-am interview with John Stapleton. Significantly, these national interviews were not organised by Labour's press office, which had offered Abbott nothing through the whole of the campaign. Stapleton's questioning reflected a growing consensus on the reasons for Labour's defeat. 'Many of your colleagues were pushed out, and I would suggest to you that they were pushed out because of the activities of many left-wing councils, particularly here in the capital.'[26] Abbott countered that gentrification in the capital was the cause of a shift in voting patterns. Nonetheless, the BBC's political editor John Cole had made the same point the night before, and Abbott soon learned that many in the Parliamentary Labour Party (PLP) blamed the London left for defeat.

PARLIAMENT

The first PLP meeting of the new parliament occurred on 17 June. Kinnock formally welcomed Abbott, Boateng, Grant and Vaz, stating that for the first time the elected party was a multiracial party. He expressed the hope that their victories would 'affect the self-image of black voters' and acknowledged that their election had been one of the successes of the campaign.[27]

However, immediately after the election, *The Times* reported that Kinnock was considering purging the party of Abbott, Grant, Boateng, Corbyn and Livingstone to counter the 'disastrous "London effect"'.[28] Considering the Atkin case, this was wholly plausible. While none was expelled, this attitude may explain press reports that Kinnock blocked Jack Cunningham's plan to promote Boateng to the frontbench as part of his environment team.

The narrative over the 'London effect' had emerged in the wake of the Greenwich by-election of February 1987. Greenwich was a Labour seat, although the majority had been declining. The SDP attacked

Deirdre Wood, Labour's candidate, as a 'loony left' feminist militant. This approach was central to the SDP's campaign. Rosie Barnes, the SDP's candidate, was presented as a conventional married mother, someone who represented ordinary people. The SDP took the seat with a majority of more than 6,000. In some ways, the SDP's campaign built on the 1983 Bermondsey by-election, in which the Liberals ran a homophobic campaign against Labour's Peter Tatchell. This model appears to have informed the SDP–Liberal Alliance campaign against Abbott in Hackney. Writing to the *New Statesman* shortly after the Greenwich by-election, Patricia Hewitt, Kinnock's press secretary, put the leader's concerns in the following way: 'The "London Effect" is now very noticeable. The "loony Labour Left" is taking its toll.'[29]

On entering Parliament, Abbott's stated ambition was to serve her constituents rather than seek promotion. As Labour's leaders were keen to hold her at arm's length, this was a sensible strategy. On the day that Abbott was sworn in, she was greeted by Lord Pitt, Labour's only black peer. Pitt made a beeline for Abbott, meeting her in New Palace Yard. Abbott was also greeted warmly by her 'little gang' of Corbyn, Bernie Grant and Tony Banks. Other Labour MPs were more wary.

In some ways, the House of Commons reminded Abbott of Cambridge, particularly the Cambridge Union. Moreover, many of the MPs had the same sense of entitlement she had encountered among Cambridge undergraduates.

Abbott had been to the Commons before, but as she began to inhabit the building, she saw it anew. 'What struck me was that everything about it, the architecture, the atmosphere, the formality spoke to somewhere that not so long ago had been at the centre of Empire.'[30] At the state opening of Parliament, Abbott chose a spot on the green benches that had once been favoured by Enoch Powell, a symbolic act of decolonisation.

Hansib Books, which published newspapers such as *West Indian World*, organised a gala reception for the new black and Asian MPs at the Royal Lancaster Hotel. Special guests included Maya Angelou, Abbott's mother, Bellos, Livingstone and Corbyn. Kinnock declined the invitation. The speakers addressed the gathering in alphabetical order, which meant that Abbott set the tone for the evening. She told the crowd that she hoped the new MPs would be a 'fist rather than four separate fingers'.[31]

By 1987, Abbott was used to working in male-dominated environments. However, she was taken aback by the atmosphere of the Commons. Tony Banks, who took it upon himself to show Abbott the ropes, took her to the Members' Smoking Room on her first day, ordering a bottle of champagne to celebrate her victory. The room was one of the places where Tories congregated. 'Afterward,' Abbott recalls, 'he said it gave him huge pleasure to see the look on all the Tory MPs' faces!'

The arrival of the new Black Sections MPs did not go unremarked by the parliamentary authorities. Abbott recalls that the Speaker, Bernard Weatherill, was clearly concerned about the arrival of the four new black and Asian MPs. As Abbott remembers, 'He thought we'd be like the Fenians. This was the height of the loony left scare, and we were the epitome of the "loony left".' A century before, Irish MPs, sometimes loosely called 'Fenians', had found ingenious ways of disrupting the Commons. On one occasion an Irish MP cut the wires which operated the division bell, leading MPs to miss an important vote; on other occasions, Irish MPs engaged in endless filibusters, often keeping Parliament sitting through the night. From what Abbott could see, the Speaker expected something similar from her, Boateng, Grant and Vaz. The antipathy towards the new MPs was recognised on the Tory benches. Jonathan Aitken remembers that it began before the 1987 election.

> There was a moment when, for the first time, it became apparent that at the next election Britain was about to have four or five black Members of Parliament. There were unpleasant rumbles in the House of Commons, saying, 'These are awful people they want to burn this place.' There was a lot of that talk; it was, perhaps, tinged a bit with racism.[32]

Aitken remembers that the Speaker was sufficiently worried that he called a meeting of a few trusted MPs to calm nerves ahead of the election.

Following the election, Weatherill wanted to make a gesture of conciliation. Assuming that Grant was the group's leader, he invited him to his rooms for a glass of port. Aitken recalls that Weatherill also planned to ask Grant to present Parliament's mace to the Leeward Islands. Grant was delighted.

The workings of the Commons were opaque, and there was no induction for new MPs. One of the immediate problems was space. Abbott had no desk, no office, no base in the Palace of Westminster. She contacted Ray Powell, the Labour whip responsible for accommodation. There was no response. Abbott went repeatedly to the whips' office, but he was never there. Having finally located Powell, she was told that she was second from bottom of the accommodation list. Dismayed, she still had the presence of mind to ask who was beneath her. Powell was candid and said that Livingstone had that honour. Livingstone recalls that Powell was 'a right-winger who rewarded loyalists and punished rebels'.[33] Evidently, Abbott and Livingstone were regarded as the least biddable MPs in the Parliamentary Labour Party.

After eight months, Abbott was assigned to an office with Joan Ruddock, Joan Lestor and Joan Walley. According to a piece on Abbott's desk that appeared in *Woman's Own*, the office was cramped and there was no word processor or typewriter. Her view comprised a blank wall, four coat pegs and a clock. The office was cut off from the sky, but it was within earshot of Big Ben. Abbott's small desk was decorated with postcards of her favourite works of art. It was also the resting place of her Filofax, a 1980s essential. Conditions were chaotic as the four MPs worked around each other. Interruptions were common. When one MP needed to speak to a constituent in confidence, the others had to leave. Abbott got more space two years later when Lestor was promoted to the shadow Cabinet and relocated.

The view that Labour's new black and Asian MPs were a liability was shared across the House. This was plain from Abbott's second appearance on *Question Time* in June 1987. Abbott was on a panel with Liberal MP Cyril Smith, Conservative minister Michael Heseltine and

Andrew Neil, editor of the *Sunday Times*. As ever, Robin Day was in the chair. The polls, Smith commented forcefully, showed that Labour was unelectable, 'and one of the reasons for it', he added, 'is Diane Abbott and people like her'.[34] The largely white audience applauded, and after a moment's delay chuckled, seeming to get some unspoken joke. Abbott called him out: 'If Mr Smith believes that having black people in Parliament for the first time is in some sense a backward step, thousands of people that voted for me in Hackney North would disagree.'

The response was immediate. For Heseltine, this was beyond the pale. Horrified at Abbott's insinuation, he appealed to Day to intervene. The audience protested vocally. 'I honestly believe', said one white man, 'that the vast majority of the audience here do not see Diane as a black person.' This went down well with the audience, as did his comment that Abbott was the panellist showing true prejudice for assuming that white people perceived race at all. Day wrapped up the discussion by apologising to the audience for calling Abbott black – his implication being that unless he had said so, none of the white people in the crowd would have been able to tell.

The Labour leadership clearly saw Abbott as a problem. A private note from Hattersley to Kinnock dated 12 July 1988 describes a conversation with radical journalist Jessica Mitford about an interview she had with Abbott.

> Amongst other things, Diane Abbott alleged that you refused to have photographs taken with black Members of Parliament, refused to visit her constituency during the election, refused to send a message of sympathy and support when there was an attack on her constituency offices and a shotgun was fired through the window. As well as these specific allegations there is a lot of talk about the general lack of sympathy from the leader.[35]

Hattersley reassured Kinnock that he had done his best 'to correct the record'.

Nonetheless, Kinnock did make some effort to welcome Abbott to the Commons. After a few weeks in Parliament, he invited Abbott and Vaz to dinner in the Members' Dining Room. 'Kinnock was obviously trying to be nice,' Abbott comments.[36] Apparently during the meal he launched into an anecdote about a black boy at school who was nicknamed 'Chalky White'. Abbott refrained from asking which definition of 'black' Kinnock had applied to his schoolmate.

Abbott set out her thoughts on the state of Kinnock's Labour Party in the autumn edition of the 1987 *Feminist Review*. Interviewed by Lynne Segal, Abbott expressed sympathy with Kinnock's desire to improve the party's media representation. However, she argued that there were problems with the approach that the party leadership failed to see. The problem with PR professionals, Abbott argued, was that they thought in terms of abstract demographic categories. This was problematic as it focused on 'nuclear families with 2.4 children living in Milton Keynes'.[37] Consequently, the party's message to families became a message to white families. Additionally, the demographic groups imagined by PR professionals were heavily stereotyped. As a result, Labour spoke to men about jobs and to women about nurseries. This, Abbott pointed out, failed to address the lives of people in Hackney, an area which had, 'the highest percentage of one-parent mothers in the country, where most women, if they're not wage-earners, are not dependent on men either. They're not women who stay at home waiting for the men to pick up money.' Abbott was also concerned that if the Labour Party started creating policy to appeal to these stereotypical demographic groups, it would inevitably swing to the right. On a practical level, Abbott reminded readers that Labour's messaging failed to win over the voters of Milton Keynes, who stuck with the Tories in 1987.

Abbott endorsed Labour's policy platform wholeheartedly. But again, she had concerns. Creating jobs, she argued, was an excellent ambition, but she was concerned that Labour would simply replicate the existing hierarchy in which, 'women and black people are a pool of unskilled and semi-skilled labour, and at the bottom of the labour pile'.[38] Similarly, she backed the plan to create a Ministry of Women but was concerned that it might simply be 'a ministry for white women'.[39] Abbott was clearly concerned that the Labour Party, like its leader, had a limited grasp of the politics of race.

The staff on the parliamentary estate also found it difficult to adjust to the presence of black and Asian MPs. 'One of the things we found when we first entered Parliament was that none of the attendants believed we were MPs.'[40] Abbott recalls that Boateng, Grant and Vaz were stopped all the time as they moved around the estate. Boateng recalls that attendants constantly confused him with Grant, despite the age gap and the fact that Grant had a beard and Boateng was clean shaven. 'They just saw black,' he comments.[41] The Serjeant at Arms and the security staff, Abbott recalls, were particularly slow to learn that Abbott, Boateng, Grant and Vaz were MPs.

Security staff were also unwilling to let black visitors into the building. Abbott was keen to hold events in Parliament for her constituents and to support black groups. The first event of this kind started late simply because the security staff would not allow Abbott's black guests into the building. On another occasion, the Serjeant at Arms presented her with a cleaning bill, even though, as far as Abbott could see, cleaning was completely unnecessary.

It was easier for black people to get in if they arrived alone. However, Abbott quickly spotted a pattern. Her black visitors were regularly sent to the Strangers' Gallery rather than to see her. A letter from Abbott, Grant and Vaz, drafted by Abbott, to the parliamentary authorities from April 1988 complains:

> Ever since my colleagues and I have been in the House there have been a series of incidents that give rise to concern. Our visitors are sometimes treated less than politely and deliberately misled … Visitors and we ourselves have been jostled. We have been challenged by attendants as to our identity in an unsubtle attempt to embarrass us. These occurrences are too frequent and have been going on for too long.[42]

Abbott and Grant took this up in the press. On 23 May 1988 they spoke to the media about racism among staff at the Commons, repeating the accusation that attendants were manhandling black MPs and their guests. Speaking to *The Times*, Grant said, 'If I don't get an apology, I won't just pick up the Mace. I'll throw the flipping thing in the Thames.'[43]

Abbott garnered a great deal of press attention following her election. Photographs of her at the state opening of Parliament were published in tabloids and broadsheets alike, some commenting on her clothes, some on her hair, some on her makeup. The *Sunday Telegraph Magazine*'s September feature on Abbott noted the interest in Abbott's style: 'Gossip columnists have made the odd remark about her hips.'[44] On this point, the author Pauline Peters remarked, 'In fact, her only truly outsized attribute is the massive chip on her shoulder.'[45] Peters, it seems, could see no basis for Abbott's claim that government and the media was dominated by rich white men from Oxford and Cambridge. Writing in the *Telegraph*, Colin Welch bemoaned the fact that 'it's illegal to call her dusky or alluring'.[46] However, press coverage was not all of this kind. *The Gleaner*, which Abbott insisted should be available in the Commons Library, defended Abbott from *The Sun*'s charge of laziness. Around this time Abbott started a regular column in the *Hackney Gazette*. She was also featured in the *Philadelphia Inquirer*, the *Washington Post* and, closer to home, *The Voice*.

Laziness was a common charge made in the press. In reality, Abbott had a larger workload than the vast majority of MPs. Corbyn recalls, 'The four black MPs were inundated with casework from all over the country. Issues of racism, of discrimination, all the issues the black community faced.'[47] As one of the first black MPs, Abbott represented a much greater community than the denizens of Hackney. 'As an MP,' Abbott comments, 'my interests have been fairly constant.'[48] Her first major campaign brought together her distaste for privatisation with her determination to champion the rights of refugees. 'Immigration, asylum,' Abbott comments, 'these were synonyms for race'.

In early August 1987, Abbott, together with Corbyn and Harry Cohen, MP for Leyton, held a press conference to protest the treatment of Tamil refugees, many of whom had fled torture. The three MPs spoke from the prow of the *Earl William*, a recently privatised car ferry, which had been hastily repurposed as Britain's first private jail and was used to house a group of Tamil refugees. The government had run out of prison space and turned to the private sector. Conditions aboard were squalid. Ipswich locals nicknamed the floating prison 'the hulk' due to its obvious disrepair. The prisoners were also denied medical care. In protest, the refugees began a hunger strike and then a lie-in. The Thatcher government refused to back down. However, 'the hulk' broke its moorings in the great storm of 1987 and more than thirty detainees escaped. The escapees were not recaptured and were granted 'temporary admission'. Those who stayed on the ship were deported, subjected to further torture, and after a protracted legal battle, won asylum in the UK two years later. In spite of the escape, Thatcher vowed to press on with prison privatisation.[49]

Corbyn recalls that he, Abbott and Cohen were there for the entire day and spent most of their time in discussion with prisoners, getting as much information as they could to bolster their legal challenge to the detention of the refugees.

The intervention forced the government to give the refugees access to basic medical care. The Home Secretary also promised to make sanitary towels available and to ensure that a space was made available to allow the women onboard some privacy. But Abbott's intervention also had more far-reaching consequences. Following the visit, the Home Secretary stripped MPs of their long-held constitutional right to halt deportations and demand the judicial review of asylum cases. Moreover, judges were instructed to disregard representations made by MPs on behalf of asylum seekers. Abbott had become an MP, only for the traditional rights of MPs in relation to asylum to be diminished.[50]

SCRUTINY

Abbott's maiden speech was given in the context of the 1987 Immigration Bill. The bill, which became law a year later, ended the right of spouses to join their partners, restricted rights of appeal and made overstaying a visa a criminal offence. Abbott pulled no punches. Beginning with the experience of her parents, she argued:

> In the quarter-century that has elapsed since 1950, to see what has happened to that notion of citizenship of Britain and its

Commonwealth – that once proud ideal – is very sad indeed. We have seen increasing restrictions placed on movement, related to what are, in effect, quasi-racial categories: new Commonwealth, old Commonwealth, patrial and non-patrial. We all know what those categories really mean.[51]

Having highlighted the administrative incompetence of the government's immigration system, Abbott continued:

Above all, in the past quarter-century we have encountered the notion that immigrants, far from being people who cross oceans in good faith seeking to work and seeking a better life, are a kind of plague or contagion. No measure is too botched up, too legally illiterate or too racist to keep them out.

In concrete terms, Abbott objected to the new rights given to immigration officers, on the basis that they were abusing the powers they already had. Abbott argued for greater accountability, not greater power. She objected to the government charging black and Asian people from the former colonies for citizenship which was rightfully theirs. She objected to the removal of the right to appeal, which cut across the basic constitutional principle that the actions of the executive should be subject to judicial review. And she objected to new police powers, arguing that they would be used against all black and Asian people, as all black and Asian people would be assumed to be immigrants. This, she claimed, was a form of 'pass law', a feature of the apartheid system, as it would force black and Asian people to carry identity documents to assuage police suspicions. What is more, Abbott argued that the real purpose of the bill was 'propaganda', to win the government some good headlines, at the cost of stoking division.

Foreshadowing the Windrush scandal, Abbott described the baleful consequences of the government's inhumane immigration regime:

Conservative members have referred to the stress that is caused by arranged marriages. If they want to know about stress, they should sit in my surgery. I have heard of girls attempting suicide because they have had to wait so long for entry clearance for their fiancés. Elderly people, who have worked all their lives here, have been unable to bring their children to this country because of the immigration laws. I have seen parents who have had to face the fact that their children would be deported.

Abbott was also determined to challenge the government over apartheid. Here, Abbott had several lines of attack. In October 1989, in a Commons debate over the Commonwealth Heads of Government conference held in Malaysia, Abbott asked:

Does the Prime Minister agree that, notwithstanding her ritual condemnation of apartheid, her performance at Kuala Lumpur demonstrates what everybody, particularly black South Africans, know – that she is and remains, at every international occasion that she attends, an indefatigable fifth columnist for apartheid?[52]

Thatcher responded with another ritual condemnation of apartheid. Abbott's view was that the Prime Minister had expended a huge amount of political capital resisting pressure from Commonwealth leaders to impose economic sanctions, indicating considerable personal support for apartheid. Moreover, Abbott argues, 'there was a continuity between the Thatcher who thought that Nelson Mandela was a terrorist and the Thatcher who thought black people were swamping Britain'.[53]

Abbott also took up the case of Trevor Monerville, a young black man who, his parents had alleged, was subjected to an appalling beating by police officers while in custody. 'Black people and the state was a long-standing concern,' Abbott comments. From her experience at the Home Office and working with the Scrap SUS campaign she was immediately willing to believe Monerville's family. Together with Brian Sedgemore, Terry Lewis, Dennis Skinner and Bob Cryer, she signed three early day motions in Parliament criticising the conduct of Stoke Newington officers. In the Commons, she pointed to the hypocrisy of Conservative MPs who claimed to support law and order, while having no commitment to justice.

While Abbott was no 'Fenian', she was willing to shake up the Commons. In March 1988 she sponsored the Crown Prerogatives (House of Commons Control) Bill, the most radical constitutional reform that had been proposed in recent years. Years before the Brexit debate over 'Henry VIII powers', Abbott backed a bill to bring all Crown prerogatives under Commons control. As became apparent after the 2016 referendum, the British constitution was still based on a distinction – recognised since the fifteenth century – between the powers of Parliament and the prerogatives of the Crown. While the former had been placed under democratic control through the Equal Franchise Act of 1928, the latter could be exercised by ministers without parliamentary authorisation. Benn put the bill before the House, supported by MPs including Abbott, Corbyn, Cohen, Banks, Grant, Skinner and Eric Heffer. The bill was the first part of the campaign group's twenty-point programme to democratise the constitution. As the Thatcher government had no intention of giving up these 'Henry VIII powers' the bill was defeated. The repercussions of this defeat were felt keenly after 2016.

While many in the Parliamentary Labour Party treated Abbott with suspicion, Tory backbencher Jonathan Aitken was pleased to see her enter the House. Aitken was on the lookout for a pair. With more than 350 Tory MPs and fewer than 250 on the opposition benches, Abbott was a scarce resource. Alec Woodall, Aitken's former pair, had left Parliament at the 1987 election. 'It's the government side', Aitken comments, 'who really need the pairs.'[54] Conscious of the need to move quickly, Aitken got hold of the list of new MPs, spotted Abbott's name and suggested the arrangement. Aitken recalls developing a friendship quickly. 'She had a good sense of humour, she's a good human being, and we just got on.' 'He targeted me. He thought,' Abbott claims, 'because he's as subject to prejudice as anyone else, that I wouldn't turn up, so I'd be a great pair, he'd be able to have lots of time off.'[55]

Abbott also found common cause with Teresa Gorman, the Conservative MP for Billericay. The two were elected at the same time and had worked together on Westminster City Council. Speaking in 1992, Abbott stated, 'Teresa, although she's a dreadful old Tory ... she's been very good on some issues. She was very good on abortion. She actually worked with Labour women on the abortion issue.'[56] Abbott and Gorman first worked together in the context of the 1988 Abortion (Amendment) Bill, which sought to limit the time in which women could seek terminations.

Nick Brown, who entered Parliament in 1983 as Labour MP for Newcastle upon Tyne East, was another MP Abbott got on well with. Although Abbott was out of favour with the leadership, Brown was on the look-out for 'bright people' to serve on the 1987 Finance Bill; MPs who could speak and not be intimidated by the House of Commons.[57] 'Diane was one of those. So, she fitted into the same category as Alistair Darling and Peter Mandelson – and I say that meaning it kindly,' he laughs, 'though I'm not sure she'd take it that way.' Brown recalls that Abbott always spoke from a radical perspective, took the party line lightly and made her own arguments. 'She was fun on the Finance Bill,' he recalls. 'Disobedient but fun.'

In 1989 Abbott joined the Treasury Select Committee. Livingstone recalls being told by Derek Foster, the Chief Whip, 'that Kinnock's office had blown a gasket' on hearing the news.[58] The leader's office only approved the selection when they were told it was a choice between Abbott and Livingstone. 'It's not that they liked me,' she explains. 'But they were going to stand up for the whip's prerogative, and they did, under enormous pressure.' Abbott recalls that joining the Treasury Select Committee was a consequence of the structure of the PLP. Before the New Labour era, the whips' office and the Leader's office were different centres of power. What is more, the whips defended their autonomy vigorously. Within the whips' office, individual whips took it in turn to nominate MPs to committees, a form of patronage which helped manage MPs. When Banks's turn came round, he nominated Abbott to the Treasury Select Committee, Parliament's most prestigious committee. Whatever Foster made of the choice, he was determined to safeguard the authority of the whips' office, and therefore threw his weight behind the decision.

Lord Carrington, who became chair of the Treasury Select Committee in 1996 while Abbott was still a member, described her as being 'always good for a laugh'.[59] Her direct manner was best illustrated by her enquiring of the Governor of the Bank of England, Eddie George, 'You're just an inflation nutter, aren't you?'[60] Abbott remained on the Treasury Select Committee until 1997.

BABY IN THE HOUSE

In the early 1990s, Parliament was organised for the convenience of men. The Commons regularly worked late into the night, and this was years before the introduction of a crèche. Abbott, who married David Thompson in 1991, gave birth to her son James in October of that year. She received no maternity leave and was required to attend Parliament and vote throughout her pregnancy. She gave birth on a Monday; the whips insisted that she work until the Thursday before, returning to Parliament eight days later. 'There was no flexibility, no support, no concern from the whips' office, you were just expected to turn up and vote.'[61]

Abbott came up with a radical solution. On 31 October, she took her son through the division lobby. Seeing Abbott carrying her son in a blue sling, her colleagues complained to the Serjeant at Arms. Abbott voted, her son asleep in her arms. The Serjeant at Arms, however, later told Abbott that she had broken the rules, and that such an infraction would not be tolerated twice. An unnamed Tory MP told *Today*, 'This is an outrageous breach of the rules. It's bad enough having David Blunkett's dog trooping through the lobby, never mind babies.'[62] Claudia Fitzherbert, writing for the *Telegraph*, proposed a crèche sited in 'the middle of the [Commons] chamber', although Fitzherbert doubted that the Speaker would have the skill to control a group of toddlers.[63] Don Dixon, one of the Labour whips, asked Abbott's critics, 'What is Diane supposed to do, leave her baby lying around on the benches?'[64]

From the Serjeant at Arms, the issue was escalated to the Speaker. Weatherill criticised Labour rather than Abbott. Speaking to the *Glasgow Herald*, he said, 'They talk a lot about sexual discrimination but don't seem to do much'.[65] In recent years, Stella Creasy, Ellie Reeves, Kemi Badenoch and Jo Swinson have followed in Abbott's footsteps, bringing their babies into Parliament. Yet, to date, Abbott's son holds the record as the youngest person to enter a division lobby in the House of Commons.

During her first years as a mother, Abbott got the impression that the whips' office would give some support to mothers who toed the line. Help, however, was not forthcoming to more independently minded MPs. Initially, Abbott brought over a cousin from Jamaica to live with the family and look after James. After she left, Abbott remembers the demands of the Commons were 'nightmarish. You spent half the time thinking you were a terrible mother, and half the time thinking you were a terrible MP.'[66] Abbott continued to bring her son into the Commons, particularly on Fridays, which was traditionally a quiet day. This shocked Nicholas Soames – not because Abbott brought in her child but because she did not have a nanny. Things changed, Abbott recalled, when Nick Brown became a whip. Abbott credits Brown as being the first Chief Whip to take childcare seriously and to do what he could to help. 'He would be lenient about letting me go home, especially if he knew I was going to vote against the Labour whip.'

PARLIAMENTARY BLACK CAUCUS

Abbott's goal was not merely to survive Parliament but to have an impact. To this end, she was involved in establishing the Parliamentary Black Caucus (PBC). The PBC was created for a number of reasons. First, Black Sections had mandated the creation of a parliamentary caucus prior to the 1987 election. A meeting with Angela Davis also seems to have influenced Abbott's thinking. Abbott interviewed the celebrated black intellectual and radical in the summer of 1987 for the *New Statesman*. Abbott jumped at the chance of meeting Davis: 'I was lost in admiration, she was one of the heroines of my youth. I felt honoured and privileged to meet her and talk to her.'[67] It was a wide-ranging interview, which considered black radicalism in America from Marcus Garvey to Jessie Jackson. Davis argued that the Congressional

Black Caucus (CBC) was the fruit of the Civil Rights era. Notwithstanding the problem of female representation, Davis argued that the CBC was 'the most progressive body in Congress'.[68] Indeed, Davis argued that one of the reasons to engage in electoral politics was to build a coalition 'not only [of] black but Chicanos, Asians, native American Indians; the women's movement; the gay movement; disabled people' and get progressives elected to decision-making bodies.

The CBC had also been one of the first institutions to formally congratulate new black and Asian MPs. Abbott had a great deal of respect for the CBC: 'It's not necessarily the most progressive group of people in the world, but they were very strong on black autonomy. They had a very strong and powerful identity as black legislators.'[69]

The first meeting of the four new MPs took place on 26 January 1988 in the Members' Dining Room and was followed by a meeting between the MPs and representatives of the ANC. A press release publicising the establishment of the PBC was circulated in March 1988. The group was modelled on the American Congressional Black Caucus. Grant took the role as chair, Vaz as treasurer, Abbott as secretary and Lord Pitt represented the caucus in the Lords. The first press release announced Boateng as vice-chair. On hearing the news, Boateng wrote to Grant to make his position clear.[70] Grant's decision to put out the press release without consultation, Boateng wrote, confirmed his 'resolve that our relationships as individuals have not yet reached the stage at which they would be capable of sustaining an effective caucus, even if one were desirable'. Boateng determined to keep collaborating with his colleagues, but not as part of the PBC.

Behind the scenes, Abbott recalls, 'Kinnock and the party machine went nuts.'[71] As secretary of the PBC Abbott was responsible for communicating the group's plans to the leader. In November 1988 she sent Kinnock a detailed statement asking for his support. Receiving no response, Abbott followed up in January. Kinnock's reply, sent almost a month later, was brief and confused. Specifically, he confused a meeting which took place in 1988 with another that took place a year earlier. This allowed him to evade Abbott's request for support. The letter offered nothing other than a meeting.[72] In the end, support from the leader's office was not forthcoming.

Abbott took the lead organising the launch. She had little luck with sponsorship. 'We were not recognised as an economic force, so corporate Britain could see no merit in being associated with anything black.'[73] Speaking to industry insiders, Abbott was told that big corporations wanted 'customers not shoplifters'. And yet, corporations were missing a trick. At the time it was estimated that black and Asian consumers had a combined spending power of almost £5 billion.

Nonetheless, the PBC were able to get sufficient support from black and Asian businesses to host a lavish launch over the last weekend in March 1989. According to *The Times*, Kinnock was 'watching closely' but had 'no objection in principle' to the formation of the PBC.[74] This was quite a change of heart, considering his former statements on 'separatist action'. However, Kinnock's hands were tied. The PBC's guests included Ron Brown, chair of the Democratic Party; Congressman Ronald Dellums, chair of the CBC; Congressman Mervyn Dymally; and former Congresswoman Shirley Chisholm. With so many respected black American politicians endorsing the PBC, Kinnock could not credibly censure the new organisation.

The PBC's guests arrived in London on 31 March. The PBC and representatives of the CBC gave a joint press conference at the House of Commons at 11 a.m. Ron Brown spoke of a 'sense of history', as black legislators from different continents met together for the first time.[75] The Democratic National Committee and Democrats Abroad then hosted a reception for members of the PBC and CBC to meet the press more informally. The day ended with a formal dinner in Parliament hosted by Lord Pitt. Here, Dellums welcomed Abbott, Grant and Vaz as honorary members of the CBC, describing them as 'kith and kin from across the water'.[76] The highlight of the next day was a joint legislative meeting, followed by another black-tie dinner, hosted by the CBC in honour of Abbott, Grant and Vaz. The weekend ended with a prayer breakfast at Grosvenor House.

The launch was an enormous success. British journalists, from tabloids and broadsheets, apparently dazzled by the American lawmakers, treated the event with uncharacteristic respect. Moreover, British papers recounted the history of the CBC, noting that originally white American politicians had derided it as 'separatist' and 'segregationist'.[77] The parallels with the British experience were there for everyone to see. The endorsement of so many senior US legislators also gave Abbott, Grant and Vaz a little more authority within the PLP. Indeed, Kinnock's papers show that from the spring of 1989 his position on Black Sections began to soften. NEC discussion papers from the end of February show that the leadership were discussing 'the creation of an affiliated organisation with the same status as socialist societies'.[78]

Jesse Jackson joined the PBC in February 1990 for the purpose of 'bridge-building' with Britain's black and Asian MPs. The meeting with Jackson led to the endorsement of the 'Jackson plan', which was modelled on the practice of the CBC. The plan allowed white MPs who represented areas with a significant ethnic minority population to join the PBC as non-voting members. This had the added benefit of making the PBC more palatable to Kinnock. Abbott relished the meeting with Jackson: 'Jessie's amazing, he's just amazing. He walked in the footsteps of Martin Luther King. And he was of the left.'[79] Wadsworth argues that pressure from Jackson helped push Kinnock towards accepting the principle of Black Sections.[80]

As a result of Jackson's visit Grant was invited to join Jackson and greet Mandela as he was released from prison. Abbott, and the rest of the PBC, stayed in Britain. She remembers watching the release live: 'He came out holding hands with Winnie, and it was really moving. One of the backdrops to my political life was the anti-apartheid struggle, more than any other international campaign. To see him walk out of prison a free man was just extraordinary.'[81] In 1994 Abbott visited South Africa as part of the United Nations observation mission, so she was in the country for Mandela's election as President.

THE WORK OF THE PBC

The PBC lobbied on a series of domestic issues, writing to newspapers about their presentation of stories, conducting research on ethnic monitoring in mental hospitals and issuing statements on government policy. In May 1989, the PBC took up the case of Martha Osamor. Following the resignation of Stuart Holland, a by-election was called in Vauxhall, the constituency which encompassed part of Brixton. Having learned from the 1987 election, Black Sections stated that they would take no part in the selection of a candidate, on the basis that they did not want the leadership to have a technical reason to block a black candidate. Bellos, Profitt and Wadsworth put themselves forward, but Osamor emerged as the frontrunner. However, a recent change in Labour Party rules meant that the candidates had to be vetted by an NEC committee chaired by Hattersley. Prior to the interview *The Guardian* reported the leadership's intention of vetoing Osamor. The finances of one of her community projects were under investigation by the local council. Notably, the investigation had been initiated by Osamor's political rivals on Haringey Council. As predicted, the NEC vetoed Osamor's candidacy. Some sources suggest that the NEC objected to her politics. Hattersley reportedly told the NEC, 'If there was ever anyone who has been used by extreme elements, it's Martha Osamor. She's a simple woman, of that sort. She could never have got elected to Parliament.'[82]

The PBC lobbied Kinnock, immediately presenting him with a detailed defence of Osamor, and the local selection process. Kinnock's response was terse. Refusing to engage with the PBC's argument, he responded, 'I am sure that you will see the NEC's short-list for Vauxhall as reflecting a serious commitment to having a candidate who will be in tune with the electors.'[83]

In spite of Kinnock's reassurances, Bellos, Profitt and Wadsworth were also excluded from the shortlist. Notably, following Osamor's removal, Bellos withdrew in solidarity.[84] Vauxhall eventually selected Kate Hoey and following Labour's lead the Conservatives and Social and Liberal Democrats both presented the citizens of Brixton with white candidates.

Kinnock was not the only obstacle to the work of the PBC. The PBC archives show a running battle between the group and the parliamentary authorities over room bookings and the use of Parliament's facilities. 'Our lives as black MPs during that period were a series of micro bureaucratic aggressions,' Abbott recalls.[85] 'Whether it was the black caucus we were organising, or an event for black women from Hackney, it was part of the climate in which we had to work.'

In September 1989 Abbott joined the CBC's annual legislative weekend in Washington, which began at the Kennedy Center. Early on, the schedule was abandoned, as a member of the CBC asked Abbott to reprise a speech on black young people that she had given in New York a few weeks earlier. She made quite an impression. There was only one black woman in Congress at the time, and delegates to the Congress were eager to hear about Abbott's path into Parliament. Following the event, Abbott was invited back semi-regularly. On one visit, Sharon Pratt, the first woman elected Mayor of Washington DC, formally proclaimed 21 February 1992 'Diane Abbott Day'.

The PBC was dissolved before the 1992 election. Initially it had received funding from the Joseph Rowntree Foundation. However, from 1991 the funding was divided between the three MPs. Without funding and facing constant opposition from the parliamentary authorities and antipathy from the Labour leadership, the PBC had none of the advantages of its American forebear. There were also differences between the PBC's members.[86] Vaz recalls that meetings could be 'rather tempestuous' and in the end the PBC simply 'fizzled out'.[87] Abbott argues that it was an idea before its time. David Lammy, who was elected as MP for Tottenham in 2000, agrees. Indeed, in recent years an informal caucus has emerged in the form of a BAME PLP WhatsApp group.[88]

Abbott's popularity in the US led to problems at home. In October 1988, concerned that Abbott was spending too much time overseas, some of her constituents mooted deselection. Graham Bash, one of those behind the plan approached Sharon Atkin, asking her to stand. She quickly informed Abbott, and the plan was nipped in the bud. However much Atkin wanted a seat in Parliament, she had no intention of challenging a friend and comrade from Black Sections.[89]

THATCHER'S FALL AND THE NEW WORLD ORDER

For all of its problems, Abbott enjoyed important aspects of life in the

Commons. 'I enjoyed the parliamentary debate, because I enjoyed making the argument. The chamber is a theatre, you have to be able to read it and understand the mood.'[90] The standard of parliamentary speeches, Abbott argues, was still quite high. Tony Benn, George Galloway and Gordon Brown were all excellent orators. Even Tory MPs, Abbott recalls, would be drawn back into the Chamber when they spoke. And, from time to time, parliamentary debate really mattered. Geoffrey Howe's resignation speech was a case in point. 'In the Chamber, it was electrifying.' What the cameras failed to see was the change that came across Thatcher's face. As Abbott remembers, as soon as Howe sat down, MPs knew that Thatcher's days were numbered.

By the autumn of 1990, Thatcher, so strong following her 1987 landslide, had become dispensable. The short-lived credit-fuelled 'Lawson boom' was followed by economic difficulties and by the end of 1990, a new recession. Inflation, the primary focus of Thatcher's initial economic policy, began to rise, reaching 7.5 per cent at the end of the decade. Moreover, local government and taxation, which had been some of Thatcher's key assets, became liabilities. The community charge, which Thatcher hoped would run Labour out of local government for good, was an important part of her undoing. Abbott was one of fifteen MPs to join the Anti-Poll Tax Federation's non-payment campaign. Not for the first time, Abbott was fighting against the government and her own frontbench. 'I knew it was a huge issue, and I knew the leadership were completely wrong.'[91] What struck Abbott was that the poll tax was hugely unpopular across the political spectrum, not just on the left.

The few days between the first ballot and Thatcher's resignation were just as compelling. 'You couldn't have had a more exciting place. History was being unfolded in a way that no one could have foreseen. If you had told people a month before that Mrs Thatcher was going to get axed by her own party, no one would have believed it.'[92] Abbott got the impression that Tory MPs who turned on Thatcher were surprised at their own courage. She detected a giddiness on the government benches: 'It was like they'd massacred matron.'

Abbott was at odds with the Labour leadership again over the Gulf

War. She set out her reasons for opposing the British involvement in Operation Desert Storm in *Socialist Campaign Group News* in October 1990, three weeks after the Commons vote. Abbott argued that all of the talk of the US and Britain acting as a global police force was a smokescreen. The fact that Britain cared nothing for the rights of small nations, she argued, was obvious from the government's response to the invasions of Grenada and Panama. Talk of sovereignty was a pretext for imperialism. The real goal of military action being 'to secure client regimes and cheap oil for the US'.[93] Abbott was involved in the grassroots campaign to stop the war, speaking at events alongside Bruce Kent, Benn, Corbyn and Grant.

Tony Banks's response was Abbott's enduring memory of the Commons vote. He was on a journey, she recalls, from the radicalism of the early 1980s to the 'new realism' of the Kinnock period. But war in Iraq was a bridge too far. Standing in the lobby, Abbott remembers Banks saying, 'I can't vote for this, I just keep thinking about those children.'[94] Abbott was struck by Banks's emotion, emotion that spurred him to put principle above loyalty to the leadership.

1992 ELECTION

Labour had high hopes for the 1992 election. John Major, the new Tory leader, lacked his predecessor's charisma. Britain was also in the midst of a recession which hit Middle England hard, due to a collapse in house prices and the rise of 'negative equity'. Moreover, Labour had re-established itself as the primary party of opposition. Following the acrimonious merger of the Liberals and the SDP in 1988, and a protracted debate over the new party's name, the Social and Liberal Democrats' poll ratings slid into single figures. The Labour leadership was also largely untroubled by the London left, which they had blamed for their poor performance in 1987. Although the polls were narrow, Labour had a consistent lead. Nonetheless, the Tories were fighting to win. Chris Patten, who was in charge of the campaign, compiled an election 'dossier' with material on Abbott. In the spirit of fair play, the Tories decided not to use the 'dossier'. Even so, the contents were leaked.

In Hackney, the campaign was less violent than in 1987, but just as chaotic. Less than a week into the campaign Verona Marfo, one of the Liberal Democrats few black candidates, resigned from the party, accusing the Lib Dems of racism. Class War and other anarchist groups formed the Anti-Election Alliance but were denied permission to hold a rally. Perhaps in homage to Major's circus background, Conservative candidate Cole Manson and his daughter engaged in some acrobatics for the press. Abbott was also battling Miss Whiplash, the Corrective Party's candidate, who, along with the other candidates, pledged to conduct a campaign without innuendo. Abbott's campaign was prosaic compared to the antics of her rivals. She attended the opening of a mosque, gave her support to a campaign to reinstate a sacked midwife, delivered leaflets and attended a women's group with Kinnock, who made a flying visit to the constituency.

On election night, Abbott increased her majority, something that she attributes to Hackney's Labour vote coming home. She took the result as confirmation that the 1987 result 'hadn't been a fluke' and that voters would not only elect but re-elect black candidates.[95] The national result, however 'was upsetting' but not wholly unexpected. 'There was a point in the 1992 campaign when you could feel it moving against Labour, even in Hackney, which is a solid Labour place.' The turning point, Abbott recalls, was the 'tax bombshell'. Prior to the campaign, John Smith, Labour's shadow Chancellor had announced a 'shadow budget' which proposed national insurance rises for people earning more than twice the average income. Tory posters dubbed this Labour's 'tax bombshell'. The 1992 campaign cast a long shadow. It was what made the Corbyn team wary of planning tax increases twenty-five years later, 'because we are all of an age when we remember the 1992 election, we all saw the impact of the "tax bombshell"'. Following Labour's unexpected defeat, Kinnock resigned as Labour leader.

OUTSIDE PARLIAMENT
Abbott's political activity was not restricted to the House of Commons. She continued to work at a grassroots level, focusing particularly on initiatives involving black women. In 1988 Maya Angelou

praised her work with young black women in Lewisham, heralding her as a 'symbol of success'.[96] Black Women Mean Business, an initiative that Abbott founded following the 1992 election, was particularly important to her. Abbott's research indicated that black women were often excluded from both formal and informal business networks. The first network of its kind, Abbott pioneered the initiative in Hackney and then expanded it to the rest of London in 1993, and then, following sponsorship from NatWest, to the entire nation in 1994. Abbott also made the most of Deputy Prime Minister Michael Heseltine's initiatives to encourage black entrepreneurs, which broke with the stereotype of black people in Britain as perpetual clients. The problem was that because of the biases implicit in business and finance there were much greater obstacles to success for black people than for white. Black Women Mean Business was an attempt to work with the aspirations of the community and to begin to overcome the structural obstacles to success.

The initiative also reflected Abbott's political concerns:

> It was a way of engaging with a part of the black community that wouldn't be coming to Labour Party meetings, they didn't feel able to engage in the formal left race agenda. But if you had an event that was about business and spoke to their aspirations they would come.[97]

The first national event for Black Women Mean Business took place on Valentine's Day 1994. The event was focused on fashion and cosmetics and participants went away with a Valentine's themed goody bag provided by the event's sponsors. Over the next few years, Abbott worked with NatWest seminars to provide information on marketing and PR, finance, emerging technology, how to run a start-up, business expansion, opportunities in Europe and global marketing. Abbott selected the focus of the seminars, which reflected the insights she had gained serving on the Treasury Select Committee and her growing connections with black women entrepreneurs.

From 1996 Abbott expanded the initiative, creating Black Women

Mean Business on the Road, which took the events to Bristol and Luton. The 1997 London event relocated to the Bank of England and Abbott approached Eddie George to appear. The two had built a rapport on the Treasury Select Committee since George's appointment as Governor of the Bank of England in 1993. George, Abbott recalls, agreed and the Bank of England, 'bent over backwards to help'.[98]

Abbott's speakers included Sandra Kay Walls, an officer in the US army; Chrystal Rose, an ITV presenter; Gloria Knight from the National Commercial Bank of Jamaica; Moira Stuart, a BBC presenter; and Kanya King, founder and chief executive officer of the MOBO Awards, all of whom Abbott invited personally. In 1998 Abbott turned things on their head and, for the first and last time, invited an all-male panel. In other years, Abbott also invited black women who had been involved in more obviously political struggles, such as Baroness Ros Howells and Jessica Huntley. In some ways, the approach was similar to the scheme she had pioneered a decade earlier with the Black Media Workers' Association and then with the ACTT, albeit in a post-industrial setting, appropriate to Britain after more than a decade of Thatcherism and the consequent industrial decline.

*　　*　　*

In 1987 Abbott achieved her life's ambition. Anthony Trollope once observed, 'It is the highest and most legitimate pride of an Englishman to have the letters M.P. written after his name.'[99] The same, Abbott maintains, is true for women. Being an MP is also the job that any working-class parent would want for their child, Abbott quips: 'clean indoor work, with no heavy lifting'.[100] The constant bureaucratic micro-aggressions and slights from her colleagues did not deter her. Nor did the fact that 'as a black woman MP you face two things: you face sexism – men not wanting to take you seriously, and people generally taking men more seriously than you. You also face racism – people feel you can't be as good, you can't be as competent.' The realities of this prejudice are illustrated by a dinner held in Parliament in the early 1990s. Abbott's brother, a civil engineer, attended an Institution of

Civil Engineers dinner at the House of Lords. Chatting over dinner, he mentioned that his sister worked in Parliament. 'So she works in the kitchen?' came the reply. Somehow it was easier to imagine a black woman working in the kitchens than in the Commons.[101]

Abbott's emergence as a national figure coincided with a change in left-wing politics. From 1983 the left suffered a series of defeats, most notably the defeat of the NUM, the abolition of the GLC, and Tony Benn's failed leadership bid in 1988. Kinnock's advocacy of 'new realism' appeared to usher in a period of consensus between Tory and Labour frontbenches: a consensus over the benefits of the market and privatisation, a consensus that held until the 2008 financial crisis. However, the election of black and Asian MPs in 1987 was a major step forward for the left. What is more, by the mid-1990s there was a second aspect to the consensus, which is not as often recognised. From the mid-1990s, all three major parties were committed, rhetorically at least, to respect diversity. The London left of the 1980s, the campaign around Black Sections in which Abbott played a leading role, and the election of Abbott, Boateng, Grant and Vaz were as crucial to the emergence of this second consensus as Thatcher, Kinnock and Blair were to the first.

CHAPTER 8

NEW LABOUR, NEW DANGER

Tony Blair's election as Labour leader was part of a sea change in Labour politics. Blair's New Labour was a party of the centre rather than of the left, a party which had made its peace with privatisation, low taxation, trade union legislation and small government.

Abbott was always suspicious of Blair's politics. During the 1994 Labour leadership election, she publicly backed the then acting party leader Margaret Beckett over Blair. She was highly critical of New Labour's command and control style of politics, opposed many of the welfare reforms and measures which tightened immigration and asylum laws and spoke out against many of the illiberal aspects of Blair and Brown's anti-terror laws.

Perhaps an exemplar of the chasm between Blair and Abbott was in their contributions to the *Islington Cookbook* in 1998. Blair provided his favourite recipe, fettuccine with olive oil, sundried tomatoes and capers; Abbott chose rice and peas.[1]

Abbott continued her role on the Treasury Select Committee during this period until being moved to the Foreign Affairs Select Committee in 1997. If this was an attempt to quieten her, it failed. She soon proved herself to be a vocal critic of the arms-to-Africa scandal and responses to the Darfur crisis. Although her decision to send her son to a private secondary school was branded 'career suicide', Abbott remained well-known both inside and outside Westminster.

RACE RELATIONS IN THE 1990S
Abbott's second parliamentary term took place against a backdrop of

continued racial tensions in the country. Although the riots of the previous decade subsided, racist attacks and murders persisted into the 1990s. In 1993 there were 291,000 racially motivated attacks recorded and this rose to 390,000 in 1995.[2] Moreover, institutional racism in the police force often hindered proper investigations into such attacks, the most high-profile example being the failed investigation into the murder of eighteen-year-old Stephen Lawrence in 1993.

The Anti-Racist Alliance (ARA) were among the groups who campaigned for justice for the Lawrence family. In 1994, Abbott succeeded Ken Livingstone as president of the ARA. However, she left the role after only three weeks. As Livingstone reports, 'She found it impossible to work with Wadsworth.'[3]

In the years following Stephen Lawrence's death, little progress had been made in bringing his killers to justice. Suspects were arrested, but all had charges dropped. The family launched an unsuccessful private prosecution, and despite an inquest ruling Lawrence had been killed 'in a completely unprovoked racist attack by five youths', the finding went beyond the bounds of their instructions.[4]

Hope for justice was reignited when Abbott, Paul Boateng and Bernie Grant accompanied Doreen Lawrence, Stephen's mother, to meet shadow Home Secretary Jack Straw. Abbott recalls that Straw was impressed by Doreen and promised her an inquiry should Labour win the next general election.

In addition to racist attacks from the public, many black people also experienced violence from those tasked with protecting them, the police. On 28 July 1993, a few months after Stephen Lawrence's murder, Joy Gardner, a forty-year-old Jamaican student, was restrained and gagged during an immigration police raid at her home. She suffered brain damage from asphyxiation and died from a cardiac arrest four days later. All three police officers who were charged with manslaughter were later acquitted.

Meanwhile, Metropolitan Police Commissioner Paul Cordon appeared to many to be more concerned with dealing with black people as the perpetrators of crime rather than victims. In 1995, he invited community leaders to a meeting on street crime, writing that 'very many of the perpetrators of muggings are very young black people, who have been excluded from school and/or are unemployed'.⁵ A few days later, the Metropolitan Police announced Operation Eagle Eye, an initiative to crack down on street crime in the capital.

Abbott was among those outraged by Condon's statement.

> There is a link between unemployment and crime, and poverty and crime, but there are no statistics which prove that black people, of whatever age, are more likely to be criminal than white people. And by linking race and crime, Paul Condon has caused deep hurt in the black community, and he's created very bad conditions really for the type of co-operation he needs in fighting crime in the capital.⁶

Criminology professor Jock Young added that street robbery was most likely to be committed by the poorest people and, 'while they are likely to be black in London, they will almost certainly be white in Newcastle'. Moreover, street crimes comprised only 4 per cent of all crime in 1994; the same proportion as fraud, which is never described as a 'white' crime.⁷

To make matters worse, the date of Condon's meeting with community leaders fell on the second anniversary of Joy Gardner's death. Gardner's mother joined protesters outside the Home Office. 'He shouldn't have wanted black people to meet with him today, not especially on the second anniversary of Joy's death,' she told reporters. 'My heart is very hurt ... it is a calculated insult to myself and my family and all the black people.'⁸

Reverend David Haslam, secretary of the Churches Commission for Racial Justice, called Condon insensitive and said the angry response was inevitable. 'The police will not be seen to be a positive agency as far as crime and the black community is concerned until they clean up racism within their own ranks.'⁹ Neither Abbott nor Grant attended Condon's meeting and said they would meet with him at a later date.

On becoming Home Secretary, Jack Straw fulfilled his promise to the Lawrence family and commissioned a public inquiry into Stephen

Lawrence's death. Sir William Macpherson chaired the inquiry and published his report in 1999. Its recommendations led to the creation of the Independent Police Complaints Commission, moves to increase ethnic diversity among the police force, and the Race Relations (Amendment) Act 2000, which required all public authorities to take action to promote racial equality.

Abbott also opposed the Asylum and Immigration Bill, arguing that it was inherently racialised and 'based on a wholly unquantified, exaggerated and apocalyptic notion of the threat that so-called bogus asylum-seekers present to the British way of life'.[10] She argued that barring the employment of undocumented migrants would make employment more difficult for all people of colour, which was particularly damaging for young black men, among whom unemployment rates were as high as 60 per cent.

'BLUE-EYED FINNS' CONTROVERSY

Ironically, it was Abbott's concern about the employment prospects of ethnic minorities that landed her in the middle of a race row. In 1996, writing in her fortnightly column for the *Hackney Gazette*, Abbott criticised the employment of 'blonde, blue-eyed Finnish girls' to fill nursing shortages at Homerton Hospital. She asked, 'Are Finnish girls, who may never have met a black person before, let alone touched one, best suited to nurse in multicultural Hackney?'[11]

She wrote: 'I am sure that these young women are charming. But they are basically here to improve their English and are unlikely to give the British health service a lifetime's commitment.' In contrast, nurses from the Caribbean 'who know the language and understand the British culture and institutions' were being driven away from the profession because of racism – pushed into night shifts and less favourable jobs – and a lack of career progression. She also accused the managers of NHS trusts of running hospitals as an 'accountancy exercise with no concern for the wider community'.

Dr Heard, the hospital's former chief executive, branded Abbott's comments 'thoughtless' and 'careless' and warned that she ran the risk of undermining the morale of staff and the public's confidence in the hospital.[12] As Abbott's comments caught national attention, she was accused of racial and gender stereotyping and slurring the professional integrity of nurses.[13]

Bernie Grant, however, stood by Abbott. 'She is quite right ... Bringing someone here from Finland who has never seen a black person before and expecting them to have some empathy with black people is nonsense. Scandinavian people don't know black people – they probably don't know how to take their temperature.'[14]

Only six miles away, in Bernie Grant's constituency, North Middlesex hospital had employed up to thirty Finnish and Irish nurses; EU citizens did not need work permits. 'What I find strange about the whole situation is that the Home Office is deporting fully trained nurses to the Caribbean and Africa while the NHS is recruiting people from Scandinavia,' he argued. Pointing to Department of Health research showing differential attainment among nurses, as well as cases of black nurses fighting deportation, Grant argued that the differential treatment of black and white nurses was 'either a case of racism or of incompetence or both'.[15]

Marc Wadsworth, who was of Jamaican and Finnish descent, felt compelled to respond. 'She had met my mother,' he laughs. 'My mother actually said at the time of the controversy, "Is she having a go at me?"'[16] He maintains that Abbott's comments were ill-advised and reflected the kind of stereotyping that they were trying to fight against. Further, Wadsworth pointed out that Lola Odusoga, a model of Finnish and Nigerian heritage, was Miss Finland. 'She's a black Finn like me.'[17]

Ironically, in Finland Abbott's comments were primarily received in good humour. The *Helsinki Sanomat*, Finland's leading daily newspaper, introduced Abbott as an MP 'known for her big mouth ... a colourful representative of a colourful district'.[18] Referring to the colours of the Finnish flag, they wrote: 'Our blue-and-white nurses crossed the British news threshold day after day. They even made it to TV and radio. Neither Finnish Presidents nor even our champion racing driver Mika Hakkinen have ever managed that.'[19]

Reprimanding the national press for taking her comments out of context, Abbott asserted 'The issue is not one of colour. The issue is that people should not be recruited from overseas in an area of mass unemployment ... I want young children leaving school in Hackney to have a future, and that means there's a responsibility on local employers to employ local people.'[20]

Reflecting on the incident years later, Abbott says:

> It was my first experience of a media pile-on. I thought it was clear if you had actually read the article what I was trying to say ... If you're a black person and you talk about race, you are the racist ... It is almost as if they really don't think a black person should be in the public space. That's the message they're trying to send to you.[21]

Abbott's comments were interpreted in a specific context which helped determine the way they were understood. It had long been taken as an article of faith that Britain was not a racist country. In the 1990s, it was also widely believed that anti-racism could be equated with being colour blind. In this context, acknowledging the problem of racism was itself an illegitimate act.

Following complaints, Scotland Yard studied the article. However, the investigation was quickly dropped. Remarkably, the party leadership stood by Abbott although she had been critical of them. They affirmed that her comments had been taken out of context, and people should read her whole article, not the edited highlights. Moreover, the story clearly did Abbott no damage among Labour Party members. Abbott retained her seat on the NEC in 1996 with an increased number of votes.

NEW LABOUR, NEW BRITAIN

Tony Blair was elected Labour leader on 21 July 1994 and coined the term 'New Labour' in his Labour Party conference speech that October. Blair's first shadow Cabinet included John Prescott as his deputy, Jack Straw as shadow Home Secretary, George Robertson as Defence Secretary, David Blunkett as Education Secretary and Harriet Harman as Work and Pensions Secretary. In return for not contesting the Labour leadership, Gordon Brown was given control of economic policy as shadow Chancellor.

Robin Cook and Michael Meacher, both more left-wing than Blair, also held key positions within as Foreign Secretary and Transport Secretary. Other left-wingers such as Clare Short remained influential in the party, and to much surprise, Abbott was elected to the NEC. Alongside Dennis Skinner, Harriet Harman, Jack Straw, Gordon Brown, David Blunkett and Robin Cook, her task was to keep the party leadership in check. However, during her three years on the NEC, Abbott's and Skinner's were often the sole dissenting voices in the era of New Labour.

'The thing about New Labour now is that even New Labour people deny that they were ever New Labour,' Abbott laughs.[22] While many on the left held onto a fundamental, class-based socialism, New Labour

[circled] around Oxbridge and people who worked for some of the so-called 'left-wing NGOs', and around the group of people who, even if their constituencies were elsewhere, lived in London. I knew about those things. I've been to Oxbridge, I've worked for a so-called 'left-wing NGO', I lived in London. So, in a sense, I knew about that type of world and that type of thinking in a way that maybe some other people on the left did not.

At the same time, as a black person, I was one removed, and that gave me a clarity about who these people were, where they were going, and what … constituted their politics when you stripped away some quasi-lefty language. I was both part of that and fundamentally not part of that. Partly because of my ideology … partly because I was a black woman.

The paragon of New Labour was Blair and Prescott's attempt at the most sensational political coup for a generation, replacing Clause IV of the Labour Party's constitution with a new statement of aims and values. Initially adopted in 1918, Clause IV outlined Labour's commitment to 'the common ownership of the means of production and exchange'.[23] Printed on the back of membership cards, it was understood to be the party's commitment to nationalisation.

Abbott felt that Clause IV's implicit opposition to privatisation and the commitment to socialism in terms of ownership was at the heart of Labour's message. However, on 4 October 1994, to the thundering applause of a Blackpool audience filled with anticipation, Blair made his inaugural speech in which he welcomed a New Labour, and new Britain, by declaring, 'This is a modern party living in an age of change. It requires a modern constitution that says what we are in terms the public cannot misunderstand, and the Tories cannot misrepresent.'[24]

Hugh Gaitskell had unsuccessfully attempted to remove Clause IV following Labour's third consecutive general election defeat in 1959. Blair succeeded where Gaitskell failed, after fifteen years in opposition, the party appeared to be willing to do whatever it took to regain power. Kinnock was keen to make the party less hostile to private enterprise and property ownership as well as more attractive to the growing population of middle-class, white-collar workers. In 1992, Gordon Brown stated that in the 'battle of ideas' 'some traditional no-go areas will lose their exemption from discussion' and in 1993, in a constituency pamphlet, Jack Straw called for Clause IV to be updated.[25] Although John Smith had dismissed the debate around Clause IV as a distraction, Blair's inaugural speech renewed old concerns.

Prescott tried to distance himself from Kinnock's desire to rid Labour of public ownership as a value, affirming that he believed in traditional values set in a modern setting. Still, he acknowledged that the changes represented a drastic shift in direction for the party, 'One thing we're sure of is that Mr Major couldn't sign up to it.'[26] Some, such as Tony Benn, felt that Labour's heart was being cut out and Labour risked losing what set it apart from other parties. Many on the right remained cynical. Michael Portillo, Secretary of State for Employment, responded, 'Weasel words will not disguise the truth. Labour's socialist instincts remain. They want higher taxes, more spending, and more government regulation and intervention.'[27]

Abbott opposed the removal of the clause. 'If all you're saying is you're going to manage the state better than the Tories, that's not much of an offer ... For a lot of people on the left, Clause IV was a line in the sand, and you had to say where you stood on it.'²⁸

Analysts remain divided over New Labour's motivations. Was it to win power, embellishing neo-liberalism with Labour branding, public relations expertise and improved market research, or was it a genuine attempt at reframing the party for the modern world? Abbott leaned towards the former view.

> You didn't feel that John Smith had come into politics to schmooze with the rich and the powerful ... You just felt with John Smith that there was a deeply moral basis to his socialism, whereas Tony Blair, well, Tony Blair said it himself; he could have joined any party.

Abbott was one of three MPs on the NEC who voted against changing Clause IV. At the 1995 special conference at Easter, Clause IV was revised.

> The Labour Party is a democratic socialist party. It believes that by the strength of our common endeavour we achieve more than we achieve alone, so as to create for each of us the means to realise our true potential and for all of us a community in which power, wealth and opportunity are in the hands of the many, not the few; where the rights we enjoy reflect the duties we owe, and where we live together, freely, in a spirit of solidarity, tolerance and respect.²⁹

Abbott felt that the new clause was 'a lot of tosh' and 'full of feel-good phrases and just vague waffle'.³⁰ The party was so enamoured with Blair, she argued, that if the leadership asked for a vote on 'the healing qualities of cabbage', it would get it.

THE ROAD TO 1997

Labour never lost its lead in the polls from Black Wednesday in September 1992. Labour's election spin doctors were poised to take party presentation in a new direction. After Labour's unsuccessful 1987 *Chariots of Fire* election campaign, Peter Mandelson, the 'shrewdest political strategist of his generation', had been working with Philip

Gould to rebrand the party as New Labour under Blair.[31] All plans were set out in a grid covering three weeks, culminating in polling day. To help Blair reach beyond traditionally Labour-supporting papers, the assistant editor of Rupert Murdoch's *Today*, Alastair Campbell, was brought in as Blair's press secretary.

Three years later, *The Sun*'s front page read: 'The Sun Backs Blair'.[32] After twenty years of supporting the Tories, the paper declared that 'the people need a leader with vision, purpose and courage who can inspire them and fire their imaginations. *The Sun* believes that man is Tony Blair.' However, Abbott and others in the party were suspicious of Labour's reliance on spin. Clare Short, for example, criticised the use of 'dark forces', spin doctors who operated in the shadows.[33]

In the run-up to the 1997 election, Labour's policy pledges had three key focuses: education, healthcare and the economy. Plans included modernising comprehensive schools with sets for different academic abilities, increasing real-term NHS spending and reducing bureaucracy. Following two economic recessions under the Tories, many welcomed Labour's promise not to increase income tax rates for five years, but to introduce a national minimum wage and commit to low and stable inflation rates.

Labour's campaign video illustrated the party's message of optimism. Backed by D:Ream's song 'Things Can Only Get Better', the video showed a diverse, joyous crowd, dancing with balloons and flowers in tow, accompanying a man to the polling station. As he casts his vote, the smiling face of the charismatic party leader Tony Blair, is revealed. The message was one of unabashed hope. 'I recall it being a very exciting campaign, but you couldn't allow yourself to hope that we would win,' says Abbott. 'You wanted to believe, but you wanted to be careful because 1992 had been a disappointment.'[34]

However, as Big Ben struck ten on 1 May 1997, millions across the country succumbed to optimism. The exit poll predicted a 'landslide likely' for Labour, but the final vote count surpassed all expectation. Labour won 418 seats, an increase of 145 seats from the previous Parliament and an astonishing majority of 179. Abbott has vivid memories of election night.

I remember going to my council count in Hackney Town Hall. It always took a long time. In its very first election in 1987, Hackney declared after the Western Isles, and in the Western Isles you had to put the ballot box in a boat, and take it to the mainland ... and we still declared after them.[35]

Still, the long wait did not dull the ecstasy of the moment that the results were announced. Abbott had retained her seat with a majority of 15,627, an increase of 5,000 and a pro-Labour swing of 8.3 per cent.[36] Ten years after she became an MP, Abbott was re-elected to Parliament.

When I finished my count, my friends and I went down to South-bank, and it was just the most amazing feeling. We parked, and we walked up. People were stopping and saying well done, well done ... It felt like I had waited my whole life for this, and more or less, I had.

As the sun cast the first colours of daylight across the sky, Blair ascended the stage to address the jubilant crowd in his victory speech at 10 Downing Street, 'A new day has dawned, has it not?'[37] Even Abbott, who was no fan of Blair's clichés, could not deny the rapture of the moment.

The Guardian stated that the election 'now joins 1945 and 1906 as the third great progressive electoral landslide of the 20th century'.[38] For the first time since 1945, the votes of women alone were enough to give Labour an overall majority. Labour also gained a significant proportion of the youth vote. As predicted, the economy played an important role in the election. The housing market crash of the early 1990s and the impact of tightened public sector spending drove many frustrated voters away from the Conservatives. Analysis of the NOP exit poll results showed that of the voters who said the economy was stronger, but their living standards had worsened, more than eight out of ten voted Labour or Liberal Democrat. Labour was also popular among mortgage payers, with high support from those with semi-detached homes, and smallest among council tenants. Blair's charisma was also a crucial boost for the party. While Blair and Major were seen as equally trustworthy, Blair was seen as a stronger leader.

Blair's leadership style was unprecedented for Labour. He ran a centralised government with a tight inner circle, which resembled Thatcher's premiership, or a presidential approach, more than it did Labour's traditional collectivism. One Blair aide stated that 'there was never any intention of having collective Cabinet government'.[39] Blair admired much of Thatcher's leadership style, and when he was pressed to be more progressive and radical he stated, 'What gives me real edge is that I'm not as Labour as you lot.'[40]

Abbott welcomed the 1998 Good Friday Agreement 'in as much as it brought peace' and supported Scottish devolution, but she remained worried that Blair would exercise his 'command and control' rule over the British nations. Indeed, Blair had caveated his support of a Scottish referendum on devolution with the assertion that 'Westminster was the ultimate constitutional authority – power devolved is power retained'.[41]

Abbott was critical of New Labour's press operation. Notably, having worked in television and as a press officer for the GLC, she knew the importance of communication. New Labour's spin doctors clearly knew what they were doing. They continued to bridge the gap between the media and politics. For example, the spin machine humanised Blair through the 'Call me Tony' campaign, which saw headlines highlighting the leader's rejection of formality and coverage of otherwise unremarkable stories, such as head-tennis matches between Blair and football managers.[42] The brilliance of New Labour's press operation was evidenced at the time of Princess Diana's death when they dubbed her the 'people's princess'.

Abbott's criticism was not so much the way that the media used but the way in which it affected government institutions. New Labour's spin doctors were unelected, and yet they exercised considerable power. Campbell started referring to himself as 'the Prime Minister's official spokesman' and was known for verbally abusing journalists who did not swallow New Labour spin.[43] In Blair's second term,

Campbell became Downing Street's director of communications and strategy, a role he often described as the 'real Deputy Prime Minister'.

Campbell also set up a Strategic Communications Unit (SCU) which was informed whenever a minister planned to deliver a speech or make an announcement. All of Labour's plans and activities were slotted into 'the grid', which covered fifty-two weeks of the year, and ensured that unfavourable announcements did not overshadow large favourable ones. SCU judgements usually involved special advisers, paid for by the taxpayer, whose loyalties laid exclusively with the ministers who employed them. Blair's government had over seventy special advisers in any one year.

The use of special advisers was hugely controversial both inside and outside the party. Critics accused the government of creating an alternative political civil service by giving government positions to political apparatchiks. For example, special advisers Alastair Campbell and Jonathan Powell were appointed press secretary and chief of staff respectively and had powers to direct press operations and impact on policy. Special advisers also came under criticism after Lobbygate in 1998, when Derek Draper boasted that he could sell access to ministers and in 2001, when, on 9/11, Jo Moore suggested that it was 'now a very good day to get out anything we want to bury'.[44]

Abbott's concerns about the institutional implications of New Labour's media operation were clearly shared by a section of the party's membership. Mandelson, who served as minister without portfolio, ran for a position on the NEC. However, 'the great operator, a great fixer, could not get himself operated and fixed on to the national executive', placing 8,000 votes behind Abbott, who placed seventh out of the seven elected members.[45] Notably, Abbott polled higher than all her left-wing peers except Dennis Skinner.

Despite Blair's mostly male inner circle, which Abbott nicknamed his 'Boys' Own Project',[46] the new Parliament contained a record number of female MPs. There were 120 women elected to Parliament, 102 of whom were on the government benches. An unprecedented total of five women also had positions on the Cabinet: Clare Short, Margaret Beckett, Harriet Harman, Mo Mowlam and Ann Taylor.

Abbott saw this as a breakthrough for women. She was particularly happy with the news of Oona King's election. 'I welcomed her because I would welcome any black woman coming into Parliament', she explained.[47] 'I think you've got to show some solidarity because it's a tough gig being an MP that's black or brown in whatever party.' King attested to this, reporting that 'Diane has been fantastic since I got here, literally threw her arms around me'.[48]

As in 1987, Abbott was second from last in line for an office position, and *The Times* reported that when Abbott realised this, 'she used the sort of language [they] wouldn't expect to hear in the kitchens'.[49] Abbott also struggled to bond with many of the new MPs.

When we all got back to Parliament, I wrote every single new woman MP a little hand-written note. But of course, not a single one replied … I remember one woman, I passed her in the corridor, she said in a kind of embarrassed mumble, 'Thank you for the letter', and that was it. It was a new group of women that came in in 1997, with a couple of exceptions, they were quite hard-core Blairites, and it was a strange atmosphere.[50]

Abbott notes that many of the female MPs who were elected in 1997 were 'not particularly radical' and were less likely to rebel against changes such as cuts to single-parent benefits than some long-standing working-class male MPs. This was one way, Abbott argues, that Blair used the constitutional changes demanded by the left to move the party to the right. The party leadership were keen to divest the party of long-serving working-class male MPs who retained a commitment to their local communities and to replace them with female MPs who were committed to the New Labour project. Over time, many female MPs who held positions of seniority were seen to have 'sold out'.[51]

In contrast, Abbott and her comrades on the left were seen as contrarians and were avoided by many ambitious Labour MPs.

In the members' tearoom, custom and practice is just to wander in and sit down next to whoever. That was the point of them; you didn't necessarily sit with your gang ... I soon realised that I would come in and, without thinking, I would sit down next to whoever was close, and some whip would zoom in and sit next to us because he was so frightened that I would wreak my toxic influence on innocent new MPs ... They thought that if we could get some influence over them, that would be a bad thing.[52]

This fear of Abbott's independent-minded radicalism cost her a seat on the Treasury Select Committee. 'Custom and practice was that parliamentary management was left to the whips, and party leaders concentrated on the actual content of our politics,' Abbott shares, 'but under Tony Blair, leaders took a very strong interest in party management.'[53] Abbott reports that Gordon Brown in particular was adamant she shouldn't be on the Treasury Select Committee, and Nick Brown, the Chief Whip at the time, 'had to go and hole up in Margaret Beckett's flat' to do the select committee assignments 'away from the eagle eye' of the leader's office.[54]

Nevertheless, after nearly a decade of experience on the committee, Abbott found she had not been re-selected. Her removal from the group was seen by some as a 'watering down of the committee', and she agreed: 'I think the main reason was that they thought I was too independent-minded.'[55]

FOREIGN AFFAIRS COMMITTEE

Following the 1997 election, Nick Brown became the Chief Whip and sent a green form around the PLP asking everyone what committee positions they wanted. Brown was adamant that the committees would be diverse and representative of the party and ensured that every committee had members from different regions, at least two women, and a 'campaign-group lefty', although Corbyn was left out for serial opposition.[56]

Brown also ensured that every MP from an ethnic minority background got their first or second choice. Brown recalls being 'spoilt for lefties for the foreign affairs team', but Abbott's experience made her the top choice for the role. Brown, Abbott recalls, had apologised when she was not re-selected, explaining, 'Diane, it was the best that I could do,' but she was excited about the new position, which she saw as 'an equally prestigious assignment'.[57]

It did not take long for Abbott to irritate Foreign Secretary Robin Cook. In 1999, regarding military action in Kosovo, she told him, 'If your only legal justification – I believe it is a slender one – for this operation is humanitarianism it would indeed be a paradox, to put it mildly, if NATO intervention had actually precipitated the very humanitarian disaster it was designed to avert.'[58] She was also one of twenty-three MPs who rebelled against endorsing a military strike in Iraq in 1998, a stance she maintained five years later in the crucial vote on the Iraq War.

Nevertheless, one of Abbott's most memorable contributions to the Foreign Affairs Committee was in the arms-to-Africa scandal. In 1997, the Sierra Leonean military ousted President Kabbah. Rakesh Saxena, an Indian banker with diamond interests in Sierra Leone, paid for the British mercenary Sandline International to provide logistical support to Kabbah. This consisted of the supply of thirty-five tonnes of Bulgarian-made AK-47 rifles and a Russian-built helicopter. On 10 March 1998, HM Customs and Excise launched an official investigation into Sandline for breach of the UN's arms embargo to Sierra Leone.

Sandline's solicitors provided evidence showing that the Foreign and Commonwealth Office officials and the British High Commissioner Peter Penfold had been aware of the arms sales. Cook denied the claims, while Tim Spicer, head of Sandline, and Peter Penfold insisted they were unaware they were breaking the law.

Abbott, with the Foreign Affairs Committee, tried to establish who knew what and when. Tony Lloyd, the minister of state responsible for Sierra Leone gave 'fumblingly inadequate answers', and Sir John Kerr, the permanent under-secretary gave evidence but later retracted it. 'We are asked to believe that he made a genuine error about when ministers knew, which is beyond belief. If he really made an error of that nature, the civil service is not what it was when I was a trainee,' Abbott said.[59]

The government announced that Sir Thomas Legg, a long-standing civil servant, was to lead an internal inquiry into the arms deal. When the Foreign Affairs Committee argued that a public inquiry with a High Court judge would be more appropriate, Cook stated that there was no 'great political scandal' to be found by a public inquiry. He was 'perfectly confident' Legg was as competent as any High Court judge.[60]

Cook refused to share telegrams concerning Sierra Leone with the committee, reporting that it would be a breach of confidentiality and erode trust. Instead, the telegrams would be looked at by Legg, and a summary would be available after he published his report. It was not until July 1998, after the Foreign Affairs Committee had published its reports that Cook gave them access.

The committee was also denied access to relevant intelligence personnel, reports and briefings and any material that was believed to fall within the Legg inquiry. When Kerr repeatedly refused to answer the committee's questions, insisting that his answers would cut across Legg's inquiry, Abbott accused him of trying to 'hide behind Legg'. Cook repeatedly denied there was a cover-up.[61]

The Foreign Affairs Committee report concluded that Spicer 'should have known the law' regarding providing arms to Sierra Leone and stated that it was 'not convinced' he had made his intentions to the Foreign and Commonwealth Office clear. It also criticised Penfold's 'ignorance and his lack of due diligence' in ascertaining the legal position on arms supplies, and Kerr for taking four weeks to inform Cook of the situation. He, and other senior officials, were berated for making 'serious errors of judgement' and for failing his duty to ministers.[62] The following year, Cook announced a £10 million assistance package to help restore peace and stability in Sierra Leone.

For Abbott, the arms-to-Africa scandal also raised questions about the role of select committees. Commenting on inconsistencies in Tony Lloyd's evidence, Abbott remarked that 'those of us who have queried it, or who have even asked questions of the minister of state, have been roundly abused for not showing sufficient loyalty towards the Labour government. We have been accused of nit-picking and self-importance.' Abbott argues that the leaders 'seem to think they can manipulate their party's members on select committees, but I think that's an abuse of the select committee system which is meant to be genuinely independent'.[63]

Abbott said that 'decisions which were once taken by Parliament are now, in effect, taken in the Cabinet, and decisions that were once taken in the Cabinet are now, in effect, taken by an inner circle around the Prime Minister of the day. We saw that under Margaret Thatcher when she was Prime Minister.' She added that this had not changed under Blair.

A few months after the inquiry, Abbott reported receiving a phone call from a journalist who claimed that the Foreign Office had 'an arsenal of personal information' to use against her. 'Since I had my son seven years ago, I have led a life of stupefying dullness,' Abbott jibed. 'But I wish them luck in their attempts.'[64]

In March 1999, *The Guardian* reported that a Foreign Office letter and a four-page dossier had been posted anonymously to Abbott. The dossier appeared to contain confidential information held by the Home Office and the Metropolitan Police, and personal details which were in a personal organiser that had been stolen from her a decade prior. Abbott said she had almost forgotten her Filofax had been stolen but became worried when its contents began to appear in local and national newspapers.[65] Abbott recalls being 'struck by the inaccuracies' in the dossier.

> To assuage me, Jack Straw invited me into his office to read the dossier … I read it quite quickly, and although some of the sources, like some of my appraisals from when I had been in the Home Office, were clearly from a legitimate source, other bits, you didn't quite know where it came from. And it wasn't wholly accurate, but then, that's not to say the state always keeps accurate information on people.[66]

Robin Cook emphatically dismissed the dossier as fake and threatened to sue those who suggested that he was behind it. Although investigations never uncovered the source of the letter and dossier, Abbott reflects that it was 'conceivable' that Cook was behind it. 'Let's put it like this: I wasn't Robin Cook's type of socialist. Robin Cook is largely regarded as the more lefty side of New Labour, but I wasn't his type of socialist.'[67]

Nor was Abbott Blair's type of socialist. Exactly what the most senior figures in New Labour made of Abbott during this period is hard to tell. Meg Hillier, who entered Parliament in 2005, says:

> I remember talking to one minister [about coming] to my constituency to talk about a policy change, they agreed, and I said it would be very good if we could have Diane there as well. [They responded], 'If Diane's coming, I'm not coming.' I was quite shocked by the vitriol. She had at the time spoken out and voted against the Labour government, and that's hard when you're in government ... I said, she is the only single black mother in Parliament, and this is an issue which particularly affects single mums.[68]

Hillier argues that there was no 'proper management of talent' in the PLP during the final New Labour parliament, and that Abbott suffered because she was not part of any of the favoured cliques. Keith Vaz, however, argues that Blair always took her seriously: 'In all the conversations I ever had with Tony he was never rolling of eyes, she comes from a position that he understands.'[69]

On this occasion, however, Abbott also became a thorn in Blair's side. On 12 November 1997, *The Times* reported Abbott had left Blair 'rattled' and 'wounded' over his government's decision to cut single-parent benefits by up to £11 a week. Abbott also directed her opposition at Social Security Secretary Harriet Harman, who had strongly fought cuts to single-parent benefits under the Tories in 1996. Harman argued that Labour's proposals were a way to tackle social exclusion and enable single parents to work. Still, for Abbott, it was simple: 'We're not in power to cut the living standards of the very poorest.'[70] Abbott's opposition to single-parent benefit cuts proved that Blair was vulnerable to principled opposition from his own benches. In that sense, Abbott was the first to show that it was possible to hold the New Labour government to account.

Abbott argues that New Labour, specifically Gordon Brown, thought in terms of Victorian notions of the deserving and undeserving poor, and this especially affected women. 'There are all sorts of reasons why women choose not to work, particularly when their children are young. If rich women stay home and have children, everyone says, "Oh, how lovely, what a great mother," but if a poor woman stays home with her child, that's terrible.'[71]

Also opposed to the cuts were left-winger Dennis Skinner and single-parents Tottenham MP Judith Church and Liverpool Wavertree MP Jane Kennedy. On 10 December 1997, the government won its vote, but the fallout was significant. Forty-seven Labour MPs rebelled, and some 100 abstained. One minister and two private parliamentary secretaries resigned their posts following the vote. Alice Mahon, a Labour rebel and aide to Culture Secretary Chris Smith, was fired after she refused to resign.[72]

Abbott also opposed many of the welfare 'reforms' that came as a result of New Labour 'thinking the unthinkable', including means testing of disability benefits, reductions in pension payments and changes to benefits for bereaved spouses. 'I think it was very important to Labour supporters to see people in the Parliamentary Labour Party who were prepared to stand up on these issues,' she explains.[73]

Abbott also opposed the privatisation of higher education in the form of university tuition fees. In 1998, Education Secretary David Blunkett announced proposals to means test tuition fees and to replace maintenance grants with loans. Abbott told the House with what Oliver Letwin described as 'passionate eloquence' that 'without access to a grant and free tuition, a working-class black sixteen-year-old [like me] could never have gone to Cambridge'.[74] She also protested increases in rents at the University of Cambridge, which she argued damaged efforts to widen access.

Abbott and her peers on the left were also critical of New Labour's economic policy. Writing in the foreword of *A Party with Socialists in It: A History of the Labour Left*, John McDonnell explained, 'Gone were most of those whose desire for transformative change had come from their experience of the harshness of our economic system. The experience of years of relative economic boom had largely eradicated from memory the inherent crisis-ridden nature of capitalism.'[75]

This New Labour generation vowed to end the battle between capitalism and socialism and, instead, focus on the battle between conservatism and progress. Rather than through wars between bosses and workers, solutions would come from stakeholding. The market economy, they asserted, was to be welcomed, not feared.

As such, only five days after Labour won the general election, Gordon Brown announced that the government was to hand over control of interest rates from the Treasury to the Bank of England. The Treasury Select Committee put forward a sponsored private member's bill with recommendations for a Monetary Policy Committee of Bank of England members who would decide the interest rate for the UK and determine other financial policy. The aim was for interest rates to be set independently of political interference. Abbott felt 'it was the wrong decision. Taken for the wrong reasons. Announced in the wrong way.'[76]

Her opposition to the private member's bill was threefold. First, economic management was inherently political as it involved judgements about the allocation of costs and benefits to different sections of the population. Monetary policy, she insisted, 'is too important to be left to bankers'. Moreover, Abbott picked holes in the academic case for an independent central bank and argued that shifting the responsibility for interest rates from politicians to bankers was anti-democratic.[77] She also had concerns over accountability. 'We cannot seriously believe that the Treasury Committee, with two and a half special advisers, can hold to account the Monetary Policy Committee and the battalions of economists behind Eddie George.'[78]

Despite her oppositions, the government concluded that the bill already contained sufficient measures for accountability, and the Bank of England Act came into force in June 1998. Speaking to the House in 1998, Abbott pointed out that the bill was 'never debated at any conference or by the national executive', arguing that this was an attempt to avoid scrutiny by backbenchers and the opposition.[79]

Abbott was also critical of New Labour's expansion of Private

Finance Initiative (PFI) schemes. While she welcomed the use of private sector finance in principle, she ridiculed 'the doctrinaire belief that the private sector has a magic answer to the problems of the public sector'.[80] In addition to 'a total lack of transparency' with private firms, Abbott argued many PFIs, such as in healthcare and housing benefit, simply did not work.[81] When savings and improvements to services occurred, they were often at the expense of staff's wages and working conditions. PFIs, she argued, were better suited to projects with a natural revenue stream, such as toll bridges, and least suited to publicly sensitive projects such as the health service.

ACQUAINTANCES OF NOTE

Former Home Secretary Charles Clarke argues that Abbott and her comrades on the left were merely contrarians, cavalier about the damage they inflicted on the most progressive government of recent times. Rather than offering 'coherent' objections to proposals, he argues, she simply maintained a 'these fuckers are doing it wrong' attitude. 'I have always had a low opinion of Diane … She was predictable in every respect. I could write her speech any day of the week before she gave it,' he says. 'I think she gets much more respect than she deserves.'[82]

Abbott argues that Clarke's dismissal of her and her colleagues as the 'awkward squad' was simply a way to diminish the significance of their work. 'It was really them saying, "So, what? These people always do this."'[83]

Fear of the dissenting left reared its head during the campaign for the first Mayor of London. In keeping with their manifesto pledge, the government created the Greater London Authority (GLA) and the position of London mayor.

When Ken Livingstone announced that he was running, Blair feared 'it would be a big disaster, and he didn't want that'.[84] Despite Livingstone gaining 75,000 votes compared to Frank Dobson's 22,000, Dobson won the candidacy as the electoral system gave more weight to the votes of London MPs, MEPs and the GLA, who were more likely to support Dobson.

Diane Abbott grew up with her father Reginald Abbott, mother Julia Abbott (née McLymont) and brother Hugh Abbott. Here, a one-year-old Abbott is pictured with her family at her brother's christening in 1954.

COURTESY OF DIANE ABBOTT

Abbott, aged seven, in her primary school uniform. Abbott stood out academically but often felt like an outsider; she and her brother were the only black students at their primary school.

COURTESY OF DIANE ABBOTT

Abbott read history at Newnham College, Cambridge, where she became a socialist. Here, she is pictured outside King's College on her graduation day in 1976.

COURTESY OF DIANE ABBOTT

Abbott worked as an equality officer at the Association of Cinematograph, Television and Allied Technicians in the 1980s. © PA/PA ARCHIVE/PA IMAGES

By the mid-1980s, Abbott was a regular speaker at political events and began to gain national attention. She is photographed here at a Labour Party conference Black Sections debate in Blackpool, 1984.

© MIKE ABRAHAMS

Abbott was elected to Westminster City Council in 1982. She is pictured here speaking during the 1985 miners debate at the Labour Party conference in Bournemouth.

© PA/PA ARCHIVE/PA IMAGES

Bernie Grant and Diane Abbott raise their hands during the debate on the creation of separate Black Sections within the Labour Party at the party's annual conference in Blackpool in 1988. Seated behind them are Paul Boateng (*left*) and Keith Vaz (*centre*).

© PA/PA ARCHIVE/PA IMAGES

A newspaper advertisement for the Conservative Party from the 1987 general election. It depicts six left-wing Labour Party members with the caption 'So this is the new moderate militant-free Labour Party'.

© THE CONSERVATIVE PARTY ARCHIVE/GETTY IMAGES

On 11 June 1987, Abbott was elected MP for Hackney North and Stoke Newington, making her the first black woman to be elected to Parliament.

© PHOTOFUSION/UNIVERSAL IMAGES GROUP VIA GETTY IMAGES

Jeremy Corbyn, Bernie Grant and Abbott toast the success of the four Black Sections MPs at a celebratory meal in late 1987.

COURTESY OF DIANE ABBOTT

Neil Kinnock photographed linking arms with Abbott and Jo Richardson at the House of Commons during a get-together with the Labour Party's female MPs in 1987.

© PA/PA ARCHIVE/PA IMAGES

ABOVE Abbott, Bernie Grant, Jeremy Corbyn and Tony Banks photographed in the House of Commons before the state opening of Parliament. © PA/PA ARCHIVE/PA IMAGES

LEFT Bernie Grant, Paul Boateng, Neil Kinnock, Keith Vaz and Abbott on the last day of the Labour Party conference in 1987.
© FOX PHOTOS/HULTON ARCHIVE/GETTY IMAGES

Abbott increased her majority in the 1992 general election. For many, it was evidence that 1987 was not a fluke; that voters would not only elect but re-elect black candidates. © ROD LEON

Abbott with her two-month-old son James at his christening in the House of Commons crypt. Also photographed are David Thompson and Canon Grey. Jonathan Aitken was named James's godfather.
COURTESY OF DIANE ABBOTT

Abbott was among the thousands of election observers deployed across South Africa during the 1994 general election. She is pictured here with other election observers in Soweto. COURTESY OF DIANE ABBOTT

Abbott and Ken Livingstone first met in the 1970s. It was Livingstone who first introduced Abbott to Corbyn and other members of the Labour left.
COURTESY OF DIANE ABBOTT

Baroness Patricia Scotland, Keith Vaz, Diane Abbott and Paul Boateng on the terrace of the Commons sharing a political joke.
COURTESY OF DIANE ABBOTT

This Week, BBC One's late-night politics show, was hosted by Andrew Neil, with Michael Portillo and Abbott featuring as regular commentators.

© JEFF OVERS/BBC NEWS & CURRENT AFFAIRS VIA GETTY IMAGES

Abbott has a deep interest in US political history and has built relationships with several African-American civil rights activists. Here, she is pictured with Reverend Jesse Jackson. COURTESY OF DIANE ABBOTT

Abbott's London Schools and the Black Child initiative addresses black educational attainment and celebrates high-achieving black children in the city. © RICHARD LOWE

The 2010 Labour leadership candidates at the start of BBC *Newsnight*'s Labour leadership debate: (*left to right*) Andy Burnham, Ed Miliband, Diane Abbott, David Miliband and Ed Balls. © KATIE COLLINS/PA ARCHIVE/PA IMAGES

Abbott's 2015 campaign for London mayor coincided with Jeremy Corbyn's campaign to become Labour leader. Events at their Bloomsbury church base were oversubscribed, with standing room only. © CAROL MOIR/ALAMY LIVE NEWS

Abbott's decision to step down from the 2017 general election campaign prompted an outpouring of affection. Here, Stephanie Ozuo presents Abbott with a self-care hamper at an Abbott appreciation event.

© STEFAN ALVERANGA-FOSTER

Vigil and protest for Rashan Charles outside Stoke Newington police station in July 2017. The fathers of Rashan Charles and Edson Da Costa were among the attendees.

© CAROL MOIR/ALAMY LIVE NEWS

Abbott and Shami Chakrabarti outside Bedford station on their way to Yarl's Wood Immigration Removal Centre. There were reports that many of the women detained there were on a hunger strike due to their living conditions and treatment. © BELL RIBEIRO-ADDY

Abbott visited Yarl's Wood in February 2018. Here, Stephanie Tonmi, a former detainee, tells Abbott about her experiences. © LEON NEAL/GETTY IMAGES

When Abbott became the shadow Home Secretary in 2016, Corbyn told her he wanted her to be the nation's aunt. She is pictured here at the 2018 Labour Party conference in Liverpool.

© PA IMAGES/ALAMY STOCK PHOTO

In 2019, Black Girl Fest organised a three-day festival themed around Michelle Obama's memoir, *Becoming*. Here, Abbott is pictured at the festival in conversation with producer Tobi Kyeremateng.

© KRYSTAL NEUVILL

In 2019, Abbott became the first black person to represent their party at Prime Minister's Questions.

© HOUSE OF COMMONS/ JESSICA TAYLOR/PA ARCHIVE/PA IMAGES

Calling the system 'tainted', Livingstone put himself forward as an independent candidate for London mayor. Abbott urged Livingstone to remain in the Labour Party as a 'health check on New Labour', and after he left the party, she campaigned for his readmittance. However, Livingstone was adamant and led a popular campaign. As Alastair Campbell noted, 'There was a sense running through it that we had really fucked it up. He was running rings round us.'[85]

On 4 May 2000, as an independent candidate, Livingstone won the London mayoral election. Thrilled, Abbott joined his advisory cabinet and became his adviser on women and equality.

> You campaign to have a political leader in London, but you don't want the one that Londoners want. The Ken for London campaign told you more about the Blair leadership than it told you about Ken … They wanted to give [the role] to Richard Branson, they wanted a businessman to do it. They didn't want it to have any real power, just some businessman to strut around. Ken made it a political role.[86]

Abbott argues that the Blair leadership was detached from the politics of London, which was characterised by an interest in women's rights, LGBTQ rights and racial justice.

> Tony Blair had gone up for a council seat in Hackney, and they rejected him, which shows the extraordinarily good sense of Hackney Labour party members … I know Ken has his difficulties now, but if you cut him open, Ken's blood bleeds Labour. He knows more about the mechanics or the issues around London politics than most people have forgotten.[87]

Ken Livingstone argues that part of Blair's frustration was that the mayoral position came with many executive powers. 'Blair just wanted the American system,' he argues. 'Take something like the congestion charge; I just signed a bit of paper. It wasn't a vote. It was terrible.'[88] They wanted these new far-reaching powers to be in the hands of Dobson, not Red Ken.

While she was busy championing Livingstone's political endeavours, Abbott was also mourning the loss of her friend and colleague Bernie Grant. On 8 April 2000, Abbott received news that he had passed away after being ill for some time. She remembers heading to Grant's home with Corbyn.

> It's a very West Indian thing; when somebody dies, everyone goes to the house ... It was extremely sad. It was definitely a voice that we missed ... I was in the house, and Paul Boateng was there. [He] was someone with whom I had had my ups and downs, but we went into the back of the garden, and we held each other, and we both cried. And Paul said, 'You know, we are the only ones that know what Bernie went through.'[89]

David Lammy, then twenty-seven years old, remembers witnessing this intimate moment between Abbott and Boateng.[90] As a young black man from Tottenham, Lammy had grown up admiring Abbott. 'If Diane walks down Tottenham High Road, she is greeted like a hero,' he explains.

At the time, there had been some dispute about who would take over from Grant as the Tottenham Labour MP. Sharon Grant, his widow, wanted to run, but Abbott felt that 'it had been a black seat, one of the first black seats, and it should have a black candidate'.[91] So, when Lammy told Abbott he had promised Sharon that he would not run, she replied, 'Rubbish, absolute rubbish, you need to run.'[92] He did and was successful.

'Bernie's loss was considerable at the time that I arrived in Parliament,' Lammy remembers. '[People] don't fully understand the sacrifice and the toil it takes being the first pushing forward in any public forum.' Though their politics have not always aligned, he holds Abbott in high esteem.

> There was immense pressure on Diane, Bernie, Keith on coming in in 1987, and Diane was somehow at the epicentre of that pressure

... I think that it's still the case that to be a black woman in British public life is rare. To be a powerful and articulate black woman surviving for so long in British public life is extremely unusual. She is the great survivor.[93]

Perhaps the most unusual of Abbott's friendships during this period was that with 'Richard Nixon super fan' Jonathan Aitken. The pair first met while working at TV-am in the 1980s. He later became her voting pair and then godfather of her son James. Indeed, it was Aitken who suggested christening James Abbott in Westminster Abbey. Their relationship, though unusual, only provoked press interest in 1999 when Aitken was imprisoned at the Old Bailey. Aitken was taken to court after it came to light that in 1993, while he was a government minister in charge of defence procurement, aides of the Saudi royal family had paid for his two-night stay in the Paris Ritz. Aitken repeatedly denied the claim until 1999, when he admitted to perjury and perverting the course of justice.

Abbott was noted to have 'maintained a deafening silence' on the Aitken case.[94] She explains, 'The issues he had which led to him going to prison were not issues I knew anything about, and I just didn't think it was appropriate to make statements about it.'

Aitken recalls that Abbott later joked, 'You're very useful as a role model; if you tell lies this is what will happen.' Aitken took his duties as godfather seriously and had dinner with his godson semi-regularly while James was at university and in the early years of his career. Although Aitken left Parliament in 1997, he and Abbott are still in touch. Indeed, Abbott attended Aitken's ordination as an Anglican minister in June 2018.

At the end of Blair's first term, New Labour was undoubtedly popular, the economic news was good, and there had been real achievements like the introduction of the minimum wage, the establishment of the Sure Start programme and legal safeguards for union rights. Abbott welcomed and supported these progressive aspects of New Labour's agenda. However, she was critical of the emphasis on PFI,

Blair's apparent disregard for the checks and balances in the parliamentary system, New Labour's desire to retain tight control even after acts of devolution and aspects of foreign policy. Abbott's criticisms of policy in Blair's first term, criticisms informed by long-standing political commitments, turned out to be extremely prescient.

CHAPTER 9

DEFENDER OF LIBERTIES

On 7 June 2001, Tony Blair became the first Labour Prime Minister to win a full second term. Abbott retained her seat with 61 per cent of the vote. However, the election was notable for a voter turnout of 59.4 per cent, which had fallen by 11.9 per cent from 1997. It was the lowest turnout in eighty years, arguably because the public expected Labour to win comfortably. Labour's second term saw an increase in the frequency and size of rebellions. In 2003, sixty-five Labour MPs rebelled in the vote on foundation hospitals, in 2004, seventy-two rebelled against the second reading of the Higher Education Bill, and in March 2003, 139 Labour MPs voted against the war in Iraq. Though the government often won a majority, rebels did manage to win several concessions, including a cap on university tuition fees, increased maintenance grants for the poorest students and limitation to indefinite detention. Abbott continued to support the progressive aspects of Blair's government and opposed the more reactionary elements of New Labour.

EDUCATION

Abbott was removed from the Foreign Affairs Select Committee in May 2001, which left her with more time to focus on constituency issues such as education. Abbott felt that poor educational achievement and disengagement in schools increased the risk of young people being unemployed and drawn into criminal activity. She argued that the abolition of the Inner London Education Authority under the Tories was a 'criminal act of educational vandalism' and contributed to many of the problems with drugs and gun crime that the city was experiencing in the 1990s and 2000s.[1] Abbott's interest in education was long-standing. In 1995, she initiated a working group called Black Men in Crisis to focus on the links between educational under-achievement, unemployment and social exclusion. Black Men in Crisis supported initiatives to address the attainment gap.

The issue of educational underachievement among black children had been documented in the 1977 House of Common's Select Committee Report on Race Relations and Immigration. In 1985, the Swann Report published the results of an independent inquiry into the education of children of ethnic minority groups and pointed to

a network of widely differing attitudes and expectations on the part of teachers and the education system as a whole, and on the part of West Indian parents, which lead the West Indian child to have particular difficulties and face particular hurdles in achieving his or her full potential.[2]

By the 1990s, there had been some improvement in the educational attainment of children from ethnic minority backgrounds, with the notable exception of African-Caribbean boys. For example, in 1996 in Birmingham 36 per cent of white students, 39 per cent of Indian students and 21 per cent of Pakistani students achieved five or more higher-grade passes in their GCSEs, compared to only 18 per cent of African-Caribbean students.[3]

In 1999, an OFSTED report found that the gap between African-Caribbean pupils and the rest of the school population continued to widen, and that 'Black Caribbean students make a sound start in primary schools, but their performance shows a marked decline at secondary level.'[4] Writing for *The Observer* in 2002, Abbott noted:

When African and Afro-Caribbean children enter the school system at five, they do as well as white and Asian children in tests. By age eleven, their achievement levels begin to drop off. By sixteen there has been a collapse. And this is particularly true of black boys –

50 per cent of all sixteen year olds get five GCSEs, grades A to E. Only 13 per cent of black boys in London achieve this standard.[5]

Moreover, black students were six times more likely to be excluded from school than white children. This was particularly concerning as school exclusion is a key driver for unemployment and social exclusion later in life and is closely linked with criminality. The 1996 Audit Commission's review of the youth justice system found that 42 per cent of young offenders had been excluded from school. In one local authority, 58 per cent of children who had been permanently excluded had offended in the year before or after their exclusion. This group was also noted to have committed 50 per cent more offences in the year after their exclusion occurred.[6] Lord Warner of Brockley, former chair of the Youth Justice Board, stated that '80 per cent of young offenders of school age are out of school, either through exclusion or refusal to attend ... mainstream schooling is not willing and not able to deal with children with challenging behaviour'.[7] Martin Narey, former head of the prison service of England and Wales, put it this way, 'The 13,000 young people excluded from school each year might as well be given a date by which to join the prison service sometime later on down the line.'[8]

Abbott argued for more black teachers, in particular, black men, to serve as role models: 'Black boys need men in the classroom. They simply do not see reading or educational achievement as masculine or "cool". Although this applies to white working-class boys, strategies for addressing male underachievement are not working with black boys.'[9]

Professor David Gillborn and Professor Gus John, who was Britain's first black education director and had worked with Abbott since the 1980s, argued, 'Black pupils, whatever their gender and social class background, too often find themselves working against teacher expectations that embody assumptions about criminality, lack of motivation and lesser "ability". These views are most entrenched in relation to black boys.'[10] John added that the use of 'sets' and tiered entry into national exams compounded the impact of teachers' low expectations.

Abbott agreed, asserting that teachers needed to be willing to challenge their own unconscious biases and attitudes about black boys
which may contribute to low educational expectations and discriminatory behaviour management. 'It seems a black boy doesn't have
to be long out of disposable nappies for some teachers to see him as
a miniature gangster rapper.'[11] Addressing these biases would enable
better identification of challenges that may present as behavioural
difficulties, such as special educational needs and experiences with
racism. Abbott felt this failure of black children was particularly tragic
because of the importance that West Indians placed on education.

> West Indians believe in education. White people told them the
> reason white people were superior to them was because they were
> educated. They believed, as well, that they were coming to Britain
> to better themselves, and they believed that the way their children
> would better themselves was by getting an education ... It is a tre-
> mendous betrayal.[12]

Abbott believed that black parents and teachers had a vital role to
play in improving the educational attainment of black children. She
pointed to the success of the Claudia Jones Saturday School in Hackney and the John Loughborough School in Tottenham. 'What all of
these schools have in common are highly motivated black teachers,
involved parents, strong discipline and boundaries, and a celebration
of the children's cultural identities,' she explained.[13]

LONDON SCHOOLS AND THE BLACK CHILD

In February 1999, prompted by the government's decision to send
a privatisation 'hit squad' into the Hackney Education Authority in
response to a poor OFSTED report, Abbott organised the first Hackney Schools and the Black Child conference. She was concerned that
black parents and educators were not being consulted about reforms
which would primarily affect black children.

'Diane's concern was really to bring about a level of consciousness
among parents in the borough about our interdependence,' Professor

John explains. 'We needed to not simply be concerned about the quality of outcomes about our children, but to understand that we collectively needed to work to improve the standard of education in the borough.'[14]

Abbott had planned for 200 people to attend, but on the day, 450 people squeezed into the room in Hackney Town Hall. Abbott remarked that people had come from all over the UK because the event was the first of its kind: a discussion on black children's education, led by black people, for black people. She also commissioned a report on black teachers, looking at issues of recruitment and retention, recognising that many felt disillusioned and disempowered. Due to the success of the conference, two more were held in November 1999 and October 2000. Both were oversubscribed.

When Ken Livingstone became the Mayor of London, he provided funding which enabled Abbott to make the conference city-wide. The first London Schools and the Black Child (LSBC) conference was held on 16 March 2002 and over 2,000 black parents, students, teachers, community organisers, school governors, local government workers and academics attended. Livingstone remarked, 'I can't think of any other idea Diane has had in the years I've known her, that has been quite as dramatically successful as this.'[15]

The first conference certainly had an impact and led to a series of educational initiatives which would go on to influence government policy. Smaller conferences brought together black parents, educationalists and teachers in Croydon, Ealing, Walthamstow and Haringey. The conference also led to the establishment of the Greater London Black Parents and Governors Network, as well as a research project on the attainment of black boys in London's schools, which was led by respected educational consultant Carol Hunte. These initiatives took full advantage of the legal changes introduced by New Labour in the Race Relations Amendment Act (2000), which placed a statutory duty on schools to promote race equality by working to eliminate unlawful racial discrimination, and promoting equality of opportunity. Specifically, schools were required to monitor the impact of their practice 'on pupils, staff and parents of different racial groups' and on the 'attainment levels' of ethnic minority students. As the GLC had done in the 1980s, Abbott and her LSBC team seized on the new 'race equality duty' to advance a progressive agenda.

Speaking at the 2003 conference, Abbott argued that one of the most significant achievements of the first conference was that it led to 'a series of roundtable discussions between Department for Education and Skills ministers, black educationalists and community activists'.[16] These discussions brought Abbott into contact with Stephen Twigg and informed the Aiming High: Raising the Achievement of Minority Ethnic Pupils initiative. In 2002, Twigg was appointed parliamentary under-secretary of state for schools. In this role, he was responsible for policies regarding ethnic minority educational achievement, and for London schools, which meant that there was considerable overlap between his brief and LSBC.

Aiming High: African Caribbean Achievement provided resources and training to create whole-school approaches to raising educational attainment among black students. Twigg published a consultation document in March 2003 and used the 2003 LSBC conference to announce that the government was going ahead with the programme. Speaking at the 2003 LSBC conference, Abbott praised the initiative as 'the first of its kind' and welcomed the £1.7 million the government had earmarked for the project's first two years.[17] 'All of this', she told the conference 'is a direct result of the black community making its voice heard at the 2002 conference.' Twigg, also addressing the conference, set out his commitment to building 'on the good practice that already exists in the community of London and elsewhere, in many schools and in local education authorities and build on what research tells us about what schools can do for their black pupils.'[18] This was one area where New Labour and Abbott were on the same page. Since the mid-1970s, Abbott had stressed the need for research and data collection to inform policy. In terms of education New Labour was also committed to an 'evidence based' approach to policy making. Twigg was concerned that existing data was used intelligently to improve educational attainment, he recalls.

Aiming High came out of a strategy that we had been pursuing for some time, and us really looking at the detail of the statistics. There was a bit of a tendency in political circles to talk about ethnic minority underachievement. But when you drilled down it was much more complicated than that, there were some minority groups, most notably Chinese and Indian children, who did much better than average, but there was a big set of challenges for black children so that's why we developed the Aiming High strategy.[19]

Carol Hunte's report to the 2003 LSBC conference shows that she and Twigg had reached the same conclusion. Hunte highlighted the findings of the national pupil database, stressing the need to disaggregate the data, and focus on the attainment of African-Caribbean pupils.

Aiming High led to real improvements. In the first two years there was a 7 per cent increase in the proportion of black students in pilot schools who achieved five GCSEs at grade A* to C. The results of black boys – the demographic group least likely to get five good GCSE passes – showed the biggest improvements: in the first two years of the project the proportion of black boys gaining five GCSEs at grades A* to C increased by 10.2 per cent. Students in other demographic groups also improved against this measure, but at a lower rate, showing that schools involved in Aiming High were closing the attainment gap. Aiming High also narrowed the attainment gap in English, Maths and Science among children aged eleven to fourteen. More generally, the academics who evaluated the programme argued that 'the Aiming High project has shown that despite decades of entrenched race inequality, there are practical things that schools can do to make real improvements'.[20] With revisions to further improve the initiative, academic reports recommended a national roll out of the scheme. Twigg recalls that 'Diane was a very important voice in shaping that strategy.'[21] The approach inspired similar initiatives, Aiming High: Raising the Achievement of Gypsy Traveller Pupils and a programme targeting the children of asylum seekers.

LSBC also led to Investing in Diversity, a programme which offered training to black teachers, preparing them for leadership roles. Again, at the 2003 LSBC conference Twigg had announced the government's commitment to 'increase the number of black and minority ethnic teachers entering the profession' and to 'Shine, a pilot targeted specifically at supporting black and minority ethnic teachers who aspire to leadership, including headship, in our schools'.[22] Shine was followed by a series of studies by the National College for School Leadership which highlighted the lack of black and minority ethnic teachers in school leadership, as well as the discrimination BME teachers faced when seeking promotion. Investing in Diversity was designed to address these barriers. Like Shine, it was funded by the London Challenge, a government initiative which, as Twigg explains, 'was all about how to improve schools across London, particularly secondary schools, when we started the London Challenge, inner London GCSE results were well below the national average'.[23] Investing in Diversity was designed by Rosemary Campbell-Stephens, who was heavily involved in LSBC and spoke at the 2003 conference. Writing in 2010, she argued that the programme should be seen in the context of the 'historical continuum of black educational activism in Britain'.[24] Indeed, Campbell-Stephens's initiative built on decades of black grassroots campaigns around education, and decades of radical scholarship on the education of black students in British schools. Investing in Diversity, she argued, was an example of 'colour conscious', rather than 'colour blind' policy.

Investing in Diversity was launched in March 2004. Campbell-Stephens established the programme in order to offer 'a "bespoke" leadership development program tailored to black and global majority educators'.[25] Black women, more than any other group, made use of the scheme, and the four people who played the largest role in running the course, including Campbell-Stephens herself, were black women. Between the establishment of the programme in 2004 and 2010, the London pilot project expanded to the north of England and Bristol, with the support of existing networks of black teachers and funding from local authorities. Almost two-thirds of the teachers who received support from Investing in Diversity gained promotions in the first three years of the course. Campbell-Stephens credits Abbott and the LSBC for ensuring that the programme gained government funding.

The 'Educational Experiences of Black Boys in London', a London Development Agency report was published at the 2004 LSBC conference. The document contained a wealth of data demonstrating that London's schools were failing young black men and pointed to the unrepresentative composition of the teaching profession. Apparently, in 2003 although almost 20 per cent of school children in London were black, less than 3 per cent of teachers were black. The report also set out a five-year strategy to begin to reverse the 'dismal academic results' of young black men. Abbott used the data in the report to begin a dialogue with teaching unions about how to make the teaching profession more representative. Her strategy of working with the teaching unions, was a continuation of the approach that she had taken years earlier working with ACTT to break down barriers to entering film and television.

Empowering black parents was an important part of the LSBC's strategy for raising standards in schools. Consequently, at the fourth LSBC conference, held in 2006, Abbott launched a new website which advised parents on the best ways to engage with schools. The 2006 conference also had workshops for black parents who wanted to become school governors.

Despite these successes, Abbott had difficulty getting press coverage for the LSBC conferences. She recalls, 'One year, we tried to get the *Evening Standard* to cover it, and the question they asked my member of staff was, "Were any of these young people gangsters?" Because unless what you're doing fits the media framework, they don't want to acknowledge it.'[26]

Abbott also sought to bring the issue of black children's educational attainment to her parliamentary peers by inviting the Education Secretary and schools' ministers to the conferences. She developed a good working relationship with Twigg and Andrew Adonis. Charles Clarke, she sighs, 'felt that he should be congratulated for talking to me at all'.[27] Professor John was among those unimpressed by the 'blooming platitudes' offered by the ministers who did attend. 'I mean I used to get vexed, never mind anybody else,' he comments.[28] He was also frustrated by the failure of the conferences to build a movement of parents around the country. 'Many individuals went on to do great things, but that has not been measured. It was a lost opportunity given the momentum that there was and the number of people who were committing themselves to being active and taking local action.'[29] Nonetheless, he asserts, 'Diane's role in galvanising support and sharing information more widely across communities through the LSBC conference is pretty historical.'[30]

The 2009 LSBC conference was the last to receive mayoral funding. The exclusion of black students, particularly of young black men, had been an ongoing concern from conference to conference, but in 2009, Abbott highlighted the issue in her opening address. She argued that 'exclusions are to education what stop and search is to criminal justice. In other words, exclusion signifies the institutional treatment that our children receive in the education system.'[31] Exclusions were another aspect of the attainment gap, as African-Caribbean children were three times more likely to be excluded from school than white children. Abbott called on the Department for Education to fulfil its duties under the Race Relations Amendment Act and eliminate discrimination in school exclusions. Abbott was critical of government initiatives that were conceived as 'universal policies – that is policies targeted at exclusions in general', as they failed to address black students.[32]

Abbott invited London's new mayor, Boris Johnson, to address the conference in 2009. Johnson professed himself 'proud to be sharing a platform with my old friend and sparring partner Diane Abbott'.[33] Abbott recalls that Johnson 'enjoyed himself'.[34] Characteristically, Johnson played to the crowd, promising support for the LSBC for 'as long as I'm lucky enough to be Mayor of London'.[35] However, despite his public promise, and despite his claim that he was 'down with the ethnics', he promptly cut the funding for the project.[36] Abbott opines that Johnson's team did not want the mayor to be associated with any initiative badged as 'black'. Indeed, at least some in Johnson's team seem to have had a fairly ambivalent attitude to black Londoners. James McGrath, who was appointed by David Cameron to keep the new mayor on message said on record, 'Well, let them [black Londoners] go if they don't like it here.'[37]

Not only did Johnson cut financial support for the LSBC; he made no attempt to work with the group when developing his own educational initiatives. Two years after defunding the LSBC, Johnson launched the Mayor's Education Inquiry, which looked at underachievement in the capital. The inquiry was chaired by Dr Tony Sewell, whose 2008 article 'Racism is not the problem' made waves claiming that 'institutional peer group culture' and low expectations among black young men was to blame for low educational achievement, rather than institutional racism in schools.[38] Despite featuring a photograph of a black young man on the cover, the Mayor's Education Inquiry, published in 2012, made no use of the data collected by the LSBC over the previous decade. Nor did Johnson's report mention the attainment gap between black students and white students. Rather the Mayor's Education Inquiry considered the attainment gap in terms of 'between pupils eligible for free school meals and pupils who are not'.[39] While the report did note that 'African Caribbean pupils were almost three times as likely to receive one or more permanent exclusions compared with all London pupils' it made no recommendations for how this issue could be addressed. In that sense, Johnson's team chose to disregard the research and data analysis that Abbott had championed in the decade since creating the LSBC.

Johnson's new initiative, the London Schools Excellence Fund, which received over £20 million from the Department for Education, did not address the achievement of young black men, of black students or of BAME students. Schools which participated in Johnson's initiative were not required to focus on the attainment of black students, nor to evaluate the impact of their measures on black students. Indeed, the final reports on the London Schools Excellence Fund made no mention of the achievement of black students or ethnic minority students more generally. Nor could it, as the project did not collect data on BAME student achievement. Some of the schools which took part deliberately took a 'colour blind' approach with the aim of raising attainment 'of children regardless of gender, ethnicity or social class'.[40]

In that sense, Johnson as mayor ignored the data collected by the LSBC, the research that Abbott had championed, and the expertise that she had brought together.

PRIVATE SCHOOL ROW

The underachievement of black boys in Hackney played a role in Abbott making a decision that almost ended her political career. In October 2003, it came to light that she had enrolled her son in the £10,000 per year City of London school.

City of London school headmaster David Levin defended the school's track record of working with schools in the state sector. 'Our one and only Prime Minister, Lord Asquith, was a scholarship boy from the East End and a single-parent family,' he told reporters.[41] Private school organisations took the opportunity to get Abbott to join their campaign to reintroduce assisted places for pupils. Still, Abbott, who had previously criticised Tony Blair and Harriet Harman for sending their children to selective schools, came under fire.

She was branded a hypocrite and a disgrace to the Labour party. Journalist Jane Shilling recommended that she write a 'handsome apology' to Harman and Blair.[42] James Abbott Thompson, then only twelve years old, phoned LBC radio to say, 'She's not a hypocrite. She just put what I wanted first.' He told listeners:

My mum didn't force me to go to private school. I took the test for the schools I wanted to go to, and I chose the school I wanted to go to. If I wanted to go to a state school, then my mum would have let me go to a state school ... It's not a flick of a coin for my mum to pay for private school.[43]

Abbott later criticised the radio show for putting her son on the air without parental permission.

On 30 October, on BBC One's *This Week*, Abbott admitted that her decision was 'inconsistent, to put it mildly' and 'indefensible'. Abbott's former husband told the *Mail on Sunday* that Abbott warned him to keep quiet about James's school, fearful of the political consequences.

While Abbott believed that private schools 'prop up the class system in society', she had to choose between her reputation as a politician and her son.[44] 'I suppose the principled thing to do would have been to send my son to a failing state school, however bad it was,' Abbott said. 'But I'm sorry, I just don't possess that level of principle.'[45]

Brian Sedgemore, MP for the neighbouring constituency, Hackney South, said Abbott could not 'understand the hurt and harm she has caused to local people in Hackney'.[46] Sedgemore, who favoured the abolition of private schools and whose son had attended a state school, said that Abbott was telling parents that 'if you haven't got £10,000 a year don't bother, and to the teachers she has virtually said, you are rubbish'. He pointed to evidence that Hackney's schools were improving, with the percentage of pupils receiving five A to C grades increasing from 31 per cent in 2002 to 40 per cent in 2003. 'Children who work hard and are supported by their parents in their education can and do succeed in Hackney schools and in schools outside the borough,' he asserted.[47]

However, Abbott was the mother of a black boy in a borough where only 9 per cent of black boys achieved five A to C grades at GCSE, compared to 42 per cent of all students nationally.[48] She told the *Sunday Mirror*: 'I do know the issues around the education of black boys in this borough ... It is a race issue because, of all the ethnic groups in London's schools, the only group falling behind is black boys.'[49] Trevor Phillips backed Abbott: 'Being the son of an MP does not exempt you from the fate of many black boys.' Kwame Kwei-Armah, an actor, director and playwright, agreed. 'I have lived in Hackney, and I guarantee that the overwhelming majority of black parents would do just what she has done if they could, regardless of what they may or may not have said in the past.'[50] Ian Peacock, the Labour education chief in Hackney and Abbott's local constituency party, also defended Abbott's choice. Indeed, it is hard to overstate the problems in London schools in the early 2000s when it came to the education of black young men. The London Development Agency's report 'The Educational Experiences of Black Boys in London Schools 2000–2003' described the situation facing African-Caribbean boys in the London schools as 'catastrophic'.[51]

At Prime Minister's Questions, Tony Blair was asked if he would send his own children to school in Hackney, to which he responded, 'It is for each individual parent to make up their own mind as to how they educate their children.'[52] William Diaz, a Labour Party member of twenty years, left the party after accusing Abbott of 'breathing life into the very institution most responsible for London's social apartheid'.[53] Michael Rosen, a children's author and poet, thanked Abbott for 'having given socialists yet another reason not to waste any time in the Labour Party'.[54] In response to Rosen, Abbott wrote:

> You are quite entitled to use my decision to send my son James to City of London School as the excuse for a withering attack on New Labour ... It is also inevitable that a political polemic about New Labour quickly turns into a personal attack on me. On this, you and the Tory media are singing from the same song sheet. What you are not entitled to do is to completely dismiss the issue of what is happening to black boys in the British education system. Because this is not a new issue.[55]

Journalist Libby Purves argued that Abbott was no worse than members of the left who manoeuvred their way into elite state schools. 'There is one school Abbott would have liked her son to go to,' she explained. 'But it is so oversubscribed that you have to live absurdly close to get your child in. Wealthier parents buy houses near it, which is a socially acceptable way for rich left-wingers to distort the system.' She continued, 'The fact is, parents are parents, and they care more about their real and present children than about some utopian future ... Windy, wordy socialism is never enough for real people living in the present.'[56] Purves's analysis acknowledged much that was unsaid in the debate over Abbott's decision. Changes in the education system since the 1980s had meant that middle-class parents could increasingly game the system through the property market. Equally, there is no contradiction between wanting a better future and having to make difficult decisions in the present. And Abbott's decision was more difficult than most. After all, none of her white critics had to grapple with the reality of institutional racism in the education system. The debate also revealed a great deal about the problems of the British press; it was far easier to attack Abbott than to do the detailed work analysing the long-term structural issues that blighted the education system at the time, work that was being done by London Schools and the Black Child.

Seven years later, in a *Daily Mirror* interview, the question of James's schooling resurfaced. Again, Abbott reiterated that she made the decision based on the educational attainment of black boys in the borough, noting that education in Hackney had improved considerably since that time.[57]

Years later, Abbott stands by supporting James's choice:

All his life, my son has had to bear the consequences of a mother who is a full-time politician. It meant I wasn't there sometimes when I should have been there. Even when I was with him, I was there in body only; my mind was somewhere else … When I was looking for a secondary school, I felt really guilty, because I thought if I spent more time on being a mother, I would know more. I wouldn't be floundering as to which is the best school … If anyone had suffered for me being an MP, it wasn't me, it was him. I felt that just once in my life, I would take a decision that was all about him and not about me, and if it proves to be career suicide, so be it.[58]

Meg Hillier, who became a Labour MP in 2005, explains that she does not talk about her family in the public sphere as she is cognisant of the backlash against Abbott.

She was not the only woman who made choices like that. When I was going through selection a lot of the Labour Party members in my constituency had gone private … I know men have sent their children to schools that women have been criticised for sending their children to, and those men get nothing.

She continues, 'I think everyone's learned the hard way from Diane. Unfortunately, she's been the trailblazer on that one.'[59]

THE WAR ON TERROR

On 11 September 2001, Abbott was leaving a meeting with the ambassador from Belize when she heard the news of an attack on New York. 'I basically watched the television for twenty-four hours. It was the most extraordinary thing. The images were terrible ... You knew it would have immense political consequences, but you couldn't be quite sure what they were.'[60]

The following month, Blair announced that British troops had joined US troops in Afghanistan. He stated that he had no doubt that al-Qaida was behind 9/11 and that they were being harboured and supported by the Taliban in Afghanistan. While Abbott agreed that 'diplomatic, legal, military and political' measures should be taken in Afghanistan, she argued that such measures should also be sustainable and effective.[61] She voted for a pause in the bombing, ridiculing the dropping of 'cluster bombs for feminism', that is to say, the creation of a greater humanitarian disaster in the quest for civil rights.

On 24 September 2002, the government published a fifty-page dossier which alleged that Iraq possessed weapons of mass destruction including chemical and biological weapons, which could be deployed within forty-five minutes of an order. Newspapers whipped the nation into a frenzy with headlines stating: 'Brits 45 mins from doom' and 'Mad Saddam ready to attack: 45 minutes from a chemical war'.[62] The same day, referring to the dossier, Blair stood before the House of Commons and made a case for military action in Iraq. Abbott was one of fifty-six Labour MPs who voted against the adjournment of the House on the issue of possible British military action in Iraq. Instead, she backed the Liberal Democrat amendment requiring a UN mandate and a vote in the House of Commons before going to war in Iraq. Abbott continued to urge caution and when Blair expressed his intention to take on North Korea, defiantly called out 'Who's next?'[63]

On 3 February 2003, Alastair Campbell published a press briefing document on Iraq's weapons programme. This briefing document, later dubbed the 'Dodgy Dossier' failed to convince Abbott. 'I have always been somebody, rightly or wrongly, who decides what they think about an issue, having looked at the information ... If you actually read [the dossier] you'd see there wasn't much substance to it.'[64]

Abbott recalls attending several parliamentary meetings with the chief weapons inspector Scott Ritter.

> I heard Scott Ritter say more than once that if anybody told you that there were still weapons of mass destruction in Iraq, you needed to get them to explain how and why ... Yet, there were MPs who didn't really want to examine the evidence and just wanted to vote with the leadership. I did what I did with Iraq and Afghanistan because I felt confident that having looked at the information, having listened to people, it was the right thing to do.[65]

In February 2003, 121 Labour MPs backed the cross-party amendment, moved by Chris Smith, which argued that the case for military action against Iraq had yet to be proven. Outside the walls of Westminster, anti-war sentiment was growing, and millions joined anti-war protests across the UK. After unsuccessful attempts at getting a UN resolution authorising military action in Iraq, President George W. Bush gave Saddam Hussein and his sons forty-eight hours to leave Iraq or face war. The following day, on 18 March 2003, the House of Commons backed military action in Iraq, 139 Labour MPs rebelled.

As British troops landed on Iraqi soil, the controversy surrounding the evidence that legitimised the war grew. BBC correspondent Andrew Gilligan reported that the intelligence in Campbell's dossier had been transformed to make it 'sexier'. This included inserting the infamous 45-minute claim. The BBC soon came under fire, Greg Dyke resigned as director general, and MI6 withdrew the 45-minute claim. When weapons inspector David Kelly was outed as the BBC's source, he came under scrutiny and was found dead on 17 July 2003. The Hutton Inquiry concluded that Kelly died by suicide, criticised the BBC's editorial policy and largely absolved Campbell and the government of any wrongdoing.

The Chilcot Inquiry into the UK's role in the Iraq War, published in 2016, largely confirmed Abbott's suspicions. Intelligence had 'not established beyond doubt' that Saddam Hussein still had weapons of mass destruction.[66] Moreover, it concluded that the UK did not face an imminent threat from Iraq, and military intervention was not a last resort at that time.

Abbott had also been closely following the events unfolding in Sudan. Since the country's independence in 1956, tensions had built between the largely Arab ruling classes and the African majority who were disproportionately affected by years of poor rainfall and food shortages. For decades, Sudan had been blighted by violent clashes between the Sudanese army, police and pro-government largely Arab Janjaweed militias, and largely non-Arab rebel groups such as the Sudanese Liberation Army and the Justice and Equality Movement. By 2004, there were reports of Janjaweed militias carrying out systematic killings and mass rapes of women and children. Over 1 million people were displaced, including hundreds of thousands who had fled to neighbouring countries.

Speaking to the Commons that summer, Abbott highlighted several underlying issues for the conflict: scarce resources, post-colonial and post-Cold War tensions, and the distribution of oil. These same precipitators, she said, underlie 'inter-communal conflict all over the world', and addressing them must accompany any immediate action taken to avert greater humanitarian crisis.[67]

Abbott's time on the Foreign Affairs Committee had left her cognisant of the need for a robust system of international law which would legitimise interventions in humanitarian crises. She also emphasised the collaborative role of the Sudanese government, the UN and regional organisations such as the African Union, in humanitarian interventions. Boldly, she asked the Commons, 'Will we stand by and allow another Rwanda in Sudan?'[68]

Abbott agreed with International Development Secretary Hilary Benn's decision to rule out military action in June 2004, but by July, Blair was asking officials to draw up plans for military intervention. The African Union and the EU sent eight human rights monitors to the region, which Abbott derided as a 'paltry' and 'hopelessly in-adequate' number for a region bigger than Britain. On 30 July, the UN Security Council Resolution 1556 placed an arms embargo on the Janjaweed and other militia and gave the Sudanese government thirty days to disarm and bring to justice the militia groups, or else they may consider sanctions. However, Abbott felt this was hopeless as the Sudanese government, which was 'the Janjawid's backer', was still allowed arms.[69]

Sudanese President Omar al-Bashir said that UN involvement was targeting the Islamic state in Sudan and warned against further interference. The following years saw increased numbers of regional troops and international peacekeepers in Darfur, peace agreements were made and broken, and the numbers raped, killed, and displaced continued to rise. During this time Abbott found herself repeating her plea for an end to the world's worst humanitarian crisis. 'If ever a situation cried out for liberal interventionism, it is that in Darfur.'[70]

THE 2005 ELECTION

Blair's lacklustre response in Darfur was a striking contrast to his involvement in Iraq. As civilian casualties in Iraq climbed, Blair's ap-proval ratings fell and he increasingly came to be seen as a liability for the Labour Party. Whereas in 1997 Blair was a considerable asset for Labour, with voters viewing him more positively than the party, after 2001 the opposite was true. In 2004, Blair announced he would lead the party for a third, but not a fourth term. It was widely speculated that Gordon Brown, who frequently appeared by Blair's side through-out the campaign, would succeed him. Labour's 2005 election cam-paign focused on the past, pointing to eight years of a strong economy and ongoing investment in public services. However, the aftermath of the 2000 fuel crisis and rising unemployment was hurting Labour's perceived ability to manage the economy.[71]

The 2005 election campaign saw the return of Alastair Campbell. Joined by 'super-Blairite' Alan Milburn, and 'all-purpose Malvolio' Peter Mandelson, their campaign tactics infamously included posters depicting Tory leader Michael Howard as a flying pig, which drew accusations of anti-Semitism. Criticising the 'testosterone-driven' and 'aggressively macho' campaign, Abbott joked that Labour's campaign slogan should be renamed: 'The Boys Are Back in Town'.[72] Meanwhile, the Liberal Democrats tried to appeal to disaffected Labour voters in their opposition to the war in Iraq. The Tories had been shifting their position on issues like public service spending and tax-spend closer to those supported by the public, as well as appealing to the right with posters asking 'Are you thinking what we're thinking? It's not racist to impose limits on immigration.'

On 5 May 2005, Labour won a historic third term. The turnout was 61.4 per cent, marginally higher than in 2001, but there was little else to celebrate: Labour now had a significantly reduced majority of sixty-six (down from 160), losing forty-seven seats across the country, including in strongholds such as Manchester, Cambridge and Bristol.

Dawn Butler was the only other black woman to be elected, winning in Brent South, which Abbott praised as 'a big step forward'. Still, she regretted that her 'personal friend' Oona King lost Bethnal Green and Bow to the former Labour MP George Galloway amid 'very controversial circumstances'. The infamously abrasive campaign saw candidates require police protection and was marred by allegations of electoral fraud and voter intimidation.[73]

The fact that schools minister Stephen Twigg lost in Enfield Southgate, the seat he had won from Michael Portillo in 1997, seemed to mark the end of an era. There were also important changes across the aisle. Michael Howard stood down as Tory Party leader and was succeeded by the 39-year-old David Cameron. Calls for Blair to announce his departure date soon followed.

BLAIR'S FINAL TERM

At the start of Blair's premiership, Abbott backed the civil liberties aspects of the New Labour agenda, including the Human Rights Act of 1998 which incorporated the European Convention on Human Rights into British law. At the same time, Abbott was concerned about the civil liberties implications of much of New Labour's anti-terror legislation, concerns she shared with Shami Chakrabarti, who was director of Liberty (formerly the National Council for Civil Liberties) for the latter part of the Blair years.

In 2000, Labour introduced the Regulation of Investigatory Powers Act, dubbed the 'snooper's charter', and the Terrorism Act, which allowed the detention of suspects without charge for up to seven days. Notably, Section 44 of the Terrorism Act allowed any area of the country to be defined as one in which police could stop and search any vehicle or person and seize articles of any kind connected with terrorism. It did not require 'reasonable suspicion' that an offence had been committed. During the Iraq War, entire counties fell under Section 44, and black and Asian men were five to seven times more likely to be stopped by police. It was also infamously used against 82-year-old Holocaust survivor Walter Wolfgang after he heckled speakers at the 2005 Labour Party conference, forcing Blair to apologise. In 2007 to 2008, only 0.6 per cent of Section 44 stop and searches ever led to an arrest, much less a charge.[74] Abbott's concerns about Section 44 were vindicated in 2009 when the European Court of Human Rights ruled that it was incompatible with the right to respect for private life under Article 8 of the Human Rights Convention.

Following 9/11, the government ramped up its anti-terror legislation. The Anti-Terrorism, Crime and Security Act 2001 increased police and security service powers and included the indefinite detention of foreign national terror suspects without trial. The then Attorney General Lord Goldsmith referred to HMP Belmarsh, where these suspects would be held, as a 'three-walled prison'.[75] The detainees could not be sent back to a place of torture, but they could voluntarily choose to return. Chakrabarti calls it 'the slightly more English, green tea version of Guantanamo'.[76] Abbott was among the minority of Labour MPs who opposed indefinite detention without trial and pushed for time limits and increased scrutiny of the process. She also opposed restrictions to unsuccessful asylum claimants' right to appeal.

Chakrabarti, whom the former *Sun* columnist Jon Gaunt once called the 'most dangerous woman in Britain', heralds Abbott as one of the MPs who consistently fought to protect civil liberties.[77] She recalls that Abbott strongly opposed the introduction of ID cards, which were linked to a national identity database. Tory MP David Davis, another champion of civil liberties, said that ID cards would be 'a massive reversal of the relationship between citizen and state'. Abbott argued they amounted to 'a new pass law in our inner cities'.[78]

'She would say, my face is my ID card,' Chakrabarti shares.[79] When the ID card bill passed, Abbott was particularly disappointed in the Labour MPs who opposed the legislation on principle but caved when it came to the vote. Chakrabarti recalls that Abbott swore she would never leave the matter of civil liberties to other people again: 'I feel that was quite a seminal moment.'

Abbott and Chakrabarti also worked closely in Hackney's DNA clinics. The Criminal Justice Act 2003 allowed police to take and keep the samples of anyone they arrested. In 2006, Blair called for the national DNA database to be expanded to include every citizen. However, Chakrabarti explains that DNA retention disproportionately affected black men.

> We knew there would be loads of young black men in Hackney who would have been stopped and searched, and they would have had their DNA taken even if they had never been charged or prosecuted … We held DNA clinics in Diane's constituency. We sent Liberty lawyers down to sit with Diane and her team in Hackney, and we, as lawyers, would write letters to the police, asking them on what basis [they retained DNA] and requesting they destroy our client's DNA, with some success.[80]

While Chakrabarti came up with the idea for the clinics, she says 'it took someone like Diane to make it work in the community … civil liberties aren't an abstract concept to her; they're about the lived experience of people and minority ethnic people in particular.'

In December 2004, the Law Lords ruled that holding suspects in HMP Belmarsh indefinitely without charge or trial was incompatible with the European Convention on Human Rights. In response, the Home Office introduced the Prevention of Terrorism Bill in February 2005, which allowed for control orders to restrict the activities of people suspected of involvement in terrorism. Although sixty-two Labour MPs rebelled, the bill passed the Commons. It ping-ponged between the Lords and Commons but eventually passed with the provision of a review after one year. Abbott was one of thirty-seven Labour rebels.

THE 7/7 ATTACKS

On 7 July 2005, Abbott was working from home when she saw a news report of explosions in London. As the story unfolded, she soon realised that there were multiple, connected explosions committed by terrorists. One of the explosions had taken place near Liverpool Street station, which was on Abbott's son's school route. She recalls being terrified until she finally received a call from him.

The 7/7 bombings killed fifty-two people, left hundreds injured, and traumatised countless more. In the wake of the attacks, anti-Muslim sentiment grew across the country. Only days after the attacks, Boris Johnson wrote in *The Spectator* that 'Islam is the problem' and suggested that Islamophobia was 'a natural reaction'.[81] At the same time, the *New York Times* published a front-page article describing London as a 'haven for radical Muslim clerics'.[82]

Abbott recalls sitting in the back of a cab a few days after the attacks when her driver started to say, 'these bombings, these bombings'. Bracing herself for Islamophobic rhetoric, she was pleasantly surprised when he continued, 'they don't understand, they think we can be frightened by a few bombs, but we're Londoners, we're Londoners'.[83]

Rachel North, a survivor of the 7/7 attacks, echoed this sentiment. 'When terrorists attack us, they try to divide us,' she wrote in *The Guardian*. 'What I learned on July 7, 2005 was that we are each other's best security. We are the guardians of each other's liberties.'[84]

Nonetheless, Abbott argues that the government used the attacks as 'an excuse for ridiculous anti-terror legislation' and attempted to increase the time limit of detention without charge to an unprecedented ninety days.[85] However, on 9 November 2005, MPs voted against the ninety-day detention by 322 votes to 291; New Labour's first defeat. Instead, MPs settled for an upper limit of twenty-eight days. Abbott later said that she voted for twenty-eight days 'under duress', with the hope that the debate on the matter would be finished.

> The time I spent [working at the NCCL] really cemented my views on the importance of civil liberties, and the importance of constraining the powers of the state. If you allow the state to behave in a lawless and unfair manner to some group that you are depicting as the other, in this case, it was Muslims, in the end, the state will behave in a lawless way to you ... Because I represented Hackney, I represented diverse communities, it was very clear that if the state had these powers, they would be using them on my constituents, people like me.[86]

In addition to eroding civil liberties and causing disproportionate harm to Muslim communities, Abbott felt that such legislation would make radicalisation more, rather than less, likely. Internment in Northern Ireland 'was the best recruiting sergeant the IRA ever had,' Abbott wrote for the *Evening Standard*.[87] 'I am certain that the disaffection this policy will cause in the Muslim community will make us all less safe.'

The 2006 local elections were disastrous for Labour; they lost 319 councillors and seventeen councils. The British National Party made gains, the Liberal Democrats saw mixed results and the Tories had their best performance since 1992. Reflecting on the election results, Abbott warned that Blair's 'headlong dash' for his 'legacy' was harming the Labour Party. She added that New Labour's entanglement with private-sector style initiatives and Blair's embrace of Bush's foreign policy was causing the 'fatal haemorrhaging' of Labour members and was putting the future of the party at risk.[88] Nick Brown asserted that Blair could not 'drift on', and Martin Salter called for a 'clear timetable' for Blair's departure. Frank Dobson damningly likened a Cabinet reshuffle to 'rearranging the deckchairs on the *Titanic*'.[89] But reshuffle he did.

That September, when Blair announced that he was to step down as Prime Minister within the year, attacks on Gordon Brown, Blair's most likely successor, started to flood in. Charles Clarke was particularly derogatory, labelling Brown a control freak with psychological issues who lacked the bottle to be Prime Minister.[90] Nonetheless, in May 2007, Blair formally endorsed Brown, making good on the agreement the pair made ahead of the 1994 Labour leadership contest.

THE BROWN YEARS

Brown became Prime Minister on 27 June 2007 amid attempted terror attacks in London and Glasgow. Two months into his premiership, Brown announced his intention to increase the upper limit for the detention of terror suspects without charge from twenty-eight to fifty-six days. The Metropolitan Police Commissioner, Sir Ian Blair, and the head of anti-terrorist operations, Peter Clarke, supported Brown's decision. In contrast, both the Home Affairs Select committee and the Joint Committee on Human Rights reported that there was no evidence that increased detention was necessary, and precaution alone was insufficient to justify this interference with personal liberty.[91] Nonetheless, in January 2008, two years after Blair's failed ninety-days proposal, the Counter-Terrorism Bill was introduced to Parliament. It extended the 28-day limit to forty-two days. Abbott comments:

> The Labour Party isn't so great on civil liberties. One of the first things I voted against the party on as a new MP was the renewal of the Prevention of Terrorism Act. A bit like all this anti-terror legislation, it was brought in specifically to deal with Irish terrorism. In order to get it through Parliament, it had to be renewed every year, and myself, Jeremy Corbyn and John McDonnell were part of a small group of people who voted not to renew it every year. So, this idea about draconian and unnecessary anti-terror legislation is not new.[92]

Frank Dobson and Abbott, the unofficial rebel leader and chief whip, guided the other rebels through the ins and outs of votes and amendments. Desperate to quell the rebellion, Brown called Abbott. 'He's never spoken more than two sentences to me, and then he rings me and tries to persuade me about this legislation,' she laughs. 'What was he thinking?'[93] Abbott recalls listening to Brown through a red mist of rage. 'His tack was that I didn't understand. The legislation was not what I thought it was.'

On 11 June 2008, in a debate on the bill, all concerned had expected the Speaker to call Dobson to make the case against the government. Unexpectedly, the Speaker called Abbott to present their case. Abbott's speech was unplanned, but it won her the Spectator Parliamentarian Speech of the Year Award and a Liberty Human Rights Award. Tory frontbencher David Davies described it as 'one of the finest speeches I have heard since being elected to the House of Commons'.[94]

Abbott began by arguing that the bill was counter-productive.

As has been said throughout this debate, the first duty of Parliament is the safety of the realm. It is because I believe that the proposals on 42-day detention will make us less safe, not more safe, that I oppose them ... What makes us free is what makes us safe, and what makes us safe is what will make us free.[95]

She then humorously directed her frustration at the Prime Minister.

Some people say that he wants to try to do something that Tony Blair could not do. Some people say that he is driven by the polls. Some people say that last year he saw an article in *The Sun* that said that he was soft on terrorism, and he has been heading down this path ever since.[96]

Abbott reprimanded Brown for resurrecting a proposal which was 'emphatically' rejected two years prior, and mocked his tactics:

People whom the Prime Minister has never spoken to in his life have been ushered into his presence twice in forty-eight hours ... People have been offered Cuba, and no doubt governorships of Bermuda have been bandied about. Any rebel backbencher with a cause is confident – if they vote the right way of course – that the

Prime Minister will make the statement, give the money or make the special visit ... It is a test of Parliament that we are willing to stand up for the civil liberties of the marginalised, the suspect and the unpopular.

That day, thirty-six Labour MPs rebelled against the proposal, but it narrowly passed after the Prime Minister won the last-minute support of the nine Democratic Unionist MPs.

Chakrabarti, who watched Abbott from the Strangers' Gallery, remembers, 'Diane made the most important speech in the House of Commons, but the most important speech in the House of Lords was made by Eliza Manningham-Buller.'[97] In her first speech in the House of Lords, the recently retired head of MI5 told the House she was aware that maiden speeches were to be short and non-controversial. 'I can do short, but non-controversial is a bit trickier in these circumstances.'[98] She explained:

In deciding what I believe on these matters I have weighed up the balance between the right to life – the most important civil liberty – the fact that there is no such thing as complete security, and the importance of our hard-won civil liberties. And, therefore, as a matter of principle, I cannot support the 42-day pre-charge detention in the bill.[99]

'It's very hard to justify unelected legislators,' Chakrabarti admits.

We don't have a written constitution, we don't have an entrenched bill of rights, and we don't have a supreme court with strike-down powers in the way that you have in the US and France. So, in our bizarre model, it has evolved, in this bizarre way, that you do get more independence in the House of Lords ... The whip rests much more lightly on their shoulders.[100]

This independence, Chakrabarti argues, is what gave many of the Lords the freedom to oppose Brown's legislation in ways many MPs dared not. The Lords defeated Brown's bill by 191 votes, and the government was forced to be content with a draft Counter-Terrorism (Temporary Provision) Bill which could be introduced 'if and when the need arises'.[101]

On reflection, Abbott comments:

> If anything, I think that analysis has been vindicated ... I made that speech because I felt very strongly about the issue of civil liberties and the way minorities are treated in this society and at the heart of our politics ... It certainly felt important that I had been able to do what I believe I had been sent to Parliament to do: be a voice for the voiceless. I felt I was a voice for the Muslim community when not many people were standing up to say, including some Muslim MPs in Parliament, that this is wrong.[102]

Following the House of Commons vote, David Davis, the shadow Home Secretary, resigned to fight a by-election on the issue of civil liberties. Meanwhile, rumours had been circling that Davis and the Liberty lead, Chakrabarti, were involved romantically. 'There was this Helen of Troy thing, the idea that I could turn David Davis,' Chakrabarti recalls.[103]

Andy Burnham confesses to starting the rumours. 'I made a daft comment,' he acknowledges. 'I was trying to make a political jibe at him to say that he'd been having too many late-night calls with Shami Chakrabarti. It was not appreciated by either of them, and Diane took it upon herself to tell me straight that it was not an acceptable comment.'[104]

For Chakrabarti, Abbott coming to her defence was one of many examples of the softer side of Abbott that many do not get the chance to see. 'There are things that are difficult to portray in adverbial politics, and that's nuance, and that's subtlety, and that's humanity ... maybe maternal is the wrong word to use, but why not?'[105]

THE FINANCIAL CRISIS

Amid the 42-day debacle, another challenge was looming. As losses from subprime mortgages were accumulating in the US, in the UK, after a decade of economic growth, house prices began to climb. On 15 September 2008, the collapse of the US housing market led to the Lehman Brothers filing bankruptcy. The knock-on effects were felt globally, including in the UK, where the stock market began to plummet. By early October, the Royal Bank of Scotland Group and HBOS had run out of money.

Gordon Brown, who had managed the economy for the past decade and professed an end to 'boom and bust', appeared to be devoid of answers. Abbott remarks, 'He had been so desperate to be leader, for years he and his allies had manoeuvred against Blair ... and as soon as he became leader, it became clear that he didn't really know what to do with it.'[106]

Chancellor Alistair Darling rejected accusations of dithering and argued that the complexity and magnitude of the problem required a thought-through solution. That solution finally came to light on 8 October 2008, when Brown announced a £500 billion rescue package to stabilise the markets and restore confidence and trust in the UK economy. 'Extraordinary times call for the bold and far-reaching solutions,' Brown told the nation.[107]

The package included £50 billion to recapitalise banks through the borrowing of capital and selling of shares to the government, as well as £250 billion to underwrite and a further £200 billion injection into the financial markets. Gilles Moec, the chief economist at the Bank of America, noted that, compared to other countries, the British plan was very comprehensive and going in the right direction. The measures were also welcomed by the opposition, but they remained wary that taxpayers' money would be lining bankers' pockets. 'Taxpayers are making an enormous investment and have potentially a huge liability. They want to see their interests protected. No one wants rewards for failure,' Cameron stated.[108]

However, Cameron's support was short-lived, and only three months later, he accused the Prime Minister of 'making a complete mess of the economy'.[109] The recession was worsening, and Brown had announced another bailout plan for the banks, which Cameron argued had a 'staggering lack of detail'. Brown retorted that the Tories 'should really grow up and face up to the big issues', adding that despite all his criticisms, Cameron had 'not one idea about how to begin to sort the problem out'.

In another boisterous Prime Minister's Questions, Cameron took repeated jibes at the government and accused them of running around like headless chickens. Brown patronisingly stated, 'The Leader of the Opposition does not understand that this is an unprecedented global banking crisis. Unprecedented means without precedent. Global means that it affects the whole of the world.'[110]

In March 2009, Brown called for a more responsible system of regulation of financial markets globally and took 'full responsibility' for his role in banking failures.[111] Abbott agreed that under-regulation was a key cause of the crisis. 'The credit crunch was not a meteor that hit us out of the sky,' she said. 'Unregulated capitalist financial institutions will create market "bubbles" which inevitably collapse. And in societies where bankers are considered the repository of all wisdom and have far more influence than ordinary people, ordinary people will pay for the losses in that process and bankers will trouser the profits.'[112]

Abbott was particularly critical of the bonus culture in banks which incentivised bankers to prioritise short-term earnings over the long-term sustainability of their institutions and the wider economy. These practices, she argued, nearly crashed the international economy. Instead, she suggested that salaries and bonuses should be determined within regulatory structures in which mega-bonuses were eliminated or replaced by a bonus over which you would have a long-term interest.

Speaking on BBC One's *This Week*, Abbott argued that preventing another financial crisis demanded three things: capital adequacy rules, separation of investment banks with 'casino-type operations' from retail banks, and preparedness to let banks close when they fail. These were simple things, which, with the benefit of hindsight, Labour could get right. Still, when Andrew Neil asked, 'Can you give an example where Gordon Brown has taken something simple and made it simpler?' Abbott laughed, 'You're taxing me, and it's late at night.'[113]

By and large, Abbott supported Brown's response to the crisis. Writing for the *Hackney Gazette*, she stated, 'So far the government is doing its best.' She pointed to tax cuts, increases in money for pensioners and child benefits, employment support and efforts to protect the savings held within British banks and building societies.[114] Former Bank of England policymaker Danny Blanchflower later credited the budget stimulus with contributing to a 3.1 per cent growth in Britain's economy between the autumn of 2009 and 2010. Under the coalition in the year afterwards, the economy grew by 0.3 per cent.[115] Andrew Rawnsley, *The Observer*'s chief political commentator, credits Brown's bailout package with saving the country from 'the apocalypse of a total banking crisis'.[116]

Abbott also welcomed Brown's decision to bring the G20 summit to London in April 2009. While wary of its benefit beyond Western Europe, she argued that 'even if the results of the G20 will not magic away the recession it is good to see countries coming together to co-operate in finding solutions'. The summit resulted in a $1.1 trillion (then £750 billion) stimulus commitment to stabilise the global economy.[117]

The G20 summit also marked President Obama's first visit to the UK. Abbott recalls that the first time she heard of Obama was when he won a primary in Iowa. She remembers bringing up the video of Obama's speech and feeling 'a real thrill' as the significance of his presidential run began to sink in. 'I was just swept away, and I followed his campaign religiously after that.'[118] Abbott felt that, given US history, it was important for a black person to be President and to have 'a black family in the White House'. She remembers repeatedly listening to the speech that Martin Luther King Jr gave the night before he was assassinated, where he described going to the mountaintop and seeing the promised land on the other side. 'This is what Martin Luther King saw,' she smiles. 'This was the other side.'

Barack Obama was elected on 4 November 2008 and inaugurated as the forty-fourth president of the United States of America on 20 January 2009. Abbott was overjoyed. Obama 'wasn't Karl Marx or anything, but he was a progressive', she says. 'If he was more left-wing, the American system could not have accepted that ... They tended to get rid of left-wing leaders.' With the gift of hindsight, Abbott maintains, 'I remain a big Obama fan despite the drones and other stuff.'

In 2009 there were also European Parliament elections and the UK local elections; both were dismal for Labour. Labour finished in third place behind the Tories and UKIP in the European elections, and behind the Tories and the Liberal Democrats in the local elections; the party's worst result since the First World War. Unable to fan the flame of hope and optimism they ignited in 1997, Labour's thirteen-year run in power seemed to be coming to an end.

Despite being a backbencher, often out of favour with the leaders of her party, Abbott made significant contributions to policy during the Blair and Brown years. Alongside other members of the 'awkward squad', Abbott persistently voted against changes that would disadvantage the most marginalised in society. She opposed restrictions to welfare and benefits; fought for better educational prospects for children, especially black boys; and stood up for the civil liberties of the marginalised, the suspect, and the unpopular, both at home and abroad.

The fallout from sending her son to a fee-paying school threatened to end Abbott's career, but her track record and reputation among her constituents meant that she was re-elected time and time again.

CHAPTER 10

SOFAS, SOUNDBITES
AND CELEBRITY

Over the years Abbott has been courted by producers keen to get the first black women in Parliament onto their television and radio programmes, and she has welcomed the opportunity to humanise the left and make left-wing ideas accessible to the public. Abbott made several guest appearances on political talk shows and debates, but it was her regular spot on BBC One's *This Week* that saw her gain something like celebrity status. The early 2000s saw Abbott transform from an outspoken backbencher to one of the top-earning MPs in the country and one of the most influential figures on the left. In 2010, Abbott's relationship with the press underwent a considerable transition when she became the shadow Minister for Public Health. Her new frontbench position meant that she had to give up her regular *This Week* appearances. When Abbott's opposition to bombings in Syria cost her a seat on the frontbench in 2013, she returned to *This Week* with fortnightly appearances. Abbott featured on several entertainment programmes, such as *Come Dine with Me* and *Celebrity Cash in the Attic*, which painted a more playful and relatable picture of the politician. Still, it was through her participation in arts and culture programmes that her personality shone through. From listening to Abbott's exposition of the brave and amoral heroine of *Vanity Fair* or sharing her childhood memory of listening to Harry Belafonte on the radio, the public came to know Abbott the person, not just the politician.

In 1993, she appeared on Channel 4's *Clive Anderson Talks Back*, and 1995 saw her first appearance on the satirical news quiz *Have I Got News For You* in which Abbott and Ian Hislop lost to Paul Merton and comedian Julian Clary. She had better luck in later appearances. Abbott also made several appearances on *A Word in Your Ear*, a game-show which saw celebrities compete in several rounds testing their observation and communication skills. Abbott teamed up with comedian Bob Carolgees and fellow Labour MP Austin Mitchell against the likes of journalist Peter Fiddick and Michael Gove, who was then an editor at *The Times*. Abbott was not only in demand on television panel shows. On Christmas Day 1996, she starred in an all-political version of Gilbert and Sullivan's operetta *Iolanthe* on Classic FM. Edwina Currie, who came to prominence as a member of Thatcher's frontbench team in the late 1980s, sang mezzo in the title role. Abbott was joined by contralto Clare Short, then Labour's shadow Minister for Overseas Development, who starred as Queen of the Fairies; and Lord Healey, former Labour Chancellor, and Lord Howe, Thatcher's Deputy Prime Minister, cameoed as comic baritones.

THIS WEEK

Abbott explains that her willingness to appear in the media was part of an attempt to humanise the left. 'There was a tendency, even then, to caricature the left as humourless, people you couldn't relate to, people that you couldn't share a joke with,' Abbott explains. 'I think, in my mind, [my media appearances were] about showing that you can be on the left and be human.'[1] Abbott became most known for her appearances on BBC One's *This Week*, which first aired in January 2003. The show was created by Vicky Flind and hosted by Andrew Neil, the former editor of the *Sunday Times*. Michael Portillo and Abbott acted as regular commentators, squeezed onto a comically small red sofa dissecting the week's politics.

The show was part of the BBC's shake-up of their political programming which increased the budget for such shows from £5 million per year to £23.5 million with the aim of growing their reach by 20 per cent. Following *Question Time*, *This Week* aired at 11.35 on a Thursday

night. 'Even I will feel challenged to watch another 45 minutes of politics immediately after the excellent *Question Time*,' said current affairs
journalist Jonathan Dimbleby at the time.[2] But the producers hoped
that the late-night slot would appeal to a non-traditional audience.
'Whether you've just rolled in from the pub or had a tough day at the
office, tuck up and tune in for the edgiest political show on TV,' read
the listing. It promised viewers a punchy, irreverent and satirical take
on the main political stories of the week.[3]

In addition to winning over the public, Flind had to convince
Abbott to take part, as she was not immediately keen on the idea of
appearing alongside Neil and Portillo. The staunch Thatcherite, the
'scrupulously polite' Tory MP and the outspoken left-winger made
an unlikely trio.[4] Abbott had first met Portillo as a teenager when
they had been members of Convergence, the student theatrical group
based in Harrow, where they had worked together in a production of
Hamlet. However, they had not kept up the acquaintance at Cambridge and had rarely interacted in Parliament. 'These weren't people
I mixed with or had much to do with,' Abbott explains. 'I hadn't had
anything to do with Michael Portillo since I was at school in fact, and
I don't particularly like Andrew Neil.'[5]

In addition to editing the *Sunday Times*, Neil was the former editor
of *The Economist* and helped to launch Sky Television. He had also
presented BBC Two's political analysis show *Despatch Box* from 1998
until 2002 when the show was axed. Neil has confessed that his presenting style was aggressive, interrogative and derogatory but argued
that it was lightened by a sense of humour. Although Neil was one of
the best-prepared and most well-researched presenters on television,
he came to be known as 'the left's least favourite television presenter'.[6]

The show's producers persuaded Abbott to take part by reassuring
her they would only need her for a few weeks. However, as it became
clear the show was a hit, Abbott became a regular.

The programme largely stuck to a regular format. Neil would open
each episode with 'Evening all,' and close with 'That's your lot for
this week.' Abbott and Portillo would each share their moment of the
week. This was followed by two filmed segments, the 'take of the week'

and a 'round-up of the week', accompanied by an in-studio discussion with the presenter and guest. Finally, there would be more light-hearted spotlight section with a celebrity guest. Guests on the show and political figures were often awarded nicknames such as 'Glitter Balls' for Ed Balls, 'Boy George' for George Osborne and 'Bojo the Clown' for Boris Johnson. Special episodes, such as the Christmas episodes, saw Abbott, Portillo and Neil don festive outfits, and Neil's dog Miss Molly made occasional appearances.

Question Time had a direct double impact on the success of *This Week*. First, as *This Week* directly followed *Question Time*, it had an audience that was already interested in politics. Portillo would often present an intellectual and detailed analysis of political issues, and Abbott, in addition to engaging with these analyses, would give viewers exclusive, first-hand accounts of what was happening within the walls of Parliament.

Second, *This Week* offered viewers a more laid-back and, in many ways, authentic discussion of politics than its more traditional counterparts. 'People told me that they liked the show because they believed Michael and I actually said what we thought. BBC executive Alan Yentob once said he thought the programme worked because we all obviously thought that politics mattered.'[7] Samir Shah, the former head of current affairs at the BBC, agrees. '[On *Question Time*], politicians just trotted out the party line, and it became less and less interesting as a programme, because you sort of knew what everyone was going to say.'[8] In contrast, Abbott often struggled to tow the party line and Portillo was reinventing himself, moving away from hard-line Thatcherism, towards a more thoughtful and reflective position. Shah explains that it was Abbott's and Portillo's willingness to speak their mind and stray from the party line that allowed for a depth of analysis and authenticity that *Question Time* failed to provide.

Abbott took advantage of the late-night slot to distance herself from the doctrines of New Labour and express radical views. Shah explains, 'They almost forget they are on telly around midnight; that show wouldn't work at seven in the evening ... It is just like a late-night, post-dinner drinks.'[9]

Memorably, in February 2008 after the shadow Chancellor John McDonnell quoted from Mao's *Little Red Book* in the Commons, Neil asked why it was acceptable to wear a Mao T-shirt but not a Hitler T-shirt. Abbott responded, 'I suppose some people would judge that on balance, Mao did more good than harm, can't say that about the Nazis.' A stunned Portillo slapped Abbott's leg and exclaimed, 'You cannot be serious, Diane!' A brief debate on the goods and evils of Mao ensued, to which Abbott finished, 'I was just putting the case for Mao.'[10]

Abbott attributes much of the show's success to the synergy between her and Portillo, whom she grew to enjoy working with. Despite sitting in opposite camps politically, Abbott and Portillo had some things in common: both were the children of immigrants, both went to grammar schools, and both were fascinated by matters of diversity. 'To my bafflement, people often remarked on the apparent chemistry between Michael Portillo and myself,' she wrote for the *New Statesman*. 'I could never see it myself.'[11] This was in part because Abbott avoided watching and listening to her media appearances, as she found it embarrassing. Nonetheless, the pair's affinity on the programme won them the nickname of 'Itchy & Scratchy'. However, the chemistry between the pair was not replicated off screen. 'We certainly don't socialise outside of the programme,' Abbott told the *Metro*. 'We move in very different circles.'[12]

Abbott found working with Neil difficult. 'Andrew Neil felt, being Andrew Neil and being very important, he wanted to be on a show with two political heavyweights,' she explains. 'He didn't regard me as a political heavyweight. I hadn't been in the Cabinet; I hadn't been on the frontbench.' Abbott argued that once Neil realised that his friends and colleagues engaged with the show more than they did with his previous endeavours, he warmed to the idea and became 'a bit more polite than he had been in the very beginning'.[13]

She recalls a conversation where Neil, who is from a lower middle-class background in Paisley, said to her, 'Do you know what? If you and I were starting out now, we would never get where we are in the media, because now, it is all about who you know.'[14]

Abbott and Neil had a major onscreen fallout in June 2010 when Abbott was running for the Labour leadership. The coalition government had just announced the budget and Abbott expected the discussion to focus on the economy. After challenging Abbott on her travel expenses claims that were in excess of £1,000 on taxis, Neil went back to the seven-year-old topic of her son's schooling.[15]

'You said, "West Indian mums will go to the wall for their children", so black mothers love their kids more than white?' Neil asked. Abbott replied, 'Andrew, we've just had I think one of the most important budgets in a generation. I've said everything I'm going to say about where I send my son to school.' 'Supposing Michael had said white mums will go to the wall for their children?' Neil persisted. 'Why would you say that West Indian mums will go to the wall for their children, I mean isn't that a racist remark?' 'I've got nothing new to say,' Abbott repeated, steering the conversation back to the budget.

'If West Indian mums are as wonderful as you say, why are there so many dysfunctional West Indian families in this country, and so many West Indian young men end up in a life of crime and gangs? … I mean you didn't want him to go to a school full of kids that are being brought up by West Indian mums.'[16]

Portillo was visibly uncomfortable, while Abbott, still composed, explained that the issue was of schooling in Hackney which had considerably improved in the years since, not the educational ability of black boys. Again, she asserted, 'I've got nothing new to say,' and Neil finally moved on to Labour's policies.

Neil later said that he gave her a 'rough ride' as he 'could not treat her any differently' to the other Labour leadership candidates. He argued that by running for Labour leadership, she was effectively saying she could be the Prime Minister and therefore should be held to higher levels of scrutiny. He did not regret interrogating Abbott about her comments: 'To this day, I don't understand it.'[17]

Neil's attack undoubtedly made good television, but he was reducing reality, in all its complexity, to abstract platitudes. Black mothers had been blamed for delinquency, for underachievement in schools, for all manner of social ills. In that context, it made perfect sense for

Abbott to remind the audience that black mothers would go to the wall for their children. Neil's comment showed just how easy it is to turn important issues regarding race into a parlour game.

Unlike most political shows, *This Week* attracted many young new viewers and had a relatively large audience from black and Asian backgrounds. Abbott recalled that the show routinely gained more viewers than more traditional political shows and its popularity amazed the BBC's management.

> I think *This Week* was important because, at its heart, it was a show about politics, and it took politics to a much wider audience than the *Newsnight*s and the *Panorama*s and so on. It was viewed by often much younger people, and it was viewed by people who didn't read *The Guardian* or watch mainstream political shows.[18]

Abbott also noted that many black people, who otherwise disengaged from mainstream politics, watched *This Week*. 'I'm always being stopped by Jamaican grannies in the street who say, "I love you on *This Week*,"' she says. She was initially sceptical, but when they quoted her views back to her, she realised that people were actually listening. 'Any programme that can stimulate conversation about the euro is achieving something,' she remarks.[19]

The programme quickly developed a fandom. 'They were like rock stars,' Shah says. 'When we did a live show, [the audience] would just whoop and scream.' Neil, in particular, was a great showman.[20]

In March 2006, *This Week* won the Hansard Society and Channel 4 award for opening up politics. Abbott and Portillo collected the award from Channel 4's headquarters. That December, the programme also won Best National Television Programme by the Plain English Campaign in their media awards. Former winners of the award included *Newsnight*, *Channel 4 News* and *Sunday AM*.

BEYOND *THIS WEEK*

Abbott also took part in several other political shows during her time as a backbencher, such as BBC One's *The Politics Show*, BBC Radio 4's

Any Questions? and radio debate show *Down With*. On *The Big Questions*, Abbott covered wide-ranging topics from political issues such as welfare and benefits to philosophical discussions on whether people could be inherently evil – Abbott asserted that some people, like Fred West, were. In one 2007 episode, in a debate on astrology, Abbott recalled working with an astrologist at TV-am who was fired nine months into the job. 'If astrology was any good, she should at least be able to prophesy she was going to get sacked,' Abbott laughed. '[Astrology] gives a lot of people harmless pleasure, but basically its rubbish.' Abbott's contemptuous remarks failed to impress co-panellist Dr Raj Sharman, a Hindu priest and astrologer, and were notably at odds with the caricature of the diplomatic Libra.[21]

Abbott also frequently appeared on BBC Radio 4's *Woman's Hour*, where she had more freedom to talk about issues that were typically brushed aside as being women's issues. For example, in 2008, Abbott debated Democratic Unionist Party MP Jeffrey Donaldson on the matter of abortion rights in Northern Ireland. Abbott headed up the cross-party parliamentary group that put forward a proposal to amend the Human Fertilisation and Embryology Bill to bring abortion rights in Northern Ireland in line with the rest of the UK. Donaldson argued the decision should come from the Northern Ireland Assembly rather than Westminster; Abbott asserted that women in Northern Ireland were being treated as second-class citizens, devoid of the choice women in the rest of the UK possessed. In other episodes, she discussed black women in politics, family life, femininity and issues such as slut-shaming and sexualised bullying in schools.

In 2010, Abbott placed thirty-sixth in the *Daily Telegraph* list of the most influential people on the left. She remained on the list for a second year, placing thirty-eighth. Explaining their choice, Iain Dale and Brian Brivati wrote:

The idea of Diane Abbott influencing anything would have provoked hollow laughter in Labour Party circles six months ago. But not now. She knew she wouldn't win the Labour leadership, but she has skilfully used her campaign to promote her own agenda and increase her political profile throughout the media. It was rumoured she might be dropped from BBC Two's *This Week* after a fallout with Andrew Neil, but happily for her, the rumours have turned out to be false.[22]

In February 2009, the BBC announced that *This Week* would be put out to the independent sector because of its commitment to reduce the number of in-house programmes made in London. The BBC News Political Programmes department considered bids from a closed tender list and eventually the current affairs production company Juniper was selected. Samir Shah, Juniper's chief executive and former head of current affairs at the BBC, became the show's executive producer, and Flind stayed on as the editor.

'When we won the contract, the BBC gave us nothing to make it. We decided, let's just make a virtue out of the fact that this is cheap as shit,' Shah laughs. 'The moment it became independent, I could be riskier. I could be a bit more mischievous.'[23] Under Juniper, *This Week*'s opening links could be more controversial; they adopted quips like welcoming viewers to their 'miserable little studio' and mocked political heavyweights such as 'Big Bad John', the Speaker of the House. Still, the programme was committed to impartiality and continued to invite guests from all points on the political spectrum. While they did receive some complaints about bias, or for Neil being too aggressive, Shah remarks that they were largely free to do what they wanted. 'If people are going to watch telly at midnight, it's because they like the show.' The programme routinely drew 1 million viewers and was often the most watched programme at that time of day.[24]

Abbott's appointment as Miliband's shadow Minister for Public Health drastically altered her relationship with the media. Bell Ribeiro-Addy, who was a member of Abbott's office at the time, explains that the press had come to rely on Abbott's commentary on hot topics and struggled to adjust to her newfound tight lip. 'A lot of MPs needed a lot of preparation before going on TV,' Ribeiro-Addy explains. 'Diane would just rock up and deliver.' Abbott's new frontbench position meant that she had to forgo her weekly late-night slot on *This Week*.[25] Shah was gutted to lose Abbott, whom he saw as a 'rarity in politics'.

'Even with Diane on the frontbench, she won't be able to tow the party line,' he laughs.

> Trying to replace Diane [was] really difficult, and the fundamental reason it is difficult is because everyone wants to tow the party line. [Abbott and Portillo] were prepared to say things that were out of step ... they cared about politics, it actually mattered. It never was, 'Let me score a political point.'[26]

Abbott made occasional guest appearances on *This Week*, such as in the Christmas episodes. However, some thought that these appearances were too frequent. In January 2012, Ulster Unionist peer Lord Laird complained that Abbott had received five payments of £839 and one of £869 for her guest appearances on *This Week* since being on the frontbench. Laird claimed that he was concerned that Abbott would 'profit financially' from the licence fee, which was, after all, public money. The BBC initially defended the payments, explaining that Abbott's role on *This Week* was that of a co-presenter rather than a guest MP or frontbencher. Laird, however, was unsatisfied and appealed. The BBC Trust's editorial standards committee conceded and ruled that she had appeared too frequently. The committee concluded that MPs 'speaking as a member of their party or expressing political views' should only receive a small disturbance fee. Abbott's appearances, they argued, should have been limited to once or twice a year.[27]

Lord Laird's righteous concern about the proper use of public money contrasted sharply with his own practice. Indeed, in 2008 and 2009, he claimed £73,000 in expenses from the public purse for his duties as a lord. Notably, he attended Parliament on only 145 occasions in 2008–09.[28] Moreover, his apparent concern for standards in public life was at odds with his own behaviour. At the very time he was making complaints about Abbott, Laird was offering to ask parliamentary questions for wealthy clients. Journalists caught him on tape offering to put questions to ministers for a retainer of £2,000 a month.[29] The details of Laird's corruption were exposed in 2013. Laird was subsequently suspended from Parliament for four months and resigned the Ulster Unionist whip. In this context, Laird discussed his campaign against Abbott, holding it up as an example of the influence he had, influence that was available for the right money.

Another conflict between Abbott's frontbench role and her life in the media arose when she was invited to take part in an episode of *Question Time* that was to be held in Scotland. The leader's office did not approve, their preference being for a Scottish MP. However, the producers were keen to reach beyond Scottish viewers and appeal to the rest of the UK. 'Lucy Powell MP tried to bully me out of going,' she remembers. 'I thought first of all, who is Lucy Powell to tell me anything? Second of all, this is ludicrous.'[30] Abbott, who was a *Question Time* regular, participated anyway.

Abbott also had a good relationship with Sky, having worked with Adam Boulton at TV-am previously. She recalls that on one occasion she had been invited to take part in a review of the papers on Sky News but was met with resistance from Healey's office. She remembers one of the Sky researchers telling her they had come under 'tremendous pressure from John Healey's office' to drop her from the programme. Abbott adds that she was also continuously reported to the leader's office for various things she had said and done. In part, she believes, this was because Healey was threatened by her. 'I was better known than he was and remain better known.'[31]

After leaving the frontbench in 2013, Abbott returned to *This Week* with fortnightly appearances, alternating with Alan Johnson. She left the programme in 2015 and did not return until the final episode aired in 2019. While Johnson, Neil and Portillo worked well together, Shah was reluctant to have three white men presenting the programme. Eventually, Liz Kendall and Miranda Green became regulars on the show. In her reflections on the programme, Abbott commented, '*This Week* was often imitated but never surpassed.'[32]

ART AND LITERATURE

Although the public grew to know Abbott through *This Week*, her humanity best shone through in her love of arts and culture. Abbott's home is furnished by books. As might be expected, her shelves are full of volumes on politics, including work by 'some dreadful right-wingers'.[33] Some bookcases are devoted to Caribbean politics and history; others, to studies of Britain and America, Robert Caro being particularly well represented.

In terms of poetry and prose, Abbott is drawn to literature in which her life is reflected. This is illustrated by her book of choice in a 1997 episode of BBC Radio 4's *A Good Read*. Abbott praised Iain Sinclair's odyssey *Lights Out for the Territory* for its vivid and familiar portrayal of the streets of London. Similarly, in a 2002 episode of Radio 4's *With Great Pleasure*, Abbott explained that she admired and saw aspects of herself in the feisty heroines in Louisa May Alcott's *Little Women*, William Congreve's *The Way of the World* and William Thackeray's *Vanity Fair*. 'I read far fewer novels than I did in my twenties,' Abbott acknowledges, 'but I still read novels by black women writers.'[34]

In 2007, Abbott made guest appearances on BBC Radio 4's *The Art of Parliament*, presented by her long-time sparring partner Michael Portillo. Abbott shared her experience of having her portrait painted. Tony Banks, the chairman of the Speaker's Advisory Committee on Works of Art, commissioned Stuart Pearson Wright, an award-winning portrait artist who has also painted J. K. Rowling and the Duke of Edinburgh. The portrait was unveiled in 2004 and depicts a striking bare-shouldered Abbott and was hung in the contemporary art display in Portcullis House.[35]

In a second episode on artwork exhibited in the parliamentary art collection, Abbott shared that she was drawn to a mural of the Battle of Trafalgar which contained a depiction of a black sailor. Abbott explained that for a long time, this was the only painting of a black person in Westminster which spoke volumes about the history that parliamentary artwork represented. 'It is very much the history of Empire,' she told Portillo. 'It is very much the history of the ruling class, it is very much a version of British history which suited a Westminster elite who, in those days, ran an Empire.'[36]

FACTUAL ENTERTAINMENT TELEVISION

By the early 2000s, Abbott was regularly invited onto reality shows, including ITV's *Dancing on Ice* and an African dance version of *Strictly Come Dancing*. Abbott laughs that she turned them down after a friend reminded her that she could not, in fact, dance. However, her reality TV moment came with BBC One's *Play It Again*. The series followed six public figures as they tried to master a musical instrument, and Abbott decided to learn to play the piano. She remembered growing up surrounded by music and stories of her professional violinist great-uncle Adrian. Abbott recalls that the producers were surprised at her choice of instrument: 'I suppose they thought I might say the bongo drums or something.'[37]

As a complete novice, Abbott spent six months learning to read music and play the piano under the tutelage of Professor Paul Roberts. She would wake at 6 a.m. to practise before commencing her daily political duties. Drawing on her time in the Black Media Workers' Association, Abbott was keen to diversify the all-white production team while working on the programme. This became especially important when plans were made to film in Jamaica and Abbott asked them to recruit black people. 'I was in a relatively privileged position because I did not need to do [the programme]. By me putting my foot down, I gave one or two other people the chance of a job.'[38]

Abbott's fears about taking a majority white production team to Jamaica were realised when the crew expressed the desire to film somewhere more 'quintessentially Jamaican' instead of her uncle's house in the suburbs of Kingston. 'They wanted a shanty town, and they couldn't understand that there were people in Jamaica who lived like that.'[39]

Nonetheless, Abbott enjoyed taking part in the programme. Although she found learning the piano challenging, her hard work culminated in a performance of Chopin's 'Prelude in E Minor' at a public recital. The episode aired in April 2007. Abbott continued to practise her scales in the months that followed; however, other priorities soon got in the way. Abbott remained grateful to Roberts for sharing his love of music with her, and in her appearance on BBC Radio 4's *Desert Island Discs* she shared a recording of Roberts playing Claude Debussy's 'Reflections in the Water' on the piano.[40]

Abbott's literary knowledge was tested on screen in 2009 when she featured on an episode of BBC Four's *The Book Quiz*. Ironically, Abbott was paired with James Delingpole, the author of *How to be Right: The Essential Guide to Making Lefty Liberals History*. The pair lost to fiction writer Jenny Colgan and the then shadow Education Secretary, Michael Gove. Abbott also competed alongside former Tory MP Edwina Currie in an episode of *Pointless Celebrities*. The pair made it to the final and Abbott donated her winnings to the Sickle Cell Society.

In 2012, she represented Newnham College, Cambridge, for a Christmas special of *University Challenge*. The Newnham team beat their all-male Nottingham opponents 155 to 110 but did not make it to the semi-finals. She also returned to *Have I Got News For You* in 2006, where she and Paul Merton narrowly lost to David Mitchell and Ian Hislop, and again in 2015, where she and Merton claimed victory against Hislop and Nish Kumar.

Abbott also competed on Channel 4's *Celebrity Come Dine with Me*. Only two politicians had previously appeared on the show, Edwina Currie and the Welsh Liberal Democrat MP Lembit Öpik, and Abbott was the first serving MP to take part. She was joined on the episode by TV presenter Terry Christian, reality TV star and former Miss England Danielle Lloyd, who admitted she did not know who Abbott was, and ballet dancer and director Wayne Sleep.[41] Abbott's dinner was characterised by ceaseless laughter, occasional wine spillage and raucous conversation. Terry gave Abbott a score of seven; Danielle did not take to the dessert and scored her six, while Wayne, who lauded Abbott's rum punch the star of the night, scored her eight. The three subsequent dinners were equally lively, and in the end, Abbott and Wayne came joint third with a score of twenty-one, Terry second with twenty-three and Danielle first with twenty-four.

Some took issue with Abbott's £3,000 fee for thirty-six hours of filming for the show. Others questioned how the frontbencher could find the time to be on reality TV. Suzanne Moore, a journalist who ran as an independent candidate against Abbott at the 2010 general election, commented, 'I guess Diane does as she pleases,' and sneered that Abbott may as well pursue a career in reality shows as her future in politics would be short-lived: 'It did wonders for George Galloway. I can't wait for Diane on *Strictly*.'[42] However, Abbott had declared her earnings in the appropriate way and, had she won, would have donated her winnings to charity. She also explained that she arranged for the filming to take place outside of her normal working hours: 'I would never have done the show if it took time away from my work in Parliament or representing my constituents.'[43]

For BBC Two's *Cash in the Celebrity Attic*, Diane Abbott welcomed Chris Hollins and antiques expert Paul Hayes into her home with the hope of selling items for charity. She was joined by her long-time friend and antique lover Marsha McDermott. Again, Abbott chose to raise money for the Sickle Cell Society, stressing the fact that the disease affects predominantly African and Caribbean people and that she wanted to raise awareness of the disease. Her aim was £250. The team came up with an eclectic collection for auction, which included paintings and prints, a solid oak bureau, a cast-iron Libra scale, and a brass key from her appearance on the ITV game show *Through the Keyhole*. At auction, the items made £239 for the charity.

An MP is a representative, and Abbott has fulfilled this role in the Commons and in the media, speaking up for the people she represents. Her engagement with the media is also profoundly democratic. In a democracy, debate is not restricted to the floor of the legislature. Debate happens in the pages of newspapers, on television and on radio, in blogs and on Twitter. Abbott was involved in this debate before she entered Parliament, and she has continued to be involved in public debate since becoming an MP. In so doing she has fulfilled her constitutional role scrutinising the government, sharing her views not only in the Commons but with the public at large through articles in newspapers, and appearances on television. Her participation in both political and non-political programmes has served to humanise the left and make politicians, and politics more widely, accessible to the public. Abbott has managed to capture the enviable attention of young people and ethnic minorities across the country, groups consistently underserved by mainstream politics, which has placed her in a unique position to spur them to action. Through the media, Abbott has appealed for citizens to play their part, keep a watchful eye on their representatives, organise themselves and make their voices heard.

CHAPTER 11

'IF NOT NOW, WHEN?
IF NOT ME, WHO?'

'**C**leggmania' hit Hackney early in the 2010 election campaign. When out canvassing, Abbott was dismayed to discover that one of her constituents was more interested in hearing Nick Clegg on the TV than talking to her MP face-to-face. Clegg's brief spell of popularity directly followed the first televised leadership debate, which was an innovation in British electoral politics. The debate, which began with feverish speculation on Twitter that there had been a last-minute rethink of David Cameron's hair, ended with a new phrase entering the lexicon: 'I agree with Nick.'[1]

Abbott argues that the Conservatives ran a shrewd campaign, with slogans such as 'Vote Blue, Go Green' disguising their real ambitions. Triangulation – a strategy of conceding ground to the Conservatives in an attempt to capture the centre ground, hurt Labour. Abbott argues it gave the impression that the parties were essentially the same. Certainly, on immigration, the main parties were singing from the same spreadsheet. The issue's salience was obvious from the fact that the first TV debate opened with a question on the subject. Cameron, using a technique pioneered by Enoch Powell, raised the spectre of 2 million immigrants entering Britain in the coming decade. He promised to reduce net migration to the tens of thousands by putting a numerical cap on migration from outside the EU. Memorably, he argued,

I was in Plymouth recently, and a forty-year-old black man actually made the point to me. He said, 'I came here when I was six, served in the Royal Navy for thirty years, I'm incredibly proud of my country. But I'm so ashamed that we've had this out-of-control system with people abusing it so badly.' So if we don't address immigration properly we are actually letting down immigrant communities, as well as everybody else.[2]

Neal Forde, the 'forty-year-old black man' whom Cameron claimed had spent thirty years in the Royal Navy, told *The Guardian* a few days later that he had been misquoted. Nonetheless, Labour was on the defensive. Abbott recalls that Ed Miliband made a series of speeches on immigration in the run-up to the election. 'I remember talking to him about it, and he said, "We've got to say these things, to get permission to be heard on everything else."'[3]

Cameron's vision was the 'Big Society'. It was this notion that held together his emollient rhetoric with the promise of swingeing cuts. In response, Abbott argued that West Indians who arrived in Britain in the 1950s knew all about the Big Society. With no state support, they had to rely on self-help and community solidarity. However, Abbott was sceptical, arguing that the Big Society was simply a way of marketing big cuts.

On election night, Abbott bucked the national trend and doubled her majority, on an increased turnout. Labour also did better than expected. After thirteen years in office, after the credit crunch, and up against a young and plausible Conservative leader, it was widely expected that the Conservatives would win outright. However, despite a 5 per cent swing, the Tories were still around twenty seats short of a majority.

The hung parliament created an opportunity for Labour. Together, Labour and the Liberal Democrats had 315 seats. This was not a majority, but it was more than the Conservatives, and could have provided the basis for a minority administration. Abbott was against a coalition, not that anyone in the Labour leadership sought her opinion. 'I was concerned about what it would mean for an already triangulated policy platform, and I didn't think you could trust the Lib Dems anyway.'[4]

Abbott was astonished by the coalition agreement. It represented a dramatic *volte-face* by the Liberal Democrats, who had fought the election opposing austerity and promising to scrap tuition fees. 'It was shocking,' Abbott recalls, 'even to someone who is deeply cynical about the Lib Dems.' Abbott spoke out against the coalition on *This Week*. Responding to news that Billy Bragg, a left-wing singer songwriter, had made some positive remarks about the new coalition, Abbott commented, 'I think Billy is being a little bit naïve. I mean one of the things about this new leadership is how post-meritocratic it is. Two posh white boys from the home counties.'[5] The comment caused a Twitter storm, which was reported in the *Daily Mail*.[6] As was the case during Abbott's debate with Cyril Smith on *Question Time* twenty years earlier, the fact that she had acknowledged and mentioned race was taken as a sign of racism. If her critics were to be believed, simply calling white people 'white' equated to bigotry. The impact of social media, Abbott opines, was part of the problem: 'New media has made it easier to stir up hostility and opposition to politicians who some people in society don't like anyway.'[7]

LEADERSHIP CONTEST

Immediately after the election, Gordon Brown stayed in No. 10 as head of government, fulfilling his constitutional duty until a new administration emerged. Nonetheless, the election result had made his position as Labour leader untenable. Labour's defeat had been expected. Therefore, even before he resigned, David Miliband, Ed Miliband, Ed Balls and Andy Burnham began gearing up for a leadership contest. In the immediate aftermath of the election, Abbott had no intention of standing. David Miliband was the first to announce his candidacy, his brother followed a day later, and over the next few days Balls and John McDonnell entered the race.

Initially, Labour MPs were given four days, from 24 to 28 May, to submit their nominations. However, after McDonnell complained that this was an 'establishment stitch-up' to ensure that only the leading figures in New Labour were able to get on the ballot the nomination period was extended to 9 June.

During the period of coalition negotiations, Abbott recalls receiving a 'trickle' of letters urging her to stand and how she was 'taken aback' at the suggestion, as she had no intention of entering the race. The two people who had the most influence on her decision were Harriet Harman, then acting Labour leader, and David Lammy. Harman, she recalls,

> arranged to meet with me and said, 'I think you should run for the leadership.' Harriet and I don't agree on everything politically, but [she] is a genuine feminist, I've known her since I worked in the National Council for Civil Liberties and she's always been a feminist. Harriet's view was that she just thought it was quite wrong for the party to have a leadership contest which was four white men.[8]

Harman's suggestion was a bolt from the blue, and Abbott was not immediately persuaded.

However, David Lammy also helped Abbott make up her mind. Before the 2010 election the two did not move in the same circles in the PLP. Nonetheless at a chance meeting in the Portcullis House café Lammy told Abbott that he would back her if she ran. 'I wanted her to run,' recalls Lammy, 'because I wanted her to make history. We needed a black candidate to get through and actually go the distance, I knew that Diane kicking through that door was important. And the candidates were all the same, they were all men who had been to Oxbridge.'[9] Lammy counted Balls and the Miliband brothers, David particularly, as his friends. But he also felt a sense of loyalty to Abbott, for her support for his candidacy in Tottenham. Knowing that she had the backing of Harman and Lammy, and mindful of what was at stake, Abbott decided to run.

Keith Vaz argues that Abbott's decision to stand had a profound impact on the race. He claims that Abbott's intervention persuaded David Miliband of the necessity of a diverse field. Vaz was a staunch supporter of Miliband and had already begun campaigning on his behalf when Abbott entered the race, so he was shocked when he bumped into Miliband and discovered his intention to nominate

Abbott. Vaz argues that Abbott's primary goal in entering the contest was to put issues which affect Britain's ethnic minority communities on the agenda.[10]

Abbott declared her candidacy on 20 May. Pundits were perplexed. Andrew Neil was one of the first to speak to Abbott after her announcement. Clearly shocked, he asked, 'Did you wake up this morning and have a rush of blood to the head? What happened?' Jane Garvey asked if Abbott was the real outsider on *Woman's Hour* as McDonnell was the only one of the six candidates not to go to Oxford or Cambridge. Abbott made her case to *ITV News* at the end of the day, explaining that her decision to run was about ensuring,

> A range of candidates for leadership which reflects the Labour movement's diversity. But above all it was about the issues. Unless you broaden the range of candidates there's a whole series of issues ranging from civil liberties to what we are doing in Afghanistan, which will simply be off the table ... Britain has changed, the Labour Party has changed. Eighteen months ago, people would have said that America wasn't ready for a black President. I believed that we are ready for a black President. My view is that we are ready for a black leader of one of the major parties. My view is, if not now when, and if not me who?[11]

Harman, Abbott argues, had assumed that Abbott would get the backing of the Campaign Group. This was not the case. Certainly, some were excited by Abbott's candidacy. But others thought that she should give McDonnell a clear run. There were some in the Campaign Group, Abbott recalls, who felt that she was not left-wing enough. 'This was news to me, after years of standing on picket lines and supporting left-wing policies.'[12] Abbott also got the impression that many of the issues that she had championed, particularly race and civil liberties, were not the top priorities of some Campaign Group MPs. Consequently, some of McDonnell's supporters visited Abbott and asked her to step aside. Entreaties of this kind merely strengthened her resolve. Initially, Kelvin Hopkins, Linda Riordan and Jon Trickett were the only Campaign Group MPs to support Abbott. Corbyn argues that the period around the nominations in 2010 'wasn't our finest hour on the Labour left'. He recalls that the response of some in the Campaign Group reflected recent history.

> In 2007, when Gordon Brown became leader, John McDonnell put himself forward and despite a very effective national campaign, did not get the necessary number of nominations. In 2010, we then had this very difficult situation where John and Diane were both nominated. I nominated John, other people nominated Diane. Then there were some very difficult conversations between them about who should do it. My view was that John had stood before and therefore had some right to do it again.[13]

Corbyn recalls that Abbott and McDonnell reached an 'uneasy compromise', agreeing that the candidate with fewest nominations should drop out and call on their supporters to back the remaining candidate.[14]

Although Abbott could not count on the support of the Campaign Group, she had the support of other MPs. Keith Vaz – the only one of the original Black Sections MPs other than Abbott still in the Commons – gave her his nomination. What is more, Lammy acted as her *de facto* campaign manager. 'What was clear to me,' Lammy recalls, 'in order to get the nominations, she needed to run a different kind of campaign, start in a different place to where John McDonnell had started.'[15] Lammy knew that Abbott needed to reach out beyond the left to get on the ballot. However, 'Diane, at that point, was not popular in the PLP ... The people who do well, are the people who lick arse, and Diane doesn't do that! She really doesn't do that!' Her group of friends and natural allies in the PLP were small. Lammy hoped to reach out, on her behalf, to other sections of the PLP.

Lammy's decision to campaign for Abbott was costly. For many years, he and Miliband had been close friends. It was a friendship that went beyond politics, the two were close socially, as were their families. 'David was pretty upset. I said to [him], "I'm going to nominate

Diane, I think she's got to be on the ballot, I've got to do this, I cannot be persuaded otherwise."' Lammy also advised Miliband that, as he had such a commanding lead, he should allow some of his supporters to nominate Abbott. Miliband, Lammy recalls, did not respond well, at least not initially. Abbott had been critical of Miliband in the past, and, for a while at least, he was not willing to forget that. 'But he came around,' says Lammy.

Lammy advised Abbott to speak to Miliband, to see if he would 'lend' her some nominations. With more than eighty MPs expected to back him, he had votes to spare. Abbott had no idea what to expect from her meeting with Miliband, but she came away with the promise that, if she got close enough, Miliband would ask some of his supporters to get her over the line. Speaking to *The Times* a few days before nominations closed, Balls said he too had appealed to some of his supporters to help widen the field.[16] An appearance by Abbott on *Woman's Hour* indicated that Balls was not alone. However, Abbott also pointed to the fact that kind words from Labour MPs rarely meant anything. 'I'm talking to too many MPs who say, "It's marvellous you're on the ballot, Diane, but I can't nominate you because I've promised Ed or Ed, or Miliband or Miliband."'[17] Abbott appealed to female voters and female members of the Labour Party, telling them that if they wanted a woman on the ballot, they should lobby their Labour MP.

Nonetheless, Harman and Miliband were working behind the scenes to support Abbott's candidacy. Stephen Twigg, who was then Harman's parliamentary private secretary, recalls that she was keen for him to nominate Abbott, 'Harriet Harman first spoke to me about nominating Diane, I was initially reluctant because I wanted to nominate David Miliband. However, both Harriet and David were persuasive in making the case for me to nominate Diane, so I did.'[18]

Meg Hillier, MP for Abbott's neighbouring constituency of Hackney South and Shoreditch, also nominated her. Hillier supported David Miliband, but felt that 'at the hustings, when she had been nominated, if I closed my eyes, all of them sounded a bit the same. I remember saying to Diane, "If it's not too much of an insult, you're the

grit in the oyster." We needed somebody to shake it up a bit.'[19] Hillier
remembers the feeling, in the David Miliband camp, that it would be
good to broaden the debate, and as her neighbour in Hackney, and as
a 'sister in the party' felt she should help Abbott across the line.

Despite their best efforts, on 8 June, the day before the nominations
closed, Abbott had secured only eleven nominations. This was well
short of the thirty-three necessary to get on the ballot; it also meant
that she was way behind her rivals McDonnell, who had secured sixteen, and Burnham who had thirty-one. Consequently, Abbott ended
the day assuming that her campaign was over.

The next morning, everything changed. Just after 10 a.m. a friend
phoned telling her that McDonnell had withdrawn. The day before,
McDonnell had asked Harman to lower the threshold so that he and
Abbott could both go forward. Once it became clear that this was
impossible, he issued a statement withdrawing, 'in the hope that we
can at least secure a woman on the ballot paper'.[20] Significantly, he did
not endorse Abbott, nor was she named in his statement.

McDonnell's withdrawal put sixteen votes back into play. Moreover,
'there was a moment', Lammy recalls, 'on the morning, where David
[Miliband], indicated to some of his followers that they could support
Diane. That's what allowed me to say to Diane, "It's on."'[21] Abbott
received Lammy's call on the train heading into Westminster. By the
time she arrived in the Commons, Denis MacShane and Chris Bryant
had nominated her, as had Miliband himself. Lammy had brought
Rushanara Ali on board and Abbott also secured the nominations
of a handful of McDonnell's former backers, including Corbyn and
Ronnie Campbell. Campbell was hesitant about supporting Abbott,
he explains, on the basis that 'if John McDonnell couldn't get the
nominations, Diane Abbott isn't going to get them. I was floating
with the idea of going with somebody else, but at the finish I decided
to nominate Diane and give her a chance.'[22] Lammy remembers that
Dennis Skinner was initially of the same mind.

However, with half an hour to the close of nominations, Abbott
was still a few votes short. Abbott and Lammy, both on their mobiles

trying to persuade waverers, ran down to the cloisters where the voting was taking place. They learned that Dennis Skinner had yet to cast his vote. Skinner was believed to be in Prime Minister's Questions (PMQs), which was due to finish after nominations closed. Down in the cloisters Harman had instructed Tony Lloyd, chair of the PLP, to keep the ballot open until PMQs was over, to give Abbott a chance to pick up her last few votes.

The PLP staff, no fans of the left, were not pleased. Nonetheless, they complied, giving Abbott another thirty minutes to pick up the last three votes. Lammy remembers constantly 'scuttling back and forth' between the Commons and the PLP office in the final minutes before nominations closed.

Having secured the extension Abbott returned to the Chamber. Campbell recalls, 'Dennis Skinner hadn't nominated her, right up to half past twelve. She came to sit in the Chamber, [and] sat beside Dennis begging him to go straight down and put a nomination in for her. She was hanging on by a thread at that moment. We all thought it was a waste of time, she wouldn't get the nominations.'[23] Nonetheless, once PMQs was over Skinner made his way to the cloisters, nominating Abbott with the words, 'There you go.'[24]

At the eleventh hour, Phil Woolas arrived. Despite coming from different wings of the party, Abbott and Woolas were on good terms and he had promised his support if Abbott got close. Jack Straw was the last to jump on board. 'I said, "Jack do you want to make history?"' Lammy recalls. Straw agreed on the understanding that his nomination was the one that put Abbott on the ballot.[25]

'David and I knew that we'd got it, and we stood there in the cloisters, and held each other, and cried. Because we knew whatever happened, the fact that a black person could even get on the ballot for the Labour leadership was something.'[26] Lammy, too, remembers the impact of that moment:

It was quite emotional. We were in the PLP office, with Phil Woolas and a couple of Labour Party staff, when they announced she had got on the ballot, and Diane and I just burst into tears. We literally just held each other and burst into tears. It was just one of those historic moments, we were aware of the weight of it.[27]

Woolas, Lammy remembers, was also swept up in the moment, 'the fact that we were weeping, made him weep'.

After the nominations closed the five candidates were ushered into Harriet Harman's office. The acting leader outlined the rules of the contest. The Miliband brothers left, followed by Burnham and Balls, but Harman invited Abbott into a side office. Abbott recalls Harman saying, 'I want you to remember, Diane, that from now on you are part of the leadership of this party, and you must never forget it.'[28] Abbott acknowledges that up until that point she had had an insurgent mentality. Harman's words had a lasting impact. Abbott realised that getting on to the ballot had given her a new role in the party.

Again, there was surprise in the media. Gary O'Donoghue, speaking on the *BBC News at One*, was one of the first to respond to Abbott's nomination. He argued that her candidacy was a shock as since becoming a regular on *This Week* it was widely assumed that she had abandoned political ambition. O'Donoghue attributed her success to McDonnell, 'whose withdrawal' he claimed, 'delivered the votes to get Diane Abbott on the ballot paper'.[29] The next day, the *Daily Mail* argued that Abbott's candidacy was the result of David Miliband's desire to fragment the left-wing vote and undermine his brother.[30] While the narratives were quite different, in both cases reporters depicted Abbott as the passive beneficiary, while McDonnell and Miliband were described as being wholly responsible for Abbott's achievement.

LEADERSHIP CAMPAIGN

The campaign schedule was packed. On the day the candidates were announced, almost forty hustings had been advertised. More were added as the campaign went on. Abbott spent a great deal of time on trains, going back and forth to Leeds, Southampton, Newcastle,

Glasgow and Cardiff. Thinking ahead to all the public appearances, she phoned a friend and asked to borrow some smart clothes.

Abbott enjoyed the campaign. The hustings were about making an argument, about engaging in debate and about meeting people; all activities she enjoyed. She also relished the chance to engage with different people from across the country.

Prior to the campaign, Abbott had never spent much time with the other contenders. They were, she says, 'the young princes of New Labour' and therefore moved in different circles. These 'young princes', Abbott quickly learned, were out of touch with the party membership. 'The thing that shocked them,' she remembers, 'was what a good response I got.'[31]

One of the first statements of support came from the University of Cambridge's Labour Club. In terms of alumni they were spoilt for choice in the election, Abbott and Burnham were both Cambridge graduates. Some of the university's Labour Club volunteered to work on Abbott's campaign, which coincided with the long summer vacation, so students from across the country could spend at least some of their holidays volunteering for one or other of the campaigns.

Bell Ribeiro-Addy was a student volunteer on Abbott's campaign. A graduate student at the time, she later became Abbott's chief of staff before being elected MP for Streatham in 2019. Ribeiro-Addy joined Abbott's campaign at the very beginning. She was one of a small group who accompanied Abbott to hustings up and down the country. The Associated Society of Locomotive Engineers and Firemen (ASLEF), she recalls, provided an early boost to the campaign. ASLEF gave Abbott an office in north London which she could use as her headquarters. Having met with all five of the candidates, the union leadership endorsed Abbott. Ribeiro-Addy remembers hearing that ASLEF were leaning toward Abbott before meeting the other candidates. The meetings confirmed their choice. Apparently, David Miliband's pitch focused on triangulation and the ASLEF officials were unimpressed. They wanted someone who supported the renationalisation of the railways. ASLEF's members were of the same mind. In fact, during the vote of affiliated organisations, ASLEF had the highest turnout of any of the unions.[32] The Musicians' Union followed the same pattern: not only did its members back Abbott, they were in the top three in terms of voting turnout.

Abbott got some flack early in the campaign, when the BBC reported that she had referred to her rivals as 'young geeks in suits'. However, speaking to *The Guardian* she put the record straight. Laura Kuenssberg, she claimed, had presented her with the phrase, and when Abbott failed to demur, reported it as her view. Abbott put it differently: 'All of them are very nice, nice suits, nice red ties, nice haircuts. They're all very nice.'[33]

LEADERSHIP HUSTINGS

The first hustings took place on the evening of the PLP vote and was organised by the *New Statesman* and the CND. Abbott remembers the magazine's staff were much more deferential to the other candidates. However, at the beginning of the debate Abbott received the largest cheer of the five candidates from the audience.

A YouGov opinion poll published at the end of July 2010 put Abbott third among both party members and trade union members, behind the Miliband brothers, but ahead of Burnham and Balls. For a moment Abbott allowed herself to wonder what would happen if she won. However, she had no illusions about her chances.

For Burnham, the campaign was the time during which he 'got to know Diane properly'.[34] They were often on the same train and spent a great deal of time together in green rooms. Burnham recalls the atmosphere before the debate was always awkward, 'as the two brothers were trying to psych each other out'. This brought Abbott, Burnham and Balls together as they joked about the family dynamic. 'The three of us were often left chatting among ourselves, as the two brothers had horns locked psychologically in another corner of the room. We were in the middle of that psycho drama!' Burnham recalls.

In policy terms, Abbott had an early impact. She remembers, 'they started off talking about immigration' rehearsing Brown's formula about the 'real concerns' of the white working class. Abbott pushed back. During the first big debate, she argued:

> Like two other candidates on this platform, I am the child of im-migrants, and I have a particular take on this issue ... I believe that this talk of immigration, which you hear on the doorsteps and is re-flected in the polling is actually a proxy for the angst of the working class, both black and white. Angst about the lack of decent housing ... Angst about job insecurity and low wages ... And if there's one thing I want to say as this campaign wears on, we as a Labour move-ment ought to be addressing those real issues rather than playing the old tune about how immigrants ... are the cause of the problems of the working class. Nothing could be more wrong, nothing could be more historically misconceived, and nothing could do more to divert us from our real mission as a Labour movement which is to address the real issues that face our people.[35]

Abbott's statement precipitated prolonged applause – in fact, the chair commented, 'the most applause of the night for that answer'. When Burnham made a case for a 'rigorous' immigration and asylums system, the audience's response was more muted. The same was true when Balls argued that immigration would only be 'politically sustainable' if it was coupled with firm controls. Several of the candidates argued that immigration was a subject that people were afraid to confront, and afraid to discuss. Here again, Abbott broke with the consensus:

> I just want to nail this myth that no one is allowed to talk about immigration ... It's a myth peddled by the Tory press. In the last thirty years, in every administration, we've had a major, and in my view largely misbegotten, immigration and asylum bill. Every Par-liament, we had a new bill. If you read the papers, every day in some paper or another, you will read about immigration. The idea that politicians don't talk about immigration at Westminster, or that the media don't talk about it is a myth.

Immigration, Abbott argued, was a defining issue for the Labour Party. Despite polls and attacks in the press, she argued that Labour should adopt a principled stance. Again, Abbott received thunderous applause. The debate moved on with Burnham acknowledging, 'Diane's got it right.' David Miliband concurred, taking on his brother, he argued, 'I don't feel this reticence … there's a lot of talking about it. I don't think it's somehow off limits.'

During the discussion on immigration, Abbott shared the experience of her parents, talking about their aspirations, how they had felt about the Labour Party and how they had felt about Britain. Abbott's approach stood in stark contrast to the recent statements made by Cameron, Brown, Balls and Ed Miliband. Cameron pointed to huge figures, making immigration about the faceless millions coming into Britain, threatening the prospects of those already here. Ed Miliband and Balls abstracted the issue in a different way, reducing immigration to a problem of policy presentation. Abbott, however, humanised the issue and made it about the experience of real people, who lived real lives. In so doing, she changed the debate. 'When they saw how a Labour audience responded to me, they dialled it back.'[36] David Miliband, she recalls, was the exception: he was the only other candidate who had no time for the 'real concerns' narrative. Miliband and Abbott came to the same conclusion from different premises. Miliband was a neo-liberal who believed in the free movement of capital, and, crucially, the free movement of labour. Abbott had taken a dim view of some of Miliband's activities in government, but she respected his refusal to 'go down the road of populist rhetoric about migration and the white working class'.[37]

Sophia Rosenfeld argues that populism is best understood as a position which starts from the assertion that 'the people' have been robbed by an 'elite'.[38] Notably, the 'elite' is usually conceived as a coalition of people with some kind of power who are in an alliance with a minority group. Importantly, populists claim that 'the people' have been robbed of the right to organise society according to 'common sense', as they see it. Rosenfeld's argument fits the New Labour years, at least to some extent. In terms of civil liberties, the European Court of Justice was the powerful 'elite' which sided with minority groups. The idea that prisoners should be given the right to vote, to take one example, was regarded as an affront to 'common sense'. New Labour's refusal to enfranchise prisoners aligned the government with the concerns of populists. Similarly, New Labour's immigration rhetoric can be understood as populist in the sense that it reflected 'common sense' views that Britain was 'full', and that 'the people' were being 'robbed' by minorities from overseas. Rather than being a bastion against populism, New Labour and Cameron's governments should be regarded, at the very least, as sympathetic to populist narratives.

Abbott was determined to counter populist narratives during the leadership campaign in 2010. Her interventions proved effective. Certainly, the discussion on immigration changed radically during the campaign. Speaking on *Question Time*, in the final major debate of the campaign, Burnham blamed New Labour's failure to build houses for the concerns about immigration, an argument that Abbott had been making since the very beginning of the contest. Ribeiro-Addy, who was with Abbott at many of the debates also noticed the shift: 'If you listened to the hustings over time, after a while, all of their answers started to lean towards Diane's. It was impressive that, although they were looking at Diane as a kind of underdog, she was changing the tone of the whole process.'[39]

Abbott changed the debate in another way too. During the *New Statesman* and CND hustings, there was a great deal of discussion about values, policy, personal qualities, morality and strategy, but very little discussion of personal biography. Even the discussion of the rivalry between the Miliband brothers did not lead to any discussion of personal history. Rather, it prompted Ed Miliband to announce that their mother was voting for Abbott (he later clarified that he was joking). Abbott was the only candidate to talk about her personal history and the experience of her parents and this went down well with the audience. Quickly, the other contenders began seasoning their arguments with references to their own experience and their families. During the Norwich hustings, which took place towards the end of the campaign, Balls made reference to his 'mum and dad' and their experience in North Norfolk, a seat which Labour had lost in 1970 and never regained.[40] Burnham told the story of 'seeing my grandmother go into care' before making the case for a national care service.[41] On the subject of immigration, David Miliband talked about being 'the first person in my family to be born in this country'.[42] Abbott, it seems, taught the 'young princes of New Labour' something about political communication.

The impact that she was having on the hustings galvanised Abbott and her team. It showed that progressive arguments, even those which were out of step with accepted wisdom, could cut through.

In addition to the hustings, Abbott set out her platform in the press, in magazines and on television. When discussing New Labour's record, Abbott agreed with David Miliband: there was a need to be proud of the record and humble about the mistakes. Writing for the Fabian Society, Abbott set out a systematic critique of New Labour. First, she argued that New Labour had been ideological rather than pragmatic. This was a counter-intuitive claim in the context of public debate, which tended to characterise Blair and Brown as arch-pragmatists. Abbott, however, argued that 'There was nothing pragmatic about New Labour's attitude to markets. They were its preferred method of delivering goods and services. Even when common sense suggested otherwise, New Labour clung to the view that markets knew better.'[43]

New Labour's commitment to markets was dogmatic in the sense that it often led to worse economic outcomes than traditional government projects. The Private Finance Initiative, to take one example, cost taxpayers more in the long run. Privatised rail services, to take another, made the rail system complex, hard for consumers to navigate and required billions of pounds in state subsidy. Much the same could be said for privatised utilities. Faith in the private sector also led to a dysfunctional housing market. By leaving the housing market to its own devices, New Labour allowed the emergence of a housing bubble in the private sector, which was not offset by investment in social housing. Consequently, by 2010 housing was becoming less and less affordable, particularly in London and particularly for young people. Finally, New Labour's faith in the market had led to the most catastrophic economic failure of all: the failure to prevent the credit crunch.

Nor was New Labour's commitment to markets pragmatic in electoral terms. Renationalising the railways was popular, but New Labour shied away from the prospect. 'It was almost as if an ideological attachment to markets mattered more to New Labour than actual popularity with the public,' Abbott argued.[44] Privatisation and marketisation were also unpopular with public sector workers, who were part of Labour's electoral coalition. They were unpopular because privatisation degraded the pay and conditions of workers, forcing many to rely on tax credits – an unacknowledged subsidy to the private sector. In schools and hospitals, the introduction of market mechanisms and league tables tied professionals up in red tape. And in 2010 public sector workers, and former public sector workers had punished Labour as a result.

Abbott's critique of New Labour contained another element, which has become counter-intuitive with hindsight. Following 2016, the New Labour era has been contrasted regularly with a new age of populism. However, Abbott's comments during the 2010 leadership campaign cast doubt on this narrative. Speaking to Polly Toynbee, Abbott criticised New Labour's 'phoney populism', saying, 'The party under New Labour was being led so far to the right that they felt like they had to throw a bone to some of their core supporters.'[45] This explained, Abbott argued, New Labour's ambivalence towards civil liberties, and New Labour's anti-immigration policies and rhetoric.

What emerged from the leadership debates was that the other candidates agreed with a great deal of Abbott's critique. David Miliband repeatedly acknowledged that New Labour was out of touch. All of the contenders agreed with Abbott that Blair had placed too much faith in the private sector. All agreed that Britain should never have gone to war in Iraq, a point that David Miliband underlined with the claim that 'the worst thing that happened to Tony Blair was George Bush'.[46] With hindsight, 'the young princes of New Labour' tacitly recognised that Abbott had been right, right about local government, right about house building, right to question Brown and

Blair. Ed Miliband argued that many of the mistakes made by New Labour could have been avoided if the government had listened to its backbenchers and its members. Abbott was perplexed by the sudden change of heart. Speaking on *Question Time* towards the end of the campaign, she quipped:

> I've listened with some bafflement to my rivals say, 'the government did this wrong', 'the government did that wrong', 'the government was out of touch'. They were all in government! I don't know when they woke up to all that was going wrong. I certainly, on the back-benches, didn't hear it at the time![47]

Abbott's team was run on a shoestring: in fact, most of the work was done by Abbott and a few friends. The other campaigns, Abbott re-calls, were run professionally. The Miliband brothers, Burnham and Balls had, after all, been contemplating running for some time, and therefore had a head start in terms of campaign infrastructure. There were other factors which also gave David Miliband an edge. 'He had the advantage that the party machine was working for him,' Abbott recalls.[48] Abbott learned from her supporters that they were receiving phone calls from David Miliband's campaign. Balls had received the same intelligence. 'In fact, Ed and I had to have a row on the phone with the general secretary, because we felt they were giving David information like mailing lists that they weren't giving to us.' Addi-tionally, at the beginning of the campaign, *The Guardian* reported that Miliband had a war chest of £200,000, compared to his brother's £15,000.[49] Abbott recalls that, initially, she was trying to run a cam-paign on £1,500. This gave David Miliband the resources to employ a team, including a phone bank to speak to party members directly, and to pay for a mailout to all members.

The lack of financial support, Burnham recalls, had an impact on the candidates.

> I have huge respect for her. Of the five of us, I didn't have a great deal of support, Diane didn't have a massive amount of support.

Seeing her going through this punishing, and it was punishing, list
of engagements, knowing that she was doing a lot of it largely on
her own. People who've never done it would never quite understand
what level of energy you have to summon up from within yourself,
and staying power. And I think it's even harder when you are doing
what Diane was doing, as the outside candidate trying to break into
the contest.[50]

Burnham was also impressed with Abbott's ability to give a 'barn-storm-
ing' performance night after night. 'You can't help but have a new
level of admiration, one politician to another.'

Over the course of the campaign, Abbott developed a riff which she
used as her final pitch to party members: 'You're looking at me, and
I know what you're thinking. You're thinking, "She doesn't look like
a leader of the Labour Party." But I'm saying to you that in 2010, in
a globalised world, this is what the leader of the Labour Party looks
like.'[51]

Abbott's coda went down well with audiences, and on occasions
where she did not use it, she recalls, 'even Ed Ball's team said they
missed it!'

By the end of the campaign, Abbott had spoken at fifty-two hustings,
and taken part in four televised debates. Voting took place throughout
the first weeks of September, with the announcement on the first day
of the annual Labour Party conference. Before the announcement, the
five candidates, each accompanied by a friend, were ushered into an
upstairs room at Manchester Central Convention Complex to hear
the result. The atmosphere was tense. Burnham recalls that the news
of Ed Miliband's victory was greeted by gasps and followed by 'an
awkward clinch' between the two brothers.[52] However, news of the
result did nothing to dispel the tension in the room. Apparently, on
being told that he would not be the next Labour leader David Milib-
and protested that he had already written his victory speech.

Abbott had anticipated the vote, at least in its broad outlines. She
expected David Miliband to pick up the largest number of votes from
the PLP and from MEPs, on the basis that Labour MPs tend to back

the candidate they think has the most chance of electoral success. However, based on her experiences at the hustings, Abbott realised that he was not nearly as popular with the grassroots. 'Not for the first time,' Abbott claims, 'the Parliamentary Labour Party was out of step with the membership.'[53] Burnham too had concluded that victory was slipping away from the frontrunner: 'You could see David giving it away. He wasn't engaging in the debate and in the contest in the way that Ed was, he wasn't connecting with members in the same way. You could feel the dynamic of the race changing.'[54]

Abbott, of course, had an impact on the result. Corbyn argues, 'Diane's votes were always going to transfer to Ed, not to David, so Diane's votes effectively put Ed in.'[55] Indeed, Abbott's votes, in every part of the electoral college, tended to go to Ed rather than David Miliband. Of the Labour MPs and MEPs who voted for Abbott as their first preference, Ed Miliband picked up four, whereas David Miliband picked up no second preference votes. In terms of the votes of constituency parties, 4,196 of Abbott's votes were redistributed to Ed Miliband, while only 1,223 votes went to his older brother. Finally, in terms of the support that she received from the unions, 7,750 of her second preferences went to Ed Miliband, compared to 3,147 which went to David Miliband.[56]

Keith Vaz agrees that Abbott's candidacy benefited Ed Miliband, albeit for different reasons:

> It was her getting on the ballot that ensured the election of Ed Miliband. She took some of the votes which would have naturally gone to David. People liked David, in the ethnic minority communities. They did not know Ed, even though Sadiq was supporting him, and most of the black MPs actually supported David … She brought people in, and those votes transferred to Ed.[57]

On this account, Abbott's candidacy encouraged more left-wingers to vote, and once Abbott was eliminated their votes helped Ed Miliband over his brother.

AFTERMATH

The campaign changed Abbott's fortunes within the party. It demonstrated that she had support in the country, and it demonstrated that she was part of the new generation of Labour's leadership. There could be no doubting the respect that she had won from her fellow contenders. Repeatedly, during the campaign, the other candidates had acknowledged that they had learned from Abbott, and that they agreed with her on important issues. Speaking at the Norwich hustings, Balls, to take one example, praised Abbott as she had 'always challenged us not to fall for false consensus, because it's easy or comfortable', concluding that her willingness to challenge consensus was the true 'Labour way'.[58] Indeed, the debates revealed that a great deal of Abbott's critique of the Blair–Brown era was shared at the top of government. Even David Miliband, who was regarded by the media as the continuity candidate, agreed with Abbott on a number of fundamental issues. This made it hard to maintain the view that Abbott was an unprincipled troublemaker, or someone who engaged in opposition for opposition's sake. Rather, the leadership contest indicated that Abbott's strategic opposition reflected genuine failings in the Blair and Brown governments.

The campaign also threw up revelations which further weakened the view that Abbott was part of a self-indulgent awkward squad. Speaking to *The Times* on 5 June, Balls acknowledged that under Blair the party leadership sought to close down debate by denigrating and misrepresenting MPs who questioned specific decisions or made the case for alternative policies.[59]

The success of Abbott's campaign also meant she could expect to have a job on Miliband's frontbench. Indeed, Abbott's new status in the party was reflected in the shadow Cabinet elections which followed the conference. Abbott placed thirty-five out of the fifty-nine candidates, gaining fifty-nine votes from her PLP colleagues, beating the likes of Ben Bradshaw, who had been in Gordon Brown's Cabinet as Minister for Culture, Media and Sport, and Mike Gapes, outgoing chair of the Foreign Affairs Select Committee. Her new status was also evident from the fact that she was in demand at the 2010 conference, and at events up and down the country. Some saw Abbott as Ed Miliband's kingmaker, others as the woman who had denied David the crown, but few doubted her impact on the party.

The 2010 leadership election had more immediate consequences for Labour MPs. Some MPs, it seems, were not aware that their voting preferences would be published. Consequently, across the PLP there were awkward conversations as MPs either justified their choices – 'the wrongs but strongs', as they were known in Abbott's office – or offered embarrassed apologies.

Abbott's campaign had wider ramifications. Ribeiro-Addy argues that David Miliband wanted Abbott on the ballot to legitimise the outcome. He wanted a field that represented the whole of the party, not just New Labour. This was undoubtedly a change from 2008 and took the party back to the example of 1994 in which Blair stood against John Prescott and Margaret Beckett. Notably, the discussion about diversity had two strands: some MPs supported Abbott because they did not want a slate that was made up exclusively of white men; others – perhaps uncomfortable with arguments about race and gender – couched their support for her in terms of wanting a 'diversity of views'. This second argument would re-emerge five years later and was crucial to Corbyn getting on to the ballot.

Abbott's presence on the ballot did not merely legitimise the process, it legitimised the left, as did the tacit acknowledgement from the other candidates that Abbott had been right to criticise key aspects of New Labour. This was a significant change in debates within the party. Since 1983 the left had been presented variously as an obstacle to electoral success, as entryists, as utopian dreamers or as obstructive and vexatious. In these guises, the left was always the problem, and the right always the solution. However, Abbott was able to show that New Labour's failings were a result of the party lurching too far to the right. She also demonstrated that had the leadership listened to the left, it would have made fewer mistakes and adopted more popular policies. Consequently, for the first time since 1983 there was widespread scepticism of the right, and a recognition that the left had a legitimate contribution to make.

The appeal of radicalism, as an antidote to the failings of New Labour, is evident from the outcome of the leadership election. In terms of the affiliated members, Abbott placed third. Moreover, opinion polling put her ahead of Burnham and Balls with the party members and trades unionists for at least part of the campaign. Abbott came away from the contest believing that there was a bigger appetite for change than the final result suggested. In that sense, even after the expulsions and even after a decade of dominance, New Labour did not have the grip on the party that might have been expected. Five years later, standing on essentially the same platform, Corbyn demonstrated the extent of the party's appetite for radicalism.

Abbott's campaign also had an impact on the radicals who had stuck with Labour during the New Labour years. Corbyn argues that Abbott's candidacy played a role in reinvigorating radicalism in the party, by putting something inspiring on the agenda,

> Anni Marjoram spoke at that year's Labour Party conference, after Ed had been elected, it must have been a Campaign Group event, and said, 'I don't regret any of those miles we went, or any of those meetings we did, at least we put something on the agenda', which was true, because the left was at quite a low ebb in the party, the membership was quite small, and the union influence was very strong, and not necessarily for the left. I think what Diane did then was to bravely lay down a marker for the rest of us.[60]

Corbyn argues that in 2015, the desire to build on Abbott's campaign was one of the main reasons he advocated another attempt to get a Campaign Group MP onto the ballot.

In some ways what Abbott achieved in 2010 was not about Labour's different factions. Abbott argues that what she witnessed reflected the desire for a better country, and a determination to embrace hope, which transcended divisions between the left and right.

CHAPTER 12

CON-DEM NATION

In the summer of 2010, after thirteen years in government, Labour found themselves in opposition, facing a Cameron–Clegg coalition. Abbott was distrustful of David Cameron and remained 'deeply cynical' about the coalition.

> I think in his heart, Cameron is an old-fashioned kind of Tory. I think deep in his heart, the only thing that Cameron believes in is that people like him, i.e. Old Etonians and similar people, should run the country ... However, I think he quite carefully tried to position himself as the continuity of a New Labour Prime Minister, certainly initially. Cameron and Osborne greatly admire Tony Blair in lots of ways.[1]

In contrast, Miliband tried to distance himself from his predecessors. 'The era of New Labour has passed. A new generation has taken over,' he announced, outlining plans for new taxes for higher-paid workers, new trade union rights for employees and a halt to public sector pension reforms. However, many Blairites did not believe it was possible to win from the left and were concerned about Labour's apparent leftward shift under a 'Red Ed'.[2] Moreover, in the first round of the election, only 31.6 per cent of Labour MPs and MEPs voted for Ed Miliband, while 41.7 per cent voted for his older brother David Miliband. Ed Miliband's narrow victory came as a result of second preference votes and union support, therefore his legitimacy as the leader was under fire. Miliband's immediate task, Abbott argued, was 'mollifying and binding in the unreconstructed Blairites in the Parliamentary Labour party, the party machine, and the media'.[3]

Miliband insisted that he was his 'own man' and that the party would not 'lurch to the left'. The idea of 'Red Ed', he argued, was 'both tiresome and rubbish'.[4] Abbott agreed that it was 'nonsense'. Far from being a fervent socialist, Miliband was part of the mainstream centre, as evidenced by his calls for responsible capitalism and his echoing of Brown's mantra of Labour being the party of the 'squeezed middle'.

When Labour lost power, its membership was just 48 per cent of what it had been in 1997.[5] The Tories had also seen a decline in membership, while parties such as the Liberal Democrats, the Green Party, UKIP and the BNP were growing. Following the election, Labour saw a brief influx of members, many of them disgruntled Liberal Democrat supporters. Still, former Cabinet minister Peter Hain's 'Refounding Labour' report concluded that the party 'still looks inward rather than outward, is stuck in its structures, and is not engaged with local communities or national civil society'.[6] As a result, Labour was 'spread pretty thinly on the ground, and with a weak base from which to develop contacts in the community and build popular support.'

Tim Bale noted that the annual party conference was less and less well attended by members, who saw it as a corporate event rather than a time to discuss and decide on policy.[7] Bell Ribeiro-Addy attests to this, recalling a women's hustings where David Miliband argued that Labour conferences should instead be a celebration of Labour ideas. 'We can't really sit there for hours and discuss policy,' she recalls him saying. 'It's great to ask the members, but sometimes leadership is not about asking, sometimes you've got to take the reins … Imagine if we had asked about the banks, imagine what the members would have said, but we got it right.' Ribeiro-Addy argues that one of the reasons so many people left the party was that they felt that their voices did not matter: 'Every opportunity was taken to strip away their decision-making powers.'[8]

In the May 2011 local elections, the Tories managed to maintain their vote share and Labour made gains at the expense of the Liberal Democrats. However, the Scottish National Party (SNP) won an overall majority in Scotland, a blow to both the Tories and Labour. Also, that month, the nation voted on the Liberal Democrat's proposal to use the alternative vote system rather than first past the post in general elections. Miliband was in favour of the change but failed to rally his party. Abbott, herself, confesses that she has never been interested in alternative vote. By allowing a free vote, Miliband managed to dodge any severe political ramifications when the referendum was lost. Equally, he failed to use the campaign to bolster his popularity.

Miliband struggled to project the same gravitas in the media as Cameron. Some criticised his age, others his physical appearance, and others still, his 'odd'-sounding voice. Miliband's appointment of Bob Roberts, the *Mirror*'s political editor, and Tom Baldwin, chief reporter for *The Times*, as director of news and head of communications respectively failed to recreate Blair's hold over the press.[9] His moment came in July 2011 amid the *News of the World* phone-hacking scandal, which exposed close links between the government and Murdoch. 'Ed was finally able to find his voice,' Abbott stated. 'It was impossible to imagine Tony Blair speaking out against Rupert Murdoch in the way that Ed did.'[10]

UNIVERSITY TUITION FEES

The Tories and Liberal Democrats faced several points of contention on forming a coalition, the most notable, perhaps, being university tuition fees. In November 2009, then Business Secretary Peter Mandelson appointed Lord Browne, the former chief executive of BP, to chair a review of higher education funding and student finance. Ahead of its publication in October 2010, it was widely speculated that Browne was to recommend increasing university tuition fees.

An NUS pledge to 'vote against any increase in fees in the next parliament and to pressure the government to introduce a fairer alternative' was signed by over 1,000 parliamentary candidates ahead of the 2010 general election. This included all fifty-seven elected Liberal Democrats. However, the Conservatives, confident Browne would recommend removing the cap on tuition fees, said they would consider the report's findings carefully.

After the general election in 2010, the coalition government agreed to await the results of the Browne review and permitted Liberal Democrat MPs to abstain if they were unable to support its conclusions. One alternative that Vince Cable proposed was replacing tuition fees with a graduate tax. Though this proposal was more appealing to many Liberal Democrats who opposed fees, Abbott worried that the proposal was just 'a rebranding exercise by Vince Cable, an attempt to placate those Liberal Democrats who campaigned against fees'.[11] Abbott's suspicions proved to be correct when Cable confessed that the graduate tax was only 'superficially attractive' and argued a pure graduate tax was not the way forward.[12] It was later revealed that, two months before the general election, the Liberal Democrats decided that they were willing to drop their opposition to tuition fees should there be a hung parliament.[13]

Lord Browne's review of university funding was published in October 2010 and proposed: the removal of the cap on tuition fees; the payment of fees through student loans for part-time students; that graduates would begin repayments once they earn over £21,000; and that unpaid student debt would be written off after thirty years, rather than twenty-five years. Other recommendations included making flat-rate maintenance loans available to all students and increasing maintenance grants for low-income students. The coalition government largely adopted Browne's recommendations but opted for a £9,000 cap on tuition fees.

Abbott was furious. 'I think the Iraq War was wrong, I think ID cards are wrong, and my view, and it's a minority view, my view is that it was wrong to introduce tuition fees in the first place, and I voted against that.'[14] Abbott argued that when Labour first introduced university tuition fees, she knew they would inevitably be increased to extortionate levels. 'It was all very well for us to introduce tuition fees in a very careful way, hedged about with all sorts of support – very judicious,' she told the House of Commons. 'But I knew that it would end in a Tory-led government ramping up fees unconscionably, leading to a more divided education system than we have ever seen.'

Abbott argued that tuition fees disproportionately impacted

students taking longer courses, such as medicine, as well as students from low and middle-income backgrounds. She argued that many families 'are not eligible for the help but cannot afford to contemplate their children going forward to pile up £40,000 of debt, not when they will have to think about their pension and their jobs, and interest rates on mortgages are rising'.[15] As the first in her family to go to university, Abbott was acutely cognisant of the debt deterrent.

> Had someone told my father, who left school at fourteen and worked all his life, that not only was I staying on into the sixth form, not only was I going on to university, but I was going to pile up upward of £40,000 debt to go to my chosen university, he would have said, 'No. You leave school, and you become a nurse like your mother,' not because he was cruel, but because he was looking out for my future. For someone from his kind of background, that level of debt would be more than they would earn in a year, and more than my father in his day would have earned in several years, which would have been completely unthinkable.'[16]

Abbott believed that as universities are for the good of the whole society, the whole society should fund them. 'No one expects that if we're at war, suddenly individuals have to put [their hands] in their pocket, and if they don't, soldiers aren't going to fight for them,' she argued. Universities should be funded through taxation, the fairest means of raising money for a social good.[17]

On 10 November 2010, the NUS and the University and College Union organised a demonstration against the proposed fee increases. Up to 50,000 demonstrators took part in the peaceful protest, but in the afternoon, several thousand broke off to surround 30 Millbank in Westminster, the Conservative Party campaign headquarters. Some 200 protesters broke into the building, lit fires, smashed windows and protested from the rooftop. In the days and weeks following, more protests occurred, including a large demonstration at Whitehall, where protesters, including schoolchildren, were kettled inside the building for several hours.[18]

Nonetheless, on 9 December 2010 proposals to increase tuition fees to £9,000 passed with 323 votes to 302; twenty-one Liberal Democrats and six Tories rebelled. Nick Clegg and Vince Cable were among the twenty-eight Liberal Democrats to vote for the new fee arrangement. Clegg and Cable had both received a university education at the tax-payer's expense, as had Cameron and Osborne. Yet they voted to deny the same right to a new generation of students. The fallout was con-siderable. One Tory and two Liberal Democrat ministerial aides quit the frontbench in protest. Demonstrations continued with the further use of kettling and batons by the police.

The coalition government also made changes to primary and second-ary education. Education secretary Michael Gove axed Labour's Build-ing Schools for the Future programme, which aimed to rebuild and modernise every secondary school in the country. Around 150 school projects were in limbo after the announcement. The situation was made worse when a list of school projects which could proceed was found to have several errors. 'His announcement was arrogant, shambolic and deeply upsetting for the schools that were told their new buildings and facilities would go ahead, only to have them snatched away a day later,' Abbott stated.[19] 'It is not just damaging for young people, but affects the possibility of growth in sectors which would have benefited from building projects and the jobs this would have created.'[20]

The Academies Act 2010 made it possible for all publicly funded schools to become academies: independent state-funded schools, which had autonomy over matters such as the curriculum, finances and staff wages. Academies would be funded centrally rather than through local authorities, freeing up money that would have otherwise funded other services, such as support for children with special educational needs. By November 2014, 55 per cent of all secondary schools were academies, including 459 sponsored schools, mostly underperforming schools changing to academy status and run by sponsors.[21]

Abbott felt that the Academies Act was a 'recipe for chaos' which would create a two-tier education system whereby academies were better funded and resourced than local-authority-maintained schools. 'There are all sorts of issues like special needs that require strong [local education authority] oversight,' she explained. 'Giving complete control to schools may seem like an attractive idea in principle, but it leaves our children's education at the mercy of a few, and most importantly, leaves schools unaccountable to anyone but their own governors.' She continued:

> Hackney's academies have always worked with other Hackney schools and were, crucially, established in Hackney because of previous serious issues with education and so were targeted to areas where investment and support were particularly critical. The new Academies Bill creates a free for all with no accountability to local councillors or parents.[22]

Educationalists involved with London Schools and the Black Child would, in the coming years, find ways of subverting the system. Where the government wanted to drive up standards through competition, London Schools would find ways of encouraging co-operation within the new system.

INTO THE SHADOW CABINET

In keeping with tradition, Labour held elections to the shadow Cabinet in October 2010. Several of the leadership contenders snatched the top spots, Yvette Cooper won the coveted first place. Refusing Business, she was made shadow Foreign Secretary. John Healey placed second and was made shadow Secretary of Health, and Ed Balls placed third and was given the Home Department rather than the expected top economics position. Instead, Alan Johnson, one of David Miliband's top men, was made shadow Chancellor. Andy Burnham placed fourth and was made shadow Education Secretary.

Placed thirty-fifth, Abbott was far from disappointed. 'I'd refreshed the brand,' she beamed. Still on a high from the election campaign, Abbott received a call from Lammy who wanted to know which job she had been offered. 'Job?' she replied. 'They haven't offered me anything.' Lammy responded, 'Diane, you just don't understand how it works, you must ring them and tell them what you want to do.'[23]

Abbott then informed Jon Trickett, the only person she knew who was close to Ed Miliband, that she would be interested in a job in international development. A few days later, Ed Miliband offered her a job as shadow Minister for Public Health. This would make Abbott a member of the shadow health team, working under John Healey. While Abbott was open to a position on the frontbench, insisting that she would remain the 'Diane Abbott this party knows', she had some reservations.

I had an interesting life as a backbencher. I was on television once a week. I could campaign for what I wanted to campaign for. I could say what I wanted to say. There was no reason in the world for me to give that up to be number five in someone's team and not be allowed to speak out on anything anymore. Because that's the discipline of being on the frontbench.[24]

Presuming Abbott sought a position of prestige, Miliband told her she would be number two in Healey's team. However, this only heightened Abbott's concerns about losing her autonomy. When she spoke with Healey about this, he laughed. The role of Minister for Public Health, he told her, would place her at number four or five on his team, not number two. Although she was relieved by this news, Abbott was disappointed in Miliband.

[The leader's office] was desperate to get my agreement because they wanted to issue the list of the new shadow Cabinet and they wanted me to be on it, and presumably, that's why Ed said, 'Oh yes, you'd be number two...' It told me something about Ed Miliband, unfortunately.

Still, Abbott, the daughter of a nurse, accepted the job and began her role in public health. Ribeiro-Addy recalls that Abbott immediately set about meeting people and communicating with public health stakeholders.

NHS REFORMS

The Health and Social Care Bill was introduced to the House of Commons in January 2011. In many ways, the bill built on Blair's move towards decentralisation in the NHS, but the scale of the changes spearheaded by Health Secretary Andrew Lansley was gargantuan.

The proposals included a new autonomous body called Healthwatch England to manage the health service, a new regulator tasked with 'promoting competition where appropriate' and the abolition of strategic health authorities and primary care trusts. Instead, the responsibility for commissioning of out-of-hospital health services would belong to geographically defined consortia of GPs who could buy from 'any willing provider'. Public health services would be commissioned by local authorities and funded by Public Health England, a new body within the Department of Health.

The government argued that the bill was patient-first, empowered health professionals and would spur innovation and change. Andrew Lansley's desire to replace democratic accountability with market mechanisms, his faith that market forces would drive up standards and drive down costs, and his desire to outsource provision was, of course, nothing new. Abbott had encountered the same approach at Westminster City Council in the early 1980s, where it cost millions of pounds in lost assets, and millions to put right the problems that had been created.

Abbott was not the only critic of Lansley's market fundamentalism. With 280 clauses and twenty-two schedules, the bill was three times the size of the 1946 Act that founded the NHS.[25] Critics argued that the proposals went too far and too fast, especially at a time when public sector staff were facing pay freezes and cuts. The introduction of several new national departments and local bodies raised questions of accountability and co-ordination. Andy Burnham argued that the bill would result in the 'wiping away of oversight and public accountability ... How will GPs be held to account for the £80 billion of public money for which they will be responsible and how will the new NHS commissioning board ... be accountable to this House and to Members of Parliament?'[26]

Another major concern was the opening of service provision to the private sector, and the promotion of competition.[27] There were concerns that private service providers would cherry-pick high-profit, low-risk services, leaving the NHS to deal with the most complex and expensive issues. There was also evidence that more competition would lead to a 'race to the bottom on price that would almost certainly threaten quality.'[28] In 2012, Dr Richard Horton, editor of *The Lancet*, called for the bill to be overturned, warning of 'unprecedented chaos from competition over quality'.[29] Moreover, there were questions over the extent to which EU competition laws would apply to the NHS. On the publication of the bill, the British Medical Association (BMA) called its first emergency meeting in nineteen years, where members voted against the changes.

There was significant opposition to the bill from within Parliament. At a time of real-term cuts, Labour argued that the NHS needed stability. The coalition government also faced opposition from their own members.

While Abbott agreed with the principle that both NHS and local government health stakeholders should work together on issues like public health, she strongly opposed Lansley's reforms.

> I thought they were terrible, and the more you spoke to stakeholders, the more you'd realise this. And all the things that have happened, the fragmentation, the introduction of the private sector, they have happened as was predicted ... We knew it was going to be disastrous, and Cameron pushed on regardless.[30]

In April 2011, the government announced that it was pausing the bill's parliamentary passage to 'listen, reflect and improve'.[31] This listening process included forming a future forum panel of advisers who recommended amendments. The government recommitted the bill to the public bill committee on 21 June 2011. Changes included multi-professional clinical commissioning groups (CCGs) in place of consortia solely run by GPs, service provision by 'any qualified provider' and a limit of 49 per cent on private income.

In October 2011, Miliband's reshuffle saw Andy Burnham return to health as shadow Health Secretary. Burnham argued that the 49 per cent limit was 'the clearest sign yet of David Cameron's determination to turn our precious NHS into a US-style commercial system' and decried hospitals would 'devote half their beds to private patients'.[32]

'I think we had been doing quite muted opposition to the Lansley reforms up until that point,' Burnham reflects. 'When I came back as shadow health in October 2011, I basically put the throttle down and went for it big time.' While some members of the shadow health team were harking back to a slightly New Labour version of health policy, Burnham shares that Abbott joined his enthusiastic opposition of the reforms. 'She was coming up with some more radical things than we had said in the government, so it was good.'[33]

One of their most pressing tasks was to garner the support of the medical sector. Abbott explains:

What would have been very helpful was if all the heads of the royal colleges had come out against the reforms, but not all of them did. The heads of the royal colleges are doctors, but they are also very much British establishment; men of a certain age, a certain class, a certain background by and large.[34]

The Academy of Medical Royal Colleges that represent medical professionals had been attending policy meetings and producing briefings to help shape the bill. Some members had participated in and submitted evidence to the future forum. Despite the changes made, many remained unsatisfied, and in December 2011, Burnham invited the heads of the colleges to Parliament. When Burnham concluded his speech, Abbott took to the stage.

I said, 'We all know how wrong these reforms are, do you really want to be in a position, in a few years' time, when you have to admit to younger doctors that you could have stopped them, and you didn't? It's no good you telling me that you'd been to tea at No. 10 Downing Street, and you've been promised a peerage, there's no good telling me that, because you have to do the right thing.' And they laughed because they knew that's exactly what had happened.[35]

In January 2012, adding to the opposition from the BMA, the Royal College of Nursing and the Royal College of Midwives, a leaked statement revealed that nineteen of the twenty royal colleges agreed they 'are not able to support the bill as it currently stands'.[36]

On 27 March 2012, after a year in Parliament, over 1,000 amendments, and continued opposition, the Health and Social Care Bill passed with a majority of eighty-eight. An Ipsos MORI poll placed Labour ahead of the Conservatives on matters of healthcare by thirty points, the party's largest lead on health since 2002.[37]

In September 2012, Lansley was moved from Health Secretary to Lord Privy Seal and Jeremy Hunt succeeded him at the Department of Health. In 2015, a King's Fund review concluded that there was insufficient evidence that the Health and Social Care Act 2012 increased privatisation of the NHS, but it did result in more marketisation, 'distracting and damaging' reorganisation and 'complex and confusing' governing and accountability systems. In 2019, many of the Act's changes were effectively undone in the NHS Long Term Plan, which promoted partnerships and integration over independence and competition.

PUBLIC HEALTH: WHOSE RESPONSIBILITY?

As shadow Minister for Public Health, Abbott had her work cut out for her. In 2008, 30 per cent of children, 57 per cent of women and 66 per cent of men were classed as overweight or obese in England.[38] One in four adults were classified as hazardous drinkers, prescriptions for alcohol dependency were increasing and, since 2001, there had been a 25 per cent rise in alcohol-related deaths.[39] Moreover, Abbott was up against a health minister who believed that public health issues demanded personal responsibility rather than 'nannying' by the state, and who clearly wanted the private sector to play a larger role in public health policy. Indeed, in 2008, while shadow Health Secretary, Lansley brought in food and alcohol industry representatives to form a public health commission to develop policy on public health. Dave Lewis, chair of Unilever for the UK and Ireland, one of the world's largest processors of industrial fats, chaired the commission. It included representatives from public health and third-sector organisations, as well as Tesco, Asda, Diageo, Compass, the Wine and Spirit Trade Association and the Fitness Industry Association. Lansley also had strong industry ties as a paid director of the marketing agency Profero.

When the Tories came into office in 2010, many of the commission members continued to develop policy as members of five Public Health Responsibility Deal (PHRD) networks which covered food, alcohol, physical activity, health at work and behaviour change. The PHRD invited industry groups to agree to a series of commitments and pledges to improve public health.

However, shortly before its launch in March 2011, six health organisations, Alcohol Concern, the British Association for the Study of the Liver, the British Liver Trust, the BMA, the Institute of Alcohol Studies, and the Royal College of Physicians, withdrew from the PHRD. They stated that the pledges were not specific, argued that the process prioritised the views of industry, and called for the government to consider regulation if businesses failed to meet their voluntary commitments. Abbott called for a Health Select Committee inquiry, arguing that the government's PHRD was 'little more than a favour to their friends in big business'.[40]

The committee echoed concerns regarding the preference for voluntary rather than statutory regulation. Further, they were 'unconvinced that [the PHRD] will be effective in resolving issues such as obesity and alcohol abuse. [...] Those with a financial interest must not be allowed to set the agenda for health improvement'. Abbott said the report was 'a damning indictment' of a 'completely ineffective' deal.[41]

THE ENABLING STATE

Rejecting the notion of the nudging or nannying state, Abbott advocated 'the enabling state'. She believed strongly in the importance of families in addressing inequalities, something she attributes to growing up as the child of immigrants: 'When you are a first-generation immigrant, family is all you have.'[42] Abbott argued by viewing families as sites of oppression, 'feminists and the left have allowed the right to dominate debates on the family'. She felt that this was a mistake, and that families, in all their forms, should be important to the left.[43] Abbott's analysis reflected the understanding of the family advanced by the black womanists who she had met through OWAAD in the late 1970s.

Abbott argued that the state ought to empower families to tackle public health issues. 'Doctors say to me that so many of the drug and alcohol problems they see stem from family difficulties,' she told *The Guardian*.[44] Abbott was also concerned about the 'rise of the alco-pop', sweet alcoholic drinks, marketed to appeal to younger drinkers at 'pocket money prices'.[45] She proposed local authorities should be allowed to ban the sale of cheap alcohol in grocery stores and off-licences and echoed calls for a 50p per unit minimum pricing.[46]

Abbott argued that many people lacked the social capital needed to exercise choice in the way that Lansley and the government imagined. Speaking at the Policy Exchange, she remarked:

> Supposing you are an old-age pensioner in Hackney who can scarcely use their mobile phone properly and does not have a computer in their house. Supposing you are a Bangladeshi mother for whom English isn't your first language. Supposing like many families in communities like mine you are not actually that literate, not actually that good at disaggregating charts and figures. What does the 'give the consumer the information and they will make the right choices' do for you? Nothing.[47]

Even worse than nothing, she argued that a focus on nudging rather than enabling risked these people falling farther behind in terms of health inequalities. This was particularly concerning for her constituency, which had some of the poorest health outcomes in the capital. As a result of market forces, Abbott argued that

> [many people] live in fresh food deserts where it's easier to place

a bet or buy chicken and chips ... than it is to buy good-quality fruit and vegetables. Too many people genuinely want to do the best for their children but are struggling against the tide of junk information about junk food where billions are spent on newspaper ads, television and increasingly online marketing, but it's billions spent on the most unhealthy foods.

Abbott stated that the government's rhetoric of 'personal responsibility' left individuals at the mercy of massive corporations. The enabling state, she claimed, could rebalance that relationship by imposing statutory duties on food corporations and help to empower consumers.

Abbott adopted the term 'McParenting' for what she described as the trend, pushed by the media, of parents substituting materialism for parental responsibility. 'Modern families are the victim not of the overbearing state', she argued, 'but of the overbearing market.'[48]

She lambasted the government's £2 million Change4Life advertising campaign, which aimed to promote healthy eating, as a 'glorified advertisement for big business' and an insult to hard-pressed British families.[49] Instead, Abbott called for more local government power to curb the spread of fast food outlets in their areas, tighter controls on the advertising of sugary foods aimed at children and for traffic light labelling on packaging. In the run-up to the 2012 London Olympics, she criticised sponsorship by brands such as McDonald's, Coca-Cola, and Dow Chemical and opposed the plans to build the world's largest McDonald's in the Olympic Park.

Tackling health inequalities, she argued, meant working with communities. 'In Hackney, more people, on a weekend, go to their church, their mosque, their temple in one weekend than attend a Labour Party conference in a year.'[50] She argued that Labour needed to overcome their 'squeamishness' regarding interacting with faith groups, to reach neglected communities.

ALIGNING PUBLIC HEALTH AND SCHOOL EDUCATION
To Abbott, empowering communities necessitated working with schools. 'Michael Gove is allergic to anything that isn't the three Rs,'

she jibed, noting the Education Secretary's preoccupation with academic rigour and discipline over other areas of the curriculum. Abbott argued that governments needed to work with schools to increase literacy among families, hold academies to the same nutritional standards as state schools, and improve food and nutritional education.

Abbott also saw the need to reform sex education in schools to improve public health outcomes. She argued that 'the answer to teenage pregnancy is better sexual health education and addressing these young women's low sense of self-esteem'.[51] For Abbott, this meant tackling the 'pornification' and sexualisation of children. While 22 per cent of young men first had sex before the age of consent at sixteen, 27 per cent of young women had. Young women were also more likely to have sexually transmitted infections than their male counterparts.[52] Abbott feared this would be exacerbated by Lansley's health reforms, which pushed sexual health into the realm of local authorities and were likely to result in cuts to sexual health services.

Abbott explained that when she was a teenager, sex and sexualisation had undergone a period of 'tremendous liberation', but in recent years, things had gone backwards. 'We see penalties paid by those who do not conform to our hypersexualised culture, and we see penalties for those who fall victim,' she stated in her speech to the Fabian Women's Network in 2013.[53] She pointed to examples of schoolchildren being pressured and coerced into sending explicit content, and then being slut-shamed and bullied when they did. In 2011, one in ten young women reported having experienced sexual abuse in childhood. Of these young women, 65.9 per cent said that the only perpetrator was under the age of eighteen.[54] Another survey of sixteen- to eighteen-year-olds found that 29 per cent had experienced unwanted sexual touching at school and 40 per cent could not recall receiving lessons or information on sexual consent.[55] Sex education in schools, Abbott argued, was out of touch, and instead, children were learning about sex and sexuality through porn.

Abbott advocated for a sex education revolution which prepared young people to 'form healthy, respectful, emotionally fulfilling relationships' and a curriculum which prioritised addressing issues of gender equality.[56] Parents and families needed to be empowered to support and educate their children and help them use technology safely and wisely, such as through blocking age-restricted content. The government needed to protect the right to choose whether to continue a pregnancy and ensure access to safe and timely abortions.

Abbott feared the government was going to 'turn the clock back for millions of women' with 'anti-choice' moves. She criticised Tory MP Nadine Dorries's proposals for abstinence-only sex education for girls, but not boys, as 'complete and utter nonsense' and opposed bills to prevent abortion providers from offering counselling. In 2012, she resigned from an all-party group on abortion counselling, stating that the group simply wanted to push through the anti-choice agenda of 'Tea Party Tories'.[57]

REFLECTIONS ON THE SHADOW HEALTH TEAM

Abbott argues that she did not get much credit for the work she did under the shadow Health Secretary John Healey. In part, she believes, this was because Healey was threatened by her. In contrast, Abbott had a good working relationship with Burnham when he replaced Healey in October 2011.

'[Abbott's] an incredibly capable person and politician,' Burnham says. 'You get the best out of Diane if you truly let her be who she is.' He continues, 'She was controversial, but that was part of her appeal. There had been too many people who had hit the frontbench, es-pecially on the Labour side, who'd become a bit nondescript and a bit platitudinous.'[58] In contrast, Abbott used her position to make an impact.

Nonetheless, Abbott's discomfort with the restraints of being on the frontbench was noticeable. As David Lammy explains, 'Diane speaking from the backbench, as a parliamentary performer is fear-less. She goes for the jugular. Always mentions Hackney.' In contrast, on the frontbench, 'She's been cautious in the sense that she has kept to the script ... Sometimes, you almost want the shackles to come off.'[59]

Abbott's neighbouring MP Meg Hillier agrees. 'She'd been quite a lone ranger and had her guard up ... But she could speak her mind.' Life on the frontbench, however, was restrictive. 'You have to toe the party line, you can't speak on anything except your portfolio, mostly ... So, it constrained her.'[60]

Frontbench duties did not stop Abbott from pursuing her extra-parliamentary concerns. Black Women Mean Business continued throughout the coalition years, and in 2013 London Schools and the Black Child celebrated its tenth conference. The event, which included the presentation of academic achievement awards, was smaller than in previous years, due to Boris Johnson's decision to defund the initiative. Still, Abbott was joined by an impressive array of guests. Singer-songwriter VV Brown addressed the winning students, as did the playwright and novelist Bonnie Greer, footballer Sol Campbell, Labour MP Chuka Umunna, the Speaker John Bercow and his chaplain Rose Hudson-Wilkin. In addition to the awards, she hosted a seminar for teachers and educational leaders. Rosemary Campbell-Stephens, the respected educationalist, praised Abbott and the London Schools and the Black Child for paving the way for the government's black achievement project Aiming High and granting £3.5 million to the Investing in Diversity in London Schools programme.[61]

Campbell-Stephens argued that Gove's discontinuation of these programmes, coupled with the hollowing out of local education authorities through his reforms, 'eradicated us from the national curriculum'.[62] As national data about the performance of black students was no longer being collected systematically, it was harder to make a case for reform or resources. Campbell-Stephens said that Gove's desire to create a 'knowledge-rich curriculum' was effectively an attack on 'multicultural' education. It was no accident that Cameron criticised schools for teaching 'Indian dance or whatever' in physical education lessons.[63]

Nonetheless, she argued that London Schools and the Black Child could play a leading role in analysing these problems and finding and sharing solutions. On that note, she shared her work in Darlington, the area with the largest number of academies in Britain. Rather than competing, the academies in Darlington had chosen to work together, signing a non-compete agreement, and deciding to use their funding collectively. Campbell-Stephens held Darlington up as an example of '*ubuntu*, which is an African-centred way of operating in the interests of the collective and of the whole'. *Ubuntu*, she argued, was an approach to education that made as much sense to the white working class in Darlington during a time of austerity as it did to black parents and black educators.[64]

THE LONDON RIOTS

> well dere woz Toxteth
> an dere woz Moss Side
> an a lat a addah places
> whe di police ad to hide
> well dere woz Brixtan
> an dere woz Chapeltoun
> an a lat a adah place dat woz burnt to di groun
> > > burnt to di groun
> > > burnt to di groun
>
> it is noh mistri
> wi mekin histri
> it is noh mistri
> wi winnin victri
> – Linton Kwesi Johnson, 'Mekkin Histri'

On 4 August 2011, Mark Duggan, a 29-year-old black man, was shot dead by police during an arrest in Tottenham. It was widely reported that Duggan had fired at the police; however, his family insisted that he was unarmed, and a later ballistics report showed that the bullet found at the scene was a police issue bullet.

On Saturday 6 August, a meeting was held between the police and local community figures at the same time that a peaceful vigil and march took place between Broadwater Farm and Tottenham police station. At the police station, the crowd demanded a response from a senior police officer, but when Inspector Ade Adelekan emerged, he was met by shouts of 'coconut' and 'coon'. There were also reports that a young woman had been hit by police with a baton, sparking anger. Abbott was at home that evening, scrolling through Twitter, when she saw that there had been some sort of disturbance in Tottenham. She turned on her television, and the footage of rioting before her immediately brought back memories of the early 1980s.

'I saw it as a classic race riot,' explained Abbott in an interview with playwright Gillian Slovo and researcher Cressida Brown. A classic race riot was sparked by the death of a black person at the hands of the police but the riot actually spoke 'to a wider a more extensive set of tensions between people and the state, whether it's what's happening in the education system, whether it's what's happening in relation to immigration'. Regarding Duggan's death, Abbott asked, 'What were people in Tottenham supposed to do? They knew perfectly well that the [Independent Police Complaints Commission] was going to come up with some kind of whitewash.'[65]

Abbott woke up on 7 August to find that the looting in Tottenham had continued overnight, and spread to Wood Green, Brixton and Enfield. A few days later, it would have spread across the UK. '[The police] wouldn't have allowed it in other parts of London, not for five hours, not for five minutes,' Abbott argued. Abbott states that police inaction and failure to pull resources from other areas meant that young people felt that they had been given 'a licence to riot'.

What began as a race riot, evolved into a looting spree fuelled by dissatisfaction and '21st-century materialism'. Abbott recalled that 'there was a lot of "I can get a new pair of trainers", and that was a different mood music than the looting that happens immediately when you have an urban riot'.[66]

The historian David Starkey asserted on *Newsnight* that 'the whites have become black'.[67] Meanwhile, David Cameron rebuked a 'sick' and 'broken' society and announced an 'all-out war' on gangs and criminality.[68]

Abbott rejected the narrative that gangs and criminality alone caused the riots. 'I don't think gangs caused the riots any more than gangs caused the apprentice riots in the Middle Ages,' she argued. 'With the exception of Iain Duncan Smith, they haven't the faintest idea of what goes on in the inner-city and are even frightened by it.' Similarly, few of the Labour leadership had any experience of politics in the city.[69]

'As was the case 26 years ago, nothing excuses violence. There is no doubt that all types of mindless thugs latched on to the disturbances,' she wrote in *The Independent*. 'But just as with the original riots, parts of the community seem to have been a tinder box waiting to explode.'[70]

An inquiry by *The Guardian* and LSE Social Research entitled 'Reading the Riots' found that in addition to opportunism there was widespread frustration at social and economic deprivation. Abbott put it this way: 'For many people who were rioting, that week was a rejection of the future that was laid out for them.'[71] Abbott recalled hearing that word spread among rioters in Hackney that the Hackney Empire theatre was off-limits. To Abbott, the protection of the theatre, a space that was highly regarded by the community, showed that 'if you can give these young people some sort of ownership and some sort of point of engagement with society, you are beginning to find a solution to these sorts of riots'.[72]

Rioters also expressed anger at the treatment of people at the hands of the police, in particular, discriminatory practices such as stop and search. 'Police take black lives lightly,' Abbott said in a 2011 interview, pointing to the disproportionately high number of black men who have died in police custody. 'It is a very frightening thing. You say goodbye to your son in the morning, the next thing you get is a phone call from the police saying they've got him and he's dead.'[73] Rather than increasing the numbers of police on the street, Abbott wanted better engagement between the police and the communities they serve and a force that better represented these communities.

Following the riots, over 3,000 people were arrested. Sixty-five per cent of those were sentenced; almost nine in ten were male and over half were under twenty.[74] Abbott did not feel the judiciary faced political pressure to administer harsh sentences.

'When the settled class of people see the urban poor rioting, they believe that society and their expectations of that society is being shaken to its very foundation,' Abbott stated. 'So, you would expect magistrates who come from the settled class of people to react, without being told, to restore order in a very broad sense by imposing exemplary sentences. This is how the magistrates work.' Abbott warned that if the social and historical issues underlying the riots are not addressed, 'the inner city will come knocking again'.[75]

DIVIDE AND RULE

On 4 January 2012 two men were found guilty of the murder of Stephen Lawrence. The pair, both in their thirties, were sentenced as juveniles as the murder took place while they were under eighteen. The long-awaited verdict grabbed the nation's attention, and many took to social media to voice their response. In a series of tweets about the verdict, journalist Bim Adewunmi bemoaned the 'lazy' generalisation of 'the black community' or 'black community leaders'. Abbott, who had over 26,000 followers at the time, replied, 'I understand the cultural point you are making. But you are playing into a "divide and rule" agenda.' After some back and forth, she tweeted, 'White people love playing 'divide & rule' We should not play their game #tacticasoldascolonialism'. Then finally, 'Ethnic communities that show more public solidarity & unity than black people do much better #dontwashdirtylineninpublic'.

It did not take long for accusations of racism to arise, and there were calls for Abbott to apologise and resign. Abbott quickly tweeted a clarification, 'Tweet taken out of context. Refers to nature of nineteenth-century European colonialism. Bit much to get into 140 characters.' The 140-character defence cut little ice. Nick Clegg called her comments a 'stupid and crass generalisation' and party sources reported Abbott had received a 'severe dressing down' from Miliband.[76] What does a severe dressing down from Miliband look like? 'Nothing,' she laughs. 'Absolutely, nothing'. It was her media officer, she explains, who bore the brunt of the media fallout.[77]

'I was probably a bit more reckless with Twitter than I am now,' she confesses. 'Partly because I learned the lesson from that tweet. But even so, I thought, isn't this a statement of fact about the way the British Empire was run? It was divide and rule.'

Darcus Howe, a long-standing ally, appeared on *Newsnight* to defend Abbott. He pointed to her long history organising with the black working class to fight racism. Although Meg Hillier thought Abbott's tweet 'ill-advised', she volunteered to go on air and defend her. During an interview on BBC Radio 4's *World at One*, she recalls, 'I think I got asked four times, "Is Diane Abbott a racist?"' When the presenters argued Abbott had a track record of racism, pointing to her comments that two posh white privately educated men are running the country, Hillier responded, 'That's fact. That's a statement of fact.'[78]

With hindsight, Abbott sees the furore in its wider context.

> If you stand back from it, you've got the Stephen Lawrence convictions which are telling you something about the society and race, so then you have to say, look, there's this black person, and she's racist … One of the things people said to me [afterwards was] it was as if they had to push back against the black community somehow.[79]

AUSTERITY

In 2010, following a global financial crisis and economic recession, the UK's deficit – the gap between government spending and income – was £167 billion. The national debt stood at 63.6 per cent of GDP. In the lead up to the 2010 election, Cameron promised a new 'age of austerity', and on assuming office, he and Clegg asserted that their most urgent issue was the economy.

In June 2010, Chancellor George Osborne's emergency budget fleshed out the coalition government's plan to eliminate the deficit and half national debt in five years. This required over £100 billion worth of spending cuts and tax increases. Describing the measures as 'tough but fair', Osborne's plans included increasing VAT to 20 per cent, welfare cuts, and public sector pay freezes. The Chancellor's hope was that by reducing the economy's reliance on the state, there would be more room for investment and trade from the private sector.[80] Acting Labour leader Harriet Harman was quick to condemn the budget as 'reckless', insisting that it would cost jobs and harm economic growth.[81] Abbott argued that cuts to public spending would hit working people twice: loss of jobs and loss of services.

By 2011, unemployment had increased to 8.1 per cent. Across the UK, real-term wages had fallen, and the cost of living was climbing. Women and ethnic minorities were particularly affected by austerity, with women of colour most likely to feel the impact of cuts.[82] There was rising foodbank use, homelessness and NHS spending failed to keep up with demand. Anthony Seldon and Mike Finn state that if NHS spending is adjusted for the ageing population, real spending per head may have even fallen during under the coalition government.[83] When it emerged that the rise in life expectancy was slowing for the first time in a century, Sir Michael Marmot, director of the Institute of Health Equity at UCL, confessed that it was 'entirely possible' that austerity was to blame.[84] To add insult to injury, economic growth flatlined, borrowing was mostly unchanged and the country narrowly avoided another recession in 2011 to 2012.

For the most part, the coalition government maintained the illusion of a united front. However, in March 2013, while Cameron was publicly defending the government's economic strategy, Business Secretary Vince Cable questioned Osborne's cuts to spending and appeared to support Labour's approach. Borrowing at low interest rates, Cable argued, was needed to invest in areas with severe impediments to growth, such as housing and infrastructure.[85] This provided a small victory for Labour who praised Cable and stated that he 'may at last be seeing sense'.[86]

In September 2013, Osborne admitted that repairing the economy would take much longer than initially thought. The government loosened its fiscal policy, and focused, instead, on a long-term economic plan which would see measures extending into the next Parliament. Abbott explains that she was unsurprised by how harsh austerity was. 'They're Tories, aren't they? You can dress yourself up as the continuity of New Labour, but in the end, they're Tories, and it's about their class interest.'[87]

In contrast, Labour tried to position itself as the party of the 'squeezed middle' and asserted the need to do away with predatory capitalism. Miliband advocated for a responsible capitalism which empowered shareholders, 'upskilled' workers and focused on

long-term success over quick returns.[88] Though appealing in principle, Labour struggled to put forward a clear economic policy and
convince the public of their economic competence. Alan Johnson,
who had joked that his first job as shadow Chancellor would be to
'pick up a primer in economics for beginners', became more known
for his gaffes than for presenting any notable challenge to Osborne's
policies.[89] After a few months in the job, he resigned due to personal
family matters.

In January 2011, Ed Balls, private school-educated, Oxford and Harvard alumnus, and former columnist at the *Financial Times* became
shadow Chancellor. Yvette Cooper took over from her husband as
shadow Home Secretary, and Douglas Alexander took over as shadow
Foreign Secretary. In 2010, Miliband had initially favoured Johnson
over Balls as Chancellor, purportedly to distance the party from the
previous government's economic policy and avoid a Blair–Brown-like
faction fight. 'We have seen that movie before and had front-row
seats. We are determined there will be no sequel,' Miliband told *The
Independent*.[90] The appointment of Balls, who was Brown's 'deputy
Chancellor' and one of the architects of Brown's infamous boom and
bust claim, drew much criticism. Stephen Williams, Liberal Democrat MP and co-chair of his party's treasury committee, mocked the
appointment of the 'deficit enthusiast' responsible for the economic
climate as shadow Chancellor.[91]

Balls hung his opposition on the cost of living crisis, 'the broken
link between the wealth of the country as a whole and people's own
finances'.[92] He was also keen to free Labour of its reputation as being
the party that spends. In June 2013, in his 'striking the right balance
for the British economy' speech, he outlined typical Labour intentions to boost infrastructure but shocked listeners when he asserted
that Tory departmental spending cuts would remain. He was reluctant
to give details about Labour's economic plans but alluded to pausing
the opening of new free schools, merging management functions in
agencies such as fire services and police forces, abolishing police commissioners, and means-testing winter fuel payments for pensioners.
However, Abbott rebuked Balls for embracing Tory austerity: 'It is

difficult to see how a Labour government that implemented cuts on that scale could last more than one term.'[93]

Although the government failed to eliminate the deficit and halve national debt in five years, the Tories continued to be the preferred party for handling the economy. In April 2014, with a year to the next general election, polls showed Cameron and Osborne were more trusted on economic management than Miliband and Balls by 40 per cent to 22 per cent.[94]

Austerity measures saw real-term spending plummet across the UK and there was a growing sentiment among pockets of the population that they were 'left behind'. For example, the SNP was gaining popularity among Scots who felt disenfranchised by Westminster. In the 2014 Scottish independence referendum, with an electoral turnout of 84.6 per cent, a sizeable 44.7 per cent voted for independence from the UK. Abbott argued that this occurred 'not because these people were "blood and soil" nationalists, but because they despaired of the Labour party actually standing up for ordinary working people'.[95]

Disillusionment also grew across England and Wales, with many Conservative voters feeling let down by the government's economic policy. Labour, who had already alienated much of their traditional voter base in favour of white-collar workers, was seen as favouring immigrants over white British 'hard-working families'. Miliband told Labour voters, 'I understand your frustration that we didn't seem to be on your side' with regards to immigration and pressures on the market and local services.[96] Using the example of his parents, Polish Jewish refugees, he stressed the importance of integration and shared his vision of 'an outward-looking country' in which immigration worked for 'all and not just some'.

Abbott supported Miliband's plans to introduce tougher standards to combat the undercutting of wages in an under-regulated labour market. This included cracking down on employers who did not pay the minimum wage, preventing recruitment agencies from solely hiring from overseas and promoting the employment, development, and training of local people. However, opinion polls indicated that many voters remained frustrated at Labour's lack of commitment to caps on immigration.

THE RISE OF UKIP

The major parties had a wake-up call in 2014 when UKIP stormed to victory in the European elections. It was the first time neither the Conservatives nor Labour won a national election since 1920. Across Europe, lay-offs of low-income workers increased support for right-wing populist parties, such as the Swedish Democrats, the French National Front and the German Golden Dawn.

Abbott notes, 'There's always been that kind of element in British politics ... You're going through an international recession, people are hurting, as we see now, they will turn to that sort of politics.'[97] UKIP was founded in 1993 in opposition to the Maastricht Treaty in 1992. While the first past the post system meant that the party struggled to gain seats in the UK, it won its first seats in the 1999 European Parliament elections, which used proportional voting. The party's 2014 success, however, was largely due to the charismatic celebrity leader, Nigel Farage.

In 2010, UKIP's membership stood at 15,000, but by 2015, this had doubled to over 30,000. The party capitalised on the growing anti-immigration sentiment and demanded a better controlled immigration system, which continued EU membership would not allow. Farage received considerable airtime from mainstream media, and UKIP councillors frequently made headlines for allegations of racism, Islamophobia and homophobia. One UKIP MEP candidate even defended his use of the n-word by stating, 'I find racist jokes funny.'[98] Despite initially dismissing the party as made up of 'a bunch of fruitcakes and loonies and closet racists', Cameron was eventually pushed to take a harsher stance on immigration and promise a referendum on continued membership in the EU.[99] 'He was frightened of losing votes to UKIP,' says Abbott.[100]

By 2014, anti-immigration rhetoric was commonplace across politics. There were whispers about quotas for 'low-skilled' EU workers and plans to cut benefits for EU migrants. Defence Secretary Michael Fallon remarked that some British towns were 'swamped' by migrants and felt 'under siege', language reminiscent of Enoch Powell in the 1960s and Thatcher in the 1970s. Home Secretary Theresa May championed Alan Johnson's vision of a 'hostile environment' by dispatching vans with the slogans 'Go home or face arrest' to London boroughs with a high immigrant population. Abbott, whose constituency was among those targeted, remarked, 'It is not so much dog-whistle politics as an entire brass band.'[101]

Abbott had asserted that 'Blue Labour wraps itself in a Hovis commercial nostalgia' which longed for a white male version of the past. It placed a 'superficial veneer' on Conservative views on topics like race and immigration.[102] By 2013, the veneer was peeling, and Miliband was being 'stampeded into moving right on race, immigration, and welfare in response to the alleged UKIP threat'.[103] In the party's official broadcast on immigration, he reassured voters that it was not prejudiced to be concerned about immigration, a line that echoed a 2005 Tory campaign slogan.

Abbott argued that though 'well-meaning', Miliband's approach risked pandering to anti-immigration rhetoric. Instead, Labour should focus on policies that would address the underlying concerns of voters, such as affordable social housing, public ownership of railways and a statutory living wage. Moreover, Abbott argued that as anti-immigration rhetoric was racialised, it risked alienating ethnic minority voters, and overlooked the fact that many 'black, brown, and foreign-looking' people were British nationals, refugees and asylum seekers.[104] She warned that Labour would enter a 'downward spiral' if they gave into 'dogwhistle' politics and 'UKIP-lite' policies.[105]

However, the party failed to heed her advice. In 2015, ahead of the general election, a photo of a red mug with the words 'Controls on immigration. I'm voting Labour' went viral. The mug, part of a collection outlining the party's five pledges, infuriated many. Abbott tweeted, 'This shameful mug is an embarrassment. But the real problem is that immigration controls are one of our five pledges at all.'

THE SYRIA BOMBINGS
On 21 August 2013, there were reports of a chemical attack on Ghouta,

Syria. Videos flooded the internet showing people suffering from what appeared to be the symptoms of nerve damage. Medics in the area also reported an influx of patients with signs of neurotoxicity. Hundreds were reported to have died. A UN report concluded that sarin, a nerve agent twenty times more toxic than cyanide, was used on the civilian population in what was considered the most significant chemical attack since 1998.

Since February 2011, there had been demonstrations, inspired by the 'Arab Spring', against President Bashar al-Assad. The government responded to the opposition with force, demonstrators retaliated, and by July 2012 the Red Cross declared Syria to be in a state of civil war. The conflict allowed the so-called Islamic State to grow in dominance.

Obama and Cameron, who agreed that Assad was behind the Ghouta attack, proposed a limited missile attack to deter Assad's use of chemical weapons. However, they did not have UN backing.

Abbott was among those concerned at the prospect of repeating the mistakes made over Iraq. 'Blair joins clamour for attack on Syria. Another reason why it's probably a bad idea,' she tweeted.[106] As with Kosovo and Iraq, Abbott argued that any military intervention should be legal, with UN backing. Moreover, she was unconvinced that a short-term bombing mission would be effective. In fact, it risked worsening the situation. She told *The Guardian*:

> I voted against the Iraq War. At the moment, I can't see anything that would make me vote for intervention in Syria. Essentially, it's a civil war. What Libya and Egypt have taught us is that these situations in the Middle East are complex. It's not good guys in white hats and bad guys in black hats.[107]

She also pointed out that intervening in Syria without UN backing would mean that the UK would have to take ownership of the aftermath.

> The danger is we get dragged into an open-ended involvement in a Syrian civil war ... We have to see the motion and the government's

rationale. The truth is, the British people have seen this movie, they know how it ends, and that's why the public is two to one against bombing Syria.

She argued against a 'unilateral US bombing raid' with 'Britain being up the rear'. The government needed to step up pressure on Russia and China, Assad's 'puppet masters' to get a UN resolution.[108]

'I know very many people who voted for the Iraq War, not because they were convinced, but out of loyalty to Tony Blair, and they regret it to this day. In the end, MPs have to do what is best for the country.'[109] Abbott kept up the pressure by speaking out against intervention at a rally in Whitehall and again on Channel 5. She asserted, 'America cannot act as the world's policeman. It is not even clear that bombing Syria would be legal … The correct way forward is with a UN-led intervention.'[110]

Although Abbott never directly threatened Miliband with resigning from the frontbench over the matter, she told *The Guardian* that should Miliband chose to back the government, it would put her in 'a very difficult position'.[111] '[My opposition] kind of triggered other people who had misgivings as well,' Abbott reflects.[112] Burnham agreed with Abbott's reasoning: 'I remember the discussions in the shadow team. We'd all lived through Iraq, and that had changed the way I was thinking. For me, it had to be utterly compelling, and I found that it wasn't at that time.'[113] Corbyn recalls that Abbott's willingness to speak out against intervention swayed opinions in the PLP. 'It was crucial,' he claims.

> Her intervention was brilliant, it dared Ed Miliband to do something about it. I was chairing a rally in Whitehall, the evening the article came out, and I said, 'We thank Diane for her bravery, and her ability to stand up on this.' She'd been arguing with Ed about it, and he was under pressure from her, probably under pressure from the right of the party to support the bombing.[114]

Chief Whip Nick Brown agrees: 'Those who called for opposing the intervention, set a standard that the rest of us could rally around.'[115]

One Labour MP with serious misgivings was Jim Fitzpatrick, a senior Labour frontbencher, who resigned hours before the vote, stating that he was 'opposed to military intervention in Syria, full stop'.[116]

Ribeiro-Addy recalls that following Abbott's interview in *The Guardian*, many MPs found that 'a lot of their constituents were emailing them, angry they were potentially going to do this and citing how people like Diane [opposed it]'.[117] Despite never having a conversation with Abbott on the topic, they reported feeling bullied by her. 'As a black person, you need to be very careful how you phrase things,' Ribeiro-Addy explains. 'They will say you are aggressive.'

On 28 August 2013, Miliband told Cameron that Labour would not support a parliamentary call for military action in Syria until a UN weapons inspection team report was issued. The government was livid. One source told *The Times* that 'No 10 and the Foreign Office think Miliband is a fucking cunt and a copper-bottomed shit'.[118]

Cameron was forced to concede and offer a second vote on military action after receipt of the UN report. There was also scepticism and opposition from some Tories and Liberal Democrats. While Parliament agreed that action was needed, they could not reach a consensus on whether the bombings would be legal and effective.

In a bid to win over MPs, the government released its Joint Intelligence Committee assessment and the government's legal position and added that Obama, who opposed the Iraq War, was in support of a strike. However, Labour remained unconvinced and pushed for a different amendment which did not attribute direct blame for the attack and required a UN Security Council vote before military action took place. This amendment was defeated by 220 to 332. The government's proposal was also defeated by 285 to 272, with thirty Tory rebels.

Although Cameron was praised for giving Parliament the say in matters of war and peace, the defeat was an embarrassment for a Prime Minister who desperately needed to prove his leadership and authority. Meanwhile, Miliband was accused of 'flip-flopping', 'moving the goal posts' and 'playing politics' with the lives of Syrians. A Downing Street spokesperson went as far as to suggest Miliband's stance gave 'succour' to the Assad regime.[119]

OFF THE FRONTBENCH

Six weeks after the Syria vote, in a shadow Cabinet reshuffle, Miliband removed Abbott from the frontbench. 'I think Ed wants more message discipline,' she remarked at the time. '[He] has been convinced that what you need in the run-up to the general election are people who literally read from the script.'[120] *The Guardian*'s Michael White questioned whether Miliband mistook dissent for disloyalty.[121]

On reflection, Abbott acknowledges that her removal from the frontbench was a long time coming, 'It was the effect of a culmination of complaints about me.'[122] Abbott recalls receiving the news of her dismissal. '[Miliband] said, "I don't want us to keep falling out." So, he sacks me,' she laughs. 'He said, "I hope you think I'm doing the right thing." So, I said, "Of course you're doing the right thing. You're the leader of the party." He still wanted reassurance,' she laughs.[123] Abbott was sorry to leave Burnham and her colleagues in public health but welcomed the freedom to better focus on issues she deemed important, such as the impact of austerity on her constituents and London as a whole.

Off the frontbench, Abbott had a freer hand holding the government to account. On 2 July 2013, Home Secretary Theresa May had announced a consultation on reforms to stop and search. Stop and search had become a dividing line between political parties, and within the Tory Party there were those who wanted to appeal to the right and defended it and argued for its extension. May had to proceed cautiously, for fear of alienating the Tory base. So, her consultation contained numerous caveats stating how effective and necessary stop and search was. Nonetheless, May's announcement acknowledged that 'when it is over-used, or when people are targeted when they do not need to be, it is a waste of police time and erodes community confidence in the police'.[124]

The clips of May's speech that were broadcast did not feature the word black, nor were the parts of her speech quoted in the press release. Nonetheless, she had acknowledged in the Commons that 'if someone is from a black or minority ethnic background, they are up to seven times more likely to be stopped and searched by the police than if they are white'.[125] Abbott and Vaz were two of the first MPs to welcome the announcement.

Since her election in 1987 Abbott had regularly organised events in Parliament dealing with stop and search, police violence against black people, about deaths in custody and about institutional racism in the police force more generally. They were part of her desire to open the Commons up to the people, to use the democratic potential of her role and the existing institution as fully as possible. Consequently, as soon as May announced that she would he holding consultations with members of the public, Abbott decided to organise an event and to invite May to hear from those who came. Abbott's staff thought the idea of inviting May was funny, it was widely assumed that she would not attend. However, Abbott was determined, and sent May an invitation. To the consternation of her staff, May agreed to come. In fact, it led to an office joke, 'Theresa is coming', a reference to HBO's *Game of Thrones*.

At the same time the invitation went to May, Abbott's staff sent out invitations to the groups campaigning around deaths in custody, groups campaigning around stop and search and black activist groups more generally. The uptake was high.

On the evening of the event, around 150 guests, the vast majority black, arrived and were shown to the committee room. May arrived, explaining that she was only able to make a brief statement and would have to leave quickly due to urgent business. May's statement was almost identical to her press release: stop and search would continue, stop and search was a vital tool, but it needed to be conducted more appropriately. Having made her statement, May motioned that she wanted to leave, but Abbott invited questions from the floor. Apparently, May's performance was impressive. One of the people who attended compared her to Thatcher, saying 'they called her the Iron Lady, May has to be made of titanium!'[126]

May clearly took the matter seriously. At the end of the consultation period she acknowledged that as many as 250,000 stops were carried out in 2013, and more than one in four of these could have been illegal. May apparently wanted legal curbs to stop and search powers included in the 2015 Queen's speech, but Cameron refused. UKIP were polling well and with an election on the horizon, this was no time to abandon populism.

The phrase 'Theresa is coming' continued to be a part of life in Abbott's office. However, its meaning changed. Anticipating a Tory leadership challenge in the near future, May's performance convinced Abbott and her staff that she was the one to beat.

LONDON MAYORAL ELECTIONS

Since the creation of the position of London mayor, only two men had held the post: Ken Livingstone and Boris Johnson. When both men announced that they would not be running in the 2016 London mayoral election, rumours about who would succeed them began.

Under the Labour electoral college, unions accounted for a third of the vote for Labour leadership, MPs and MEPs accounted for another third and party members comprised the remaining third. This proved particularly controversial after Miliband's leadership win in 2010 and again in 2013, when Unite was accused of attempting to rig the Labour candidate selection in the Falkirk by-election. In 2014, Labour members voted in favour of Miliband's proposals to require union members to opt in to be Labour members, instead of automatic affiliation, and a one-member, one-vote system for leadership elections. This included mayoral candidate selections.

Abbott was among those rumoured to be standing for selection as Labour's candidate for London mayor. She had doubled her majority in the 2010 general election and in July 2014, she ranked first in an *Evening Standard* poll which asked people intending to vote Labour at the 2015 general election who they would back for London mayor.[127] 'It was something she could win,' Ribeiro-Addy states, recalling the excitement around the campaign.[128]

Abbott finally confirmed that she would be running to be the Labour candidate for Mayor of London on 30 November 2014. 'A great many people have been pressing me for some time to throw my hat in the ring. In the end I decided that because London needs a genuinely independent candidate. London needs a candidate that will fight to make London more affordable for ordinary Londoners,' she said on *ITV News London*.[129]

Her campaign centred on issues such as transport, housing and immigration. She said she would freeze public transport fares for four years and introduce a legal minimum wage for London due to the high cost of living in the city. Regarding housing, she proposed greater rent control to tackle exploitation, special rates of capital gains tax for non-domicile investors, who she argued sent 'ripples of gentrification' across London, and more freedom for councils to borrow to build housing. Although she initially opposed Ed Ball's proposal for a mansion tax, she later supported it as long as it did not hurt the 'asset-rich, income poor' and helped fund investment in genuinely affordable homes.[130]

In a speech at the London School of Economics, Abbott attacked the 'toxic anti-immigration culture' which, she claimed, Labour in Westminster had become complicit with, but no London mayor should. 'The mayor should not be a party glove puppet,' she asserted.[131] She also outlined proposals to 'drive an assault on health inequality', such as the introduction of a London health commissioner who would work in partnership with the NHS and Public Health England. She also called for the Education Maintenance Allowance (EMA) to be restored in London.

Abbott positioned herself as the 'genuinely independent' candidate, 'a candidate that is not in the pocket of party leadership'.[132] Pointing to her opposition to military action in Iraq and Syria and the rise in tuition fees, Abbott asserted she had 'shown the capacity to stand up and be counted when it matters'.[133] This capacity to stray from the party line gained Abbott the support of student leaders from organisations including the NUS and London Young Labour, who asserted, 'Diane is always true to her word: that's her character.'[134]

Despite an overall disappointing result at the May general election, Labour increased its seats in London from thirty-eight to forty-five, gaining 43.7 per cent of the vote. This gave new optimism for the mayoral election. In June 2015, after gaining at least five Constituency Labour Party nominations and passing selection interviews, Abbott, former Olympics Minister Tessa Jowell, Tooting MP and former Transport Minister Sadiq Khan, Tottenham MP David Lammy, Harrow West MP and former shadow minister Gareth Thomas and transport journalist Christian Wolmar were confirmed as contenders for the Labour mayoral candidate.

The favourites were Tessa Jowell and Sadiq Khan. Tessa Jowell had served as an MP for twenty-three years and played a key role in securing the 2012 Olympics for London. The ardent Blairite argued that her appeal to non-Labour voters made her best placed to challenge the Tory Zac Goldsmith. Having stepped down from the frontbench in 2012, Jowell had ample time to focus on her campaign. 'Tessa Jowell was the big money, the very big money,' Ribeiro-Addy shares. '[But] Sadiq was probably the one to beat.'[135]

Sadiq Khan had resigned as shadow Justice Secretary and shadow Minister for London to run for mayor. He had gained the support of many of the Labour-affiliated unions, Margaret Hodge, Oona King, Michael Cashman and Abbott's long-time friend, Ken Livingstone. 'It was a surprise because we weren't told beforehand; it was disappointing because it was Ken,' Ribeiro-Addy states.[136] 'It wasn't about issues, but about what people were willing to do when they got into office.' By mid-May, Jowell was the favourite to win, followed by Khan, then Lammy and then Abbott with odds of 33–1.[137]

On 3 June 2015, Corbyn was nominated by the PLP to run for the Labour leadership. His authentic, down-to-earth style and radical left-wing politics hugely appealed to young people who flocked to hear him speak at hustings across the country. The Labour Party saw a surge in people paying the £3 membership fee, allowing them to vote in the leadership election. It also allowed them to vote in the mayoral election, a huge benefit for long-time Corbyn supporter Abbott.

Ribeiro-Addy reports that Corbyn's team did not allow him to formally endorse Abbott, fearful it would harm his campaign. Nonetheless, when Corbyn spoke at Abbott's campaign event, her supporters greeted him with equal enthusiasm. As Labour councillor Claudia Webbe wrote in August 2015, 'For supporters of Jeremy Corbyn, Diane Abbott is the logical choice for Mayor of London.'[138]

Despite coming from different wings of the party, all six candidates took a left-wing stance on issues such as housing, transport and policing, supposedly to better appeal to Londoners. This was particularly frustrating for Abbott and her team. Ribeiro-Addy remembers Abbott used the hustings to contrast the candidates' proposals with their voting records. On one occasion, Ribeiro-Addy recalls, Abbott held up a newspaper article that Khan had written which contradicted the left-leaning ideas he was spouting.

After months of campaigning and five hustings across London, the ballots closed on 10 September 2015. Bookies put Abbott's chances of winning the candidacy at 20–1, Khan 3–1, and Jowell 2–1.[139] The following day it was announced that Khan had won the Labour nomination for mayoral candidate. He defeated Jowell on the final ballot by 58.9 per cent to 41.1 per cent. Abbott placed third.[140] 'Diane said if there's anything that showed her who her friends were, it was the mayoral selection,' Ribeiro-Addy shares.[141]

Abbott used her role as shadow Minister for Public Health to expose the costs of austerity. Working with Andy Burnham, she used her time on the frontbench to challenge the power of the food and alcohol industry, empower families and advocate for the enabling role of the state in improving the health of the nation, especially that of young people. In some ways, Abbott found Miliband's frontbench stifling, but she stood her ground on issues such as opposing military action in Syria, putting pressure on other Labour MPs to do the same. Abbott's dissent may have cost her a seat on the frontbench, but she continued to advocate for issues important to her constituents, education, austerity and anti-immigration sentiment and this culminated in her bid to be the Labour candidate for London mayor.

CHAPTER 13

JEZ WE CAN!

Pledge mugs were one of the innovations of the 1997 election campaign. As Britain went to the polls, Labour supporters could sip a caffè latte from one of five official mugs, bearing slogans such as 'Fast track for young offenders' and 'Cut NHS waiting lists'. Almost two decades later, Ed Miliband was still using the New Labour playbook. Pledge cards were printed, bearing the leader's signature, and Labour's five canonical commitments were printed on vermilion mugs. As Britain went to the polls in 2015, Labour supporters could sip their macchiato from a 'Controls on immigration. I'm voting Labour' mug. During the 2010 leadership campaign, Abbott had dragged Ed Miliband away from hard-line rhetoric on immigration. The 2014 local and European Elections pushed immigration back up the agenda. By 2015 Miliband was promising to strengthen Britain's borders with more border guards and additional immigration checks.

During the 2010 leadership campaign, there had been discussion of bold new policies. Abbott had promised the renationalisation of the railways, scrapping Trident and the mutualisation of publicly owned banks and Andy Burnham had advocated a national care service. By 2015, the leadership debates were a dim memory, and political debate had narrowed. Writing in *The Times*, Hugo Rifkind tried to summon up a memory of the contest. It was, he recalled, 'a showdown between a guy everybody thought should win ... and that other guy nobody liked, who had hair like Hitler ... hair that looked like it wished to rule for 1,000 years'.[1] Implausibly, Rifkind assured his readers 'and truly, kids, I swear this did happen' that Abbott had been one of the contenders. By 2015 the wide-ranging debate of the leadership race had faded and political debate had narrowed to the deficit, the NHS and immigration. Europe, which would come to dominate politics in the coming years, was way down the list.[2]

David Cameron's pledge to 'ring-fence' NHS spending seems to have neutralised the issue for the Tories. Cameron had a commanding lead on economic competence. Immigration was not a major talking point in the campaign. Indeed, less than 4 per cent of discussion on television and in the press related to immigration.[3] This may have reflected Labour's success in neutralising the issue. Equally, polling showed that although voters believed immigration was a major issue facing the nation, they did not regard it as an issue for their families, a fact that indicates that Abbott was right to argue that Labour could have won the argument on principle, by making immigration an issue about the experience of real people rather than about quotas and numerical caps.

Labour's defeat led to a renewed debate about the party's future. Forty-eight hours after the result was announced, Peter Mandelson told Andrew Marr that Labour had lost as it had deserted the centre ground. 'The scale of the sort of challenge we face and the need for re-thinking and re-modernisation of the party is akin to the sort of scale of challenge we faced in the late 1980s.'[4] Mandelson had good reason to be concerned. In the 2015 election Labour had been wiped out in Scotland, the collapse in the Liberal Democrat vote had not benefited Labour and after five years of austerity Cameron had increased both his party's vote and won the first Tory majority in Parliament since 1992. Other than the election of 1983, Labour had had its worst result in recent history. Mandelson's comments reflected the fact that, according to all the norms of modern politics, Labour was likely to spend another decade out of power.

Mandelson's solution was for Labour to become 'New New Labour'.[5] He was not the only senior figure in the party to reach this conclusion. Earlier that morning, Tony Blair, writing in *The Observer*, had admonished Labour and stated that 'the route to the summit lies through the centre ground'.[6] Mandelson and Blair made no pronouncements on policy, after all, Blair argued, 'the centre ground is as much a state of mind as a set of policies'. This was one of the problems for those wishing to cleave to the centre. Dominating the centre ground sounded like an excellent strategy, but neither Mandelson nor Blair suggested anything concrete. In the 1990s they had defined the centre ground with radical policies: a minimum wage, devolution, a reduction in class sizes, guaranteed nursery places, incorporating the European Convention on Human Rights into British Law and dramatic increases in health spending. In 2015, beyond platitudes, Mandelson and Blair could do nothing to give 'the centre ground' shape. Another problem with Blair's argument was that it assumed that 'the centre ground' was broadly constant, that the values and approaches which had characterised the centre in the mid-1990s, had not been affected by the Iraq War, the expenses scandal, the credit crunch, austerity or the emergence of a new generation of voters who lived with the consequences of privatisation and marketisation. Indeed, Blair and Mandelson made their case before the publication of analysis indicating that a generational shift was underway.

Abbott was the first on Labour's left to respond to Mandelson and Blair. Speaking to the BBC, Abbott argued that it was no time to return to the past. Rather, Labour needed to have a strong anti-austerity message. When asked how this would appeal to the middle class, Abbott stated that many middle-class voters were 'worried about their children's future', and that more than £12 billion of cuts would hit the middle class as well as the working class. Abbott ruled herself out of the leadership race. Nonetheless, she had highlighted one of the issues that would define the next few years. Decades of *laissez-faire* housing policy had created a housing crisis, austerity had saddled many young people with tens of thousands of pounds of debt, and deregulation was destroying job security, particularly for the young. The new generation, on current trends, would be poorer than their parents, would work longer hours, accrue more debt, would rent rather than own property and would live more precarious lives. New Labour's approach offered no solutions to these problems, nor did empty talk about the centre ground. What is more, while Mandelson and Blair blamed the 2015 result on Miliband's shift to the left, Abbott argued, 'the roots of this defeat are not actually in the five years Ed Miliband spent as leader … the roots of this defeat, particularly in Scotland, go back a lot further'.[7] Published in 2016, Philip Cowley and Dennis Kavanagh's authoritative study of the 2015 election indicated that Abbott had better understood the dynamics of the election than Mandelson and Blair.[8] First, Cowley and Kavanagh dismissed the claim that voters thought Labour had lurched too far to the left. Mandelson and Blair were correct, however, that voters did not trust Labour with the economy. But what they missed was that this judgement was based on perceptions of New Labour's record. Indeed, voters blamed New Labour, rather than Cameron or Osborne, for the financial crash and the austerity that followed.

LEADERSHIP ELECTION

Another defeat precipitated another leadership election. Liz Kendall was the first to announce her candidacy. Speaking to Andrew Marr, Chuka Umunna refused to rule himself out and received an equivocal endorsement from Mandelson. Yvette Cooper and Andy Burnham stepped forward a few days later. By mid-May it looked like Labour had a diverse field, far more so than in the early stages of the 2010 campaign. In that sense, Abbott's candidacy five years earlier foreshadowed much more diverse fields in 2015 and 2020. Early opinion polls put Andy Burnham and Umunna out in front among Labour members and Labour voters. Umunna, who was the second black person to stand for the Labour leadership after Abbott, withdrew in mid-May.

The Campaign Group was divided. 'Most of them', Abbott recalls, 'weren't that enthusiastic because they knew we were going to lose.'[9] 'John McDonnell's view', Corbyn recalls, 'was that we had no chance of getting on the ballot paper, so why embarrass ourselves?'[10] However, Abbott was aware that Labour activists were in favour of the left running a candidate, and Corbyn agreed. Speaking at a Labour Representation Committee event prior to the weekly Campaign Group meeting, he made the case that left-wing MPs should run. His argument was that they had a duty to build on Abbott's 2010 campaign.

Even so, at the weekly Campaign Group meeting, which took place as usual in Parliament's Room W1, Abbott remembers, 'no one was fighting to do it, so we literally went round the table'.[11] Abbott ruled herself out, she had done her bit in 2010. McDonnell too had tried in the past and thought someone else should have a go. Jon Trickett and Ian Lavery were unwilling to stand. Corbyn recalls that it was a small meeting and therefore options quickly narrowed. 'We were going around the table and they said, "What about you?"'[12] Accepting that it was his turn, Corbyn agreed. He remembers:

> At that point, Diane, what a bloody so-and-so, she had her phone open already, and she'd already written a tweet, she just pressed send. So, we came out of the meeting, and there were all these journalists in the corridor – it was Diane's bloody tweet! She's very sharp with her phone![13]

Abbott had two reasons for putting out the tweet. She wanted to firm up Corbyn's candidacy, as she could see that he did not want to run. Second, she wanted Corbyn, rather than anyone else in the Campaign Group, to be the candidate. Abbott's tweet meant that she was effectively Corbyn's first campaign manager, or perhaps the Corbyn team's first leak.

Like Abbott before him, Corbyn had a struggle getting on the ballot. Nonetheless, as McDonnell, who chaired Corbyn's campaign, points out, 'We were able to remind people that they had nominated Diane, and that for the health of the party, it's better to have a spread of candidates to demonstrate the broad church nature of the party.'[14] Moreover, Abbott's campaign in 2010 allowed McDonnell

> to use the argument in the PLP that there was sizable support for a left candidate out there, who would be extremely disappointed if they didn't have the chance, not only to vote for a left candidate, but to hear the arguments. It prepared the path for the argument that we could put to the PLP to get the nominations ... It gave us confidence that we could run a candidate and get a reasonable vote.

The argument was that if we could get 25 or 30 per cent of the vote, we could demonstrate that the left had significant support inside the party. Diane laid the trail for that, no doubt about it.

Like Abbott, Corbyn saw his attempt to secure the nominations go down to the wire. He gained the nominations necessary with minutes to spare. Like Abbott, Corbyn received a large number of nominations from MPs who were not sympathetic to his politics but were happy to help as they knew he had no chance of winning. Margaret Beckett later described herself as 'a moron' for lending him her support.[15] Other MPs doubtless felt the same.

The Labour leadership campaign coincided with the selection process for Labour's mayoral candidate. Abbott was one of the first MPs to endorse Corbyn's candidacy. The question of who the candidates were backing for leader came up repeatedly during the campaign for the mayoral nomination. At the penultimate hustings, which took place in late July in Wood Green, Abbott endorsed Corbyn, 'Jeremy Corbyn is my oldest friend in politics, I was the first MP to nominate him, I was proud to do so, and I will be voting for Jeremy Corbyn.'[16]

Some of the other candidates were less willing to commit. Tessa Jowell said that she was not endorsing anyone but advised party members to vote for the candidate that they could imagine as the next Prime Minister. David Lammy and Sadiq Khan both made much of the fact that they had nominated Corbyn but professed themselves undecided.

As soon as Corbyn was on the ballot, Abbott began emailing her supporters, and using campaign events to promote his leadership bid. The two campaigns ran an impromptu joint event at Bloomsbury Central Baptist Church at the end of July. Corbyn recalls that the meeting was initially planned to be a 'Diane4London' event, at which he was to speak on her behalf. On the night, it became a joint event. Corbyn recalls, 'I turned up there and was introduced as the person brave enough to stand as leader of the Labour Party and got a fantastic reception. Diane and I both got a great reception.'[17]

The queue for the event snaked up to New Oxford Street. An

overspill room was hastily opened, and stewards urged the crowd to 'share like good socialists' as the pews filled. Ribeiro-Addy remembers the anticipation as large numbers of people queued up around Bloomsbury Baptist Church, the campaign base, eager to meet Abbott and Corbyn, her guest speaker. 'It was a bit of a revival!' she laughs. 'A baptism of left philosophy.' Abbott outlined her plan for London, Corbyn his plans for Britain. The evening ended with a standing ovation for both candidates.[18]

At the beginning of the contest no one in the Campaign Group expected Corbyn to win. 'He was up against the brightest and the best of New Labour,' Abbott recalls, and he had little, if any, institutional support.[19] Bookies put Corbyn's odds of victory at 100–1 against. But the atmosphere at Bloomsbury Central Baptist Church was like nothing Abbott had experienced before. Her team also picked up on a different atmosphere.

Ribeiro-Addy recalls, 'We'd done rallies all over the country, but the enthusiasm with which people were registering, people were just beyond excited.' Abbott remembers, 'to everyone's amazement, including some of the people who nominated him, he cut through'.[20]

As the campaign went on, Abbott's team got updated membership lists, to use in her mayoral campaign. She also kept an eye on her constituency party membership list. As they got longer, she and her campaign team could see something big was happening. There was also an influx of registered supporters. These were not full party members, but for a small fee, they could vote in the election. From what Abbott's team could make out, people who were still in two minds about Labour were registering but were holding back from joining the party until the outcome of the leadership election was declared. As the membership list in London was growing at what one of her staffers described as 'a crazy rate' and as London was a progressive city, Abbott and her team started to believe that Corbyn was in with a chance.

On 10 August, a YouGov poll put Corbyn way ahead in the leadership race, which clearly worried Labour's grandees. Writing in *The Guardian*, Blair appealed to party members, 'If Jeremy Corbyn becomes leader it won't be a defeat like 1983 or 2015 at the next election.

It will mean rout, possibly annihilation.'[21] Blair's prophecy became a dividing line in the mayoral campaign. Asked by LBC's Iain Dale if Blair was right, Jowell dismissed the question as a distraction. 'You're doing an Yvette Cooper, Andy Burnham, and Liz Kendall. That's what they did in the Labour leadership debate in this studio. They wouldn't give me a direct answer. Diane'll give me a direct answer,' Dale retorted. Dale was right. Live on air she put £20 on Corbyn being Prime Minister in 2020.[22]

In mid-August #LabourPurge started trending on Twitter, as activists keen to cast their vote found they had been dropped from membership lists or expelled from the party. Controversy over Miliband's pledge mugs was one reason given for the expulsions. Labour members who had complained about the 'Controls on immigration. I'm voting Labour' mug on Twitter, or who had praised the Green Party parody mug bearing the slogan 'Standing up for migrants. I'm voting Green' were among those likely to be expelled. Abbott took up the case, defending members who had criticised the mugs. If it was a crime, she pointed out, she was as guilty as any.

During the summer of 2015, Abbott argues, it became clear that 'New Labour's brightest and best' were failing to win over the membership. In part, Abbott argues, Blair's approach to government meant that New Labour was unsustainable. First, 'modernisation' stripped party members of their right to make policy. Second, it stripped the conference and the NEC – the institutions which represented the membership – of power. This meant that the leadership and policy making became increasingly disconnected from ordinary Labour members. Third, Blair determined to change the composition of the PLP. Labour MPs, historically, came up through unions or local government and therefore had genuine local roots. In the name of professionalisation, the leadership increasingly imposed candidates on local parties. Consequently, as Abbott argues, 'He removed a swathe of people, the old Labour right. Whatever I may have thought of them, they had genuine roots in the communities they sought to serve.'[23] Blair's preferred MPs tended to be middle class, university educated and media savvy. These changes in the makeup of the PLP meant that many of the MPs who made it into Parliament in the 2000s did not really understand the needs of the communities they 'represented' or the impact of the policies they championed. Corbyn, by contrast, had come up through local government and through union work. He was also constantly involved with grassroots campaigns. This was not lost on the press. The *Guardian* headline 'Jeremy Corbyn profile: "He talks like a human being, about things that are real"', published in mid-August, reflected this.[24] The fact that it was newsworthy to find a Labour MP who could talk to ordinary people about things that really mattered says a lot about the generation of MPs who had emerged in the Blair–Brown era.

Blair, Mandelson and Cooper all dismissed Corbyn on the basis that he would not win a general election. However, as the other leadership contenders struggled to connect with ordinary party members, none of them looked like credible winners. Therefore, the electability argument failed to cut through.

The result of the leadership contest was announced in September 2015, at the Queen Elizabeth II Conference Centre. The hall was full of faces from Labour's recent past. John Prescott sat in the centre, Keith Vaz and Margaret Beckett in the front row, Harriet Harman and Khan behind the empty seats which had been reserved for the leadership hopefuls. Abbott, uncharacteristically, was on the right.

The event started with a video montage of the campaign, which was accompanied by a piece of light orchestral music worthy of *Kinnock: The Movie*. Abbott was namechecked and received a round of applause when Khan – who had recently been confirmed as Labour's candidate for London mayor – congratulated her on a well-fought campaign. The theme of the event was unity. Tom Watson, Labour's newly elected deputy leader told the party to abandon faction fighting and unite behind the new leader. Corbyn's victory also appeared to be a moment of unity. Cooper and Kendall were the first to congratulate him. Unlike Miliband five years earlier, Corbyn's victory was decisive. Indeed, with 59.5 per cent of the vote in the first round, Corbyn won more convincingly than Blair.

Corbyn's victory was a shock to the party and the country. It was also a shock to the left. 'Initially,' Abbott remembers, 'we hadn't expected to win at all. It became clear that Jeremy was doing better than expected but you didn't expect the margin, and you didn't quite expect the victory.'[25] Corbyn had been polling well, but after the failure of the polls in the recent election, that meant nothing. The weight of recent history was against him. Abbott recalls that 'the left of the party had been marginalised and excluded since the Kinnock years' and therefore, even for Corbyn's supporters it was hard to believe that he might have won. The result was electrifying: 'Some of us were ecstatic! Now suddenly we were running the party.'[26] When Abbott first entered Parliament in 1987, she and Corbyn had been blamed for Labour's defeat. Now almost thirty years later everything had been reversed.

For Abbott, Corbyn's victory was a necessary reorientation of the party, which brought the leadership back into line with party members. She argues that it reflected a rejection of the market fundamentalism of the later New Labour period, and the desire for a radical alternative to austerity.

Corbyn's victory guaranteed nothing. Bookies put his odds of fighting an election as Labour leader at 6–4. The commentariat were of the same mind. Indeed, as delegates entered the conference centre, ninety minutes before the result was announced, Michael Crick was already asking Labour's big hitters if they were planning to run when Corbyn was forced out.

Within minutes of the result, Tristram Hunt had quit the shadow Cabinet. He was the first of many who refused to serve the new leader. Over the course of the next two hours Cooper and Kendall, Rachel Reeves and Emma Reynolds had announced that they would not join Corbyn's shadow Cabinet, as had lesser-known figures such as Chris Leslie.

Abbott remembers being wary of 'a coup' from the outset. Corbyn's victory, she observes, 'had completely upturned the party establishment, the party as an institution, the big donors, but also the left media establishment. A lot of *Guardian* commentators were completely gutted. They were deeply hostile, so you had to expect a coup at any time.'[27] This was not paranoia; Abbott's perspective reflected the briefings being given by Labour MPs to the press. Two weeks after Corbyn's victory, and on the eve of Labour's annual conference, the *Financial Times* reported, 'The political death notices are already being prepared and one question is on the lips of those gathering by the English seaside: "How long can he last?"' The paper quoted one 'moderate Labour MP' saying, 'We have to give him time to fail … There can't be a coup now: we would have blood on our hands.'[28]

BACK TO THE FRONTBENCH

Corbyn's victory meant that for the first time in her political career, Abbott could expect a position in the shadow Cabinet. Corbyn's first shadow Cabinet, Abbott recalls, was an exercise in conciliation. The new leader worked with Rosie Winterton, then Chief Whip, to include people who represented the breadth of opinion in the PLP. Winterton proved important in winning over some of the Corbyn sceptics in the PLP. The first Cabinet contained Hilary Benn as shadow Foreign Secretary and Lord Falconer as shadow Justice Secretary. Only four of Corbyn's first shadow Cabinet members could be described as his natural allies. McDonnell was given a prominent job as shadow Chancellor. But to balance that, and to make room for MPs from other wings of the party, Abbott was given a more junior position. She had indicated an interest in several roles and in the end she was appointed shadow Secretary of State for International Development. This was a disappointment for Abbott, but she recognised it reflected the need to reach an accommodation with the PLP.

As a member of the shadow Cabinet, Abbott had, in theory, a certain authority in the PLP. However, the position came with constraints. Her statements required approval from Labour's press office at Southside, where Corbyn had few allies, and she was expected to speak only on matters concerning her brief and her constituency. Nonetheless, there was a tension between the formal constraints and the attitude of the leader. Abbott's staff quickly got the impression that Corbyn had no intention of placing limits on what she could say in public.

CONFERENCE SEASON

Abbott addressed the 2015 Labour conference as part of the shadow Cabinet. It was thirty-one years since she first addressed conference. Her 2015 conference speech required a similar balancing act. First, she spoke as conciliator, praising Clare Short and Gordon Brown for their action on development during the New Labour years. Corbyn and Benn, who sat next to each other on the platform applauded. Then she praised Cooper, who had stood against Corbyn in the leadership election, pointing to her success in forcing the Cameron government to take humanitarian action to help refugees crossing the Mediterranean. Having reached out across the party, Abbott set out a series of radical positions. On the question of migration and asylum she stated, 'you cannot out-UKIP UKIP, and we shouldn't even try'.[29] Second, she advocated 'women-centred development policies'. A new commitment to development had been part of Cameron's agenda. However, a few weeks before Abbott's speech Cameron had announced that £25 million of the foreign aid budget would be used to build a prison in Jamaica so that the UK could then deport Jamaican prisoners. Abbott pledged to expose this misuse of public money.

Abbott's speech also contained a surprise. She pledged to vote against an extension of British military action in Syria. Abbott's speech had been checked prior to the conference by party officials. Her comments on Syria were planned but had not been part of her submission. Apparently, party officials were furious. Nonetheless, Abbott's statement went down well with the conference. What is more, it was a statement of her personal opinion, not of party policy, and obviously had the backing of the leader. It was the first indication that Abbott was going to be a spokesperson for the leadership, as well as international development.

The Conservative Party conference, which took place in early October, was radical in a different way. It convinced many commentators that Corbynism was already dead. Prior to the conference the *Financial Times* reported one of Cameron's allies commenting that Corbyn's victory was 'proof that God is a Conservative'.[30] Cameron, still buoyant from his unexpected election victory in May, gave a speech which was widely viewed as a bid for the vacant 'centre ground'. Remarkably, Cameron acknowledged the reality of racism in Britain. In a much-quoted section he stated,

> We can talk all we want about opportunity, but it's meaningless unless people are really judged equally. Think about it like this. Opportunity doesn't mean much to a British Muslim if he walks down the street and is abused for his faith. Opportunity doesn't mean much to a black person constantly stopped and searched by the police because of the colour of their skin.[31]

Cameron also made a virtue of the diversity of his frontbench team, describing Sam Gyimah as 'the black British son of a single parent'; Priti Patel as 'the daughter of Gujarati immigrants who arrived in our country from East Africa with nothing except the clothes they stood up in'; and noting that Sajid Javid's 'father came here from Pakistan to drive the buses'. Cameron also argued that the Conservatives should be the champions of opportunity for all, including women, gay men, lesbian women and people with disabilities. Thirty years earlier, these words would have been written off as 'loony left' extremism. But in 2015, coming from the Tory leader they were covered as a bold one nation vision, which showed that the Conservatives were now the party of moderation, compared to Corbyn's Labour which, having abandoned 'the centre ground' would face inevitable annihilation at the polls.

Cameron had positioned the Conservative Party firmly within the existing consensus. In terms of economic policy, the government was committed to free markets, in terms of social policy Cameron had reasonable liberal credentials and in terms of foreign policy, if not presentation, he was pro-European. This was the territory that Blair had occupied in the 1990s and 2000s and the political space to which Mandelson, Blair and many in the PLP thought Labour should return.

The Tory conference was widely regarded as heralding a new era of Conservative dominance. Keynote speeches stuck to the Cameron script. For once Conservative ministers really had stopped banging on about Europe, and focused on the need to improve opportunity, improve education and safeguard the NHS. All, that is, except one. Theresa May's tough rhetoric on immigration struck a discordant note. Reports circulated that her hard-line speech was a signal that she was out of step with the rest of the leadership. Some even claimed that she had been allowed to give the speech in order to destroy her chances of succeeding Cameron, to clear the path for George Osborne. Whatever the case, May's speech merely served to emphasise the moderation and modernity of the Tory team, compared to Labour's new leadership who were presented as a bunch of extremists who were stuck in the past.

The media narrative showed a particular view of recent history. Cameron was regarded as a moderate statesman because he had adopted, rhetorically at least, the equality agenda which Abbott and Corbyn had fought for in the 1980s. Corbyn and Abbott, however, were still regarded as 'loony left', in no small part, because of their campaigns, decades earlier, on precisely these issues. The reaction to Cameron's speech also showed a double standard. Cameron could describe a young woman he had met as a 'young black girl' and be applauded as a moderate. However, when Abbott described Cameron and Clegg as 'posh white boys' she was attacked as a racist. What was a virtue for Cameron was a vice for Abbott.

TENSIONS IN THE SHADOW CABINET
Concern that Labour had abandoned 'the centre ground' was also felt in the PLP. Abbott recalls that in the first nine months of the new parliament, 'for those of us who supported the Corbyn project, it was really very uneasy'.[32] Many of Corbyn's opponents had honed their faction-fighting skills during the New Labour years and knew how to hurt the leadership. Leaks were common. 'Sometimes', Abbott recalls, 'you'd be in the shadow Cabinet and you'd look at your phone, and you'd see someone was leaking what was being said, before the meeting had even finished.' If the leaked report on anti-Semitism in the Labour Party is to be believed, this faction fighting targeted Abbott.

Shadow Cabinet discord was particularly evident in the debate about Syria. Corbyn's opposition to military action was leaked at the very beginning of the shadow Cabinet meeting before any attempt had been made to reach a compromise. Corbyn offered to try to reach an agreement with Benn in a face-to-face meeting, but Benn refused. Some in the shadow Cabinet made it clear that they had no respect for Corbyn and had no respect for the choice of Labour members. 'It was a difficult and unhappy atmosphere,' she recalls.[33] Abbott argues that Corbyn had every intention of working constructively with the PLP and went out of his way to avoid confrontation and to foster compromise. However, some accepted jobs in the shadow Cabinet and then gave every impression of wanting to undermine Corbyn's leadership. In a sense, this was a continuation of the tactics Abbott had encountered on first entering Parliament, whereby some in the PLP had attempted to make her life unbearable, presumably in the hope of forcing her out.

In the lead up to the Commons vote on military action in Syria Abbott put the leadership's case to the media. Speaking on *Channel 4 News* and on Sky News a week before the debate, she made the case for a free vote. She also asked Labour MPs to consult with their members and look carefully at the government's proposals. This was a sensible strategy. Polling showed that around 70 per cent of Labour members opposed the bombing. The government's case was also extremely shaky. After all, Cameron's position was both that ISIS presented a near-apocalyptic threat to Britain and the world, and that the intervention of a tiny force of British bombers would lead to their defeat. In that sense, Abbott was able to appeal to Labour MPs in a way that side-stepped faction fighting.

Abbott's interventions on Syria were not popular with the party bureaucracy. After public statements on Syria, her office would routinely receive calls from Labour headquarters at Southside telling her to stick to her brief. Abbott's response was twofold. First, she argued that war was the biggest obstacle to international development, and therefore the bombing of Syria was central to her brief. Second, she spoke with the backing of the leader.

Government plans to extend RAF bombing in Syria precipitated the first big show down between Corbyn and the Labour frontbench. In private, there were disagreements over how the new leadership should approach the issue. McDonnell advocated giving the PLP a free vote. This would allow the frontbench to vote in different lobbies, without breaching collective responsibility, thus avoiding a shadow Cabinet split. Abbott took a different view: 'I felt strongly you should whip the vote. If people wanted to resign, they weren't supporters of Jeremy anyway, so it would have been better for them to go.'[34] Corbyn, she remembers, was still determined to try, and hoped that over time he could build a relationship of trust with his critics. Consequently, he compromised.

An hour before the vote, Abbott was on television again countering Cameron's comments that Corbyn and his supporters were 'terrorist sympathisers'. Speaking from her experience she argued, 'I'm a London MP, I remember 7/7, I spent hours frightened, I didn't know where my relatives were, if they were caught up in it. I'm very far from a terrorist sympathiser.'[35] Abbott also made the case that the proposed airstrikes 'will not work, they will not make British people safe … We know that the Americans have been bombing Syria for a year, and ISIS is stronger.'[36]

The parliamentary debate took place on 2 December. It was a grave matter, and tension in the Chamber was heightened by the fact that Corbyn and Benn, who were sitting next to each other immediately behind the despatch box, were planning to make diametrically opposing cases. Abbott who was sitting close by on the frontbench, regarded Benn's speech as 'wholly disloyal'.[37] By conceding a free vote, Corbyn had tried to draw the sting out of the disagreement. Benn, by contrast, used his speech to establish dividing lines. Keir Starmer had made a forensic and dispassionate case against extending intervention. David Lammy and Beckett had both advanced measured and thoughtful arguments on different sides of the debate, demonstrating that it was possible for Labour MPs to disagree well. Benn, however, raised the emotional pitch of the debate with a series of doubtful historical comparisons between 21st-century Syria, the Spanish Civil War and the Second World War. Following the leadership campaign, some of

Corbyn's opponents had criticised him for reducing complex political problems to simple moral issues.[38] On 2 December this was Benn's strategy. Indeed, he began his speech with the observation that 'the question that confronts us in a very complex conflict is, at its heart, very simple'.[39] Abbott was unimpressed. 'The thing about Hilary Benn is he sounds like an effective speaker because he sounds like his father.'[40] However, although the tone and cadences gave the speech an air of authority, Abbott claims, 'the content was vacuous'. Benn's speech also gave Foreign Secretary Philip Hammond the opportunity to present Corbyn as someone who wilfully endangered the lives of British citizens.

The overwhelming majority of the Labour Party opposed the extension of airstrikes, and when the vote was taken, around 60 per cent of Labour MPs felt the same. The shadow Cabinet, however, was out of step with the party and with the PLP. Eleven out of twenty-four voted with the government. Nonetheless, the government won.

The controversy over Syria showed that Abbott had a key role in the new leadership. Again and again she was sent to speak to journalists to make the leadership's case. Whenever there was controversy, one of Abbott's aides recalls, 'she was the leadership's main line of defence, for television interviews, or to make sure there was a Corbynista view in the papers. She helped give the Corbyn leadership a voice, but it attracted more criticism her way.'[41] In late 2015, Corbyn's team was small and inexperienced. Within the shadow Cabinet, Corbyn had few supporters, and among his supporters, Abbott was the only truly experienced media performer. Formally, she was shadow Secretary of State for International Development, but in reality, she was the media face of the new leadership, or as McDonnell puts it, 'our key message carrier'.[42]

EUROPEAN UNION REFERENDUM

The 2016 referendum campaign was quite different. Cameron, the architect of the referendum, had assumed Labour would do most of the heavy lifting on the pro-EU campaign. Abbott, however, was never invited to play a key role. She opines that as the Remain campaign wanted to win over voters with 'real concerns' about immigration, they were not keen to have a black woman front and centre in the campaign. Abbott did, however, speak at a number of Remain events. In Hackney, the events were straightforward: not only was Abbott a popular MP but the locals were overwhelmingly pro-European. In other areas, it was harder work. Indeed, she argues that the Labour Party had underestimated the strength of feeling among Labour voters in the north.

Abbott did not play a major role in the Remain campaign, but she was a hate figure among some Brexiteers. Social media played an important role in the referendum, and the long campaign which followed. Indeed, in the wake of the result, websites and Facebook groups, such as BrexitCentral, Leave.EU, Brexit News and Kipper Central sprang up to keep up the pressure for a British exit.

Brexit was not motivated by race – contributors to BrexitCentral and Leave.EU were certain of that. For Brexit News regulars, Black Lives Matter, Eurocrats, the African-Caribbean Leukaemia Trust, the BBC and the National Black Police Association were the real racist organisations. It was in this context that posts about Abbott proliferated. Following the Brexit vote Abbott was the most vilified 'racist' on Brexit News. Published in October 2016, the Kipper Central article 'Diane Abbott and her Racist Black Supremacist Ideology' made the case against Abbott at length citing 'some of the horrific anti-white things she has said'.[43]

After the polls closed, Abbott spoke to CNN, predicting that the result would be close, but that Remain would win, a view later echoed by Nigel Farage. Returning home around midnight, she followed the count on the radio. As results came in it was clear that the pro-EU vote was down, but for a while Abbott assumed that voters in London would push Remain over the line. The final result was a shock. Prior to the vote it was widely assumed that the length of Cameron's time in office would be determined by the size of the Remain victory. Nonetheless, the speed of Cameron's resignation was breath-taking. On the morning of 24 June, members of the government went to ground, leaving Mark Carney to steady the markets.

The result caused major problems for Labour, since the late 1980s it had been an overwhelmingly pro-European party. Corbyn's statement that the result should be respected, and Article 50 triggered, horrified many Labour MPs. The PLP's reaction was delayed, but forty-eight hours after the polls closed reports began circulating that Benn was co-ordinating a move against Corbyn. Corbyn sacked Benn on the Sunday, and resignations began. Some, including Andy Burnham, remained loyal. Indeed, in the midst of the resignations, he tweeted, 'I have never taken part in a coup against any leader in the Labour Party and I am not going to start now'. But over the next few days the bulk of Labour's frontbench resigned.

Abbott recalls that Corbyn was taken aback. 'It was awful, Jeremy didn't expect it to happen. He had tried to reach out to people.'[44] Abbott recalls that Corbyn was determined to build rapport with those in his shadow team who were not his natural allies. Moreover, in supporting Remain, Corbyn was in step with the vast majority of the PLP. Initially, the charge against Corbyn was that he had failed to run an effective campaign to support Britain's continued membership of the EU. Critics cited his statement that he was 'seven, or seven and a half' out of ten in favour of the EU as evidence that his heart had never been in the campaign. Others pointed to his refusal to share a stage with Cameron, and his ambivalence to Stronger In's 'campaign grid', which Andrew Cooper, one of Stronger In's chief strategists de-scribed as the Remain campaign's 'Bible'.[45]

Abbott argues that criticisms of Corbyn's approach to the campaign were misplaced, 'Jeremy, contrary to what everyone said, did a lot of campaigning around Brexit.'[46] Indeed, he spoke at rallies across the country, launched Labour's ad campaign, took part in a televised debate with Faisal Islam on Sky News, wrote two op-eds one for the *Mirror*, and one for *The Observer* and made more than 120 media appearances over the thirty-three days of the campaign. Certainly Corbyn did not stick to the 'grid', but given his antipathy to this kind of media management, this was hardly a surprise. Equally, it is difficult to imagine Cameron, Osborne or Tim Farron appearing on Channel 4's *The Last Leg* arguing,

I want to see a Europe that is about social cohesion, that is about better human rights, that is about workers' rights, that is also about taking a European response to help victims of wars who are going through the most appalling situation on the borders of Europe at the moment, particularly Syrian refugees, there has to be a humanitarian response.[47]

Abbott states that the Leave victory owes more to Cameron's miscalculations. 'Cameron was focused, almost entirely, on internal party matters, and holding his party together.'[48] Fundamentally, she argues that a referendum was not necessary. There was no over-riding national or constitutional imperative for an in/out referendum in mid-2016. The only reasons for holding the referendum and for its timing were to do with the politics of the Conservative Party. Cameron had made two promises: to hold a referendum and not to serve a full second term as Prime Minister. What is more, he knew that he could only make a real start on his agenda once the issue of Europe had been settled. Therefore, he had to hold a referendum early in his government, in a context where there had been what Abbott describes as 'long-standing anti-EU propaganda in the tabloid press, a hostility to the so-called establishment, and a concern about migration'.[49] Abbott claims that years of anti-EU narratives in the press proved 'difficult to unpick' in the short campaign. In terms of migration, Cameron had played on the issue in 2010 and 2015 for electoral advantage and conspicuously failed to deliver on his 'ambition for Britain' to cut net migration to the tens of thousands. Turning to the desire to kick back against 'the establishment' Abbott states that some voters saw the referendum as 'an anti-Cameron vote because it was Cameron's referendum'.[50] And in 2016, after six years of austerity, which had only deepened following the 2015 election, there were plenty of reasons to register anti-Cameron feeling. Cameron's message during the referendum was that Britain's economy was booming, and that voters should back Remain to protect the recovery. But recovery had been joyless and living standards were still lower than they had been in 2008. Rather than presenting a good reason for staying in, Cameron's pitch served to emphasise the gap between the Prime Minister and ordinary voters.

Nonetheless, for Corbyn's critics in the PLP, his actions during the campaign were irrelevant, as was the context in which the campaign took place. The most salient fact was that Corbyn's heart was not in it, and from that, all else followed. Discussion of what was in Corbyn's heart could never be settled. But, for those who were already against Corbyn's leadership, the content of his heart was crucial in making the case that he had to go. Additionally, the argument that Corbyn's performance was responsible for Remain's failure was crucial to his opponents' position. It proved beyond doubt that he could not win a national election. The context of the result and the UK's long and fraught relationship with Europe were irrelevant to the point that his critics were determined to make.

On Corbyn's behalf, McDonnell announced that although the leader had wanted to retain his top team, he respected the resignations and would appoint a new frontbench. In the ensuing reshuffle, Abbott was promoted to shadow Secretary of State for Health.

McDonnell asserts that the 2016 'coup' was merely the most public expression of the determination to keep the leadership 'under siege'.[51] During this time, he claims, Abbott was crucial to the survival of the leadership and the proper functioning of the official opposition,

> There was a concerted attempt from day one to try and undermine Jeremy and get rid of him, but Diane was a stalwart supporter all the way through, she was steady as a rock, and was not averse to calling people out. [She provided] advocacy on the media, and alongside that, she was trying to ensure that our parliamentary performance was holding the government to account, and making sure that we were developing the policies that went into the 2017 manifesto. She was integral to all that.[52]

LEADERSHIP CHALLENGE

The PLP meeting on 27 June was tense. Abbott recalls that the prevailing mood among Labour MPs was one of disbelief, 'everyone was very shocked, because most Labour MPs were Remainers, including very many of them who represented constituencies that had voted to leave. They were particularly shocked.'[53] Labour MPs confronted Corbyn demanding that he stand down. A day later 172 Labour MPs voted that they had no confidence in the leader, compared to just forty who backed Corbyn. Meetings with the likes of Kate Green, John Healey, Lisa Nandy and Owen Smith provided no resolution, nor did attempts to broker a deal with Watson. Crucially, Corbyn's legitimacy came from his victory in a ballot of the members, not support from the PLP. Therefore, Corbyn and his supporters believed they could ride out the storm.

While she had not expected a leadership challenge in the immediate aftermath of the referendum, Abbott argues that the resignations simply revealed what was already there. 'We knew that the right in the PLP had never accepted Jeremy's legitimacy, and were looking for an excuse. Although, some people were genuinely concerned, it was an excuse.'[54] Abbott regarded the challenge as wrong. At that moment of crisis, she argues the party should have come together. It was also unprecedented. Kinnock and Hugh Gaitskell had both faced leadership challenges, but never mass resignations and never a vote of no confidence. The action, Abbott points out, also had no democratic basis. 'They had no mandate, it wasn't that constituency parties were asking their MPs for a vote of no confidence. It could only damage the party.' However, from what Abbott could see, Corbyn's opponents were not seeking to use democratic methods of winning the leadership. Rather, 'what they were trying to do was destroy him as a person'. The constant attacks, she argues, were designed to weaken his resolve, destroy his confidence, to ramp up the pressure until he was forced to resign. 'That is consciously what they were doing.' Abbott was having none of it. She advised Corbyn, 'If you feel the urge to step down, just call me.' Corbyn's resolve held, the pressure tactics failed.

After a fortnight-long standoff, Angela Eagle launched a formal challenge. Speaking at her campaign's launch she stated, 'I'm not a Blairite, I'm not a Brownite, and I'm not a Corbynista. I am my own woman.'[55] This was crucial. Corbyn had been criticised for appointing men to the top positions in the shadow Cabinet, and some commentators argued that it showed the left of the party that he did not take women's issues seriously.

Abbott played a significant role during the 2016 leadership campaign, handling the bulk of the media. Speaking on *Good Morning Britain*, Abbott welcomed Eagle's challenge as a chance to clear the air.

> What's going on is that there's a small group of Labour MPs who didn't accept the leadership result last summer, and this has snowballed, and we've had all this posturing and huffing and puffing in the past few weeks. But now, Angela says she's challenging the leadership, she's completely within her rights to do so, but I'm surprised that she's not insisting that Jeremy be on the ballot.[56]

Abbott's approach to Eagle's challenge was twofold. First, she talked about policy. Eagle, she reminded viewers, had voted for the Iraq War and voted for tuition fees, so there was a clear policy difference between Corbyn and his challenger. In that sense, Abbott labelled Eagle the 'Empire Strikes Back candidate' who represented a return to the politics of triangulation.[57] Second, Abbott questioned Eagle's claim that she was the more electable of the two. She had, after all, come fourth out of five candidates in the 2015 deputy leadership election. Abbott challenged Eagle to prove she was a winner, by winning a leadership contest against Corbyn. This line of argument pointed at one of the contradictions in the campaign against Corbyn: his opponents argued that he was unelectable, but they did not want to fight an election against him.

Like Eagle, Owen Smith argued that Corbyn was unelectable. Despite considerable support from the PLP at the beginning of her campaign, Eagle dropped out of the race and backed Smith following his victory in an indicative vote of PLP members. Smith, however, proved gaffe-prone. And Smith's gaffes, at least according to some commentators, had a sexist edge. Smith's claim that he was 'normal' because he had a wife and kids, was, according to the *New Statesman*, an 'incendiary observation, particularly in light of the fact that his key opponent in the Labour leadership race is a gay woman, Angela

Eagle.'[58] Indeed, Anoosh Chakelian went as far as to call it his 'Andrea Leadsom moment'. Corbyn's critics in the PLP had accused him of ignoring talented women in the creation of his first shadow Cabinet. Yet they had backed Smith over Eagle, a turn of events that led some to conclude the concern over sexism, at least among some of the PLP, was merely strategic.

Smith's pitch had little to do with policy. Rather, he accused Corbyn of ignoring an abusive culture that, he claimed, was prevalent in the party. Speaking to the BBC, he argued, 'I think Jeremy should take a little more responsibility, for what's going on in the Labour Party. After all, we didn't have this sort of abuse and intolerance, misogyny, anti-Semitism, in the Labour Party before Jeremy Corbyn became the leader.'[59]

The idea that Labour had been free of prejudice prior to September 2015 was news to Abbott and went way beyond anything that Corbyn's harshest critics had alleged. The statement indicated that Smith was either ignorant of the prejudices in the party or was denying misogyny and anti-Semitism existed in the party prior to 2015. Both options were extremely problematic.

After Smith emerged as the PLP's preferred candidate, Abbott again presented the leadership's case to the media. In some ways, countering Smith was far easier than countering Eagle. Not only was Smith gaffe-prone, his work for Pfizer and Amgen, two American-owned multinational pharmaceutical companies, raised concerns among Labour members. Speaking on Radio 4's *Today* programme she argued that Smith was the wrong person to take on the Tory's new leader.

> The Tories had just had a former PR man/lobbyist as their leader – David Cameron – they've now moved beyond that. Owen Smith is a great bloke and so on, but I don't believe that someone whose history is having been a special adviser and a pharmaceutical company lobbyist is going to enthuse the [Labour] base.[60]

There were other obstacles, however; legal challenges to Corbyn's presence on the ballot, legal challenges in regard to which party members could vote. Corbyn won in the High Court on the first issue but lost the second at the Court of Appeal.

Abbott states that Corbyn's allies had no doubt that they would win any vote of the membership. However, when the PLP selected Smith they knew it would be easy. Abbott campaigned for Corbyn but stayed in London for the better part of the campaign, as she was handling the media on behalf of the leadership. A year after his first victory, Corbyn was re-elected with an increased share of the vote. Immediately following the result, Abbott, in her role as the leadership's *de facto* spokesperson, addressed reporters. Her message was that 'the coup' had damaged Corbyn's opponents in the eyes of ordinary Labour members, and that MPs should respect the democratic decision of members and give Corbyn a chance. She urged the PLP to unite and fight the Tories, rather than their own leader.

Abbott's speech at the 2016 Labour Party conference exemplified this approach. She praised Heidi Alexander, who had backed the bombing in Syria and had resigned from the shadow Cabinet in June, for her work defending junior doctors, and devoted the bulk of her address to a critique of Jeremy Hunt's health policies.

The 2016 leadership election diminished the credibility of Corbyn's critics. Their primary complaint was that he was unelectable. His opponents claimed a wealth of strategic expertise, their trump card was that they knew how to win. Yet the campaign to oust Corbyn had failed at every stage. The PLP initially united behind Eagle, only to endorse Smith. In so doing they conspicuously failed to back a winner. Having initiated the campaign, Corbyn's opponents failed to make the case against him. They failed in their own terms.

Nonetheless, following Corbyn's second victory, Abbott recalls that there was a recognition that opposition from within the PLP was not going away.

The forces ranged against us were still formidable. Having failed to force Jeremy out, they pedalled the idea that they would have a breakaway from the PLP, leaving Jeremy the leader of some kind of rump, and then they would be the official opposition, they would get the short money, this rumour kept coming and going.[61]

Rumours of a breakaway were part of a larger reconsideration of the history of the 1980s. Although it was common to brand Corbyn and Abbott as stuck in the past, many of their opponents turned to the Thatcher era for inspiration. Broadsheets of all stripes likened Corbyn to Foot, Corbynism to the manifesto of 1983 – 'the longest suicide note in history'. Up against Theresa May, a Conservative Prime Minister with a level of authority over her party not seen since Thatcher, the parallels were too good to miss. So, inevitably the debate turned to the SDP. Speculation that Labour MPs would split and set up an 'SDP 2.0' began as soon as Corbyn was elected, and there was a flurry of interest in the SDP in newspapers and on television early in 2016. In the midst of the 2016 leadership election there was another burst of speculation. Rumours circulated that if Corbyn was re-elected 150 Labour MPs were planning to break away and set up 'Continuity Labour'. On the day that Eagle withdrew from the race, Lord Rodgers, one of the original Gang of Four, told *The Guardian*:

> Even a week ago, I would have said that somehow the Labour party will scrabble along [intact]. I think now it is a possibility there will be a split … I have a feeling these [anti-Corbyn] guys will declare themselves to be a parliamentary party. If they're really disciplined, they will have more MPs than Corbyn, and become the opposition to the government.[62]

Shirley Williams also argued that Brexit, which cut across traditional party lines, meant that there was a real chance of a realignment, if Labour MPs were willing to break with Labour and Corbyn.

Speculation about a 'new centre party' had been ongoing throughout the leadership election. In August, *The Economist* argued that 'True Labour' could succeed where the SDP had failed. According to *The Economist*, if all the Labour MPs who rejected Corbyn's leadership quit, the party would 'become [a] rump of administratively incapable hard-liners, while True Labour (as we might call it) will inherit almost all of the party's political talent'. Then, 'True Labour's role would then not be to compete amicably with Mr Corbyn's "Labour" but to marginalise or, ideally, destroy it by appropriating the Labour mantle through sheer weight, dynamism and persuasiveness.'[63]

The 2016 'coup' had a significant impact on Labour's poll ratings. At the beginning of 2016, Labour was trailing by around ten points. From March to June, however, the gap had narrowed. The two parties were either neck-and-neck or the Tories had a lead of a few points. Moreover, before Benn's sacking Labour had won every by-election, it had won the London mayoral election, and in the local elections, although Labour had lost eighteen seats, it had increased its vote share, and narrowly beaten the Conservatives. Corbyn's critics complained that the party should have done better. However, following the 'coup' Labour's position declined, by the end of July, the Tory lead, which was averaging 3 per cent in the period from the beginning of March until Benn's sacking, shot up. For the rest of the year, the Conservative lead was regularly in double figures, averaging almost 11 per cent.

Faction fighting was not the only reason for Labour's slide in the polls. May's victory in the Conservative leadership contest meant that Labour was up against a popular Prime Minister. An Ipsos MORI poll conducted in August, during Labour's leadership election, found that 54 per cent of voters were satisfied with May's leadership. Corbyn's ratings were much lower, a mere 25 per cent.

Nonetheless, the six months following Corbyn's second leadership victory were a period of relative stability. Benn and Cooper devoted their energies to their select committee work, Hunt left politics to become director of the V&A. Corbyn was able to promote radical MPs who had entered Parliament in 2015 such as Angela Rayner, Rebecca Long-Bailey and Clive Lewis, as well as Baroness Shami Chakrabarti, who became shadow Attorney General. Although there had been concerns that Momentum would organise a deselection campaign to allow Corbyn to remake the PLP in his own image, not a single Labour MP was deselected. Corbyn gained a hold on the shadow Cabinet not by forcing people out, but by promoting those who were willing to serve.

Within the shadow Cabinet, Abbott played an authoritative role. Chakrabarti argues, 'People listen when Diane speaks. She speaks surprisingly succinctly for a senior politician. It's a very authoritative senior voice in the shadow Cabinet.'[64] McDonnell agrees. Within the shadow Cabinet, she was 'forthright, as she always is. She was a stalwart supporter of Jeremy all the way through, and she was not averse to calling people out.'[65] Corbyn agrees that Abbott was one of his strongest supporters

> when the shadow Cabinet were not, how should I put it ... not overly sympathetic to its leader, she was always supportive and positive. In the shadow Cabinet, she would often speak up, to people attacking me, she would say, 'Don't underestimate the views of party members, who overwhelmingly support Jeremy.'[66]

SHADOW SECRETARY OF STATE FOR HEALTH

Abbott was able to use this brief period of relative quiet to challenge the government's management of the NHS and develop health policy. Abbott proved to be a radical shadow Health Minister. In September 2016 she opened the parliamentary debate over the NHS Sustainability and Transformation Plans with a plea for openness. Abbott argued that the initiative which sounded 'anodyne and managerial' was shrouded in secrecy in order to disguise major cuts and planned privatisation of some health services.[67] She appealed to the government to publish their plans. If the Tories genuinely believed that they were better for patients, what did they have to hide?

Abbott's view that the government had good reason to keep their plans a closely guarded secret proved correct. In June 2017, following a series of freedom of information requests, the BMA finally obtained information about the scale of the cuts, the extent of proposed privatisation and the amount that would be spent on salaries for the managerial staff who would run the system. As a result, the BMA ceased working with the government on reforms. Rather than triangulate, Abbott committed Labour to reversing the cuts, ending privatisation of healthcare, and restoring transparency.

In highlighting the secrecy of the Department of Health Abbott put her finger on an important trend. In February 2017 it was reported that Jeremy Hunt had tried to cover up a report that a private company lost over 700,000 letters containing test results, child protection notes and medical histories. More generally, privatisation of NHS services allowed the government to evade freedom of information requests on the basis that either the government did not have the private providers' data or that it was commercially sensitive.

SHADOW HOME SECRETARY

In October, Burnham, who had served as Corbyn's shadow Home Secretary since 2015, resigned to focus on the Manchester mayoral race. With a reshuffle imminent, Vaz advised Abbott to seize the moment and go for a promotion, 'She said, "What job do you think I should have?" I said, "There's only one job: shadow Home Secretary. We've never had a black shadow Home Secretary, and you know all about it."' Vaz was so determined that Abbott should shadow one of the great offices of state that he texted Corbyn, telling him to make the appointment. 'Frankly,' Vaz argues, 'for reasons of symbolism there was no one else who could do it.' For Vaz, the promotion was a long time coming. Nobody else apart from Corbyn would have made her shadow Home Secretary, but it was time. 'Immigration and policing were big parts of the portfolio and for Diane those policy issues were in her DNA.'[68]

Shadow Home Secretary was the only role that Abbott wanted. 'Everything the Home Office covers, be it security, be it policing or immigration, it's all about the relationship between the state and the individual.'[69] These were policy areas that Abbott had been concerned about throughout her political career, and areas where she believed reform was essential. 'Also,' she adds, 'if you are interested in the politics of race the Home Office and its different functions are very much part of that.'[70] There were some, Abbott felt, even within her own party, who were perturbed by the appointment of a black woman as shadow Home Secretary. But this was part of the job's appeal.

Corbyn and Vaz came from different wings of the party, but they shared the view that Abbott should be promoted to the role. Corbyn recalls, 'I thought she was the ideal choice for it because of her experience representing an inner-city community, her experience on asylum and immigration issues, and her experience on human rights and justice issues.'[71]

Corbyn told Abbott that he wanted her to be the nation's aunt and believes that 'she did that very well'.[72] Previous Home Secretaries had increased prison numbers, had made a virtue of standing up against the European Court of Justice or had worked with schools, hospitals and employers to create a 'hostile environment' for migrants. Abbott's emphasis on a principled approach to asylum and immigration, and a human rights-based approach to justice meant that she, with Corbyn's support, could be different from many of her predecessors.

Abbott came to the role as one of Britain's most energetic defenders of human rights. Shami Chakrabarti recalls that as director of Liberty, 'we worked together so closely. She was just our go-to person on every civil liberties campaign, a complete champion of the Human Rights Act.'[73] In recent years, the Home Office had been a great populist platform, through which the governing party could pose as the defender of the decent majority, by making a virtue of locking up or deporting whichever minority group was out of favour at the time. For Chakrabarti, Abbott was a break from this populism, because her politics had a radically different basis: 'Her politics was rooted in the diversity of the community she represented, and in the need for race equality. So she very much came to human rights from that trajectory.'

Moreover, Abbott's appointment came at a crucial juncture. Prior to 2010, Cameron had committed the Conservative Party to scrapping the Human Rights Act and replacing it with a British bill of rights. The 2015 Conservative Party manifesto repeated the commitment to 'scrap the Human Rights Act' explaining that the British Bill of Rights would 'reverse the mission creep that has meant human rights law being used for more and more purposes, and often with little regard for the rights of wider society'.[74] Chakrabarti points out:

The British Bill of Rights was a way to undermine the Human Rights

Act. It was a way to suggest that there could be a red, white and blue alternative to something that was essentially universal human rights. When they [the coalition] published a paper on it, the truth was laid bare. The plan was that some people's rights would count more than others. British nationals would be more worthy of rights than foreign nationals. Prisoners won't have rights, and suspects won't have rights, so what's left?[75]

Abbott's appointment, then, was a signal that the Labour Party would not back down on the defence of human rights, even the rights of stigmatised minorities. One of her first actions as shadow Home Secretary was to write to Amber Rudd and demand to visit Yarl's Wood Immigration Removal Centre, the privately run detention camp in which women and young people are held as they await rulings on their immigration status. May had stopped the UN's Special Rapporteur on violence against women from visiting Yarl's Wood in 2014. Abbott had to lobby continually for more than a year to gain access to the detention centre.

The Home Office is a notoriously large brief, and therefore the minister delegates parts of the brief to their team. Abbott retained responsibility for immigration, rather than allocating it to anyone else. Following the referendum, this meant that Abbott took a lead on developing Labour's response to the end of freedom of movement.

ABBOTT AND THE PRESS

The six months following Corbyn's second leadership victory was a period of relative calm. But they were still difficult. Since Corbyn's election as Labour leader Abbott had become a lightning-rod. Anyone wanting to damage Corbyn could attack Abbott in the knowledge that the two were close personally and politically. One of her aides argues that this was certainly true in terms of Corbyn's critics in the PLP, 'Particularly in the first year and a half, being in the shadow Cabinet, and being so close to Jeremy, when they couldn't get him, they would get her. That was the right of the party and the media.'[76]

There was also a renewed interest in Abbott and Corbyn's romantic relationship. Sometimes their relationship was presented as a sordid affair, with extremely unpleasant undertones. In early 2016 there were a series of articles exploring the 'explosive revelations' contained in Rosa Prince's biography *Comrade Corbyn*.[77] The *Telegraph*, for example, printed a short section of Prince's book under the title 'Revealed: Jeremy Corbyn "showed off naked Diane Abbott to impress Left-wing friends"'. The extract from Prince's book, however, gave no support for the paper's claim that 'Corbyn "showed off" a naked Diane Abbott'. A day later the *Daily Mail* ran essentially the same story, again based on *Comrade Corbyn*, under the headline 'Jeremy Corbyn "showed off a naked Diane Abbott to impress his Left-wing activist friends" after breakdown of his first marriage'.[78] *The Times* followed suit with 'How Corbyn revealed Abbott was his lover'.[79] The publication of *Comrade Corbyn* meant that stories about their relationship, which had already circulated in September 2015 could be revisited. Stories of this kind ran and ran. Indeed, in February 2019, following the publication of another biography, the *Daily Mail* returned to this theme under the headline '"She was shocked when we entered": Jeremy Corbyn drove two friends to his flat because he WANTED them to see new girlfriend Diane Abbott naked in his bed, biography reveals'.[80] A month later, *The Sun* ran with 'CORB BLIMEY! Jeremy Corbyn "invited two left-wing friends to his flat to show off naked girlfriend Diane Abbott"', which embellished the story with the statement that Corbyn's friends 'stumbled in to find Abbott lying naked on the bed', a detail not supported by any accounts of the event.[81]

Sometimes, reports of their relationship were coupled with the suggestion that Abbott had only been given a job in the shadow Cabinet because the two had lived together briefly almost forty years ago. It was an indication that after thirty years in Parliament, having run for the Labour leadership, and having served on Miliband's frontbench, Abbott was still not regarded as either a serious or a legitimate political actor in her own right.

Corbyn the Musical: The Motorcycle Diaries was one of the stranger examples of the popular fascination with the relationship between Abbott and Corbyn. Scored by composer Jen Green, with words and lyrics by Rupert Myers and Bobby Friedman, the show opened at the Waterloo East Theatre in April 2016, staring Natasha Lewis as Abbott, Martin Neely as Corbyn and David Muscat as both Vladimir Putin and Boris Johnson. At the time the show opened Friedman explained to CNBC International, 'We came up with the idea last year when we heard the story about Diane Abbott and Jeremy Corbyn potentially going on a motorbike journey across East Germany.'[82] Set in a future where Corbyn is Prime Minister and facing a nuclear stand-off with Russia, the play centres on 'a 1970s motorbike journey in East Berlin with Diane Abbott' during which the pair 'encounter some people and get involved in some romantic and embarrassing events that lead to this nuclear crisis'.

#PRAYFORDIANE

Following the failure of 'the coup' there were no overt organised attempts from within the PLP to end Corbyn's leadership. There was still opposition from the backbenches, and attacks on Abbott continued as a proxy war against Corbyn. It was in this context that #PrayForDiane began trending on Twitter. The beginning of February 2017 was a watershed moment. May put a bill to the Commons which would allow the government to trigger Article 50. Labour MPs were whipped to respect the result of the referendum. Abbott did not vote for the bill due to illness and there was considerable scepticism in the PLP about Abbott's illness. Vaz who met Abbott in the Commons on the day of the vote recalls, 'She was with me, in the Chamber on the day of the debate, and she was absolutely not well. I said to her, "What are you doing here? You should be at home."'[83] The government was set to win the vote easily, so Vaz advised Abbott to go home and recover. 'Then they all started attacking her because she missed the stupid vote.'

The vote took place on the Wednesday, and early on Thursday morning #PrayForDiane and #ShowDianeWeCare were trending on Twitter. #PrayForDiane was an organised campaign to cast doubt on Abbott's claim that she was ill. On the morning after the vote, an anonymous Labour MP sent the following email to their colleagues:

I'm very worried about Diane's illness and I know many colleagues will share my concern. Can we organize a PLP collection for flowers? I've tried to get colleagues to donate informally, but I've only raised 64p and can only think this is because they are too traumatized and worried to focus on it properly at the moment.

I want to get #PrayForDiane trending on twitter. Those not comfortable with a faith-based message could perhaps tweet #ShowDianeWeCare.

Is there anything else we should be doing?[84]

Labour MP Chris Leslie, speaking on television on Thursday morning, sarcastically stated that he wished Abbott would 'get well soon'.[85] The *Daily Mail* threw its weight behind the campaign with a Facebook post 'Let's get #PrayForDiane trending', linked to a piece quoting an unnamed 'furious Labour backbencher' who claimed:

No-one believes she was ill. People who are seriously ill came down and voted and she went AWOL. She didn't have the balls to vote for the Bill. People are very angry at her. Others have resigned, but she won't because she is a mate of Jeremy's. It's exactly what you expect from them. It is one rule for Corbyn's mates and another for everyone else.[86]

McDonnell defended her, stating that as the bill was going to pass with a big margin she had been excused. But for Abbott's critics in the PLP the obvious explanation lay in the nature of the relationship between Abbott and Corbyn. Again, Corbyn's critics attacked the leader through Abbott. According to *The Times*, the PLP was plunged into chaos due to Abbott's actions and Corbyn's refusal to take disciplinary action.[87]

Attacks on Abbott may also reflect another dynamic at work in the Labour Party. Abbott had first felt the wrath of powerful figures in the party in 1985 when she had stood against Livingstone in Brent East. At the time, Abbott had written in *West Indian World* that white members of the Labour Party were happy to tolerate black women as long as they had no power. Much the same could be said following her promotion to the shadow Cabinet. MPs who had sat with Abbott on the Labour benches for years, and seemed to have accepted her as a backbencher, were now running media campaigns against her, mocking her, accusing her of bad faith, and of having a position in the party based exclusively on patronage. Writing in 1985, Abbott had argued, 'Most white people find it difficult to accept a black woman in a position of authority.'[88] The experience of the first eighteen months or so of Corbyn's leadership indicated that most of the largely white PLP would not accept her presence in the shadow Cabinet.

The MPs who led the attack on Abbott remained anonymous. More generally, attacks on the leadership stopped short of an organised attempt to topple Corbyn. In the short term, talk of a new centre party came to nothing, although it continued to excite columnists, and provided inspiration for Steve Waters' *Limehouse*, which opened to rave reviews at the Donmar Warehouse in March 2017. Rather than break away, some in the PLP contented themselves with anonymous briefings. Others subscribed to the 'Sibthorpe Doctrine', the idea that Corbynism should be allowed to crash and burn; that the electoral rout to which Corbynism would inevitably lead was the only way to bring the membership back to their senses. The iron law of 1983, that a left-wing Labour Party would be decimated at the polls, and the fact that the Conservative poll lead was growing in the spring of 2017, seems to have convinced many in the PLP that they should play a waiting game, and there was good reason to assume they would not have to wait long.

CHAPTER 14

FOR THE MANY, NOT THE FEW

With a commanding lead in the polls, a small majority in the Commons, and the 1980s as the go-to point of historical comparison, there was considerable speculation that Theresa May would call a snap election in May 2017. If the comparisons between Corbyn and Foot were correct, May could expect not just a victory but a landslide. The Fixed-Term Parliaments Act was no obstacle as opposition parties could not credibly demur. The real obstacle was May herself, who had repeatedly ruled out a snap election.

Corbyn's inner circle differed over the likelihood of a snap election. With a poll lead averaging more than 15 per cent, Seumas Milne believed that May had every reason to go to the polls. Abbott took a different view. May would take a hit for so obviously breaking a promise, and Philip Hammond's austere March budget contained nothing that pointed to an imminent election. When it became clear that the Prime Minister had missed the date for holding an election in May, Abbott told her team she was certain that there would be no election before the autumn. After eighteen months of constant pressure, it looked like Abbott would finally get a break.

The announcement early on 18 April that May was making an unscheduled address to the nation led to renewed speculation about an early general election. Abbott was in a meeting in Westminster Hall with Caribbean high commissioners when one of her staff received the news from the leader's office. Initially, Abbott's team assumed that it was going to be a statement on Brexit. However, at around 11 a.m. when the Prime Minister's lectern appeared without the official crest, options narrowed. Suddenly, a general election seemed inevitable. Journalists reached the same conclusion, and Abbott was inundated with requests for interviews. Responding as quickly as she could she rushed to College Green. However, in the first hour after the announcement none of Labour's frontbench team had appeared before the cameras. Some Labour MPs, however, began having informal conversations with journalists. The *Mirror*'s Kevin Maguire told the BBC that although 'Labour's never gone into an election in such a bad position since 1983 … one Labour source described it to me as a silver lining, that if Labour lose, Jeremy Corbyn will go.'[1]

Prior to Abbott's arrival on College Green, Corbyn, who was away campaigning in Bristol, was the only member of the shadow Cabinet to appear in front of the cameras. Other parties were out of the blocks faster. Alistair Carmichael and Tim Farron had appeared on television for the Liberal Democrats; Iain Duncan Smith, Crispin Blunt, Nigel Evans and Malcolm Rifkind for the Conservatives; and Jonathan Bartley for the Greens. As Abbott arrived, Stephen Kinnock was the only Labour MP in sight and he was not attracting much interest. Abbott had agreed to do three interviews, but with no one else from Labour's top team available, she spoke to nineteen journalists in ninety minutes.

By that evening, journalists wanting to hear from Labour still had few options. Most recycled Corbyn's interview from the morning, others interviewed Peter Mandelson. However, for journalists who wanted a live reaction from the current Labour leadership their only option was to speak to Abbott, who had returned to College Green.

Channel 4 News unveiled a new poll putting the Conservatives on 44 per cent, with Labour trailing on 23 per cent, which would, as Krishnan Guru-Murthy speculated, give the Tories a majority of more than 100 seats. However, after a day in which the election of 1983 was discussed ceaselessly Abbott reached for a different example. Countering Guru-Murthy's claim that Abbott and Corbyn were finished, she argued, 'First of all, this won't be the first time the polls have called an election wrong. Secondly, as I say, if you think back to 1974, "Who Governs Britain?", the public said, "You certainly don't!" and delivered a hung parliament and Ted Heath had to step down.'[2]

This was an unnecessary election, Abbott claimed, and the British people would punish the party that called it. This was not simply a line for the cameras. In private, Bell Ribeiro-Addy, Abbott's chief of staff, recalls that she was hopeful that Labour would cut through and make gains. There was reason for hope. May was criticised from all sides for breaking her promise not to hold an early election. Her claim that she had called the election in the national interest also looked implausible. Commentators agreed; the decision smacked of opportunism. To make matters worse, the election was called on the same day that it became clear that the police were investigating the expenses claims of at least twenty Conservative MPs. May was also getting bad press for calling an election only to rule out a head-to-head debate with Corbyn. Moreover, once the election began in earnest, broadcasting rules kicked in requiring impartiality on television and this gave Corbyn's team a chance to get their message across.

But even though there was cause for hope, Abbott recalls that 'it was worrying going into the election'.[3] Within the PLP, Abbott recalls, the mood was despondent. It had become clear that private polls conducted by the Conservatives showed that the party was expecting to lose seats to the Liberal Democrats in the south-west but to make big gains in Labour's heartlands. National polls certainly looked bad for Labour, but John Rentoul, *The Independent*'s chief political commentator, went further. Speaking to the BBC he claimed that opinion polls were 'flattering the Labour Party', adding, 'The last time Labour touched as low as 23 per cent in a national opinion poll was just before the 1983 general election when Margaret Thatcher won a 144 seat majority, and I think Labour's in a weaker position today than it was then.'[4] Tom Blenkinsop was the first Labour backbencher to give up the ghost. He announced that he would rather stand down than fight and lose. Nonetheless, Labour's message was resolute. Speaking to ITV, the BBC, Channel 4 and a host of other broadcasters, Abbott both welcomed the contest and pledged that she would fight to win.

Abbott's resolution was not shared by many in the PLP. She remembers that on the last day before dissolution walking through the tea room and seeing Labour MPs in a state of mourning, 'They were convinced they weren't coming back, they were convinced we were going down to a dreadful defeat.'[5]

Local elections in May seemed to confirm Labour's worst fears. Writing in the *New Statesman*, Stephen Bush claimed, 'It's hard to overstate the scale of the Conservative victory.'[6] The Conservatives topped the poll with 38 per cent of the vote, Labour's vote a mere 27 per cent. The results indicated that UKIP's vote had collapsed to the benefit of the Tories. The result seemed to prefigure a wipe-out, or at least a historic defeat for Labour.

Nonetheless, 2017 was not the election the pundits were expecting. May had hoped for a Brexit election in which she could lead the bulk of Cameron's coalition and UKIP, the Tories 'lost tribe', to a decisive victory. However, as Labour accepted the referendum result, and as Farron's campaign had been blown off course by theological controversies, domestic issues came to the fore. On Sunday 30 April, Andrew Marr quizzed May on foodbanks and the health service. He invited her to acknowledge that it was wrong that nurses had to rely on foodbanks. May was evasive. Her comment, 'there are many complex reasons why people go to foodbanks', led to twenty-four hours of bad press.[7]

LBC INTERVIEW

Two days later, Abbott got in trouble when discussing police numbers with Nick Ferrari on LBC. Ferrari asked how much it would cost to employ 10,000 police officers. Abbott was unable to give a figure. Notably, Abbott did seven interviews on the morning of 2 May, six of them without difficulty. It was only in the Ferrari interview that she stumbled.

Shortly after May's interview, her comments about foodbanks were all over the internet. The same happened following Abbott's LBC interview. At this point, obvious biases came into play. Forty-eight hours after Abbott's LBC interview aired, the top comments on YouTube's most prominent version of the interview included claims that the shadow Home Secretary was a 'racist bint', a 'communist anti-white bitch', an 'imbecile', a 'stupid racist dumb bitch', and a 'retarded liberal woman'.

The response to May's interview was far more muted. Comments, again on the most viewed version of May's interview after forty-eight hours, included the observation 'she can't answer a single and simple question', or 'she obviously doesn't care about poor people', or 'she is not strong and stable she is stubborn and arrogant'. The top comments on Abbott's interview were racialised and gendered in a way that the top comments on May's interview were simply not. Equally, the comments on Abbott's interviews routinely stressed her intellectual capacity, or lack of it. So, Abbott, a Cambridge graduate, was perceived by many of her detractors as an 'imbecile', or a 'retard'. But May's intellect, as someone who had had a similar education at Oxford, was rarely questioned.

Turning to the packaging of the interviews, YouTube's most viewed version of May's interview was twenty minutes long. It contained the entire interview, in which May's awkward evasion, was only a small part. The top videos dealing with Abbott's interview were far shorter, and focused, almost exclusively, on Abbott's moments of discomfort. Indeed, the most viewed footage of Abbott's LBC interview, forty-eight hours on, was truncated so drastically that it started mid-sentence. May's moment of discomfort, then, was viewed in the context of a broadly assured performance, whereas Abbott's was put front and centre.

In the more toxic corners of the internet, such as the English Defence League-affiliated Twitter account #BurnDianeAbbott, the abuse was far worse. Speaking in Parliament after the campaign, Abbott told fellow MPs, 'I've had death threats, I've had people tweeting that I should be hung if "they could find a tree big enough to take the fat bitch's weight" ... I've had rape threats, been described as a pathetic, useless, fat, black piece of shit [and an] ugly, fat black bitch.'

For Abbott, online abuse was nothing new. Prior to the campaign, Conservative councillor Alan Pearmain had tweeted an image of an orangutan photoshopped to look as though it was wearing lipstick, with the caption, 'Forget the London look, get the Diane Abbott look.'[8] Pearmain defended the Tweet on the basis that 'people will take offence about everything, won't they?'[9] The Tory councillor, who was suspended a couple of months after posting the tweet, explained to the BBC that he was prepared to apologise, but he also wanted to 'ask her to explain some of the comments I've read that she's made'.[10] Pearmain's tweet was posted around the time that Tory MP Anne Marie Morris was reinstated, following a six-month suspension for using the n-word in Parliament.

Following the referendum the scale of online abuse experienced by MPs reached another level. Significantly, the abuse on Twitter was not equal opportunity malice, it had a strong racial and gender bias. According to Amnesty International, '20 BAME MPs received almost half (41 per cent) of the abusive tweets, despite there being almost eight times as many white MPs in the study.'[11] Abbott was the MP most likely to receive abuse. Indeed, Amnesty reported that 'in the six weeks leading up to 2017's snap general election ... 45.14 per cent of abusive tweets were aimed at her'. In terms of online abuse Amnesty concluded that 'the type of abuse she receives often focuses on her gender and race, and includes threats of sexual violence'.

Where new media led, old media followed. Zoe Strimpel, writing in the *Telegraph*, reassured readers, 'It's not racist to point out that Diane Abbott is a bungling disappointment.'[12] Strimpel wrote, 'Without descending into nasty comments about her voice, her expression, or her odd mixture of seeming cluelessness and arrogance, it's worth simply reviewing a few of the mistakes that have made her campaign such a disaster.' The *Evening Standard* quickly published a 'full transcript' of the interview, which, in reality, cut out around one third of the discussion. Steerpike, in *The Spectator* published edited highlights with a short gloss, and *The Sun* published a selection of tweets including one from the wits in the Liberal Democrat press office under the headline, 'Labour's Diane Abbott mocked mercilessly online after her car-crash interview round on police funding.'[13]

However, the response was not uniform. Prior to the election, journalist and academic Maya Goodfellow, writing in the *New Statesman*, had presented an analysis of the way in which comments on social media exposed deep-rooted prejudices against black women. Following the LBC interview, radical blogs, such as Consented, began posting articles in Abbott's defence. Young black women played a prominent role in establishing a counter-narrative. Speaking on *Channel 4 News* Edem Barbara Ntumy, then a leader of the NUS Black Students Campaign, argued:

> Even in my party people are falling into this trap – it's a clear amalgamation of sexism and racism tapping into something deep in this country. It speaks to something wider in the Labour Party of people thinking that because they're in the Labour Party they're beyond reproach to sexism and racism. Diane gets so much abuse because of who she is, and what she stands for. I don't think you can separate those two things.[14]

Danielle Dash's 'Diane Abbott & Unrelenting Misogynoir', and Fiona Rutherford's essay on BuzzFeed also made the case for Abbott and against her critics.[15] Anoosh Chakelian, Lily Allen and Paul Mason followed in their wake. Shortly after the result, Paula Akpan's 'Diane Abbott and misogynoir: a woman scorned, a woman vindicated' on gal-dem set a trend which was followed by the likes of Stephen Bush, Jack Monroe on Cooking on a Bootstrap, and Owen Jones.[16]

The response to the LBC interview took Abbott's team by surprise. Ribeiro-Addy recalls that Abbott was doing a string of appearances that morning, so as soon as she had finished with Ferrari, they were on to the next interview. It took an hour or so for the story to gain traction, and in that time, Abbott had done two more interviews both without incident. Ribeiro-Addy remembers that by this point in the campaign, the whole team were exhausted. Abbott was constantly on air. As many in the PLP were unwilling to speak to the national media, her schedule was packed. She was also having to speak on the whole gamut of Labour's policy, which required mastering a mass of data.

May, apparently, did not want the Tory campaign to feature the interview. Why her wishes were ignored is not clear, but ignored they were. The Conservatives seized on Abbott's LBC interview and built it into their campaign. Tim Ross and Tom McTague reported that 'Tory focus groups found that the idea of Abbott taking control of national security was horrifying for voters'.[17] According to Tim Shipman, 'The Tories seized on Abbott's performance, pumping out social media videos.'[18] Apparently, senior Conservatives believed that the 'car-crash' interview was achieving 'cut-through' and decided to feature it heavily. BuzzFeed, which published an analysis of stories trending on social media a week before polling day, concluded that '10 per cent of the most viral right-wing news stories during this election [were] attacks on Abbott' and that there had been an increasing focus on her in Tory attack ads as the campaign went on.[19] Additionally, one-third of emails sent by the Conservatives to their supporters during the campaign mentioned 'the so-called threat of Abbott becoming home secretary'.[20]

Abbott began featuring in Tory campaign ads alongside Farron, Nicola Sturgeon and Corbyn – even though she was not a party leader. Equally Tory ministers, including Boris Johnson and Amber Rudd, began to drop her name into interviews, regardless of the subject matter. May, who had been against using the LBC interview, took up the anti-Abbott messaging during her *Question Time* appearance.[21]

The anti-Abbott messaging was not just for voters; apparently in the Conservative campaign headquarters 'the walls were decorated with a cartoon of Corbyn and Abbott dancing like the lead characters in the film *La La Land*'.[22] Evidently, humiliating Abbott was good for morale at Tory head office. The election of 2017 joined the elections of 1987 and 1992 where Abbott became the focus of Tory campaigning.

The Liberal Democrats also ran a negative campaign around Abbott. A senior figure on the Liberal Democrat team told *Business Insider* that during focus groups, 'people have been saying "who's that woman in Labour who can't do numbers?" and when we show them a picture of Dianne [*sic*] Abbott they point at the picture and say "that's her!" … She's really cutting through'.[23]

Lord Ashcroft's final report on the state of public opinion, published a month after the Nick Ferrari interview noted that the LBC interview had indeed cut through. Labour MPs, some anonymously, also briefed journalists during the campaign that, Abbott was coming up on the doorsteps. Remarkably, weeks after her appearance on LBC, the interview was still dominating discussion.

The *Daily Mail* reported that 'Tory strategists have dubbed Corbyn, Abbott and McDonnell the "toxic trio", believing that their hard-Left views will repel Middle England'.[24] For a while shop.conservatives.com stocked a tea towel featuring the famous 1987 Tory campaign poster, 'So this is the new moderate Militant-Free Labour Party'. For less than £20 consumers could dry their dishes with a picture of Abbott's face. The *Mail* was one of the Conservative's key message carriers. On the eve of polling day the paper ran a front page featuring the 'toxic trio', with the headline 'Labour's apologists for terror: The *Mail* accuses this troika of befriending Britain's enemies and scorning the institutions that keep us safe'.[25]

Some accounts of the 2017 election implied that Abbott retired from the campaign soon after the LBC interview, and that for the last month she played little role in the campaign.[26] However, this does not reflect the reality. Abbott continued her media work throughout the rest of May and into early June. Press coverage, however, focused relentlessly on the LBC interview. Indeed, some journalists used every new interview to revisit Abbott's performance on LBC. And any time another politician came unstuck, the LBC interview was recounted as a comparator. Consequently, while the right-wing press were early adopters of the anti-Abbott narrative, other papers followed suit. More than three weeks after the LBC interview, Matthew Norman in *The Independent* was still using Abbott's performance as the basis for an opinion piece, stating that she would win the election for the Tories.[27] Norman used the LBC interview as the lens which pulled subsequent interviews, her political career, in fact her entire life into focus. Similarly, at the end of May *The Guardian*'s John Crace was still referring to Abbott as 'Dozy Diane', a nickname he had first used in discussion of the LBC interview.[28]

The press reaction was self-perpetuating. Stories about Abbott proliferated. Abbott's name was clickbait, so online editions could re-package the story several times a day. As it dominated the papers, the

LBC interview became a story on television news. The press reaction fed on itself in another sense too. Where Abbott had been treated with a degree of respect by reporters at the beginning of the campaign, after the LBC interview her reception by interviewers became more hostile. Perhaps having read countless abusive tweets and articles claiming that she was not on top of her brief, journalists began to believe that Abbott was unfit for frontline politics.

Despite this, Abbott continued to appear on television and radio. Commentators may not have liked her opposition to Trident and they may not have been sympathetic to her change of heart on Irish republicanism, but Abbott's media performances were those of an experienced politician. Some in the Labour campaign team wanted to take her off the front line, but she had the support of Corbyn, Shami Chakrabarti, Bell Ribeiro-Addy and the rest of her team. She also had a job to do. At the end of May, Abbott was still speaking regularly on television, radio and in the papers. Despite claims that she was ruining Labour's chances it was clear that Corbyn's team were experiencing a bump in the polls.

In addition to radio and television, McDonnell recalls that Abbott played a big role:

> on the stump, around the country. The key issue for us was how do we get our message across, not just using the media, social media, but also speaking on platforms. The meetings that Diane and others were doing was giving confidence to our members. It was as a result of the mass campaign on the ground that we came so close, she was a key motivator for our rank and file.[29]

Whatever Tory and Liberal Democrat spin doctors said about key demographics like 'Mondeo Man' and '*Holby City* Woman', large swathes of Labour's members wanted to hear from her. Abbott was well known and regarded as one of the few high-profile MPs who had been loyal to Corbyn. Therefore, McDonnell claims, she was regarded as being on the side of ordinary members, which is why so many activists turned out to see her on the campaign trail.

The campaign was full of surprises. Labour's leaked manifesto proved to be popular. Radical commitments on the renationalisation of the railways; the creation of public water and power utilities, owned and managed locally; a huge investment in green energy; and the creation of a national investment bank, played well with the public, despite the fact that they reflected a big step away from the post-Thatcher free market consensus. Picking up where the GLC left off, the manifesto promised to use government procurement to force businesses which received state contracts to act ethically. Labour reached out to former Liberal Democrat voters promising to scrap tuition fees and reintroduce a maintenance grant.

Theresa May proved to be a poor campaigner. The Conservative social care plan, dubbed 'the dementia tax' went down badly with the Tory base, as did May's apparent U-turn. The Liberal Democrats also fared badly. Farron became immured in a theo-ethical debate over the status of gay sex and turned on the Liberal Democrat base with a scathing attack on 'muesli-eating *Guardian* readers' during a televised debate.[30]

Media coverage of Abbott's LBC interview was at odds with the dynamic of the campaign. Again and again pundits told readers that Abbott's performance was handing victory to the Tories. However, all the while Labour's poll numbers were climbing. At the very time Abbott was one of the party's main media performers, Labour was catching up with the Tories in the polls. Of course, this did not fit the established narrative that May was the most popular Tory leader since Thatcher, and that Labour was heading to a defeat on the scale of 1983. Nor did it fit narratives about black women in public life.

Abbott was forced to pull out of frontline campaigning on the morning of 6 June, forty-eight hours before the polls closed. The announcement came on the *Woman's Hour* Twitter account at 8.42 a.m., 'A change in the #WHdebate line-up this morning: @HackneyAbbott taken ill. @UKLabour say finding a replacement. Tune in at 9am.'[31]

A tweet from a commuter, circulated around 11 a.m. showed Abbott at Oxford Circus Tube station, which led some commentators to conclude that she was fit and well. Minutes later, George Osborne, one-time Tory Chancellor and then editor of the *Evening Standard* tweeted a cartoon of Abbott as Home Secretary pulling out of an anti-terror meeting due to ill health. However, the Conservatives did not have it all their way. May had pulled out of *Woman's Hour* a couple of days earlier and survived unscathed in the Tory press. Many on Twitter picked up on the double standard.

Ribeiro-Addy argues that this double standard soon became undeniable. Abbott was certainly not the only senior politician to stumble over figures. Speaking on the *Today* programme, Philip Hammond stated that HS2 would cost £32 billion. The Chancellor was £20 billion out. Hammond was also unable to recall the correct figure until prompted by John Humphrys. Damian Green was flummoxed on BBC television when asked how much pensioners would lose after the election from proposed benefit reforms. Andrew Mitchell had no idea what the minimum wage was. Worse still, he engaged in an embarrassing guessing game with the BBC's Victoria Derbyshire. His opening offer was 'it's less than nine pounds', then he dropped to 'about six pounds, I think,' before asking, 'What is it, £8?'[32] The answer he was searching for was £7.50, for those over twenty-five. Amber Rudd, to take another example, accidentally admitted on *Woman's Hour* that the government had cut police numbers. Britain's political elite were not only lost when it came to numbers. Having arrived in West Bridgford, Theresa May began an interview with 'I'm pleased to come to this … er … this particular town…' And yet none of these led to the avalanche of coverage which followed Abbott's LBC interview, let alone the abuse. White politicians, it seems, are allowed to make mistakes.

The fascination with the LBC interview reveals a great deal about perceptions of Abbott in the press and in public discourse more generally. Her thirty years in Parliament were disregarded, as commentators picked over forty seconds of an interview in which she had momentarily forgotten her figures. In 1997, Abbott reviewed Patricia Williams's *Seeing a Colorblind Future* for *The Times*. Abbott recalled her arrival at a May ball in her last year at Cambridge, as an example of the 'small aggressions of unconscious racism' discussed by Williams.[33] *Seeing a Colorblind Future* argued that these aggressions were rooted in 'an assumption that being white is the norm and ultimately superior'. Abbott was out of place at a Cambridge May ball because she was black. She was out of place as the spokesperson for a potential party of government in 2017 for the same reason. What had been a small aggression based on unconscious racism at Cambridge, when transposed to the larger canvas of the national media, had become widespread and relentless abuse.

Deborah Gabriel, an activist scholar and senior lecturer at Bournemouth University, argued that the abuse should be understood in terms of broader patterns. First, black women tend to be objectified in the British media. Gabriel pointed out that much of the coverage of Abbott referenced her relationship with Corbyn, and in so doing played 'on historical conceptions of Black women as concubines'.[34] Such narratives, Gabriel claimed, served to dehumanise Abbott, and delegitimise her in the public square. Gabriel also pointed to the fact that 'racialised discourse need not be explicitly racist to be discriminatory, marginalising or oppressive'.

Lisa Amanda Palmer's paper 'Diane Abbott, misogynoir and the politics of Black British feminism's anticolonial imperatives' argued that the response to Abbott in 2017 reflected long-standing narratives about black women, which had been intensified following the recent revival of white English nationalism.[35] She argued, 'Misogynoir creates invisibility for Black women's pain and hypervisibility for what are deemed as inherent flaws in Black womanhood by speaking to the specific violence that Black women experience due to anti-Blackness.' Palmer's work located the creation of images – such as the picture of the orangutan circulated by Pearmain – in the context of images of 'monstrous bodies' created in the period of enslavement and colonialism to depict black women.[36] She also situated the threats of rape and lynching in a long history of violence and fantasies of violence toward black women. Moreover, she juxtaposed 'monstrous' depictions of Abbott with the fascination regarding her relationship with Corbyn, showing the way that in much British discourse 'Black women's bodies [are] a contradictory site of sexual desirability and repulsiveness'.[37] In terms of the LBC interview, Palmer argued that the mockery of Abbott's mental capacity also had deep roots. The 'white man's burden', an essential aspect of colonialism, was based on the notion that white men had a superior capacity for reason, and therefore a right to exercise authority over the people they sought to subjugate. In this sense, Palmer's analysis pointed to the fact that the abuse that Abbott received was not merely equal opportunity bullying. Describing it as such misses the specific nature of misogynoir which reflects historic relationships of power and domination.[38]

On election day, Operation Black Vote published an 'Urgent Statement in Support of Diane Abbott MP', which deplored 'the racism, misogyny and hatred suffered' by her during the campaign.[39] The statement, which was signed by activists, academics, clergy and public figures of all kinds argued, 'We note the current hysteria of sections of the British media which has a disturbing tendency to apply a wholly different standard of critical news values when reporting on senior black political figures, and in particular, black women.' In comparison, white privilege allowed white politicians to make mistakes in public without paying such a heavy price.

Keith Vaz also argues that the abuse that Abbott received during the 2017 election campaign was exceptional, 'This wasn't just nastiness, they tried to destroy her. Underlying it all is a racism that exists in some sections of the British media that will never be eradicated.'[40] Vaz argues that while he has experienced this racism, 'she has put up with more'.

Vaz was an important source of support for Abbott during the 2017 campaign. He concluded that she was showing signs of hypoglycaemia – low blood sugar, which can lead to physical fatigue and lapses in concentration. As a diabetic himself, and the chair of the All-Party Parliamentary Group for Diabetes for a decade, Vaz was familiar with the symptoms and the significance of stress as a trigger. Leaving his campaign in Leicester on election day 2017 he rushed to London to try to persuade Abbott to see a doctor.

Abbott had received similar advice from her brother, who also has diabetes. Vaz's agent was horrified. It was unheard of to break off campaigning on polling day to travel to another constituency 100 miles away and ordered Vaz back to Leicester. Properly managed, Vaz explains, symptoms disappear, but left untreated the consequences can be serious. Vaz talked to Abbott on polling day and advised her that once the count was over, she should take some time off. She told him that Karie Murphy, Jeremy Corbyn's chief of staff had come to her flat apparently on Corbyn's instructions to tell her to stand down as shadow Home Secretary. She had tried to get hold of Corbyn. It was only the arrival of her own chief of staff Ribeiro-Addy that made her stay in the post. Vaz also counselled her to stand firm.[41]

News that Abbott was stepping back from the campaign due to ill-health evoked an emotional reaction from her supporters. Two north Londoners launched a GoFundMe fundraiser to send Abbott a care package which included music albums, jars of coconut oil, champagne, books, 'Bouji af Candles' and homemade fried plantain. Recognising the disproportionate abuse Abbott received, Sophie Duker, one of the organisers, wrote: 'We know she gon' be back though, rising from the ashes like Solange to take her Seat At The Table. And by table we mean Cabinet. And by seat we mean the position of Home Secretary, haters.'[42]

Over 500 people donated to the fundraiser, generating £5,935 in less than one week. A total of £83.18 was spent on Abbott's care package and the remaining funds were distributed evenly between three Hackney charities: Project Indigo, The Crib, and the Refugee Women's Association. The pair also collaborated with artist Leyla Reynolds who designed 'Queen Di' T-shirts and sweatshirts, with funds donated to Women Against Rape.

Meanwhile, Stephanie Ozuo and Tiss Saccoh started the Twitter hashtag #AbbottAppreciation, which prompted an outpouring of support and statements of solidarity for the MP. Abbott tweeted, 'Touched by all the messages of support. Still standing! Will rejoin the fray soon. Vote Labour!' Later that day, she tweeted a clip from her 1987 BBC election night interview with the caption, 'Defending Hackney since 1987 #VoteLabour'.

Wanting to take #AbbottAppreciation offline Ozuo and her peers organised an event for Abbott at the Queen of Hoxton in Shoreditch.

As Abbott arrived, she was greeted by ecstatic cheers and applause. Keith Vaz, Patrick Vernon, Clive Lewis and Eleanor Smith were among the 100 people who turned up to support Abbott. 'Diane broke the glass ceiling,' Vaz told the audience. 'Everything she has done in the last thirty years, she has taken steps no one else was able to take.'[43] On the night, Hackney resident and *The Voice UK* 2014 winner Jermain Jackman thanked Abbott for inspiring him to enter politics and sang a moving rendition of 'You Raise Me Up'. Abbott thanked the audience before stating,

> People always talk about strong black women and I'm sick of hearing that because everyone is human ... Contrary to what you've heard about strong black women, even strong black women cry, even strong black women feel alone, even strong black women wonder, 'Is this all really worth it?' Even strong black women think, 'Maybe I should just bail out.'[44]

Reflecting on the event, Abbott says:

> It was really touching because it can be isolating in politics. There were all these twenty-somethings who had gotten together to try and show that people cared about me and supported me. That was one of the most moving things. In the end, I have always felt that my role in life is to make it easier for young black women that come after me, so I hope that I have managed to make it easier.[45]

As the event ended, Ozuo presented Abbott with a care package. She tearfully told the MP, 'We have come here to really show you our appreciation and how much we love you. I, as a black woman, I cannot tell you how much this means to me. I'm not as visible as you, but I get it, I see it, and I know.'[46]

Activists involved in Black Lives Matter also rallied to Abbott during the campaign. Siana Bangura, a writer, producer, performer and activist involved with Black Lives Matter comments, 'A lot of black women and black girls made care packages for her at that time.'[47] Bangura argues that the 2017 election changed perceptions of Abbott in black communities,

> Since her vindication at the last election, it feels like there's a warmer reception to her. I'd always thought of her as being a character who there are really mixed reviews about even in the black community. She's always been outspoken, so she's always got a lot of stick, that's from everybody, not just from white people, to be honest. But in this particular election, it was so clear that she was being bullied horrifically … it was very clear that there was quite a specific campaign against her, and it feels like the landscape was warmer to her after her vindication.

The award-winning writer Reni Eddo-Lodge also argues that there has been a change in the way that Abbott has been viewed in recent years: 'I think there has been a renaissance of respect for Diane, a groundswell, in the last couple of years. It's respect for the work that she's doing now, which she was also doing in the 1990s.'[48]

ELECTION NIGHT

Election night in 2017 started with a surprise, as the BBC exit poll projected a hung parliament. Predictions of May's majority had been dropping steadily during the campaign, from over 100 seats, to around eighty, to forty, but few expected anything other than a Tory majority. Briefly, in the middle of the night, it even looked like Labour might emerge as the largest party.

The evening was a vindication for Abbott. Labour had fought a campaign from the left. For the first time in a long time, Labour had made a principled argument about immigration and asylum. Rather than collapsing, Labour gained 40 per cent of the popular vote. To put that in context, it was a higher share than Blair achieved in 2005, higher than Harold Wilson achieved in either of the elections of 1974 and it was better than anything achieved by Kinnock, or Brown or Callaghan. Indeed, it was comparable with Blair's victory of 2001. In terms of seats, Labour were in a much better position in 2017 than they had been two years earlier. In 2015 Labour had lost seats, meaning that, barring a miracle, the party could not expect to win a majority at the next election. However, following 2017, there was a realistic prospect that with one more push, Labour could win next time round.

The racism of the campaign also seems to have backfired. BAME members of Momentum rallied behind Abbott, joining the campaign to get the vote out and to get the BAME vote out. In the seventy-five seats with the largest BAME populations Labour's share of the vote shot up 11.5 per cent. Labour attracted fifty-four percentage points of BAME voters in 2017, an increase on 2015. Indeed, as Cowley and Kavanagh pointed out, the 2017 election was the 'second consecutive election in which the Conservatives had increased their share of the vote, whilst falling behind among BAME voters.'[49]

The 2017 election was also a personal victory. Elected in 1987 with a majority of 7,500, thirty years later Abbott's majority had grown to 35,139; a personal record, and an indication that her constituents wanted to stand with her at the end of an appalling campaign. Speaking at the count, she was defiant:

The Conservative Party fought a campaign characterised by the politics of personal destruction and yet the British people have seen past that, and in Hackney they have supported our Labour campaign which was a positive campaign addressing the issues that concerned people here in Hackney. Whether it is the state of the NHS, whether it's the housing crisis, whether it's the benefit cuts, we fought a positive campaign here in Hackney and we have been vindicated.

You know, they said if Labour fought this general election on a progressive manifesto we would be swept away by a Conservative landslide. They said, if we fought this general election under the leadership of Jeremy Corbyn we would be annihilated. But I am proud to say even at this point we have seen how the British people of all ages, of all classes, all creeds and all colours have rallied to a positive message, and rallied to the leadership of Jeremy Corbyn.[50]

CHAPTER 15

LEVEL PEGGING

Between 10 p.m. on Thursday 8 June 2017 and 7 the next morning, British politics was turned on its head. The night before, May was secure, while Corbyn was reckoned to be on the way out. The morning after, pundits were agreed that the Labour leader was safe until the next election. May, however, had thrown away her majority. There was talk of a leadership bid. Johnson was reportedly 'on manoeuvres'.[1]

The narratives that had dominated the media for two years fell away. The endless talk of 1983 stopped. Comparisons between Corbyn and Foot would no longer do. Trying to tell the story of the election without the analogical language of the early 1980s, the BBC fell back on graphics and numbers, which elevated the Labour leader to the ranks of Blair and Wilson. Labour's campaign, in which Abbott and Corbyn had played the most prominent part, had increased the Labour vote by 9 per cent, a bigger swing than Blair had achieved in 1997. Labour also became the most successful socialist party in Europe, achieving a higher share of the vote than the French Socialist Party in January, and the Social Democratic Party of Germany in March of the same year.

With May struggling to negotiate a deal with the Democratic Unionist Party, Abbott remembers that the feeling in the Labour leadership was positive.[2] The election had been a vindication. What is more, in the eighteen months following the election Labour and the Conservatives were neck and neck in the polls. With the Conservatives bitterly divided over Brexit, there was the possibility that the government might fall and an election could propel Labour into office.

The narrative around Abbott also went into reverse. After polling day there was something of a reassessment of Abbott in newspapers and magazines and among established radio and television journalists. On 15 June, Abbott announced that she had been diagnosed with Type-2 diabetes. Speaking to Anushka Asthana and Heather Stewart in her first interview since the end of the campaign, she explained that her condition was now being managed properly. She also used the interview to discuss the abuse directed at her throughout the campaign. From what she had seen of the Tory campaign, Abbott concluded 'clearly I was part of Lynton Crosby's grid', a reference to the Conservative campaign plan.[3] In the run-up to the election she said, 'you felt you were in a kind of vortex – as I became aware of what was happening – the Facebook ads, the Tories name-dropping me for no reason'. Of the elections that she had fought, Abbott claimed that 2017 had been the nastiest, 'It was an extraordinary campaign. You fight seven general election campaigns, in Hackney, and suddenly you are this target.' Abbott claimed that the Tories had to explain why she had been singled out. However, a Conservative spokesperson saw things differently. 'Was her response to "vicious" campaigning also in response to whether Labour were vicious? ... no one knows more about the difficulties of diabetes than the prime minister.'[4] The Tories refused to take all the blame, nor would they allow Abbott to monopolise public sympathy.

At the end of June, Johnson's 'car-crash interview' on Radio 4's *PM* reignited the debate over Abbott's treatment during the campaign. Asked about measures set out in the Queen's speech to combat institutional racism in the justice system Johnson said,

> Well, there are measures in the... err um, I believe, in the, er, the bill on the courts, which I, I, I, think is supposed to er, address some of those issues. And I think one, one thing in particular that... er, we are, we are looking at is, erm... measures to... hang on a second...[5]

Writing for fashion magazine *Elle*, Louise Donovan compared the treatment of Abbott with that of Johnson and concluded that while the media 'viciously hounded Abbott', Johnson was allowed to 'wiggle out of almost anything'.[6] Former Deputy Prime Minister John Prescott apparently reached the same view. He tweeted, 'THE worst interview by a politician EVER. I expect @BBCNews & @itvnews will cover it & it'll be in every newspaper [thinking face emoji].'[7] Chuka Umunna followed suit, tweeting, 'This is pretty damn embarrassing but I guarantee he won't have the opprobrium heaped on him that @HackneyAbbott received.'[8]

In the new media environment, less progressive figures had also noticed the politics of unequal consequences. Louise Donovan stopped short of saying that Johnson could get away with murder. A year earlier, however, Donald Trump joked, 'I could stand in the middle of Fifth Avenue and shoot someone, and I wouldn't lose any voters, okay. It's incredible.'[9] His quip pointed to the fact that he was so insulated by his status that he could get away with almost anything. Comparisons between Abbott and Johnson indicated that a similar relationship between privilege and bias was at work in British politics.

GRENFELL TOWER

Two days after Abbott's return to public life, fire engulfed Grenfell Tower in North Kensington. Before the death toll was known, a series of concerning details emerged. The 1970s brutalist tower had recently been clad in flammable material. The building had no sprinklers, and the fire service did not have the equipment necessary to reach the higher floors. It soon emerged that the 'stay put' advice that was issued by the fire service had compounded the problem. In the immediate aftermath of the fire, the first thought was for the victims and survivors, then for residents of other towers clad in similar material. There was also the question of the local and central government system which had created the conditions for the fire, and now seemed unable to respond. Media reports presented the fire as a symbol of Britain's divisions.

Located in North Kensington, Grenfell Tower was just over a mile from Edbrooke Road and the house in which Abbott had lived as a child. Even after she had moved to Harrow she visited 'North Ken' and 'the Grove' frequently to visit family and friends, as she explains:

'I knew the area well, it was a very Caribbean area when I was a child.'[10] Grenfell Tower was built between 1972 and 1974 and was located less than a mile from Frank Crichlow's Mangrove restaurant, which at the time was both the heart of the black community in Notting Hill, and the front line in a running battle between the local black community and the police. As Andrew O'Hagan described, North Kensington is a place 'where poor people have always had a hard time, and where immigrants, in particular, have always been subject to ill-treatment, lack of choice, and racism. Whatever else has gone on, the memory of "No Irish. No Blacks. No Dogs" hasn't been erased.'[11]

Abbott first heard about the fire on the television.

When I saw the tower up in flames, and when I saw some of the victims, you felt there but for the grace of God. I related to it because I knew the area well. I related to it because it was a very diverse community. And I related to it because it shone a light on the gulf between rich and poor in London.[12]

On the morning after the fire, Corbyn visited the remains of the building, meeting survivors. May visited the site a day later surrounded by a security team. Government ministers stressed that there should be no rush to judgement, either about the causes of the fire or about what should be done to help survivors. They were also at pains to stress how deeply they felt. Speaking on Sky News on 16 June, Andrea Leadsom stated that in Parliament, 'You could absolutely feel the sympathy and the horror and the real sense of tragedy. And I think MPs from right across the House … are just desperately wanting to help residents.'[13] Michael Gove struck a similar tone. Asked what action the government was going to take, Gove responded, 'I feel distraught about this, I want everything possible to be done, there are people who are friends of mine with whom I've worked, who have been directly affected.'[14] Gove and Leadsom spoke movingly about their own grief and how much they wished something would be done. Neither gave the impression that it might be their job as government ministers to intervene. In the absence of government action, local synagogues, mosques and churches opened their doors and worked together to meet the immediate needs of the community. May's commitment to rehouse all of the Grenfell survivors locally within three weeks was the only specific promise that emerged in the first few days after the tragedy.

Abbott took a different tack. Rather than stressing her personal grief, she met with local people and began developing an analysis of what had gone wrong. Speaking on *Channel 4 News* from a church building in Kensington, she argued that the local council's response had been slow and chaotic.[15] The cause of this, she argued, was that 'the Royal Borough of Kensington and Chelsea outsourced the management of the block, and then seemed to think they had outsourced the care and concern for the people'. Labour proposed a radical solution, empty houses owned by absentee landlords should be bought by the government and used to rehome the 300 families.

In the ensuing months, Abbott attended community meetings in the area regularly, listening to survivors and speaking to residents of neighbouring blocks. Speaking at a Stand Up to Racism event at the end of the year, Abbott argued that above all else, Grenfell was about people, specifically those people who the government wanted to remove from public view. Moreover, she argued that Grenfell was no accident. It was the consequence of a whole approach to government. 'Grenfell' she argued 'is the culmination of policies of deregulation, outsourcing and austerity'.[16]

Under Blair, the government had encouraged the deregulation of building and the 'commercialisation of safety'. O'Hagan argued that this allowed companies to 'flout regulations and fake tests and call it normal practice'.[17] Deregulation also meant that there was no comprehensive view of how new building materials worked in combination. With the establishment of the coalition, the Department of Energy and Climate Change invited manufacturers to advise government, and in some cases to generate policy. One of these companies was Celotex, the firm which manufactured the Grenfell cladding. At a local level too, the emphasis was on outsourcing. This was nothing new, indeed, since the Victorian period Kensington and Chelsea Council had preferred to allow charities to deal with the problems of housing, and to establish community trusts to manage public spaces. However, this created problems. Local councils were accountable to the people. Charities and trusts often worked hand in hand with the council but were technically independent and therefore difficult to hold to account. Moreover, the managers of the charity trusts, many of whom were appointed directly by the council were middle-class, white professionals, while the communities they served were overwhelmingly poor, working class and black.

In a sense, the system that led to the Grenfell disaster was the model for Cameron's 'Big Society'. Cameron was a resident of Notting Hill, and a beneficiary of their services. The regime of outsourcing and working with semi-autonomous trusts had won the Royal Borough of Kensington and Chelsea numerous awards. Public services met targets, and official reports praised the management of local housing. On paper the council was the model of efficiency. The fact that the targets bore no relation to the experience of the tenants, and that the official reports were written by the people running the services was neither here nor there.

As Abbott argued, running social housing as a business led to multiple failures. The refurbishment of the tower supervised by the Kensington and Chelsea Tenant Management Organisation Ltd resulted in the installation of fire retardant cavity barriers that were the wrong size, the creation of gaps around windows which fed the fire with oxygen, poorly fitted fire doors that would not close and the installation of flammable cladding.[18] Abbott would later refer to what was going on in Grenfell and Kensington more generally as 'social apartheid'.[19] Not only was the borough divided between the rich south and the poor north, there was division between the people who relied on public services and the people who made the decisions about those services. Both divisions were, in large part, divisions between black and white.

The issues surrounding Grenfell became increasingly contested as 2017 went on. In December the *Daily Mail* published an article stating that 'Far-left activists' were attempting to 'hijack Grenfell'.[20] Justice4Grenfell, the *Mail* claimed, was side-lining survivors, and 'self-appointed activists' from the Socialist Worker, from trade unions and from disability rights groups were circulating false claims about the number of people killed.

INTIMIDATION IN PUBLIC LIFE

Following the election, there was a recognition that something had gone very wrong in the 2017 campaign. May committed the government to an investigation, and on 12 July MPs assembled for a debate in Westminster Hall. White MPs listened in silence as Abbott explained how the dynamics of politics had changed since the advent of social media. She argued that although she was an advocate of 'robust debate', MPs needed to recognise the 'mindless abuse' which had gone on during the election campaign,

> I have had rape threats and been described as a 'pathetic useless fat black piece of shit', an 'ugly, fat black bitch', and a 'n*****' over and over again. One of my members of staff said that the most surprising thing about coming to work for me is how often she has to read the word 'n*****'. It comes in through emails, Twitter and Facebook.[21]

Abbott used her speech to challenge a number of misconceptions. First, while acknowledging that all MPs received abuse, she argued that her colleagues needed to recognise that it 'is much worse for women', and that such abuse was often racialised. Second, she disabused her colleagues of the notion that the harassment had been unique to the 2017 election, or purely the result of social media.

> It is certainly true that the online abuse that I and others experience has got worse in recent years, and that it gets worse at election time, but I do not put it down to a particular election. I think the rise in the use of online media has turbocharged abuse. Thirty years ago, when I first became an MP, if someone wanted to attack an MP, they had to write a letter – usually in green ink – put it in an envelope, put a stamp on it and walk to the post box. Now, they

press a button and we read vile abuse that, thirty years ago, people would have been frightened even to write down.[22]

In the wake of Abbott's speech, May professed herself 'horrified by stories from colleagues about the scale and nature of the intimidation, bullying and harassment they suffered during the general election campaign'.[23] However, May's statements did not acknowledge that there had been a racial element to the abuse. Right-wing papers were in no doubt about the culprit. The *Daily Mail*, for example, covered May's comments with the headline, 'May calls on Corbyn to condemn the "bullying and harassment" of MPs after politicians come forward to tell of the death threats and abuse they received during the election campaign'.[24] May had not attacked Corbyn during her press conference, and Corbyn had condemned the abuse throughout the campaign, but this was incidental to the *Mail*'s point.

May's condemnation of 'abuse and bullying and harassment' also failed to acknowledge the way in which the Tory campaign targeted Abbott. Labour MPs Ian Lavery and Cat Smith, however, issued a statement on 12 July criticising the Conservative campaign for doing exactly this. They argued:

> The Conservatives ran a negative, nasty campaign, propagating personal attacks, smears and untruths, particularly aimed at one of the most prominent women MPs, and indeed the first black woman MP, Diane Abbott ... The Conservative Party perpetrated this on an industrial scale by spending millions of pounds to post highly personalised and nasty attack adverts on voters' Facebook timelines without their permission.[25]

Moreover, Lavery and Smith pointed to a pattern: 'Last year Zac Goldsmith MP ran an extremely negative, divisive and racially discriminatory campaign against Sadiq Khan.' Goldsmith's 2016 London mayoral campaign had been criticised for trying to target Hindu voters, and for trying to link Khan to extremism.

Amnesty International's report in September quantified the extent of the abuse and there was also some small public redress.[26] Ofcom formally reprimanded LBC for allowing a caller to describe Abbott as a 'retard' twice on air during the campaign.[27] At the end of the year Lord Bew's report 'Intimidation in Public Life: A Review by the Committee on Standards in Public Life' concluded that 'Intimidation is disproportionately likely to be directed towards women, those from ethnic and religious minorities, and LGBT candidates. A failure to tackle such abuse will perpetuate inequalities in Britain's public life and restrict the diversity of those representing the public.'[28]

For all the discussion of standards in public life, the LBC interview continued to haunt public perceptions. In December, Star Sports Bookmakers posted a tweet of a white man wearing blackface, apparently impersonating Abbott, as part of its campaign around the World Darts Championships.[29] The tweet played on both narratives of black womanhood and on the notion that Abbott was incapable of basic maths. A spontaneous pushback on Twitter forced the bookmakers to apologise.

Theresa May welcomed Lord Bew's report in February 2018 in a speech celebrating the centenary of the Representation of the People Act, and the enfranchisement of women aged over thirty.[30] May paid tribute to Emmeline Pankhurst and 'the heroic campaigners of the past, who fought to include the voices of all citizens in our public debate'. Nonetheless, May expressed fear that 'public debate today is coarsening', that in the country of John Milton and J. S. Mill, public debate was 'becoming oppressively hostile'.

May's framing of the report stressed the dangers of 'abuse', 'sexism, bullying, undemocratic behaviour and outright personal attacks' as well as the problems which occur when 'disagreement mutates into intimidation'.[31] By linking Lord Bew's report to the campaign for women's suffrage May was able to focus public attention on the real abuse faced by women in public life. At the same time, by concentrating on women, May side-stepped racism. Indeed, all of her examples of women who had been subjected to abuse were white. Her speech did acknowledge that BAME candidates in the 2017 election had been 'disproportionately targeted in terms of scale, intensity and vitriol', but she did not discuss racism, nor anti-Semitism. May used the word 'race' twice, once to celebrate the progress that had been made and once to set out a vision for the future.[32]

This framing of the report allowed May to score some party political points. By focusing on white women, she was able to emphasise the progressive credentials of the Conservative Party. Having discussed the 1918 Act, she reminded her audience, 'gender equality at the ballot box was not achieved for another ten years, and I am proud to say under a Conservative government'.[33] She also reflected on the fact that Emmeline Pankhurst was 'selected as the Conservative candidate for Whitechapel and St Georges', that the Conservatives could claim two female Prime Ministers, and of her own work as 'co-founder of Women2Win'. May's determination to fight for standards in public life was allied with a determination to place the Conservative Party on the right side of history.

May also characterised abuse in a way that was wholly at odds with Abbott's statement in Westminster Hall. Abbott had drawn a distinction between robust public debate on the one hand, and 'mindless abuse' that had 'been characteristically racist and sexist' on the other. May, by contrast, argued that the problem was that 'disagreements about policy or questions of professional competence' led to 'vitriol and hostility.'[34] In so doing, May ignored the nature of the abuse that Abbott had highlighted. The tweets that Abbott had read out had nothing to do with policy disagreements or conflicting ideological commitments, they were personal attacks based on hatred of black women. But May's speech had nothing to say about such abuse. Moreover, while May's view that it was legitimate to discuss 'professional competence' was wholly plausible in the abstract, it ignored the way in which discussion purporting to be about 'professional competence' had reflected biases against black women, and the way in which discussions of this kind had been used as a 'dogwhistle'.

By linking the report to women's suffrage and by emphasising the sexist abuse hurled at white women, May had managed to place the Conservative Party on the side of decency. At the same time by minimising the report's findings on race, and by refusing to mention

Abbott she side-stepped difficult questions about the nature of the Conservative campaign and her complicity in dogwhistle politics. Indeed, as Abbott received more abuse than any other woman, her absence from a speech about the abuse of women was surely no accident.

May's speech highlighted two of the shortcomings of Bew's report. First, Bew had not used the term 'racism' and although he had recognised racial abuse, the report's three references to the issue had done nothing to clarify what was at stake. Consequently, the report was no defence against dog-whistle politics and coded attacks on black people. Second, Bew expected politicians to put aside party political divisions and work together. May's speech showed that she, at least, had no intention of damaging the Conservative brand in her fight for decency. Indeed, Bew's hope that politicians might work together ignored the fact that dog-whistle politics had an electoral advantage for the Conservatives. What is more, in a situation where one of the major parties had long benefited from dog-whistle politics it was naïve to think that there would be change. May's approach to restoring decency to public life was reflected in a Respect Pledge, which all Tory candidates would be required to sign. The pledge, like May's speech, contained no reference to racism.

May's speech also presented a highly edited account of British history. For the Prime Minister, Britain was the nation of Milton, a champion of free speech; Mill, an advocate of personal liberty; and Pankhurst, a campaigner for women's rights. There was no sense that Britain was also the homeland of slave trader Edward Colston or Reginald Dyer, 'the Butcher of Amritsar', or arch-imperialist Cecil Rhodes or Edward Long, slave owner, colonial administrator, and 'one of the most vociferous and influential supporters of the slave trade and slavery'.[35]

ANTI-SEMITISM

With hindsight, one surprising feature of May's speech was the absence of any reference to anti-Semitism. May had attacked Labour for 'tolerating anti-Semitism and supporting voices of hate' in her 2016 conference speech, branding Labour 'the nasty party'.[36] Concerns about anti-Semitism in the Labour Party had been ongoing since April 2016. A series of social media posts by Naz Shah, Labour MP for Bradford West were the initial catalyst for concern. Shah admitted that her posts were anti-Semitic, apologised and was suspended from the Party. Shortly thereafter Ken Livingstone was suspended for comments made in Shah's defence on BBC London's *Vanessa Feltz Show*. Addressing anti-Semitism in the Labour Party following Livingstone's suspension, Abbott stated, 'I take anti-Semitism extremely seriously, so does the party, that's why every single, of I think twelve, allegations of anti-Semitism since Jeremy became leader has resulted in suspension. Ken was suspended within hours.' Abbott acknowledged that 'Ken's remarks were extremely offensive', she pledged that Labour would specify anti-Semitism explicitly as an offence in the party rulebook but denied that the 'Labour Party is riddled with anti-Semitism'.[37]

The Chakrabarti Inquiry of June 2016 had acknowledged an 'occasionally toxic atmosphere' in the party, and that while Labour was 'not overrun by anti-Semitism, Islamophobia or other forms of racism', acknowledged that 'there is too much clear evidence (going back some years) of a minority of hateful or ignorant attitudes and behaviours festering within a sometimes bitter incivility of discourse'.[38] Labour was criticised again in October 2016 when the Home Affairs Select Committee accused the party of incompetence over the handling of allegations of anti-Semitism, and of helping to create a 'safe space' for people with 'vile attitudes towards Jewish people'.[39] Lord Bew's report, published at the end of 2017, also presented evidence that 'anti-Semitic abuse has put off candidates from standing for public office', and noted the findings of the All-Party Parliamentary Group Against Antisemitism that although anti-Semitic abuse in Britain was nothing new, the growth of social media meant that 'candidates are more exposed and open to abuse which is taking place on a larger scale than even five years ago'.[40]

A rule change in September 2017, which was designed to make it easier for Labour to discipline members guilty of anti-Semitic abuse failed to win back public trust. In 2018 Corbyn apologised 'for the hurt that has been caused to many Jewish people' acknowledging that Labour had been 'too slow in processing disciplinary cases'.[41]

Discussion over the International Holocaust Remembrance Alliance Working Definition of Antisemitism led to a confrontation between Margaret Hodge and the Labour leader, during which Hodge called Corbyn 'a racist' and 'an antisemite'.[42] Abbott comments, 'It was a particularly painful set of allegations for Jeremy. Jeremy's not a racist, he's not an anti-Semite. Anti-racism is very much his *raison d'être*. So, it was particularly painful for him.'[43] By late 2018 public opinion was shifting. A ComRes poll showed that almost a third of voters now regarded Labour as 'the nasty party'.[44]

ANTI-RACISM

Shortly after the publication of the ComRes poll, Abbott received tributes from an unexpected quarter. May's 2018 conference address revisited the theme of her speech celebrating the centenary of women's suffrage. However, her emphasis was different.

> In the last few years, something's changed for the worse, I feel it, and I'm sure you do. Rigorous debate between political opponents, is becoming more like a confrontation between enemies. People who put themselves forward to serve are becoming targets. Not just them, their families as well. We all saw the sickening pictures of a far-left extremist shouting abuse at Jacob Rees-Mogg's children. And it's not only Conservatives who are facing abuse. The first black woman ever to be elected to the House of Commons receives more racist and misogynist messages today than when she first stood over thirty years ago. You do not have to agree with a word Diane Abbott says to believe passionately in her right to say it, free from threats and abuse.[45]

The Conservative faithful applauded. A day earlier, Sajid Javid had been warmer still. May urged the Tories to respect Abbott's right to engage in debate. Javid went further. In Britain, he claimed,

> we see people from diverse backgrounds succeeding in all walks of life and in all levels. This progress is happening in our politics too.

That requires role models and pioneers. People on all sides, including people that we wouldn't normally praise in our party conference. People like Diane Abbott. Yes, Diane Abbott. We might disagree with the shadow Home Secretary on almost all her policies. But it takes guts and determination to become the first black woman to be elected to the House of Commons. And we should pay tribute to that.[46]

Speaking on *Peston* shortly after May's speech, Dawn Butler, shadow Women and Equalities Minister, stated:

I actually found it a little bit sinister … because they [the Conservatives] were responsible for the spike in abuse that Diane saw over the general election, because they had her picture plastered all over billboards, and they had really ugly messaging framed around her … if it was accompanied by an apology I would have accepted that and said OK, but it was very sinister because it was Javid one day and the Prime Minister the next day.[47]

Abbott put out a tweet saying much the same: 'Some nice words from Tory leaders like Theresa May and Sajid Javid. Makes you wonder who was responsible for the Tory party's relentless personal attacks in the general election campaign 2017 #CPC18.'[48]

While May stopped well short of an apology, her speech signalled a matter of political import. Early in the summer, Johnson had caused a storm. In a piece in the *Telegraph* he had likened women who wear the niqab and the burka to 'letter boxes' and 'bank robber[s]', stating that schools, universities, banks and businesses should be able to prohibit students and staff from wearing 'these odd bits of headgear'.[49] He had also likened the relationship between *Telegraph* readers who wanted a total ban, and women who want to wear the burka or the niqab to that of 'a parent confronted by a rebellious teenager'. Although Johnson styled himself a follower of J. S. Mill, critics accused him of being illiberal.[50] May was quick to condemn the essay. It is conceivable that she used her reference to Abbott to signal her moderation against Johnson's harder line.

Six months after the Tory conference, Amber Rudd also acknowledged the extent of abuse that Abbott received. Speaking to Jeremy Vine on BBC Radio 2, and referring to Lord Bew's report, Rudd acknowledged that women in public life received more abuse than men. 'It's definitely worse if you're a woman, and it's worst of all if you're a coloured woman. I know that Diane Abbott gets a huge amount of abuse, and I think that's something we need to continue to call out.'[51]

Abbott responded with a tweet, 'The term "coloured", is an outdated, offensive and revealing choice of words.'[52] Rudd took to Twitter to apologise: 'Mortified at my clumsy language and sorry to @HackneyAbbott. My point stands: that no one should suffer abuse because of their race or gender.'[53]

Rudd's comment reflected a degree of historical ignorance. As Avtar Brah has asserted, 'coloured' was a term used in Britain in the decades after the war to describe migrants from the Caribbean, from Africa and from south Asia, but it reflected a colonial vocabulary. As Brah has argued, it 'was not a simple descriptive term. It had been the colonial code for a relationship of domination and subordination between coloniser and colonised.'[54] In the metropolis, the term went along with 'racist practices of stigmatisation, inferiorisation, exclusion, and/or discrimination in arenas such as employment, education, housing, media, the criminal justice system, immigration … and the health services'.[55] Rudd's comment also reflected an attempt to rewrite history. Rather than being the person, or a representative of the party, who was targeting Abbott with racist dogwhistles, Rudd was one of those who was continuing to 'call out' racist and sexist abuse.

Rudd's comment points to a continuity in British politics from the Thatcher period to the age of Brexit: the paradox of anti-racism. Britain is both a country where everyone deplores racism, and a country where racism persists.[56] Rudd was both the minister who oversaw the illegal deportation of black people while directing the 'hostile environment' policy and someone who was determined to stand shoulder to shoulder with Abbott and call out racist and sexist abuse. Abbott first addressed this paradox in an interview given to *Socialist Action* in November 1985, when she had argued that black people could not make alliances with white people simply 'because they claim to be anti-racist'.[57] However, the historical parallel is not exact. In 1985 Abbott had been talking about 'anti-racists' in the Labour Party. By 2019 this brand of 'anti-racism' had spread to other parties.

BREXIT

The outcome of the 2017 election had implications for Brexit. Gina Miller's 2017 victory in the Supreme Court established that the government could not use Crown prerogatives to trigger Article 50. By implication the case established that Parliament should play a role in the Brexit process. As May had lost her majority in the Commons, there was the possibility that the government might lose control of Brexit. In addition, although Labour and Conservatives had both promised to work towards the British exit from the EU during the 2017 campaign, a significant proportion of MPs elected in 2017 had backed Remain in 2016. This gave hope to some Remainers that Parliament might legislate for a new referendum which could prevent Brexit.

Of all the major political parties, Labour faced the greatest difficulties. Labour voters were divided. The PLP and the membership, however, were overwhelmingly pro-Remain. May was in a very different position. Her base was much more committed to Brexit, and having failed to win a majority in 2017, she fell back on the referendum result as her claim to democratic legitimacy.

Exactly what Brexit would look like was up for grabs. May's famous statement 'Brexit means Brexit' gave nothing away, nor did slogans such as 'red, white and blue Brexit'. When it came to Brexit the English language struggled to describe what was going on. May proposed a 'Great Repeal Bill'. While this echoed the language of reform of the Victorian era and therefore had some rhetorical appeal, it wholly misrepresented the purpose of the bill, which rather than repealing EU law would copy large chunks of it into British law.

Influenced by Tony Benn, Abbott had initially been sceptical of European institutions, believing them to be undemocratic. However, she had campaigned for Remain, represented a solidly pro-European constituency, and believed in the principle of the free movement of people.

Corbyn's February 2018 announcement that Labour were backing British membership of a customs union was taken as an indication that the party wanted a 'soft Brexit'. For once, Corbyn and his team were in the centre ground. Following the referendum Nick Clegg had argued for a Norway-style Brexit, as the 'most sensible and softest' approach to leaving the EU, and in the aftermath of the 2017 election, Yvette Cooper and Harriet Harman called for a cross-party approach, which they hoped would lead to a 'soft Brexit'.[58] Indeed, a few weeks before Corbyn set out Labour's position Anna Soubry and Ken Clarke had come out in favour of a customs union with the EU.

May's Chequers plan unveiled in July took a much 'harder' position. Not 'hard' enough for David Davis or Johnson, who quit the cabinet two days after its publication. As shadow Home Secretary, Abbott took the lead on Labour's post-Brexit immigration policy. Most commentators agreed that the Brexit vote was, at root, a vote about immigration. With this in mind, Abbott took charge of an extremely significant aspect of policy. From March to September 2018, she gave a series of speeches and interviews in which she set out Labour's approach to immigration.

As shadow Home Secretary, Abbott consulted relevant stakeholders and reviewed existing policy, but her work on immigration began with her own experience of the system. 'What most influenced my thinking was thirty years of dealing with immigration casework, and seeing how the Home Office worked,' she explains.[59]

Speaking in February and March, Abbott went back to first principles. She argued that too often immigration policy had been devoid of humanitarian values. Labour's approach, she promised, would start from a recognition of 'migrants' basic humanity' and from there, 'build a system which is both fair and efficient'. This meant scrapping the 'false and unworkable net migration target'; ending the hostile environment; ending the policy of breaking up families; and ending the indefinite detention of asylum seekers. Amber Rudd, then Abbott's opposite number, was unable to respond with immigration proposals of her own. In fact, on 2 February, the Home Office announced further delays to the government's already long-overdue immigration white paper.

YARL'S WOOD

Abbott's first speech came days before her visit to Yarl's Wood Immigration Removal Centre. She had first requested to visit the detention centre on her appointment as shadow Home Secretary in October 2016. For Abbott, the detention centre was bound up with many of her central concerns: the politics of human rights, the relationship between the individual and the state and the politics of race, as 'most of the women in Yarl's Wood are women of colour'.[60]

Shami Chakrabarti, shadow Attorney General from September 2016 until March 2020, was part of the campaign to ensure Abbott visited Yarl's Wood. For more than a year Chakrabarti recalls that Abbott's requests were 'fobbed off.' In 2017 Chakrabarti intervened,

> I just thought with my old Liberty hat on, this is outrageous, and we need to do something a bit more public, and if necessary, threaten legal action. This is a liberal democracy based on the rule of law. The idea that the shadow Home Secretary shouldn't be allowed to visit Yarl's Wood, or any place of detention, is just wrong.[61]

In December 2017, Chakrabarti and her team wrote to the Home Office on Abbott's behalf. Two months later, they were granted permission to visit Yarl's Wood.

The Yarl's Wood detention centre and the legal regime that governs it has a complex history. The Immigration Act 1971 allowed the Home Office to detain migrants indefinitely, giving the government a power unique among European democracies. Following New Labour's 1998 white paper 'Fairer, Faster and Firmer – A Modern Approach to Immigration and Asylum' new detention centres opened across the country. In 1988, there had been fewer than fifty detainees, mostly held at the airports to which they arrived. Three decades later, approximately

30,000 people were being placed in detention annually, the majority held in privately run immigration removal centres.[62]

Abbott recalls that when immigration removal centres were introduced, MPs were assured that detainees would be held for no more than a few days. Having visited Yarl's Wood in 2002 after a fire, Abbott recalls being assured by David Blunkett that detainees would be held for no more than twenty-eight days. But quickly it became the norm for people to be held for months and even years without a release date in sight. In 2017 Abbott told the Commons, 'The use of immigration detention has mushroomed, and the length of time has expanded, and that has shone a light on the lack of due process. We should never forget that none of these people, as matters stand, has committed a crime.'[63]

Published Home Office policy included a reference to the presumption of liberty, that is to say, liberty is the default position and detention must be justified. However, between 2006 and 2008, the Border and Immigration Agency had applied 'a near blanket ban on release'. When this came to light, the presumption of detention was included in published policy until it was ruled unlawful.

As well as being inhumane, Abbott believed the government's approach was 'wholly ineffective'. Amnesty argued that over the years, more and more people had been detained only to be released back into the community; these low removal rates make such a large detention estate hard to justify.

Yarl's Wood also raised the moral problem of detaining children. Abbott argued that this was 'wrong in principle, and it was almost certainly in breach of a number of human rights conventions'.[64] In 2010, the Children's Commissioner for England reported that children at Yarl's Wood were detained for 'unacceptable' lengths of time and faced 'extremely distressing' conditions.[65] Abbott also worked closely with Bail for Immigration Detainees, a group which raised the issue of children, many British citizens, taken into care because their parents had been detained or deported.

Yarl's Wood frequently made headlines due to protests. Serco and

G4S, the companies responsible for the running of the detention centre and the provision of healthcare, respectively, were under constant scrutiny as detainees, campaigners and whistle-blowers reported multiple incidents of sexual assault by staff. Chakrabarti explains that the Home Office, Serco and G4S all pointed the finger at each other: 'It's like a triangle. Nobody's responsible, and everybody's responsible. And that's what contracting out of places of detention is like; you contract out responsibility.'[66]

Following a Channel 4 exposé, Nick Hardwick, the Chief Inspector of Prisons, called Yarl's Wood a 'place of national concern' and asserted that pregnant women and those with mental health issues should only be held in exceptional cases.[67] He added that extremely vulnerable people, such as survivors of trauma and torture, should not be detained. Women for Refugee Women found that over 70 per cent of women in Yarl's Wood had experienced rape and/or sexual violence prior to their detention.[68] His successor, Peter Clarke, added that he was concerned the Home Office did not include rape in their legal definition of torture.

At the same time, the All-Party Parliamentary Group on Refugees and the All-Party Parliamentary Group on Migration published a joint inquiry, which concluded that 'the UK detains too many people, for too long a time, and that in far too many cases people are detained completely unnecessarily'.[69] The inquiry called for a detention time limit of twenty-eight days, prioritisation of community-based resolutions and for the government to introduce a wider range of alternatives to detention. Shortly before the report was published, the Home Secretary commissioned the Shaw review into the welfare of vulnerable persons in detention. Published in January 2016, it stated that detention 'undermines welfare and contributes to vulnerability' and made sixty-four recommendations for reform.[70] These included a reduction in the use and length of immigration detention, as well as exemptions for vulnerable people, such as survivors of sexual violence, those with severe mental health problems and learning disabilities and all pregnant women.

The Immigration Minister James Brokenshire said the government accepted the 'broad thrust' of Shaw's report and would introduce reforms to reduce the frequency and duration of detention. Significantly, the coalition government rejected the call for a time limit. Shaw's second review of vulnerable people in detention in 2018 found many of his key recommendations had not been implemented. While there had been a fall in the number of people detained, the number of people held in immigration removal centres for between two and six months had increased.

As shadow Home Secretary, Abbott was in a position to make policy in an area in which she had been campaigning for over thirty years. Her visit to Yarl's Wood would also give her an opportunity to put the unjust detention of women back in the headlines.

VISITING YARL'S WOOD

In late February 2018 Abbott, Chakrabarti, Ribeiro-Addy and anti-racism campaigner Denis Fernando travelled by train to Bedford. Abbott put out tweets at regular intervals as they approached Bedford station, and as they made their way to the detention centre. Chakrabarti led the way to the large glass doors. The reception, which was almost all glass, gave the impression of openness, in contrast to the tiny windows hidden in the dark brick of the accommodation wings. Nonetheless, as soon as she was inside Abbott remembers that the building felt like a prison.

The day before the visit, Abbott was informed she would not be able to speak with the women held in the centre. This was intolerable, so Abbott 'had to have a row' with the Home Office to make sure they knew she would be speaking to the women held there. However, on arrival, she was escorted by staff from the Home Office, Serco and G4S to a boardroom, and was given the impression that the centre's top brass wanted to keep her there. As Chakrabarti recalls, 'A bunch of executives were very nice to us, and they offered us food and drink, when we knew people were on hunger strike.'[71] Although the executives tried to keep her in the boardroom, Abbott was determined to meet the women and families held in Yarl's Wood. The feeling was reciprocated. Abbott recalls that the women held there had been following her tweets. As a result, when she finally extracted herself from the boardroom, she found women waiting to see her. Chakrabarti explains:

> The women were all very excited that Diane was coming and were desperate to have somebody that they trusted to bear witness to what they were facing. Eventually, when we started walking round, the women were so relieved, so excited to see Diane. They started congregating in the corridors and the authorities didn't know how to cope.[72]

In the end the authorities were forced to open the sports hall. Here, women shared their experience of being detained. Chakrabarti continues:

> The place was packed with all these women who wanted to speak to Diane. There were hundreds of women, and they were just desperate to speak with Diane. They wanted her to know their names. It was incredibly moving, quite upsetting. They told her their stories. Some of those women had lived in Britain their whole lives.

Abbott invited women to tell their stories, one after another. Chakrabarti remembers, 'All we could do was listen, and listen. The authorities were incredibly twitchy about us being there.'

Some of the women that Abbott spoke to had been in the UK for decades and had assumed that they were British citizens. Now, they were awaiting deportation to countries where they knew no one. Others shared the turmoil of being detained without a release date. Some told of how they had arrived at Yarl's Wood with serious medical conditions, had their NHS operations cancelled and received nothing more than aspirin from detention centre medics.

Abbott's next port of call was the medical centre, which was run by G4S. A 2015 Channel 4 documentary had revealed that dozens of pregnant women had been detained for several months, some being held for over a year, as well as uncovering the provision of poor healthcare services and frequent self-harm and suicide attempts.[73] Chakrabarti recalls an interaction with a young doctor who was incredibly rude. 'You could tell he had a huge problem with who she was and what she represented, and the audacity of her being there. He was so aggressive.' The medic was piqued that Abbott had brought politics into the detention of women and children. For this doctor, working in a building full of surveillance cameras, it was outrageous that Abbott should want to scrutinise G4S's work. Chakrabarti recalls, 'I remember saying to Diane afterwards, "Goodness me, if he talks to us like that, how does he talk to the women detained here, who are his patients?"'

Yarl's Wood staff had denied that women in the centre were on hunger strike. However, Abbott soon learned the truth. She was given a letter from a detainee that read, 'The fact that you are currently refusing food and/or fluid ... may, in fact, lead to your case being accelerated.' Bringing the matter to Parliament, Abbott questioned the use of punitive deportations for women who 'dared to go on hunger strike'.[74]

Caroline Nokes, then Minister of State for Immigration, said the letter was only given to women after an extensive welfare review and was, in fact, part of Home Office guidance, with consultation with NHS England, Medical Justice, the Immigration Law Practitioners' Association and other NGOs. She did not specify whether these organisations supported the practice; Medical Justice later commented that they were consulted but had deemed the approach 'wholly inappropriate and contrary to clinical best practice'.[75]

On one level, the visit to Yarl's Wood merely confirmed what Abbott had gleaned from official reports. At the same time, seeing the women and seeing their desperation was shocking. Abbott committed Labour to closing the detention centre and reviewing the entire system. 'One of the problems with detention centres', Abbott notes, 'is that they are run like they are prisons, and they behave like they are prisons, but they are not prisons, because nobody in detention has committed a crime.'[76]

May's rhetoric on women's rights in her centenary address was a stark contrast to what Abbott found at Yarl's Wood. 'The women of Yarl's Wood are desperate, and we owe them a duty of care,' Abbott told the Commons.[77] She recalled some of the women had believed that they were British until they tried to get a passport and then ended up in detention. This was an aspect of another unfolding injustice, the Windrush scandal.

THE WINDRUSH SCANDAL

It was in the context of the Windrush scandal that Abbott made her next important statement on Brexit and immigration. Speaking in May 2018, at the Institute for Public Policy Research think tank Abbott pledged that a future Labour government would close down Yarl's Wood and end the government's reliance on private contractors such as G4S and Serco. Following Sajid Javid's admission that sixty-three citizens could have been wrongly deported due to the government's hostile environment policy, Abbott promised, 'The next Labour government will repeal all those parts of the immigration legislation that were introduced to support it. We will rescind all Home Office instructions to carry it out, and we will remove all obligations on landlords, employers and others to enact it.'[78]

The 'Windrush generation' refers to the group of Caribbean migrants who came to the UK between 1948 and the early 1970s. This wave of migration was in response to campaigns from the UK government, which was desperate to fill labour shortages following the Second World War. Initially, migrants from the Commonwealth had 'United Kingdom and Colonies' citizenship under the British Nationality Act 1948. The Immigration Act 1971 then gave anyone who had settled in the UK on or before 1 January 1973 indefinite leave to remain in the UK and the Immigration and Asylum Act 1999 gave people from Commonwealth countries special protections against deportation.

However, the Home Office had not kept records of this group of migrants from the 'Windrush generation', nor had it provided them with documents to prove their immigration status. In the years that followed, immigration legislation tightened, the definition of British nationality narrowed, and the extent of evidence needed to verify immigration status was expanded.

As early as 2006, the Home Office was aware of a group of Commonwealth citizens who arrived in the UK on or before 1 January 1973 who would have difficulty providing documentary evidence of their indefinite leave to remain in the UK. Home Office internal guidance made it clear that, 'If there is no conclusive documentary evidence of settlement on 1 January 1973, they may be deemed to have been settled on that date if other evidence is reasonably persuasive (e.g. that they married here and raised a family before that date).'[79]

Nonetheless, in the years that followed, an increasing number of people who believed they were British found themselves with uncertain immigration status after having applied for a passport or a new job. Abbott remembers that it was one of her constituency immigration caseworkers who alerted her to the issue. 'She was concerned because there was a pattern to some of these cases, it was like they were looking for reasons to deport people,' she explains.[80]

Abbott notes that, in many ways, Tory policy on immigration built on the approach of New Labour. Despite this, the introduction of Theresa May's hostile environment in 2012, and the Immigration Acts of 2014 and 2016 marked a step-change in legislation. In addition to enhancing Home Office powers, the 2014 Act removed long-standing Commonwealth residents' protections from enforced removal and introduced a 'deport first, appeal later' policy.[81] Its 2016 counterpart extended these powers.

Abbott stated that, 'the 2014 act created a system of internal security border guards – obliging everyone from teachers, medical professionals, and social workers to landlords and employers to report on people they suspected of being an illegal immigrant'.[82] Banks, building societies and the Driver and Vehicle Licensing Agency were required to check the immigration status of applicants and refuse 'disqualified persons'.[83]

Similarly, the government's 'right to rent' scheme in 2016 required landlords and letting agents to check the immigration status of their tenants or face fines and criminal sanctions. Abbott was among those concerned that this would lead to racial profiling and discrimination in the housing and renting sector. Moreover, Abbott argued that the checks would disproportionately affect people who merely looked like they may be immigrants, such as black people.

Speaking to the Commons, Abbott said:

> When my parents first came to this country, landlords would routinely tell prospective black tenants that the room was gone. Does not the legislation bring us back to the situation in which people, rather than go through the rigmarole, will see a black face and say, 'The room is gone'?[84]

The hostile environment also increased data sharing between the government and public services to trace undocumented migrants. This included deals with the NHS, schools and job centres.[85]

The Legal Action Group's 2014 report on the 'surprised Brits' who found themselves with irregular immigration status recommended the government create a specialist unit to fast-track these cases, ensure they get legal advice, maintain their ability to work and access services until their cases are resolved and change the standard of evidence for providing residency. In April 2018, the Green Party's Caroline Lucas asked if the government had acted on these recommendations; in July 2018, the Immigration Minister Caroline Nokes admitted that no specific action had been taken.

In August 2017, *The Guardian* published an article detailing the case of 21-year-old Shane Ridge.[86] Born and raised in the UK, he received a letter from the Home Office which informed him that he was not a British citizen and needed to leave the UK within ten days. His mother was born in Australia during a family holiday, but as she and his father never married, Ridge did not have an automatic right to British citizenship. The Home Office later apologised for their error and the distress caused, but soon, similar cases started to catch the media's attention. Eight-year-old Anthony Bryan and ten-year-old Paulette Wilson arrived in the UK from Jamaica in 1965 and 1968 respectively. In 2015, Wilson was told to report to immigration officials monthly before she was detained in Yarl's Wood. In 2017, Bryan was held in a detention centre twice and threatened with deportation when he could not provide documentary evidence of his right to live in the UK.

In December 2017, *The Independent* reported that more than sixty MPs, academics and campaign groups had signed an open letter to Home Secretary Amber Rudd about the impact of hostile environment measures on bank account checks.[87] The Immigration Act 2014 required banks to refuse current account applications from 'disqualified persons' as determined by a Home Office database. Building on this, the 2016 Act required banks to check the immigration status of existing customers. However, an examination of the existing measures found that one in ten people were wrongly included in the 'disqualified persons' lists.[88] This meant thousands of people were at risk of having their accounts closed erroneously.[89] It also came to light that in 2016 Caribbean representatives had asked to meet with the government to discuss the cases affecting the Windrush generation but had received no response.

Meanwhile, reports of members of the Windrush generation who had been denied access to public services, detained, refused re-entry or removed from the country grew, as did the calls for immigration amnesty and an end to the hostile environment.

On 16 April, Rudd apologised for the scandal, stating that she was 'concerned that the Home Office has become too concerned with policy and strategy and sometimes loses sight of the individual'.[90] She announced the creation of a taskforce of twenty people to help those affected prove their right to live in the UK. Meanwhile, detentions and deportations of people from the Windrush generation was put on hold. However, Rudd was unable to specify what level of evidence would be demanded of the individuals and failed to commit to a statutory instrument that would restore the rights that the Windrush generation had secured prior to the Immigration Act 2014.

The Home Affairs Select Committee also questioned Rudd about Home Office targets for detention and deportations. Rudd initially denied that there were numerical targets, but an inspection report from 2015 contradicted her claims. *The Guardian* then gave details of a private letter from Rudd to Theresa May where she set out her 'ambitious but deliverable' plans to increase forced and voluntary removals by 10 per cent.[91] To make matters worse, on 27 April, a leaked 2017 memo from the Home Office Immigration Enforcement Agency, referenced a target of 12,800 enforced returns for 2017 to 2018. The memo boasted that they had exceeded their target and progress was being made towards Rudd's 10 per cent promise. Rudd vehemently denied seeing the memo, which had been copied to her office and insisted that she was unaware of numerical deportation targets.

Abbott argued that these numerical targets might have contributed to the mistreatment of the Windrush generation. She explained, 'The danger is that that very broad target put pressure on the Home Office officials to bundle Jamaican grandmothers into detention centres.'[92] Abbott was one of the first people to call for Rudd's resignation. 'I think she needs to consider her position. There are so many things that have gone wrong,' she said. 'This has caused so much misery and has ruined so many people's lives and there is so much unity in the House of Commons on both sides of the chamber about this subject.'[93]

On Radio 4 Abbott said that she had 'reminded [Rudd] that Lord Carrington, when he resigned over the Falklands War said it was a matter of honour' and 'asked her to consider her honour'. On 29 April 2018, Rudd resigned, stating that there were targets and that she should have known about them. Abbott felt that Rudd did the honourable thing but insisted that May was the architect of the scandal through her hostile environment policies which meant that members of the Windrush generation were no longer protected from being deported.

Ribeiro-Addy argues that Abbott is not given enough credit for her role in Rudd's resignation. 'People say she's just harking on. No, she's making meaningful interventions,' Ribeiro-Addy states. '[Rudd was] Theresa May's right hand, and to have forced [her resignation] is something that people would not give her enough credit for, but it shows you, again, that she's relentless in what she's doing.'[94]

After thirty years of persistent campaigning on immigration, the country's leaders were finally listening. Sajid Javid succeeded Rudd as Home Secretary, announced a temporary suspension of bank account checks and launched a Windrush compensation scheme the following year. Ribeiro-Addy reflects,

> You have Sajid Javid leaning in on everything she says. All of a sudden, he wants to limit detention … He's allowed people to have bank accounts and things like that. He's making changes to the hostile environment slowly and quietly so as not to cause himself too much embarrassment, but so as to detract from Diane's criticisms … Some people think that the answer to everything is, 'We'll do it in government.' That can't be the answer to everything; we are a campaigning party. Diane very much believes that, which is why before we are in government, we will do everything we can to change things with a view as to what we'll do in government.[95]

Ribeiro-Addy's comment reflects a consistent aspect of Abbott's approach to politics. Since the late 1970s she has consistently had one foot in Labour politics and the other in grassroots campaigns. This remained true following her election as an MP and following her appointment to the shadow Cabinet. In the context of Grenfell, in the context of Yarl's Wood and in the context of the Windrush scandal, Abbott has consistently combined working in Parliament with campaigning with grassroots organisations.

By September 2019, 8,124 people had received documentation proving their right to remain in the UK through the Windrush taskforce; 9,284 had their application refused. The Home Office Historical Cases Review Unit identified that 164 Caribbean Commonwealth nationals who had arrived in the UK before January 1973 had been wrongfully detained or removed from the UK since 2002. Wendy Williams's independent review of the Windrush scandal found that of the eighty-three people who had been wrongfully removed, fourteen had died, and another fourteen could not be contacted. Data gaps mean that the number of people affected remains unknown.[96] By July

2020, more than 1,200 compensation claims had been made by those affected by the Windrush scandal but only sixty payments, totalling £360,000, had been made. Abbott chastised the government's 'crocodile tears'.[97] Speaking on the seventieth anniversary of Windrush, Abbott explained:

> The Windrush generation has had a number of important effects, but none has been more important than forcing people to look at migrants as people – people with families, people with histories and people just like other people. If we could only extend the humanisation of the debate on migration from the Windrush generation to migrants of all generations and all times, we would achieve what I am committed to seeing – namely, a very different type of conversation on migration.[98]

Abbott unveiled Labour's post-Brexit immigration policy in September 2018, six months after Rudd's resignation. This was not just another speech; it was an example of the 'type of conversation on migration' that Abbott envisaged. Abbott spoke in Portcullis House in the Harold Wilson Room, a picture of Labour's former Prime Minister immediately behind her. In the days of Black Sections, Wilson had been criticised for treating immigration as a purely electoral issue. Now in 2018, Abbott wanted to reconnect immigration policy with humanitarian values. In making a speech on immigration, she was also returning to the theme of her maiden speech, which she had given thirty-one years earlier. In that sense, the speech reflected decades of thought on immigration. In terms of more recent history, Abbott spoke not just in the midst of the Windrush scandal, but soon after footage of children kept in cages on the US–Mexican border had shown the world the inhumanity of Trump's immigration regime. The day of her speech, a poll for Opinium/*Observer* had put Labour within one point of the Conservatives.[99] Abbott was still in opposition but facing a minority government that was divided on Brexit and led by an unpopular Prime Minister. Consequently, there was a realistic chance that her immigration policies would one day become law.

Abbott began by stating that Labour would 'uphold the right to a family life' for all migrants.[100] This reflected both an ongoing commitment to the universal rights entrenched in the European Convention on Human Rights, and a rejection of an immigration regime which routinely separated children from their parents. Turning to the Windrush scandal, Abbott promised that a future Labour government would treat 'the Windrush generation as they should be treated – as British citizens' and redress for all those who were deported, including those who, she claimed, had been 'bullied or threatened into "voluntary removal"' by the Home Office.

Before setting out her alternative, Abbott addressed the roots of Britain's broken immigration system. Here, she paused to reflect on her own biography, noting that even when she had joined the civil service in the late 1970s it was clear that the immigration system was unjust and poorly managed. The problem that Abbott pointed to was the 'othering' of immigrants,

> The most important factor is that official policy, ministerial rhetoric, and media coverage fails to treat migrants as people. They have been numbers. They have been a problem. They have been a 'flood' and a 'tidal wave'. According to Philip Hammond they have been marauding. A former Tory Prime Minister referred to migrants 'swarming' into this country. If you believe this rubbish, it's little wonder the current Prime Minister calls for 'deport first, and appeal later'.[101]

This populist motive lay at the root of failed policy. Cameron's pledge to get net migration down to the tens of thousands was, Abbott argued, 'plucked out of the air'. Moreover, the legislation that Cameron and May could have introduced to stop immigration from outside the EU was never drafted. The contradiction between rhetoric and policy, Abbott argued, pointed to a deeper motive, 'its actual purpose is to allow a permanent campaign against migrants and immigration in general'. Immigration, was in turn, used to explain the steepest fall in living standards since the Great Depression, the housing crisis, cuts in welfare budgets, and the pay freeze. 'Go Home' vans, bogus targets, the demonisation of migrants, indefinite detention and the hostile environ-ment had the effect of scapegoating migrants. 'These' Abbott argued, 'were the policies of Enoch Powell. He was thrown out of the Tory Cabinet for advocating them. Now, they are Tory government policy.'[102]

Instead of the 'deport first, appeal later' system introduced under the coalition, Abbott promised a 'fair and reasonable management of migration that puts our collective prosperity first'. It would also be a policy which recognised the contribution that immigrants made. There was, Abbott argued, no economic benefit in excluding skilled and unskilled workers when there were record shortages of doctors and nurses, and where without seasonal agricultural workers crops would be left to rot. Moreover, Labour would not relegate migrants to the status of second-class citizens. In practice, this meant rejecting populist rhetoric about migrants, and replacing the regime of de-tention centres and 'Go Home' vans, with a 'Streamlined work visa [which] allows us to offer rights of work and residency to a range of professions, workers and those creating employment who want to come here. It will be available to all those we need to come here, whether it is doctors, or scientists, or care workers, or others.'

While Abbott outlined Labour's post-Brexit immigration policy, the government's own proposals continued to be delayed. Abbott's proposals had the benefit of being compatible with a high degree of EU market access, another indication that Labour was seeking a 'soft-Brexit'.

Brexit continued to be a source of tension in the Conservative Party. Following the publication of the draft Brexit withdrawal agreement in November 2018 Raab resigned as Secretary of State for Exiting the European Union. Partly due to Brexit, partly due to the consequences of ongoing austerity, May's government performed poorly in the polls. Between Raab's resignation and the end of January 2019 the Tories had an average lead of 0.5 per cent.[103]

QUESTION TIME

During 2018 Abbott remained a regular on *Question Time*. In May, she clashed with Raab over Grenfell. In November there was consensus on the panel as Abbott, Conservative frontbencher Kwasi Kwarteng, and right-wing 'thought leader' Jordan B. Peterson all agreed that stop and search was an ineffective tool in the campaign against knife crime.

It was Abbott's appearance on 17 January 2019 that really made waves. In the week leading up to the programme six polls had been published. Kantar put Labour ahead on 38 per cent, with the Tories three points behind; ComRes/*Daily Express* had Labour on 39 per cent, with the Tories two points behind; ComRes/*Sunday Mirror* had the Conservatives one point ahead; NCPolitics put the Tories on 41 per cent, two points ahead of their rivals; BMG/*Independent* had the two parties tied; YouGov/*Times* was the outlier putting the Conservatives five points ahead.[104] Against this background, it was entirely reasonable for Abbott to say of the two main parties, 'in the polls, overall, we're level pegging'.[105] Fiona Bruce, in the chair, however, stepped in immediately to 'correct' Abbott, siding with journalist Isabel Oakeshott's wholly erroneous statement that Labour was 'way behind … miles behind'. Bruce interrupted Abbott twice to assure the audience that she was 'definitely' wrong.[106] The audience clearly enjoyed the moment and laughed heartily; Rory Stewart beamed.

This was not the only aspect of the show which demonstrated bias. The introductions at the top of the show were far from even-handed. Stewart's introduction covered his ministerial career past and present, as well as his governorships in Iraq. Abbott's introduction was short on detail and stressed her relationship with Corbyn rather than her experience or achievements. By linking her position as shadow Home Secretary to her relationship with Corbyn, there was an implication that Abbott owed her job to a personal relationship, rather than merit. Indeed, according to several audience members, this was precisely the point made by Fiona Bruce before the show. Equally, Abbott was interrupted twice as often as Stewart, even though Stewart spoke more often, and for more of the show. In spite of her long, pioneering and successful career, in spite of all of her experience in parliament and working with grassroots campaigns, Abbott was treated with less respect than other panellists.

Anti-politics and a generalised distrust is part of the zeitgeist. Yet, even in an age of distrust Abbott's experience on *Question Time* demonstrates that some public figures have an easier time than others. Oakeshott got polling data wrong and enjoyed the full support of the chair. Stewart, who had recently apologised for making up statistics, was treated with considerable respect.[107] But as a black woman, Abbott was treated dismissively.

The following week, Bruce issued a 'clarification'. She had been talking about 'a poll that came out on the day of the programme' she explained.[108] Speaking on Abbott's behalf she claimed that 'the shadow Home Secretary mentioned some earlier polls'. The clarification may have saved Bruce some embarrassment, but it hardly explained what had happened. Two polls came out on the day of the show: one put the Tories two points ahead; the other gave Labour a 1 per cent lead. Both supported Abbott's contention that the two parties were essentially neck-and-neck; neither justified Bruce publicly 'correcting' Abbott and supporting Oakeshott's claim that Labour was 'miles behind'. Bruce's 'clarification' also failed to address the bias in terms of interruptions, or the comments made at Abbott's expense before the show. While Bruce's 'clarification' clarified nothing, the context suggests an explanation for what happened. The dominant media narrative of the 2017 election was that Abbott made mistakes with figures, and that she had once had a romantic relationship with Corbyn. Bruce gave every indication of accepting these narratives uncritically.

Labour's request for footage of the pre-show comments led Bruce to acknowledge that she had made a 'light-hearted' comment about Corbyn and Abbott's personal relationship. The BBC refused, however, to provide the footage. Nor was an apology forthcoming. Apparently, black staff in the BBC newsroom put pressure on executives to apologise, but with no success.

Back in November, a white man in the *Question Time* audience had defended stop and search on the basis that 'if you've got nothing to hide, you've got nothing to lose'.[109] No innocent person, he argued, should be afraid of state surveillance. Abbott's approach to politics flips this logic on its head. If the state has nothing to hide, then the state has nothing to lose. Any government that is pursuing humane policies which benefit citizens should welcome surveillance. May had praised 'free and open debate' as the driver of 'progressive, democratic change' in her speech celebrating the centenary of women's suffrage. Yet, under May, the commitment to open government remained largely rhetorical. Information about deportation targets was kept secret, UN inspectors were denied access to Yarl's Wood, and Jeremy Hunt refused to divulge his plans to extend privatisation in the NHS. The secrecy that shrouded government ministries also characterised other institutions. Outsourcing and the creation of semi-autonomous trusts had the consequence of placing the provision of many services in Kensington and Chelsea beyond public scrutiny. Hiding the reality of immigration policy, of life in detention centres and of 'social apartheid' allowed the government to maintain the illusion that Britain was a country built on the values of Milton, Mill and Pankhurst. As a campaigning politician, Abbott was determined to keep government under surveillance. Like the suffragettes so much admired by May, Abbott was concerned with deeds, not words.

CHAPTER 16

BREXIT BRITAIN

Early on the morning of 18 February 2019, journalists rushed to County Hall to hear a statement on the 'future of British politics'. Rumours circulated that a handful of MPs were making the long-antic-ipated break with Labour. Once the headquarters of the GLC's radical left-wing experiment in local democracy, County Hall now boasted a luxury hotel, an aquarium and a Namco Funscape amusement arcade. It also housed the Etc conference centre. This was the launch pad of The Independent Group (TIG). Luciana Berger was the first MP to speak. As the group of seven took to the podium, race quickly emerged as a theme. Berger opened the press conference stating, 'I cannot remain in a party that I have today come to the sickening conclusion is institutionally anti-Semitic.'[1] Chuka Umunna, the last to speak, put his decision in the perspective of a century of British history.

> When our democracy is failing, the British people have overcome the hurdles, over history, to build a better future. We demanded elected MPs take precedent over unelected Lords, we insisted that working men and women had the vote, we said our parliament should better reflect and look like the country in terms of gender and ethnicity, and now we have got to change our politics again.[2]

Like Theresa May a year earlier, Umunna claimed the mantle of the suffragettes. He also stood in the tradition of Herbert Asquith's Liberals. More radical still, he claimed TIG was the inheritor of Abbott, Bellos, Boateng, Grant and Vaz: the heir of Black Sections.

Chris Leslie broadened the attack on Labour by excoriating 'Jeremy Corbyn [and] the team around him' for its 'betrayal on Europe' and the 'appalling culture … intolerant, closing down of debate, abuse and hatred, online as you're seeing this morning, and offline in party meetings, and the anti-Semitism'.[3] The team around Corbyn, the people guilty of 'betrayal' included Abbott. But the 'appalling culture' and 'abuse and hatred' apparently did not include the #PrayforDiane campaign, of which he had been a part.

It was an odd time to be colonising the 'centre ground'. If centrism was a combination of economic liberalism, social liberalism and a commitment to the EU, the territory occupied by Blair, William Hague and Cameron, then the 'centre' had collapsed. The European Research Group were increasingly equating 'free trade' with 'World Trade Organization terms', which would mean tariffs on British goods. Outside the European Research Group, May and Corbyn had both, in their different ways, moved their parties away from economic liberalism. Brexit had also highlighted a division between social liberals, those comfortable living in diverse communities, and social conservatives who wanted a more homogeneous Britain. And following the referendum, no issue was more divisive than Europe. Nonetheless, the 'Etc Declaration', as it was dubbed in a nod to the Limehouse Declaration of 1981, crystallised some of the issues which dominated 2019.

MOJITOGATE

As the Brexit debate became increasingly intractable, the Mental Health Foundation published research indicating that the resultant feelings of powerlessness were leading to increased stress for many Britons.[4] Thankfully, Abbott was able to provide a moment of light relief. In April, she was snapped drinking an M&S mojito on a Transport for London (TfL) train. What was light relief for some was a moral outrage for others. Tory MP for Harrow East Bob Blackman argued:

> It's up to a shadow Home Secretary to set an example by obeying the rules – not openly flout them. Diane should be prosecuted by

TfL for this. She can have no excuse. Not only is she a London MP but this very sensible rule has been in place for over a decade now.[5]

The story broke in *The Sun* under the headline 'COCKTAIL PARTY: Labour's Diane Abbott breaks the law by swigging can of mojito on the train home'.[6] The alert citizen who took the photo commented, 'She kept her head down and was staring at her phone but kept slurping from the can. It was 1 p.m., so a bit early to be drinking – especially in public.' *The Sun*'s enterprising journalists sought out Mick Neville, a retired Scotland Yard detective chief inspector, to establish the legal position. Neville told *The Sun*, 'TfL should be looking into this and sending her a fine. She should face action as a deterrent to others.'

For Susan Hall, Tory member of General London Assembly's Police and Crime Committee, 'MojitoGate' was about standards in public life, 'As someone who aspires to be Home Secretary, Diane Abbott should know better. How can she have any credibility if she's willing to break the law? This is typical of a Labour politician; one rule for them and another for everyone else.'[7]

The *Mail* used the story to rehearse the events of the 2017 LBC interview on police numbers, and to publish a timeline of 'Abbott's other gaffes and controversies'.[8]

While the *Mail* and *The Sun* presented 'MojitoGate' as a matter of grave public concern, others took a different view. On Twitter, some, like Rylan Clark-Neal and David Lammy, clearly saw the funny side.

Abbott apologised immediately. Marks and Spencer did well out of the incident. Within forty-eight hours stores across London had sold out of the 'ready to drink' mojito. Instagram lit up with people posting photos of themselves drinking mojitos on buses, Tubes and trains. Others who were late to the party had to content themselves with posting photos of empty shelves #TheAbbottEffect.

According to Kevin Craig of *PRWeek*, the real issue which #MojitoGate threw into sharp relief was M&S's failure to capitalise on a marketing opportunity.[9] Pepsi's misstep in appropriating Black Lives Matter notwithstanding, 'riding the crest of #MojitoGate', he argued, could have allowed M&S to embrace a new era of marketing and brand identity.

BREXIT CRISIS

By early 2019 Brexit was provoking a political and constitutional crisis. The 'first meaningful vote' had led to a historic defeat for the government. The scale of the defeat was unprecedented. Before the Fixed-Term Parliaments Act, defeat on a major issue might have occasioned the fall of a government.

Brexit was a complex problem, not least because of the timetable. Article 50 established a two-year window, by the end of which the UK and the EU had to agree on the terms of withdrawal. Without a withdrawal agreement, Britain risked leaving the single market and the customs union and reverting to World Trade Organization rules, an event which some experts predicted would have catastrophic economic consequences.

Negotiations with the EU were one part of a highly complex picture. Theresa May had to negotiate with the different wings of her own party, she had to retain the goodwill of the Democratic Unionist Party, in order to present a bill that would get past Parliament. Britain's constitution made matters more difficult still. The exact relationship between royal prerogatives and the power of Parliament remained contested, as did the role of the Speaker and the Supreme Court. All of this was compounded by allegations of bad faith. May had been a Remainer, Corbyn was regarded, in some Remain circles, as a closet Leaver. Allegations of betrayal became an established part of the discourse. And betrayal over Brexit was treachery of the worst kind. To disregard the referendum result was to betray the will of the British people, and side with foreign powers.

Debate within the shadow Cabinet, as Abbott recalls, reflected the complexity of the situation and the divisions that existed across Britain. 'It was very difficult, because there were people in the shadow Cabinet with diametrically opposed views ... which reflected the different views out in the country.'[10] Abbott represented a constituency which had voted overwhelmingly to Remain, and supported Britain's continued membership of the EU. At the same time, 'there were members of the shadow Cabinet that were very strong Brexiters'. This included some people 'around Jeremy who felt very strongly about Brexit and had a lot of influence on him. Jeremy's challenge was to balance those two sets of views'.

More often than not Corbyn's attempts to seek compromise, however, were regarded as being a betrayal. Many Remainers wanted Labour to endorse a 'people's vote'. In the spring of 2019, the Liberal Democrats conflated opposition to the government with opposition to Brexit. Labour's willingness to advocate a 'jobs-first Brexit', they claimed was a 'betrayal' as it equated to support for an incompetent Tory government. The 'Magnificent Seven', the original members of TIG, made much the same point at their launch in February, as did the 'Three Amigos' and the 'Lone Ranger' who joined TIG in the week after the initial launch.[11]

The creation of TIG did not perturb Abbott. 'I'm old enough to remember the SDP. History repeats itself first as tragedy then as farce.'[12] Abbott argues that TIG emerged from a media bubble. 'They were entirely swept up in the media narrative that there were all these people out there who wanted to support an SDP Mark II.' They were also caught up in the belief, rooted in another media narrative, that Corbyn was poised to enable Brexit, that he would through action or omission allow May to get her bill through Parliament. According to some sources, the original plan was to wait for this act of 'betrayal', and then to launch and pick up horrified Labour Remainers and former Liberal Democrats who were still disillusioned with the coalition. Rumours from Umunna's office indicated that TIG was forced to launch ahead of plan, as it was feared that the backers of Progressive Centre UK would withdraw their funding if Umunna stayed with Labour. Whatever the truth of these rumours the new centre party did not do well. TIG, latterly Change UK, failed to flesh out the centre ground in terms of policy. Indeed, the original eleven had radically different views. For Heidi Allen, interim party leader, these disparate political positions were an attractive part of TIG's point of difference. Speaking at a meeting in her constituency, she argued,

Here's the weird thing about us Gang of Eleven: we quite like each other. If you meet somebody in a pub or in a restaurant is the first thing you say to them, 'how do you vote?' before I decided if you're going to be my friend or not. Life just isn't like that is it?'[13]

This approach also reminded Abbott of the SDP, particularly their slogan 'Take the politics out of politics'. TIG's strategy began to unravel when it became clear that Labour was not facilitating Brexit. One scenario, much discussed, was that the Labour leadership would covertly authorise a small rebellion, just large enough to get May's deal through the Commons, while allowing the leadership a degree of plausible deniability. This failed to happen. Indeed, in a party that was divided over Brexit, Labour's whipping operation was extremely effective. Abbott attributes this in no small part to Nick Brown, Labour's Chief Whip. What is more, the profundity of the issues raised by Brexit concentrated minds in the PLP. 'People understood this was about the future of the party. We couldn't afford to have people peeling off. So, there were people who really were Brexity like Dennis Skinner who voted with the whip because it was about loyalty to the party.'[14]

Change UK also failed to anticipate the Liberal Democrat revival. In May the Liberal Democrats achieved 20 per cent of the vote in the European elections. Change UK's campaign was lacklustre. According to some commentators, Umunna's heart was no longer in it. Change UK gained 3.4 per cent of the vote, just ahead of the unreconstructed UKIP. Looking back at Change UK, Abbott comments, 'It was a fiasco, a fiasco fuelled by a hatred of the politics that Jeremy represented.'

In March 2019 when Labour gave a qualified endorsement to a 'people's vote' Corbyn was attacked from a different quarter. Writing in *The Spectator*, Brendan O'Neill claimed, 'In siding with the so-called People's Vote lobby, Corbyn has betrayed Labour's traditional working-class base … He has betrayed his party's own manifesto … He has betrayed his old Labour mentors, most notably his hero Tony Benn … And he has betrayed himself.'[15]

For TIG and the Liberal Democrats, endorsing a people's vote was not enough. Would Labour support a people's vote in all eventualities? Would Corbyn campaign for Remain in a people's vote? Did Labour want a general election then a people's vote, or a people's vote then a general election? What did Corbyn really think? Was he working covertly to push Britain over the 'cliff edge'? And why was Labour's position so confusing?

Abbott argues that talk of 'betrayal' and 'treachery' obscured Corbyn's aim. 'He got criticised for equivocating, but what he was always trying to do was to bring people together.'[16] Labour's electoral coalition also pushed the party toward a compromise position. Labour's northern 'heartlands' had voted to Leave, Labour's southern metropolitan voters wanted to Remain. May gambled that she could embrace Brexit and build a new coalition with UKIP voters. Tim Farron abandoned Liberal Democrat Leavers in the south-west, hoping to pick up metropolitan Remainers in the south-east. Labour, alone, was trying to represent the whole country. In the eighteen months after the referendum this meant embracing a soft Brexit, and from the spring of 2019 it meant embracing a second referendum, which would allow the public to choose between a workable Brexit option and Remaining on existing terms.

Abbott was sympathetic to the view that the people needed a say over any Brexit deal. In November 2017, she wrote to two of her constituents stating, 'I will argue for the right of the electorate to vote on any deal that is finally agreed.'[17] However, after the letters were published in *The Guardian*, she gave an interview to Andrew Marr, clarifying that in a parliamentary democracy, it was for MPs, representing the electorate, to have a say.[18] On this point, she was at odds with May who had to be forced into agreeing to a 'meaningful vote'.

Abbott was not, however, against a second referendum in principle. Indeed, on *Question Time* in January 2019, she argued that there was nothing inherently undemocratic about a new vote.[19] However, she cautioned that as things stood, she thought there was a good chance that Leave would win again, and with an increased majority. Her claim reflected several of the political dynamics that had followed the referendum. First, Remainers had done little to establish an argument for staying in the EU which went beyond the economic predictions that had failed to win over voters during the referendum. Indeed, Remainers had devoted their attention to the campaign for a second referendum, and to a campaign against the Labour leadership rather than to laying the foundation for winning a second vote. Second, following the referendum, there had been no sharp rise in unemployment, no market crash. Living standards continued to stagnate, but that was not obviously a result of Brexit. This led many Leavers to double down on their claim that Brexit would not damage the economy, and that claims to the contrary were merely 'project fear'. Third, the fact of Leave's victory in 2016 shifted the debate. In any future referendum campaign, Leavers could claim that democracy was being betrayed. Moreover, should Parliament agree to a second referendum, Remain would not, unlike in 2016, have the support of the government or the Conservative frontbench. In short, while Remainers were convinced they could win a second vote, Abbott's view was that it would be an uphill struggle.

In this context, and with very little room for compromise, taking 'no deal off the table' seemed to be an option that could command a degree of agreement. Soft Brexiters in both main parties and Remainers agreed that 'no deal' was the worst outcome, and therefore in the spring of 2019 averting no deal became Labour's immediate goal. Yvette Cooper's amendment on 29 January proposed just this and won the backing of the Labour leadership. In essence, the Cooper amendment proposed that if a withdrawal agreement had not been approved the government would be legally bound to seek an extension of the process until the end of 2019. Speaking to the BBC shortly before the vote, Tory rebel Dominic Raab, dismissed the Cooper amendment claiming, 'Opening up this Pandora's Box at this eleventh hour would take us back to square one … It's just another garden path that MPs want to throw into the mix.'[20] The Cooper amendment was defeated narrowly.

Among Brexiters, 'no deal' had its supporters. Some claimed it was the ideal Brexit end state, as it marked a return of true sovereignty.

Others, using the same logic as nuclear deterrence, argued that, although it would never be used, 'no deal' was an important threat which would force the EU to give Britain a good deal. This was George Eustice's view. The Minister of State for Agriculture, Fisheries and Food resigned after May allowed a vote on extension, arguing,

> I think it would be highly dangerous for our country to go cap in hand to the European Union at the eleventh hour and beg for an extension. We would be literally over the barrel of a gun. We have to have the confidence and courage to walk away without an agreement.[21]

Theresa May was defeated in rebellion after rebellion, her government unable to get its legislative business through the House. Labour sought a general election, both as the appropriate constitutional solution to the problem, and in the hope of forming a government. But the Tories were in no mood to go to the polls. May was less popular than ever, the Brexit Party were riding high, and there was the possibility of a Corbyn government.

This impasse led to constitutional innovation. At the end of March 2019 parliamentarians took control of the timetable of the House of Commons for a series of 'indicative votes', an attempt to find a position on Brexit that was acceptable to the Commons. Abbott voted for a 'permanent and comprehensive' customs union; for a second referendum; for Labour's proposed 'soft Brexit'; and for 'common market 2.0', a form of 'soft Brexit' proposed by Conservative Nick Boles and Labour's Lucy Powell. Abbott also voted against no deal. In so doing, she went through the voting lobbies with Yasmin Qureshi, Nick Brown, Yvette Cooper, Naz Shah, Rebecca Long-Bailey, Emily Thornberry, Keir Starmer, Ed Miliband, John McDonnell and Tom Watson. Her voting pattern was the mirror image of that of Jacob Rees-Mogg, Priti Patel, Dominic Raab and Boris Johnson.

In May, Abbott confirmed that Labour backed a people's vote. The European election had seen Labour and the Conservatives falling behind Farage's Brexit Party and a reinvigorated Liberal Democrats.

A week later, Abbott presented Labour's position on the *Today* programme on Radio 4.[22] Her argument was that, as regular constitutional means had failed to deliver either a general election or a resolution to Brexit, a people's vote was now the only way out of the impasse. Corbyn had also pledged a second referendum on any Brexit deal. However, this was not enough for the 'Follow Back, Pro EU' lobby. Endorsing a second referendum was not enough, the real question was not about policy, but identity. As Liberal Democrat Tom Brake put it, Labour were 'still a party of Brexit'.[23]

For Corbyn, the challenge of Brexit was to 'bring the party together somehow, which is what I tried to do all the way through. It's not been easy'.[24] Behind closed doors, he remembers that Abbott

> believed strongly in a second referendum, and was very much part of the second referendum, Remain grouping within the shadow Cabinet ... she was strongly Remain. Not necessarily because she loves the European Union, but her view was, it was a question of the attitude of openness to the rest of the world, and we'd be seen to be cutting ourselves off. And her constituency were overwhelmingly Remain.

While they took different positions in private, Corbyn recalls that they never fell out over Brexit.

For Labour's opponents, the niceties of compromise smacked of betrayal. As Chris Leslie, now deputy leader of TIG, explained, the question was actually very simple. Brexit was bad, and 'Corbyn's refusal to be honest about that fact is a deep betrayal of the people Labour used to represent.'[25]

GRASSROOTS

As ever, Abbott kept in touch with grassroots organisations. In the midst of Brexit, she continued to support Justice4Grenfell, as well as the campaign around the Windrush scandal. Abbott has spoken at events supported by Black Lives Matter UK since the foundation of the group in Britain in 2016. Siana Bangura, an activist involved with the campaign, explains that working with MPs is not at the centre of their strategy, 'We're very much grassroots, we work with the community in the black radical tradition.'[26] She explains that activists have been working with the United Families and Friends Campaign, a coalition of families of those who have been killed in police custody, following police contact, or in mental health institutions. Nonetheless, Bangura argues that radicals involved with Black Lives Matter recognise the value of using a range of tactics. Abbott, Bangura argues, 'has always said black lives matter, and she's always pioneered.'

In May 2019, Abbott spoke at Black Girl Festival (BGF). Nicole Crentsil, one of BGF's founders explains that the idea for the festival came from 'Angela Davis in Conversation', which was part of the 2017 Women of the World event held on the Southbank, 'The space was incredibly filled with black women who were really eager and excited to hear Angela Davis. I remember being really inspired by the space.'[27] Also influenced by the work of black feminists such as Stella Dadzie and Beverley Bryan and the example of OWAAD, Crentsil and Paula Akpan brought their experience as event producers to bear on a project to create a festival that was 'specifically tailored towards black women'. Akpan argues that, as a black queer woman, one of the lessons they learned from OWAAD was the need to create an event that truly recognised the 'intersectionality of black women's various overlapping identities'.[28]

The result was the first BGF, a three-day event which took place in Shoreditch in 2017. The crowd-funded initiative which attracted over 4,000 people to a 350-seater venue, was the first event of its kind in the UK. After this success, the festival became an annual event, featuring a mix of talks, entertainment, workshops, panels, as well as a marketplace which showcases the work of black female designers.

In addition to the annual events, in 2019 Black Girl Fest organised a three-day festival in April, themed around Michelle Obama's memoir *Becoming*. Speakers included the novelist Dorothy Koomson and authors of *Slay in Your Lane: The Black Girl Bible* Yomi Adegoke and Elizabeth Uviebinené, as well as talks on black British feminism and creative writing, and workshops on mental health. Crentsil and

Akpan argue that BGF has attracted an inter-generational crowd, and for this reason they decided to use BGF as a forum for dialogue between different generations. Crentsil says she wanted to invite Abbott to speak as part of a desire to focus on black history. Equally, in a context where Abbott was facing constant abuse, the invitation was an expression of 'appreciation and love for what she has done' not least in terms of advancing the representation of black women.[29] Akpan adds, 'For any kind of black woman living in the UK, you can relate to Diane Abbott's experiences, of being a very visible black woman, and experiencing so much misogynoir, although people try and dismiss it, you know it's entirely disproportionate.'[30]

Abbott spoke on 11 April 2019; the final day of the festival. The day before, Theresa May had agreed an extension of the Article 50 process with the European Council, which meant that Britain was likely to remain in the EU until 31 October. As a result, May made an unscheduled statement on Brexit, which meant that for some time the organisers of BGF had no idea if Abbott would still be able to attend the event. Abbott arrived later than expected for a conversation with film-maker and theatre producer Tobi Kyeremateng. The two discussed growing up in Britain, linking Abbott's experiences with OWAAD, the Scrap SUS campaign, and in the Labour Party with the experiences of young black women in contemporary Britain. Unlike an event like *Question Time*, Akpan argues, the fact that Abbott was 'sat in a room with just black women, using language and talking about experiences that everyone in the room understands' meant that she could be candid and told her own story in a way that was rarely reflected in the press.[31]

Abbott was also keen to draw parallels between her experiences as a young woman and the contemporary world, noting, 'The issues I was concerned about in my twenties, police harassment, harassment of black people by the state, the sort of oppression black women suffer, these are still very live issues today.'[32] The issues that had emerged in recent years which had not been as prominent in Abbott's early years as an activist included climate change, which she argued would disproportionately affect people of colour. With this in mind, she argued, it was important that black women's voices were heard in the environmental movement in order to bring a 'black perspective'.

BACK BORIS

The campaign to succeed Theresa May as Conservative leader crystallised several of the issues surrounding Brexit, as well as social issues more generally. Towards the end of May 2019, the Prime Minister announced that she would step down as Tory leader on 7 June and make way for the new Prime Minister by the end of July. There was no shortage of contenders for the unenviable job. Rory Stewart, Esther McVey, Dominic Raab, Andrea Leadsom, Sajid Javid, Jeremy Hunt and Michael Gove were just some of the best-known politicians to chance their arm.

A leadership election had clearly been on the cards for some time. However, for much of 2019 Abbott assumed that Johnson would never win the backing of his colleagues. 'If anybody knows about Boris Johnson's flaws, it's Conservative MPs.'[33] Johnson was known to be gaffe-prone, his many articles took contradictory positions and were peppered with highly problematic language, he had been attacked for mendacity, and he did not appear to know how many children he had fathered. It was clear, Abbott argued, that, prior to the European election, there was considerable hostility to the idea of a Johnson premiership on the Tory benches. Senior figures such as Alan Duncan and Nicky Morgan were known to be extremely concerned about the prospect of Johnson becoming Prime Minister. Ultimately, Abbott argues, Tory MPs backed him because he looked like a winner. Indeed, some Tories argued that having beaten Livingstone in London, he was ideally placed to beat Corbyn at a general election.

The three big questions that the Tory hopefuls had to answer were: What kind of Brexit did they want? When would Britain leave? And how would Brexit be achieved? On the first question, contenders, using the new vocabulary which had emerged in the last eighteen months proposed everything from 'Canada dry', through 'super Canada-plus', to 'Norway minus'. On the second, Johnson said he would rather 'die in a ditch' than allow Britain to stay in the EU beyond 31 October.[34]

Gove initially appeared to suggest that he would be prepared to keep Britain in the EU until the end of 2020, but later clarified that he was thinking of a short delay to allow 'a little more time' to get an exit deal with the EU.[35]

The trickier question was how Britain might leave. Without a majority in Parliament, and having used up the good will of the European Commission, how was it possible to get a deal that would be acceptable to Parliament? Stewart campaigned for a citizens' assembly to decide on the shape of a withdrawal agreement. The other constitutional innovation was Raab's suggestion that Parliament be prorogued until after 31 October. This would prevent Parliament from stopping the legal default: British exit on the 31 October with no deal. Raab's advocacy of prorogation reflected the view of 'Spartans' and 'Brexit ultras' in the ERG, who believed that Parliament had become an impediment to democracy. At the end of March, Steve Baker, in a highly emotional outburst, told the ERG, 'I could tear this place [Parliament] down and bulldoze it into the river.'[36] Within a few months Baker became deputy chairman of the European Research Group.

The 'Spartan' position reflected constitutional and political debates which had been going on for decades, in which Abbott had played an important part. In terms of the constitution, Spartans wanted to use prerogative powers against Parliament. Prerogatives were powers exercised by government that emanated from the Queen, not from a democratic election. Abbott had sponsored a bill in 1987, in her first few months in Parliament, to remove prerogative powers from the Crown and transfer them to Parliament. Concern about prerogative powers had been dismissed as eccentric at the time, but thirty years later, their significance was clear.

While Abbott had argued that the existence of 'Henry VIII powers' showed that the constitution still had undemocratic elements, Spartans argued that there was a democratic basis for using the prerogative powers against Parliament. This too was an argument that had its roots in the 1980s. In stripping local government of its power, Thatcher had argued that she was acting in accord with the will of the people. In establishing nuclear-free zones, in subsidising public transport, in introducing equal opportunity policies, Thatcher argued, 'loony left' councils were not merely defying the government, they were acting undemocratically. Thatcher had won a mandate at the general election which trumped any mandate that could be claimed by Livingstone in London or Linda Bellos in Lambeth. The same was true in Thatcher's battle with the unions. Unions claimed to represent their members, but Thatcher represented the will of the British people.

Theresa May had made a similar argument in March 2019. However, when she referred to 'the biggest democratic exercise in our history' she was not referring to a general election; she was describing the 2016 referendum.[37] May claimed the mantle of the referendum, and argued that Parliament, which had engaged in 'political games and … arcane procedural rows' was obstructing the decision of the people.

The Brexit Spartans went further. The government should claim the mandate of the referendum to shut down parliament and take Britain out of the European Union. In essence, Brexit ultras proposed that the government should treat Parliament as Thatcher had treated local government decades before.

Johnson's appointment as Prime Minister changed the dynamics of the Brexit debate. May was committed to Brexit, but not at any cost. Johnson's rhetoric had always been harder, and he was regarded as a risk taker. Therefore, his appointment increased the chances of Britain leaving without a deal. This sharpened minds and, over the summer, there was talk of a 'government of national unity' (GNU). Jo Swinson ruled out Liberal Democrat backing for a Corbyn-led government, even a Corbyn-led government which would 'take no deal off the table'. Rather, she stated that Ken Clarke and Harriet Harman were ready to lead a GNU to stop Brexit.[38] Swinson's plan unravelled quickly. Harman refused the invitation immediately. Clarke accepted. Yet he was an odd choice, as he was on record as saying that a second referendum would be 'folly'. Clarke quickly made it clear that as interim Prime Minister his preferred option would be to 'sort Brexit out' by taking Britain out of the EU with 'a negotiated deal'. While he was open to discussion about a referendum, he believed a Brexit deal was the option 'that would carry the majority of the House of Commons and help reunite the public'.[39]

Following the collapse of Swinson's plan, Caroline Lucas published a letter in *The Guardian* inviting ten senior female MPs to form a government.[40] Speaking to the BBC, she explained, 'I've approached women, basically the women who are in the most senior positions in their political parties, across Westminster'.[41] Lucas invited MPs such as Swinson from the Liberal Democrats; Yvette Cooper and Emily Thornberry from Labour; Heidi Allen formerly of TIG; Plaid Cymru's Liz Saville Roberts; Nicola Sturgeon and Kirsty Blackman from the SNP; and Conservative Justine Greening. However, Lucas's list of 'the most senior' women in Parliament did not include Abbott, nor any other black or Asian MPs. Speaking to the *Feminist Review* in 1987, Abbott had argued that the danger with a women's ministry was that it might become 'just a ministry for white women' which would 'marginalise Black women's issues'.[42] Much the same could be said of Lucas's women's Cabinet.

Interviewed by Victoria Derbyshire for the BBC, Lucas initially claimed that she had formulated her list 'simply because they are the leaders or deputy leaders of their parties at Westminster ... they all happen to be white'.[43] She added that she was proposing 'a practical way of breaking through that log-jam' and therefore she had approached 'women who are in the senior positions in parties across Westminster'. However, this explanation was unconvincing. Lucas's list included Cooper, Thornberry, Allen, and Greening, none of whom were either the leaders or deputy leaders of parties at Westminster. In terms of seniority, Abbott was on a par with Thornberry, and as shadow Home Secretary far more senior than Cooper, Allen and Greening.

Lucas offered no apology at this stage. Rather, she declared herself keen 'to open this up as soon as possible to more women, more diversity, that would certainly be my dream'. Why it had not been possible for her to achieve her 'dream' and formulate a more diverse list initially, she did not say.

Lucas apologised later in the day, issuing a Facebook post which acknowledged that she should 'have reached out further and thought more deeply about who, and what kind of politics, an all-white list represents'.[44] Lucas's new explanation was that she had wanted to invite 'two representatives from the main opposition party to represent the diverse views within it' and had therefore gone for Thornberry and Cooper. Again, her logic did not quite stack up. Abbott and Cooper came from different wings of the Labour Party, and therefore Abbott could have been invited on that basis.

While opposition MPs were trying to construct a GNU, Johnson and his team were preparing for a prorogation. Johnson was appointed Prime Minister on 24 July, the day before Parliament's summer recess. During the recess, Johnson advised the Queen to prorogue Parliament for five weeks. He presented prorogation as a routine matter to allow the government to prepare for the Queen's speech. However, there were other ways of reading the decision. For Jacob Rees-Mogg, it was a challenge to the government's opponents. The *Express* detected a political motive, 'Johnson [was] "paving way for people vs Parliament" election in Brexit showdown.'[45]

Abbott reached the conclusion early in the recess that Johnson would opt for prorogation. 'It's quite frightening, because what Boris and the people around him are showing is they're really careless of the rule of law,' she said at the time.[46] Once again, Gina Miller stepped in with legal action. The Supreme Court's ruling came during the Labour Party conference after two weeks of prorogation. The government's argument and the Supreme Court's decision both paralleled ongoing debates about race. The government's case was that it had acted within its constitutional rights, did not intend to disrupt the proper functioning of Parliament, and that advice had been given to the Queen in good faith. Johnson defended his various comments about 'watermelon smiles' and 'flag-waving piccaninnies' in much the same way.[47] Free speech was his right, he had intended no offence, and that in his heart he was a decent liberal, a disciple of J. S. Mill.

The Supreme Court, however, reached a different conclusion. First, Lady Hale argued that Crown prerogative did not constitute an absolute right. Rather, since 1611 the courts had had a supervisory role over acts of government that stemmed from prerogative powers. Hale's second argument reflected the intervention of Shami Chakrabarti, the shadow Attorney General. Specifically, Hale argued that regardless of the intention, prorogation was illegal because it had the effect of stopping Parliament performing its constitutional role. In so doing, the Supreme Court adopted the analysis of Chakrabarti's team that the court should be concerned with the effects of proroga- tion rather than the intentions behind it. This aspect of the court's decision reflected modes of argument that Abbott and other black activists had been using in Britain since the 1970s. In terms of discus- sions over racism, Abbott had argued, since her time at the NCCL if not before, that institutions and policies should be judged not on the intentions or the good character of their authors, but on their consequences. This was why she supported 'ethnic record keeping', this is why she supported open government, so that the effects of education policy, of health policy, of immigration policy, of all areas of government action could be examined, to establish their impact on black people and white.

During an emergency Cabinet meeting Rees-Mogg apparently de- scribed the ruling as a 'constitutional coup'.[48] Evidently, his study of history had not acquainted him with early modern legal and consti- tutional cases. Unlike Abbott, Rees-Mogg did not have the benefit of a Cambridge history degree, or the understanding of legal principles that flowed from years of engagement in black radical politics. The ruling did not, in Abbott's view, draw the sting of a government that is blasé about the rule of law. Cameron and May had campaigned to end universal human rights, but Johnson's Cabinet appeared to be more ambitious: 'Following on from their failed attempt at prorogation, they keep hinting that they are going to "come for the lawyers" or "come for the judges". There's something quite frightening about such carelessness with the rule of law.'[49]

PMQS

The return of Parliament at the end of September allowed Abbott to achieve another first. In October 2019, she became the first black person to represent their party during Prime Minister's Questions. The decision was taken the week before. 'It was Jeremy's idea,' Abbott recalls. Abbott was nervous prior to the event. In one sense, it was 'just another day at work'.[50] But in another, PMQs was the big set piece, and since the 2016 referendum it had become a much more prominent part of public life. Abbott was keenly aware that 'you are speaking not just to Parliament, you are speaking to the country'.[51]

Abbott was up against Dominic Raab. Boris Johnson had made a habit of missing PMQs – in fact, since his appointment in July, he had only attended once. Initially, the mood was light. Raab, perhaps uncertain of protocol, interrupted Abbott during her first question. He explained his mistake by saying that he had been overcome by eagerness to pay tribute to Abbott. Apparently unmoved by this flattery, Abbott used her first question to address the issue of the abuse of women in public life. Quoting Paula Sherriff, Labour MP for Dewsbury, Abbott pointed to a worrying new trend: the people hurling abuse at BAME MPs and at female MPs were increasingly using the words of the Prime Minister. More worrying still, Johnson had dismissed such concerns, only a week earlier, as being 'humbug'.[52] Raab agreed with Abbott that abuse was a problem, but he appealed to Abbott as a 'passionate champion of free speech' to recognise that the Prime Minister had a right to speak out on matters of substance. Abbott had always drawn a clear line between 'robust debate' and 'mindless abuse'; May had conflated the two; now Raab was appealing to 'robust debate' to justify Johnson's use of language.[53]

Abbott's next question related to abortion. This reflected Abbott's ongoing use of her position in the Commons to champion women's rights. Abbott asked Raab to condemn 'deliberately disturbing bill-boards' showing foetuses which had been put up by pro-life groups in Stella Creasy's constituency.[54] She also asked the government to drop the 'rape clause', a four-page form which forced victims of rape to prove what had happened to them before they could receive financial support. Raab was non-committal, although he took issue with Abbott's use of language; the government's commitment to 'free speech' only went so far. Nonetheless, he certainly tried to moderate his tone. Where he disagreed with Abbott, he described his criticisms as 'gentle' reminders.

Reactions to Abbott's performance at PMQs varied. The BBC was even-handed, saying both politicians had acquitted themselves well. For the *Express*, the take-home message was that a Labour government would go on another spending spree which would 'trap' poor people on benefits. The *Mirror* focused on Raab's initial gaffe, and the *Telegraph* credited Abbott with doing 'better than expected ... but that isn't saying much'.[55] Anticipating that an election was coming, papers predictably divided along party lines. On a personal level, Abbott remembers being struck 'by how many people saw it' and congratulated her, 'for a lot of people, it was quite symbolic to have a black woman doing PMQs'.[56]

The parliament that returned at the end of September was quite different from the one Johnson had inherited from May at the beginning of the summer. In early September, Johnson had expelled twenty-one Tory MPs who had supported the Benn Act, which Abbott regarded as a 'scorched earth' approach to party management. As a result, there was no longer any sense in which Johnson commanded a majority in the House. Rather, the Tories were kept in place by a combination of the Fixed-Term Parliaments Act and the unwillingness of opposition MPs to coalesce around an alternative.

Johnson's new Cabinet was quite a change. For the first time in his career, Rees-Mogg was elevated to the Cabinet. Javid became Chancellor, Priti Patel Home Secretary, and Kwasi Kwarteng was appointed Minister of State for Business. For Abbott, this was a deliberate strategy, 'to give himself the appearance of being progressive. In practice, he's not proved to be progressive. And Sajid has learned that the price of being Boris's token Asian man is humiliation, humiliation that Sajid was not prepared to tolerate.'[57]

At the end of September, there had been talk of a caretaker government led by Corbyn. The SNP backed the idea, as did Caroline Lucas. However, parliamentary arithmetic and the political interests of the Liberal Democrats meant that the plan came to nothing. Parliament's return did, however, mean that the legislature could force the executive to abide by the provisions of the Benn Act. Government ministers and members of the European Research Group had implied that they had a cunning legal work-around which would allow them to ignore the Benn Act. In the end, the government sent a photocopy of an unsigned document, and a second letter arguing against further extension. Abbott had long claimed that some of her parliamentary colleagues treated politics like a debate in the Oxford or Cambridge Union. This was a case in point. What Johnson's strategy lacked in legal finesse, it made up for in political impact. Johnson would break his promise; he would neither leave the EU on 31 October, nor be found dead in a ditch, but he had signalled to the Brexit faithful that he had done everything in his power to take Britain out of the EU at the end of October.

Gridlock in Parliament pointed to a general election, but there were signs of movement in late October. The government's grudging compliance with the Benn Act took, for a time at least, no deal off the table. Additionally, a version of the Withdrawal Agreement finally passed the Commons on 22 October. The paradoxes of Brexit, how-ever, persisted. Johnson, who had pledged not to have an election was now demanding an election, on the basis that the Commons, which had just passed the Withdrawal Agreement was obstructing Brexit. The Liberal Democrats, who had consistently opposed an election and were long-standing advocates of a second referendum, had reversed on the first issue and were now advocating a straight revocation of Article 50. Labour, who had campaigned for a general election consistently since 2017, did not want to give Johnson an election on his terms. A shift in the Liberal Democrats' position proved decisive and on 29 October all the major parties voted for an early election.

ELECTION 2019

For Abbott, the ensuing campaign was 'exceptionally dirty'.[58] In some ways the election picked up where the 2017 campaign had left off. Again, Abbott was a prominent part of the campaign. And as soon as Abbott set out on the election trail articles were published reminding readers, in great detail, of her 2017 LBC interview. However, politi-cians were determined to learn from the mistakes of 2017. Johnson embraced the triple lock on pensions, dropped the 'dementia tax' and campaigned on an anti-austerity platform. The complex issues raised by Brexit were reduced to slogans. As the campaign went on 'get Brexit done' became simply 'get it done'. The Liberal Democrat slogan 'revoke' was pithier still. Against slogans of this kind, Labour's policy appeared extraordinarily complex.

Race featured in the campaign. Johnson dealt with his record in a variety of ways. First, he defended his right to free speech.[59] He assured his supporters that his critics were seeking offence in what were, in reality, quite innocuous remarks. He did, however, apologise for his comments on Muslim women. Johnson also joined Abbott in the ranks of politicians who have achieved notable firsts, by becoming the first sitting Prime Minister to shut himself in a fridge on the campaign trail.

Dominic Cummings, apparently, argued that Britain wanted change, and that change could take one of two forms, Brexit or Corbyn. Perhaps, one of the reasons why Brexit triumphed is that Johnson's vision chimed with accepted and highly romantic narratives of Britain's past. For Johnson, Britain was the nation that rescued Europe during the Second World War; the nation that had led the way in the abolition of slavery; that defended individual rights around the world; a dynamic nation that had been stifled by EU red tape. Britain could look to the future with hope, not least because after Brexit, Britain could become a world leader again, and British values could make Britain and the world a better place. Johnson's vision of hope, and his narrative of history were attractive, precisely because Yarl's Wood, the horrors of Grenfell Tower, the injustices of the Windrush scandal and years of austerity were either ignored, or presented as aberrations, which could be dealt with as soon as Britain took back control.

After the Grenfell Tower fire, Kim Taylor-Smith, deputy leader of Kensington and Chelsea Council, stated that he still had no idea why the council had failed so badly. But this was no obstacle to a brighter future, as Taylor-Smith stated, 'I try not to dwell on history. The important thing is to focus on tomorrow and getting it right.'[60] This seems to have been Johnson's approach to Britain as a whole.

Abbott takes a different view. Corbynism offered real hope because it reckoned with British history as it is, rather than history as we might like it to be. Chakrabarti argues that one thing that Abbott brought to the shadow Cabinet was a sense of history, a history of the Labour movement, situating the reform that Britain needs in a broader story. For Corbyn too, 'Diane had the historical perspective on what we were doing.'[61] History both to identify the problems the country faced and as an inspiration for solutions. The politics that Abbott fought for in 2019 reflected theoretical perspectives that she had discussed in the context of OWAAD, an understanding of the British state that had been sharpened through her work with the Scrap SUS campaign, the example of policies developed by the GLC and likeminded councils in the 1980s, the successes and disappointments of New Labour and a hard-headed analysis of the consequences of colonialism, neo-liberalism and austerity. While Labour were ultimately unsuccessful electorally, Abbott argues that Labour's radicalism after 2015 shifted public debate, and the policies which the party advocated remain the best template for the politics of the future.

CONCLUSION

LEGACY

'I can't believe it's been thirty-three years since the four of us walked through the doors of Parliament, where no one who looked like us had been before. We've been working together for more than forty years, forty years in the struggle for racial, social and economic justice. Diane, we've seen ups and downs, victories, defeats – more victories than defeats – but throughout that time you've been steadfast. You've been true to what you believe in, and you've been brave ... Diane Abbott, ayeeko, ayeeko, which means simply, well done, well done.'

PAUL BOATENG, 11 JUNE 2020[1]

In one sense, Abbott's time at the Home Office epitomised her career. On graduating, she entered the civil service on a 'Quixotic quest' to 'do good'. But the conservative character of Whitehall ran counter to her desire for progressive reform. At the NCCL, in the Labour Party, in Parliament and even on the Labour frontbench, progressive change was always hard won. Abbott has achieved undoubted successes, her election in 1987 being the most obvious example. And yet, in many accounts of recent history, in histories of the Labour Party, and in the memoirs of leading politicians, Abbott rarely gets more than a passing mention.

Campaigner, former leader of Lambeth Council and equality law specialist Linda Bellos argues that the omission of black people from historical narratives is both wilful and conscious; someone,

471

somewhere decided their stories were not worth preserving. 'Black things go missing because they are so held in contempt that people cannot be bothered [to include them],' Bellos claims. 'I want to say that because I want to wake them up. They have a duty of care to everybody who contributes to this society.'[2] Bellos's comment points to the fact that all too often British history is regarded as the history of white people, that 'white' is used as a synonym for British or English, and that 'black' is a synonym for outsider. Bellos did significant work countering this trend. Indeed, she was responsible for the establishment of Black History Month in the UK in the 1980s.

The reaction to research surrounding 'Cheddar Man' indicates how accurate Bellos's observation is. In 2018, DNA analysis of a 10,000-year-old skeleton of Cheddar Man led to the revelation that the first 'modern Britons' may have had dark brown skin, dark curly hair and blue eyes. For some, the mere suggestion that early Europeans may not have been white sparked accusations that the findings were part of liberal propaganda and a government hoax. For others, while Cheddar Man could not be thought of as black, his existence confirmed that equating Britishness with whiteness was not only reductive but ahistorical. As early as the sixteenth century, black people living in the UK could be found working as traders and merchants, sailors and musicians, they were getting married, being baptised and testifying in court. After centuries of slavery and colonisation, black people fought in British wars, crossed the Atlantic to rebuild British services, and, despite continued oppression, continue to advance British society. The introduction of Black History Month to the UK, the establishment of the Black Cultural Archives, the Black in the Day project and the celebration of Windrush Day are all attempts to embed black people in British historical narratives. In many ways, this book is a continuation of this effort. It is a deliberate and conscious act to recognise, record and revere black British stories.

Jeremy Corbyn praises Abbott for always being the first. 'The first black woman councillor, the first black woman MP, the first black shadow Home Secretary, the first black person to [shadow] one of the great officers of state.'[3] In 2019, standing in for Corbyn, Abbott became the first black person to represent their party at Prime Minister's Questions. John McDonnell agrees: 'To be the first black woman in the history of this country in Parliament and to hold significant office within a major political party, it is a huge breakthrough. If you look at the history of this country over the last century, it is an earth-shattering breakthrough.'[4]

Sharon Grant witnessed first-hand the pressures placed on those first black MPs, including her late husband, Bernie Grant.

[There were] so many expectations; people wanted them everywhere. They were expected to do all the normal things MPs do plus deal with the frustrations in the black community that had built up over so many years. The amount of pressure really was tremendous. All of them had a very difficult time and managed to survive it and do something positive.[5]

David Lammy agrees: 'People don't fully understand the sacrifice and the toil it takes being a first, pushing forward in that way in a public forum.'[6] All politicians, all public figures, face scrutiny and abuse. Nevertheless, the criticism and vitriol hurled at Abbott is unparalleled and speaks volumes about the race and gender biases inherent in British politics and wider society. During the 2017 election campaign, Abbott received 45 per cent of all of the abusive tweets sent to female MPs. In 2019, a leaked Labour report revealed insidious anti-black racism in the party, including dehumanising and disparaging remarks directed at Abbott and Dawn Butler.[7] And despite Abbott being Cambridge-educated with extensive political experience, attempts to denigrate her intelligence and aptitude persist.

'Remember, she is very bright. She could have been a senior civil servant; she could have had a private sector career and done well,' Nick Brown asserts.[8] 'But the core to her being are a sense of injustice, her commitment to social justice and her love of politics.' He continues, 'I think her courage and her resilience and the underlying strength of purpose that you must have to put up with all of this has been an example to others.'

McDonnell agrees that Abbott's unwavering principles have fuelled her. 'The person who's stayed there the longest, fought it through, seen it through ... is Diane Abbott. It's phenomenal,' he marvels. 'Many others would have buckled.' Andy Burnham says much the same: 'You cannot help but be in awe of it, that strength of character. Even though getting flak from everywhere, that ability to plough on and to succeed.'[9]

Lammy too attests to Abbott's tenacity.

I think that it's still the case that to be a black British woman in public life is rare. To be a powerful, articulate black woman surviving for so long in British public life is extremely unusual ... I think that she has done so much heavy lifting on behalf of the communities she's from and on behalf of the community she represents in Hackney and wider that words fail me. She's the great survivor.[10]

Commenting on Abbott's longevity at a celebration of her thirty-three years in Parliament, Michael Portillo stated, 'You were the first black female MP; you are the longest-serving black MP. These are enormous achievements.'[11]

For decades, Abbott sat on the backbenches, one of a small group of left-wing MPs who were in Parliament but out of power. Resolute in her socialist values, she consistently stood up for trade unions and supported grassroots campaigns such as those in Orgreave, Hillsborough, and Shrewsbury. Ansel Wong, the cultural archivist who played a key role in the establishment of UK Black History Month and the Notting Hill Carnival, describes Abbott as a committed advocate who used her platform to support grassroots work. 'She was accepted as one of us, [and] she was accepted as an important voice in the corridors of power ... She is the vanguard of some of those policies and procedures and therefore we had that sense of belonging, that sense of satisfaction that she had that role.' He continues, 'She did not always agree with our points of view. Nevertheless, you had to show that due respect to her and what she stood for.'[12]

Abbott has been assiduous in her opposition to restrictive welfare reforms, draconian immigration and asylum law and illiberal anti-terror legislation. When looking back at some of the key parliamentary votes throughout her career, Abbott, though often in the minority, was invariably vindicated. 'She is completely relentless,' Bell Ribeiro-Addy asserts.

> As you will see from the things she has supported over time, her strategy, as it should be with all campaigners, is to keep going, keep the message consistent, make the point again and again and again until they buy it. And history's proven that she's been on the right lines, so they always get it in the end.[13]

'I'll tell you a secret,' McDonnell laughs. 'When you're rushing into Parliament, and there's a vote going on, sometimes, you're never completely sure what the vote's about ... I always look for Diane and Jeremy and make sure we're in the same lobby, and I know I'll never go wrong.'[14]

Abbott is also much admired for her loyalty to her friends and constituents. 'She's fiercely loyal to the people she loves and cares about,' says Lammy. 'Amongst our group of minority ethnic parliamentarians, Diane is hugely respected. We seek her advice.'[15] Shami Chakrabarti feels the same. 'She's a political icon. She is admired by so many underdogs and outsiders ... If I want to get brownie points with anybody that's serving tea or serving a drink, I just sit with Diane Abbott. The admiration that people have, it is really touching.' She continues,

> There are all these contradictions because on the one hand there is the scary lefty Diane Abbott. Yet, there will be some liberal Tory and other women who would really like to have a selfie with Diane Abbott just because she's the first black woman in the House of Commons, she's had to put up with so much, and she's still here. She's principled, and she's brave, and she's a role model. And these words are all hackneyed, but they're not hackneyed when we're talking about Hackney Abbott. It's the best of Britain, isn't it? ...

That despite all the problems with being in this supposedly naturally conservative country dominated by an establishment and little England, it can produce a Diane Abbott.[16]

Abbott has often stated that she is not in the habit of pulling the ladder up behind her. Much of her career has focused on improving access to education, addressing differential attainment in schools and tackling social exclusion, especially among black boys and men. Still, Abbott's life and career carry particular significance for many young black British women.

For Edem Barbara Ntumy, a black activist and founder of Sassy Apparel, Abbott's achievements should be understood in their historical context.

> Diane's legacy is one of socialist triumph against the odds and doing the correct thing even if it meant falling out of favour with the Labour Party leadership. This is evident when she organised Black Sections, ran for leader of the Labour Party and her voting record in Parliament on key issues such as immigration and abortion rights. Whilst neoliberal identity politics takes root in society, Diane has been accountable to the communities she represents, keeping her feet firmly on the ground and on the pulse when it comes to the struggle for equality, peace and justice.[17]

History is important to other black women activists. 'Understanding black Britain and black British history is really important; we didn't really learn it in school, and it's also incredibly linked to our own identities,' Nicole Crentsil explains. Crentsil and Paula Akpan, the founders of Black Girl Fest, are grateful to Abbott for the barriers that she broke for them. They assert that Abbott's presence and longevity have encouraged many young black people, across the political spectrum, to engage with politics. 'That saying, "You cannot be what you don't see", often it rings very true,' Akpan explains. 'Because if we didn't have her, I would think there's no space for me in this arena.'[18]

Abbott entered Parliament at a time when fewer than 5 per cent of MPs were women, and none were black. By contrast, in the 2019 general election, a record 10 per cent of all elected MPs, and half of all new Labour MPs were from ethnic minority backgrounds. Speaking in the House of Commons as she stood in at PMQs, Dominic Raab praised Abbott: 'She has blazed a trail, she has made it easier for others to follow in her footsteps. That is something that I and every honourable member in this House can take pride in paying tribute to.'[19]

'She was a catalyst,' says MP Ronnie Campbell. 'She opened the door for black people coming in.'[20] 'I think she's in that rare category of people who are true pioneers, who actually do cut a path through the undergrowth and lay a path for other people,' Burnham adds. 'There are a lot more women from black and ethnic minority backgrounds that I'm sure have taken confidence that they can do it because they've seen Diane do it.'[21]

Dawn Butler agrees and states that black female politicians owe Abbott 'a great debt of gratitude'.[22] Claudia Webbe and Bell Ribeiro-Addy were among the black women elected to Parliament in 2019. 'I wouldn't even have thought about doing this job, I wouldn't have been able to do this job, if I didn't learn everything in Diane's office,' argues Ribeiro-Addy.[23] Webbe concurs:

While we still have much to do, we are indebted, and it is right for us to be indebted to Diane for breaking down many of the barriers facing black women in particular in politics today … Diane's leadership has demonstrated to us that we don't have to accept an unjust status quo, that it's possible to fight against systems of oppression, and that together we can achieve real change.[24]

For writer Reni Eddo-Lodge, Abbott is not just another politician.

The thing I really admire about Diane is that she has provided a model of participating in party politics without ever compromising on core values. I think that's rare. Part of the reason why I personally chose not to go into party politics was, I think sometimes it can be a bit hostile to people with independent minds. What I see in

Diane is, no matter what the leadership of the Labour Party, she has her core values, and despite where the tide goes, she sticks to those, and I respect that … Over the last thirty years we've seen a lot of black politicians come and go, who treat racism as the elephant in the room, even though there are still so few black people in Parliament. I always admire how even when it's not been popular, she's challenged it.[25]

US Congresswoman Terri Sewell draws parallels between Abbott and Shirley Chisholm, the first black women to be elected to Parliament in the UK and Congress in the US respectively.

Not only were they the first women of African descent to walk the halls of the nation's legislature … Both of them were keenly aware of the importance of promoting social justice, and both ran on that platform. Both were amazing ambassadors, not only for their race, but for their gender.

Sewell, who worked on Abbott's election campaign in 1987, thanks Abbott for inspiring her and encouraging her to run for Congress.

While I played a very small part in her getting elected, she played a very big part in my even believing in my ability to one day run for the highest legislative office in my country… I was really following in the very big footsteps that she'd left all the way across the Atlantic … Her advice was to be authentically who you are. The issues that you care about that you champion, make sure those issues are aligned with the people that you want to represent and to be steadfast in your commitment.[26]

Abbott's steadfastness was rewarded in 2010 when her Labour leadership bid propelled her onto the party's frontbench. Labour's transformation, first under Ed Miliband and then Jeremy Corbyn, has brought her brand of politics back into the mainstream debate. As shadow Home Secretary, Abbott played a central role in shaping

Labour's response to the Windrush scandal, the Grenfell Tower fire and the party's policy on immigration and asylum. What is more, the growth of radicalism since 2010, whether that be in Momentum, the Black Lives Matter campaign or ongoing campaigns to decolonise Britain's universities, has led to renewed interest in the history of black radicalism in Britain, a history in which Abbott has played an important part.

11 June 2020 marked thirty-three years since Abbott, Grant, Vaz and Boateng were elected to Parliament. 'The Labour Party owes Diane a great debt,' Labour party leader Keir Starmer declared.

> In thirty-three years, progress has been made, but this year, the anniversary comes as worldwide events have exposed the fact that racism, discrimination and social injustice are all rife within our society. The reality of anti-black racism, the impact of Covid-19, particularly on black and Asian communities, and society's in-built racial inequalities have shown that we've still got a long way to go.[27]

To date, the Covid-19 pandemic has claimed over 800,000 lives across the globe, 40,000 in the UK. In Britain, black and Asian communities have borne the brunt of the pandemic with higher rates of severe illness and death than white counterparts. A Public Health England report pointed to several factors: ethnic minorities are more likely to live in urban and deprived areas, live in overcrowded households and work in manual and caring jobs. The report also stated that co-morbidities, such as cardiovascular disease, might mean black and Asian people are more likely to die following an infection. However, an unpublished Public Health England report listed another factor contributing to the excess deaths among ethnic minorities, racism. The leaked report also recommended safeguards to protect those from ethnic minority backgrounds from infection. As Abbott noted, 'It is not that the virus discriminates but that this government and wider society do.'[28]

In June 2020, the USA experienced its biggest race riots since the assassination of Martin Luther King Jr in 1968. The cause: the murder of George Floyd by the police. Abbott was among 166 MPs who called for the UK to stop its export of riot gear, teargas and rubber bullets to the USA, and over 700,000 individuals signed a petition calling for the same. While many in the UK try to paint police brutality as being an American issue, a 2015 inquest report found that over 1,500 people had died in police custody or following police contact in the UK since 1990. A third of these were from an ethnic minority background.

As Abbott stated:

> The British political class need not think that it could not happen here. All the elements that have generated a wave of civil unrest in America are present in the UK: the terrible coronavirus death toll amongst black people; a history of a disproportionate use of force against black people by the state; institutional racism generally; and a national leader who shows no understanding or empathy about issues of race.[29]

The summer of 2020 saw tens of thousands gather in towns and cities across the UK in anti-racism demonstrations. Protesters in Bristol captured the nation's attention when they tore down a statue commemorating the slave owner, Edward Colston. After dragging it through the streets, they tossed it into the harbour amid cheers and jubilation. The following month, the artist Marc Quinn secretly erected a sculpture atop the empty plinth. The sculpture depicted Jen Reid, a protester who had been photographed standing on the plinth, fist raised. When the news broke that demonstrators had toppled the statue of Colston, Boris Johnson lamented that the protest had been 'hijacked by extremists intent on violence', and MPs such as Priti Patel and Rishi Sunak condemned the events in Bristol as 'utterly disgraceful' and 'criminal'.[30] Abbott, however, contended:

> The real disgrace and the horror which echoes down the centuries is the slave trade itself #BlackLivesMatter.
>
> The history of Empire, the history of British slaveholders like Bristol's Edward Colston, and the history of colonialism is an intrinsically violent one … The thousands of BAME deaths from Covid is also a form of violence.[31]

Siana Bangura praises Abbott for relentlessly speaking up about the conditions of black people in the UK when it is unfavourable to do so. She also applauds MPs like Abbott for pushing important bills through Parliament and argues that they have an essential role to play in directing public funds into public services like the NHS and local communities. Still, she asserts that legislation and policy is only one part of the fight.

> There is always a difference between what we have *de jure* versus *de facto*; what is written in law versus what happens in practice … We have the Race Relations Act, but we're still saying black lives matter, so there's a disconnect between what is in law and what happens in practice. It is always powerful to have people in places of power like Diane Abbott who are on your side, but it's not the only story. It all has to be simultaneous with grassroots community work.[32]

Abbott joined the civil service in 1976 because she wanted power. It was the same desire which led her to black grassroots politics, and ultimately to Parliament. Thirty-three years later, she is still there. 'I used to think that if I could look in the mirror when I was forty and say, well I tried, I'd be happy,' Abbott reflects. 'Well, I can look in the mirror now, definitely, and say, I tried, I tried my best.'[33]

The omission of black people from historical narratives is wilful and conscious. In any true history of the past thirty years, Abbott's name should be writ large. As Corbyn asserts, 'There is power in ideas, there is power in organisations, there is power in activism.'[34] Abbott has been a constant voice of hope to the marginalised and a persistent thorn in the side of the powers that be. Her words are recorded in Hansard, her influence felt in progressive reform and her work reflected in the success of those who come after her. Therein lies her power.

ACKNOWLEDGEMENTS

SAMARA LINTON

There are many people who have made this book possible, too many to mention. Nevertheless, I will use these pages to thank a few by name.

First and foremost, I must thank Diane Abbott for sharing her story with me. I have long admired Diane because of her status as the first black woman MP but also because in many ways, her story parallels my own. I, too, am the daughter of Jamaican immigrants, attended a grammar school in north London, and was one of the only black women in my Cambridge college. I can only hope that my story will continue to parallel Diane's, that I too will be known as a woman who speaks up for those who are silenced; defends those deemed unworthy; and speaks truth to power. I would like to thank Bell Ribeiro-Addy for her invaluable support and her contributions to this biography, and Olivia Beattie at Biteback for her support.

Robin, my writing partner, thank you for the opportunity to document this piece of history. I am grateful for your continued patience, feedback and encouragement and editorial brilliance. Lucy, I am indebted to you. From my early days as a university student, you have never ceased to provide love, wisdom and a listening ear. Thank you for opening up your home to me and my family, such kindness will never be forgotten.

Sister Josseth, thank you for your love and prayers. Thank you to the numerous people who supported me and my family as we adjusted to life in the UK: Sister Nelson, our church mothers and fathers, pastors and intercessors. I am grateful to Ms Daniels who saw the potential in me, an eight-year-old Jamaican immigrant, and pushed me beyond the curriculum. I am grateful to Mr Phillips and Mrs Silcock for nurturing my love of writing and exposition. Dr Sophia Mehnaz, Dr Reena Sani and Dr Ajith Azad, thank you for going above and beyond in your support. I am grateful to trailblazers like Professor Chinegwundoh who have dedicated their lives to helping and empowering their communities, to people like Dami who know how to brighten up even the darkest of days.

Thank you to the countless people who have supported me in my career shifts and changes, people like Tom Ilube, Sandra Thompson and Mugabi Turya. Zosia Kmietowicz, Sangeeta Chattoo, Gemma Mulreany, Jess Austin and Roisín Dervish-O'Kane, thank you for valuing my words and giving me the platforms on which to share them.

Thank you to my friends, my best fans and critics: Wandy, Tobi, Lwazi, Tiggy, Naomi, Ella Watts, Ella Green, Rhianna, Robyn, Precious, Mike, Jackson, Ada, Tanya, Lolly, Fausta, Naomi and Megan. Rianna, without you and *The Colour of Madness*, I would never have dreamed of writing a book like this. Rue, thank you for keeping me going, for reminding me to eat lunch and celebrate small wins. Nicki, thank you for being a big sister to me when I needed one the most.

I thank God for blessing me with my family. My grandparents 'Sir Rob' and Hilda, Grandpa and Grandma Linton, thank you for your journeys. Without your strength and determination to create a better life for your children, I would not be here today. My sister Anna, thank you for your unconditional love; you give me a reason to keep going. I am grateful to my parents, Fitz and Rosie; you have always encouraged me to interrogate assumed knowledge, affirmed me when I felt like giving up, and have never faltered in loving me. I thank you for your continued prayers, which, no doubt, have carried me through. Robert and Sarai, thank you for bringing joy into my life. May you grow up to be people who speak truth to power and bring light wherever you go.

ROBIN BUNCE

Four people have been at the heart of this book: Diane Abbott who gave generously of her time, and opened her personal archive; Bell Ribeiro-Addy, who has also been extremely generous to the authors, reading the drafts and spending time with us; and Samara Linton, an excellent writer, researcher and a great writing partner, someone with whom I have discussed politics in all its forms for many years now. Your comments on my sections improved them no end.

Paul Field also deserves special mention. Paul and I wrote *Renegade: The Life and Times of Darcus Howe* together a decade ago. This project was as much his idea as anyone else's. Paul's work arranging interviews early on, and his encyclopaedic knowledge of politics, past and present, have enriched this book greatly. Sadly, Paul had to withdraw from writing due to the pressure of other projects. Thank you, Paul, for your energy, expertise and friendship.

Thank you to everyone who agreed to speak to us on the record: Andy Burnham, Ansel Wong, Linda Bellos, Shami Chakrabarti, Nicole Crentsil, Paula Akpan, Charles Clarke, David Lammy, Gus John, Harry Goulbourne, Jeremy Corbyn, Jill Lewis, John McDonnell, Judith Kampfner, Julian Henriques, Linton Crawford, Marc Wadsworth, Meg Hillier, Mark Goldie, Mia Morris, Michael Ward, Paul Dimoldenberg, Peter Kahn, Peter Tatchell, Reni Eddo-Lodge, Ronnie Campbell, Russell Profitt, Samir Shah, Diane's friends from school and former teachers, Stephen Twigg, Steve Bell, Terri Sewell, Elaine Foster, Emily Evans, Graham Bash, Andrew Hosken, Jonathan Aitken, Ken Livingstone, Kwasi Kwarteng, Michael Attwell, Nick Brown, Elizabeth Anionwu, Sharon Grant, Siana Bangura, Tim Gopsil, Keith Vaz, Paul Boateng and Narendra Makanji. Your help was invaluable. Thank you to Ayo Sanusi and everyone in Diane's office. And thank you to those who spoke to us off the record, you know who you are.

I'd like to express my warmest thanks to all of the librarians and archivists who helped with this project. The staff of the Black Cultural Archives in Brixton, the Churchill Archives in Cambridge, the British Film Institute Archive, the Hull History Centre; as well as the staff at Cambridge University Library, Westminster City Council Archives, the Bishopsgate Institute Library, the British Library, at Homerton College Library and the Seeley Historical Library in Cambridge, where Diane studied as an undergraduate, all have been unfailingly helpful. Their expertise and advice have been invaluable throughout this project.

The staff at the George Padmore Institute in Stroud Green Road have been especially helpful. In fact, without the ongoing aid of Sarah Garrod, little of the work that I have done over the past ten years would have been possible. Thank you also to Anne Thomson at Newnham College Archive for her kindness and expert assistance.

I am no less obliged to Olivia Beattie at Biteback, to James Lilford, an excellent editor, and Sophie Scard of United Agents, without whom this project would have got nowhere.

I must also record my gratitude to Rohan McWilliam, who commented on several chapters, and whose conference, organised with the Labour History Research Unit, and subsequent book, *Labour and the Left in the 1980s*, was an important influence on this project. I am also grateful to Rohan for sharing his 'Labour Renewal Project' paper with me. Similarly, thank you to Deirdre Osborne for your advice and help. Thank you to Jennifer Davis for inviting me to speak at the migration and radicalism seminar, alongside the excellent David Feldman and Edward Anderson. Thank you to Andrew Gilbert of the Open University for sharing some of his resources with me, and for his thoughts on recent Conservative social policy. Thank you to Edem Barbara Ntumy for discussing her work on Black Sections and to Nathaniel Adam Tobias Coleman, and Adam Elliott-Cooper for their generosity sharing their analysis of politics and philosophy. In Cambridge, this project has been supported by the Principal, Fellows and staff of Homerton College. Particular thanks, to Melanie Keene, Catherine MacKenzie, Beth Singler and Chris Brooke, for discussing this project. Thank you to Duncan Bell, of Cambridge's Department of Politics and International Studies, whose invitation to teach on a course dealing with the politics of the future has enriched my understanding of the Empire and British discourses around race. Thank you to my former students Frances Rayner and Zoe Cormack, who asked why we only studied dead white men. In so doing they prompted me to think about black history. I would like to offer my thanks to Sundeep Lidher, for her kind words about my work and, along with Malachi MacIntosh, for the invitation to collaborate on Our Migration Story. Keith MacKenzie-Ingle, Andrew Heywood, Chris Taylor, Graham Thomas, Richard Sakwa, David McLellan and Scott Mandelbrote have also been important intellectual influences, and enormously kind, encouraging me to write and research.

I owe particularly heartfelt thanks to my friend Brandon High for reading and commenting on the first draft of the book. Your encouragement, expertise and suggestions were helpful in equal measure. And to my other dear friends for their help and encouragement during this process. Susie Hart, who was behind the cover's colour scheme, Jamie Hailstone, Kate Woodrow, Sami Savonius-Wroth, Alistair and Harriet Rouse, Niamh McNabb, Katherine Butler Schofield your support has been invaluable. Farrukh Dhondy's encouragement and advice was always a tonic. Thank you to Richard Kueh, who I had the pleasure of seeing *Limehouse* with back in the spring of 2017. Thank you to Patrick Greene, Jaime Prater and Trip McCrossin for their radical erudition. And thank you to Leila Howe, Tamara Howe, Margaret Peacock, Michael Cadette and Claudius Hilliman, all the members of Darcus Howe Legacy.

Above all, I owe my gratitude to my family, my mum and dad, my wife Lucy and daughter India, without whose love and support none of this would have been completed.

ENDNOTES

INTRODUCTION

1   Interview with Diane Abbott, 12 December 2019.
2   Ibid.
3   Boris Johnson, 'Boris Johnson compares Jeremy Corbyn to Stalin for his "hatred" of wealth creators as he launches election campaign', *Daily Telegraph*, 5 November 2019.
4   Diane Abbott, lecture given at London School of Economics, 22 October 2014.
5   David Cameron, 'I've put the bulldozing of sink estates at the heart of turnaround Britain', *Sunday Times*, 10 January 2016.
6   Diane Abbott, NUS Black Students' Campaign event, House of Commons, 15 December 2013.
7   Ibid.
8   Ibid.
9   Ibid.

CHAPTER 1: THE DAUGHTER OF IMMIGRANTS

1   Diane Abbott, NUS Black Students' Campaign event, House of Commons, 15 December 2013.
2   Interview with Diane Abbott, 25 October 2018.
3   Ibid.
4   *Play it Again*, BBC One, 22 April 2007.
5   Ibid.
6   *This Week*, BBC One, 19 April 2007.
7   Interview with Diane Abbott, 25 October 2018.
8   *Conversations: Diane Abbott*, BBC, 12 April 2016.
9   See: David J. Smith, *Racial Disadvantage in Britain: The PEP Report* (Harmondsworth: Penguin, 1977), p. 104; and Peter Fryer, *Staying Power: The History of Black People in Britain* (London: Pluto, 1984), p. 387.
10 'Black Women and Nursing: A Job Like No Other', *Race Today* (August 1974), vol. 6, no. 8, p. 227.
11 Beverley Bryan, Stella Dadzie, Suzanne Scafe, *Heart of the Race: Black Women's Lives in Britain* (London: Verso Books, 2018), p. 92.
12 Interview with Diane Abbott, 25 October 2018.
13 David Kynaston, *Austerity Britain, 1945–51* (London: Bloomsbury, 2010), p. 346.
14 Yasmin Alibhai-Brown, *Who Do We Think We Are? Imagining the New Britain* (London: Allen Lane, 2000), p. 56.
15 David Olusoga, *Black and British: A Forgotten History* (London: Pan Macmillan, 2016) p. 495.
16 C. F. H. Wegg-Prosser, 'Housing in Paddington', *The Times*, 18 August 1950.
17 Kenneth Leech, 'Housing and Immigration, Crisis in London', *RACE* (1967), vol. 8, no. 4, pp. 329–44.
18 Mark Stephens, 'Social Housing in the United Kingdom', in Jie Chen, Mark Stephens and

Yanyun Man (eds), *The Future of Public Housing: Ongoing Trends in the East and the West* (Heidelberg: Springer Science, 2013), p. 204.

19 Ibid., p. 205.

20 Interview with Diane Abbott, 25 October 2018.

21 Camilla Schofield, *Enoch Powell and the Making of Postcolonial Britain* (Cambridge: Cambridge University Press, 2013).

22 Douglas K. Midgett, 'West Indian Ethnic Identity in Great Britain', in Helen I. Safa, Brian M. du Toit (eds), *Migration and Development: Implications for Ethnic Identity and Political Conflict* (The Hague: Moulton, 2011), p. 68.

23 John Davis, 'Containing Racism? The London Experience, 1957–1968', in Robin D. G. Kelley and Stephen Tuck (eds), *The Other Special Relationship: Race, Rights, and Riots in Britain and the United States* (New York: Palgrave Macmillan, 2013), pp. 125–46.

24 Ibid., p. 126.

25 Ibid., pp. 130–31.

26 Interview with Diane Abbott, 25 October 2018.

27 Ibid.

28 Diane Abbott speaking at Stand Up To Racism Conference, 'Grenfell: Institutional Racism and the Social Cleansing of our Cities', 22 October 2017.

29 *Conversations: Diane Abbott*.

30 Tony Travers, *London Boroughs at 50* (London: Biteback, 2015), p. 214.

31 Interview with Diane Abbott, 25 October 2018.

32 Interview with Marilyn Macey, 7 August 2019.

33 Interview with Diane Abbott, 25 October 2018.

34 *Desert Island Discs*, BBC Radio 4, 23 May 2008.

35 Interview with Diane Abbott, 25 October 2018.

36 Ibid.

37 Interview with Diane Abbott, 25 October 2018.

38 Interview with Madeleine Watkins, 8 June 2019.

39 Interview with Maxine Longmuir, 8 June 2019.

40 Fiona Santon, 'Harrow County School for Girls', https://www.jeffreymaynard.com/Harrow_County/HCSG/HCSG_Fiona_Santon.htm (accessed June 2020).

41 Private correspondence with Ann West, 12 June 2019.

42 Interview with Maxine Longmuir.

43 Interview with Madeleine Watkins.

44 Interview with Madeleine Watkins.

45 Interview with Maxine Longmuir.

46 *Desert Island Discs*, BBC Radio 4, 23 May 2008.

47 Interview with Maxine Longmuir.

48 Interview with Maxine Longmuir.

49 Interview with Cathy Wilkey, 30 October 2019.

50 Interview with Diane Abbott, 25 October 2018.

51 Interview with Diane Abbott, 25 October 2018.

52 Interview with Maxine Longmuir.

53 Interview with Madeleine Watkins.

54 Interview with Madeleine Watkins.

55 Newnham College Archive, University of Cambridge.

56 Interview with Diane Abbott, 25 October 2018.

57 Ibid.

58 Harrow County School for Girls Magazine, 1968–69.

59 Ibid.

60 Ibid.

61 Richard Titmuss, 'The Limits of the Welfare State', *New Left Review* (1964), vol. 27, pp. 28–37.

62 Enoch Powell, *Freedom and Reality* (London: B. T. Batsford, 1969), p. 215.

63 Ibid., p. 219.
64 Ibid., p. 215.
65 Paul Corthorn, *Enoch Powell: Politics and Ideas in Modern Britain* (Oxford: Oxford University Press, 2019), p. 86.
66 Interview with Diane Abbott, 25 October 2018.
67 Camilla Schofield, *Enoch Powell and the Making of Postcolonial Britain*, pp. 247–9.
68 Interview with Cathy Wilkey, 30 October 2019.
69 Interview with Maxine Longmuir.
70 Newnham College Archive.
71 Interview with Liz Turner, 17 June 2019.
72 Ibid.
73 Private correspondence with Ann West, 12 June 2019.
74 Harrow County School for Girls Magazine, 1971.
75 Interview with Gill Cook, 19 August 2019.
76 Newnham College Archive.
77 Harrow County School for Girls Magazine.
78 Interview with Cathy Wilkey.
79 Harrow County School for Girls Magazine.
80 Ibid.
81 Interview with Gill Cook.
82 Interview with Diane Abbott, 25 October 2018.
83 *Hamlet* Programme, April 1971, Diane Abbott's private archive.
84 Harrow County School for Girls Magazine.
85 Interview with Diane Abbott, 25 October 2018.
86 School Magazine, private archive.
87 Newnham College Archive.
88 Interview with Diane Abbott, 25 October 2018.
89 Ibid.
90 See Rosie Wild, '"Black was the colour of our fight." Black Power in Britain 1955–1976', PhD thesis, University of Sheffield, 2008.
91 Kimberly Springer, Ana Laura Lopez de la Torre, Anna Collin and Tanisha C. Ford (eds), *Do You Remember Olive Morris?* (Gasworks & Remembering Olive Collective, 2009).
92 Interview with Diane Abbott, 25 October 2018.
93 Ibid.
94 Robin Bunce and Paul Field, *Darcus Howe: A Political Biography* (London: Bloomsbury, 2013) pp. 105–36.
95 Interview with Cathy Wilkey.
96 Interview with Gill Cook.
97 Interview with Diane Abbott, 25 October 2018.
98 Ibid.

CHAPTER 2: CAMBRIDGE: THE MAKING OF DIANE ABBOTT

1 Interview with Diane Abbott, 15 November 2018.
2 Ibid.
3 Ibid.
4 Newnham College Archive.
5 *Alternative Prospectus*, 1973, Cambridge Students' Union.
6 Helen Connor and Sara Dewson et al., 'Social Class and Higher Education: Issues Affecting Decisions on Participation by Lower Social Class Groups, Institute for Employment Studies', 2001, p. 6.
7 Paul Bolton, 'Briefing paper: Oxford "elitism"', House of Commons Library, 31 July 2019.
8 Interview with Diane Abbott, 15 November 2018.
9 Interview with Gill Sutherland, 28 October 2019.

10 Interview with Diane Abbott, 15 November 2018.
11 Newnham College Archive.
12 Ibid.
13 Margaret Birney Vickery, *Buildings for Bluestockings: The Architecture and Social History of Women's Colleges in Late Victorian England* (London: Associated University Presses, 1999), pp. 55–6.
14 'Naughty goings on at Newnham: Have the women of the all-women Cambridge college always been so raucous?', *Daily Mail*, 5 February 2010.
15 Interview with Diane Abbott, 15 November 2018.
16 Interview with Jill Lewis, 5 August 2018.
17 Newnham College Archive.
18 'Naughty goings on at Newnham: Have the women of the all-women Cambridge college always been so raucous?'
19 Interview with Diane Abbott, 15 November 2018.
20 Interview with Judith Kampfner, 25 November 2019.
21 *Alternative Prospectus*, 1973, Cambridge Students' Union.
22 Ibid.
23 Interview with Judith Kampfner.
24 Interview with Diane Abbott, 15 November 2018.
25 Newnham College Archive.
26 Interview with Diane Abbott, 15 November 2018.
27 'CUCA keeps quiet on Powell meeting', *Stop Press with Varsity*, 19 October 1974, p. 12.
28 'The Black Cantabs database', https://www.blackcantabs.org/the-database (accessed July 2020).
29 Enoch Powell, *Freedom and Reality*, p. 215.
30 Interview with Diane Abbott, 15 November 2018.
31 Interview with Jill Lewis, 5 August 2018.
32 Newnham College Archive.
33 Interview with Jill Lewis.
34 Interview with Diane Abbott, 15 November 2018.
35 Interview with Gill Sutherland.
36 Interview with Judith Kampfner.
37 History faculty archive, Cambridge University.
38 History faculty archive, Cambridge University.
39 Private correspondence with Mark Goldie, 6 August 2019.
40 *Alternative Prospectus*, 1975, Cambridge Students' Union.
41 Private correspondence with Mark Goldie.
42 Newnham College Archive.
43 Interview with Gill Sutherland.
44 Interview with Diane Abbott.
45 *Alternative Prospectus*, 1975, Cambridge Students' Union.
46 Newnham College Archive.
47 Ibid.
48 Interview with Diane Abbott, 15 November 2018.
49 Ibid.
50 Newnham College Archive.
51 *Alternative Prospectus*, 1975, Cambridge Students' Union.
52 Interview with Diane Abbott, 15 November 2018.
53 Interview with Gill Sutherland.
54 Ibid.
55 Robert Fogel and Geoffrey Elton, *Which Road to the Past: Two Views of History* (New Haven: Yale University Press, 1983), p. 3.
56 Interview with Gill Sutherland.

57 Newnham College Archive.
58 Interview with Diane Abbott, 15 November 2018.
59 Newnham College Archive.
60 Ibid.
61 Diane Abbott, 'Making sense of what's in black and white', *The Times*, 17 April 1997.
62 Interview with Diane Abbott, 15 November 2018.
63 Interview with Gill Sutherland.
64 Interview with Diane Abbott, 15 November 2018.
65 Newnham College Archive.
66 Interview with Diane Abbott, 15 November 2018.
67 Ibid.
68 Ibid.

CHAPTER 3: 'BECAUSE I WANT POWER'
1   Interview with Diane Abbott, 15 November 2018.
2   Newnham College Archive.
3   Graham Wood, 'Opening the door on Abbott', *The Times*, 6 October 1990.
4   Interview with Diane Abbott, 3 May 2019.
5   'Jenkins found guilty of harshness', *The Times*, 2 September 1976.
6   Marie Gottschalk, *The Prison and the Gallows: The Politics of Mass Incarceration in America* (Cambridge: Cambridge University Press, 2006), p. 190.
7   Interview with Diane Abbott, 3 May 2019.
8   Ibid.
9   Ibid.
10 Ibid.
11 Chris Moores, *Civil Liberties and Human Rights in Twentieth-Century Britain* (Cambridge: Cambridge University Press, 2017), pp. 144–218.
12 Private correspondence with Patricia Hewitt, 16 May 2019.
13 'Cobden – NCCL race relations project', *Rights!*, March/April 1979.
14 The National Council for Civil Liberties Archives.
15 Stuart Hall, Chas Critcher, Tony Jefferson, John Clarke and Brian Roberts *Policing the Crisis: Mugging, the State and Law and Order* (Basingstoke: Palgrave Macmillan, 2013), p. 214.
16 Ibid., pp. 215–320.
17 Chris Moores, *Civil Liberties and Human Rights in Twentieth-Century Britain*, p. 145.
18 Interview with Farrukh Dhondy, 5 May 2018.
19 Diane Abbott, 'Race Relations conference', *Rights!*, May/June 1979.
20 Wendy Laverick and Peter Joyce, *Racial and Religious Hate Crime: The UK From 1945 to Brexit* (Basingstoke: Palgrave Macmillan, 2019), p. 66.
21 Interview with Diane Abbott, 3 May 2019.
22 Diane Abbott, 'Race Relations conference'.
23 Ibid.
24 Diane Abbott, 'Draft of document on Equal Opportunity Policies and Ethnic Record Keeping', July 1979, National Council for Civil Liberties Archives.
25 Ibid.
26 'Minutes of Race Relations Sub-Committee, NCCL meeting, 14 May 1979', National Council for Civil Liberties Archives.
27 Diane Abbott, 'Draft of document on Equal Opportunity Policies and Ethnic Record Keeping'.
28 Ibid.
29 Interview with Diane Abbott, 3 May 2019.
30 Interview with Paul Boateng, 25 April 2019.
31 Letter from Asquith Gibbes, 22 June 1979, National Council for Civil Liberties Archives.
32 Interview with Diane Abbott, 3 May 2019.
33 Private correspondence with Jenny Bourne, 23 April 2019.

34 'Sus: Organ of the Steering Committee BPOCAS', 1 June 1978, National Council for Civil Liberties Archives.
35 Interview with Diane Abbott, 3 May 2019.
36 Beverley Bryan, Stella Dadzie, Suzanne Scafe, *The Heart of the Race*, p. 160.
37 Interview with Diane Abbott, 3 May 2019.
38 Diane Abbott, 'Race Relations Officer's Report to the Cobden Trust', 17 June 1979, The National Council for Civil Liberties Archives.
39 Ibid.
40 *Race Card*, Channel 4, 31 October 1999.
41 Beverley Bryan, Stella Dadzie, Suzanne Scafe, *The Heart of the Race*, p. 141.
42 Ibid., p. 144.
43 Interview with Diane Abbott, 3 May 2019.
44 'Introductory Talk: Black Women in Britain', OWAAD circular, National Council for Civil Liberties Archives.
45 Beverley Bryan, Stella Dadzie, Suzanne Scafe, *The Heart of the Race*, p. 149.
46 Stella Dadzie interview, British Library, 2011.
47 Interview with Mia Morris.
48 Interview with Diane Abbott, 3 May 2019.
49 Hazel V. Carby, 'White Woman Listen! Black Feminism and the Boundaries of Sisterhood', in Centre for Contemporary Cultural Studies, *The Empire Strikes Back: Race and Racism in 70s Britain* (London: Hutchinson, 1982) pp. 212–35.
50 Margaretta Jolly, *Sisterhood and After: An Oral History of the UK Women's Liberation Movement, 1968–Present* (Oxford: Oxford University Press, 2019) p. 179.
51 Interview with Elizabeth Anionwu, 1 September 2018.
52 Interview with Mia Morris.
53 Interview with Diane Abbott, 3 May 2019.
54 Stella Dadzie interview, British Library, 2011.
55 Interview with Ken Livingstone, 30 May 2018.
56 Ibid.
57 'Whose side are you on?', *Socialist Organiser*, May 1979.
58 Interview with Diane Abbott, 3 May 2019.
59 Matthew Lewin, 'Election line-up', *Hampstead Express*, from 27 April 1979.
60 Ken Livingstone, 'The trade unions are key', *Socialist Organiser*, May 1979.
61 John Carvel, *Citizen Ken* (London: Chatto & Windus, 1984), p. 69.
62 Interview with Diane Abbott, 3 May 2019.
63 Interview with Ken Livingstone.
64 Interview with Diane Abbott, 3 May 2019.
65 Interview with Jeremy Corbyn.
66 'Haringey councillors demand inquiry into police "power"!', *West Indian World*, 1 February 1979.
67 Interview with Diane Abbott, 3 May 2019.
68 Rosa Prince, *Comrade Corbyn* (Biteback: London, 2018) pp. 53–6.
69 Interview with Jeremy Corbyn, 10 February 2020.
70 Ibid.
71 Interview with Diane Abbott, 3 May 2019.
72 Darcus Howe, 'Enter Mrs Thatcher', *Race Today*, 1978, p. 58.
73 *FOWAAD!*, November 1979, p. 3.
74 Interview with Diane Abbott, 3 May 2019.

CHAPTER 4: THE FOURTH ESTATE

1 Diane Abbott, NUS Black Students' Campaign event, House of Commons, 15 December 2013.
2 Interview with Michael Attwell, 26 March 2020.
3 Interview with Diane Abbott, 3 May 2019.

4   Ibid.

5   Ibid.

6   Interview with Tim Gopsill, 27 March 2020.

7   Diane Abbott, 'And now this', *The Leveller* (1979), no. 43, p. 10.

8   Diane Abbott, 'One battle won – but the war?', *The Leveller* (1980), no. 38, p. 28.

9   Ibid.

10 Diane Abbott, 'Who rules the airwaves?', *The Leveller* (1981), no. 49, p. 20.

11 Interview with Michael Ward, 16 April 2018.

12 Richard Heffernan and Mike Marqusee, *Defeat from the Jaws of Victory: Inside Kinnock's Labour Party* (London: Verso, 1992), p. 10.

13 *London Labour Briefing* (1980), Trial Issues, p. 1.

14 Interview with Jeremy Corbyn, 10 February 2020.

15 Jeremy Corbyn, 'Target 1982', *London Labour Briefing* (1980), no. 7, p. 1.

16 Ibid.

17 Interview with Diane Abbott, 3 May 2019.

18 Ibid.

19 Private correspondence with Paul Dimoldenberg, 17 March 2020.

20 Richard Heffernan and Mike Marqusee, *Defeat from the Jaws of Victory*, p. 14.

21 Diane Abbott, 'The slipway to centrism', *The Leveller* (1981), no. 50, p. 7.

22 Ibid.

23 Ibid.

24 'Briefing on the Social Democrats', *London Labour Briefing*, 1982.

25 Diane Abbott, 'Plays', *The Leveller* (1981), no. 52, p. 20.

26 Interview with Diane Abbott, 3 May 2019.

27 Ibid.

28 Brian Alleyne, *Radicals Against Race: Black Activism and Cultural Politics* (Oxford: Berg, 2002), p. 57.

29 John La Rose, *The New Cross Massacre Story* (London: New Beacon Books, 2011), p. 62.

30 Interview with Diane Abbott, 3 May 2019.

31 Robin Bunce and Paul Field, *Darcus Howe: A Political Biography*, p. 188.

32 Trevor Phillips and Mike Phillips, *Windrush: The Irresistible Rise of Multi-Racial Britain* (London: HarperCollins, 1998), p. 328.

33 Diane Abbott and Ben Provost, 'The New Cross March – "Suddenly we realised what it was to feel powerful"', *The Leveller* (1981), no. 52, p. 16.

34 Ibid.

35 Ibid.

36 Ibid.

37 'The Day the Blacks Ran Riot in London', *The Sun*, 3 March 1981.

38 Interview with Diane Abbott, 3 May 2019.

39 Diane Abbott and Ben Provost, 'The New Cross March'.

40 Phillips and Phillips, *Windrush*, p. 347.

41 Lord Scarman, *The Scarman Report: The Brixton Disorders, 10–12 April 1981* (London: Penguin, 1986), p. 95.

42 Robin Bunce and Paul Field, *Darcus Howe: A Political Biography*, pp. 210–11.

43 Interview with Diane Abbott, 3 May 2019.

44 Interview with Diane Abbott, 3 May 2019.

45 Interview with Ansel Wong, 16 September 2019.

46 Interview with Diane Abbott, 3 May 2019.

47 Interview with Diane Abbott, 3 May 2019.

48 Interview with Ansel Wong, 3 May 2019.

49 Interview with Diane Abbott, 3 May 2019.

50 Ibid.

51 Ken Livingstone, *If Voting Changed Anything, They'd Abolish It* (London: Collins, 1987), p. 149.

52 Ibid.
53 Interview with Linda Bellos, 'The GLC Story Oral History Project', 7 March 2017, http://glcstory. co.uk/wp-content/uploads/2017/03/LindaBellostranscript.docx-1.pdf (accessed June 2020).
54 Interview with Michael Ward.
55 Lynda Lee-Potter, *Daily Mail*, 2 November 1985.
56 Jonathan Davis and Rohan McWilliam, *Labour and the Left in the 1980s* (Manchester: Manchester University Press, 2018), p. ix.
57 Interview with Diane Abbott, 3 May 2019.
58 Ken Livingstone, *If Voting Changed Anything, They'd Abolish It*, p. 151.
59 Interview with Diane Abbott, 3 May 2019.
60 Interview with John McDonnell, 6 April 2020.
61 Alan Freeman, 'Constructing alliances', *Socialist Action*, 15 November 1985, p. 5.
62 Interview with Ansel Wong.
63 Interview with John McDonnell.
64 Interview with Diane Abbott, 3 May 2019.
65 *Sunday Express*, 27 September 1981.
66 Interview with Diane Abbott, 3 May 2019.
67 James Curran, *Culture Wars: The Media and the British Left* (London: Routledge, 2018), pp. 5–39.
68 Margaret Thatcher, *The Path to Power* (London: HarperCollins, 1995), p. 405–6.
69 *Daily Mail*, 2 November 1984.
70 *Daily Telegraphy*, 23 January 1985.
71 *Daily Mail*, 19 May 1983.
72 Frank Chapple, *Daily Mail*, 27 March 1986.
73 Interview with Diane Abbott, 3 May 2019.
74 Interview with John McDonnell.
75 Interview with Diane Abbott, 3 May 2019.
76 Ibid.

CHAPTER 5: WESTMINSTER
1   Interview with Diane Abbott, 18 March 2019.
2   Interview with Paul Dimoldenberg, 12 February 2019.
3   Andrew Hosken, *Nothing Like a Dame: The Scandals of Shirley Porter* (London: Granta Books, 2006), p. 64.
4   Interview with Paul Dimoldenberg.
5   Labour election flyer for the Harrow Road Ward, May 1982, Paul Dimoldenberg's private archive.
6   Ibid.
7   Ibid.
8   Andrew Hosken, *Nothing Like a Dame*, pp. 47–8.
9   Penny Chorlton, 'Blacks fail to make impact in local elections', *The Guardian*, 15 May 1982.
10 Interview with Paul Dimoldenberg.
11 Minutes of council meeting, 24 January 1983, Westminster Council Archives.
12 Interview with Diane Abbott, 18 March 2019.
13 Interview with Paul Dimoldenberg.
14 Daniel Cordle, 'Protect/Protest: British nuclear fiction of the 1980s', *The British Journal for the History of Science* (December 2012), vol. 45, no. 4, pp. 653–69, p. 655.
15 Minutes of extraordinary council meeting, 30 March 1983, Westminster Council Archives.
16 Hansard, House of Commons debate, 24 March 1983, vol. 39, cc. 1083–99.
17 Interview with Paul Dimoldenberg.
18 Ken Livingstone, *If Voting Changed Anything, They'd Abolish It*, p. 217.
19 C. Phillips and I. Ross, *The Nuclear Casebook: An Illustrated Guide* (Edinburgh: Polygon Books, 1983), p. 35.

20 Andrew Hosken, *Nothing Like a Dame*, p. 75.
21 Ibid., p. 88.
22 Interview with Diane Abbott, 18 March 2019.
23 Andrew Hosken, *Nothing Like a Dame*, p. 112.
24 Paul Dimoldenberg, *The Westminster Whistleblowers: Shirley Porter, Homes for Votes and Twenty Years of Scandal in Britain's Rottenest Borough* (London: Politicos, 2006), p. 15.
25 Sue Bruley, *Women in Britain Since 1900* (Macmillan, 1999), p. 161.
26 Andrew Hosken, *Nothing Like a Dame*, p. 112.
27 Interview with Jeremy Corbyn, 10 February 2020.
28 Diane Abbott, 'Wanted: a black NEC member', *Tribune*, 28 September 1984.
29 Interview with Paul Dimoldenberg.
30 Paul Dimoldenberg, *The Westminster Whistleblowers*, pp. 27–35.
31 Andrew Hosken, *Nothing Like a Dame*, p. 103.
32 Ibid., p. 291.
33 Interview with Paul Dimoldenberg.
34 Private correspondence with Jenny Bourne, 23 April 2019.
35 Interview with Diane Abbott, 18 March 2019.
36 Lionel Morrison, *A Century of Black Journalism in Britain: A Kaleidoscopic View of Race and the Media (1893–2003)* (London: Truebay, 2007), p. 57.
37 Roxy Harris, Sarah White, Sharmilla Beezmohun (eds), A *Meeting of the Continents: The International Book Fair of Radical Black and Third World Books* (London: New Beacon Books, 2005), p. vi.
38 Sound recording of 'Forum on Black Films in Britain', GB 2904 BFC/01/06/03/01, George Padmore Institute Archive.
39 Interview with Diane Abbott, 18 March 2019.
40 Michael Leapman, *Treachery? The Power Struggle at TV-Am* (London: Allen & Unwin, 1984), pp. 112–3.
41 Peter Jay, *The Crisis for Western Political Economy and Other Essays* (London: Deutsch, 1984), p. 237.
42 Interview with Diane Abbott, 18 March 2019.
43 Ibid.
44 Ibid.
45 Interview with Jonathan Aitken, 16 May 2018.
46 Interview with Diane Abbott, 18 March 2019.
47 'Diary', *Tribune*, 14 June 1985.
48 'Labour Party conference (2.10.1985)', British Film Institute Archive.
49 Ibid.
50 Ibid.
51 'Profile: Diane Abbott', *The Equal Opportunities Review* (1985), vol. 1, no. 3, p. 19.
52 Ibid., p. 20.
53 James Curran, Ivor Gaber, Julian Petley, *Culture Wars: The Media and the British Left* (London: Routledge, 2018), pp. 72–6.

CHAPTER 6: THE REPRESENTATION OF THE PEOPLE

1   Hansard, House of Commons debate, 24 March 1983, vol. 39, c. 504.
2   *Election*, ITN, 10 June 1983.
3   David Kogan, *Protest and Power: The Battle for The Labour Party* (London: Bloomsbury, 2010), p. 49.
4   Richard Heffernan and Mike Marqusee, *Defeat from the Jaws of Victory*, p. 35.
5   Off-air recording of BBC footage of the Labour Party conference, 3 October 1984, British Film Institute Archive.
6   Muhammad Anwar, *Race and Politics: Ethnic Minorities and the British Political System* (London: Routledge, 2013), p. 126.

7   Private correspondence with Russell Profitt, 23 January 2019.
8   Ben Bousquet interview, British Library, 1986.
9   Interview with Paul Boateng, 10 February 2020.
10 Muhammad Anwar, *Race and Politics*, pp. 126–7.
11 Interview with Diane Abbott, 18 March 2019.
12 Interview with Paul Boateng.
13 Private correspondence with Russell Profitt, 23 January 2019.
14 Interview with Narendra Makanji, 24 August 2018.
15 Diane Abbott, 'Black Sections', *Socialist Action*, 25 May 1984.
16 'Commemorating 25 years of the Labour Party Black Sections', Hansib Publications, 2008, p. 10.
17 Muhammad Anwar, *Race and Politics*, p. 118.
18 Ibid.
19 Interview with Diane Abbott, 18 March 2019.
20 Muhammad Anwar, *Race and Politics*, p. 119.
21 Hilary Wainwright, *Labour: A Tale of Two Parties* (London: Hogarth, 1987), p. 191.
22 Terri A. Sewell, *Black Tribunes: Black Political Participation in Britain* (London: Lawrence & Wishart, 1993), p. 99.
23 Hilary Wainwright, *Labour: A Tale of Two Parties*, p. 188.
24 Pnina Werbner, *Black and Ethnic Leaderships: The Cultural Dimensions of Political Action* (London: Routledge, 2009), p. 45.
25 Hilary Wainwright, *Labour: A Tale of Two Parties*, p. 163.
26 Interview with Keith Vaz, 21 February 2018.
27 Interview with Paul Boateng.
28 Interview with Paul Boateng.
29 Narendra Makanji interview, British Library, 1986.
30 Ibid.
31 Pnina Werbner, *Black and Ethnic Leaderships*, pp. 34–5.
32 T. Carver and P. Thomas (eds), *Rational Choice Marxism* (London: Springer, 2016), p. 209.
33 Richard Heffernan and Mike Marqusee, *Defeat from the Jaws of Victory*, p. 37.
34 Terri A. Sewell, *Black Tribunes*, p. 18.
35 Dalton Barrett, 'Which way forward?', *The Voice*, 31 March 1984.
36 'Kinnock rejects "Black Sections minefield"', *The Guardian*, 11 April 1984.
37 'Black rebellion may split Labour Party', *Daily Mail*, 11 June 1984.
38 'Council backs 5 women for Labour NEC places', *The Guardian*, 26 June 1984.
39 'Black Sections – Neil Kinnock', *New Life*, 29 June 1984.
40 Ian Aitken, 'Kinnock within whisker of NEC defeat', *The Guardian*, 27 September 1984.
41 Open letter signed by 30 MPs, including Tony Benn and Eric Heffer, *Tribune*, 28 September 1984.
42 'Black Sections Yes!', *Socialist Action*, 1984, p. 10.
43 Off-air recording of BBC footage of the Labour Party conference, 3 October 1984, British Film Institute Archive.
44 Ibid.
45 Interview with Paul Boateng.
46 Nicholas Harman, 'The black and the red', *Sunday Times*, 16 December 1984.
47 Marian Fitzgerald, 'Political Parties and "The Black Vote"', December 1983, Neil Kinnock Archives.
48 Ibid.
49 Letter from Neil Kinnock to Jo Richardson, 23 July 1984, Neil Kinnock Archives.
50 Harry Goulbourne (ed.), *Black Politics in Britain* (Aldershot: Avebury, 1990), p. 172.
51 Interview with Diane Abbott, 18 March 2019.
52 Interview with Jeremy Corbyn, 10 February 2020.
53 Interview with Diane Abbott, 18 March 2019.
54 Alan Rusbridger, 'Diary', *The Guardian*, 9 February 1985.

55 Ibid.
56 Interview with Diane Abbott, 18 March 2019.
57 Interview with Jeremy Corbyn, 10 February 2020.
58 Interview with Diane Abbott, 18 March 2019.
59 Diane Abbott, 'Working within the Labour Party', *West Indian World*, 20 March 1985.
60 Ibid.
61 Interview with Keith Vaz.
62 Narendra Makanji interview, British Library, 1986.
63 Interview with Diane Abbott, 18 March 2019.
64 'Black group campaign "repellent"', *The Times*, 14 June 1985.
65 *Tribune* interview with Neil Kinnock, KNNK 26/2/19, 10 September 1985, Neil Kinnock Archive.
66 Letter from Roy Hattersley to Neil Kinnock, 7 May 1985, Roy Hattersley Archive.
67 Off-air recording of BBC footage of the Labour Party conference, 3 October 1984, British Film Institute Archive.
68 Ibid.
69 Ibid.
70 Interview with Farrukh Dhondy 10 June 2020.
71 Interview with Narendra Makanji, 24 August 2018.
72 Interview with Peter Kahn, 14 November 2018.
73 Interview with Cathy Warnock, 30 October 2018.
74 Interview with Peter Kahn.
75 Interview with Cathy Warnock.
76 Interview with Graham Bash, 17 January 2018.
77 Interview with Marc Wadsworth, 21 February 2018.
78 Hackney Trades Union Council meeting minutes, 5 October 1985, Hackney Archives.
79 Hackney Trades Union Council meeting minutes, 7 November 1985, Hackney Archives.
80 Interview with Cathy Warnock.
81 Interview with Diane Abbott 18 March 2019.
82 Colin Hughes, 'Ousted MP says votes "switched"', *The Times*, 10 December 1985.
83 Tim Cooper, 'Black woman MP for Hackney?', *Hackney Gazette*, 10 December 1985.
84 'Ousted MP to challenge vote "riddle"', *The Sun*, 10 December 1985.
85 John Warden, 'Labour chooses black activist to stand as MP', *Daily Express*, 9 December 1985.
86 Ibid.
87 *Hackney Gazette*, 17 December 1985.

CHAPTER 7: IN THE BELLY OF THE BEAST

1   Off-air recording of *VOTE '87*, ITV, 11 June 1987, British Film Institute Archive.
2   'Kinnock calls off attack on Tebbit', *Daily Express*, 16 December 1985.
3   Michael Leapman, *Kinnock* (London: Unwin Hyman, 1987), p. 73.
4   Interview with Diane Abbott, 14 December 2017.
5   Off-air recording of *Question Time*, BBC One, 12 June 1986, British Film Institute Archive.
6   Ibid.
7   *The Guardian*, 26 Mar 1987.
8   Interview with Sharon Grant, 18 March 2019.
9   Letter from Roy Hattersley to Bernie Grant, Bernie Grant Archive.
10 Off-air recording of *Today*, BBC Radio 4, 8 April 1987, Neil Kinnock Archive.
11 Annotated document 'Possible Constitutional Action in relation to Linda Bellos and Sharon Atkin', April 1987, Neil Kinnock Archive.
12 Interview with Sharon Grant.
13 Interview with Diane Abbott, 14 December 2017.
14 Ibid.
15 *Bandung File*, Channel 4, 7 June 1987.

16 Interview with Diane Abbott, 14 December 2017.
17 Interview with Jeremy Corbyn, 11 March 2020.
18 John Burnell online speaking event, 10 June 2020.
19 Peter Kenyon online speaking event, 10 June 2020.
20 'Libel writs fly in political dogfight', *Hackney Gazette*, 22 May 1987.
21 'Hard left and the true blue vie for deprived Hackney', *The Times*, 18 May 1987.
22 Ibid.
23 Interview with Terri Sewell, 29 April 2018.
24 Off-air recording of *VOTE '87*, ITV, 11 June 1987, British Film Institute Archive.
25 Interview with Paul Boateng, 10 February 2020.
26 Off-air recording of *Good Morning Britain*, 12 June 1987, British Film Institute Archive.
27 Tony Benn, *The End of an Era: Diaries 1980–90* (London: Cornerstone Digital), p. 578.
28 R. W. Johnson, 'Now for a real alliance?', *The Times*, 7 July 1987.
29 Patricia Hewitt letter, *New Statesman*, 13 March 1987.
30 Interview with Diane Abbott, 14 December 2017.
31 'Hansib honours four black tribunes', *Caribbean World*, 24 July 1987.
32 Interview with Jonathan Aitken, 16 May 2018.
33 Ken Livingstone, *You Can't Say That: Memoirs* (London: Faber & Faber, 2011), p. 321.
34 Off-air recording of *Question Time*, BBC One, 18 June 1987, British Film Institute Archive.
35 Letter from Roy Hattersley to Neil Kinnock, 12 July 1988, Roy Hattersley Archive.
36 Interview with Diane Abbott, 14 December 2017.
37 Lynne Segal, 'Lynne Segal Interviews Diane Abbott', *Feminist Review* (1987), no. 27, p. 56.
38 Ibid., p. 57.
39 Ibid., p. 59.
40 Interview with Diane Abbott, 14 December 2017.
41 Interview with Paul Boateng.
42 Draft Letter regarding House of Commons policemen and attendants, appended to the minutes of the Parliamentary Black Caucus, 26 April 1988, Bernie Grant Archive.
43 'MPs complain about "Commons staff racism"', *The Times*, 24 May 1988.
44 Pauline Peters, 'Westminster Abbott', *Sunday Telegraph Magazine*, 20 September 1987.
45 Ibid.
46 *Daily Telegraph*, 12 November 1987.
47 Interview with Jeremy Corbyn, 11 March 2020.
48 Interview with Diane Abbott, 14 December 2017.
49 The details of the escape are given in Louise Pirouet, *Whatever Happened to Asylum in Britain? A Tale of Two Walls* (London: Berghahn Books, 2001), p. 35.
50 Ibid., p. 33.
51 Hansard, House of Commons debate, 16 November 1987, vol. 122, cc. 816–7.
52 Hansard, House of Commons debate, 26 October 1989, vol. 158, c. 1059.
53 Interview with Diane Abbott, 14 December 2017.
54 Interview with Jonathan Aitken.
55 Interview with Diane Abbott, 14 December 2017.
56 *Work Talk*, BBC Radio 4, 26 October 1992.
57 Interview with Nick Brown, 26 October 2018.
58 Ken Livingstone, *You Can't Say That*, p. 317.
59 Lord Carrington interview, British Library, 2012.
60 Lucy Ward, 'The Guardian Profile: Diane Abbott', *The Guardian*, 16 March 1999.
61 Interview with Diane Abbott, 14 December 2017.
62 *Today*, 13 November 1991.
63 Claudia Fitzherbert, 'Time for a baby in the House', *Daily Telegraph*, 24 October 1991.
64 Ibid.
65 'Plea for baby to come too', *Glasgow Herald*, 22 October 1991.

66 Interview with Diane Abbott, 14 December 2017.
67 Ibid.
68 'Revolution by other means', *New Statesman*, 14 August 1987.
69 Interview with Diane Abbott, 14 December 2017.
70 Letter from Paul Boateng to Bernie Grant, 31 March 1988, Bernie Grant Archive.
71 Interview with Diane Abbott, 14 December 2017.
72 Letter from Neil Kinnock to Diane Abbott, 21 February 1989, Neil Kinnock archive.
73 Interview with Diane Abbott, 14 December 2017.
74 Martin Fletcher, 'Times Diary', *The Times*, 10 March 1989.
75 The *Caribbean Times*, 7 April 1989.
76 Ibid.
77 'US thumbs up to black caucus', *The Voice*, 4 April 1989.
78 Private and confidential memo on 'Black and Asian Organisations in the Labour Party', presented to the NEC on 22 Feb 1989, Neil Kinnock archive.
79 Interview with Diane Abbott, 14 December 2017.
80 Interview with Marc Wadsworth, 21 February 2018.
81 Ibid.
82 Richard Heffernan and Mike Marqusee, *Defeat from the Jaws of Victory*, p. 268.
83 Letter from Neil Kinnock to Bernie Grant, 17 May 1989, Bernie Grant Archives.
84 Interview with Linda Bellos, 1 September 2018.
85 Interview with Diane Abbott, 14 December 2017.
86 Charles E Jones, 'A Dream Deferred: The Abortive Efforts of the Parliamentary Black Caucus in Great Britain', in Georgia Anne Persons (ed.), *Race and Ethnicity in Comparative Perspective* (London: Transaction, 1999), pp. 37–52.
87 Interview with Keith Vaz.
88 Interview with David Lammy, 13 July 2018.
89 Interview with Graham Bash, 17 January 2018.
90 Interview with Diane Abbott, 14 December 2017.
91 Ibid.
92 Ibid.
93 *Socialist Campaign Group News* in October 1990.
94 Interview with Diane Abbott, 14 December 2017.
95 Ibid.
96 Lorraine Griffiths, 'How are we doing?', *The Voice*, 16 August 1988.
97 Interview with Diane Abbott, 14 December 2017.
98 Ibid.
99 John Halperin, *Trollope and Politics: A Study of the Pallisers and Others* (London: Macmillan, 1977), p. 67.
100 *Work Talk*, BBC Radio 4, 26 October 1992.
101 Interview with Diane Abbott MP conducted as part of the Bernie Grant Trust project 'Taken for Granted', October 2011.

CHAPTER 8: NEW LABOUR, NEW DANGER

1 Mais, *Islington Cookbook* (London: National Society for the Prevention of Cruelty to Children, 1998).
2 'National Analytical Study on Racist Violence and Crime', Commission for Racial Equality, 2010.
3 Interview with Ken Livingstone, 30 May 2018.
4 'Trial by the *Daily Mail*', *The Guardian*, 14 February 1997.
5 Nicholas Timmins, 'Mugging: criminal or political offence?', *The Independent*, 4 August 1995.
6 'Paul Condon accused of racism', LBC/IRN, 28 July 1995.
7 Nicholas Timmins, 'Mugging: criminal or political offence?', *The Independent*, 4 August 1995.

8   'Paul Condon accused of racism'.
9   Ibid.
10 Hansard, House of Commons debate, 11 December 1995, vol. 300, cc. 765–6.
11 'Finnish this recruitment', *Hackney Gazette*, 14 November 1996.
12 'Matters of Opinion: MP is no help to morale', *Hackney Gazette*, 5 December 1996.
13 'Matters of Opinion: Docs join Abbott blast', *Hackney Gazette*, 28 November 1996.
14 John Rentoul, 'Diane Abbott is sorry (For the record Miss Finland is also black)', *The Independent*, 29 November 1996.
15 Ibid.
16 Interview with Marc Wadsworth.
17 *The Independent*, 29 November 1996.
18 'Diane Abbott: Finland responds', *The Spectator*, 7 December 1996.
19 Ibid.
20 'Abbott denies attack on nurses was racist', *The Herald*, 27 November 1996.
21 Interview with Diane Abbott, 14 December 2017.
22 Interview with Diane Abbott, 17 May 2018.
23 Ian Adams, *Ideology and Politics in Britain Today* (Manchester: Manchester University Press, 1999), p. 144.
24 Rob Sewell, *In the Cause of Labour: History of British Trade Unionism* (London: Wellred Books, 2003), p. 368.
25 James E. Cronin, *New Labour's Pasts: The Labour Party and Its Discontents* (Harlow: Pearson, 2004), p. 383.
26 "'Defining moment" as Blair wins backing for Clause IV', *The Independent*, 14 March 1995.
27 Ibid.
28 Interview with Diane Abbott, 14 December 2017.
29 Steven Fielding, *The Labour Party: Continuity and Change in the Making of New Labour* (Basingstoke: Palgrave, 2003), p. 77.
30 Andrew Roth, 'Diane (Julia) Abbott', Parliamentary Profiles, Bishopsgate Institute, http://internetserver.bishopsgate.org.uk/files/Parliamentary%20Profiles%20Archive/A-D%5CABBOTT,%20Diane/ABBOTT,%20Diane.pdf (accessed July 2020).
31 Philip Webster, 'Mandelson learns "touch of humility"', *The Times*, 30 September 1997.
32 *The Sun*, 18 March 1997.
33 Colin Brown, 'Short hits at "dark forces" behind Blair', *The Independent*, 8 August 1996.
34 Interview with Diane Abbott, 14 December 2017.
35 Ibid.
36 'Election '97 results', *The Times*, 3 May 1997.
37 John Charmley, *A History of Conservative Politics Since 1830* (Basingstoke: Palgrave Macmillan, 2008), p. 254.
38 'A political earthquake', *The Guardian*, 2 May 1997.
39 D. Kavanagh and A. Seldon, *The Powers Behind the Prime Minister: The Hidden Influence of Number Ten* (London: HarperCollins, 1999), p. 245.
40 Alastair Campbell, *Diaries: Volume Three: Power and Responsibility* (London: Hutchinson, 2011), p. 385.
41 Alastair Campbell, *Diaries: Volume One: Prelude to Power, 1994–1997* (London: Hutchinson, 2010), p. 477.
42 'Campbell's top spins', *The Guardian*, 29 August 2003.
43 Simon Jeffery, 'Alastair Campbell: highs and lows', *The Guardian*, 29 August 2003.
44 *The Guardian*, 8 August 2001.
45 Philip Webster, 'Mandelson learns "touch of humility"', *The Times*, 30 September 1997 and David Boothroyd, 'The Labour Party Elections 1998', United Kingdom Election Results, www.election.demon.co.uk (accessed July 2020).
46 'Labour rebel attacks "Boy's Own" reshuffle', BBC News, 28 July 1998.
47 Interview with Diane Abbott, 14 December 2017.

48 Valerie Grove, 'I'm Top Shop Girl, all through', *The Times*, 30 May 1997.
49 'Office Politics', *The Times*, 28 May 1997.
50 Interview with Diane Abbott, 14 December 2017.
51 William Rees-Mogg, 'Why Tory Meldrews are such a turn-off', *The Times*, 9 March 2001.
52 Interview with Diane Abbott, 14 December 2017.
53 Ibid.
54 Ibid.
55 'Abbott to Lose Place on Treasury Select Committee', BBC News, 21 March 1997.
56 Interview with Nick Brown.
57 Interview with Diane Abbott, 14 December 2017.
58 Ibid.
59 Hansard, House of Commons debate, 18 May 1998, vol. 312, c. 636.
60 Ibid., c. 611.
61 'Arms-to-Africa: "Minister knew of Customs probe"', BBC News, 9 June 1998.
62 'Foreign Affairs – Second Report', Foreign Affairs Committee, February 1999, https://publications.parliament.uk/pa/cm199899/cmselect/cmfaff/116/11602.htm (accessed June 2020).
63 Hansard, House of Commons debate, 18 May 1998, vol. 312, c. 633.
64 Ibid, 2 March 1999, vol. 326, c. 922.
65 David Hencke, 'MPs demand full enquiry into plot to smear Cook', *The Guardian*, 17 March 1999.
66 Interview with Diane Abbott, 14 December 2017.
67 Ibid.
68 Interview with Meg Hillier, 10 December 2018.
69 Interview with Keith Vaz, 21 February 2018.
70 Interview with Diane Abbott, 14 December 2017.
71 Ibid.
72 'Blair suffers in benefits revolt', BBC News, 11 December 1997.
73 Ibid.
74 Hansard, House of Commons debate, 16 March 1998, vol. 308, c. 1035.
75 Hansard, House of Commons debate, 28 January 1994, vol. 236, c. 561. John McDonnell in Simon Hannah, *A Party with Socialists in It: A History of the Labour Left* (London: Pluto Press, 2018), p. xi.
76 Diane Abbott, 'The Case against the Maastricht Model of Central Bank Independence', in Mark Baimbridge, Brian Burkitt and Philip Whyman (eds), *The Impact of the Euro: Debating Britain's Future* (Basingstoke: Macmillan, 2000), pp. 226–31.
77 Hansard, House of Commons debate, 11 June 1997, vol. 295, c. 1055.
78 Hansard, House of Commons debate, 11 November 1997, vol. 300, c. 765.
79 Hansard, House of Commons debate, 26 October 1998, vol. 320, c. 62.
80 Ibid, 17 July 2001, vol. 372, c. 36WH.
81 Ibid.
82 Interview with Charles Clarke 27 February 2019.
83 Interview with Diane Abbott, 14 December 2017.
84 Alastair Campbell, *Diaries: Volume Three*, p. 220.
85 Ibid.
86 Interview with Diane Abbott, 14 December 2017.
87 Ibid.
88 Interview with Ken Livingstone, 30 May 2018.
89 Interview with Diane Abbott, 14 December 2017.
90 Interview with David Lammy, 13 July 2018.
91 Interview with Diane Abbott, 14 December 2017.
92 Interview with David Lammy.
93 Interview with Diane Abbott, 14 December 2017.
94 Andrew Roth, 'Diane (Julia) Abbott'.

CHAPTER 9: DEFENDER OF LIBERTIES

1   Hansard, House of Commons debate, 29 January 2003, c. 264WH.
2   Anthony Rampton, 'West Indian Children in Our Schools', Committee of Inquiry into the Education of Children from Ethnic Minority Groups, June 1981.
3   Kaushika Amin, *Black and Ethnic Minority Young People and Educational Disadvantage* (Runnymede Trust, 1997).
4   'Raising the attainment of minority ethnic pupils', OFSTED, 1999.
5   Diane Abbott, 'Teachers are failing black boys', *The Observer*, 6 January 2002.
6   'Misspent Youth: Young People and Crime', Audit Commission, 1996.
7   Written evidence, Select Committee for Home Affairs, 22 May 2007.
8   'Priority Review: Exclusion of Black Pupils "Getting it. Getting it right"', Department for Education and Skills, September 2006.
9   Diane Abbott, 'Teachers are failing black boys'.
10 'Towards a Vision of Black Excellence', London Schools and the Black Child Awards 2002, Conference Report (Greater London Authority, March 2003), www.blackeducation.info/upload/docs (accessed July 2020).
11 Diane Abbott, 'Teachers are failing black boys'.
12 Interview with Diane Abbott, 7 June 2019.
13 Diane Abbott, 'Teachers are failing black boys'.
14 Interview with Gus John, 20 March 2018.
15 'Towards a Vision of Black Excellence', London Schools and the Black Child Awards 2002, Conference Report.
16 Diane Abbott, London Schools and the Black Child II, 10 May 2003.
17 Ibid.
18 Stephen Twigg, London Schools and the Black Child II, 10 May 2003.
19 Interview with Stephen Twigg, 21 May 2020.
20 Leon Tikly, Jo Haynes, Chamion Caballero, David Gillborn and John Hill, 'Evaluation of Aiming High: African Caribbean Achievement Project', Department for Education, 2006.
21 Interview with Stephen Twigg.
22 Stephen Twigg, London Schools and the Black Child II, 10 May 2003.
23 Interview with Stephen Twigg.
24 Lauri Johnson and Rosemary Campbell-Stephens, 'Investing in Diversity in London Schools: Leadership Preparation for Black and Global Majority Educators', *Urban Education* (November 2010), vol. 45, no. 6, p. 842.
25 Ibid., p. 847.
26 Interview with Diane Abbott, 7 June 2019.
27 Ibid.
28 Interview with Gus John.
29 Ibid.
30 Ibid.
31 Diane Abbott, London Schools and the Black Child VI, 7 February 2009.
32 Ibid.
33 Boris Johnson, London Schools and the Black Child VI, 7 February 2009.
34 Interview with Diane Abbott, 7 June 2019.
35 Boris Johnson, London Schools and the Black Child VI.
36 Andy McSmith, 'Boris boasts on radio: "I'm down with the ethnics"', *The Independent*, 18 April 2008.
37 Marc Wadsworth, 'McGrath's gaffe', *The Guardian*, 23 June 2008.
38 Tony Sewell, 'Racism is not the problem', *The Guardian*, 5 September 2008.
39 Tony Sewell, 'The Mayor's Education Inquiry Final Report', Mayor of London, October 2012.
40 London Schools Excellence Fund, 'Self-Evaluation Toolkit Final Report', September 2015.
41 David Charter, 'Head defends MP's choice of school', *The Times*, 3 November 2003.
42 Jane Shilling, 'Welcome to the real world', *The Times*, 31 October 2003.

43 Glen Owen, 'Abbott's son counters hypocrite accusation', *The Times*, 29 October 2003.
44 Patrick Wintour, 'Abbott defends indefensible in sending son to private school', *The Guardian*, 1 November 2003.
45 Adam Lusher, 'Private school may well cost me my seat, admits Abbott', *Daily Telegraph*, 2 November 2003.
46 Matthew Tempest, 'Abbott defiant in private school row', *The Guardian*, 5 November 2003.
47 Patrick Wintour, 'Abbott's school choice a kick in the teeth for teachers, says Labour MP', *The Guardian*, 4 November 2003.
48 Michele Kirsch, 'Why black boys fail? Don't ask me', *The Times*, 10 September 2004.
49 *Sunday Mirror* interview cited in Charles Begley, 'Abbott says choice of school is a race issue', *The Independent*, 2 November 2003.
50 Kwame Kwei-Armah, 'Is what Diane Abbott did really so bad?', *The Guardian*, 4 November 2003.
51 Lauri Johnson and Rosemary Campbell-Stephens, 'Investing in Diversity in London Schools, p. 845.
52 'Blair defends Diane Abbott', *Evening Standard*, 5 November 2003.
53 William Diaz, 'Diane Abbott disgraces Labour', *The Guardian*, 2 November 2003.
54 Michael Rosen, 'Education: Dear Diane Abbott…', *Socialist Review* (2003), Issue 280.
55 Diane Abbott, 'Education: Dear Michael Rosen…', *Socialist Review* (2004), Issue 283.
56 Libby Purves, 'Why Diane Abbott made the right decision', *The Times*, 4 November 2003.
57 'Diane Abbott: I sent my son to private school so he wouldn't end up in a gang', *Daily Mirror*, 21 June 2010.
58 Interview with Diane Abbott, 7 June 2019.
59 Interview with Meg Hillier.
60 Interview with Diane Abbott, 7 June 2019.
61 Hansard, House of Commons debate, 1 November 2001, vol. 374, c. 1079.
62 'Brits 45 mins from doom', *The Sun*, 25 September 2002 and 'Mad Saddam ready to attack: 45 minutes from a chemical war', *Daily Star*, 25 September 2002.
63 Greg Hurst, 'Blair vows to take on North Korea next', *The Times*, 30 January 2003.
64 Interview with Diane Abbott, 7 June 2019.
65 Ibid.
66 John Chilcot, *Chilcot Report: Executive Summary* (London: Canbury Press, 2016), p. 540.
67 Hansard, House of Commons debate, Wednesday 9 June 2004, c. 69WH.
68 Ibid.
69 Diane Abbott, 'Food aid is not enough – we must act now to halt the rape of Darfur', *The Times*, 21 July 2004.
70 Hansard, House of Commons debate, 5 June 2007, vol. 461, c. 191.
71 Paul Whiteley, Harold D. Clarke, David Sanders, Marianne C. Stewart, *Affluence, Austerity and Electoral Change in Britain* (Cambridge, 2014), pp. 23–53.
72 Diane Abbott, 'Forget Blair's babes, it's the return of the heavy mob'. *The Times*, 13 February 2005.
73 Hugh Muir, 'Galloway claims Labour tried to rig Bow election', *The Guardian*, 9 June 2005.
74 Shami Chakrabarti, *On Liberty* (London: Penguin, 2015), pp. 26, 29.
75 'Justice report: Secret evidence', *Justice* (June 2009), https://justice.org.uk/wp-content/uploads/2015/07/Secret-Evidence-10-June-2009.pdf (accessed June 2020).
76 Interview with Shami Chakrabarti, 20 March 2019.
77 Jon Gaunt cited in Shami Chakrabarti, 'Why I'm defending the shock-jock who branded me "dangerous"', *The Guardian*, 27 November 2008.
78 Shami Chakrabarti, *On Liberty*, p. 7.
79 Interview with Shami Chakrabarti.
80 Ibid.
81 Boris Johnson, 'Just don't call it war', *The Spectator*, 16 July 2005.
82 Elaine Sciolino and Don van Natta Jr, 'For a decade, London thrived as a busy crossroads of terror', *New York Times*, July 10, 2005.

83 Interview with Diane Abbott, 7 June 2019.
84 Rachel North, 'We are each other's best security', *The Guardian*, 11 July 2008.
85 Interview with Diane Abbott, 7 June 2019.
86 Ibid.
87 Diane Abbott, 'Beware of Blair's fervour', *Evening Standard*, 9 November 2005.
88 Diane Abbott, 'What we in Labour really fear now', *The Times*, 10 May 2006.
89 'Blair set for Cabinet reshuffle', BBC News, 5 May 2006.
90 Rachel Sylvester, Alice Thomson and Toby Helm, 'Clarke attack on Brown "the deluded control freak"', *Daily Telegraph*, 9 September 2006.
91 'Nineteenth Report from The Joint Committee on Human Rights Session', 2006–07 Hl Paper, 157, HC 394.
92 Interview with Diane Abbott, 7 June 2019.
93 Ibid.
94 'Diane Abbott's 42-days speech', *The Guardian*, 12 June 2008.
95 Hansard, House of Commons debate, 11 June 2008, vol. 483, c. 379.
96 Ibid.
97 Shami Chakrabarti, *On Liberty*, p. 68, and interview with Shami Chakrabarti.
98 Hansard, House of Lords, 8 July 2008, vol. 478, c. 647.
99 Ibid.
100 Interview with Shami Chakrabarti.
101 Ibid.
102 Interview with Diane Abbott, 7 June 2019.
103 Interview with Shami Chakrabarti.
104 Interview with Andy Burnham, 22 November 2018.
105 Interview with Shami Chakrabarti.
106 Interview with Diane Abbott, 7 June 2019.
107 Jon Swaine, 'Gordon Brown hails £500 billion bank rescue plan' *Daily Telegraph*, 8 October 2008.
108 Ibid.
109 Hansard, House of Commons debate, 21 January 2009, vol. 486, c. 745.
110 Hansard, House of Commons debate, 18 March 2009, vol. 48p, c. 901.
111 Patrick Wintour and Nicholas Watt, 'Brown: I should have done more to prevent bank crisis', *The Guardian*, 17 March 2009.
112 'Diane Abbott: You ask the questions', *The Independent*, 8 February 2010.
113 *This Week*, BBC One, 19 March 2009.
114 Diane Abbott, 'G20 vision of hope', *Hackney Gazette*, 3 April 2009.
115 Aditya Chakrabortty, 'Gordon Brown did not save the world but he saved the UK', *The Guardian*, 6 February 2012.
116 Andrew Rawnsley, 'The weekend Gordon Brown saved the banks from the abyss', *The Observer*, 21 February 2010.
117 Diane Abbott, 'G20 vision of hope', *Hackney Gazette*, 3 April 2009.
118 Interview with Diane Abbott, 7 June 2019.

CHAPTER 10: SOFAS, SOUNDBITES AND CELEBRITY

1 Interview with Diane Abbott, 17 May 2018.
2 Jason Deans and Claire Cozens, 'A new manifesto for viewers', *The Guardian*, 19 September 2002.
3 Interview with Samir Shah, 26 May 2020.
4 Michael Gove, *Michael Portillo: The Future of the Right* (London: Fourth Estate, 1995), p. 207.
5 Interview with Diane Abbott, 17 May 2018.
6 Diane Abbott, 'Diane Abbott bids farewell to Andrew Neil's flagship programme This Week', *New Statesman*, 21 February 2019.
7 Ibid.

8   Interview with Samir Shah.
9   Ibid.
10 *This Week*, BBC One, 21 February 2008.
11 Diane Abbott, 'Diane Abbott bids farewell to Andrew Neil's flagship programme This Week'.
12 Andrew Williams, '60 SECONDS: Diane Abbott', *The Metro*, 18 April 2007.
13 Interview with Diane Abbott, 17 May 2018.
14 Ibid.
15 *This Week*, BBC One, 24 June 2010.
16 Ibid.
17 *Richard Bacon*, BBC Radio 5 Live, 11 January 2011.
18 Interview with Diane Abbott, 17 May 2018.
19 Ibid.
20 Interview with Samir Shah.
21 *The Big Questions*, BBC One, 30 December 2007.
22 'Top 100 most influential left-wingers: 50–26', *Daily Telegraph*, 29 September 2010.
23 Interview with Samir Shah.
24 Ibid.
25 Interview with Bell Ribeiro-Addy, 22 August 2018.
26 Interview with Samir Shah.
27 Josh Halliday, 'BBC Trust finds broadcaster breached rules over fees for MP Diane Abbott', *The Guardian*, 30 August 2012.
28 'Expense claims: Lord Laid most expensive peer', BBC News, 11 December 2009.
29 Claire Newell, Holly Watt and Daniel Foggo, 'Lord suggests best way to "bribe" colleagues', *Daily Telegraph*, 2 June 2013.
30 Interview with Diane Abbott, 17 May 2018.
31 Ibid.
32 Diane Abbott, 'Diane Abbott bids farewell to Andrew Neil's flagship programme This Week'.
33 Interview with Diane Abbott, 17 May 2018.
34 Ibid.
35 *The Art of Parliament*, BBC Radio 4, 17 October 2007.
36 Ibid.
37 Interview with Diane Abbott, 17 May 2018.
38 Ibid.
39 Ibid.
40 *Desert Island Discs*, BBC Radio 4, 23 May 2008.
41 *Celebrity Come Dine with Me*, Channel 4, 10 January 2011.
42 'No votes for Diane Abbott's cooking as she competes in Celebrity Come Dine With Me', *Hackney Gazette*, 11 January 2011.
43 Ibid.

CHAPTER 11: 'IF NOT NOW, WHEN? IF NOT ME, WHO?'

1   Jonathan Freedland, 'Leaders' TV debate: "I agree with Nick" was the night's real catchphrase', *The Guardian*, 16 April 2010.
2   *The First Election Debate*, ITV1, 15 April 2010.
3   Interview with Diane Abbott, 31 July 2018.
4   Ibid.
5   *This Week*, BBC One, 20 May 2010.
6   Paul Revoir, 'Diane Abbott in race row after calling Cameron and Clegg "two posh white boys"', *Daily Mail*, 23 May 2010.
7   Interview with Diane Abbott, 31 July 2018.
8   Ibid.
9   Interview with David Lammy, 13 July 2018.
10 Interview with Keith Vaz, 21 February 2018.

11 *ITV News*, ITV, 20 May 2010.
12 Interview with Diane Abbott, 31 July 2018.
13 Interview with Jeremy Corbyn, 11 March 2020.
14 Ibid.
15 Interview with David Lammy.
16 David Bebber, 'Ed Balls says he's the one to lead new Labour to victory', *The Times*, 5 June 2010.
17 *Woman's Hour*, BBC Radio 4, 29 May 2010.
18 Interview with Stephen Twigg, 21 May 2020.
19 Interview with Meg Hillier, 10 December 2018.
20 Hélène Mulholland and Allegra Stratton, 'John McDonnell withdraws from Labour leadership race in favour of Diane Abbott', *The Guardian*, 9 June 2010.
21 Interview with David Lammy.
22 Interview with Ronnie Campbell 23 August 2018.
23 Interview with Ronnie Campbell.
24 Interview with Diane Abbott, 31 July 2018.
25 Interview with David Lammy.
26 Interview with Diane Abbott, 31 July 2018.
27 Interview with David Lammy.
28 Interview with Diane Abbott, 31 July 2018.
29 *BBC News at One*, BBC One, 9 June 2010.
30 James Chapman, 'David Miliband accused of helping Diane Abbott into Labour leadership race to damage his brother's chances', *Daily Mail*, 10 June 2010.
31 Interview with Diane Abbott, 31 July 2018.
32 Peter Dorey and Andrew Denham, '"O, brother, where art thou?" The Labour Party leadership election of 2010', *British Politics* (September 2011), vol. 6, no. 3, pp. 286–316.
33 'Diane Abbott: "I'm the only candidate who's not a continuity candidate"', interview with Polly Toynbee, *The Guardian*, 11 August 2010, YouTube, https://www.youtube.com/watch?v=rMROqV2zlm4 (accessed July 2020).
34 Interview with Andy Burnham, 22 November 2018.
35 Diane Abbott, Labour leadership debate, *New Statesman* and CND, 9 June 2010, footage of the debate is available here: https://www.youtube.com/watch?v=NLn2aJAXNa8 (accessed July 2020).
36 Interview with Diane Abbott, 31 July 2018.
37 Ibid.
38 Sophia Rosenfeld, *Democracy and Truth: A Short History* (Pennsylvania: University of Pennsylvania Press, 2018), pp. 115–35.
39 Interview with Bell Ribeiro-Addy, 22 August 2018.
40 Ed Balls, Sky News hustings, Norwich, 5 September 2010.
41 Andy Burnham, Sky News hustings, Norwich, 5 September 2010.
42 David Miliband, Sky News hustings, Norwich, 5 September 2010.
43 Diane Abbott, Ed Balls, Andy Burnham, David Miliband and Ed Miliband, 'The Labour Leadership: How Important is it that the Party has a distinctive ideology?', Fabian Society, 2010, p. 5.
44 Ibid., p. 6.
45 'Diane Abbott: "I'm the only candidate who's not a continuity candidate"'.
46 *Question Time*, BBC Two, 16 September 2010.
47 Ibid.
48 Interview with Diane Abbott, 31 July 2018.
49 Owen Bowcott, Hugh Muir and Allegra Stratton, 'David Miliband well ahead on cash for Labour leadership fight', *The Guardian*, 23 July 2010.
50 Interview with Andy Burnham.
51 Interview with Diane Abbott, 31 July 2018.

52 Interview with Andy Burnham.
53 Interview with Diane Abbott, 31 July 2018.
54 Interview with Andy Burnham.
55 Interview with Jeremy Corbyn.
56 Dorey and Denham, "'O, brother, where art thou?'".
57 Interview with Keith Vaz.
58 Ed Balls, Sky News hustings, Norwich, 5 September 2010.
59 David Bebber, 'Ed Balls says he's the one to lead new labour to victory', *The Times*, 5 June 2010.
60 Interview with Jeremy Corbyn.

CHAPTER 12: CON-DEM NATION
1   Interview with Diane Abbott, 31 July 2018.
2   Anthony Seldon and Mike Finn (eds), *The Coalition Effect, 2010–2015* (Cambridge: Cambridge University Press, 2015), p. 531.
3   Diane Abbott, 'Ed Miliband has won over his Blairite critics. Now he must win over the public', *The Observer*, 25 September 2011.
4   Andrew Porter and Robert Winnett, 'Ed Miliband: New Labour is dead', *Daily Telegraph*, 26 September 2010.
5   Hugh Pemberton and Mark Wickham-Jones, 'Labour's lost grassroots: The rise and fall of party membership', *British Politics* (December 2013), vol. 8(2), pp. 181–206.
6   Peter Hain, 'Refounding Labour: A party for the new generation', The Labour Party, March 2011.
7   Tim Bale, *Five Year Mission: The Labour Party Under Ed Miliband* (Oxford: Oxford University Press, 2015), p. 74.
8   Interview with Bell Ribeiro-Addy, 22 August 2018.
9   Tim Bale, *Five Year Mission*, p. 99.
10 Diane Abbott, 'Ed Miliband has won over his Blairite critics'.
11 Diane Abbott, 'Diane urges caution on graduate tax', 15 July 2010, https://www.dianeabbott.org.uk/news/news/press/item612 (accessed July 2020).
12 Sean Coughlan, 'Vince Cable ditches graduate tax option for England', BBC News, 9 October 2010.
13 Nicholas Watt, 'Revealed: Lib Dems planned before election to abandon tuition fees pledge', *The Guardian*, 12 November 2010.
14 Diane Abbott, lecture given at Liverpool John Moores University, 7 November 2012.
15 Ibid.
16 Hansard, House of Commons debate, 3 November 2010, vol. 517, cc. 308WH–310WH.
17 Interview with Diane Abbott, 31 July 2018.
18 Matthew Taylor, Paul Lewis and Peter Walker, 'Student protest largely peaceful despite the images', *The Guardian*, 24 November 2010.
19 'Diane condemns Lib-Con's slashing of school funding', London Schools and the Black Child, 12 July 2010, http://3782-28669.el-alt.com/news/press/news.aspx?p=102581 (accessed July 2020).
20 Ibid.
21 Anthony Seldon and Mike Finn (eds), *The Coalition Effect*, p. 264.
22 'New academies plan with bring chaos, says MPs', *Hackney Citizen*, 6 August 2010.
23 Interview with David Lammy, 13 July 2018.
24 Interview with Diane Abbott, 31 July 2018.
25 Nicholas Timmins, *Never Again? The Story of the Health and Social Care Act 2012: A Study in Coalition Government and Policy Making* (London: The Institute for Government and the King's Fund, 2012).
26 Hansard, House of Commons debate, 12 July 2010, vol. 513, cc. 664–5.
27 Clive Peedell, 'Further privatisation is inevitable under the proposed NHS reforms' *British Medical Journal* (2011), vol. 342, issue 7807.
28 Nicholas Timmins, *Never Again?*.

29 Press Association, 'NHS shakeup spells "unprecedented chaos", warns Lancet editor', *The Guardian*, 24 March 2012.

30 Interview with Diane Abbott, 31 July 2018.

31 Hélène Mulholland, 'Government to "pause, listen, reflect and improve" NHS reform plans', *The Guardian*, 6 April 2011.

32 Sam Lister, 'NHS private income cap to be lifted', *The Independent*, 27 December 2011.

33 Interview with Andy Burnham, 22 November 2018.

34 Interview with Diane Abbott, 31 July 2018.

35 Ibid.

36 Randeep Ramesh and Denis Campbell, 'Royal medical colleges toughen stance against NHS reforms', *The Guardian*, 25 January 2012.

37 'Labour increases its lead on healthcare and education', Ipsos MORI, 28 September 2012, https://www.ipsos.com/ipsos-mori/en-uk/labour-increases-its-lead-healthcare-and-education (accessed July 2020).

38 'Statistics on Obesity, Physical Activity and Diet – England, 2010', NHS Digital, 10 February 2010, https://digital.nhs.uk/data-and-information/publications/statistical/statistics-on-obesity-physical-activity-and-diet/statistics-on-obesity-physical-activity-and-diet-england-2010 (accessed July 2020).

39 Ibid.

40 Maeve McClenaghan, 'Analysis: Unhealthy Friendships with the Department of Health', The Bureau of Investigative Journalism, 25 November 2011.

41 'Twelfth report of session 2010–12', Health Select Committee, vol. 1, p. 6.

42 Diane Abbott, Policy Exchange speech, 12 May 2012.

43 Deirdre Osborne, 'Determination, Dedication, Dynamism: An Interview with Diane Abbott', *Women: A Cultural Review* (2013), vol. 24, pp. 169–78.

44 Patrick Wintour, 'Diane Abbott outlines plan to curb fast food shops', *The Guardian*, 3 January 2013.

45 Diane Abbott, Policy Exchange speech.

46 Patrick Wintour, 'Diane Abbott outlines plan to curb fast food shops'.

47 Diane Abbott, Policy Exchange speech.

48 Ibid.

49 'Families encouraged to eat healthily on the cheap', BBC News, 2 January 2012 and Sean O'Hare, 'Government blasted for spending £2m on Morph-style Change4Life health adverts that warn against fast food', *Daily Mail*, 7 January 2013.

50 Diane Abbott, Policy Exchange speech.

51 Diane Abbott, 'Why I'm marching at a pro-choice rally', *The Guardian*, 8 July 2011.

52 Sarah Boseley, 'Quarter of UK women had underage sex, report finds', *The Guardian*, 15 December 2011.

53 Diane Abbott, 'Fabian Women's Network speech – the sexualisation of women and girls in British society', 24 January 2013.

54 Lorraine Radford et al., 'Child abuse and neglect in the UK today', NSPCC, 2011.

55 'YouGov Poll Exposes High Levels Sexual Harassment in Schools', End Violence Against Women, 2010.

56 Ibid.

57 Sarah Boseley, 'Diane Abbott resigns from abortion counselling working group', *The Guardian*, 26 January 2012.

58 Interview with Andy Burnham.

59 Interview with David Lammy.

60 Interview with Meg Hillier, 10 December 2018.

61 Rosemary Campbell-Stephens, London Schools and the Black Child conference, 1 June 2013, Institute of Education, London.

62 Ibid.

63 John Paul Ford-Rojas, 'David Cameron challenged to take part in "Indian dance" class', *Daily Telegraph*, 10 August 2012.
64 Rosemary Campbell-Stephens, London Schools and the Black Child conference.
65 'The Riots', interview with Diane Abbott, British Library, 26 September 2011.
66 Ibid.
67 *Newsnight*, BBC Two, 12 August 2011.
68 Allegra Stratton, 'David Cameron on riots: broken society is top of my political agenda', *The Guardian*, 15 August 2011.
69 'The Riots', interview with Diane Abbott.
70 'Diane Abbott: A tinder box waiting to explode', *The Independent*, 8 August 2011.
71 'Diane Abbott slams David Cameron for blaming gangs for riots', London Schools and the Black Child, 24 October 2011, http://www.blackeducation.info/news/press/news.aspx?p=102590 (accessed July 2020).
72 Interview with Diane Abbott, 31 July 2018.
73 'The Riots', interview with Diane Abbott.
74 'England riots: Who's been prosecuted?', BBC News, 4 July 2012.
75 'The Riots', interview with Diane Abbott.
76 'Nick Clegg: Diane Abbott "has been stupid and crass"', *Daily Telegraph*, 5 January 2012 and Andrew Sparrow, 'Diane Abbott apologises over Twitter racism row', *The Guardian*, 5 January 2012.
77 Interview with Diane Abbott, 31 July 2018.
78 Interview with Meg Hillier.
79 Interview with Diane Abbott, 31 July 2018.
80 Polly Curtis, 'Budget 2010: Public sector faces deepest ever spending cuts', *The Guardian*, 22 June 2010.
81 Hansard, House of Commons debate, 22 June 2010, vol. 512, col. 182.
82 'Intersecting inequalities: The impact of austerity on Black and Minority Ethnic women in the UK', Women's Budget Group and Runnymede Trust, 10 October 2017.
83 Anthony Seldon and Mike Finn (eds), *The Coalition Effect*, p. 316.
84 Nick Triggle, 'Life expectancy rises "grinding to halt" in England', BBC News, 18 July 2017.
85 Vince Cable, 'When the facts change, should I change my mind?', *New Statesman*, 6 March 2013.
86 Andrew Grice, 'David Cameron and Vince Cable at war over route to recovery', *The Independent*, 6 March 2013.
87 Interview with Diane Abbott, 31 July 2018.
88 'Full Transcript: Ed Miliband Speech on a new economy', *New Statesman*, 17 November 2011.
89 Phil Mason and Matthew Parris, *Is That Mic Off? More Things Politicians Wish They Hadn't Said* (London: The Robson Press, 2012).
90 Tim Bale, *Five Year Mission*, p. 40.
91 Nick Collins, 'Alan Johnson: what they said', *Daily Telegraph*, 21 January 2011.
92 Ed Balls, 'Why Labour won't stop talking about the cost of living crisis', *The Guardian*, 14 April 2014.
93 Diane Abbott, 'Labour is doomed if it buys into Tory austerity, so let's spell out an alternative', *The Guardian*, 16 April 2014.
94 Tom Clark, Rowena Mason and Katie Allen, 'Support for Tories falls three points after post-budget bounce', *The Guardian*, 14 April 2014.
95 Diane Abbott, 'How Labour can prevent core voters defecting to UKIP', *The Guardian*, 10 October 2014.
96 'Labour conference: Ed Miliband speech in full', *The Guardian*, 28 September 2010.
97 Interview with Diane Abbott, 31 July 2018.
98 Harriet Brewis, 'UKIP MEP candidate Carl Benjamin says "Personally I find racist jokes funny" after offensive video is uncovered', *Evening Standard*, 26 April 2019.

99 Ros Taylor, 'Cameron refuses to apologise to UKIP', *The Guardian*, 4 April 2006.

100 Interview with Diane Abbott, 31 July 2018.

101 Matthew Taylor, Mirren Gidda and Rajeev Syal, '"Go home" ad campaign targeting illegal immigrants face court challenge', *The Guardian*, 26 July 2013.

102 David Shariatmadari, Alice Salfield and Andy Gallagher, 'Diane Abbott: "Blur Labour is a blind alley" – video', *The Guardian*, 1 August 2011.

103 Diane Abbott, 'How Labour can prevent core voters defecting to UKIP', *The Guardian*, 10 October 2014.

104 Diane Abbott, 'There must be no right turn on immigration', *New Statesman*, 5 March 2013.

105 Rajeev Syal, 'Diane Abbott warns Labour on immigration', *The Guardian*, 21 April 2013.

106 @HackneyAbbott, 27 August 2013.

107 Diane Abbott, 'Diane Abbott voices opposition to Syria intervention', *The Guardian*, 27 August 2013.

108 Tamara Cohen, 'Miliband "slams into reverse gear"', *Daily Mail*, 28 August 2013.

109 Interview with Diane Abbott, 31 July 2018.

110 *5 News*, Channel 5, 28 August 2013.

111 Abbott, 'Diane Abbott voices opposition to Syria intervention'.

112 Interview with Diane Abbott, 31 July 2018.

113 Interview with Andy Burnham.

114 Interview with Jeremy Corbyn, 11 March 2020.

115 Interview with Nick Brown, 26 October 2018.

116 Press Association, 'Labour frontbencher opposed to Syria military action "full stop" resigns', *The Guardian*, 29 August 2013.

117 Interview with Bell Ribeiro-Addy.

118 Tim Bale, *Five Year Mission*, p. 190.

119 Nicholas Watt and Nick Hopkins, 'Syria divisions laid bare as Tories savage Ed Miliband', *The Guardian*, 29 August 2013.

120 Sidoine Chaffer-Melly, 'Labour tells new health spokeswoman to drop her support for homeopathy', *The Independent*, 13 October 2013.

121 Michael White, 'Ed Miliband and Diane Abbott: better to keep your enemies close?', *The Guardian*, 9 October 2013.

122 Interview with Diane Abbott, 31 July 2018.

123 Ibid.

124 'Home Secretary launches consultation into stop and search', Home Office, 2 July 2013, https://www.gov.uk/government/news/home-secretary-launches-consultation-into-stop-and-search (accessed July 2020).

125 Hansard, House of Commons debate, 2 July 2013, vol. 565, col. 773.

126 Member of Diane Abbott's constituency team, 23 July 2020.

127 Nicholas Cecil, 'Diane Abbott is Labour voters' choice for Mayor of London, poll reveals', *The Evening Standard*, 23 June 2014.

128 Interview with Bell Ribeiro-Addy.

129 *ITV News London*, ITV, 30 November 2014.

130 Dave Hill, 'Diane Abbott: defending Hackney North with half an eye on City Hall', *The Guardian*, 28 April 2015.

131 Diane Abbott, London School of Economics speech, 22 October 2014.

132 Dave Hill, 'Diane Abbott: defending Hackney North with half an eye on City Hall'.

133 Maya Goodfellow, 'Diane Abbott: "Londoners want a Mayor who is not just directed by party bosses"', *LabourList*, 3 March 2015.

134 Stephen Bush, 'Student leaders back Diane Abbott for Mayor of London', *New Statesman*, 14 August 2015.

135 Interview with Bell Ribeiro-Addy, op. cit.

136 Ibid.

137 Dave Hill, 'Can Labour be stopped from winning back the London mayoralty?', *The Guardian*, 14 May 2015.
138 Claudia Webbe, 'For supporters of Jeremy Corbyn, Diane Abbott is the logical choice for Mayor of London', *LabourList*, 20 August 2015.
139 @LadPolitics, 10 September 2015.
140 Patrick Wintour, 'Sadiq Khan elected as Labour's candidate for mayor of London', *The Guardian*, 11 September 2015.
141 Interview with Bell Ribeiro-Addy.

CHAPTER 13: JEZ WE CAN!
1   Hugo Rifkind, 'It's not how you look, Ed. It's how you think', *The Times*, 29 July 2014.
2   William Jordan, 'Health overtakes immigration as an issue for voters', YouGov, 15 April 2015.
3   Daniel Jackson, Einar Thorsen, Darren Lilleker and Nathalie Weidhase (eds), 'UK Election Analysis 2019: Media, Voters and the Campaign: Early reflections from leading academics', The Centre for Comparative Politics and Media Research, December 2019, p. 13.
4   'Labour "back to 1980s" after election loss – Mandelson', BBC News, 9 May 2015.
5   Ibid.
6   Tony Blair, 'Labour must be the party of ambition as well as compassion', *The Observer*, 9 May 2015.
7   BBC News, 8 May 2015.
8   Philip Cowley and Dennis Kavanagh, *The British General Election of 2015* (Basingstoke: Palgrave Macmillan, 2016), p. 368.
9   Interview with Diane Abbott, 31 July 2018.
10 Interview with Jeremy Corbyn, 11 March 2020.
11 Interview with Diane Abbott, 31 July 2018.
12 Interview with Jeremy Corbyn.
13 Ibid.
14 Interview with John McDonnell, 26 May 2020.
15 Matt Bolton and Frederick Harry Pitts, *Corbynism: A Critical Approach* (London: Emerald, 2018), p. 296.
16 Diane Abbott, mayoral hustings, Wood Green, 24 July 2015.
17 Interview with Jeremy Corbyn.
18 '"The Policies Labour Needs to Win with Diane Abbott & Jeremy Corbyn" at the Bloomsbury Central Baptist Church, 28th July 2015', London City Nights, 29 July 2015.
19 Interview with Diane Abbott, 31 July 2018.
20 Interview with Bell Ribeiro-Addy.
21 Rowena Mason, 'If Jeremy Corbyn wins leadership Labour faces "annihilation", says Tony Blair', *The Guardian*, 13 August 2015.
22 *Drivetime*, LBC, 13 August 2015.
23 Interview with Diane Abbott, 31 July 2018.
24 'Jeremy Corbyn profile: "He talks like a human being, about things that are real"', *The Guardian*, 12 August 2015.
25 Interview with Diane Abbott, 31 July 2018.
26 Ibid.
27 Ibid.
28 George Parker and Jim Pickard, 'Jeremy Corbyn: how long can he last?', *Financial Times*, 25 September 2015.
29 Diane Abbott, Labour Party conference speech, Brighton, 28 September 2015.
30 George Parker and Jim Pickard, 'Jeremy Corbyn: how long can he last?'.
31 Rafael Behr, 'David Cameron speech at Tory conference: what he said – and what he meant', *The Guardian*, 7 October 2015.
32 Interview with Diane Abbott, 31 July 2018.

33 Ibid.
34 Ibid.
35 *Channel 4 News*, Channel 4, 2 December 2015.
36 Ibid.
37 Interview with Diane Abbott, 31 July 2018.
38 Philip Cowley and Dennis Kavanagh, *The British General Election of 2015*, p. 72.
39 Hansard, House of Commons debate, 2 December 2015, vol. 603, c. 483.
40 Interview with Diane Abbott, 31 July 2018.
41 Member of Diane Abbott's parliamentary office team, 24 July 2018.
42 Interview with John McDonnell.
43 'Diane Abbott and her Racist Black Supremacist Ideology', Kipper Central, 17 December 2016, https://kippercentral.com/2016/10/01/diane-abbott-racist-black-supremacist/ (accessed July 2020).
44 Interview with Diane Abbott, 31 July 2018.
45 Tim Shipman, *All Out War: The Full Story of Brexit* (London: William Collins, 2017), p. 64.
46 Interview with Diane Abbott, 31 July 2018.
47 *The Last Leg*, Channel 4, 11 June 2016.
48 Interview with Diane Abbott, 31 July 2018.
49 Ibid.
50 Ibid.
51 Interview with John McDonnell.
52 Ibid.
53 Interview with Diane Abbott, 31 July 2018.
54 Ibid.
55 Joe Murphy, 'Labour leadership: I'm not a Corbynista, I'm my own woman, says Angela Eagle', *Evening Standard*, 11 July 2016.
56 *Good Morning Britain*, ITV1, 11 July 2016.
57 Ibid.
58 Anoosh Chakelian, '"I've got a wife and children": Owen Smith's Andrew Leadsom moment', *New Statesman*, 18 July 2016.
59 'Labour leadership: Female MPs urge Corbyn to tackle abuse', BBC News, 22 July 2016.
60 *Today*, BBC Radio 4, 20 July 2016.
61 Interview with Diane Abbott, 31 July 2018.
62 Andy Beckett, 'The fight for Labour's soul – what the party's brutal 1981 split means today', *The Guardian*, 19 July 2016.
63 Bagehot, 'Why a "True Labour" splinter party could succeed where the SDP failed', *The Economist*, 12 August 2016.
64 Interview with Shami Chakrabarti, 20 March 2019.
65 Interview with John McDonnell, 26 May 2020.
66 Interview with Jeremy Corbyn.
67 Hansard, House of Commons debate, 14 September 2016, vol. 614, c. 948.
68 Interview with Keith Vaz, 21 February 2018.
69 Interview with Diane Abbott, 31 July 2018.
70 Ibid.
71 Interview with Jeremy Corbyn.
72 Ibid.
73 Interview with Shami Chakrabarti, 20 March 2019.
74 Conservative Party manifesto 2015, p. 73.
75 Interview with Shami Chakrabarti.
76 Member of Diane Abbott's parliamentary office team, 24 July 2018.
77 James Kirkup and Rosa Prince, 'Revealed: Jeremy Corbyn "showed off" naked Diane Abbott to impress left-wing friends', *Daily Telegraph*, 29 January 2016.
78 Katie Louise Davies, 'Jeremy Corbyn "showed off a naked Diane Abbott to impress his Left-wing activists friends" after breakdown of his first marriage', *Daily Mail*, 30 January 2016.

79 Nadeem Badshah, 'How Corbyn revealed Abbott was his lover' *The Times*, 30 January 2016.

80 Tom Bower, '"She was shocked when we entered": Jeremy Corbyn drove two friends to his flat because he WANTED them to see new girlfriend Diane Abbott naked in his bed, biography reveals', *Daily Mail*, 9 February 2019.

81 Thomas Burrows, 'CORB BLIMEY! Jeremy Corbyn "invited two left-wing friends to his flat to show off naked girlfriend Diane Abbott"', *The Sun*, 21 February 2019.

82 'Corbyn the Musical', CNBC International, 21 April 2016.

83 Interview with Keith Vaz.

84 Tom McTague, '#PrayForDiane: Labour MPs mock Corbyn ally', POLITICO, 2 February 2017.

85 Sebastian Whale, 'Diane Abbott gets grief (and get well wishes) from Labour MPs', *Total Politics*, 2 February 2017.

86 Tim Sculthorpe, James Tapsfield, Martin Robinson and Daniel Martin, 'Drinks in the Red Lion pub... then Diane Abbott gets a "migraine" and misses crucial Brexit vote', *Daily Mail*, 2 February 2017.

87 Lucy Fisher, 'Migraine is pain in neck for party', *The Times*, 6 February 2017.

88 Diane Abbott, 'Working within the Labour Party', *West Indian World*, 20 March 1985.

CHAPTER 14: FOR THE MANY, NOT THE FEW

1 *BBC News*, BBC, 18 April 2017.

2 *Channel 4 News*, Channel 4, 18 April 2017.

3 Interview with Diane Abbott, 29 February 2020.

4 *BBC News*, BBC, 18 April 2017.

5 Interview with Diane Abbott, 29 February 2020.

6 Stephen Bush, 'Nine thoughts on the local elections', *New Statesman*, 5 May 2017.

7 *The Andrew Marr Show*, BBC One, 30 April 2017.

8 'Labour fury at senior South Ribble Tory's comment on racist tweet', *Lancashire Post*, 9 February 2017.

9 'Suspended Tory admits inappropriate Diane Abbott tweet', BBC News, 10 February 2017.

10 Ibid.

11 'Black and Asian women MPs abused more online', Amnesty International UK, https://www.amnesty.org.uk/online-violence-women-mps (accessed July 2020).

12 Zoe Strimpel, 'It's not racist to point out that Diane Abbott is a bungling disappointment', *Daily Telegraph*, 6 June 2017.

13 Natasha Clark, '"DON'T LET HER HELP WITH THE MATHS HOMEWORK!" Labour's Diane Abbott mocked mercilessly after her car-crash interview round on police funding', *The Sun*, 2 May 2017.

14 *Channel 4 News*, Channel 4, 6 June 2017.

15 Danielle Dash, 'Diane Abbott & Unrelenting Misogynoir', 5 June 2017, http://www.danielledash.com/a-quick-read/dianeabbott (accessed July 2020) and Fiona Rutherford, 'Diane Abbott said the abuse she faced during the election campaign made her feel "very low"', BuzzFeed, 22 June 2017.

16 'Misogynoir' is a term created originally by Moya Bailey, a black American queer feminist. It is used to connote the ways in which racism affects the experience of misogyny by black women. See Paula Akpab, 'Diane Abbott and misogynoir: a woman scorned, a woman vindicated', gal-dem, 9 June 2017, https://gal-dem.com/diane-abbott-misogynoir-woman-scorned-woman-vindicated/ (accessed July 2020) and Jack Monroe, 'We need to talk about Diane Abbott. Now.', 7 June 2017, https://cookingonabootstrap.com/2017/06/07/we-need-to-talk-about-diane-abbott-now-explicit-content/ (accessed July 2020).

17 Tim Ross and Tom McTague, *Betting the House: The Inside Story of the 2017 Election* (London: Biteback, 2017), p. 208.

18 Tim Shipman, *Fall Out: A Year of Political Mayhem* (London: William Collins, 2017), p. 222.

19 Tom Phillips and Jim Waterson, 'Not even right-wingers are sharing positive stories about Theresa May on Facebook', BuzzFeed, 3 June 2017.

20 Jim Waterson and Emily Dugan, 'How the Conservatives are focusing their campaigning on Diane Abbott', BuzzFeed, 6 June 2017.

21 *Question Time*, BBC One, 2 June 2017.

22 Tim Shipman, *Fall Out*, p. 222.

23 Adam Payne and Adam Bienkov, 'Dianne Abbott is putting people off from voting Labour', *Business Insider*, 2 June 2017.

24 Jason Groves, 'It's a clear choice, says Theresa – me or chaos', *Daily Mail*, 6 June 2017.

25 'Labour's apologists for terror: The *Mail* accuses Corbyn troika befriending Britain's enemies and scorning the institutions that keep us safe', *Daily Mail*, 6 June 2017.

26 Tim Ross and Tom McTague's otherwise excellent *Betting the House*, to take one example, claims, 'For a time, Diane Abbott took a prominent role but disappeared from view after a series of disastrous interviews in which she failed to explain how much Labour's policy of recruiting 10,000 extra police would cost.' *Betting the House*, p. 208.

27 Matthew Norma, 'Diane Abbott is no fool – but she keeps blundering into every trap set by the Tories, and she's become a liability', *The Independent*, 28 May 2017.

28 John Crace, 'Angry Amber v Dozy Diane: conscious meets unconscious on Marr', *The Guardian*, 28 May 2017.

29 Interview with John McDonnell, 26 May 2020.

30 *Question Time*, BBC One, 31 May 2017.

31 @BBC Woman's House, 6 June 2017.

32 *Victoria Derbyshire*, BBC Two, 6 June 2017.

33 Diane Abbott, 'Making sense of what's in black and white', *The Times*, 17 April 1997.

34 Deborah Gabriel, 'The othering and objectification of Diane Abbott MP', Election Analysis, http://www.electionanalysis.uk/uk-election-analysis-2017/section-8-personality-politics-and-popular-culture/the-othering-and-objectification-of-diane-abbott-mp/ (accessed July 2020).

35 Lisa Amanda Palmer, 'Diane Abbott, misogynoir and the politics of Black British feminism's anticolonial imperatives: "In Britain too, it's as if we don't exist"', *The Sociological Review* (December 2019), vol. 63, no. 3. p. 512.

36 Ibid., p. 515.

37 Ibid.

38 Lisa Amanda Palmer is a scholar whose work is informed by writers such as Hazel Carby, Beverley Bryan, Stella Dadzie and Suzanne Scafe. In that sense she is working within the tradition of black feminism which goes back to OWAAD, and beyond, the tradition to which Abbott too belongs.

39 'Urgent statement in support of Diane Abbott MP', Operation Black Vote, 8 June 2017, https://www.obv.org.uk/news-blogs/urgent-statement-support-diane-abbott-mp (accessed July 2020).

40 Interview with Keith Vaz.

41 Ibid.

42 'The Diane Abbott Care Package', The-Dots, https://the-dots.com/projects/the-diane-abbot-care-package-234639 (accessed July 2020).

43 Chelsea Mendez, 'Diane Abbott "appreciation night" sees veteran Hackney MP honoured at Queen of Hoxton for "breaking glass ceiling"', *Hackney Gazette*, 26 June 2017.

44 Ibid., and Nadine White, '"Even Strong Black Women Cry," Diane Abbott Tells Supporters', *The Voice*, 25 June 2017.

45 Interview with Diane Abbott, 29 February 2020.

46 Chelsea Mendez, 'Diane Abbott "appreciation night" sees veteran Hackney MP honoured at Queen of Hoxton for "breaking glass ceiling"'.

47 Interview with Siana Bangura, 13 June 2020.

48 Interview with Reni Eddo-Lodge, 25 June 2020.

49 Philip Cowley and Dennis Kavanagh, *The British General Election of 2017* (Basingstoke: Palgrave Macmillan, 2018), p. 422.

50 Diane Abbott, Hackney Town Hall, 8 June 2017.

CHAPTER 15: LEVEL PEGGING

1   @jimwaterson, 9 June 2017.
2   Interview with Diane Abbott, 29 February 2020.
3   Anushka Asthana and Heather Steward, 'Diane Abbott reveals illness and hits out at "vicious" Tory campaign', *The Guardian*, 13 June 2017.
4   Ibid.
5   *PM*, BBC Radio 4, 21 June 2017.
6   Louise Donovan, 'Boris Johnson gets away with car crash interview, yet Diane Abbott is forced to step down', *Elle*, 27 June 2017.
7   @johnprescott, 21 June 2017.
8   @ChukaUmunna, 21 June 2017.
9   Reuters, 'Donald Trump: "I could shoot somebody and I wouldn't lose any voters"', *The Guardian*, 24 January 2016.
10 Interview with Diane Abbott, 29 February 2020.
11 Andrew O'Hagan, 'The Tower', *London Review of Books* (June 2018), vol. 40, no. 11.
12 Ibid.
13 Sky News, 16 June 2017.
14 *Good Morning Britain*, ITV1, 16 June 2017.
15 *Channel 4 News*, Channel 4, 31 July 2017.
16 Diane Abbott, Stand Up to Racism conference, 22 October 2017.
17 Andrew O'Hagan, 'The Tower'.
18 'Phase 1 report', Grenfell Tower Inquiry, October 2019, https://www.grenfelltowerinquiry.org.uk/phase-1-report (accessed July 2020).
19 May Bulman, 'Grenfell victims were subject to "social apartheid" in north Kensington, Labour's Diane Abbott says', *The Independent*, 13 June 2018.
20 Arthur Martin and Fionn Hargreaves, 'Far-left activist in bid to hijack Grenfell: Fire victims hit out at rabble-rousers to exploit deaths of 71', *Daily Mail*, 12 December 2017.
21 Hansard, 12 July 2017, vol. 627, cc. 158WH–159WH.
22 Ibid.
23 Steven Swinford, 'Theresa May announces independent review into "horrific" election abuse suffered by MPs', *Daily Telegraph*, 12 July 2017.
24 Kate Ferguson, 'May calls on Corbyn to condemn the "bullying and harassment" of MPs after politicians come forward to tell of the death threats and abuse they received during the election campaign', *Daily Mail*, 10 July 2017.
25 Jamie Grierson, 'Labour attacks Tories over "smear" campaign before abuse debate', *The Guardian*, 12 July 2017.
26 'Black and Asian women MPs abused more online', Amnesty International UK.
27 'Ofcom broadcast and on demand bulletin', Ofcom, 11 September 2017, pp. 23–25.
28 'Intimidation in Public Life: A Review by the Committee on Standards in Public Life', Committee on Standards in Public Life, December 2017, p. 79.
29 Zoe Drewett, 'Bookies take days to apologise for black face Diane Abbott tweet', *Metro*, 17 December 2017.
30 Theresa May', 'PM speech on standard in public life', 6 February 2018, https://www.gov.uk/government/speeches/pm-speech-on-standards-in-public-life-6-february-2018 (accessed July 2020).
31 Ibid.
32 Ibid.
33 Ibid.
34 Ibid.
35 Catherine Hall, 'Whose Memories? Edward Long and the Work of Re-Remembering', in Katie Donington, Ryan Hanley and Jessica Moody (eds), *Britain's History and Memory of Transatlantic Slavery: Local Nuances of a 'National Sin'* (Liverpool: Liverpool University Press, 2016), p. 129.
36 'Theresa May's keynote speech at Tory conference in full', *The Independent*, 5 October 2016.

37 'Diane Abbott defends Labour over anti-Semitism row', BBC News, 1 May 2016.
38 Shami Chakrabarti, 'The Shami Chakrabarti Inquiry', 20 June 2016, https://labour.org.uk/wp-content/uploads/2017/10/Chakrabarti-Inquiry-Report-30June16.pdf (accessed July 2020).
39 Daniel Boffey and Harriet Sherwood, 'Jeremy Corbyn accused of incompetence by MPs over antisemitic abuse', *The Guardian*, 16 October 2016.
40 'Intimidation in Public Life', Committee on Standard in Public Life, December 2017.
41 Pippa Crerar, 'Corbyn "sorry for hurt inflicted on Jewish people by antisemitism row"', *The Guardian*, 5 August 2018.
42 Margaret Hodge, 'I challenged Corbyn on antisemitism a year ago. Things have only got worse', *The Guardian*, 17 July 2018.
43 Interview with Diane Abbott, 19 February 2020.
44 Justin Cohen,' 'Jewish News poll: Labour now shares "nasty party" label with Tories', *Jewish News*, 22 September 2018.
45 'READ IN FULL: Theresa May's speech to the 2018 Conservative party conference', Politics Home, 3 October 2018.
46 Media Mole, 'Theresa May and Sajid Javid praise Diane Abbott – but the Tory campaign attacked her', *New Statesman*, 3 October 2018.
47 *Peston*, ITV1, 4 October 2018.
48 @HackneyAbbott, 3 October 2018.
49 Boris Johnson, 'Denmark has got it wrong. Yes, the burka is oppressive and ridiculous – but that's still no reason to ban it', *Daily Telegraph*, 5 August 2018.
50 Ibid. Notably, around 2018 the American 'alt-right' had claimed J. S. Mill as an intellectual forebear. See for example, 'What is a Classical Liberal?', The Rubin Report, https://www.youtube.com/watch?v=Bsba-dNApvw (accessed July 2020).
51 *Jeremy Vine*, BBC Radio 2, 7 March 2019.
52 @HackneyAbbott, 7 March 2019.
53 @AmberRuddUK, 7 March 2019.
54 Avtar Brah, *Cartographies of Diaspora: Contesting Identities* (London: Routledge, 2005), p. 96.
55 Ibid., p. 97.
56 S. Sayyid, 'Post-racial paradoxes: rethinking European racism and anti-racism', *Patterns of Prejudice* (January 2017), vol. 51, no. 1, pp. 9–25.
57 'Constructing alliances', *Socialist Action*, 15 November 1985, p. 5.
58 Toby Helm, 'Nick Clegg says May should go for a Norway-style trade deal', *The Guardian*, 14 January 2017.
59 Interview with Diane Abbott, 29 February 2020.
60 Ibid.
61 Interview with Shami Chakrabarti, 20 March 2019.
62 'What is immigration detention?', Association of Visitors to Immigration Detainees, http://www.aviddetention.org.uk/immigration-detention/what-immigration-detention (accessed July 2020).
63 Hansard, House of Commons debate, 14 March 2017, vol. 623, cc. 62WH–63WH.
64 Hansard, House of Commons debate, 17 June 2010, vol. 511, c. 221WH.
65 Karen McVeigh, 'Yarl's Wood children face "extreme distress", report reveals', *The Guardian*, 17 February 2010.
66 Interview with Shami Chakrabarti.
67 Jamie Grierson, 'UK prisons inspector seeks time limits on detention of migrants without trial', *The Guardian*, 11 August 2015.
68 Marchu Girma et al., 'Detained: women asylum seekers locked up in the UK', Women for Refugee Women, 29 January 2014 and 'I am Human: refugee women's experiences of detention in the UK', Women for Refugee Women, 14 January 2015.
69 'Inquiry into the use of Immigration Detention', 17 May 2016, https://detentioninquiry.com/ (accessed July 2020).
70 Stephen Shaw, 'Review into the Welfare in Detention of Vulnerable Persons', Home Office, 14 January 2016.

71 Interview with Shami Chakrabarti.
72 Ibid.
73 *Yarl's Wood: Undercover in the secretive immigration centre*, Channel 4, 2 March 2015.
74 Hansard, House of Commons debate, 6 March 2018, vol. 637, cc. 182–3.
75 'Medical Justice: Working for health rights for detainees, Annual Review, 2018–19.
76 Interview with Diane Abbott, 29 February 2020.
77 Hansard, House of Commons debate, 26 February 2018, vol. 636, c. 545.
78 Diane Abbott, 'Labour vows to end May's "hostile environment" and overhaul the UK's detention system', https://labour.org.uk/press/labour-vows-end-mays-hostile-environment-overhaul-uks-detention-system/ (accessed July 2020).
79 Wendy Williams, 'Independent Report: Windrush Lessons Learned', 19 July 2018, https://www.gov.uk/government/publications/windrush-lessons-learned-review (accessed July 2020).
80 Interview with Diane Abbott, 29 February 2020.
81 '"Deport first, appeal later" policy ruled unlawful', BBC News, 14 June 2017.
82 Diane Abbott, 'The death of Paulette Wilson must mark the end of the hostile environment', *The Guardian*, 25 July 2020.
83 David Holt, 'An inspection of the "hostile environment" measures relating to driving licences and bank accounts', Independent Chief Inspector of Borders and Immigration, October 2016.
84 Hansard, House of Commons debate, 22 October 2013, vol. 569, c. 178.
85 'Hostile environment data-sharing', Liberty, https://www.libertyhumanrights.org.uk/campaign/challenge-hostile-environment-data-sharing/ (accessed July 2020).
86 Nadia Khomami, 'Man born and raised in UK told he is not a British citizen', *The Guardian*, 29 August 2017.
87 May Bulman, 'Home Office urged to stop "harmful" immigration checks on bank accounts by more than 60 MPs and campaign groups', *The Independent*, 19 December 2017.
88 David Holt, 'An inspection of the "hostile environment" measures relating to driving licences and bank accounts'.
89 May Bulman, 'Home Office urged to stop "harmful" immigration checks on bank accounts by more than 60 MPs and campaign groups', *The Independent*, 19 December 2017.
90 Amelia Gentleman, 'Amber Rudd "sorry" for appalling treatment of Windrush-era citizens', *The Guardian*, 16 April 2018.
91 Nick Hopkins, 'Amber Rudd letter to PM reveals "ambitious but deliverable" removals target', *The Guardian*, 29 April 2018.
92 Benjamin Kentish, 'Amber Rudd summoned back to parliament for questioning as calls grow for resignation', *The Independent*, 28 April 2018.
93 Rob Merrick, 'Amber Rudd should resign over "lives ruined" by the Windrush deportation scandal, suggests Diane Abbott', *The Independent*, 18 April 2018.
94 Interview with Bell Ribeiro-Addy, 22 August 2018.
95 Ibid.
96 Wendy Williams, 'Windrush Lessons Learned Review', Home Office, 19 March 2020.
97 Diane Abbott, 'The death of Paulette Wilson must mark the end of the hostile environment'.
98 Hansard, House of Commons debate, 14 June 2018, vol. 642, c. 1180.
99 'Political polling 11th September 2018', Opinium, 16 September 2018, https://www.opinium.com/resource-center/political-polling-11th-september-2018/ (accessed July 2020).
100 'Diane Abbott's speech on Labour's plans for a simpler, fairer immigration system', 13 September 2018, https://labour.org.uk/press/diane-abbotts-speech-labours-plans-simpler-fairer-immigration-system/ (accessed July 2020).
101 Ibid.
102 Ibid.
103 Anthony Wells, 'Voting Intention since 2010', UKPOLLINGREPORT, http://ukpollingreport.co.uk/voting-intention-2# (accessed July 2020).
104 'Opinion Poll by Kantar Public, 10–14 January 2019', Kantar, '*Daily Express* voting intention and Brexit poll January 2019', ComRes/*Daily Express*, Matt Singh, 'Voting intention: Did the

last week hurt the Conservatives', Number Cruncher Politics, 19 January 2019, 'Sunday Mirror/ Sunday Express voting intention and Brexit poll January 2019', ComRes/Sunday Mirror/Sunday Express, 'BMG's Westminster Voting Intention Results: January 2019', 15 January 2019 and Des Freedman, 'Question Time's attacks on Diane Abbott are part of a pattern', Counterfire, 21 January 2019, https://www.counterfire.org/articles/analysis/20097-question-time-s-attacks-on-diane-abbott-are-part-of-a-pattern (accessed July 2020).

105 Question Time, BBC One, 17 January 2019.
106 Ibid.
107 'Rory Stewart apologises after making up Brexit stat', BBC News, 15 November 2018.
108 Question Time, BBC One, 24 January 2019.
109 Question Time, BBC One, 8 November 2018.

CHAPTER 16: BREXIT BRITAIN

1 John Johnston, 'Read the FULL resignation statements as Labour MPs quit to form 'The Independent Group', Politics Home, 18 February 2019.
2 Ibid.
3 Ibid.
4 'Millions have felt "powerless", "angry" or "worried" because of Brexit – results of our new poll', Mental Health Foundation, 21 March 2019, https://www.mentalhealth.org.uk/news/millions-have-felt-powerless-angry-or-worried-because-brexit-results-our-new-poll (accessed July 2020).
5 Brendan Carlin, '"She can have no excuse": Diane Abbott should be prosecuted for flouting drink ban on Overground train, Conservative MPs claim', Daily Mail, 20 April 2019.
6 Chris Pollard, Tom Wells and Chloe Kerr, 'COCKTAIL PARTY: Labour's Diane Abbott breaks the law by swigging can of mojito on the train home', The Sun, 20 April 2019.
7 Ibid.
8 Henry Martin and Emer Scully, '"I sincerely apologise": Shadow Home Secretary Diane Abbott says sorry for breaking the law after she is caught drinking M&S mojito on a train in London', Daily Mail, 20 April 2019.
9 Kevin Craig, 'M&S missed a PR opportunity with Diane Abbott #Mojitogate', PRWeek, 25 April 2019.
10 Interview with Diane Abbott, 29 February 2020.
11 David Singleton, '"Three Amigos" set out their reasons for walking out on the Tories', Total Politics, 20 February 2019.
12 Ibid.
13 Heidi Allen, Long Road Sixth Form College, Cambridge, 16 March 2019.
14 Interview with Diane Abbott, 29 February 2020.
15 Brendan O'Neill, 'Jeremy Corbyn's Brexit Betrayal is Complete', The Spectator, 26 February 2019.
16 Interview with Diane Abbott, 29 February 2020.
17 Jessica Elgot, 'Diane Abbott says she would back referendum on final Brexit deal', The Guardian, 28 November 2017.
18 Andrew Marr, BBC One, 17 December 2017.
19 Question Time, BBC One, 17 January 2019.
20 PM, BBC Radio 4, 29 January 2019.
21 'Minister George Eustice quits over Brexit delay vote', BBC News, 1 March 2019.
22 Today, BBC Radio 4, 28 May 2019.
23 'Brexit: Labour to back Remain as it calls for a new EU referendum', BBC News, 9 July 2019.
24 Interview with Jeremy Corbyn, 11 March 2020.
25 Jonathon Read, 'Critics say Jeremy Corbyn's new Brexit position is more fence sitting', New European, 9 July 2019.
26 Interview with Siana Bangura, 13 June 2020.
27 Interview with Paula Akpan and Nicole Crentsil, 26 April 2019.
28 Ibid.

29 Ibid.
30 Ibid.
31 Ibid.
32 Diane Abbott, BGF *Becoming* Festival, 11 April 2019.
33 Interview with Diane Abbott, 29 February 2020.
34 'PM: "I'd rather be dead in a ditch than delay Brexit"', BBC News 5 September 2019.
35 Michael Gove, 'The real horror of a Halloween No Deal Brexit? Handing the keys to Number 10 to Jeremy Corbyn', *Daily Mail*, 5 June 2019.
36 David Wilcock, 'I could tear this place down and bulldoze it into the river', *Daily Mail*, 27 March 2019.
37 Theresa May, 'PM statement on Brexit', Downing Street, 20 March 2019, https://www.gov.uk/government/speeches/pm-statement-on-brexit-20-march-2019 (accessed June 2020).
38 'Jo Swinson: Clarke and Harman prepared to lead emergency government', BBC News, 16 August 2019.
39 Danielle Sheridan, 'Ken Clarke: I am willing to become caretaker prime minister to "sort Brexit out"', *Daily Telegraph*, 16 August 2019.
40 Jessica Elgot and Peter Walker, 'Caroline Lucas calls for emergency female cabinet to block no-deal Brexit', *The Guardian*, 11 August 2019.
41 'Brexit: Caroline Lucas criticised over all-female cabinet plan', BBC News, 12 August 2019.
42 Lynne Segal, 'Lynne Segal Interviews Diane Abbott', *Feminist Review* (1987), no. 27, p. 59.
43 Brexit: Caroline Lucas criticised over all-female cabinet plan', BBC News.
44 Lucy Campbell and Rowena Mason, 'Caroline Lucas apologises for omitting BAME women from proposal', *The Guardian*, 12 August 2019.
45 Ciaran McGrath, 'Boris Johnson "paving way for people vs Parliament" election in Brexit showdown', *Daily Express*, 30 August 2019.
46 Interview with Diane Abbott, 29 February 2020.
47 Adam Forrest, 'Boris Johnson says describing black people as having "watermelon smiles" was "wholly satirical"', *The Independent*, 30 June 2019.
48 George Parker, Jane Croft, Sebastian Payne and Laura Hughes, 'Boris Johnson flies home to face the anger of MPs', *Financial Times*, 25 September 2019. Rees-Mogg refused to confirm that he had made this statement, but also refused to deny the words were his, telling Christopher 'Chopper' Hope that historians would have to wait for the release of Cabinet papers to find out the truth of what he said, Chopper's Brexit Podcast, 30 September 2019.
49 Interview with Diane Abbott, 29 February 2020.
50 Ibid.
51 Ibid.
52 Hansard, House of Commons debate, 25 September 2019, vol. 664, c. 794.
53 Hansard, House of Commons debate, 2 October 2019, vol. 664, cc. 1215–18.
54 Ibid.
55 Tom Harris, 'Diane Abbott did better than expected at PMQs – but that isn't saying much', *Daily Telegraph*, 2 October 2019.
56 Interview with Diane Abbott, 29 February 2020.
57 Ibid.
58 Interview with Diane Abbott, 12 December 2019.
59 Johnson's appeal to 'free speech' should be understood in the context of alt-right campaigns in defence of freedom of speech. Remarkably, the campaign seems to have emerged following 'Gamergate' of mid-2014. Harassment of prominent women in the video games industry led to an anti-feminist movement, primarily on YouTube, in which alt-right YouTubers accused online feminists of suppressing free speech. These debates came originally into the mainstream through concerns about 'no platforming' on campus.
60 'Grenfell: The End of an Experiment?', *London Review of Books*, 30 May 2018, https://www.youtube.com/watch?v=kXSR-Jd25Ds (accessed July 2020).
61 Interview with Jeremy Corbyn.

CONCLUSION

1   Paul Boateng, Stay Home for Labour online event, 11 June 2020.
2   Interview with Linda Bellos, 1 September 2018.
3   Interview with Jeremy Corbyn, 11 March 2020.
4   John McDonnell, Stay Home for Labour online event, 11 June 2020.
5   Interview with Sharon Grant, 18 March 2019.
6   Interview with David Lammy, 13 July 2018.
7   Yomi Adegoke, 'The leaked Labour report reveals a shocking level of racism and sexism towards its black MPs', *i*, 19 April 2020.
8   Interview with Nick Brown, 26 October 2018.
9   Interview with Andy Burnham, 22 November 2018.
10 Interview with David Lammy.
11 Michael Portillo, Stay Home for Labour online event, 11 June 2020.
12 Interview with Ansel Wong, 16 September 2019.
13 Interview with Bell Ribeiro-Addy, 22 August 2018.
14 John McDonnell, Stay Home for Labour online event, 11 June 2020.
15 Interview with David Lammy.
16 Interview with Shami Chakrabarti, 20 March 2019.
17 Private correspondence with Edem Barbara Ntumy, 11 June 2020.
18 Interview with Paula Akpan and Nicole Crentsil, 26 April 2019.
19 Hansard, House of Commons debate, 2 October 2019, vol. 664, c. 1215.
20 Interview with Ronnie Campbell 23 August 2018.
21 Interview with Andy Burnham, 22 November 2018.
22 Dawn Butler, Stay Home for Labour online event, 11 June 2020.
23 Bell Ribeiro-Addy, Stay Home for Labour online event, 11 June 2020.
24 Claudia Webbe, Stay Home for Labour online event, 11 June 2020.
25 Interview with Reni Eddo-Lodge, 25 June 2020.
26 Interview with Terri Sewell, 29 April 2018.
27 @Keir_Starmer, 11 June 2020.
28 'The virus does not discriminate, but this government does', Labour Outlook, 28 May 2020, https://labouroutlook.org/2020/05/28/the-virus-does-not-discriminate-but-this-government-does-by-diane-abbott/ (accessed July 2020).
29 Diane Abbott, 'British politicians must act decisively to fight institutional racism here in the UK', *LabourList* 2 June 2020, https://labourlist.org/2020/06/british-politicians-must-act-decisively-to-fight-institutional-racism-here-in-the-uk/ (accessed July 2020).
30 Peter Walker, Alexandra Topping and Steven Morris, 'Boris Johnson says removing statues is "to lie about our history"', *The Guardian*, 12 June 2020 and 'UK anti-racism protests: "Justice will follow" the "thuggery", Patel says', BBC News, 8 June 2020.
31 @HackneyAbbott, 8 June 2020.
32 Interview with Siana Bangura, 13 June 2020.
33 Diane Abbott, Stay Home for Labour online event, 11 June 2020.
34 Interview with Jeremy Corbyn.

INDEX